4 NOW READ THE CHAPTER AGAIN, SLOWLY AND CA[REFULLY]... [atten]tion to the key terms, which are printed in bold type and de[fined in the mar]gins. Highlight the three or four most important points in each major section, and copy them into your notes. Be sure to include the page number where they appear for reference later. Look for answers to any questions you jotted in the margins. Study the artwork in the chapter, too, because the figures present important data and summarize key points; write your own brief note detailing each figure's main point in the margin. Read the photo captions carefully and test your judgment by tackling the questions posed in each.

5 USE THE EXTRA STUDY FEATURES IN EACH CHAPTER TO MAKE YOUR STUDY AN ACTIVE LEARNING EXPERIENCE.

● Try to answer the boxed "Thinking Critically" questions in the margins; if you can't, review the section you just read and try again before you move on.

● The "Myth-Fact" boxes correct common misconceptions about criminal justice; test the accuracy of your thinking against these myths.

● The "CJ Online" activities direct you to Internet sites to research real-world data and criminal cases. Make notes to help you recall what you learn there.

● Use the "Careers in Criminal Justice" boxes as a study break. These boxes introduce you to real people working in the field of criminal justice and the day-to-day challenges they encounter on the job.

6 AFTER REREADING THE CHAPTER, REREAD THE SUMMARY. Be sure you understand each of the main points and have completely mastered all the concepts listed under each chapter objective. These represent the minimum you need to know after your careful reading of the chapter. If you feel weak in any area, stop, reread, and review. Make sure your notes are complete and that you have not overlooked anything important.

7 STUDY THE KEY TERMS AGAIN. Try writing the definitions on a separate sheet of paper without looking them up first. You can refresh your memory of the key terms by looking at the page number where each first appears (see the list following the summary) or by skimming the chapter again and looking for the definitions in the margins. Make sure you are very familiar with the vocabulary of criminal justice before you go on.

CONTINUED ON INSIDE BACK COVER

A CONCISE INTRODUCTION TO

CRIMINAL JUSTICE

Acknowledgments

This book, like any book, is the product of a collaborative effort. I would like to acknowledge and thank the many people who helped to make this edition possible. First, my thanks go to **Keith N. Haley** of Tiffin University, for his major contributions to the law enforcement chapters, and to **Kevin I. Minor** and **H. Preston Elrod** both of Eastern Kentucky University, for their significant contributions to the chapters on corrections and the juvenile justice system, respectively. I would also like to thank **John O. Smykla** of the University of West Florida for his help with Chapter 9: "Community Corrections", and **Donna M. Bishop** of Northeastern University, for her assistance with Chapter 10 "Juvenile Justice." In addition, for their insightful reviews, criticism, helpful suggestions, and information, I would like to thank:

James R. Acker
State University of New York at Albany

Brandon Applegate
University of Central Florida

Richard L. Ashbaugh
Clackamas Community College

Gregg Barak
Eastern Michigan University

David Barlow
Fayetteville State University

Michael Barrett
Ashland University

Denny Bebout
Central Ohio Technical College

Anita Blowers
University of North Carolina at Charlotte

Robert J. Boyer
Luzerne County Community College

William D. Burrell
Probation Services Division, State of New Jersey

Michael Cain
Coastal Bend Community College

Vincent J. Capozzella
Jefferson Community College

Jonathan Cella
Central Texas Community College

Charles Chastain
University of Arkansas at Little Rock

Daryl Cullison
Columbus State Community College

Hank DiMatteo
New Mexico State University

Vicky Dorworth
Montgomery College

Joyce K. Dozier
Wilmington College

Mary Ann Eastep
University of Central Florida

Randy Eastep
Brevard Community College

Robert R. Eiggins
Cedarville College

John W. Flickinger
Tiffin University

Kenneth A. Frayer
Schoolcraft College at Radcliff

David O. Friedrichs
University of Scranton

Rodney Friery
Jacksonville State University

Alex Greenberg
Niagara County Community College

Bob Hale
Southeastern Louisiana University

David O. Harding
Ohio University at Chillicothe

Stuart Henry
San Diego State University

Joseph Hogan
Central Texas College

Thomas E. Holdren
Muskingum Technical College

James Houston
Grand Valley State University

James L. Hudson
Clark State Community College

W. Richard Janikowski
University of Memphis

Lamar Jordan
Southern Utah University

Don Knueve
Defence College

Peter C. Kratcoski
Kent State University

Gregory C. Leavitt
Green River Community College

Gavin Lee
University of Central Florida

Vivian Lord
University of North Carolina at Charlotte

Karol Lucken
University of Central Florida

Richard Lumb
State University of New York at Brockport

Kathleen Maguire
Hindelang Criminal Justice Research Center

Bradley Martin
University of Findlay

Richard M. Martin
Elgin Community College

Alida Merlo
Indiana University of Pennsylvania

Dale Mooso
San Antonio College

James Newman
Rio Hondo College

Sarah Nordin
Solano Community College

Les Obert
Casper College

Nancy Oesch
Florida Metropolitan University

Angela Ondrus
Owens Community College

Mary Carolyn Purtill
San Joaquin Delta College

Jerome Randall
University of Central Florida

Matthew Robinson
Appalachian State University

Joseph B. Sanborn, Jr.
University of Central Florida

Martin D. Schwartz
Ohio University

Lance Selva
Middle Tennessee State University

David Slaughter
University of Central Florida

James E. Smith
West Valley College

Jeffrey B. Spelman
North Central Technical College

Clayton Steenberg
Arkansas State University

Gene Stephens
University of South Carolina

James Stinchcomb
Miami-Dade Community College

David Streater
Catawba Valley Community College

William L. Tafoya
University of Illinois Chicago

Henry A. Townsend
Washtenaw Community College

Roger D. Turner
Shelby State Community College

Ronald E. Vogel
California State University at Long Beach

Harold Williamson
Northeastern Louisiana University

Ross Wolf
University of Central Florida

Peter Wood
Mississippi State University

I would also like to thank **Jack Bohm,** Leawood, Kansas; **Richard Bohm,** New York, New York; and **Lorie Klumb,** Denver, Colorado, for their help with this book.

A CONCISE INTRODUCTION TO

CRIMINAL JUSTICE

ROBERT M. BOHM
University of Central Florida

Boston   Burr Ridge, IL   Dubuque, IA   Madison, WI   New York   San Francisco   St. Louis
Bangkok   Bogotá   Caracas   Kuala Lumpur   Lisbon   London   Madrid   Mexico City
Milan   Montreal   New Delhi   Santiago   Seoul   Singapore   Sydney   Taipei   Toronto

The McGraw·Hill Companies

Higher Education

Published by McGraw-Hill, a business unit of The McGraw-Hill Companies, Inc., 1221 Avenue of the Americas, New York, NY, 10020. Copyright © 2008 by The McGraw-Hill Companies, Inc. All rights reserved. No part of this publication may be reproduced or distributed in any form or by any means, or stored in a database or retrieval system, without the prior written consent of The McGraw-Hill Companies, Inc., including, but not limited to, in any network or other electronic storage or transmission, or broadcast for distance learning.

Some ancillaries, including electronic and print components, may not be available to customers outside the United States.

This book is printed on acid-free paper.

1 2 3 4 5 6 7 8 9 0 DOW/DOW 0 9 8 7

ISBN: 978-0-07-340150-8
MHID: 0-07-340150-1

Publisher: *Phillip A. Butcher/Frank Mortimer*
Sponsoring Editor: *Katie Stevens*
Freelance Developmental Editor: *Craig S. Leonard*
Senior Marketing Manager: *Lori DeShazo*
Editorial Coordinator: *Teresa Treacy*
Senior Project Manager: *Christina Thornton-Villagomez*
Art Editor: *Emma Ghiselli*
Design Manager: *Gino Cieslik*
Senior Photo Research Coordinator: *Alexandra Ambrose*
Photo Researcher: *Judy Mason*
Permission Editor: *Karyn L. Morrison*
Media Producer: *Christie Ling*
Production Supervisor: *Randy Hurst*
Composition: *9.5/12 New Astor by Techbooks—India*
Printing: *45# Pub Matte Plus by R.R. Donnelley/Willard*

Credits: The credits section for this book begins on page 429 and is considered an extension of the copyright page.

Library of Congress Cataloging-in-Publication Data

Bohm, Robert M.
  A concise introduction to criminal justice / Robert Bohm.—1st ed.
    p. cm.
  Includes index.
  ISBN-13: 978-0-07-340150-8 (softcover : alk. paper)
  ISBN-10: 0-07-340150-1 (softcover : alk. paper)
  1. Criminal justice, Administration of—United States. 2. Crime—United States.
3. Criminal law—United States. I. Title.
HV9950.B625 2007
364.973—dc22

                                                             2006028887

The Internet addresses listed in the text were accurate at the time of publication. The inclusion of a Web site does not indicate an endorsement by the authors or McGraw-Hill, and McGraw-Hill does not guarantee the accuracy of the information presented at these sites.

www.mhhe.com

Dedication

To my wife, Linda Taconis, with love.

ROBERT M. BOHM is professor of Criminal Justice and Legal Studies at the University of Central Florida in Orlando. He has also been a faculty member in the Departments of Criminal Justice at the University of North Carolina at Charlotte (1989–1995) and at Jacksonville State University in Alabama (1979–1989). From 1973 to 1974, he worked for the Jackson County Department of Corrections in Kansas City, Missouri, first as a corrections officer and later as an instructor/counselor in the Model Inmate Employment Program, a Law Enforcement Assistance Administration sponsored–work-release project. He received his PhD in Criminology from Florida State University in 1980. He has published numerous journal articles and book chapters in the areas of criminal justice and criminology. Besides being the author of *A Concise Introduction to Criminal Justice* (McGraw-Hill, 2008), he is the coauthor (with Keith N. Haley) of *Introduction to Criminal Justice,* 4th ed. update (McGraw-Hill, 2007), the editor of *The Death Penalty in America: Current Research,* the author of *A Primer on Crime and Delinquency Theory,* 2nd ed., and *Deathquest II: An Introduction to the Theory and Practice of Capital Punishment in the United States,* 2nd ed., and an editor (with James R. Acker and Charles S. Lanier) of *America's Experiment with Capital Punishment: Reflections on the Past, Present, and Future of the Ultimate Sanction,* 2nd ed., and *Demystifying Crime and Criminal Justice* (with Jeffery T. Walker). He has been active in the American Society of Criminology, the Southern Criminal Justice Association, and especially the Academy of Criminal Justice Sciences, having served as Trustee-at-Large (1987–90), Second Vice President (1990–91), First Vice President (1991–92), and President (1992–93). In 1989, he was selected as the *Outstanding Educator of the Year* by the Southern Criminal Justice Association. In 1999, he was elected a Fellow of the Academy of Criminal Justice Sciences and, in 2001; he was presented with the Founder's Award of the Academy of Criminal Justice Sciences.

CONTENTS

PART THREE

The Courts 151

CHAPTER FIVE

The Administration of Justice 153

CHAPTER EIGHT

Prison Life, Inmate Rights, Release, and Recidivism 291

CHAPTER NINE

Community Corrections 319

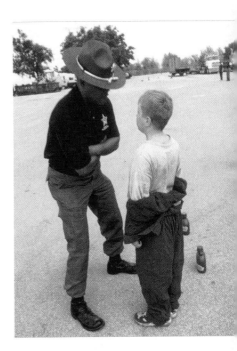

I am convinced that a good education in criminal justice can significantly improve the performance of most criminal justice personnel by equipping them, as this text does, to think critically, act ethically, and solve problems effectively. *A Concise Introduction to Criminal Justice* is not just for students interested in pursuing a career in criminal justice, however. It is also for students who simply want to learn more about this important social institution, which is vital to a free and democratic society.

All citizens need to know their legal rights and responsibilities. The better informed citizens are, the better able they are to protect themselves. A major theme of this book is that much of what the public "knows" about criminal justice in the United States is myth—that is, either wrong or significantly misunderstood. Consequently, in addition to presenting current, accurate information about criminal justice in the United States and generally accepted interpretations of historical and modern developments, this book "sets the record straight" in areas where, I believe, many people are being misled.

With the help of a quality education in criminal justice, people will feel more comfortable and better equipped to participate in criminal justice policy formulation. They will also be more effective in solving problems in their communities. They will have the critical thinking skills they need if they are to be constructive participants in a democratic nation and to have greater control over their own destinies.

Organization

A Concise Guide to Criminal Justice has been created to meet the demand for a more succinct examination of the criminal and juvenile justice systems in the United States, one that focuses almost exclusively on the police, courts, and corrections. The book is divided into ten chapters. The first chapter provides an overview that introduces criminal justice as an institution of social control, briefly describes the concepts of crime and the criminal law, outlines the stages in the criminal justice system, explains the standards of proof used in criminal justice, presents the crime control and due process models of criminal justice, and previews a main theme of the book: myths of criminal justice. Chapters 2, 3, and 4 are dedicated to the law enforcement component of criminal justice—its history, structure, roles, ethical issues, and challenges. Chapters 5 and 6 focus on the administration of justice, sentencing, appeals, and the court process as a whole. Chapters 7, 8, and 9 address the corrections system, jails, prisons, alternative sanctions, community corrections, and release of prisoners back into the community. Finally, Chapter 10 examines juvenile justice: its historical development, the processing of juvenile offenders, and correctional programs. Integrated into several chapters are discussions of criminal justice's new expanded role in the "war against terrorism."

Pedagogical Aids

Most of the pedagogical aids that have made Bohm and Haley's *Introduction to Criminal Justice* such a success are included in *A Concise Introduction to Criminal Justice*. They include:

- *10 Steps to Student Success.* This unique roadmap to student success is printed on the text's inside front and back covers and gives students all the tips and tools they need to excel in their first criminal justice course.
- *Careers in Criminal Justice.* These minibiographies highlight some of the most exciting career options available to criminal justice majors and keep the book relevant for students.
- *CJ Online.* These inserts enable students to explore chapter topics on the Net in a directed fashion.
- *FYI.* These sidebars present eye-opening additional information to retain students' interest and keep them thinking about what they are reading.
- *Myth vs. Fact.* These inserts debunk common misconceptions about the system and alert students to the need to question what they see in the media.
- *Thinking Critically.* These sections throughout the chapter challenge students to think about and apply chapter concepts.

I am especially proud of the comprehensive end-of-chapter review sections. In these sections, I provide every kind of review and study tool students could need:

- *Summary*—a terrific study tool, because it is organized into sections that mirror the chapter-opening objectives exactly.
- *Key Terms*—a comprehensive list of the terms defined in the chapter, complete with page references to make it easy for students to go back and review further.
- *Review Questions*—study questions that allow students to test their knowledge and prepare for exams.
- *In the Field Activities*—unique experiential exercises that enable students to broaden their understanding of chapter material by taking it to the next level.
- *On the Net Activities*—still more Internet-based exercises for today's Net-oriented learner.
- *Critical Thinking Exercises*—unique scenario-based activities that challenge students to apply what they've learned in the chapter.

Supplements Package

As a full-service publisher of quality educational products, McGraw-Hill does much more than just sell textbooks. The company creates and publishes an extensive array of print, video, and digital supplements for students and instructors. This first edition of *A Concise Introduction to Criminal Justice* is accompanied by a comprehensive supplements package:

FOR THE STUDENT

- *Reel Justice CD-ROM*—this unique interactive movie takes the concept of active learning to a whole new level, enabling students to take on the role of one of the story's characters and influence key plot turns by making choices for that character. The movie, centered on a domestic violence incident that takes place in a college town, allows students to explore course concepts and terminology in a relevant and meaningful context. Movie segments are augmented by a robust array of review and assessment features. With this breakthrough learning tool, students can explore a wide variety of criminal justice issues firsthand—criminal responsibility; theories of crime causation; civil versus criminal law; police roles, functions, and ethics; the courts; and more—and master course concepts more completely than they could by just reading any text.
- *Online Learning Center Web site*—an innovative, text-specific Web site featuring interactive cases—online access to articles from the popular and scholarly press, weekly updates, daily news feeds, and a search engine—as well as flashcards that can be used to master vocabulary, quizzes with feedback that

students can use to study for exams, downloadable state supplements, and more.

FOR THE INSTRUCTOR

- *Instructor's Resource CD*—a single CD with an easy-to-use interface providing access to a wide array of important ancillaries:
  - *Instructor's Manual/Testbank*—detailed chapter outlines, key terms, overviews, lecture notes, and a complete testbank.
  - *Reel Justice Instructor's Guide*—teaching tips and notes that make it easy to integrate the *Reel Justice* CD into your course.
  - *Computerized Testbank*—easy-to-use computerized testing program for both Windows and Macintosh computers.
  - *PowerPoint Slides*—complete, chapter-by-chapter slide shows featuring text, art, figures, and tables.
- *Online Learning Center Web site*—password-protected access to downloadable state supplements and other important instructor support materials and additional resources.
- *Reel Justice Lecture Launcher Videotape*—so even if you can't require students to use the CD, you can use the movie footage to jumpstart lectures in an exciting fashion.
- *NBC News Lecture Launcher Videotape*—unique video featuring brief clips from NBC News programs that can also be used to jump-start lectures.
- *Full-Length Videotapes*—a wide variety of videotapes from the *Films for the Humanities and Social Sciences* series is available to adopters of the text.
- *Course Management Systems*—whether you use WebCT, Blackboard, e-College, or another course management system, McGraw-Hill will provide you with a cartridge that enables you either to conduct your course entirely online or to supplement your lectures with online material. And if your school does not yet have one of these course management systems, we can provide you with PageOut, an easy-to-use tool that allows you to create your own course Web page and access all material on the Online Learning Center.
- *Primis Online*—a unique database publishing system that allows instructors to create a customized text from material in this text or elsewhere and deliver that text to students electronically as an e-book or in print format via the bookstore.

In closing I would like to acknowledge the help and support I received from the McGraw-Hill staff: publishers Phil Butcher and Frank Mortimer, editors Craig Leonard and Katie Stevens, project manager Christina Thornton-Villagomez, Gino Cieslik for the design, Alexandra Ambrose and Judy Mason for photo research, Teresa Treacy, editorial coordinator, and the rest of the team.

Robert M. Bohm

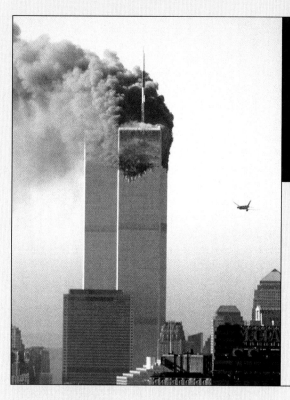

CRIMINAL JUSTICE IN THE UNITED STATES: AN OVERVIEW

CHAPTER OUTLINE

Criminal Justice: An Institution of Social Control

Crime and Criminal Law

Criminal Justice: The System

    Police

    Courts

    Corrections

Standards of Proof in Criminal Justice

Two Models of Criminal Justice

    The Crime Control Model

    The Due Process Model

    Crime Control versus Due Process

Myths about Criminal Justice

CHAPTER OBJECTIVES

After completing this chapter, you should be able to:

1. Identify institutions of social control and explain what makes criminal justice an institution of social control.

2. Define crime.

3. Describe the purpose of criminal justice.

4. Distinguish between substantive law and procedural law.

5. Summarize how the criminal justice system responds to crime.

6. Describe the standards of proof used in criminal justice and identify the criminal justice activities that correspond to each standard.

7. Point out major differences between Packer's crime control and due process models.

8. Explain how myths about crime and criminal justice affect the criminal justice system.

CHAPTER-OPENING PREVIEWS

Detailed chapter-opening objectives and outlines help students focus on the chapter's most critical concepts.

CAREERS IN CRIMINAL JUSTICE BOXES

Boxed inserts highlight the wide array of career options available to the criminal justice major.

---

10 PART ONE   The Foundations of Criminal Justice

are guided by prevailing philosophical rationales, by organizational considerations, and by presentence investigation reports. Decisions are also influenced by judges' own personal characteristics. Presentence investigation reports are used in the federal system and in the majority of states to help judges determine appropriate sentences.

Currently, five general types of punishment are used in the United States: fines, probation, intermediate punishments (various punishments that are more restrictive than probation but less restrictive and less costly than imprisonment), imprisonment, and death. As long as a judge imposes one or a combination of the five punishments and the sentence length and type are within statutory limits, the judge is free to set any sentence.

CAREERS IN CRIMINAL JUSTICE

Law Enforcement/Security

BATF Agent
Border Patrol Agent
Campus Police Officer
Crime Prevention Specialist
Criminal Investigator
Criminal Profiler
Customs Officer
Deputy Sheriff
Deputy U.S. Marshal
Drug Enforcement Officer
Environmental Protection Agent
FBI Special Agent
Federal Agency Investigator
Fingerprint Technician
Forensic Scientist
Highway Patrol Officer
INS Officer
Insurance Fraud Investigator
Laboratory Technician
Loss Prevention Officer
Military Police Officer
Park Ranger
Police Administrator
Police Dispatcher
Police Officer
Polygraph Examiner
Postal Inspector
Private Investigator
Secret Service Agent
State Trooper

Courts/Legal

Arbitrator
Attorney General
Bailiff
Clerk of Court
Court Reporter
District Attorney
Judge
Jury Assignment Commissioner
Jury Coordinator
Juvenile Magistrate
Law Clerk
Law Librarian
Legal Researcher
Mediator
Paralegal
Public Defender
Public Information Officer
Trial Court Administrator
Victim Advocate

Teaching/Research

Agency Researcher
Community College, College, or
    University Lecturer or Professor

Corrections/Rehabilitation

Activity Therapy Administrator
Business Manager
Case Manager
Chaplain
Chemical Dependency Manager
Child Care Worker

Children's Services Counselor
Classification Officer
Client Service Coordinator
Clinical Social Worker
Community Liaison Officer
Correctional Officer
Dietary Officer
Drug Court Coordinator
Field Administrator
Fugitive Apprehension Officer
Home Detention Supervisor
Human Services Counselor
Job Placement Officer
Juvenile Detention Officer
Juvenile Probation Officer
Mental Health Clinician
Parole/Probation Officer
Presentence Investigator
Prison Industries Superintendent
Program Officer/Specialist
Programmer/Analyst
Psychologist
Recreation Coordinator
Rehabilitation Counselor
Researcher
Residence Supervisor
Sex Offender Therapist
Social Worker
Statistician
Substance Abuse Counselor
Teacher
Vocational Instructor
Warden or Superintendent
Youth Service Worker/Coordinator
Youth Supervisor

PLENTIFUL VISUALS

Photographs with thought-provoking captions and questions, as well as figures and tables on almost every page of the text bring material to life.

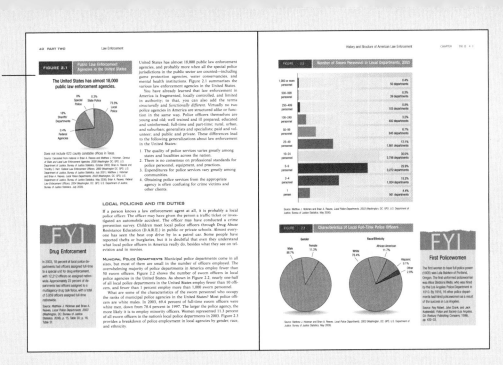

CJ ONLINE INSERTS

Web sites that students can visit to explore chapter topics on the Net in greater depth.

FYI SIDEBARS

Margin notes that present eye-opening information and keep students thinking about what they are reading.

THINKING CRITICALLY SECTIONS

End-of-section critical thinking questions throughout every chapter challenge students to apply chapter concepts.

MYTH VS. FACT BOXES

Boxed inserts debunk common misconceptions about criminal justice and alerts students to the need to question what they see in the media.

EAST-TO-USE CHAPTER REVIEWS

Clear, concise chapter summaries, key terms lists, and review questions provide students with essential study materials.

UNIQUE END-OF-CHAPTER EXERCISES

End-of-chapter critical thinking, experiential, and Internet activities challenge students to explore and think critically about chapter issues.

REEL JUSTICE INTERACTIVE MOVIE CD-ROM

A unique interactive movie that takes the concept of active learning to a whole new level, enabling students to take on the role of one of the story's characters and influence key plot turns by making choices for that character.

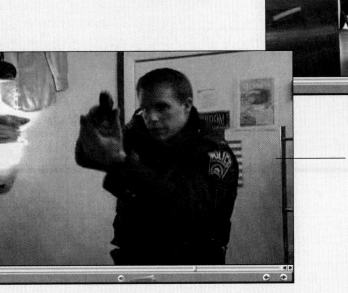

The movie, centered on a domestic violence incident that takes place in a college town, allows students to explore course concepts and terminology in a relevant and meaningful context. Movie segments are augmented by a robust array of review and assessment features.

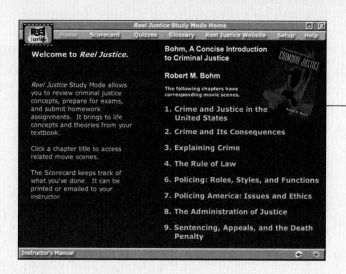

With this breakthrough learning tool, students can explore a wide variety of criminal justice issues firsthand—criminal responsibility, theories of crime causation, civil vs. criminal law, police roles, functions, and ethics, the courts, and more—and master course concepts more completely than they could by just reading any text.

ONLINE LEARNING CENTER WEB SITE

Book-specific website features unique interactive cases as well as chapter quizzes, online access to a wealth of popular press and scholarly articles, flashcards that can be used to master vocabulary, and many other chapter review tools.

PART ONE

THE FOUNDATIONS OF CRIMINAL JUSTICE

CHAPTER ONE

Criminal Justice in the United States: An Overview

CRIMINAL JUSTICE IN THE UNITED STATES: AN OVERVIEW

CHAPTER OUTLINE

CHAPTER OBJECTIVES

After completing this chapter, you should be able to:

1. Identify institutions of social control and explain what makes criminal justice an institution of social control.

2. Define crime.

3. Describe the purpose of criminal justice.

4. Distinguish between substantive law and procedural law.

5. Summarize how the criminal justice system responds to crime.

6. Describe the standards of proof used in criminal justice and identify the criminal justice activities that correspond to each standard.

7. Point out major differences between Packer's crime control and due process models.

8. Explain how myths about crime and criminal justice affect the criminal justice system.

institution of social control An organization that persuades people, through subtle and not-so-subtle means, to abide by the dominant values of society.

Criminal Justice: An Institution of Social Control

In the United States, there are a variety of responses to crime. When a child commits a criminal act, even if that act does not come to the attention of the police, parents or school authorities nevertheless may punish the child for the offense (if they find out about it). Attempts to prevent crime by installing burglar alarms in automobiles and homes are other ways of responding to crime. Throughout this book, we focus on the criminal justice response to crime.

Like the family, schools, organized religion, the media, and the law, criminal justice is an **institution of social control** in the United States. A primary role of such institutions is to persuade people, through subtle and not-so-subtle means, to abide by the dominant values of society. Subtle means of persuasion include gossip and peer pressure, whereas expulsion and incarceration are examples of not-so-subtle means.

As an institution of social control, criminal justice differs from the others in two important ways. First, the role of criminal justice is restricted officially to persuading people to abide by a limited range of social values: those whose violation constitutes crime. Thus, although courteous behavior is desired of all citizens, rude behavior is of no official concern to criminal justice, unless it violates the criminal law. Dealing with noncriminal rude behavior is primarily the responsibility of the family. Second, criminal justice is generally society's "last line of defense" against people who refuse to abide by dominant social values and commit crimes. Usually, society turns to criminal justice only after other institutions of social control have failed.

penal code The criminal law of a political jurisdiction.

jurisdiction A politically defined geographical area.

criminal law One of two general types of law practiced in the United States (the other is civil law); "a formal means of social control [that uses] rules . . . interpreted [and enforced] by the courts . . . to set limits to the conduct of the citizens, to guide the officials, and to define . . . unacceptable behavior."

substantive law The body of law that defines criminal offenses and their penalties.

Crime and Criminal Law

The conventional definition of *crime* is a violation of the criminal law or of the **penal code** of a political jurisdiction. The term **jurisdiction,** as used here, means a politically defined geographical area (for example, a city, a county, a state, or a nation). **Criminal law** is one of two general types of law practiced in the United States; the other is civil law.

Criminal law is "a formal means of social control [that] involves the use of rules that are interpreted, and are enforceable, by the courts of a political community. . . . The function of the rules is to set limits to the conduct of the citizens, to guide the officials (police and other administrators), and to define conditions of deviance or unacceptable behavior."[1] The purpose of criminal justice is to enforce the criminal law.

There are two types of criminal law: substantive and procedural. **Substantive law** is the body of law that defines criminal offenses and their penalties. Substantive laws, which are found in the various penal codes, govern what people legally may and may not do. Examples of substantive laws are those that prohibit and penalize murder, rape, robbery, and other crimes. **Procedural law,** sometimes called *adjective* or *remedial* law, governs the ways in which the substantive laws are to be administered. It covers such subjects as the way suspects can legally be arrested, searched, interrogated, tried, and punished. In other words, procedural law is concerned with **due process of law,** or the rights of people suspected of or charged with crimes. Later chapters of this book examine the procedural law in more detail.

Criminal Justice: The System

Criminal justice in the United States is administered by a loose confederation of more than 50,000 agencies of federal, state, and local governments. Those agencies consist of the police, the courts, and corrections. Together they are commonly referred to as the *criminal justice system.* Although there are differences in the ways the criminal justice system operates in different jurisdictions, there are also similarities.

The following paragraphs provide a brief overview of a typical criminal justice response to criminal behavior. Figure 1.1 is a graphic representation of the process. It includes the variations for petty offenses, **misdemeanors** (less serious crimes), **felonies** (serious crimes), and juvenile offenses. A more detailed examination of the criminal justice response to crime and delinquency will be provided in later chapters of this book.

POLICE

The criminal justice response to crime begins when a crime is reported to the police or, far less often, when the police themselves discover that a crime has been committed. Sometimes solving the crime is easy—the victim or a witness knows the perpetrator, or where to find him or her. Often, an arrest supported by witness statements and crime scene evidence is sufficient to close a case, especially with a less serious crime. More often, though, the police must conduct an in-depth investigation to determine what happened in a particular crime. Even when the police start with a known crime or a cooperative victim or witness, the investigation can be lengthy and difficult.

If police investigation of the crime is successful, a suspect is arrested. An **arrest** is the seizing and detaining of a person by lawful authority. After an arrest has been made, the suspect is brought to the police station to be booked. **Booking** is the administrative recording of the arrest. It typically involves entering the suspect's name, the charge, and perhaps the suspect's fingerprints or photograph in the police blotter.

COURTS

Soon after a suspect has been arrested and booked, a prosecutor reviews the facts of the case and the available evidence. Sometimes a prosecutor reviews the case before arrest. The prosecutor decides whether to charge the suspect with a crime or crimes. If no charges are filed, the suspect must be released.

Crimes and Torts

Violations of the criminal law are crimes; violations of the civil law are torts. Although crime is committed against individuals, it is considered an offense against the state, that is, the political jurisdiction that enacted the law. A tort, on the other hand, is considered a private matter between individuals.

Myth   Fact

Myth	Fact
The agencies that administer criminal justice in the United States form a unified system: the criminal justice system.	There is no single "criminal justice system" in the United States. Instead, there is a loose confederation of many independent criminal justice agencies at all levels of government. Moreover, instead of operating together as a system, agencies of criminal justice in the United States interact but generally operate independently of one another, each agency often causing problems for the others.

procedural law The body of law that governs the ways substantive laws are administered; sometimes called *adjective* or *remedial* law.

due process of law The rights of people suspected of or charged with crimes; the procedures followed by courts to ensure that a defendant's constitutional rights are not violated.

misdemeanors Less serious crimes generally punishable by a fine or by incarceration in jail for not more than 1 year.

felonies Serious offenses punishable by confinement in prison for more than 1 year or by death.

FIGURE 1.1 Overview of the Criminal Justice System

Procedures vary among jurisdictions.

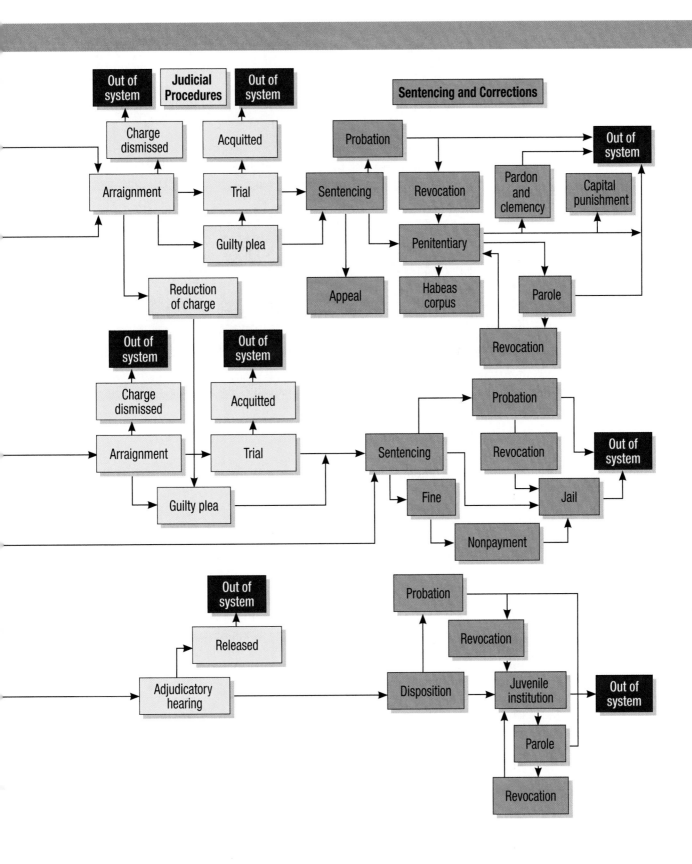

Getting fingerprints is generally a part of the booking into jail process. Pictured here is an inmate being fingerprinted with a technologically advanced "Printrat Livescan Finger Machine." *Why are inmates fingerprinted?*

arrest The seizing and detaining of a person by lawful authority.

booking The administrative recording of an arrest. Typically, the suspect's name, the charge, and perhaps the suspect's fingerprints or photograph are entered in the police blotter.

defendant A person against whom a legal action is brought, a warrant is issued, or an indictment is found.

initial appearance A pretrial stage in which a defendant is brought before a lower court to be given notice of the charge(s) and advised of her or his constitutional rights.

summary trial An immediate trial without a jury.

probable cause A standard of proof that requires evidence sufficient to make a reasonable person believe that, more likely than not, the proposed action is justified.

bail Usually a monetary guarantee deposited with the court to ensure that suspects or defendants will appear at a later stage in the criminal justice process.

preliminary hearing In a felony case, a pretrial stage at which a judge determines whether there is probable cause.

grand jury A group of citizens who meet to investigate charges coming from preliminary hearings.

PRETRIAL STAGES After the charge or charges have been filed, the suspect, who is now the **defendant,** is brought before a lower-court judge for an **initial appearance.** At the initial appearance the defendant is given formal notice of the charge or charges against him or her and advised of his or her constitutional rights (for example, the right to counsel). In the case of a misdemeanor or an ordinance violation, a **summary trial** (an immediate trial without a jury) may be held. In the case of a felony, a hearing is held to determine whether the defendant should be released or whether there is probable cause to hold the defendant for a preliminary hearing. **Probable cause** is a standard of proof that requires trustworthy evidence sufficient to make a reasonable person believe that, more likely than not, the proposed action is justified. If the suspect is to be held for a preliminary hearing, bail is set if the judge believes release on bail is appropriate. **Bail,** usually a monetary guarantee deposited with the court, is meant to ensure that the defendant will appear at a later stage in the criminal justice process.

In about half of all states, the initial appearance is followed by a preliminary hearing. Preliminary hearings are used only in felony cases. At the **preliminary hearing,** a judge determines whether there is probable cause to believe that the defendant committed the crime or crimes with which he or she is charged. If the judge finds probable cause, the defendant is bound over for possible indictment in a state with grand juries or for arraignment on an information in a state without grand juries.

Grand juries are involved in felony prosecutions in about half the states. A **grand jury** is a group of citizens who meet in closed sessions for a specified period to investigate charges coming from preliminary hearings and to fulfill other responsibilities. Thus, a primary purpose of the grand jury is to determine whether there is probable cause to believe that the accused committed the crime or crimes with which the prosecutor has charged her or him. The grand jury can either indict or fail to indict a suspect. If the grand jury fails to indict, the prosecution must be dropped. In states that do not use grand juries, prosecutors charge defendants with a document called an *information.*

Arrestees can spend up to 48 hours or more in a jail holding cell before a judge decides whether an arrest was justified. *What problems could occur as a result of this practice?*

An **information** outlines the formal charge or charges, the law or laws that have been violated, and the evidence to support the charge or charges.

Once an indictment or information is filed with the trial court, the defendant is scheduled for arraignment. The primary purpose of **arraignment** is to hear the formal information or indictment and to allow the defendant to enter a plea. About 90 percent of criminal defendants plead guilty to the charges against them, in an arrangement called *plea bargaining*. **Plea bargaining** is the practice whereby the prosecutor, the defense attorney, the defendant, and, in many jurisdictions, the judge agree on a specific sentence to be imposed if the accused pleads guilty to an agreed-upon charge or charges instead of going to trial.

TRIAL If a defendant pleads not guilty or not guilty by reason of insanity, a trial date is set. Although all criminal defendants have a constitutional right to a trial (when imprisonment for 6 months or more is a possible outcome), only about 10 percent of all criminal cases are disposed of by trial. Approximately 5 percent of criminal cases involve jury trials. The remaining cases that are not resolved through plea bargaining are decided by a judge in a **bench trial** (without a jury). Thus, approximately 90 percent of all criminal cases are resolved through plea bargaining, about 5 percent through jury trials, and about 5 percent through bench trials. (See Figure 1.2.) In most jurisdictions the choice between a jury trial and a bench trial is the defendant's to make.

If the judge or the jury finds the defendant guilty as charged, the judge begins to consider a sentence. In some jurisdictions the jury participates to varying degrees in the sentencing process. The degree of jury participation depends on the jurisdiction and the crime. If the judge or jury finds the defendant not guilty, the defendant is released from the jurisdiction of the court and becomes a free person.

CORRECTIONS

Judges cannot impose just any sentence. Many factors restrict sentencing decisions. Judges are limited by the U.S. Constitution's Eighth Amendment (prohibiting cruel and unusual punishments) and statutory provisions. They

information A document that outlines the formal charge(s) against a suspect, the law(s) that have been violated, and the evidence to support the charge(s).

arraignment A pretrial stage to hear the information or indictment and to allow a plea.

plea bargaining The practice whereby a specific sentence is imposed if the accused pleads guilty to an agreed-upon charge or charges instead of going to trial.

bench trial A trial before a judge without a jury.

FIGURE 1.2	Criminal Case Dispositions

Bench Trial 5%

Jury Trial 5%

Plea Bargain 90%

are guided by prevailing philosophical rationales, by organizational considerations, and by presentence investigation reports. Decisions are also influenced by judges' own personal characteristics. Presentence investigation reports are used in the federal system and in the majority of states to help judges determine appropriate sentences.

Currently, five general types of punishment are used in the United States: fines, probation, intermediate punishments (various punishments that are more restrictive than probation but less restrictive and less costly than imprisonment), imprisonment, and death. As long as a judge imposes one or a combination of the five punishments and the sentence length and type are within statutory limits, the judge is free to set any sentence.

CAREERS IN CRIMINAL JUSTICE

Law Enforcement/Security

BATF Agent
Border Patrol Agent
Campus Police Officer
Crime Prevention Specialist
Criminal Investigator
Criminal Profiler
Customs Officer
Deputy Sheriff
Deputy U.S. Marshal
Drug Enforcement Officer
Environmental Protection Agent
FBI Special Agent
Federal Agency Investigator
Fingerprint Technician
Forensic Scientist
Highway Patrol Officer
INS Officer
Insurance Fraud Investigator
Laboratory Technician
Loss Prevention Officer
Military Police Officer
Park Ranger
Police Administrator
Police Dispatcher
Police Officer
Polygraph Examiner
Postal Inspector
Private Investigator
Secret Service Agent
State Trooper

Courts/Legal

Arbitrator
Attorney General
Bailiff
Clerk of Court
Court Reporter
District Attorney
Judge
Jury Assignment Commissioner
Jury Coordinator
Juvenile Magistrate
Law Clerk
Law Librarian
Legal Researcher
Mediator
Paralegal
Public Defender
Public Information Officer
Trial Court Administrator
Victim Advocate

Teaching/Research

Agency Researcher
Community College, College, or
    University Lecturer or Professor

Corrections/Rehabilitation

Activity Therapy Administrator
Business Manager
Case Manager
Chaplain
Chemical Dependency Manager
Child Care Worker

Children's Services Counselor
Classification Officer
Client Service Coordinator
Clinical Social Worker
Community Liaison Officer
Correctional Officer
Dietary Officer
Drug Court Coordinator
Field Administrator
Fugitive Apprehension Officer
Home Detention Supervisor
Human Services Counselor
Job Placement Officer
Juvenile Detention Officer
Juvenile Probation Officer
Mental Health Clinician
Parole/Probation Officer
Presentence Investigator
Prison Industries Superintendent
Program Officer/Specialist
Programmer/Analyst
Psychologist
Recreation Coordinator
Rehabilitation Counselor
Researcher
Residence Supervisor
Sex Offender Therapist
Social Worker
Statistician
Substance Abuse Counselor
Teacher
Vocational Instructor
Warden or Superintendent
Youth Service Worker/Coordinator
Youth Supervisor

Defendants who are found guilty can appeal their convictions either on legal grounds or on constitutional grounds. Examples of legal grounds include defects in jury selection, improper admission of evidence at trial, and mistaken interpretations of law. Constitutional grounds include illegal search and seizure, improper questioning of the defendant by the police, identification of the defendant through a defective police lineup, and incompetent assistance of counsel. The appellate court can either *affirm* the verdict of the lower court and let it stand; modify the verdict of the lower court, without totally reversing it; reverse the verdict of the lower court, which requires no further court action; or reverse the decision and *remand,* or return, the case to the court of original jurisdiction for either a retrial or resentencing. A defendant sentenced to prison may be eligible for parole (in those jurisdictions that grant parole) after serving a portion of his or her sentence. **Parole** is the conditional release of prisoners before they have served their full sentences. Generally, the decision to grant parole is made by a parole board. Once offenders have served their sentences, they are released from criminal justice authority.

parole The conditional release of prisoners before they have served their full sentences.

THINKING CRITICALLY

1. Do you think the criminal justice system "works" in the United States? Why or why not?

2. What improvements do you think should be made to the criminal justice system?

3. Do you think judges should be limited in the sentences they are allowed to impose? Why or why not?

Standards of Proof in Criminal Justice

As mentioned previously, a purpose of both an initial appearance and a preliminary hearing is for a judge to make a probable cause assessment—to determine whether there are reasonable grounds to believe a person has committed a crime. Probable cause is one among a number of standards of proof for various criminal justice activities. The amount of proof necessary depends on the activity in question. Figure 1.3 shows various standards of proof, along a continuum of certainty, and the criminal justice activities that correspond to them.

Toward one end of the continuum is the standard of proof with the least certainty: *mere suspicion.* **Mere suspicion** is equivalent to a "gut feeling." In other words, a law enforcement officer may have a feeling that something is wrong—an uncanny knack that some experienced law enforcement officers possess—but be unable to state exactly what it is. With only mere suspicion, law enforcement officers cannot legally even stop a suspect.

mere suspicion The standard of proof with the least certainty; a "gut feeling." With mere suspicion, a law enforcement officer cannot legally even stop a suspect.

| FIGURE 1.3 | Standards of Proof and Criminal Justice Activities |

Mere suspicion	Reasonable suspicion	Probable cause	Preponderance of evidence	Clear and convincing evidence	Beyond a reasonable doubt	Absolute certainty
None	Stop and frisk	Search or arrest; determine whether a person committed crime at initial appearance and preliminary hearing	Determinine "good faith" exception to exclusionary rule; show waiver of right to counsel "knowingly and intelligently"	Make successful claim of insanity in federal courts	Determine guilt in a criminal trial	None

reasonable suspicion A standard of proof that is more than a gut feeling. It includes the ability to articulate reasons for the suspicion. With reasonable suspicion, a law enforcement officer is legally permitted to stop and frisk a suspect.

frisking Conducting a search for weapons by patting the outside of a suspect's clothing, feeling for hard objects that might be weapons.

preponderance of evidence Evidence that more likely than not outweighs the opposing evidence, or sufficient evidence to overcome doubt or speculation.

A standard of proof with greater certainty is *reasonable suspicion.* **Reasonable suspicion** is more than a gut feeling. It includes the ability to articulate reasons for the suspicion. For example, if a law enforcement officer observes a person in front of a bank wearing a heavy trench coat on a hot summer day, the officer might have a reasonable suspicion that something is wrong. The officer could state that idling in front of a bank while wearing a heavy trench coat on a hot summer day is suspect behavior. Until recently, an anonymous tip, as long as there were other reliable indicators, could be the basis for reasonable suspicion. However, in *Florida* v. *J.L.* (2000), the Supreme Court ruled that an uncorroborated anonymous tip was unconstitutional.[2] On the other hand, the Court, in *Illinois* v. *Wardlow* (2000), confirmed that running from the police when they enter a high-crime area is reasonably suspicious behavior.[3] With reasonable suspicion, a law enforcement officer is legally permitted to stop and frisk a suspect (*Terry* v. *Ohio*, 1968). **Frisking** a suspect means conducting a search for weapons by patting the outside of a suspect's clothing, feeling for hard objects that might be weapons. Only if an officer feels something that may be a weapon may he or she search inside a pocket or an article of clothing. If evidence of a crime is discovered, the officer is permitted to make an arrest.

Besides being used in initial appearances and preliminary hearings, *probable cause* is also the standard of proof needed to conduct a search or to make an arrest. The conventional definition of probable cause in the context of a search or an arrest is the amount of proof necessary for a reasonably intelligent person to believe that a crime has been committed or that items connected with criminal activity can be found in a particular place. Although its meaning is not entirely clear—what is "reasonably intelligent"?—probable cause has a greater degree of certainty than reasonable suspicion. For probable cause, law enforcement officers must have some tangible evidence that a crime has been committed, but that evidence does not have to be admissible at trial. Such evidence might include a tip from a reliable informant or the pungent aroma of marijuana in the air.

The line between probable cause and reasonable suspicion, or even mere suspicion, is a fine one and a matter of interpretation. In practice, there are many gray areas. Consequently, criminal courts and the judicial officers who are authorized to approve search warrants have been given the responsibility of determining whether a standard of proof has been met in a particular situation. The way courts and judicial officers determine whether a standard of proof has been met will be discussed in detail in Chapter 2. For much of the public, one of the frustrating aspects of criminal justice is that offenders who are factually guilty of their crimes sometimes escape punishment because a judicial officer did not have probable cause to issue a warrant, or a police officer did not have probable cause to make an arrest or have reasonable suspicion to stop and frisk the suspect.

The next standard of proof along the continuum of legal certainty is *preponderance of evidence.* **Preponderance of evidence** is evidence that more likely than not outweighs the opposing evidence, or sufficient evidence to overcome doubt or speculation. It is the standard of proof necessary to find a defendant liable (responsible) in a civil lawsuit. (Civil courts do not "convict.") This standard is also used in determining whether the *inevitable-discovery rule* applies. That is, the prosecution must prove by a preponderance of the evidence that evidence actually uncovered as a result of a constitutional violation would inevitably have been discovered through lawful means, independent of the action constituting the violation. Finally, preponderance of evidence is the standard of proof in criminal proceedings by which the state must show that the right to counsel has been waived "knowingly and intelligently." The inevitable-discovery rule and the right to waive counsel are described more fully in later chapters.

Next along the continuum of certainty is **clear and convincing evidence,** which is evidence indicating that the thing to be proved is highly probable or reasonably certain. It is the standard of proof required in some civil cases and, in federal courts, the standard of proof necessary for a defendant to make a successful claim of insanity.

Of greater certainty still is proof **beyond a reasonable doubt,** the standard of proof necessary to find a defendant guilty in a criminal trial. Reasonable doubt is the amount of doubt about a defendant's guilt that a reasonable person might have after carefully examining all the evidence. In the case of *Sandoval* v. *California* (1994), the Court upheld the following definition of *reasonable doubt:*

> It is *not a mere possible doubt;* because everything relating to human affairs, and *depending on moral evidence,* is open to some possible or imaginary doubt. It is that state of the case which, after the entire comparison and consideration of all the evidence, leaves the minds of the jurors in that they cannot say they feel an abiding conviction, *to a moral certainty,* of the truth of the charge. [Emphasis in original.]

Thus, to convict a criminal defendant in a jury trial, a juror must be convinced of guilt by this standard. However, what is considered reasonable varies, and reasonableness is thus a matter of interpretation. Therefore, the procedural laws in most jurisdictions require that all jurors agree that a defendant is guilty beyond a reasonable doubt before that defendant can be convicted. No criminal justice activity requires absolute certainty as a standard of proof.

clear and convincing evidence The standard of proof required in some civil cases and, in federal courts, the standard of proof necessary for a defendant to make a successful claim of insanity.

beyond a reasonable doubt The standard of proof necessary to find a defendant guilty in a criminal trial.

THINKING CRITICALLY

1. Do you think different standards of proof should govern different criminal justice activities, or do you think one standard should be applied to all criminal justice activities? Why or why not? If the latter, what standard of proof should it be?

2. Do you think the standards of proof that currently govern criminal justice activities should govern criminal justice activities during the war on terrorism, or should different standards of proof be used? Why or why not?

Two Models of Criminal Justice

In his influential 1968 book entitled *The Limits of the Criminal Sanction,* legal scholar Herbert Packer describes the criminal justice process in the United States as the outcome of competition between two value systems.[4] Those two value systems, which represent two ends of a value continuum, are the basis for two models of the operation of criminal justice—the crime control model and the due process model. Figure 1.4 depicts this continuum. From a political standpoint, the **crime control model** reflects traditional conservative values, while the **due process model** embodies traditional liberal values.[5]

crime control model One of Packer's two models of the criminal justice process. Politically, it reflects traditional conservative values. In this model, the control of criminal behavior is the most important function of criminal justice.

due process model One of Packer's two models of the criminal justice process. Politically, it embodies traditional liberal values. In this model, the principal goal of criminal justice is at least as much to protect the innocent as it is to convict the guilty.

FIGURE 1.4	Two Models of the Criminal Justice Process

Due Process Model

Traditional liberal values

Crime Control Model

Traditional conservative values

Consequently, when politically conservative values are dominant in society, as they are currently, the principles and policies of the crime control model seem to dominate the operation of criminal justice. During more politically liberal periods, such as the 1960s and 1970s, the principles and policies of the due process model seem to dominate criminal justice activity.

The models are ideal types, neither of which corresponds exactly to the actual day-to-day practice of criminal justice. Rather, they both provide a convenient way to understand and discuss the operation of criminal justice in the United States. In practice, the criminal justice process represents a series of conflicts and compromises between the value systems of the two models. In the following sections, Packer's two models are described in detail.

THE CRIME CONTROL MODEL

In the crime control model, the control of criminal behavior is by far the most important function of criminal justice. Although the means by which crime is controlled are important in this view (illegal means are not advocated), they are less important than the ultimate goal of control. Consequently, the primary focus of this model is on efficiency in the operation of the criminal justice process. Advocates of the crime control model want to make the process more efficient—to move cases through the process as quickly as possible and to bring them to a close. Packer characterizes the crime control model as "assembly-line justice." To achieve "quick closure" in the processing of cases, a premium is placed on speed and finality. Speed requires that cases be handled informally and uniformly; finality depends on minimizing occasions for challenge, that is, appeals.

To appreciate the assembly-line metaphor used by Packer and to understand how treating cases uniformly speeds up the process and makes it more efficient, consider the way that McDonald's sells billions of hamburgers. When you order a Big Mac from McDonald's, you know exactly what you are going to get. All Big Macs are the same, because they are made uniformly. Moreover, you can get a Big Mac in a matter of seconds most of the time. However, what happens when you order something different, or something not already prepared, such as a hamburger with ketchup only? Your order is taken, and you are asked to stand to the side because your special order will take a few minutes. Your special order has slowed down the assembly line and reduced efficiency. This happens in criminal justice, too! If defendants ask for something special, such as a trial, the assembly line is slowed and efficiency is reduced.

As described in Chapter 5 ("The Administration of Justice"), even when criminal justice is operating at its best, it is a slow process. The time from arrest to final case disposition can typically be measured in weeks or months. If defendants opt for a jury trial, as is their right in most felony cases, the cases are handled formally and are treated as unique; no two cases are the same in their circumstances or in the way they are handled. If defendants are not satisfied with the outcome of their trials, then they have the right to appeal. Appeals may delay by years the final resolution of cases.

To increase efficiency—meaning speed and finality—crime control advocates prefer plea bargaining. As described previously and in Chapter 5, plea bargaining is an informal process that is used instead of trial. Plea bargains can be offered and accepted in a relatively short time. Also, cases are handled uniformly because the mechanics of a plea bargain are basically the same; only the substance of the deals differs. Additionally, with successful plea bargains, there is no opportunity for challenge; there are no appeals. Thus, plea bargaining is the perfect mechanism for achieving the primary focus of the crime control model—efficiency.

The key to the operation of the crime control model is "a presumption of guilt." In other words, advocates of this model assume that if the police have expended the time and effort to arrest a suspect and the prosecutor has formally charged the suspect with a crime, then the suspect must be guilty. Why else would police arrest and prosecutors charge? Although the answers to that question are many (see the discussions in Chapters 4 and 5 of the extralegal factors that influence police and prosecutorial behavior), the fact remains that a presumption of guilt is accurate most of the time. That is, most people who are arrested and charged with a crime or crimes are, in fact, guilty. A problem—but not a significant one for crime control advocates—is that a presumption of guilt is not accurate all of the time; miscarriages of justice do occur (see the discussion in Chapter 5). An equally important problem is that a presumption of guilt goes against one of the oldest and most cherished principles of American criminal justice—that a person is considered innocent until proven guilty.

Reduced to its barest essentials and operating at its highest level of efficiency, the crime control model consists of an administrative fact-finding process with two possible outcomes: a suspect's exoneration or the suspect's guilty plea.

Gary Ridgway, the so-called Green River Killer, was allowed to plead guilty to 48 counts of murder in exchange for helping authorities find some of his victims' remains. The plea bargain allowed him to escape the death penalty. He was sentenced to 48 consecutive life sentences without parole instead. *Was the plea bargain in this case justified? Why or why not?*

THE DUE PROCESS MODEL

Advocates of the due process model, by contrast, reject the informal fact-finding process as definitive of factual guilt. They insist, instead, on formal, adjudicative fact-finding processes in which cases against suspects are heard publicly by impartial trial courts. In the due process model, moreover, the factual guilt of suspects is not determined until the suspects have had a full opportunity to discredit the charges against them. For those reasons, Packer characterizes the due process model as "obstacle-course justice."

What motivates this careful and deliberate approach to the administration of justice is the realization that human beings sometimes make mistakes. The police sometimes arrest the wrong person, and prosecutors sometimes charge the wrong person. Thus, contrary to the crime control model, the demand for finality is low in the due process model, and the goal is at least as much to protect the innocent as it is to convict the guilty. Indeed, for due process model advocates, it is better to let a guilty person go free than it is to wrongly convict and punish an innocent person.

The due process model is based on the doctrine of legal guilt and the presumption of innocence. According to the **doctrine of legal guilt,** people are not to be held guilty of crimes merely on a showing, based on reliable evidence, that in all probability they did in fact do what they are accused of doing. In other words, it is not enough that people are factually guilty in the due process model; they must also be legally guilty. Legal guilt results only when factual guilt is determined in a procedurally regular fashion, as in a criminal trial, and when the procedural rules, or due process rights, designed to protect suspects and defendants and to safeguard the integrity

doctrine of legal guilt The principle that people are not to be held guilty of crimes merely on a showing, based on reliable evidence, that in all probability they did in fact do what they are accused of doing. Legal guilt results only when factual guilt is determined in a procedurally regular fashion, as in a criminal trial, and when the procedural rules designed to protect suspects and defendants and to safeguard the integrity of the process are employed.

of the process are employed. The conditions of legal guilt—that is, procedural, or due process, rights—are described in later chapters of this book. They include:

- Freedom from unreasonable searches and seizures.
- Protection against double jeopardy.
- Protection against compelled self-incrimination.
- A speedy and public trial.
- An impartial jury of the state and district where the crime occurred.
- Notice of the nature and cause of the accusation.
- The right to confront opposing witnesses.
- Compulsory process for obtaining favorable witnesses.
- The right to counsel.
- The prohibition of cruel and unusual punishment.

In short, in the due process model, factual guilt is not enough. For people to be found guilty of crimes, they must be found *both* factually and legally guilty.

This obstacle-course model of justice is championed by due process advocates because they are skeptical about the ideal of equality on which American criminal justice is supposedly based. They recognize that there can be no equal justice where the kind of trial a person gets, or whether he or she gets a trial at all, depends substantially on how much money that person has. It is assumed that in an adversarial system of justice (as described in Chapter 5 and employed in the United States), an effective defense is largely a function of the resources that can be mustered on behalf of the accused. It is also assumed that there are gross inequalities in the financial means of criminal defendants. Most criminal defendants are indigent or poor, and because of their indigence, they are frequently denied an effective defense. Although procedural safeguards, or conditions of legal guilt, cannot by themselves correct the inequity in resources, they do provide indigent defendants, at least theoretically, with a better chance for justice than they would receive without them.

Fundamentally, the due process model defends the ideal of personal freedom and its protection. The model rests on the assumption that preventing tyranny by the government and its agents is the most important function of the criminal justice process.

CRIME CONTROL VERSUS DUE PROCESS

As noted earlier, which of the models dominates criminal justice policy in the United States at any particular time depends on the political climate. Currently, the United States is in the midst of a prolonged period—beginning in the mid-1970s—in which politically conservative values have dominated the practice of criminal and juvenile justice. Thus, it should come as no surprise that the crime control model of criminal justice more closely resembles the actual practice of criminal and juvenile justice in the United States today. At the time Packer wrote and published his book, however, politically liberal values and, thus, the principles and policies of the due process model, dominated the operation of criminal and juvenile justice.

In any event, neither model is likely to completely represent the practices of criminal justice. Even though the current operation of criminal and juvenile justice reflects the dominance of the crime control model, elements of the due process model remain evident. How long this trend will continue is anybody's guess. Many suspect that the American people will eventually get tired of seeing their tax dollars spent on programs and a process that is not providing them with the safety from criminal behavior that they so desperately desire.

However, if Packer's model of criminal justice is correct, a shift in criminal justice practice will come only after a shift in the values held by American political leaders and, of course, American citizens.

Myths about Criminal Justice

THINKING CRITICALLY

1. What do you think are some of the fundamental problems with the crime control model? What are the benefits of this model?

2. What do you think are some of the fundamental problems with the due process model? What are the benefits of this model?

A major theme of this book is to expose and correct misconceptions the American public has about criminal justice. Much of the public's understanding of criminal justice is wrong; it is based on myths. **Myths** are "simplistic and distorted beliefs based upon emotion rather than rigorous analysis" or "at worst . . . dangerous falsifications."[6] More specifically, myths are "credible, dramatic, socially constructed representation[s] of perceived realities that people accept as permanent, fixed knowledge of reality while forgetting (if they were ever aware of it) [their] tentative, imaginative, creative, and perhaps fictional qualities."[7] For example, during the Middle Ages in Europe, people commonly believed that guilt or innocence could be determined through *trial by ordeal*. The accused might have been required to walk barefoot over hot coals, hold a piece of red-hot iron, or walk through fire. The absence of any injury was believed to be a sign from God that the person was innocent. Although we may now wonder how such a distorted and simplistic belief could have been taken as fact and used to determine a person's guilt or innocence, people did not consider the belief a myth during the time that it was official practice. The lesson to be learned from this example is that a belief that is taken as fact at one time may in retrospect be viewed as a myth. In this book, we attempt to place such myths about criminal justice in perspective.[8]

myths Beliefs based on emotion rather than analysis.

Throughout this text, we present generally accepted beliefs about the justice system that can be considered myths because they can be contradicted with facts. In some instances it can be demonstrated that the perpetuation and acceptance of certain myths by the public, politicians, and criminal justice practitioners has contributed to the failure to significantly reduce predatory criminal behavior and to increase peace. It is also possible that acceptance of these myths as accurate representations of reality or as facts results in the waste of billions of dollars in the battle against crime.

1. Identify institutions of social control and explain what makes criminal justice an institution of social control.

Institutions of social control include the family, schools, organized religion, the media, the law, and criminal justice. Such institutions attempt to persuade people to abide by the dominant values of society. Criminal justice is restricted to persuading people to abide by a limited range of social values, the violation of which constitutes crime.

2. Define crime.

The conventional definition of crime is a violation of the criminal law or of the penal code of a political jurisdiction.

3. Describe the purpose of criminal justice.

The purpose of criminal justice is to enforce the criminal law.

4. Distinguish between substantive law and procedural law.

There are two types of criminal law: substantive and procedural. Substantive law is the body of law that defines criminal offenses and their penalties. Substantive laws, which are found in the various penal codes, govern what people legally may and may not do. Examples of substantive laws are those that prohibit and penalize murder, rape, robbery, and other crimes. Procedural law, sometimes called adjective or remedial law, governs the ways in which the substantive laws are to be administered. It covers such subjects as the way suspects can legally be arrested, searched, interrogated, tried, and punished. In other words, procedural law is concerned with due process of law, or the rights of people suspected of or charged with crimes.

5. Summarize how the criminal justice system responds to crime.

The typical criminal justice response to the commission of a crime involves the following: investigation; arrest (if the investigation is successful); booking; the formal charging of the suspect; an initial appearance; a preliminary hearing (for a felony); either indictment by a grand jury followed by arraignment, or arraignment on an information; either a plea bargain or a trial; sentencing; possible appeal; and punishment (if the defendant is found guilty).

6. Describe the standards of proof used in criminal justice and identify the criminal justice activities that correspond to each standard.

The standards of proof, along a continuum of certainty, and the criminal justice activities that correspond to them are as follows. The standard of proof with the least amount of certainty is mere suspicion. Mere suspicion is equivalent to a "gut feeling." With only mere suspicion, law enforcement officers cannot legally even stop a suspect. A standard of proof with greater certainty is reasonable suspicion. It includes the ability to articulate reasons for the suspicion. With reasonable suspicion, a law enforcement officer is legally permitted to stop and frisk a suspect. The standard of proof needed to conduct a search or make an arrest is probable cause. Probable cause is the amount of proof necessary for a reasonably intelligent person to believe that a crime has been committed or that items connected with criminal activity can be found in a particular place. It is also the standard of proof used by judges at initial appearances and preliminary hearings to determine whether there are reasonable grounds to believe a person has committed a crime. The next standard of proof along the continuum of legal certainty is preponderance of evidence, which is evidence that more likely than not outweighs the opposing evidence, or sufficient evidence to overcome doubt or speculation. It is the standard of proof necessary to find a defendant liable in a civil lawsuit, in determining whether the inevitable-discovery rule applies, and in criminal proceedings by which the state must show that the right to counsel has been waived knowingly and intelligently. Next along the continuum is clear and convincing evidence, which is evidence indicating that the thing to be proved is highly probable or reasonably certain. It is the standard of proof in some civil cases and, in federal courts, the standard necessary for a defendant to make a successful claim of insanity. Of greatest certainty is proof beyond a reasonable doubt, which is the standard of proof necessary to find a defendant guilty in a criminal trial. Reasonable doubt is the amount of doubt about a defendant's guilt that a reasonable person might have after carefully examining all the evidence.

7. Point out major differences between Packer's crime control and due process models.

From a political standpoint, the crime control model of criminal justice reflects traditional conservative values, while the due process model embodies traditional liberal values. In the crime control model, the control of criminal behavior is by far the most important function of criminal justice. Consequently, the primary focus of this model is on efficiency in the operation of the criminal justice process. The goal of the due process model, on the other hand, is at least as much to protect the innocent as it is to convict the guilty. Fundamentally, the due process model defends the ideal of personal freedom and its protection, and rests on the assumption that the prevention of tyranny on the part of government and its agents is the most important function of the criminal justice process.

8. Explain how myths about crime and criminal justice affect the criminal justice system.

The acceptance and perpetuation of myths, or simplistic beliefs based on emotion rather than rigorous analysis, can harm the criminal justice system by contributing to the failure to reduce crime and to the waste of money in the battle against crime.

KEY TERMS

institution of social control, p. 4
penal code, p. 4
jurisdiction, p. 4
criminal law, p. 4
substantive law, p. 4
procedural law, p. 5
due process of law, p. 5
misdemeanors, p. 5
felonies, p. 5

arrest, p. 5
booking, p. 5
defendant, p. 8
initial appearance, p. 8
summary trial, p. 8
probable cause, p. 8
bail, p. 8
preliminary hearing, p. 8
grand jury, p. 8

information, p. 9
arraignment, p. 9
plea bargaining, p. 9
bench trial, p. 9
parole, p. 11
mere suspicion, p. 11
reasonable suspicion, p. 12
frisking, p. 12
preponderance of evidence, p. 12

clear and convincing evidence, p. 13
beyond a reasonable doubt, p. 13
crime control model, p. 13
due process model, p. 13
doctrine of legal guilt, p. 15
myths, p. 17

REVIEW QUESTIONS

1. What is an institution of social control?
2. Why is criminal justice sometimes considered society's "last line of defense"?
3. What is the difference between a crime and a tort?
4. What three agencies make up the criminal justice system?
5. What is a jurisdiction?
6. What is the difference between an arrest and a booking?
7. Who decides whether to charge a suspect with a crime?
8. What is the difference between a misdemeanor and a felony?
9. What is a defendant, and when does a suspect become a defendant?

10. What is the difference between an initial appearance and a preliminary hearing?
11. Define bench trial, summary trial, bail, grand jury, arraignment, plea bargaining, and parole.
12. What is frisking, and what standard of proof is necessary for a law enforcement officer to do it?
13. Why does Packer use the metaphors of assembly-line justice and obstacle-course justice to characterize his crime control and due process models of criminal justice?
14. What are the bases (that is, the presumptions or doctrines) of Packer's crime control and due process models of criminal justice?
15. What is a lesson to be learned from myths about criminal justice?

1. Criminal Justice in the Movies There are numerous science fiction movies or videos that depict criminal justice in the future. Examples are *Blue Thunder, Escape from New York, Demolition Man, Blade Runner, Minority Report,* and the *RoboCop series.* Watch one or more of those movies or videos, and consider how plausible they seem. Have any of the innovations of these futuristic justice systems become a part of the current American justice system?

2. Crime Control versus Due Process Read a book-length treatment of a criminal case and identify the features of the case that exemplify elements of both the crime control model and the due process model. Decide which one of Packer's two models of criminal justice best describes the case as a whole. Examples of books that describe criminal cases are Truman Capote's *In Cold Blood,* Vincent Bugliosi's *Helter Skelter,* Norman Mailer's *The Executioner's Song,* and Hal Higdon's *The Crime of the Century: The Leopold and Loeb Case.*

1. Criminal Justice in Other Countries Learn about the criminal justice systems of other countries by visiting the Web site of the U.S. Justice Department's *The World Factbook of Criminal Justice Systems* at www.ojp.usdoj.gov/bjs/abstract/wfcj.htm.

2. Criminal Law Learn more about the criminal law by visiting the Web site of the Legal Information Institute of the Cornell Law School at www.law.cornell.edu/wex/index.php/Criminal_law.

1. Plea Bargaining Shirley Smith pleaded guilty to third-degree murder after admitting she had put rat poison in drinks her husband ingested at least 12 times during the course of their 13-month marriage. Sentenced to a maximum of 20 years in prison, she would have to serve at least 10 years before she could be considered for parole. The prosecutor defended the plea bargain against much public criticism. The prosecutor claimed that the costs of a murder trial and subsequent appeals were not paramount. However, the prosecutor did acknowledge that the case could have been the most expensive in county history, exhausted his entire $2 million budget for the fiscal year, and required a tax increase to cover the costs. As an elected official, the prosecutor attempted to seek justice while exercising a sense of fiscal responsibility.

a. Do you think the prosecutor made the correct decision to plea bargain? Defend your answer.

b. In potentially expensive cases, should the prosecutor seek a referendum on the matter (to determine whether residents are willing to pay additional taxes to try a defendant rather than accept a plea bargain)?

2. Standards of Proof A police officer, on a downtown beat that he had been patrolling for many years, observed two strangers on a street corner. He saw them proceed alternately back and forth along an identical route, pausing to stare in the same store window, which they did for a total of about 24 times. Each completion of the route was followed by a conference between the two on a corner, at one of which they were joined by a third man who left swiftly. Suspecting the two men of "casing a job, a stickup," the officer followed them and saw them rejoin the third man a couple of blocks away in front of a store. The officer approached the three, identified himself as a police officer, and asked their names. The men "mumbled something," whereupon the police officer spun one of them around, patted down his outside clothing, and found a pistol in his overcoat pocket, but he was unable to remove it. The officer ordered the three men into the store. He removed the one man's overcoat, took out the revolver, and ordered the three men to face the wall with their hands raised.

He patted down the outer clothing of the other two men and seized a revolver from the outside overcoat pocket of one of them. He did not put his hands under the outer garments of the third man because he discovered nothing in his pat-down that might have been a weapon, or under the outer garments of the other two men until he felt the guns. The police officer transported the three men to the police station, where the two with revolvers were charged with carrying concealed weapons. Their defense attorney moved to suppress the weapons.

a. If you were the judge, would you grant the defense motion to suppress the weapons as evidence? Why or why not?

To access more information and resources, including study questions, chapter summaries, and links, go to: www.mhhe.com/bohm1.

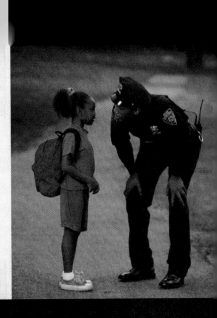

PART TWO

LAW ENFORCEMENT

HISTORY · OF CIVIC · SERVICES
IN THE · CITY · OF · NEW · YORK

Stadt Huys

POLICE   **No. 1**

1658

On October 4, 1658 a paid Rattle Watch of eight men to do the duty from 9 o'clock at night until morning drum beat was established, the duty being imposed upon each of the citizens by turns, and each householder was taxed 15 stivers for its support.

Thief

Felon

The Rattle Watch

CHAPTER TWO

HISTORY AND STRUCTURE OF AMERICAN LAW ENFORCEMENT

CHAPTER OUTLINE

CHAPTER OBJECTIVES

After completing this chapter, you should be able to:

1. Briefly describe the jurisdictional limitations of American law enforcement.

2. Trace the English origins of American law enforcement.

3. Discuss the early development of American law enforcement.

4. Describe the major developments that have occurred in American policing.

5. Describe the structure of American law enforcement.

6. Explain the relationship between the FBI and the Department of Homeland Security.

7. Discuss the development and growth of private security in the United States.

jurisdiction The right or authority of a justice agency to act in regard to a particular subject matter, territory, or person.

The Limited Authority of American Law Enforcement

The United States has almost 18,000 public law enforcement agencies at the federal, state, and local levels of government. The vast majority of those agencies, however, are local, serving municipalities, townships, villages, and counties. The authority of each agency—whether it is the FBI, a state highway patrol, or a county sheriff's department—is carefully limited by law. The territory within which an agency may operate is also restricted. The city police, for example, may not patrol or answer calls for service outside the city's boundaries unless cooperative pacts have been developed. **Jurisdiction,** which is defined as a specific geographical area, also means the right or authority of a justice agency to act in regard to a particular subject matter, territory, or person. It includes the laws a particular police agency is permitted to enforce and the duties it is allowed to perform. The Oklahoma Highway Patrol, for example, has investigative and enforcement responsibilities only in traffic matters, while the Kentucky State Police have a broader jurisdiction that includes

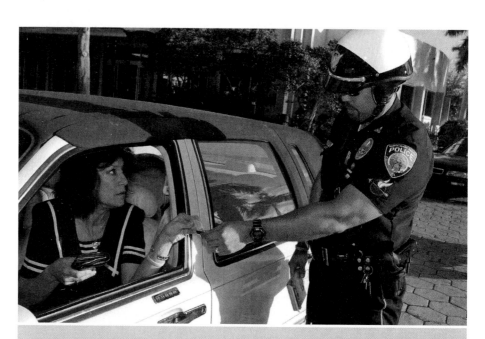

The only police contact most citizens have is in a traffic situation in a local or state jurisdiction. *Should citizens have more contact with the police in non–law enforcement situations? Why or why not?*

the authority to conduct criminal investigations throughout the state. Each of the 69 federal law enforcement agencies, large and small, has a specific jurisdiction, although one criminal event may involve crimes that give several federal agencies concurrent jurisdiction. For example, in a bank robbery, if mail of any sort is taken, both the Postal Inspection Service and the FBI are likely to investigate the case.

Beyond the statutes that create and direct law enforcement agencies, the procedural law derived from U.S. Supreme Court decisions also imposes limitations on the authority of those agencies. Giving arrested suspects the familiar *Miranda* warnings before questioning is a good example of the Court's role in limiting the authority of the police. In addition, police civilian review boards, departmental policies and procedures, and civil liability suits against officers who have abused their authority curtail the power of the police in the United States.

Thus, there is a great difference between law enforcement with limited authority, operating under the rule of law in a democratic nation, and law enforcement in countries where the law is by decree and the police are simply a tool of those in power. Even in comparison with other democratic nations of the world, however, the United States has remarkably more police agencies that operate under far more restrictions on their authority. To understand the origin of those unique qualities of law enforcement in the United States, it is necessary to look first at the history of law enforcement in England, the nation that provided the model for most of American criminal justice.

THINKING CRITICALLY

Why do you think it is important that law enforcement agencies have limited authority?

English Roots

If you are the victim of a crime, you might expect that a uniformed patrol officer will respond quickly to your call and that a plainclothes detective will soon follow up on the investigation. Because there are thousands of police departments in local communities across the nation, you might also take for granted that the police handling your case are paid public servants employed by your city or county. Such was not always the case in the United States—nor in England, where the basic concepts of American law enforcement and criminal justice originated. The criminal justice system in England took hundreds of years to develop, but eventually the idea arose of a locally controlled uniformed police force with follow-up plainclothes investigators.

THE TITHING SYSTEM

Before the twelfth century in England, justice was primarily a private matter based on revenge and retribution.[1] Victims of a crime had to pursue perpetrators without assistance from the king or his agents. Disputes were often settled by blood feuds, in which families would wage war on each other.

By the twelfth century, a system of group protection had begun to develop. Often referred to as the **tithing system** or the frankpledge system, it afforded some improvements over past practices. Ten families, or a *tithing*, were required to become a group and agree to follow the law, keep the peace in their areas, and bring law violators to justice. Over even larger areas, 10 tithings were grouped together to form a *hundred*, and one or several hundreds

tithing system A private self-help protection system in early medieval England, in which a group of 10 families, or a tithing, agreed to follow the law, keep the peace in their areas, and bring law violators to justice.

shire reeve In medieval England, the chief law enforcement officer in a territorial area called a shire; later called the sheriff.

posses Groups of able-bodied citizens of a community, called into service by a sheriff or constable to chase and apprehend offenders.

constable-watch system A system of protection in early England in which citizens, under the direction of a constable, or chief peacekeeper, were required to guard the city and to pursue criminals.

constable The peacekeeper in charge of protection in early English towns.

constituted a *shire*, which was similar to a modern American county. The shire was under the direction of the **shire reeve** (later called the *sheriff*), the fore-runner of the American sheriff. The shire reeve received some assistance from elected constables at the town and village levels, who organized able-bodied citizens into **posses** to chase and apprehend offenders.[2] County law enforcement agencies in the United States still sometimes use posses to apprehend law violators. The Maricopa County (Arizona) Sheriff's Department, for example, has a 3,000-member volunteer posse, whose members are trained and often former deputies.[3]

THE CONSTABLE-WATCH SYSTEM

The Statute of Winchester, passed in 1285, formalized the **constable-watch system** of protection. The statute provided for one man from each parish to be selected as **constable**, or chief peacekeeper. The statute further granted constables the power to draft citizens as watchmen and require them to guard the city at night. Watchmen were not paid for their efforts and, as a result, were often found sleeping or sitting in a pub rather than performing their duties. In addition, the statute required all male citizens between the ages of 15 and 60 to maintain weapons and to join in the *hue and cry*, meaning to come to the aid of the constable or the watchman when either called for help. If they did not come when called, the male citizens were subject to criminal penalties for aiding the offender. This system of community law enforcement lasted well into the 1700s.

Two features of this system are worthy of note. First, the people were the police, and second, the organization of the protection system was local. These two ideas were transported to the American colonies centuries later.

THE BOW STREET RUNNERS

In 1748, Henry Fielding, a London magistrate, founded a group of professional law enforcement agents to apprehend criminals and recover stolen property in the entertainment district of London, known as Bow Street Covent Garden. This publicly funded detective force, named the Bow Street Runners, was by far the most effective official law enforcement organization of its day. Efforts to duplicate it in other parts of London proved unsuccessful, but Fielding's work in organizing the first British detective force, and his writing addressing the shortcomings of the criminal justice system, had a great deal of influence. They helped pave the way for a more professional and better-organized response to the crime problems that were dramatically increasing in London by the end of the eighteenth century.[4]

THE LONDON METROPOLITAN POLICE

Because of the Industrial Revolution, urban populations in cities like London swelled with an influx of people from the countryside looking for work in factories. A major result of this social transformation was that England began experiencing increasing poverty, public disorder, and crime. There was no clear consensus about what to do. Several efforts to establish a central police force for London had been opposed by people who believed that police of any kind were a throwback to the absolute power formerly wielded by English kings. Parliament eventually responded, in 1829, with the London Metropolitan Police Act. It created a 1,000-officer police force with professional standards to replace the patchwork of community law enforcement systems then in use. Members of the London Police became known as *bobbies* or *peelers*,

Henry Fielding

Henry Fielding, founder of the Bow Street Runners, is perhaps better known for his literary accomplishments. His most famous work is *Tom Jones*, which first appeared in 1749 and is considered by many literary scholars as the first "satisfactory" novel written in English.

Source: William H. McNeill, History Handbook of Western Civilization (Chicago: The University of Chicago Press, 1965), p. 526.

TABLE 2.1	Robert Peel's Principles of Policing

1. The police must be stable, efficient, and organized along military lines.
2. The police must be under governmental control.
3. The absence of crime will best prove the efficiency of police.
4. The distribution of crime news is essential.
5. The deployment of police strength both by time and area is essential.
6. No quality is more indispensable to a policeman than a perfect command of temper; a quiet, determined manner has more effect than violent action.
7. Good appearance commands respect.
8. The securing and training of proper persons is at the root of efficiency.
9. Public security demands that every police officer be given a number.
10. Police headquarters should be centrally located and easily accessible to the people.
11. Policemen should be hired on a probationary basis.
12. Police records are necessary to the correct distribution of police strength.

after Robert Peel, the British Home Secretary who had prodded Parliament to create the police force.

To ensure discipline, the London Police were organized according to military rank and structure and were under the command of two magistrates, who were later called commissioners. According to Peel, the main function of the police was to prevent crime, not by force but by preventive patrol of the community. Londoners, who resented such close scrutiny, did not at first welcome this police presence in the community. Eventually, though, the bobbies (the term was originally derogatory) showed that the police could have a positive effect on the quality of life in the community. Peel's military approach to policing, as well as some of his other principles, remain in effect today throughout the world. **Peel's Principles of Policing** are outlined in Table 2.1.[5]

THINKING CRITICALLY

Do you think any of the early English systems of law enforcement (e.g., tithing) could work today? Why or why not?

Peel's Principles of Policing A dozen standards proposed by Robert Peel, the author of the legislation resulting in the formation of the London Metropolitan Police Department. The standards are still applicable to today's law enforcement.

The London Metropolitan Police discover another victim of Jack the Ripper. *What do you suppose were some of the unique problems encountered by the first "bobbies" or "peelers"?*

The Development of American Law Enforcement

The United States has more police departments than any other nation in the world. The major reason for this is that local control is highly regarded in the United States. Thus, like many other services, even small communities that can barely afford police service provide it locally. This practice is primarily responsible for the disparity in the quality of American police personnel and service. The struggle to improve American law enforcement began even before formal police departments came into existence.

EARLY AMERICAN LAW ENFORCEMENT

The chance for a better life, free of government intervention, was key in the decision of many colonists to cross the Atlantic and settle in the New World. American colonists from England brought with them the constable-watch system with which they were familiar, if not completely satisfied. Boston established a night watch as early as 1634. Except for the military's intervention in major disturbances, the watch system, at least in the cities, was the means of preventing crime and apprehending criminals for the next two centuries. As in England, the people were the police. Citizens could pay for watch replacements, and often the worst of the lot ended up protecting the community. In fact, Boston and other cities frequently deployed the most elderly citizens and occasionally sentenced minor offenders to serve on the watch.[6] Later, in rural and southern areas of the country, the office of sheriff was established and the power of the posse was used to maintain order and apprehend offenders. In essence, two forms of protection began to evolve—the watch in the villages, towns, and cities and the sheriff in the rural areas, unincorporated areas, and counties. Communities in the North often had both systems.

LAW ENFORCEMENT IN THE CITIES

As had happened in England, the growth of the Industrial Revolution lured people away from the farms to cities. Large groups of newcomers, sometimes immigrants from other countries, settled near factories. Factory workers put in long days, often in unsafe and unhealthy working conditions. Some workers organized strikes, seeking better working conditions, but the strikes were quickly suppressed. As the populations of cities swelled, living conditions in some areas became overcrowded and unhealthy.

Major episodes of urban violence occurred in the first half of the nineteenth century because of the social and economic changes transforming American cities. Racial and ethnic tensions often reached a boiling point, resulting in mob disturbances that lasted for days. The drinking establishments located throughout working-class districts of cities were particular sources of trouble. Regular heavy drinking led to fights, brawls, and even full-scale riots.

Unlike London, which organized its police force in 1829, American citizens resisted the formation of police departments, relying instead on the constable-watch system, whose members lit streetlights, patrolled the streets to maintain order, and arrested some suspicious people. Constables often had daytime duties, which included investigating health hazards, carrying out orders of the court, clearing the streets of debris, and apprehending criminals against whom complaints had been filed. Neither the night watch nor the constables tried to prevent or discover crime, nor did they wear any kind of

The "Leatherheads"

In Dutch-influenced New York in the seventeenth century, the first paid officers on the night watch were known as *leatherheads* because they wore leather helmets similar in appearance to the helmets worn by today's firefighters. The leatherheads were not known for their attention to duty and often spent entirely too much of their watch schedule inside.

Source: Carl Sifakis, "Leatherheads: First New York Police," *The Encyclopedia of American Crimes* (New York: Smithmark Publishers, Inc., 1992).

uniform. This weak protection system was unable to contain the increasing level of lawlessness.

MUNICIPAL POLICE FORCES In 1844, New York City combined its day and night watches to form the first paid, unified police force in the United States. Close ties developed between the police and local political leaders. As with the first police in London, citizens were suspicious of the constant presence of police officers in their neighborhoods. Also, citizens had little respect for the New York police because they thought they were political hacks, appointed by local officials who wanted to control the police for their own gain. During the next several years, the struggle to control the police in New York built to a fever pitch.[7]

In 1853, the New York state legislature formed the Municipal Police Department, but within 4 years that force was so corrupt from taking bribes to overlook crime that the legislature decided to abolish it. It was replaced by the Metropolitan Police, which was administered by five commissioners appointed by the governor. The commissioners then selected one superintendent. Each commissioner was to oversee the oth-

A street arrest in 1878 Manhattan, New York. *What problems did the police of this era encounter?*

ers, as well as the superintendent, and keep them all honest. The new structure was an improvement, in the minds of the legislature, that would prevent corruption in the top level of the department. But when the Metropolitan Police Board called on Mayor Fernando Wood to abolish the Municipal Police, he refused. Even after New York's highest court upheld a decision to disband the Municipals, the mayor refused. The Metropolitans even tried to arrest Mayor Wood, but that failed attempt resulted in a pitched battle between the two police forces. When the National Guard was called in, Mayor Wood submitted to arrest but was immediately released on bail.

During the summer of 1857, the two police forces often fought over whether to arrest certain criminals. A particularly troubling practice was one police force's releasing from custody the criminals arrested by the other force. Lawbreakers operated freely during the dispute between the two police forces. Criminal gangs had a free hand to commit robberies and burglaries during most of that summer. The public became enraged over this neglect of duty and the increased danger on the streets of New York City. Only when another court order upheld the decision to disband the Municipal Police did Mayor Wood finally comply.

Following the course charted by New York City, other large cities in the United States soon established their own police departments. In 1855, Boston combined its day and night watches to form a city police department. By the end of the decade, police departments had been formed in many major cities east of the Mississippi. The duties of the officers did not vary substantially from the duties of those who had served on the watch. After the Civil War, however, peace officers began to take on the trappings of today's police. They began to wear uniforms, carry nightsticks, and even carry firearms, although many citizens resisted giving this much authority to the police.

TANGLE OF POLITICS AND POLICING Until the 1920s in most American cities, party politics prevented the development of professional police departments.

Local political leaders understood that controlling the police was a means of maintaining their own political power and of allowing criminal friends and political allies to violate the law with impunity. In fact, in some cities, the police were clearly extensions of the local party machine, which attempted to dominate all activity in a community. If local politicians gave police applicants a job, it became the hired officers' job to get out the vote so that the politicians could keep their positions. The system was so corrupt in some cities that police officers bought their jobs, their promotions, and their special assignments. In collaboration with local politicians, but often on their own, the police were more than willing to ignore violations of the law if the lawbreakers gave them money, valuables, or privileges.

A BRIEF HISTORY OF BLACKS IN POLICING For most of American history blacks who have wanted to be police officers have faced blatant discrimination and have generally been denied the opportunity.[8] The first black police officers in the United States were "free men of color." They were hired around 1805 to serve as members of the New Orleans city watch system. They were hired primarily because other people did not want the job. In addition to serving on the watch, they were responsible for catching runaway slaves and generally policing black slaves in New Orleans.

By 1830, policing had become more important in New Orleans, and the "free men of color" lost their jobs on the city police force to others who wanted them. Not until after the Civil War were black Americans allowed to be police officers again. During Reconstruction, black Americans were elected to political office and hired as police officers throughout the South. This did not last long. By 1877, the backlash to Reconstruction drove black Americans and their white Republican allies from elective offices, and black police

By the early 1900s, most American cities had organized, uniformed police forces similar to the police force of Newport, Rhode Island, pictured circa 1910. *How do current police officers differ from those depicted in the photo?*

officers throughout the South lost their jobs. By 1890, most southern cities had all-white police departments. The few black police officers in the southern cities that retained them generally could not arrest white people and were limited to patrolling only areas and communities where other black Americans lived. By 1910, there were fewer than 600 black police officers in the entire United States, and most of them were employed in northern cities.

It was not until the 1940s and 1950s that black police officers began to be hired again in most southern cities. They were hired primarily to patrol black communities, to prevent crime, and to improve race relations. Still, few black Americans ever rose to command positions in their departments. Indeed, prior to the 1950s, only two black Americans had ever been promoted to the command position of captain: Octave Rey of New Orleans and John Scott of Chicago. Both served relatively short tenures in the position: Rey from 1868 to 1877 and Scott from 1940 to 1946.

LAW ENFORCEMENT IN THE STATES AND ON THE FRONTIER

The development of law enforcement on the state level and in the frontier territories was often peculiar to the individual location. Without large population centers that required the control of disorderly crowds, law enforcement was more likely to respond to specific situations—for example, by rounding up cattle rustlers or capturing escaped slaves. Still, out of this kind of limited law enforcement activity, the basic organizational structure of police units with broader responsibilities was born.

SOUTHERN SLAVE PATROLS In the South, the earliest form of policing was the plantation **slave patrols.**[9] They have been called "the first distinctively American police system."[10] The slave patrols were created to enforce the infamous slave codes, the first of which was enacted by the South Carolina legislature in 1712. Eventually all the Southern colonies enacted slave codes. The slave codes protected the slaveholders' property rights in human beings, while holding slaves responsible for their crimes and other acts that were not crimes if committed by free persons. Under some slave codes, enslaved people could not hold meetings, leave the plantation without permission from the master, travel without a pass, learn to read and write, carry a firearm, trade, or gamble. Both the slave codes and the slave patrols were created in part because of a fear of bloody slave revolts, such as had already occurred in Virginia and other parts of the South.

Generally consisting of three men on horseback who covered a beat of 15 square miles, a slave patrol was responsible for catching runaway slaves, preventing slave uprisings, and maintaining discipline among the slaves. To maintain discipline, the patrols often whipped and terrorized black slaves who were caught after dark without passes. The slave patrols also helped enforce the laws prohibiting literacy, trade, and gambling among slaves. Although the law required that all white males perform patrol services, the large plantation owners usually hired poor, landless whites to substitute for them. The slave patrols lasted until the end of the Civil War, in 1865. After the Civil War, the Ku Klux Klan served the purpose of controlling blacks just as the slave patrols had before the Civil War.

The plantation slave patrols have been called "the first distinctively American police system." *Have any elements of the slave patrols influenced contemporary American policing? If yes, what are they?*

slave patrols The earliest form of policing in the South. They were a product of the slave codes.

FYI

Nat Turner Rebellion

Perhaps the most publicized slave revolt was the Nat Turner Rebellion of 1831 in Virginia. Turner and five other slaves killed Joseph Travis, Turner's owner, and his family. Approximately 70 more rebels joined Turner, whose immediate plan was to capture the county seat, where munitions were stored. Turner was unsuccessful in his plan, but during the siege, he and his rebels killed 57 whites. Turner was tried, convicted, and hanged, along with 16 other rebels. In response to the revolt, white mobs lynched nearly 200 blacks, most of whom were innocent.

Source: John Duff and Peter Mitchell, *The Nat Turner Rebellion: The Historical Event and the Modern Controversy* (New York: Harper & Row, 1971).

FRONTIER LAW ENFORCEMENT In the remote and unpopulated areas of the nation, and particularly on the expanding frontier, justice was often in the hands of the people in a more direct way. Vigilantism was often the only way that people could maintain order and defend themselves against renegades and thugs.[11] Even when formal law enforcement procedures were provided by the sheriff or a marshal, courts in many communities were held only once or twice a year, leaving many cases unresolved. This idea of self-protection remains very popular in the South and the West, where firearms laws in many states permit people to carry loaded weapons in a vehicle, or even on their persons if they have completed a qualification and licensing procedure.

STATE POLICE AGENCIES Self-protection did not prove sufficient as populations and their accompanying problems increased. As early as 1823, mounted militia units in Texas protected American settlers throughout that territory. Called *rangers,* these mounted militia fought Native Americans and Mexican bandits. The Texas Rangers were officially formed in 1835, and the organization remains in existence today as an elite and effective unit of the Texas Department of Public Safety.[12]

The inefficiency and unwillingness of some sheriffs and constables to control crime, along with an emerging crime problem that exceeded the local community's ability to deal with it, prompted other states to form state law enforcement agencies. In 1905, Pennsylvania established the first modern state law enforcement organization with the authority to enforce the law statewide, an authority that made it unpopular in some communities where enforcement of state laws had been decidedly lax.[13] The advent of the automobile and the addition of miles of state highways extended the authority of state police agencies. Some form of state law enforcement agency existed in every state by the 1930s.

CJ ONLINE

Texas Rangers
To learn more about the history of the Texas Rangers, visit the Texas Ranger Hall of Fame and Museum Web site at **www.texasranger.org/Index.htm.** *Why do you think the Texas Rangers have elite status?*

The Texas Rangers, organized in the early 1800s to fight Native Americans, patrol the Mexican border, and track down rustlers, were the first form of state police. *Why and how do you think the Rangers have endured for so long?*

PROFESSIONALISM AND REFORM

You will recall that the people themselves were once the police, as they served on the watch. Being an adult citizen was about the only qualification. No training was required, and it was common practice for citizens who did not want to serve to hire replacements, sometimes hiring sentenced offenders. Because of the few services and the little order the watch provided, not much else seems to have been required. Even when organized police forces were developed in the 1840s and 1850s in the United States, qualifications for the job mattered little beyond the right political connections or the ability to purchase one's position outright.

Not until the latter part of the nineteenth century did qualifications for the position of police officer begin to evolve. In the 1880s, Cincinnati posted two qualifications to be a police officer.[14] First, an applicant had to be a person of high moral character—an improvement over earlier times. Three citizens had to vouch for the applicant's character at a city council meeting. If deemed acceptable by the council, the applicant was immediately taken to a gymnasium and tested for the second qualification, foot speed.

Both Cincinnati and New York began police academies in the 1880s, but the curriculum was meager and recruits were not required to pass any examinations to prove their competence. The lack of adequate standards and training for police officers was recognized as a major stumbling block to improved policing. A group of reformers within policing allied themselves with the Progressives, a movement for political, social, and economic change. Among the reformers was August Vollmer, who became chief of police of Berkeley, California, in 1909. During his tenure as chief from 1909 to 1932, Vollmer attempted to create a professional model of policing. With Vollmer and a succession of internal reformers who followed, a new era of professional policing began.

Vollmer and his followers advocated training and education as two of the key ingredients of professionalism in policing. He also believed strongly that the police should stay out of politics and that politics should stay out of policing. Vollmer believed that the major function of the police was fighting crime, and he saw great promise in professionalizing law enforcement by emphasizing that role.[15] He began to hire college graduates for the Berkeley Police Department, and he held college classes on police administration.

Within a few decades, this professional model, sometimes called the reform model, had taken root in police departments across the country. To eliminate political influences, gain control of officers, and establish crime-fighting priorities, departments made major changes in organization and operation. Those changes included the following:

- Narrowing of the police function from social service and the maintenance of order to law enforcement only.
- Centralization of authority, with the power of precinct captains and commanders checked.
- Creation of specialized, centrally based crime-fighting units, as for burglary.
- A shift from neighborhood foot patrol to motorized patrol.
- Implementation of patrol allocation systems based on such variables as crime rates, calls for service, and response times.
- Reliance on technology, such as police radios, to both control and aid the policing function.
- Recruitment of police officers through psychological screening and civil service testing.
- Specific training in law enforcement techniques.

CONFLICTING ROLES

Throughout their history, Americans have never been sure precisely what role they want their police officers to play. Much of the ambivalence has to do with American heritage, which makes many Americans suspicious of government authority. At one time or another, local police have acted as peacekeepers, social workers, crime fighters, and public servants, completing any task that was requested. Often, the police have been asked to take on all those roles simultaneously.

For most of the nineteenth century, distrust of government was so strong and the need to maintain order in the cities so critical that the police operated almost exclusively as peacekeepers and social service agents, with little or no concern for enforcing the law beyond what was absolutely necessary to maintain tranquility.[16] In this role, the police in many American cities administered the laws that provided for public relief and support of the poor. They fed the hungry and housed the homeless at the request of the politicians who controlled them. Later, other social service agents, such as social workers, began to replace them, and a reform effort developed to remove policing from the direct control of corrupt politicians. As a result, the police began to focus on crime-fighting as early as the 1920s. Having the police enforce the law fairly and objectively was thought to be a major way of professionalizing law enforcement. This approach also fit the professional model of policing advocated by Vollmer and other reformers.

By the end of the 1960s, strong doubts about the role of the police emerged again. The role they had been playing encouraged them to ferret out crime and criminals through such practices as aggressive patrol, undercover operations, and electronic surveillance. In some neighborhoods, the police came to be viewed as armies of occupation. Some confrontations between police and

Brutal tactics by some police officers to suppress civil rights protests during the 1960s led to calls for improved standards of police conduct and training. *Have new standards of conduct and training ended brutal police tactics?*

citizens resulted in violence. The civil rights movement produced a series of demonstrations and civil disorders in more than 100 cities across America, beginning in 1964. As in the labor struggles of the late nineteenth and early twentieth centuries, the police were called in to restore order. Some police officers suppressed the demonstrations with brutal tactics. The anti–Vietnam War movement during the 1960s sparked protests all over the country, especially on college campuses. Again, police officers were called upon to maintain and sometimes to restore order. Thousands of students were sprayed with tear gas, and some were beaten and even killed by police.

By the end of the 1960s, it was clear that police standards and training had to be improved. To many observers, fast response and proactive patrols did not seem effective in reducing crime, and officers increasingly were seeing their work world through the windshield of a cruiser. The likelihood of establishing rapport with the people they served was remote as officers dashed from one crime scene to another.

Four blue-ribbon commissions studied the police in the United States. The names of the four commissions and the years in which they released their reports are as follows:

> National Advisory Commission on Civil Disorders, 1967.
> President's Commission on Law Enforcement and the Administration of Justice, 1967.
> National Advisory Commission on Criminal Justice Standards and Goals, 1973.
> American Bar Association's Standards Relating to Urban Police Function, 1973.

All four reports made the same major recommendations: They pointed out the critical role police officers play in American society, called for careful selection of law enforcement officers, and recommended extensive and continuous training. The reports also recommended better police management and supervision, as well as internal and external methods of maintaining integrity in police departments.

In an attempt to follow many of the specific recommendations of the reform commissions' reports, police selection became an expensive and elaborate process. It was designed to identify candidates who had the qualities to be effective law enforcement officers: integrity, intelligence, interpersonal skills, mental stability, adequate physical strength, and agility. Attempts were also made to eliminate discriminatory employment practices that had prevented minorities and women from entering and advancing in law enforcement. Finally, it became more common for police officers to attend college, and some police agencies began to set a minimum number of college credit hours as an employment qualification.

COMMUNITY POLICING

By the 1970s, research began to show that a rapid response to crime does not necessarily lead to more arrests and that having more police officers using methods made popular under the professional or reform model does not significantly reduce crime.[17] What was emerging was the view that unattended disorderly behavior in neighborhoods—such as unruly groups of youths, prostitution, vandalism, drunk and disorderly

Myth | Fact

Myth: Random patrol, as opposed to directed patrol, reduces crime. It is important to have police out in patrol cars, scouting neighborhoods and business districts.

Fact: There is not much value to such random patrols other than perhaps helping people feel safe. They would probably feel even safer if the police were walking a beat. However, little research supports the idea that officers who ride around for 3 to 5 hours of their shifts are repressing crime. Even being available to respond to calls from the public is not a strong argument for such patrols. Only a small percentage of reported crimes and other incidents require a rapid response.

vagrants, and aggressive street people—is a signal to more serious criminals that residents do not care what goes on in their community and that the criminals can move in and operate with impunity.

The 1970s and 1980s saw some experimentation with community- and neighborhood-based policing projects.[18] Those projects got mixed results, and many were abandoned because of high costs, administrative neglect, and citizen apathy. However, higher crime rates, continued community deterioration, and recognition of the failure to control crime caused law enforcement to again question the role it was playing. The enforcer role still was not working well enough. It appeared senseless simply to respond to calls for service and arrive at scenes of crime and disorder time and time again without resolving the problems or having any lasting effect on the lives of the residents of the community. Out of this failure and frustration came the contemporary concept of **community policing.**

community policing A contemporary approach to policing that actively involves the community in a working partnership to control and reduce crime.

Under a community policing philosophy, the people of a community and the police form a lasting partnership, in which they jointly approach the problems of maintaining order, providing services, and fighting crime.[19] If the police show they care about the minor problems associated with community disorder, two positive changes are likely to occur: citizens will develop better relations with the police as they turn to them for solutions to the disorder, and criminals will see that residents and the police have a commitment to keeping all crime out of the neighborhood. Once again, the emphasis has shifted from fighting crime to keeping peace and delivering social services. The goal is eradicating the causes of crime in a community, not simply responding to symptoms.

In the early 1990s, many communities across the nation began implementing community policing strategies. Community policing called for a shift from incident-based crime fighting to a problem-oriented approach, in which police would be prepared to handle a broad range of troublesome situations in a city's neighborhoods. There was greater emphasis on foot patrol so that officers could come to know and be known by the residents of a neighborhood. Those citizens would then be more willing to help the police identify and solve problems in the neighborhood. Many other aspects of community policing will be discussed more fully in Chapter 3.

THINKING CRITICALLY

1. Which of the major changes in the organization and operation of police departments listed on page 35 do you think brought about the most significant change? Why?
2. What do you think are the key benefits of community policing? Why?

The Structure of American Law Enforcement

Describing American law enforcement and its structure is especially difficult today because of its ongoing restructuring and transformation, from community policing at the local level to the new Department of Homeland Security at the federal level and increasing privatization at all levels. It is also difficult to describe because law enforcement agencies are so diverse. To begin with, you must decide which law enforcement agency you are talking about. For example, Oklahoma Highway Patrol officers cruise the highways and back roads, enforcing traffic laws, investigating accidents, and assisting motorists over seemingly endless miles of paved and unpaved routes. They do not ordinarily investigate criminal violations unless the violations are on state property. In contrast, a sheriff and three deputies in rural Warren County, Georgia, conduct criminal investigations, serve subpoenas, and investigate accidents. In the towns of Astoria, Homer, and Newman, Illinois, only one employee, the chief of police, works in each department, and that person is responsible for all law enforcement, public order, and service duties. About 60 sworn law enforcement officers at the University of Texas in Austin are also a part of American law enforcement.[20]

Altogether, tens of thousands of law enforcement officers at the federal, state, county, and municipal levels protect life and property and serve their respective publics. They are employed by government, private enterprise, and quasi-governmental entities. Their responsibilities are specific and sometimes unique to the kind of organization that employs them. Examples of these organizations are airports, transit authorities, hospitals, and parks.

At the state level, there are highway patrols, bureaus of investigation, park rangers, watercraft officers, and other law enforcement agencies and personnel with limited jurisdictions. Colleges and universities employ police officers, and some of those forces are comparable to many medium-sized police departments in the United States.

At the federal level, there are about 69 law enforcement agencies if all of the small agencies with very specific jurisdictions are included. The Federal Bureau of Investigation (FBI), the U.S. Secret Service, and the Drug Enforcement Administration (DEA) are three of the better-known agencies. The U.S. Marshals Service, the Bureau of Alcohol, Tobacco, Firearms and Explosives (ATF), and U.S. Immigration and Customs Enforcement (ICE) are other federal law enforcement agencies, as are the Internal Revenue Service's Criminal Investigation Division, the U.S. Postal Inspection Service, the U.S. Customs and Border Protection (CBP), and several dozen other agencies. As of September 2004, federal law enforcement agencies employed more than 105,000 full-time personnel authorized to make arrests and carry firearms.[21]

As the aforementioned list of law enforcement agencies suggests, explaining the law enforcement mandate and its execution in the United States is difficult. The structure of American police services is different from those of other countries. Japan and many other nations have only one police department. The

Secret Service
To learn more about the U.S. Secret Service, visit their Web site at **www. treas.gov/usss.** *Based on what you have learned from the Web site, do you think that you would be interested in a career with the Secret Service? Why or why not?*

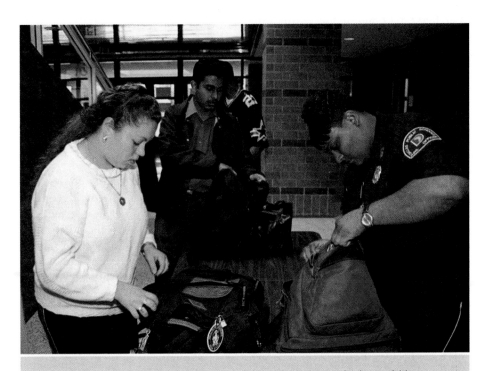

Before entering some schools, students have their bags checked every day by special law enforcement officers with limited jurisdiction. *Is this practice necessary? Why or why not?*

FIGURE 2.1 | Public Law Enforcement Agencies in the United States

The United States has almost 18,000 public law enforcement agencies.

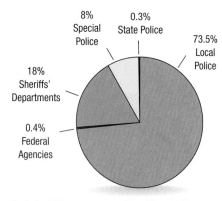

8% Special Police
0.3% State Police
73.5% Local Police
18% Sheriffs' Departments
0.4% Federal Agencies

Does not include 623 county constable offices in Texas.

Source: Calculated from material in Brian A. Reaves and Matthew J. Hickman, *Census of State and Local Law Enforcement Agencies, 2000* (Washington DC: GPO, U.S. Department of Justice, Bureau of Justice Statistics, October 2002); Brian A. Reaves and Timothy C. Hart, *Federal Law Enforcement Officers, 2000* (Washington DC: GPO, U.S. Department of Justice, Bureau of Justice Statistics, July 2001); Matthew J. Hickman and Brian A. Reaves, *Local Police Departments, 2003* (Washington, DC: GPO, U.S. Department of Justice, Bureau of Justice Statistics, May 2006); Brian A. Reaves, *Federal Law Enforcement Officers, 2004* (Washington, DC: GPO, U.S. Department of Justice, Bureau of Justice Statistics, July 2006).

United States has almost 18,000 public law enforcement agencies, and probably more when all the special police jurisdictions in the public sector are counted—including game protection agencies, water conservancies, and mental health institutions. Figure 2.1 summarizes the various law enforcement agencies in the United States.

You have already learned that law enforcement in America is fragmented, locally controlled, and limited in authority; to that, you can also add the terms *structurally* and *functionally different*. Virtually no two police agencies in America are structured alike or function in the same way. Police officers themselves are young and old; well trained and ill prepared; educated and uninformed; full-time and part-time; rural, urban, and suburban; generalists and specialists; paid and volunteer; and public and private. These differences lead to the following generalizations about law enforcement in the United States:

1. The quality of police services varies greatly among states and localities across the nation.
2. There is no consensus on professional standards for police personnel, equipment, and practices.
3. Expenditures for police services vary greatly among communities.
4. Obtaining police services from the appropriate agency is often confusing for crime victims and other clients.

LOCAL POLICING AND ITS DUTIES

If a person knows a law enforcement agent at all, it is probably a local police officer. The officer may have given the person a traffic ticket or investigated an automobile accident. The officer may have conducted a crime prevention survey. Children meet local police officers through Drug Abuse Resistance Education (D.A.R.E.) in public or private schools. Almost everyone has seen the beat cop drive by in a patrol car. Some people have reported thefts or burglaries, but it is doubtful that even they understand what local police officers in America really do, besides what they see on television and in movies.

MUNICIPAL POLICE DEPARTMENTS Municipal police departments come in all sizes, but most of them are small in the number of officers employed. The overwhelming majority of police departments in America employ fewer than 50 sworn officers. Figure 2.2 shows the number of sworn officers in local police agencies in the United States. As shown in Figure 2.2, nearly one-half of all local police departments in the United States employ fewer than 10 officers, and fewer than 1 percent employ more than 1,000 sworn personnel.

What are some of the characteristics of the sworn personnel who occupy the ranks of municipal police agencies in the United States? Most police officers are white males. In 2003, 69.4 percent of full-time sworn officers were white men, down from 78.4 percent in 1997. The larger the police agency, the more likely it is to employ minority officers. Women represented 11.3 percent of all sworn officers in the nation's local police departments in 2003. Figure 2.3 provides a breakdown of police employment in local agencies by gender, race, and ethnicity.

Drug Enforcement

In 2003, 18 percent of local police departments had officers assigned full-time to a special unit for drug enforcement, with 12,212 officers so assigned nationwide. Approximately 23 percent of departments had officers assigned to a multiagency drug task force, with a total of 5,959 officers assigned full-time nationwide.

Source: Matthew J. Hickman and Brian A. Reaves, *Local Police Departments, 2003* (Washington, DC: Bureau of Justice Statistics, 2006), p. 15, Table 30; p. 16, Table 31.

FIGURE 2.2   Number of Sworn Personnel in Local Departments, 2003

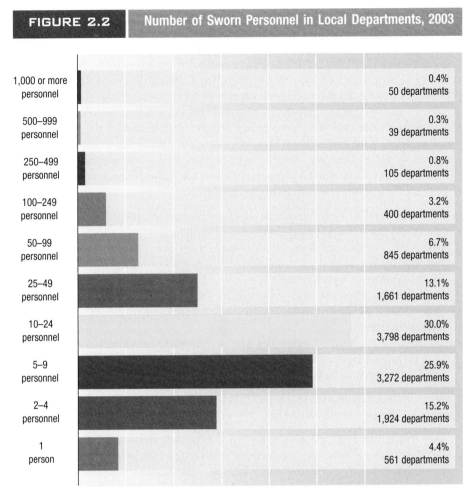

1,000 or more personnel	0.4% 50 departments
500–999 personnel	0.3% 39 departments
250–499 personnel	0.8% 105 departments
100–249 personnel	3.2% 400 departments
50–99 personnel	6.7% 845 departments
25–49 personnel	13.1% 1,661 departments
10–24 personnel	30.0% 3,798 departments
5–9 personnel	25.9% 3,272 departments
2–4 personnel	15.2% 1,924 departments
1 person	4.4% 561 departments

Source: Matthew J. Hickman and Brian A. Reaves, *Local Police Departments, 2003* (Washington, DC: GPO, U.S. Department of Justice, Bureau of Justice Statistics, May 2006).

FIGURE 2.3   Characteristics of Local Full-Time Police Officers

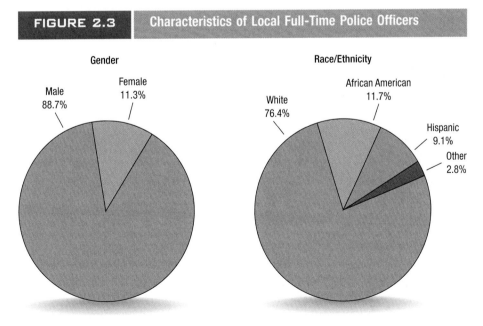

Gender

Male 88.7%
Female 11.3%

Race/Ethnicity

White 76.4%
African American 11.7%
Hispanic 9.1%
Other 2.8%

Source: Matthew J. Hickman and Brian A. Reaves, *Local Police Departments, 2003* (Washington, DC: GPO, U.S. Department of Justice, Bureau of Justice Statistics, May 2006).

First Policewomen

The first woman to have full police power (1905) was Lola Baldwin of Portland, Oregon. The first uniformed policewoman was Alice Stebbins Wells, who was hired by the Los Angeles Police Department in 1910. By 1916, 16 other police departments had hired policewomen as a result of the success in Los Angeles.

Source: Roy Robert, John Crank, and Jack Kuykendall, *Police and Society* (Los Angeles, CA: Roxbury Publishing Company, 1999), pp. 432–33.

Policewomen

It took a long time for policewomen to gain the opportunity to perform the same roles and duties as their male counterparts. From the early 1900s until 1972, when the Equal Employment Opportunity Commission began to assist women police officers in obtaining equal employment status with male officers, policewomen were responsible for protection and crime prevention work with women and juveniles, particularly with girls. The Los Angeles Police Department created the City Mother's Bureau in 1914 and hired policewomen to work with delinquent and predelinquent children whose mothers did not want formal intervention by a law enforcement agency. Policewomen were also used to monitor, investigate, and punish young girls whose behavior flouted social and sexual conventions of the times.

A high school diploma or higher educational achievement was required by 99 percent of the local police departments of the nation in 2003. Eight percent of local police departments in 2003 required some college courses (up from 6 percent in 1990), but only 9 percent of the agencies required recruits to have a minimum of two years of college. Just 1 percent required new recruits to have a 4-year college degree.[22]

LOCAL POLICE DUTIES The local police are the workhorses of the law enforcement system in America. They have many duties and tasks that will never be included in police detective novels or in movies about law enforcement. Their duties have been categorized in several different ways. One general grouping lists these four categories of local police duties:

1. *Law enforcement*—examples are investigating a burglary, arresting a car thief, serving a warrant, or testifying in court.
2. *Order maintenance or peacekeeping*—examples are breaking up a fight, holding back a crowd at a sporting event, or intervening in a domestic dispute before it gets violent.
3. *Service*—examples are taking people to the hospital, escorting funeral processions, delivering mail for city officials, or chasing bats out of a caller's house.
4. *Information gathering*—examples are determining neighborhood reactions to a proposed liquor license in the community, investigating a missing child case, or investigating and reporting on a dangerous road condition.

Some police academies teach recruits the duties of a police officer through the use of the acronym *PEPPAS:*

P—Protect life and property (patrol a business district at night, keep citizens from a fire scene, or recover and return lost property).

E—Enforce the law (ensure traffic laws are obeyed, warn jaywalkers of the inherent danger, make out criminal complaints, or seize illegal weapons).

P—Prevent crime (give home security advice, patrol high crime areas, or work as a D.A.R.E. officer in schools).

P—Preserve the peace (disband disorderly groups, have a visible presence at sporting events, or intervene in neighbor conflicts).

A—Arrest violators (apprehend fleeing suspects, give citations to alcohol permit holders who sell to minors, or conduct drug raids).

S—Serve the public (give directions to travelers, deliver emergency messages, or administer first aid).

Myth Fact

Myth	Fact
The police spend most of their time and resources apprehending law violators and combating crime.	Only about 10 percent of police time and resources is devoted to apprehending law violators and combating crime. Most of their time and resources is spent "keeping the peace," which means maintaining a police presence in the community, for example, by routine patrolling.

There are literally dozens of other duties that the police of a city, town, or village carry out, and much of the work falls into the category of helping out when no one else seems to be available. Because the police are on duty 24 hours a day in nearly every community, they are often called on to perform services that have nothing to do with law enforcement. That round-the-clock availability also significantly affects the structure, work life, and activity of a police agency.

ORGANIZATIONAL STRUCTURE How a police agency is structured depends on the size of the agency, the degree of specialization, the philosophy the leadership has chosen (such as community policing), the political context of the department (the form of municipal government), and the history and preferences of a particular community. Most medium- to large-staffed police

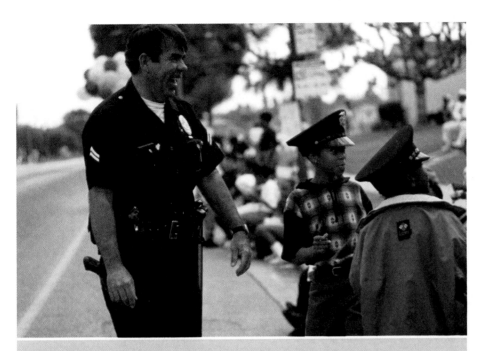

Local police departments, which make up the bulk of law enforcement agencies in America, are responsible for law enforcement, order maintenance, service, and information gathering. *How important is public relations for local police departments? Why?*

agencies are subdivided into patrol, criminal investigation, traffic, juvenile, and technical and support services. Subspecialties include robbery, gangs, training, bombs, property, victims' services, jail, and mounted patrol.

The Dallas (Texas) Police Department, with 2,977 sworn officers and 556 nonsworn employees, is large, sophisticated, and very specialized. For example, it has a separate detective unit for each major category of crime. Evidence technicians collect and preserve evidence during the preliminary investigation of a crime. An entire contingent of officers is assigned to traffic regulation and enforcement duties. Bicycle patrol officers work the popular West End entertainment and restaurant section downtown. The Dallas police even have sworn officers who serve as crime analysts and collect, analyze, map, and report crime data to enable better prevention and repression of crime by means of scientific deployment of officers and other strategies. Figure 2.4 presents the organizational structure of the Dallas Police Department.

Most police agencies in the United States do not have or need elaborate organizational structures. Police officers on the beat are generalists, and when special circumstances arise, such as a homicide or a complex financial investigation, they can usually rely on state bureaus of investigation to assist them. Moreover, local cooperation pacts among departments in a particular region often provide for sharing resources and specialized assistance when needed.

The infrequent need for homicide investigation skills in communities under 30,000 people, for example, makes it impractical to train one or more officers in the methods of conducting a thorough death investigation. An officer so trained might have to wait an entire career to put into practice the acquired skills, and it is most likely that by the time they were needed, the officer would have forgotten them. The lack of a trained specialist for the infrequent complex investigation, however, is one of the major reasons criminal investigation services in small communities are not equal to those in larger police departments.

FIGURE 2.4 Dallas Police Department Organization Chart

The question has been raised whether larger, regional police departments would be more efficient providers of police services, but as you have already discovered, policing in America is a local concern, and that is not likely to change.

The police are organized militarily with regard to accountability, discipline, rank, dress, and decorum. Many people believe that the military structure of a chain of command may be dysfunctional because police work is so varied. Some people believe that a military structure is best suited for situations where the objectives are simple and few, which is not the case in municipal policing. Some commentators think the military structure impedes the flow of communication and the development of good community relations because people are suspicious of the police or even fear them in some neighborhoods. Despite these criticisms, most police departments retain this organizational structure, which originated in the hiring of military leaders as the first police chiefs. Attempts to change the military structure of policing have generally failed. One reason is that police officers have often resisted any type of reorganization.

THE POLITICAL CONTEXT OF POLICING A police department of any size is part of a larger government entity. Municipalities generally operate under one of four forms of municipal government:[23]

> *Strong Mayor-Council*—Voters elect the mayor and the city council; the mayor appoints heads of departments.
> *Weak Mayor-Council*—Voters elect the mayor and the city council; the city council appoints heads of departments.
> *City Manager*—Voters elect the city council and, in some cities, a mayor; the city council selects the city manager, who appoints heads of departments.
> *Commission*—Voters elect a board of commissioners, who become the heads of departments; the commission or the voters may choose one commissioner to be mayor.

As you can see, the forms of municipal government vary in the amount of control citizens have over the municipality's leaders, the source of the executive authority of the chief of police, and the degree of insulation a chief of police has from interference by the executive head of the city (mayor or city manager) or the city council. Each form has advantages and disadvantages. At one time it was thought that city manager government was the system under which the police were most likely to develop professionally, be free of political meddling from city lawmakers, and be insulated from local corruption. Although many progressive and effective police departments operate under a city manager form of government, other municipal forms of government have records of both success and failure in local police effectiveness and integrity.

You have probably noticed from reading newspapers and listening to radio and television that chief executives of local police agencies have different titles, depending on the locale. Popular titles are chief of police (Kansas City), director of police (Dayton, Ohio), and commissioner (New York City).

COUNTY LAW ENFORCEMENT

A substantial portion of law enforcement work in the United States is carried out by sheriffs' departments. In 2003, the nation had 3,061 sheriffs' departments, employing 330,274 full-time personnel. About 53 percent of the personnel were sworn peace officers. Sheriffs frequently employ part-time personnel who work as special deputies, assisting with posses, disasters, county fairs, traffic control, and other duties. Sheriffs' departments represent about 17 percent of all the law enforcement departments in the United States. In 2003, the cost to

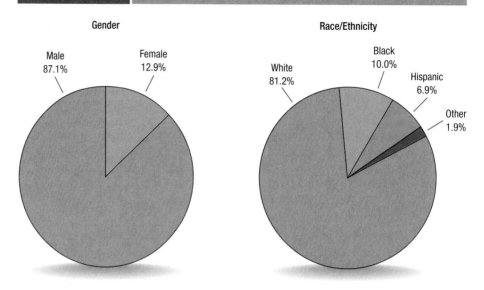

| FIGURE 2.5 | Characteristics of Sheriffs' Personnel, 2003 |

Source: Matthew J. Hickman and Brian A. Reaves, *Sheriffs' Offices, 2003* (Washington, DC: Bureau of Justice Statistics, May 2006).

Female Sheriffs

Before 1992, no woman had ever been elected to the position of sheriff in the United States. The first two were elected in 1992: the first was Jackie Barrett in Fulton County, Georgia, and the second was Judy Pridgen in Saline County, Arkansas.

provide county law enforcement was $22.3 billion, 18 percent more than in 2000 after adjusting for inflation.[24]

Sheriffs' personnel are 81.2 percent white, 10.0 percent black, 6.9 percent Hispanic, and 1.9 percent other. Women make up 12.9 percent of the sworn personnel working for sheriffs' departments.[25] (See Figure 2.5.)

As are most municipal police departments, most sheriffs' departments in America are small. Figure 2.6 shows the number of departments and their respective sizes. More than one-half of all sheriffs' departments employ fewer than 25 sworn personnel.

Sheriffs' departments often have employment qualifications similar to those of municipal police agencies. A high school diploma or higher educational achievement was required by 99 percent of sheriffs' departments in 2003. Four percent of sheriffs' departments in 2003 required some college courses (the same as in 1990), and 5 percent of the departments required recruits to have a 2-year college degree. Fewer than one-half of 1 percent of departments required new recruits to have a 4-year college degree.[26]

COUNTY LAW ENFORCEMENT FUNCTIONS The sheriff and department personnel perform functions that range from investigation to supervision of sentenced offenders. Even in the smallest departments, sheriffs are responsible for investigating crimes and enforcing the criminal and traffic laws of the state. They also perform many civil process services for the court, such as serving summonses, warrants, and various writs. In addition, they provide courtroom security and confine and transport prisoners. The larger the sheriff's department, the more confinement and corrections responsibilities it has. Sheriffs' departments frequently operate the county jail, which houses hundreds and even thousands of prisoners, depending on the particular county. In some counties, the sheriff's department shares law enforcement duties with a separate police department.

POLITICS AND COUNTY LAW ENFORCEMENT Most sheriffs are directly elected and depend on an elected board of county commissioners or supervisors for their funding and some oversight of their operations. Sheriffs generally have

FIGURE 2.6	Number of Sworn Personnel in Sheriffs' Departments, 2003

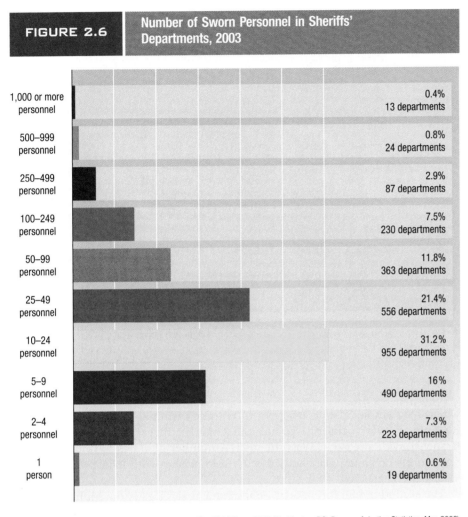

1,000 or more personnel	0.4% 13 departments
500–999 personnel	0.8% 24 departments
250–499 personnel	2.9% 87 departments
100–249 personnel	7.5% 230 departments
50–99 personnel	11.8% 363 departments
25–49 personnel	21.4% 556 departments
10–24 personnel	31.2% 955 departments
5–9 personnel	16% 490 departments
2–4 personnel	7.3% 223 departments
1 person	0.6% 19 departments

Source: Matthew J. Hickman and Brian A. Reaves, *Sheriffs' Offices, 2003* (Washington, DC: Bureau of Justice Statistics, May 2006).

a freer hand in running their agencies than do police chiefs. In many counties, local politics govern the operation of the sheriff's department, and the sheriff must operate as a partisan politician to remain in office. The authority to appoint special deputies and to award patronage jobs contributes to the sheriff's power and influence in a county.

STATE LAW ENFORCEMENT

Filling the complement of law enforcement agencies in a particular state are one or more state law enforcement agencies, which provide criminal and traffic law enforcement, as well as other services peculiar to the needs of that state government. In 2003, the 49 primary state law enforcement agencies (Hawaii has no state police agency) had 82,419 full-time employees, of which 57,611 or 70 percent were full-time sworn officers. Seventeen state agencies employ more than 1,000 personnel. The California Highway Patrol is the largest state law enforcement agency, with nearly 10,000 personnel, of which about two-thirds are sworn officers.[27]

For the most part, each state has chosen one of two models for providing law enforcement services at the state level. The first model is the **state police model,** in which the agency and its officers have essentially the same enforcement powers as local police in the state and can work cases and enforce the law anywhere within the state's boundaries. One of the best-known state police agencies is the Texas Rangers, part of the Texas Department of Public Safety,

state police model A model of state law enforcement services in which the agency and its officers have the same law enforcement powers as local police but can exercise them anywhere within the state.

State police agencies in every state except Hawaii have statewide jurisdiction and may be set up according to state police or highway patrol models. *Are state police agencies necessary? Why or why not?*

highway patrol model A model of state law enforcement services in which officers focus on highway traffic safety, enforcement of the state's traffic laws, and the investigation of accidents on the state's roads, highways, and property.

which also employs state troopers to enforce criminal and traffic laws. The Rangers usually focus on special and complex investigations, such as the Branch Davidian case in Waco in 1993. A number of states have placed some restrictions on state police activities to avoid clashes with local politicians and local police agencies.

The second model for state law enforcement services is the **highway patrol model,** in which officers focus almost exclusively on highway traffic safety, enforcement of the state's traffic laws, and investigation of accidents on the state's roads and highways. Even highway patrols, however, may retain responsibility for investigating criminal violations on state property and in state institutions or for conducting drug interdictions.

States that employ the highway patrol model often have other state law enforcement agencies with narrow service mandates, such as the following:

- Bureaus of criminal investigation (to investigate white-collar and organized crime, narcotics, etc.).
- State criminal identification services.
- Forest, game, and watercraft protection services.
- Alcoholic beverage control and enforcement.
- Crime laboratory and criminalistics services.
- Driver's license examinations.
- Drug interdiction activities.
- Peace officer training and certification.

Both state police and highway patrol agencies help regulate commercial traffic, conduct bomb investigations, protect the governor and the capitol grounds and buildings, and administer computerized information networks for the state, which link up with the National Crime Information Center (NCIC) run by the FBI.

Some tension always seems to exist between state police agencies and local law enforcement over legal jurisdiction and recognition for conducting investigations and making arrests. Recall that policing in America and the political system that governs it are local. Much of the resentment by locals over state interference is similar to the suspicions and doubts concerning federal involvement at the local level.

A significant function performed by a special category of state law enforcement officers is university or campus policing. Some of the large state and private universities and colleges have full-blown police agencies with many special subdivisions. They are very much like municipal police departments—and rightly so, because a community's problems with crime and public order do not end at the university gate.

FEDERAL LAW ENFORCEMENT

Everyone has heard of a few of the better-known federal law enforcement agencies. The FBI, the U.S. Secret Service, and even the T-men and T-women of the Treasury Department have had their own television shows, creating wider public recognition of those agencies. The unrelenting war on drugs has brought to the attention of the American public the activities of the Drug Enforcement Administration (DEA). There are also other, lesser-known federal police agencies. Their law enforcement jurisdictions are narrowly defined by specific statutes, and their work is unlikely to come to the attention of most American citizens.

Three major differences exist between federal law enforcement and the local and state police agencies with which we are likely to be more familiar. First, federal agencies such as the FBI operate across the entire nation and even have agents serving abroad. Second, federal police agencies do not, as a rule, have the peacekeeping or order maintenance duties typical in local policing. Finally, some federal law enforcement agencies have extremely narrow jurisdictions. (The U.S. Supreme Court Police, for example, provide protective and investigative services for the Supreme Court only.)

FEDERAL LAW ENFORCEMENT PERSONNEL As of September 2004, federal agencies employed nationwide about 105,000 full-time personnel authorized to make arrests and carry firearms—an increase of about 13 percent since

Department of Homeland Security

As of June 2002, agencies in Justice (55 percent) and Treasury (23 percent) Departments were the largest employers of federal officers with arrest and firearm authority; however, the Homeland Security Act made the Departments of Homeland Security (41 percent) and Justice (36 percent) the major employers in 2004.

Source: Brian A. Reaves and Lynn M. Bauer, *Federal Law Enforcement, 2002* (Washington, DC: GPO, U.S. Department of Justice, Bureau of Justice Statistics, August 2003), p. 5.; Brian A. Reaves, *Federal Law Enforcement Officers, 2004* (Washington, DC: U.S. Department of Justice, Bureau of Justice Statistics, July 2006).

Federal law enforcement agencies investigate violations of federal law, enforce laws that involve interstate crimes, and conduct activities to prevent and control domestic and international terrorism. *How do the jobs of federal law enforcement agents differ from the jobs of other law enforcement officers?*

June 2002 and 52 percent since the end of 1993.[28] Another 1,500 federal officers worked in U.S. territories, and some were employed in foreign countries. (Data for the Transportation Security Administration's Federal Air Marshals were not available because of security concerns, but see FYI later in this chapter.) Approximately 60 percent of federal officers were employed by the four largest agencies: U.S. Customs and Border Protection, the Federal Bureau of Prisons, the Federal Bureau of Investigation, and U.S. Immigration and Customs Enforcement.[29] (Note that on March 1, 2003, the former Immigration and Naturalization Service, the border and agency functions of the U.S. Customs Service, and the Federal Protective Service were reorganized into the Bureau of Immigration and Customs Enforcement in the new Department of Homeland Security, which is described in detail in the next section.) Table 2.2 shows the major employers of federal officers authorized to make arrests and carry firearms. Nearly 40 percent of federal law enforcement officers have criminal investigation and enforcement duties; about 20 percent engage in police response and patrol; 16 percent do inspections related to immigration or custom laws; another 16 percent perform corrections or detention-related

TABLE 2.2	Gender and Race or Ethnicity of Federal Officers with Arrest and Firearm Authority, Agencies Employing 500 or More Full-Time Officers, September 2004

| | | **PERCENTAGE OF FULL-TIME FEDERAL OFFICERS WITH ARREST AND FIREARM AUTHORITY** | | | | | | |
| | | | | **RACE/ETHNICITY** | | | | |
AGENCY	**NUMBER OF OFFICERS***	**FEMALE**	**TOTAL MINORITY**	**AMERICAN INDIAN**	**BLACK OR AFRICAN AMERICAN**	**ASIAN OR PACIFIC ISLANDER**	**HISPANIC OR LATINO, ANY RACE**	**OTHER RACE**
U.S. Customs and Border Protection	28,200	15.3%	46.8%	0.6%	5.0%	4.2%	36.9%	0%
Federal Bureau of Prisons	15,361	13.3	39.7	1.3	24.2	1.5	12.7	0
Federal Bureau of Investigation	12,414	18.5	17.2	0.4	5.8	3.6	7.4	0
U.S. Immigration and Customs Enforcement	10,691	13.7	33.9	0.6	8.6	2.7	22.0	0
U.S. Secret Service	4,780	10.5	19.6	0.6	11.2	2.6	5.2	0
Drug Enforcement Administration	4,500	8.9	19.4	0.4	7.6	2.5	8.9	0
Administrative Office of the U.S. Courts	4,166	44.2	32.2	0.5	15.3	1.6	14.1	0.6
U.S. Marshals Service	3,233	10.2	20.0	0.7	7.3	2.3	9.6	0.1
U.S. Postal Inspection Service	2,999	19.6	36.4	0.5	21.6	4.7	9.6	0
Internal Revenue Service, Criminal Investigation	2,791	30	24.0	0.8	10.2	4.5	8.1	0.4
Veterans Health Administration	2,474	6.9	40.1	0.9	26.8	2.5	10.0	0
Bureau of Alcohol, Tobacco, Firearms & Explosives	2,398	13.3	19.9	1.1	9.3	2.1	7.5	0
National Park Service— Ranger Division	1,547	18.2	10.3	2.1	2.5	2.4	3.0	0.3
U.S. Capitol Police	1,535	18.8	34.7	0.3	28.9	1.2	4.2	0
Bureau of Diplomatic Security	825	11.8	20	0.7	9.7	3.4	5.5	0.7
U.S. Fish and Wildlife Service	713	8.7	13.6	3.5	1.7	1.4	7.0	0
National Park Service— U.S. Park Police	612	11.4	18.8	0	10.9	2.8	5.1	0
USDA Forest Service	604	17.5	17.4	6.5	3.3	1.3	6.30	

Note: Data on gender and race or ethnicity of officers were not provided by the Administrative Office of the U.S. Courts. Detail may not add to total because of rounding or because of personnel classified as "other" race. *Includes employees in U.S. Territories.

Source: Brian A. Reaves, *Federal Law Enforcement Officers, 2004* (Washington, DC: GPO, U.S. Department of Justice, Bureau of Justice Statistics, July 2006), Table 4.

roles; 5 percent have court-related duties; and 4 percent are directly involved with security and protection.[30] Combined, the federal law enforcement agencies spent approximately $20 billion on police protection in 2003 (the latest year for which data were available), which represented an increase of about 46 percent since 2000 (pre-9/11).[31]

Of the federal officers with arrest and firearm authority in 2004, about 84 percent were men and 16 percent were women—an increase in women from 14 percent in 1996. The Administrative Office of the U.S. Courts employed the largest percentage of women (44 percent), while the Veteran's Health Administration employed the fewest women (7 percent).[32] About one-third of federal officers were members of a racial or ethnic minority—an increase from 28 percent in 1996. Approximately 18 percent of them were Hispanic or Latino, about 11 percent were non-Hispanic blacks, 3 percent were Asians or Pacific Islanders, and 1 percent were American Indians. U.S. Customs and Border Protection had the largest minority percentage (approximately 47 percent, of which about 37 percent were Hispanic or Latino.) The agency with the fewest minorities was the National Park Service, Ranger Activities Division (with 10.3 percent). The largest percentage of black officers (about 29 percent) was employed by the U.S. Capitol Police, the Forest Service employed the largest percentage of American Indians (about 7 percent), and the Postal Inspection Service employed the largest percentage of Asians and Pacific Islanders (4.4 percent).[33] Table 2.2 also shows the gender and race or ethnicity of federal officers with arrest and firearm authority that were working for agencies that employed 500 or more full-time officers in 2004.

TRAINING FEDERAL LAW ENFORCEMENT OFFICERS The Federal Law Enforcement Training Center (FLETC) is the largest law enforcement-training establishment in the United States.[34] It provides some or all of the training for a majority of federal law enforcement agencies, as well as for many state, local, and international law enforcement agencies. Notable exceptions are the FBI and DEA, which train their special agents at their respective academies in Quantico, Virginia. Until 2003, when it became a part of the Department of Homeland Security, FLETC was a bureau of the Treasury Department with an annual budget of about $200 million.

The FLETC got its start in the late 1960s, when a federal government study disclosed that the training of most federal law enforcement personnel was inadequate at worst and substandard at best. With only a few exceptions, part-time instructors, on an irregular basis, conducted most training in inferior facilities. Much of the training duplicated the training of other federal agencies or was inconsistent with it. A government task force recommended that a federal law enforcement training center be established to provide the training for most federal law enforcement personnel. The center would have a professionally trained, full-time staff that offered consistent and high-quality programs in state-of-the-art facilities.

FLETC first opened in Washington, D.C., in 1970. That year it graduated 848 students. In 1975, its first full year of operation at its current headquarters location on a 1,500-acre campus in Glenn County ("Glynco"), Georgia (near Brunswick, Georgia), it graduated more than 5,000 students. At year-end 2005, more than 19,000 students graduated from the FLETC at Glynco, including 566 state and local officers. Another 4,910 students graduated from the FLETC Office of Artesia Operations (OAO) in New Mexico, which was opened in 1989 to provide training for the Bureau of Indian Affairs and agencies with a large number of officers in the western United States. It also hosts the new U.S. Border Patrol Academy. A temporary satellite training campus was opened in Charleston, South Carolina, in 1995, to

Offices of Inspector General

Offices of inspector general (IG) investigate criminal violations and prevent and detect fraud, waste, and abuse related to federal programs, operations, and employees. In September of 2004, there were 57 statutory federal IG offices, 27 of which employed criminal investigators with arrest and firearm authority. Overall, these agencies employed nearly 3,000 officers. The largest IG employer of federal officers authorized to arrest and carry firearms in 2004 was the Department of Health and Human Services (with 374 officers).

Source: Brian A. Reaves, *Federal Law Enforcement, 2004* (Washington, DC: GPO, U.S. Department of Justice, Bureau of Justice Statistics, July 2006) p. 5.

CJ ONLINE

Federal Law Enforcement Training Center
To learn more about the FLETC, visit its Web site at **www.fletc.gov.** Access its "Catalog of Training Programs." *Which programs, if any, would be of interest to you? Why?*

THINKING CRITICALLY

1. What do you think are the pros and cons of working at the local, state, and federal levels of law enforcement?

2. Do you think that any one of the three major areas of law enforcement (local, state, federal) is more prestigious? Why?

train an increasing number of INS and border patrol agents. In 2003, the Charleston facility became the third FLETC-residential campus and, in 2004, all of the Border Patrol training operations were moved to FLETC-Artesia. Besides some of the same training programs offered at FLETC-Glynco and FLETC-Artesia, the FLETC-Charleston facility specializes in maritime law enforcement training. In 2005, the facility graduated nearly 1,850 officers. A fourth training facility that was developed in 2002 in Cheltenham, Maryland, is used primarily for in-service and requalification training for officers and agents in the Washington, D.C., area. It also serves as the home for the U.S. Capitol Police Training Academy. In 2005, it graduated 15,591 students. FLETC also provides training at other temporary sites in the United States and in foreign countries.

Because basic training requirements for federal officers vary by agency and by position within agencies, FLETC provides more than 150 different agency-specific training programs. About half of the instructors are permanent employees, while the other half are federal officers on short-term assignment from their respective agencies. Depending on the agency, classroom instruction ranges from about 8 to 22 weeks for criminal investigators and from 4 to 26 weeks for patrol officers. Field training requirements range from 2 weeks to 6 months for patrol officers and up to 2 years for investigators.

The Department of Homeland Security

The U.S. Congress responded to the terrorist attacks of September 11, 2001 (described in Chapter 4), by enacting the Homeland Security Act of 2002.[35] Among other provisions, such as allowing commercial pilots to carry guns in cockpits, the act established the Department of Homeland Security

CAREERS IN CRIMINAL JUSTICE

FBI Special Agent

My name is Michelle L. Rankin and I am an FBI special agent in the Washington, D.C. field office, Public Corruption Unit (PCU). The Washington, D.C., field office is the second-largest field office in the FBI. I thoroughly enjoy my career with the FBI.

The PCU investigates allegations of bribery involving public officials, including extortion or using the mail to defraud the public. Examples include the issuance of licenses, permits, contracts, or zoning variances; judicial case fixing; and law enforcement corruption.

The PCU's responsibilities are divided into two squads. My squad focuses on the District of Columbia government. The other squad concentrates on the executive branch of

the federal government in the Washington, D.C., area. Twelve agents are assigned to my squad, along with non-agent support specialists.

Prior to transferring to the PCU, I worked on a special inquiry squad, conducting background investigations for White House staff and presidential appointees. It was in this capacity that I had the opportunity to interview Attorney General Janet Reno as well as other prominent politicians.

People often ask about training at the FBI Academy. The program is 16 weeks of rigorous and intellectually challenging work. You have to study 12–15 major subject areas and you often have 3 hours of homework for the next day's classes; you may also have an exam in another

(DHS). According to the legislation, this new executive department was created to

1. Prevent terrorist attacks within the United States.
2. Reduce the vulnerability of the United States to terrorism.
3. Minimize the damage, and assist in the recovery, from terrorist attacks that do occur within the United States.
4. Carry out all functions of entities transferred to the department, including by acting as a focal point regarding natural and manmade crises and emergency planning.
5. Ensure that the functions of the agencies and subdivisions within the department that are not related directly to securing the homeland are not diminished or neglected except by an explicit act of Congress.
6. Ensure that the overall economic security of the United States is not diminished by efforts, activities, and programs aimed at securing the homeland.
7. Monitor connections between illegal drug trafficking and terrorism, coordinate efforts to sever such connections, and otherwise contribute to efforts to interdict illegal drug trafficking.

The act also stipulates that "primary responsibility for investigating and prosecuting acts of terrorism shall be vested not in the Department, but rather in Federal, State, and local law enforcement agencies with jurisdiction over the acts in question."

The creation of the DHS represents the most dramatic transformation of the U.S. government since 1947, when President Harry S. Truman combined the various branches of the U.S. military into the Department of Defense. On an even grander scale, President George W. Bush has combined 22 previously separate domestic agencies into the new department to protect the country from future threats. To head the new department, President Bush selected former Pennsylvania governor Tom Ridge. On February 15, 2005, Michael Chertoff was sworn in as the second secretary of the DHS.

course the next day. Some agents realize that the FBI is not what they thought it was. Others find it difficult to be away from family and friends.

I have a BA in Criminal Justice from California State University at San Bernardino. While working on a Certificate in Crime and Intelligence Analysis through the California State University system and the California Department of Justice, I began to volunteer with the Riverside County Sheriff's Department. I eventually obtained a full-time position as an analyst there. Later I went to the Santa Clara Police Department as a certified crime and intelligence analyst. I designed and directed their crime analysis unit for 4 years. I left Santa Clara in 1999 to become an FBI agent.

To become an FBI special agent, applicants must be between the ages of 23 and 37. The FBI prefers to hire people who are already successful in some other field. Prior work experience need not be in law enforcement. The FBI hires agents from four career categories: law; accounting; foreign languages; and "diversified"—which includes criminal justice. You need to have a minimum of 3 years of work experience in your chosen field before applying to be an agent. When hired, new FBI special agents start at a GS-10, step 1 pay grade, which is now approximately $40,000 per year before overtime.

My advice to someone who wants to become an FBI agent is to maintain the highest standards of conduct in your life. Your first job out of college does not have to be in criminal justice, but be sure to be successful in whatever you do.

After reading this account, what do you think is a key quality of a good FBI agent?

A UH-60 Black Hawk helicopter from the Department of Homeland Security's new Bureau of Immigration and Customs Enforcement patrolling restricted airspace over the New York metropolitan area to detect unauthorized intrusions. *Is this an effective defensive strategy against terrorism? Why or why not?*

CJ ONLINE

Department of Homeland Security
To learn more about the Department of Homeland Security, visit its Web site at **www.dhs.gov/dhspublic.** *Based on what you have learned, do you think the DHS will be effective in preventing terrorism on American soil?*

The new department, which has been reorganized since its inception, comprises the following major components:

The *Directorate for Preparedness* works with state, local, and private sector partners to identify threats, determine vulnerabilities, and target resources where risk is greatest, thereby safeguarding our borders, seaports, bridges and highways, and critical information systems. The components of the Preparedness Directorate include the following:

- *Cyber and Telecommunications* has primary responsibility for working with other federal agencies in completing comprehensive plans for executing responsibilities to prevent and mitigate cyber-based attacks.
- *Chief Medical Officer* has primary responsibility for working with other federal agencies in completing comprehensive plans for executing responsibilities to prevent and mitigate biologically based attacks.
- *Fire Administration* reduces deaths and economic losses from fires and related emergencies through public education, training for fire protection personnel, and enhanced technology.
- *Grants and Training* assists states, local communities, regional authorities, and tribal jurisdictions to prevent, deter, and respond to terrorist and other threats to national security through funding, training, and exercises designed to increase preparedness and responsiveness.
- *Infrastructure Protection* identifies and assesses current and future threats to the nation's physical and informational infrastructure, issuing timely warnings to prevent damage to the infrastructure that supports our community and economic life.
- *Office of National Capital Region Coordination* oversees and coordinates federal programs for and relationships with the National

Capital Region (NCR) to ensure adequate planning, information sharing, training, and execution of domestic preparedness activities. The NCR includes the District of Columbia and 11 local jurisdictions in the State of Maryland and the Commonwealth of Virginia.

The *Directorate for Science and Technology* is the primary research and development arm of the DHS. It provides federal, state, and local officials with the technology and capabilities to protect the homeland.

The *Directorate for Management* is responsible for department budgets and appropriations, expenditure of funds, accounting and finance, procurement, human resources, information technology systems, facilities and equipment, and the identification and tracking of performance measurements.

The *Office of Intelligence and Analysis* is responsible for using information and intelligence from multiple sources to identify and assess current and future threats to the United States.

The *Office of Operations Coordination* is responsible for monitoring the security of the United States on a daily basis and coordinating activities within the department and with governors, DHS advisers, law enforcement partners, and critical infrastructure operators in all 50 states and more than 50 major urban areas nationwide.

The *Directorate for Policy* is the primary policy formulation and coordination component for the DHS. It provides a centralized, coordinated focus to the development of departmentwide, long-range planning to protect the United States. The components of the Policy Directorate include the following:

- The *Office of Policy* is the primary office within the Policy Directorate responsible for the formulation and coordination of departmentwide policies designed to protect the United States.
- The *Office of Immigration Statistics* contributes to the formulation of department policies through the development, analysis, and dissemination of statistical information on immigration in the United States.
- The *Office of International Affairs* is responsible for coordinating the development of DHS policies that have implications for the international community in accordance with U.S. foreign policy.
- The *Office of the Private Sector* fosters communication between the private sector and the department and provides guidance to the secretary on proposed policies and regulations and their potential impact on private sector organizations and the nation's economic security.
- The *Office of Strategic Planning* provides a central focus for the formulation of departmentwide, long-range planning and strategic goals to safeguard the homeland.
- The *Senior Asylum Officer* is responsible for policies and practices affecting refugees and others seeking asylum in the United States.

The *Domestic Nuclear Detection Office* works to enhance the nuclear detection efforts of federal, state, territorial, tribal, and local governments, and the private sector and to ensure a coordinated response to such threats.

Federal Emergency Management Agency (FEMA) prepares the nation for hazards, manages federal response and recovery efforts following any national incident, and administers the National Flood Insurance Program.

Transportation Security Administration (TSA) protects the nation's transportation systems to ensure freedom of movement for people and commerce.

Customs and Border Protection is responsible for protecting our nation's borders in order to prevent terrorists and terrorist weapons from entering the United States, while facilitating the flow of legitimate trade and travel.

TSA and Federal Air Marshals

The Transportation Security Administration (TSA) was created in response to 9/11. One of its first actions was to significantly expand the Federal Air Marshals program to provide security on commercial aircraft. Although exact numbers are not available, there are an estimated 3,000 to 4,000 Federal Air Marshals.

Source: Brian A. Reaves, *Federal Law Enforcement Officers, 2004* (Washington, DC: Bureau of Justice Statistics, July 2006), p. 11, Exhibit B.

Immigration and Customs Enforcement (ICE), the largest investigative arm of the DHS, is responsible for identifying and shutting down vulnerabilities in the nation's border, economic, transportation, and infrastructure security.

Federal Law Enforcement Training Center provides career-long training to law enforcement professionals to help them fulfill their responsibilities safely and proficiently.

Citizenship and Immigration Services is responsible for the administration of immigration and naturalization adjudication functions and establishing immigration services policies and priorities.

The *U.S. Coast Guard* protects the public, the environment, and U.S. economic interests—in the nation's ports and waterways, along the coast, on international waters, or in any maritime region as required to support national security.

The *U.S. Secret Service* protects the president and other high-level officials and investigates counterfeiting and other financial crimes, including financial institution fraud, identity theft, computer fraud; and computer-based attacks on our nation's financial, banking, and telecommunications infrastructure.

The *Office of the Secretary* oversees activities with other federal, state, local, and private entities as part of a collaborative effort to strengthen our borders, provide for intelligence analysis and infrastructure protection, improve the use of science and technology to counter weapons of mass destruction, and to create a comprehensive response and recovery system. Within the Office of the Secretary there are multiple offices that contribute to the overall DHS mission.

- The *Privacy Office* works to minimize the impact on the individual's privacy, particularly the individual's personal information and dignity, while achieving the mission of DHS.
- The *Office for Civil Rights and Civil Liberties* provides legal and policy advice to DHS leadership on civil rights and civil liberties issues, investigates and resolves complaints, and provides leadership to Equal Employment Opportunity Programs.
- The *Office of Inspector General* is responsible for conducting and supervising audits, investigations, and inspections relating to the programs and operations of the department, recommending ways for the DHS to carry out its responsibilities in the most effective, efficient, and economical manner possible.
- The *Citizenship and Immigration Services Ombudsman* provides recommendations for resolving individual and employer problems with the United States Citizenship and Immigration Services in order to ensure national security and the integrity of the legal immigration system, increase efficiencies in administering citizenship and immigration services, and improve customer service.
- The *Office of Legislative and Intergovernmental Affairs* serves as primary liaison to members of Congress and their staffs, the White House and executive branch, and to other federal agencies and governmental entities that have roles in assuring national security.
- The *Office of the Federal Coordinator for Gulf Coast Rebuilding* was created to help assist the region with long-term planning and coordinating the federal government's response to rebuild the Gulf Coast region devastated by Hurricanes Katrina and Rita.
- *Office of the General Counsel*
- *Office of Counternarcotics Enforcement*
- *Office of Public Affairs*

Advisory Panels and Committees

- The *Homeland Security Advisory Council* provides advice and recommendations to the secretary on matters related to homeland security. The council is composed of leaders from state and local government, first-responder communities, the private sector, and academia.
- The *National Infrastructure Advisory Council* provides advice to the secretary of the DHS and the president on the security of information systems for the public and private institutions that constitute the critical infrastructure of our nation's economy.
- The *Interagency Coordinating Council on Emergency Preparedness and Individuals with Disabilities* was established to ensure that the federal government appropriately supports safety and security for individuals with disabilities in disaster situations.

The organization chart of the Department of Homeland Security is shown in Figure 2.7.

HOMELAND SECURITY AND THE FBI Before the creation of the Department of Homeland Security, the FBI had primary responsibility for locating terrorist groups and preventing terrorist acts in the United States. It had many successes. According to FBI data, for example, the agency prevented 130 terrorist acts between 1980 and 1999.[36] However, following the al Qaeda attacks on New York

FIGURE 2.7   **Department of Homeland Security Organization Chart**

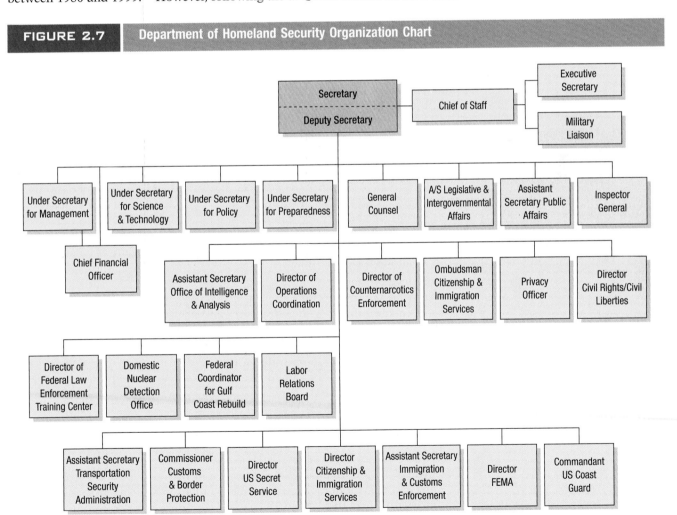

Source: Department of Homeland Security at www.dhs.gov/dhspublic.

and Washington, the FBI was heavily criticized for missing clues and intelligence failures.[37] For example, Senator John Edwards of North Carolina, who had oversight responsibility for the FBI as a member of both the Intelligence and Judiciary Committees, remarked, "The FBI is clearly broken, and we can accept no further delay in the effort to fix it." He added, "The FBI should do what it does best: law enforcement [rather than] collecting information, fitting it into a bigger picture and sharing that information with people who can act on it."[38] To root out terrorists within the United States, legislators on Capitol Hill called for the creation of a new domestic intelligence-gathering agency similar to the MI-5 in Great Britain.

FBI director Robert Mueller defended his agency. He responded, "Establishing a new domestic intelligence agency would constitute a step backward in the war on terror, not a step forward." He maintained that rather than "create a new agency from whole cloth, the public would be better served by improving what the FBI is already doing."[39]

Director Mueller won a reprieve for the FBI and quickly began implementing fundamental changes. First, he shifted the top priority of the FBI from being a federal police agency to being an intelligence and counterterrorism agency. In doing so, he no longer allows local field offices to establish their own distinct agendas. Second, he restructured the management hierarchy at FBI headquarters in Washington to support counterterrorism efforts. Figure 2.8 shows the FBI's post-9/11 organization chart with the new emphasis on counterterrorism. Third, he reassigned about one-quarter of the FBI's 11,000 agents to work on counterterrorism. That represents a doubling of the number of agents handling terrorism cases and a quadrupling of the number of strategic analysts at FBI headquarters. Fourth, he established a National Joint Terrorism Task Force at FBI headquarters that includes staffers from federal, state, and local agencies. They are responsible for coordinating the flow of information with task forces in each of the bureau's 56 field offices. Fifth, to more directly address the global threat of al Qaeda and other terrorist groups, he planned on opening FBI offices in Kabul, Afghanistan; Sarajevo, Bosnia; Jakarta, Indonesia; Tashkent, Uzbekistan; and Belgrade, Serbia. He also planned on expanding FBI offices in Ottawa, Canada; Seoul, South Korea; London, Berlin, and Moscow. Since the tragic events of 9/11 about 500 FBI agents and 200 support personnel have been working outside the United States on terrorism investigation. Already working outside the United States were FBI agents known as permanent legal attaches, or "legats." The job of legats is to feed information gathered from interviews back to the United States for further investigation. Unlike CIA agents, legats, who will work more closely with the CIA, do not operate covertly and are involved more with investigations than with gathering intelligence. In sum, through the efforts of Director Mueller, the FBI will remain an independent agency, albeit with a new top priority, and retain its traditional responsibility of intelligence gathering and analysis. However, it will now closely coordinate its antiterrorism activities with the CIA and the new DHS.

THE WAR ON TERRORISM: A PRELIMINARY EVALUATION

Advocates of the Department of Homeland Security are confident that the DHS will have the financial, intelligence, and tactical resources necessary to prevent and control domestic terrorism. At this writing, the DHS is assessing the threats against the United States and coordinating the resources of law enforcement and other kinds of agencies that are necessary to defeat terrorism at home. One of its first efforts was the creation of a color-coded warning

FBI Fights Terrorism

To learn more about the FBI's efforts to combat terrorism, visit its Web site at **www.fbi.gov.** Click on "Terrorism" and then click on "Counterterrorism Website." *From what you have learned, do you think the FBI will be effective in combating terrorism?*

The Homeland Security Department's color-coded national threat alert system is intended to help citizens better prepare for potential terrorist attacks. *Do you believe the system is effective? Why or why not?*

FIGURE 2.8 | **Federal Bureau of Investigation**

Source: www.fbi.gov/filelink.html?file=/aboutus/todaysfbi/orgchart.pdf.

system to alert citizens to the likelihood of a terrorist attack. The hope is that as the warning level is raised, the vigilance of Americans will increase and information will be discovered that will prevent a terrorist act.

The war on terrorism is an ongoing battle with no end in sight. Nevertheless, there already have been some successes. For example, since September

11, 2001, as a result of cooperation among law enforcement agencies, more than 3,400 members of al Qaeda or their associates have been captured and detained in more than 100 countries.[40] In addition, most of al Qaeda's top leadership has been killed or captured.[41] The financial resources of terrorist groups have also been successfully attacked. Leaders of 173 countries have ordered the freezing of more than $136 million terrorist-related financial assets.[42] In the United States, under the authority of Executive Order 13224, which was issued by President Bush on September 23, 2001, about 350 terrorist groups and entities have been listed as possible targets for the freezing of their U.S.-based assets.[43] Further, any American citizen who contributes money or other aid to any of the 350 organizations and entities automatically becomes suspect. Most important, the United States, as of October 2006, has not experienced a repeat of the 9/11 tragedy. On the other hand, Osama bin Laden (probably) and other key al Qaeda leaders were still at large (as of October 2006) despite the best efforts of the United States and its coalition partners and a reward of up to $25 million authorized by then secretary of state Colin Powell for information leading to their capture.[44]

A major problem in the war on terrorism is lax and poorly enforced immigration policies. Both the United States and Canada have some of the most lenient immigration policies in the world, and the result has been that terrorists and their supporters have found safe haven in both nations. A recent study found that 15 out of 80 identified international terrorist groups have members or significant supporters in Canada.[45] Another study of both legal and illegal immigration in the United States discovered that the 19 terrorist hijackers of September 11, 2001, could not have accomplished their mission without the failures of U.S. immigration agencies. It is widely believed that "we unlocked our doors, spread out the welcome mat, and allowed these foreign visitors to plot death and destruction in the comfort of our home. And they can do it again in a heartbeat."[46] It is hoped that through the efforts of the DHS, law enforcement agencies at all levels of government, and vigilant American citizens, acts of terrorism can be prevented in the future.

American Private Security

Private security is a huge enterprise that complements public law enforcement in the United States. The Department of Labor's Bureau of Labor Statistics projects the continued growth of private security employment well into this century.[47] It has been estimated that twice as many people work in private security as in public law enforcement. Until recently, substantially more money was being spent on private security than on public policing, but that gap has been narrowing somewhat because of the increases in spending on public law enforcement during the 1990s and the federalizing of airport security (through the Transportation Security Administration) in the wake of the 9/11 terrorist assault.

A common way to categorize private security employment is to classify the agencies and personnel as either contract or proprietary. **Contract security** companies offer protective services for a fee to people, agencies, and companies that do not employ their own security personnel or that need extra protection. A state university, for example, may employ private security officers to work at a football game. Contract security employees are not peace officers. **Proprietary security** agents and personnel provide protective services for the entity that employs them. They are also not classified as sworn peace officers. For example, the Ford Motor Company employs its own security forces at its

contract security Protective services that a private security firm provides to people, agencies, and companies that do not employ their own security personnel or that need extra protection.

proprietary security In-house protective services that a security staff provides for the entity that employs it.

large manufacturing plants. Primarily for cost reasons, the number of contract security jobs is likely to increase faster than the number of proprietary security jobs.

PRIVATE SECURITY OFFICERS

Private security officers, or "guards," are hired to provide protection.[48] They typically work 8-hour shifts, 5 days a week. In 2004, they were paid between about $14,000 and $43,000 annually. The average salary for a private security officer in 2004 was $20,320. Managers and corporate officers made more. More than half of private security officers in 2004 worked for investigation and security services, such as armored car services.

Because of relatively low wages, private security officers frequently work part-time or have another "primary" job and use their security job wages to supplement their incomes. In 2004, there were more than one million private security officers. A private security officer's duties vary and depend on the employers' particular needs. Private security officers generally specialize in one of the following areas:

Private security is assuming an increasing role in maintaining order, investigating crime, and apprehending criminals. *Is this a positive trend? Why or why not?*

- Protecting people, records, merchandise, money, and equipment in department stores; also working with undercover store detectives to prevent theft by customers or store employees and helping in the apprehension of shoplifting suspects before the police arrive.
- Patrolling the parking lots of shopping centers and theaters, sometimes on horseback or bicycles, to deter car theft and robberies.
- Maintaining order and protecting property, staff, and customers in office buildings, banks, and hospitals.
- Protecting people, freight, property, and equipment at air, sea, and rail terminals as well as other transportation facilities; also screening passengers and visitors for weapons and explosives using metal detectors and high-tech equipment, ensuring that nothing is stolen while being loaded or unloaded, and watching for fires and criminals.
- Protecting paintings and exhibits by inspecting people and packages entering and leaving public buildings such as museums or art galleries.
- Protecting information, products, computer codes, and defense secrets and checking the credentials of people and vehicles entering or leaving the premises of factories, laboratories, government buildings, data-processing centers, and military bases.
- Performing crowd control, supervising parking and seating, and directing traffic at universities, parks, and sports stadiums.
- Preventing access by minors, collecting cover charges at the door, maintaining order among customers, and protecting property and patrons while stationed at the entrance to bars and places of adult entertainment such as night clubs.
- Protecting money and valuables during transit in armored cars; also protecting individuals responsible for making commercial bank deposits from theft or bodily injuries.
- Observing casino operations for irregular activities, such as cheating or theft, by employees or patrons.

REASONS FOR GROWTH

A number of factors have stimulated the phenomenal growth of private security since the 1970s.

DECLINING REVENUES FOR PUBLIC POLICING In virtually all major cities and in state governments in the United States, the competition for limited funds to operate public services is fierce. Public police agencies have experienced their share of across-the-board government belt-tightening, and that has caused limitations and even freezes on the hiring of additional police officers. (That trend has been decreasing recently.) As a result, police departments have curtailed services no longer deemed critical. Often, businesses have filled the service gap by employing private security personnel.

THE PRIVATE NATURE OF CRIMES IN THE WORKPLACE A business depends on a positive reputation to remain competitive. Widespread employee theft, embezzlement scandals, and substance abuse harm an organization's public image and may cause potential customers to question the quality of a company's products and services. By employing private security personnel to prevent and repress crime in their facilities, businesses can either hide the crimes that occur or minimize the negative publicity.

BETTER CONTROL AND ATTENTION TO THE PROBLEM By employing in-house security personnel or by contracting with an outside firm, the management of a business can direct security personnel to do precisely what is needed to prevent crime, minimize substance abuse, and discipline wayward employees. Public police would have to combine the concerns of a business with the priorities of the citizens of the community.

FEWER CONSTITUTIONAL LIMITATIONS Some of the constitutional restrictions that would limit the actions of public police officers working undercover to curtail drug trafficking in an industrial plant, for example, would not restrict private security personnel employed directly by that industry. U.S. Supreme Court prohibitions that restrict a public police officer's right to search and seize property, for instance, would not limit the actions of a private security agent.

ISSUES INVOLVING PRIVATE SECURITY

A number of unresolved problems and issues impinge on the potential for development of the private security industry. Some of them put the industry at odds with public law enforcement.

LEGAL STATUS AND AUTHORITY Private security officers' legal status and authority derive from the rights of the owner who employs them to protect property on the premises. These rights are essentially the same ones you have to protect your life and property at home.

If this view prevails, private security personnel face few constitutional limitations in investigating crime, obtaining evidence, employing reasonable force, searching personal property stored in corporate spaces, and interrogating suspects. Although this is not a unanimous view among courts, it is the most prevalent one. However, private security officers and their employers face the possibility of being held civilly or criminally liable for violating an individual's civil rights or for false arrest.

PUBLIC POLICING IN A PRIVATE CAPACITY Although some police departments prohibit moonlighting, thousands of police officers still work in a private capacity during their off-duty hours. Some police agencies even cooperate with private agencies in scheduling their officers for off-duty assignments. With regard to their legal status and authority, are these officers considered public police or private security personnel? The private organization that employs them believes that off-duty police officers are better qualified, have more authority to arrest, and will have a greater deterrent effect on the crimes and disturbances of the peace the employer is trying to prevent.

An equally important question is, Who is liable should moonlighting officers abuse their authority or make a mistake? At present, it seems police agencies that take an active role in scheduling off-duty assignments accept greater liability than the police departments that do not. Many agencies limit the assignments officers are allowed to accept and the number of hours they are permitted to work.

QUALIFICATIONS AND TRAINING Many superbly qualified people work in private security at all levels throughout the United States, but those people are not the norm. Although the minimum qualifications for private security personnel at all levels of employment are increasing, they lag far behind those of the public police. Few states enforce any educational, physical, or background integrity qualifications for private security personnel. In most states, the training required to become a private security officer is less than a week long. However, private security officers at nuclear power plants, for example, receive months of training before they are placed on the job under close supervision. In some states, armed security officers must attend a firearms course, including

CAREERS IN CRIMINAL JUSTICE

U.S. Immigration and Customs Special Agent

My name is José Pagan and I became a U.S. Customs special agent/criminal investigator in 1987. During my career, I have served as a federal law enforcement officer in the U.S. Virgin Islands, Puerto Rico, and Orlando, Florida, where I have been assigned since December 2000.

I have had the opportunity to conduct and participate in numerous narcotic interdiction investigations, as well as become a liaison officer between U.S. Customs and other federal and international law enforcement agencies.

As a U.S. Customs special agent, I have learned the value of organization and sound criminal investigation procedures as the primordial law enforcement tools. The investigation of crimes, regardless of type (passion, violence, financial, fraud, narcotic smuggling, counterfeiting, etc.), depends on sound standardized investigatory procedures. I have also mastered many investigative techniques. Among these techniques are interviewing skills such as detecting and utilizing flaws in elicited responses from a suspect, as well as observing behavior that could assist me in assessing the subject's veracity.

By utilizing proven criminal investigation procedures, in conjunction with the officer's experience, crime investigation becomes a scientific, measurable, and reliable method of protecting the public. Even in the investigation

of the most heinous crimes, a reliable investigation, based on facts properly discovered and presented in an orderly, organized, and logical fashion, will always portray a fair, just, and clear case for the jury.

I have participated in operations such as the marine interdiction of narcotics and illegal aliens, as well as serving dozens of search warrants, all of which have demanded a great deal of physical exertion (added to the emotional stress that an assertive law enforcement action creates on the officers). Cases such as joint international investigations of narcotic smuggling have given me the opportunity to learn other countries' law enforcement techniques, customs, and points of view. At the same time, counterfeiting cases offer the opportunity to learn about the U.S. and international trade systems, as well as teaching the true impact that unfair trade practices have on the U.S. economy.

There are no typical days at the office in this career. On any given day, I could be on a vessel, sailing to prevent narcotic smuggling into the United States, or interviewing the operations manager of a large company whose product has been counterfeited.

What parts of the U.S. Customs special agent's role do you find most and least appealing? Why?

Laws Governing Private Security

There are no federal laws governing the private security industry. No training is required for unarmed guards in 29 states and the District of Columbia. Private security officers do not have to be licensed in 22 states. In 16 states, background checks are not required.

Source: Mimi Hall, "Private Security Guards: Homeland Defense's Weak Link," *USA Today,* January 23, 2003, p. 1A.

a section on the laws applicable to the use of deadly force, and must successfully complete a practical firearms qualification test. In nearly all states, public police officers who work off duty in a private policing capacity are exempt from any private security training, even if the nature of their private police work is substantially different from their police department functions.

The qualifications of proprietary security officers are generally higher than those of contract security officers, demonstrating corporate demand for high-quality security services even when they cost more.

DIMINISHED PUBLIC RESPONSIBILITY The current mixture of public and private protection is a matter of concern to many. What does it say about a government's ability to govern and provide for the general welfare—let alone what it says about American society—that ever more frequently it is shifting responsibility for protecting life and property to private security enterprises? To some, it seems to mean that public police officers and the governments that employ them have defaulted on a major portion of the social contract.

PRIVATE SECURITY'S ROLE IN THE FIGHT AGAINST TERRORISM Private security officers are often the first line of defense against terrorism in the United States and other nations. They guard government buildings, utilities, schools, courts, corporate headquarters, office complexes, laboratories, and transportation facilities, to name only a few. Unfortunately, with relatively few exceptions, most of the nation's more than one million security officers are unlicensed, untrained, and do not undergo background checks (see the nearby FYI entitled "Laws Governing Private Security").

The private security industry and its officers have been given more protection responsibilities as the threat of domestic terrorism in the United States has increased. Public law enforcement alone cannot begin to meet the protection responsibilities necessary to prevent terrorism. This means that the private security industry, comprising 11,000 companies throughout America, will have to begin improving its selection standards and training if the nation's people, visitors, and assets are to be protected. As unbelievable as it is, hundreds of security guards employed to protect the Statue of Liberty were found in 2002 to have no licenses and their ranks included ex-convicts.

Because it is so difficult to find enough capable private security officers, the proprietary security firms, motivated by large profits, have been employing hundreds if not thousands of unqualified and unmotivated applicants. For many of the guards, the position is a second or low-paying job that they can easily quit if they find a better-paying job or simply choose to do so. More troublesome is that foreign and domestic terrorists could easily obtain a private security position and inflict physical and emotional havoc on the nation by initiating some terrorist activity inside a vulnerable site.

Seldom is throwing money at a problem a solution in and of itself; yet, if the private security industry is to fulfill its obligation to protect the homeland, it is going to need more financial resources. It may be necessary, for example, to provide government subsidies for training and background checks and a significant increase in the amount of cooperation between the public police and the private security industry. That sort of investment and training can bring positive results. Following the 1993 World Trade Center bombing, the security officers at the World Trade Center were provided in-depth and regular follow-up training on such topics as emergency evacuation procedures and building layout. On September 11, 2001, security officers helped thousands of building workers safely out of the World Trade Center before the twin towers fell.

THINKING CRITICALLY

1. What do you think are some of the benefits and drawbacks of being a private security officer?

2. Do you think that stricter qualification standards should be established for private security personnel? Why or why not?

1. Briefly describe the jurisdictional limitations of American law enforcement.

   The authority of public law enforcement agencies in the United States, whether they are local, state, or federal agencies, is carefully limited by law. The territory within which each may operate is also restricted.

2. Trace the English origins of American law enforcement.

   Many institutions of American law enforcement evolved from the English tradition. The medieval tithing system and the constable-watch system were early methods of community protection that led to the development of the positions of sheriff and constable. The Bow Street Runners in the city of London in the 1750s were an early group of crime fighters who patrolled neighborhoods and pursued lawbreakers. The London Metropolitan Police, founded in 1829, became the model for municipal police departments in the United States.

3. Discuss the early development of American law enforcement.

   Americans at first adopted the British system of community protection. When the constable-watch system proved inadequate in meeting the peacekeeping needs of the nation's major cities, municipal police forces were established in the mid-1800s. They soon became entangled with local politics. In the states and on the frontier, law enforcement reflected regional differences. In the South, the earliest policing was the plantation slave patrols. On the frontier, vigilantism and later, local sheriffs or U.S. marshals dealt with lawbreakers. In some states, state police agencies, such as the Texas Rangers, were established to enforce laws statewide.

4. Describe the major developments that have occurred in American policing.

   During the period of professionalism and reform that lasted from about 1920 to 1970, the police became professional crime fighters, relying on the centralization of authority, motorized patrols, specialization, and technological aids. In the 1960s, the crime-fighting role of the police came into conflict with the social and political upheavals of the time, causing critics to call for improved standards and training. By the early 1990s, some police agencies began to turn to community policing, attempting to eliminate crime problems in neighborhoods and return to their role as peacekeepers. At the start of the twenty-first century, the prevention and repression of domestic terrorism has also become a major priority of police in America.

5. Describe the structure of American law enforcement.

   Law enforcement agencies are found at all levels of government in the United States. Most law enforcement officers work for local governments and are responsible for enforcing laws, maintaining order, providing service, and gathering information. In rural areas, the county sheriffs' department is responsible for law enforcement. Every state, except Hawaii, has a state law enforcement agency. The law enforcement agencies of the federal government are concerned primarily with violations of federal laws, especially violations that cross state boundaries; maintaining homeland security; and preventing domestic terrorism.

6. Explain the relationship between the FBI and the Department of Homeland Security.

   Since 9/11 the FBI has undergone fundamental changes. The biggest change is that it has shifted its top priority from being a federal police agency to being an intelligence and counterterrorism agency. Although it remains an independent agency in the Justice Department, it will now closely coordinate its antiterrorism activities with the CIA and the Department of Homeland Security.

7. Discuss the development and growth of private security in the United States.

   The private security industry has grown rapidly over the past 35 years for a number of reasons: revenues for public policing have declined (until recently); crimes in the workplace are often private, costly, and embarrassing; employers have better control of private security officers; and fewer constitutional limits restrict private security officers.

REVIEW QUESTIONS

1. What is meant by *jurisdiction?*

2. What was the *tithing system?*

3. Who were the Bow Street Runners?

4. In what year was the London Metropolitan Police founded?

5. Who was Robert Peel?

6. What system of English policing did the colonists bring to America?

7. What were the *slave codes?*

8. What group is considered to be the first state police agency?

9. How did August Vollmer change policing?

10. How did police response to the demonstrations and civil disorders of the 1960s affect policing?

11. What is *community policing?*

12. What are the four main functions of local police?

13. Why do county sheriffs have more political clout than police chiefs?

14. What is the difference between a *state police model* and a *highway patrol model* of state law enforcement?

15. Name some federal law enforcement agencies.

16. Distinguish between *contract* and *proprietary private security services.*

17. What are some successes and problems in the war on terrorism?

18. How do the employment qualifications for private security personnel in the United States compare and contrast with the qualifications to be a police officer, deputy sheriff, state police officer, or federal agent?

IN THE FIELD

1. **Your Local Law Enforcement** Identify all the local law enforcement agencies in your area. Divide up the list among your classmates and arrange to visit your assigned agency. On the day that you visit, find out how many calls the department received and/or how many crimes the agency personnel investigated in the 24-hour period prior to your visit, what types of calls were received or crimes were investigated, and how the agency handled the situation. Categorize the actions of the agency personnel into law enforcement, order maintenance, service, or information gathering. Identify the category with the most action. Share your findings with others in the class. What conclusions can you draw about the operation of the local law enforcement agencies in your area?

2. **Local and Private Police** Describe the possibilities you see for local police departments and private security agencies to work together more closely. To prepare for this activity, interview a local police official and a private security manager, either by telephone or in person, asking them what obstacles prevent closer cooperation between local policing and private security.

1. **Local Police Jobs** Go to the following links for sites dedicated to law enforcement careers and select two municipal police departments, one large and one small, and one county sheriffs' department that list the agency's employment qualifications on their Web page:

   www.govtjobs.com/safe/index.html
   www.jobs4police.com
   www.lawenforcementjobs.com
   www.policecareer.com
   www.policeemployment.com
   www.wpoaca.com/job.html

   Then find the qualifications for a private security officer through other applicable career sites provided at www.securityjobs.net or www.bls.gov/oco/ocos159.htm. Make a list of the similarities and differences between police and

deputy sheriff qualifications and private security officer qualifications. Given your background and abilities, for which type of work would you be best suited? Why? Compile your findings in a two-page report and present it to the class.

2. **Federal Law Enforcement** To learn about the responsibilities of some of the lesser-known federal law enforcement agencies, access their Web sites: (1) *Food and Drug Administration, Office of Criminal Investigations,* www.fda.gov/ora/inspect_ref/iom/ChapterText/980.html; (2) *National Park Service, U.S. Park Police,* www.nps.gov/personnel/parkpolice.htm; (3) *U.S. Fish and Wildlife Service, Division of Law Enforcement,* www.le.fws.gov; and (4) *U.S. Capitol Police,* www.fedquest.com/opmrefs/tei51.htm. Which agency seems the most interesting? Why?

1. **Neighborhood Watch** You live in a middle-class community of single-family homes close to the center of a midsize city. Over the past 5 years, everyone in your neighborhood has noted the rise in burglaries and many people feel that it is not safe to walk around the neighborhood after dark. You think that setting up a neighborhood watch would help lower the burglary rate and make people feel safer. Prepare an oral presentation of your ideas for a community meeting. Use the following questions as a guide.
   a. How would you go about organizing a night watch?
   b. How would you select volunteers?
   c. What training, if any, would volunteers have to have?
   d. How would you maintain interest and participation in the watch?

2. **Public Officer or Private Citizen?** An off-duty police officer was seated in a restaurant when two men entered, drew guns, and robbed the cashier. The officer made no attempt to prevent the robbery or apprehend the robbers. Later the officer justified the conduct by stating that an officer, when off duty, is a private citizen with the same duties and rights as all private citizens. Do you agree? Explain.

To access more information and resources, including study questions, chapter summaries, and links, go to: www.mhhe.com/bohm1.

CHAPTER THREE

POLICING: ROLES, STYLES, FUNCTIONS, AND LEGAL CONSTRAINTS

CHAPTER OUTLINE

CHAPTER OBJECTIVES

After completing this chapter, you should be able to:

1. Identify characteristics of police work.

2. Distinguish among James Q. Wilson's three operational styles in policing.

3. List the four major functions of police departments.

4. List the drug enforcement strategies of local police agencies.

5. Explain the main components of community policing.

6. Identify the four steps in a community policing approach to problem solving.

7. Describe the procedural rights in the Fourth Amendment.

8. Describe the procedural rights in the Fifth Amendment.

Policing in America

The police are at the forefront of the criminal justice process and, for most people, the only personal experience they have with that process is contact with a local police officer. Most people have never been in a courthouse for a criminal matter or in a jail or prison for any reason. This chapter examines what the police do, and the qualities they need to do it.

THE ROLES OF THE POLICE

Our expectations of police behavior depend on where we live and when we consider the question. For example, we saw in the last chapter that Cincinnati wanted its police officers in the 1880s to be fleet-footed and honest. In Dallas, Miami, and New York City, citizens may expect police officers to have a working knowledge of Spanish. In Alaska, we would expect police officers to be self-reliant, enjoy the outdoors, and not mind working by themselves in lonely surroundings. In essence, what we expect from the police depends on how we view their role in society.

A **role** consists of the rights and responsibilities associated with a particular position in society. A related concept is **role expectation,** the behavior and actions that people expect from a person in a particular role. Suppose, for example, that teenagers living in a wealthy neighborhood have been caught drinking alcohol. Their parents probably expect police officers to warn the young people and bring them home. In a less affluent neighborhood, on the other hand, the expectation of community residents might be that the police will arrest the teenagers and bring them into juvenile court. This example illustrates a problem that often arises in our attempt to understand the police role in America. When the public's expectations differ from the official police role, the public may become disenchanted and sometimes hostile toward law enforcement officers. Such negative feelings cause officers personal frustration and role conflict. **Role conflict** is the psychological strain and stress that results from trying to perform two or more incompatible responsibilities. A common source of role conflict for the police is the expectation that they should be social or helping agents at the same time they are expected to be control agents by arresting law violators.

What we expect from police officers, then, depends on how we view the police role—a role that has been described as complex, ambiguous, changing, and repressive. Obviously, not everyone views the role of the police in the same way, but a definition that includes the majority of perspectives is possible. The police:

1. Are community leaders in public safety? (By nature, this makes the work potentially dangerous.)
2. Possess broad discretion.
3. Solve sociological and technological problems for people on a short-term basis.
4. Occasionally serve in a hostile or dangerous environment.[1]

---

role The rights and responsibilities associated with a particular position in society.

role expectation The behavior and actions that people expect from a person in a particular role.

role conflict The psychological stress and frustration that results from trying to perform two or more incompatible responsibilities.

Police officers are expected to respond to traffic accidents. *How might such experiences affect them?*

Think about some of the common situations in which police officers find themselves when people call and want something "fixed." One example would be an officer's response to freeway accidents where vehicles are overturned and burning and people are trapped inside. Such situations require leadership, informed and quick decisions, the solving of numerous immediate problems, and the use of extreme caution to prevent further injury to citizens or the police officer. Another example would be intervention in a long-running family dispute that has suddenly turned violent. Such a situation requires caution, quick thinking, and the solving of a number of problems in an effort to ensure the safety of all parties. Still another typical role of a police officer is to provide protection at protests and strikes. Those potentially volatile circumstances clearly illustrate the key elements of the police role. Of course, sometimes an officer's role may be simply to solve problems in the course of providing service, as when retrieving a citizen's dropped keys from below a sewer grate.

CHARACTERISTICS OF POLICE WORK

Police work requires a combination of special characteristics. Personnel with the following qualities are best able to carry out the difficult service role mandated for law enforcement officers.

QUICK DECISION MAKING Sometimes police officers must make on-the-spot decisions about whether to use force, how to maneuver a patrol car, or whether to stop a suspect. Making the wrong decision can be fatal for the officer or the other person. All of the work in a lengthy investigation can be ruined by a single procedural law violation if an officer unintentionally makes a wrong decision.

THE INDEPENDENT NATURE OF POLICE WORK The position of peace officer in all states in the United States is a position of honor and trust. After patrol officers attend roll call, stand inspection, check out their equipment, and depart into the streets in their patrol cars, they work virtually unsupervised until the end of their tour of duty.

Figure 3.1 shows the Law Enforcement Officer's Code of Ethics, which was written as a guide for working police officers. It offers some professional

FIGURE 3.1	Law Enforcement Officer Code of Ethics

The purpose of the Code of Ethics is to ensure that all peace officers are fully aware of their individual responsibility to maintain their own integrity and that of their agency. Every peace officer, during basic training, or at the time of appointment, shall be administered the [following] Code of Ethics.

As a law enforcement officer, my fundamental duty is to serve mankind; to safeguard lives and property; to protect the innocent against deception, the weak against oppression or intimidation, and the peaceful against violence or disorder; and to respect the constitutional rights of all men to liberty, equality, and justice.

I will keep my private life unsullied as an example to all; maintain courageous calm in the face of danger, scorn, or ridicule; develop self-restraint; and be constantly mindful of the welfare of others. Honest in thought and deed in both my personal and official life, I will be exemplary in obeying the laws of the land and the regulations of my department. Whatever I see or hear of a confidential nature or that is confided to me in my official capacity will be kept ever secret unless revelation is necessary in the performance of my duty. I will never act officiously or permit personal feelings, prejudices, animosities, or friendships to influence my decisions. With no compromise for crime and with relentless prosecution of criminals, I will enforce the law courteously and appropriately without fear or favor, malice or ill will, never employing unnecessary force or violence, and never accepting gratuities.

I recognize the badge of my office as a symbol of public faith, and I accept it as a public trust to be held so long as I am true to the ethics of the police service. I will constantly strive to achieve these objectives and ideals, dedicating myself to my chosen profession—law enforcement.

Canons

1. The primary responsibility of police officers and organizations is the protection of citizens by upholding the law and respecting the legally expressed will of the whole community and not a particular party or clique.

2. Police officers should be aware of the legal limits on their authority and the "genius of the American system," which limits the power of individuals, groups, and institutions.

3. Police officers are responsible for being familiar with the law and not only their responsibilities but also those of other public officials.

4. Police officers should be mindful of the importance of using the proper means to gain proper ends. Officers should not employ illegal means, nor should they disregard public safety or property to accomplish a goal.

5. Police officers will cooperate with other public officials in carrying out their duties. However, the officer shall be careful not to use his or her position in an improper or illegal manner when cooperating with other officials.

6. In their private lives, police officers will behave in such a manner that the public will "regard (the officer) as an example of stability, fidelity, and morality." It is necessary that police officers conduct themselves in a "decent and honorable" manner.

7. In their behavior toward members of the public, officers will provide service when possible, require compliance with the law, respond in a manner that inspires confidence and trust, and will be neither overbearing nor subservient.

8. When dealing with violators or making arrests, officers will follow the law; officers have no right to persecute individuals or punish them. And officers should behave in such a manner so the likelihood of the use of force is minimized.

9. Police officers should refuse to accept any gifts, favors, or gratuities that, from a public perspective, could influence the manner in which the officer discharges his or her duties.

10. Officers will present evidence in criminal cases impartially because the officer should be equally concerned with both the prosecution of criminals and the defense of innocent persons.

Source: Commission on Peace Officer Standards and Training, *Administrative Manual* (State of California: POST, 1990), p. c.-5.

TABLE 3.1	Law Enforcement Officers Assaulted in the United States, 2004

CIRCUMSTANCES AT SCENE OF INCIDENT	TOTAL
Total	**59,373**
Percent of Total	**100%**
Disturbance calls (family quarrel, man with guns, etc.)	18,234
	30.7%
Burglaries in progress of pursuit of burglary suspects	850
	1.4%
Robberies in progress or pursuit of robbery suspects	544
	0.9%
Other arrest attempts	9,674
	16.3%
Civil disorders (mass disobedience, riot, etc.)	734
	1.2%
Handling, transporting, custody of prisoners	7,748
	13.0%
Investigation of suspicious persons and circumstances	5,532
	9.3%
Ambush (no warning)	189
	0.3%
Mentally deranged	1,079
	1.8%
Traffic pursuits and stops	6,568
	11.1%
All others	8,221
	13.8%

Source: United States Department of Justice, Federal Bureau of Investigation, *Law Enforcement Officers Killed and Assaulted, 2004;* www.fbi.gov/ucr/killed/2004/table67.htm.

direction in a line of work with many opportunities to go astray. The independent nature of police work increases the chances of malfeasance and corruption—topics to be discussed in the next chapter.

"DIRTY WORK" Most people agree that police work needs to be done, but police work is sometimes distasteful—for example, dealing with people who have committed horrible acts and viewing mangled, broken, and decomposed bodies. Oftentimes, the police must deal with people at their worst—angry, drunk, in trouble, victimized, violent, and so forth. The distasteful part of policing has been referred to as "dirty work."[2]

DANGER Police officers in the United States spend a substantial amount of their time trying to resolve conflicts, frequently in hostile environments.[3] Table 3.1 identifies dangerous circumstances in which officers find themselves. Contrary to the media image, police officers are often afraid on the job, and far too many are injured or killed. The data reveal that disturbance calls (for example, a family quarrel or a man with a gun) and arrests of suspects are the most dangerous circumstances for police officers. Because of the danger field officers face, many departments require them to wear body armor while on duty. Table 3.2 shows the percentage of local police departments, by size of population served, that required field officers to wear body armor while on duty in 2003.

| | PERCENTAGE OF AGENCIES REQUIRING FIELD OFFICERS TO WEAR ARMOR WHILE ON DUTY | | |
POPULATION SERVED	TOTAL	AT ALL TIMES	IN SOME CIRCUMSTANCES
All Sizes	71%	59%	12%
1,000,000 or more	63%	44%	19%
500,000–999,999	79	60	19
250,000–499,999	68	56	12
100,000–249,999	68	50	18
50,000–99,999	69	52	17
25,000–49,999	74	61	13
10,000–24,999	74	63	11
2,500–9,999	80	69	11
Under 2,500	63	52	11

TABLE 3.2 Body Armor Requirements for Field Officers in Local Police Departments, by Size of Population Served, 2003

Source: Matthew J. Hickman and Brian A. Reaves, *Local Police Departments, 2003* (Washington, DC: GPO, U.S. Department of Justice, Bureau of Justice Statistics, May 2006), p. 25, Table 56.

Killed in the Line of Duty

Today, more than 800,000 sworn officers put their lives on the line for our protection each day. The first known line-of-duty death was that of U.S. Marshal Robert Forsyth, who was shot and killed on January 11, 1794, while serving court papers in a civil suit. Wilmington, Delaware, police matron Mary T. Davis was the first female officer killed on duty. She was beaten to death in 1924 while guarding a prisoner in the city jail.

operational styles The different overall approaches to the police job.

Despite the use of body armor and other precautions, each year police officers are killed while on duty. In 2005, for example, 55 officers were feloniously killed in the line of duty, many fewer than the 142 officers killed feloniously in 2001, and 2 fewer than the 57 officers killed feloniously in 2004. However, 2001 was an unusual year. Among the 142 officers feloniously killed were the 72 federal, state, and local officers killed during the tragedy of September 11—the most officers killed in the United States on a single day. In 1999, only 42 officers were feloniously killed in the line of duty, which was the lowest recorded figure in more than 35 years.[4]

Of the 55 officers feloniously killed in the line of duty in 2005, 15 were killed during traffic pursuits and stops, 8 died in arrest situations, 8 were ambushed by their assailants, 7 were murdered answering disturbance calls, 7 while investigating suspicious persons or circumstances, 4 while conducting investigative activities, 3 during tactical situations, 2 while handling mentally deranged individuals, and 1 while handling and transporting prisoners.[5] Accidents, such as automobile accidents, during the performance of official duties claimed the lives of an additional 67 officers in 2005, down from 82 in 2004, 80 in 2003, 76 in 2002, 78 in 2001, and 84 in 2000.[6]

From 1972 through 2005, 4,905 law enforcement officers were killed in the line of duty: 2,787 were feloniously killed and 2,118 were accidentally killed. The most officers killed in any one year were 220 in 2001, while the least in any year was 107 in 1999. In general, and with the exception of 2001, the number of law enforcement officers killed while on duty has declined since the early 1970s.[7]

OPERATIONAL STYLES

After police officers are trained and begin to gain experience and wisdom from their encounters with veteran police officers and citizens on the street, it is believed that they develop **operational styles** that characterize their overall approach to the police job. If these styles actually exist, it means that the effort of the police department to systematically train and deploy officers with the same philosophy and practical approach to policing in the community has not been entirely successful. The research on operational styles shows that they vary both between departments and among officers of the same department.

One of the earliest scholars to report on the existence of policing styles was political scientist James Q. Wilson, who found the following three styles in a study of eight police departments:

1. *Legalistic style.* The emphasis is on violations of law and the use of threats or actual arrests to solve disputes in the community. In theory, the more arrests that are made, the safer a community will be. This style is often found in large metropolitan areas.
2. *Watchman style.* The emphasis is on informal means of resolving disputes and problems in a community. Keeping the peace is the paramount concern, and arrest is used only as a last resort to resolve any kind of disturbance of the peace. This style of policing is most commonly found in economically poorer communities.
3. *Service style.* The emphasis is on helping in the community, as opposed to enforcing the law. Referrals and diversion to community treatment agencies are more common than arrest and formal court action. The service style is most likely to be found in wealthy communities.[8]

Sociologist John Broderick, who also studied operational styles among the police, classified police officers by their degree of commitment to maintaining order and their respect for due process. The following are the categories he used:

1. *Enforcers.* The emphasis is on order, with little respect for due process.
2. *Idealists.* The emphasis is on both social order and due process.
3. *Optimists.* The emphasis is on due process, with little priority given to social order.
4. *Realists.* Little emphasis is given to due process or social order.[9]

Another classification is based on the way officers use their authority and power in street police work. The two key ingredients of this scheme are passion and perspective. *Passion* is the ability to use force or the recognition that force is a legitimate means of resolving conflict; *perspective* is the ability to understand human suffering and to use force ethically and morally. According to political scientist William Muir's styles of policing, police officers may be classified as the following:

1. *Professionals.* Officers have the necessary passion and perspective to be valuable police officers.
2. *Enforcers.* Officers have passion for the job, for enforcing the law, for taking decisive action; their inner drive or value system allows them to be comfortable using force to solve problems.
3. *Reciprocators.* Officers lack the passion to do the job; they have a difficult time taking action, making arrests, enforcing the law; their values make it difficult for them to use force to solve problems.
4. *Avoiders.* Officers have neither passion nor perspective, resulting in no recognition of people's problems and no action to resolve them.[10]

Are there identifiable styles of policing? What value do these styles hold for us? In any area of human endeavor, classifications have been constructed. We have developed classifications for leaders, prisoners, quarterbacks, and teachers. These classifications give us a framework of analysis, a basis for discussion. But can they be substantiated when we go into a police agency to see if they actually exist?

THINKING CRITICALLY

1. Which characteristics do you think are the most important for police officers to have? Why?

2. Is there an operational style of policing that you think is the most effective? If so, which one?

3. Do you think it is possible to identify styles of policing? If so, how can it be done? If not, what obstacles prevent identification?

Social scientist Ellen Hochstedler examined the issue of policing styles with 1,134 Dallas, Texas, police officers and was not able to confirm the officer styles identified in the literature by Broderick, Muir, and others. Her conclusion was that it is not possible to "pigeonhole" officers into one style or another because the way officers think and react to street situations varies, depending on the particular situation, the time, and the officers themselves.[11]

Police Functions

The list of functions that police are expected to carry out is long and varies from place to place. In the following sections, the major operations of police departments and the services they provide are examined.

CAREERS IN CRIMINAL JUSTICE

Ohio State Highway Patrol Officer

My name is Lieutenant Brenda Sue Collins. I have had an exciting career with the Ohio State Highway Patrol and have worked in a variety of assignments since 1985. Currently I am the post commander for the Fremont post of the State Highway Patrol, responsible for the leadership of all operational and staff personnel serving at the Fremont post. I have also served as a cadet dispatcher (my first job with the patrol), a highway trooper, an academy instructor, an officer in the Traffic and Drug Interdiction Unit, a supervisor in the recruiting section, and a public information officer. I am married to Captain Richard Collins, a district commander of the patrol stationed in Findlay.

An Ohio State Highway Patrol Officer's major responsibility is to patrol the roadways and keep them safe. That responsibility includes investigating vehicle crashes, gaining obedience to the traffic laws by enforcement and other means, giving assistance to motorists 24 hours a day, keeping the roadway free of obstructions, enforcing the extensive commercial vehicle laws, and checking for signs of criminal activity during vehicle stops. One of the toughest parts of the patrol officer's job is to make death notifications to family members of loved ones who have been killed in a fatal crash.

I graduated in the 116th Academy class and was assigned to the Portsmouth post as a trooper where I was somewhat of a novelty with the citizens since there were not that many female highway patrol officers. But when people see that you do your job effectively and professionally just like your male counterparts, the novelty soon wears off. Now we have about 130 female troopers out of a total of approximately 1,400 troopers.

I attended Ohio University, where I studied forensic chemistry and law enforcement, and Ohio State University in Marion. The OSHP provides tuition assistance that varies depending on the grades you receive in courses.

Being married to another highway patrol officer really has its advantages. First, you can learn from each other because you have worked in different assignments and have experienced common things at different times in your career. Richard and I also know the language and values of the highway patrol, therefore allowing us to communicate a lot more clearly than a married couple working at entirely different jobs. The only disadvantage that I can see is that when both of you are senior officers in the patrol, you have to deal with the issue of promotions. As a married couple we are not allowed to serve in the same posts of the patrol, but can be in adjacent districts if there are openings for our rank. Consequently when promotional opportunities come up for one or the other of us, we have to think of what kind of disruption that will cause in our home life.

The advice I would offer to somebody who wants to be a highway patrol officer is to work in a job you really want until the highway patrol officer's job becomes available. The selection process is long and difficult. I would suggest that you investigate and really find out what a highway patrol officer's job is like. The job entails round-the-clock duty in all sorts of weather, including the worst weather. In fact, you may be the only one out on the highways during bad weather. You are more likely to stick with it when you know these things up front.

What characteristics of your personality do you think would make you best suited to be a highway patrol officer?

PATROL

Police administrators have long referred to patrol as the backbone of the department. It is unquestionably the most time-consuming and resource-intensive task of any police agency. More than half of the sworn personnel in any police department are assigned to patrol. In Houston, Chicago, and New York, for example, patrol officers make up more than 65 percent of the sworn personnel in each department.

Patrol officers respond to burglar alarms, investigate traffic accidents, care for injured people, try to resolve domestic disputes, and engage in a host of other duties that keep them chasing radio calls across their own beats and the entire city and county when no other cars are available to respond. Precisely how to conduct patrol activities, however, is a matter of much debate in the nation today. Indeed, it seems that there are many ways to police a city.

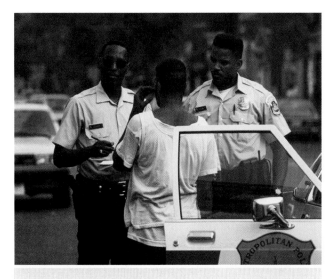

Street patrol is the most resource-intensive task of any police agency. *Are there acceptable alternatives to street patrol? If yes, what are they?*

PREVENTIVE PATROL For decades, police officers patrolled the streets with little direction. Between their responses to radio calls, they were told to be "systematically unsystematic" and observant in an attempt to both prevent and ferret out crime on their beats. In many police departments, as much as 50 percent of an officer's time is uncommitted and available for patrolling the beats that make up a political jurisdiction. The simultaneous increases in the official crime rate and the size of police forces beginning in the 1960s caused police managers and academics to question the usefulness of what has come to be known as **preventive patrol,** or random patrol. To test the usefulness of preventive patrol, the now famous Kansas City (Missouri) Preventive Patrol Experiment was conducted in 1972.

The Kansas City, Missouri, Police Department and the Police Foundation set up an experiment in which 15 patrol districts were divided into three matched groups according to size, record of calls for service, and demographic characteristics. In the first group, the "control beats," the police department operated the same level of patrol used previously in those beats. In the second group of districts, the "proactive beats," the police department doubled or even tripled the number of patrol officers normally deployed in the area. In the third group of districts, the "reactive beats," the police department deployed no officers at all on preventive patrol. Officers only responded to calls for service and did no patrolling on their own. At the end of the 1-year study, the results showed no significant differences in crime rates among the three groups of patrol districts. In other words, a group of districts that had no officers on preventive patrol had the same crime rates as groups that had several times the normal level of staffing engaged in patrol activity. The number of officers made no difference in the number of burglaries, robberies, vehicle thefts, and other serious crimes experienced in the three groups of police districts. Perhaps even more important is that the citizens of Kansas City did not even notice that the levels of patrol in two of the three districts had been changed.[12]

preventive patrol Patrolling the streets with little direction; between responses to radio calls, officers are "systematically unsystematic" and observant in an attempt to both prevent and ferret out crime. Also known as *random patrol.*

Myth   Fact

Adding more police officers will reduce crime.

Short of having a police officer on every corner, evidence indicates no relationship between the number of police officers and the crime rate.

The law enforcement community was astounded by the results of the study, which showed that it made no difference whether patrol officers conducted preventive, or random, patrol. The research was immediately attacked on both philosophical and methodological grounds. How could anyone say that having patrol officers on the street made no difference?

One of the criticisms of the study was that no one in the community was told that there were no officers on patrol in reactive districts. What might have happened to the crime rates had the community known no officers were on patrol? Moreover, during the course of the study, marked police cars from other departments and districts crossed the reactive districts to answer calls but then left when the work was completed. Thus, there appeared to be a police presence even in the so-called reactive districts.

This study has forced police executives and academics to reconsider the whole issue of how patrol is conducted, once considered a closed issue. Police administrators have begun to entertain the possibility of reducing the number of officers on patrol. Innovations in patrol methods have also been proposed.

directed patrol Patrolling under guidance or orders on how to use patrol time.

DIRECTED PATROL In **directed patrol,** officers are given guidance or orders on how to use their patrol time. The guidance is often based on the results of crime analyses that identify problem areas. Evidence shows that directed patrol can reduce the incidence of targeted crimes such as thefts from autos and robberies.[13]

GIS crime mapping A technique that involves the charting of crime patterns within a geographic area.

CRIME MAPPING One technological innovation in crime analysis that has aided directed patrol is Geographic Information Systems (GIS) crime mapping. **GIS crime mapping** is a technique that involves the charting of crime patterns within a geographic area. Crime mapping makes it possible to keep a closer watch on crime and criminals through the generation of crime maps capable of displaying numerous fields of information. If, for example, a series of armed robberies of dry cleaning stores had been committed over a period of several weeks in three adjacent police beats, police crime analysts would be able to record, analyze, determine a definite pattern to these robberies and then make a reasonable prediction as to when and where the next robbery in the series is likely to occur. The patrol and investigation forces could be deployed at a prescribed time to conduct surveillance of the prospective target dry cleaning store or stores with a good chance the robber can be arrested. This use of crime mapping is referred to as "resource reallocation" and is probably the most widely used crime-mapping application. Figure 3.2 is an example of a crime map.

Crime mapping is also used as a tool to help evaluate the ability of police departments to resolve the problems in their communities. This is the primary purpose of the New York City Police Department's CompStat process, for example.[14] Begun in 1994, CompStat is a divisional unit responsible for statistical analysis of daily precinct crime reports frequently using crime mapping. The information produced by CompStat is used by the chief of police to judge the performance of precinct commanders and by precinct commanders to hold their officers accountable.

Crime mapping is likely to be used increasingly in crime scene investigations and the forensic sciences. For example, a GIS-based system has been created that can determine the origin of gunshots through sound triangulation. Crime mapping will also be combined with other technologies such as aerial photography so that geocoded data can be superimposed on aerial photographs rather than computer-generated maps. This should aid community-policing efforts by making census data, liquor license locations, drug-market data, and probationer addresses, for example, readily available in a more useful form. Another technology that will be combined with crime mapping is Global Positioning Systems (GPS) technology. Such technology would allow

GIS Crime Mapping
To learn more about GIS crime mapping and how it works, visit the GIS Lounge at **www.gislounge.com/features/ aa101100.shtml.** *Why is crime mapping important?*

FIGURE 3.2	Crime Map of Violent Crimes in the City of Phoenix, Arizona, January 1, 2004 through December 31, 2004

This crime map shows the number of violent crimes in the city of Phoenix, Arizona, during 2004. *What can be learned about the causes of crime from crime mapping?*

beat officers to track and monitor probationers and parolees in the area, for example. It is currently used in some departments to help manage the department's fleet of vehicles.[15]

AGGRESSIVE PATROL In nearly all police departments, some patrol officers have used aggressive patrol tactics and have been rewarded as high performers because they made many arrests for both minor and serious offenses. When the entire patrol section is instructed to make numerous traffic stops and field interrogations, the practice is referred to as **aggressive patrol. A field interrogation** is a temporary detention in which officers stop and question pedestrians and motorists they find in suspicious circumstances. Such procedures have been found to reduce crime in targeted areas.[16]

aggressive patrol The practice of having an entire patrol section make numerous traffic stops and field interrogations.

field interrogation A temporary detention in which officers stop and question pedestrians and motorists they find in suspicious circumstances.

Field interrogation has been found to reduce crime in targeted areas. *What are some of the problems with field interrogations?*

Patrolling

In 2003, 59 percent of local police departments, including more than 75 percent of those serving 250,000 or more residents, routinely used foot patrol. All local police departments used automobiles for routine patrol. In addition, approximately 40 percent of departments, including more than 95 percent of those serving 500,000 or more residents, used bicycle patrol on a regular basis.

SOURCE: Matthew J. Hicks and Brian A. Reaves, *Local Police Departments, 2003* (Washington, DC: Bureau of Justice Statistics, 2006), p. iii.

At least two problems can occur as a result of aggressive patrol. First, random traffic stops and field interrogations inconvenience innocent citizens. To avoid conflict, the police must be certain that those tactics are necessary, and they must explain the necessity to the public. Second, it is often difficult to get all officers on each work shift and in each patrol division motivated to use aggressive patrol tactics. Many officers are reluctant to carry out their duties in an aggressive way. Nevertheless, with crime rates high and research confirming that aggressive patrol can reduce crime, aggressive patrol tactics are likely to continue.

FOOT PATROL   For some time, there has been renewed interest in having police officers patrol their beats on foot. Is there value in this practice, or is it just nostalgia for a more romantic period in law enforcement? The use of motorized patrols has allowed the police to respond rapidly to citizen calls and to cover large geographical areas. Yet, officers working a busy shift, perhaps responding to more than two dozen calls, come to feel as if they are seeing the world through a windshield. Moreover, it is now generally accepted that rapid response time is useful in only a small portion of the incidents and crimes to which the police are asked to respond.

Challenging conventional wisdom about rapid response, two cities—Flint, Michigan, and Newark, New Jersey—launched substantial programs in foot patrol. In Newark, the results of the foot patrol experiment showed that foot patrol had little or no effect on the level of crime. However, positive effects were identified:

1. Newark residents noticed whether foot patrol officers were present.
2. They were more satisfied with police service when foot patrol officers delivered it.
3. They were less afraid than citizens being served by motorized patrol.[17]

In Flint, Michigan, the extensive neighborhood foot patrol experiment also had positive results:

1. Flint residents had a decreased fear of crime.
2. Their satisfaction with police service increased.
3. There were moderate decreases in crime.
4. There were decreased numbers of calls for police service.

TABLE 3.3	Types of Patrol Used on a Routine Basis by Local Police Departments, by Size of Population Served, 2003

POPULATION SERVED	PERCENTAGE OF AGENCIES USING EACH TYPE OF PATROL ON A ROUTINE BASIS					
	AUTO-MOBILE*	FOOT	BICYCLE	MOTOR-CYCLE	MARINE	HORSE
ALL SIZES	100%	59%	38%	14%	4%	2%
1,000,000 or more	100	75%	100%	81%	63%	63%
500,000–999,999	100	79	95	100	41	63
250,000–499,999	100	76	83	93	32	59
100,000–249,999	100	57	83	89	14	18
50,000–99,999	100	54	64	63	14	7
25,000–49,999	100	47	60	49	8	2
10,000–24,999	100	53	58	21	5	2
2,500–9,999	100	61	43	8	3	—
Under 2,500	100	61	18	3	2	—

*As of 2000, all local police departments surveyed reported routine use of automobile patrols.—Less than 0.5%.

Source: Matthew J. Hickman and Brian A. Reaves, *Local Police Departments, 2003* (Washington, DC: GPO, U.S. Department of Justice, Bureau of Justice Statistics, May 2006), p. 13, Table 24.

Citizens would wait to talk to their neighborhood foot patrol officer about a problem instead of calling the police department through 911 and speaking with an officer they were not likely to know. One astounding result of the Flint program was that the foot patrol officers became so popular that citizens saw them as real community leaders. They often became more influential than some elected officials. Evidence of the degree of satisfaction with the foot patrol program in Flint was that the community voted three times to continue and expand foot patrol at a time when the city was experiencing one of the nation's highest unemployment rates.[18] Perhaps even more important, the findings of foot patrol research provided the seeds of a much broader concept for law enforcement: community policing, which we will discuss later in this chapter. Table 3.3 shows the percentage of agencies, by size of population served, that used various types of patrol on a routine basis in 2003.

INVESTIGATION

The role of the detective has generally been glorified by media sources in both fiction and nonfiction accounts. Homicide investigation, in particular, has captured the imagination of fiction readers worldwide. Most police officers aspire to be investigative specialists by attaining the position of detective. But it should be noted that detectives represent only one unit in a police department that conducts investigations. Investigators work in a variety of capacities in a police agency:

1. Traffic homicide and hit-and-run accident investigators in the traffic section.
2. Undercover investigators in narcotics, vice, and violent gang cases.
3. Internal affairs investigators conducting investigations of alleged crimes by police personnel.
4. Investigators conducting background checks of applicants to the police department.
5. Uniformed patrol officers investigating the crimes they have been dispatched to or have encountered on their own while on patrol.
6. Detectives of Criminal Investigation Divisions who conduct investigations into reports of criminal activity made by patrol officers.

Crime Assessment

For less serious crimes, many police departments use solvability-factor score sheets or software programs to assess information collected at crime scenes. The assessment, which is done by the responding officer, a case-screening officer, or a felony-review unit, determines which cases are likely to be solved, given the initial information obtained. Promising cases are turned over to detectives for follow-up investigation. The rest are often closed on the basis of the preliminary investigation and are reopened only if additional information is uncovered.

SOURCE: Alfred Blumstein and Joan Petersilia, "NIJ and Its Research Program," *25 Years of Criminal Justice Research* (Washington, DC: The National Institute of Justice, 1994), p. 13.

WHAT IS CRIMINAL INVESTIGATION? Criminal investigation has been defined as a lawful search for people and things to reconstruct the circumstances of an illegal act, apprehend or determine the guilty party, and aid in the state's prosecution of the offender.[19] The criminal investigation process is generally divided into two parts: the preliminary, or initial, investigation and the continuing, or follow-up, investigation. Most of the time the preliminary investigation in both felony and misdemeanor cases is conducted by patrol officers, although for homicides and other complex, time-consuming investigations, trained investigators are dispatched to the crime scene immediately. The continuing investigation in serious crimes is ordinarily conducted by plainclothes detectives, although small and medium-sized agencies may require patrol officers or a patrol supervisor to follow up on serious criminal offenses.

INVESTIGATIVE FUNCTIONS In any type of investigation in a police agency, all investigators share responsibility for a number of critical functions. They must:

1. Locate witnesses and suspects.
2. Arrest criminals.
3. Collect, preserve, and analyze evidence.
4. Interview witnesses.
5. Interrogate suspects.
6. Write reports.
7. Recover stolen property.
8. Seize contraband.
9. Prepare cases and testify in court.

The specific application and context of those functions vary considerably, depending on whether the investigation is of the theft of expensive paintings, for example, or the rape of an elderly widow living alone.

Criminal investigation is a time-consuming task that requires much attention to detail. *What aspects of criminal investigations are the most time-consuming and why?*

THE ROLE OF THE DETECTIVE At first glance, the role of the detective seems highly desirable. To a patrol officer who has been rotating work shifts for several years, seldom getting a weekend off, detectives in the police department seem to have a number of advantages:

1. They do not have to wear uniforms.
2. They have anonymity during work hours if they choose it.
3. They have steady work hours, often daytime hours with weekends off.
4. They have offices and desks.
5. They enjoy the prestige associated with the position.
6. In many agencies, detectives receive higher compensation and hold a higher rank.
7. Perhaps most important, they enjoy more freedom than patrol officers from the police radio, geographical boundaries, and close supervision.

All these advantages add up to a high-status position, both within the police department and in the eyes of the public.

PRODUCTIVITY Despite all the advantages of being a detective, investigators are often faced with insurmountable obstacles and stressful work conditions. Notifying the next of kin in a homicide is one of the worst tasks:

> Of all the dirty tasks that go with the dirty work of chasing a killer, notifying the next of kin is the job that homicide detectives hate most. It's worse than getting up at 3 A.M. on a February night to slog through a field of freezing mud toward a body that needed burying two days ago. Worse than staring into the flat cold eyes of a teenager who bragged about dragging a man through the streets to his death. Worse than visiting every sleazy dive in town until you finally find the one person who can put the murderer away and having that person say as cool as a debutante with a full dance card, "I don't want to get involved."[20]

Detectives have the cards stacked against them most of the time. Unless they discover, during the preliminary investigation, a named suspect or a description or other information that leads to a named suspect, the chances of solving the crime are low. Property crimes with no witnesses are particularly hard to solve. In 2004, for example, the clearance rates for crimes against persons were 62.6 percent for murder, 55.6 percent for aggravated assault, 41.8 percent for forcible rape, and 26.2 percent for robbery. In crimes against property, the clearance rates were 12.9 percent for burglary, 18.3 percent for larceny-theft, and 13.0 percent for motor vehicle theft. Clearances for crimes against persons are generally higher than for property crimes because crimes against persons receive more intensive investigative effort and because victims and witnesses frequently identify the perpetrators. In 2004, for example, the nationwide clearance rate for violent crimes was 46.3 percent and for property crimes, 16.5 percent.[21] Studies have found that much of what a detective does is not needed and that an investigator's technical knowledge often does little to help solve cases.[22] In one study, for example, fewer than 10 percent of all arrests for robbery were the result of investigative work by detectives.[23] Nevertheless, police agencies retain detectives and plainclothes investigators for a number of reasons:

1. Detectives have interrogation and case presentation skills that assist in prosecution.
2. Technical knowledge, such as knowing about burglary tools, does help in some investigations and prosecutions.

Myth

Improvements in detective work and criminal investigation will significantly raise clearance rates or lower the crime rate.

Fact

"Cleared" crimes generally solve themselves. The offender either is discovered at the scene or can be identified by the victim or a witness. Investigation rarely solves "cold" or "stranger" crimes.

DNA

In approximately one-third of DNA examinations, the suspect's DNA cannot be matched with biological evidence from the crime scene. Thus, potential suspects can be eliminated from consideration early in the investigative process, allowing investigators to focus their efforts more effectively on other suspects or cases.

CJ ONLINE

DNA Evidence
The National Commission on the Future of DNA Evidence is a program sponsored by the National Institute of Justice. Visit the program's Web site at **www.ojp. usdoj.gov/nij/dna/.** *How big a role should DNA play in criminal investigations?*

Myth Fact

Fingerprints are crucial in solving crimes.

Although fingerprints are useful in cases involving known suspects, they are rarely helpful in solving crimes where the suspect is unknown (the vast majority of criminal cases) because of the difficulty of obtaining usable prints at the crime scene.

3. Law enforcement executives can assign detectives to a major, high-profile case to demonstrate to the public that they are committing resources to the matter.

The major studies of investigative effectiveness emphasize the value of improving the suspect-identification process. Once a suspect is identified by name or some other clearly distinguishing characteristic, the chances of making an arrest are increased substantially.

RECENT IDENTIFICATION DEVELOPMENTS IN CRIMINAL INVESTIGATION Two of the most significant advances in criminal investigation have been the development of fingerprinting and DNA profiling. Fingerprinting has resulted in the arrest and conviction of millions of criminal suspects who otherwise might never have been brought to justice. DNA profiling holds even greater promise.

DNA Profiling DNA (deoxyribonucleic acid) is a molecule present in all forms of life. A unique genetic profile can be derived from blood, hair, semen, or other bodily substances found at the scene of a crime or on a victim. Not only can bodily substances found at a crime scene be matched with DNA samples from a suspect to give an extremely high probability of identifying the perpetrator, but it is believed that soon DNA from a sample as small as a flake of dandruff will yield a positive, unique identification, with no need to consider mathematical probabilities.

DNA profiling has three distinct functions: linking or eliminating identified suspects to a crime; identifying "cold hits" where a sample from a crime scene is matched against numerous cases in a DNA database and a positive match is made; and clearing convicted rapists and murderers years after they began serving their sentences. DNA profiling would be very useful, for example, in cases where a murderer's blood was found at the scene of a crime after a deadly struggle or in a rape case where seminal fluid could be obtained from the victim.

A serious issue at present is whether DNA databases ought to be assembled and from whom the samples should be taken. Many states permit the taking of DNA samples from arrested and convicted subjects. Some enthusiasts believe that DNA samples should be taken from all suspects in crimes, while a smaller number believe the samples should be collected from all people at birth. Currently, the most complete DNA database is the Combined DNA Index System (CODIS), which is managed by the Federal Bureau of Investigation. CODIS comprises DNA profiles that have been entered into local, state, and other national databases. The profiles are from either biological evidence left at crime scenes or individuals convicted of violent crimes and other felonies. Undoubtedly the more collected samples in a database, the more likely a match is going to be found. But privacy concerns and the potential for misuse of DNA samples are likely to hinder any more intrusive measures on the part of agents of the justice system.

Automated Fingerprint Identification System An expensive but invaluable tool in criminal investigation is the Automated Fingerprint Identification System (AFIS). This relatively new technology allows investigators to sort through thousands of sets of stored fingerprints for a match with those of a suspect in a crime. In fact, many of the current attempts to match prints would not have been made without AFIS, because the old process would have taken thousands of hours. Large metropolitan police agencies use it to identify 200–500 suspects a year who would have escaped apprehension before the implementation of AFIS. The initial and maintenance costs for an AFIS, however, are expensive. The FBI's AFIS is the world's largest, with more than 47 million prints on file. The Florida Department of Law Enforcement's system, by contrast, has only about 2.6 million prints on file.[24]

CYBERCRIME The use of computer technology to commit crime is of increasing concern to law enforcement officials. The FBI reports that the losses from **cybercrime** each year total $10 billion even though two-thirds of computer crime victims fail to notify the authorities. Some of the reasons for not reporting computer crime are the fear of loss of the public's confidence in the organization, the attention to vulnerability that a crime report would attract, and the shame of not providing adequate security to protect trusted assets.

cybercrime The use of computer technology to commit crime.

Since so little hardware and expense is involved, any person with a computer and modem connection to the Internet has the potential to attack computer systems and people online. The knowledge to carry out these attacks is often available online at hacker Web sites, message boards, and chat rooms. The cybercriminal can be as unsophisticated as a teenage amateur hacker just out for some fun or a talented computer specialist possessing skills on par with technical experts employed by the nation's top security organizations. Each of these types of computer criminal can wreak destructive havoc on a computer system, invade the privacy of thousands of citizens, and engage in the theft of millions of dollars' worth of trade secrets or steal large sums of money. At present, unfortunately, most law enforcement agencies in America are ill prepared to detect, investigate, and prosecute cybercriminals.[25]

A variety of offenses can be committed using computer and Internet technology.

1. Sex Crimes—Predators search the Internet looking for sexually explicit content as well as child pornography. Much of the sexually explicit and pornographic content is in JPEG and MPEG formats, which allow it to be downloaded to a person's hard drive easily.[26] Downloading much of this material is illegal in a number of states. The origin of some of this content is often from other nations of the world, thus complicating investigation and prosecution.

2. Illegal Access, Destruction, and Manipulation of Data—Cybercriminals break into computer systems and obtain data that are illegal for them to have, such as credit card numbers, bank records, and software codes. In October of 2000, someone illegally entered Microsoft's computer system and stole software codes for some of its future products. Hackers often illegally enter computer systems and introduce viruses or worms that infect that computer system and any other storage device that interacts with it. Computer data can also be illegally manipulated in a variety of ways. Computer records can be altered at financial, business, and educational institutions. Millions of dollars have been illegally transferred to the accounts of cybercriminals since the inception of electronic data storage. The crime of identity theft often involves cybercrime.

   In a survey involving 114 state and local law enforcement agencies, it was revealed that these agencies lacked the adequate training, equipment, and staff to confront present and future incidents of cybercrime.[27] Cooperative efforts are now under way among law enforcement, business, high-tech, and national security organizations to better prepare the nation's police agencies to combat cybercrime.

CJ ONLINE

Combating Cybercrime
To learn more about what the U.S. government is doing to combat cybercrime, visit the U.S. Department of Justice cybercrime Web site at **www.usdoj.gov/criminal/cybercrime.** *Do you think that there is anything more the government can do to prevent cybercrime?*

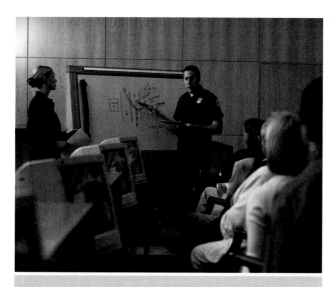

Scientific traffic accident investigation requires technical expertise. *Should all patrol officers be trained to conduct traffic investigations? Why or why not?*

Extent of Drug Use

According to the Substance Abuse and Mental Health Services Administration's *2004 National Household Survey on Drug Abuse*, 19.1 million Americans ages 12 and older (7.9 percent) reported using an illegal drug in the month before the survey was conducted. More than 12 percent reported illegal drug use during the past year, and 41.7 percent reported use of an illegal drug at least once during their lifetime. The most common illegal drugs used by current users over the age of 12 were marijuana (14.6 million users, or 6.1 percent of the population), cocaine (2.0 million users, or 0.8 percent of the population), and hallucinogens, which include LSD, PCP, and MDMA (929,000 users, or 0.4 percent of the population). There were an estimated 166,000 current heroin users (0.1 percent). Approximately 40 percent of those over the age of 12 reported lifetime use of marijuana, 14.2 percent reported lifetime use of cocaine, and 14.3 percent reported lifetime use of hallucinogens.

Source: 2004 National Survey on Drug Use and Health: Results, www.oas.samhsa.gov/NSDUH.htm#NSDUHinfo(2k4Results.pdf).

TRAFFIC

When loss of life, serious injury, suffering, and property damage are all considered, the regulation and control of vehicle and pedestrian traffic are important, if not the most important, police responsibilities. Each year, nearly twice as many people are killed in automobile accidents on the streets and highways of the nation as are murdered.

A large percentage of this highway death and suffering is attributable to alcohol. Enforcement of DUI (driving under the influence) laws is critical to the safety of a community. In addition, automobile insurance rates are based to some degree on a community's level of traffic enforcement. Thus, if the police neglect traffic regulation and enforcement, they are likely to hear about it from both insurance companies and premium payers.

Some of the debate about traffic enforcement concerns whether the major enforcers of traffic regulations should be specialized personnel or uniformed patrol officers. Some traffic responsibilities are already delegated to specialized personnel, such as enforcement of parking regulations and investigations of hit-and-run accidents and traffic fatalities. In some agencies, special traffic accident investigation crews are assigned to all traffic accident investigations. Otherwise, patrol officers investigate accidents and attend to other traffic-related duties as a normal part of their everyday workload.

Traffic units exist in nearly all medium-to-large police agencies. Some of their more important functions are:

- To educate motorists in a community about traffic safety and proper driving procedures.
- To enforce traffic laws, particularly when violations of those laws cause traffic accidents.
- To recommend traffic engineering changes that will enhance the flow of traffic and promote safety.

Enforcing traffic laws may also reduce criminal activity because stopping vehicles for traffic violations both day and night is likely to put police officers in contact with criminals.

Many veteran officers consider working in the traffic division "clean" police work because it does not normally involve responding to radio calls that take them to the scene of fights, domestic disturbances, or other distasteful incidents, such as those involving drunks. Traffic officers in large police agencies are usually well schooled in scientific accident investigation, a skill that makes them employable in the private sector, usually doing traffic reconstruction for insurance companies. The Traffic Institute at Northwestern University is one of the major schools that prepare officers for sophisticated accident investigation, although many state peace officer and highway patrol academies now have comparable training programs.

DRUG ENFORCEMENT

Over the last several decades, drug enforcement has become an increasingly important responsibility of police departments across the nation. Although the war on drugs is a priority of state and federal law enforcement agencies as well, it has been at the local level that many of the battles have been fought. Approximately 90 percent of local police departments regularly engaged in drug enforcement in 2003 (the latest year for which data were available), and nearly all police departments that served 100,000 or more residents did so.[28]

Eighteen percent of local police departments in 2003 had a special drug enforcement unit with one or more officers assigned to it full-time. Larger departments were much more likely than smaller departments to have special drug enforcement units and more full-time officers assigned to them. For example, all departments serving one million or more residents had such units, and a majority of departments serving at least 50,000 residents had them. The average number of full-time officers assigned to drug enforcement units was 6, but departments serving one million or more residents averaged 233 full-time officers. In departments serving less than 10,000 residents, only an average of 1.5 full-time officers were assigned to the special drug enforcement unit in those departments that had one.

In 2003, approximately one in four local police departments had one or more officers assigned full time to a multiagency drug enforcement task force. Again, larger departments were more likely than smaller departments to participate in these task forces and assign full-time officers to them. More than 75 percent of local police departments serving 50,000 or more residents participated in a multiagency drug enforcement task force in 2003, and nearly two-thirds of the departments serving 25,000 or more residents participated in them. About 6,000 local police officers were assigned full-time to a task force in 2003. The average number of officers assigned ranged from 39 in departments serving one million or more residents to about 1 or 2 in departments serving fewer than 50,000 residents.

Although all levels of government are waging the war on drugs, the focus of the remainder of this section is the drug enforcement strategies of local police (and sheriffs') agencies. The particular strategies employed by individual agencies vary widely, but the most common strategies are street-level enforcement, midlevel investigations, major investigations, crop eradication, smuggling interdiction, problem-oriented and community policing strategies, drug demand reduction, and asset forfeiture. It is important to note at the outset that none of these strategies has had much of a long-term effect on the U.S. drug problem.

STREET-LEVEL ENFORCEMENT Patrol officers, officers assigned to special drug enforcement units, and plainclothes officers do most of the street-level enforcement. Their tactics include surveillance, interruption of suspected transactions, raids of "shooting galleries" and "crack houses," buy-and-bust operations, and "reverse stings," in which plainclothes officers offer to sell drugs to willing customers. Street-level enforcement is responsible for most drug arrests and seizures. However, typically, the people arrested are either drug users or small-time dealers, and the seizures are for small amounts of drugs.

MIDLEVEL INVESTIGATIONS Informants or undercover police officers are frequently employed in midlevel investigations. The primary purpose of these investigations is to identify and make cases against midlevel dealers. Although midlevel dealers generally occupy relatively low-level positions in a drug distribution network and are easily replaced, they often are the highest-ranking drug traffickers that local police agencies can catch. The basic tactic used in these investigations is for undercover officers to gain the confidence of street-level dealers and work their way up to midlevel dealers by requesting to buy larger quantities of drugs than the street-level dealer can provide. Another tactic is for an informant to simply introduce an undercover officer to a midlevel dealer. Street-level dealers often become informants when they are arrested and agree to inform on their suppliers in return for some consideration in prosecution.

Drug Arrests

In 2004, 12.5 percent of all arrests reported to the FBI were drug arrests (about 1.7 million). According to the National Institute of Justice's Arrestee Drug Abuse Monitoring (ADAM) program, approximately 64 percent of both male and female arrestees tested positive for at least one of the following drugs: cocaine, opiates, marijuana, methamphetamine, and PCP. Marijuana was the drug most commonly used by male arrestees, followed by cocaine, opiates, methamphetamine, and PCP. Cocaine was the drug most commonly used by female arrestees, followed by marijuana, methamphetamine, opiates, and PCP.

SOURCE: Federal Bureau of Investigation, *Crime in the United States 2004* at www.fbi.gov/ucr/cius_04/persons_arrested/index.html; "Drug Data Summary," Office of National Drug Control Policy, Drug Policy Information Clearinghouse, March 2003, at www.whitehousedrugpolicy.gov.

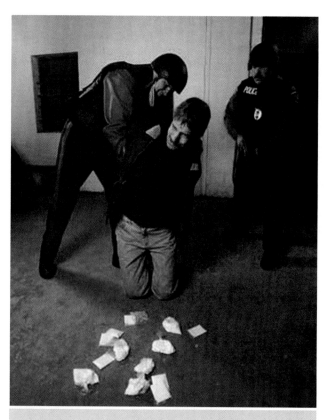

Drug busts can be dangerous. *As a law enforcement officer, would you be willing to participate in drug busts? Why or why not?*

MAJOR INVESTIGATIONS The goal of major investigations is to arrest drug kingpins and shut down the organizations responsible for producing, importing, and distributing large quantities of illegal drugs. Major investigations are conducted primarily by federal and state law enforcement agencies, but sometimes the largest local police agencies are involved as well. Most local police agencies do not have the resources to engage in major investigations, which often require long-term commitments, extensive travel, and specialized expertise. In some cases, however, local police agencies participate in major investigations as part of a multiagency task force.

CROP ERADICATION Crop eradication is a tactic employed by federal, state, and local law enforcement agencies. However, the only crop targeted by local police agencies is cannabis (marijuana) because it is the only major illegal drug grown in the United States. Because cannabis eradication intervenes at the beginning of the trafficking process, in theory it should have the greatest potential for eliminating or at least significantly reducing marijuana availability and use. In practice, however, a number of problems reduce the effectiveness of the eradication strategy. First, large quantities of marijuana are generally grown in remote, largely inaccessible areas. This makes locating and destroying crops by hand difficult, time-consuming, labor-intensive, and dangerous. Second, spraying crops with chemicals can be hazardous to people, water supplies, animals, and other vegetation. Third, even when crop eradication is successful in one area, a new crop can easily be grown in another area. The huge profits that can be made from a marijuana crop create a powerful incentive not to be deterred by eradication efforts.

Myth

Drug interdiction and eradication are effective strategies.

Fact

Despite the regular seizure of huge quantities of illegal drugs, federal, state, and local law enforcement efforts net only about 10 to 15 percent of the total supply. As for drug interdiction, if correctional officials cannot keep illegal drugs out of maximum security prisons, how effective is the government going to be in keeping illegal drugs from entering the country?

SMUGGLING INTERDICTION Federal law enforcement agencies have the primary responsibility for smuggling interdiction, but local police agencies can play a role. Local police officers in jurisdictions near the U.S. borders or those in jurisdictions with international airports or even small airports and airfields can be on the lookout for drug smugglers.

PROBLEM-ORIENTED AND COMMUNITY POLICING STRATEGIES Problem-oriented policing is a strategy that focuses on the underlying problems that cause crime rather than focusing on each specific criminal event. The strategy involves identifying the underlying problems, analyzing them in detail, applying solutions to them, and then evaluating the effectiveness of the solutions. The problem-oriented approach to drug enforcement has been adopted by many local police agencies to address drug problems in public housing projects, drug abuse among teenagers, and drug abuse in abandoned buildings. The strategy makes sense because it promotes careful analysis of a community's unique drug problem before action is taken, advocates customizing responses and targeting resources, and recommends working with other public and private agencies in the problem-solving process.

Community policing, which is addressed in more detail later in the chapter, is both a philosophy and a set of methods. The philosophy is that citizens and the police must form a partnership and work collectively to identify problems, propose solutions, implement action, and evaluate results in the community. Methods include foot patrol, storefronts and other ministations in the community, door-to-door contact with citizens, community organizing, ombudsperson-like activities, provision of social services, and problem-oriented policing. Community policing can contribute to drug enforcement in several ways. For example, foot patrol and problem-oriented policing can reduce street-level dealing. Successful community policing may increase public support for drug enforcement efforts by encouraging citizens to report drug crimes and identify drug dealers. Community organizing may empower citizens to resist drug dealers and drug abusers who invade their communities. The provision of enhanced social services, whether provided by police officers or through police ombudspersons, may help individuals resist the temptation of illegal drugs.

DRUG DEMAND REDUCTION Local police agencies can play a role in drug demand reduction strategies in at least four ways. First, through visible drug enforcement efforts, the police may discourage some people from using drugs in the first place because of a fear of arrest. Second, the police may stop some people from continuing to use drugs by arresting them so that they can get court-ordered treatment or by diverting them to drug treatment programs. Third, through public education programs, especially in the schools, the police may get young people to resist the temptations of drugs or the peer pressure to use them. Fourth, the police can lend their stature and credibility to efforts to increase funding for drug treatment, prevention, and education programs.

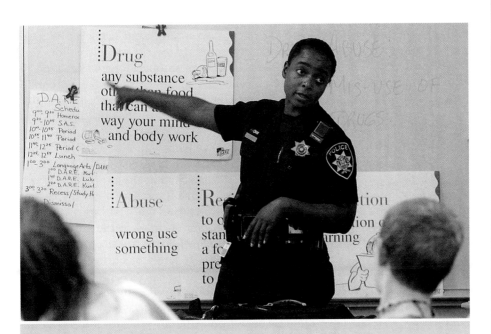

D.A.R.E. programs are taught in more than 80 percent of the nation's school districts. *Why haven't these programs been more effective in reducing illegal drug use among the nation's youth?*

Money Spent on Drugs

In 2000, Americans spent an estimated $36 billion on cocaine, $11 billion on marijuana, $10 billion on heroin, $5.4 billion on methamphetamine, and $2.4 billion on other illegal substances.

SOURCE: "Drug Data Summary," Office of National Drug Control Policy, Drug Policy Information Clearinghouse, March 2003, at www.whitehousedrugpolicy.gov.

D.A.R.E. Programs

D.A.R.E. (Drug Abuse Resistance Education) is the nation's largest and best-known substance abuse prevention program. It was developed in 1983 by Los Angeles police chief Daryl Gates and is now taught in more than 80 percent of the school districts nationwide. It is a school-based collaborative effort among police departments, schools, parents, and community leaders to teach children how to recognize and resist the direct and subtle pressures that influence them to experiment with alcohol, tobacco, marijuana, and other drugs. Usually addressing children in the fifth or sixth grade, a specially trained uniformed police officer comes to the school 1 day a week for 17 weeks and teaches the children for about an hour. The D.A.R.E. curriculum is integrated with other regular subjects. Although D.A.R.E. programs are hugely popular, no scientific study, among the many evaluations that have been conducted, has discovered any statistically significant difference in drug-usage rates between students who had taken D.A.R.E. and those who had not.

SOURCE: Drug Abuse Resistance Education at www.dare.com; The Drug Reform Coordination Network, "A Different Look at D.A.R.E." at www.drcnet.org/DARE.

ASSET FORFEITURE A huge incentive for local police departments to participate in drug enforcement activities is *asset forfeiture*. Asset forfeiture for crimes is an ancient practice that is referred to in the Bible. It was part of English common law and helped instigate the American Revolution. Partly because of asset forfeiture abuses, the due process clause of the Fifth Amendment was included in the U.S. Constitution to guarantee that property could not be taken from citizens without a judicial hearing.

Congress enacted the first drug-related civil asset forfeiture law in 1970, as part of the Comprehensive Drug Abuse and Prevention Act. The law authorized the government to seize and forfeit illegal drugs, manufacturing and storage equipment, and vehicles used to transport drugs. A major rationale for the law was the belief that drug traffickers should not benefit financially from their illegal activities or be able to use property or money obtained illegally in future drug crimes. In 1978 and throughout the 1980s, Congress passed several more antidrug laws that enhanced the government's power to seize and forfeit property.

It is important to note that the government can seize a person's property under both criminal and civil law. A reason why civil asset forfeiture has been the preferred tool in drug enforcement is that property can only be forfeited under criminal law if the property owner has been convicted of a crime (beyond a reasonable doubt). Under civil forfeiture law, on the other hand, the government is only required to have probable cause to seize a person's property. Furthermore, until the passage of the Civil Asset Forfeiture Reform Act of 2000 (CAFRA), an owner under civil forfeiture law had to be proactive to get his or her property back: An owner had to prove in a civil proceeding by a preponderance of the evidence that the property was not used in a crime. CAFRA shifted the burden of proof so that, today, the government has to prove by a preponderance of evidence that the property should be forfeited.

Assets can be forfeited under either federal or state law. When federal agencies are involved in a successful drug enforcement operation, they can return up to 80 percent of forfeited assets to other participating state or local law enforcement agencies. The amount of money or property returned depends on the particular agency's level of involvement in the case. Federal law requires that all funds returned to state and local law enforcement agencies be used for law enforcement activities. Each state has its own formula for how forfeited assets are to be distributed and used. For example, some states require all forfeitures to be used for drug enforcement activities; some states require forfeited assets to be given to the state educational system; and other states require the proceeds from forfeitures to be deposited in the state treasury to be used at the legislature's discretion.

Prior to CAFRA, critics pointed to many problems with civil asset forfeiture laws. First, as noted previously, civil asset forfeiture laws placed the burden of proof on the owner of the property seized to show that the property was not used in a drug-related crime. Not only was it difficult to prove a negative—that the property was *not* used in a drug-related crime—the government had to prove almost nothing. CAFRA shifted the burden of proof to the government.

Second, the costs involved in a civil asset forfeiture proceeding could be prohibitively high. For example, to contest a federal forfeiture, a property owner had to post a bond equal to 10 percent of the seized property's value. This requirement placed a burden on the poor. CAFRA abolished the bond requirement. The poor were further handicapped in civil asset forfeiture proceedings because the government was not obligated to provide counsel, as the Sixth Amendment required in criminal trials. In many cases, property owners simply forfeited the seized property because of the high costs of getting it back. In some cases, the costs of getting property back were higher than the value of the seized property itself. CAFRA provides for court-appointed

Civil Forfeiture

Civil forfeiture is based on the legal fiction that the property that facilitates or is connected to a crime has itself committed a wrong and can be seized and tried in civil court. Such judicial hearings are referred to as *in rem* proceedings, meaning "against the thing."

SOURCE: Scott Ehlers, *Policy Briefing: Asset Forfeiture* (Washington, DC: GPO, The Drug Policy Foundation, 1999), p. 4.

counsel for indigent owners if (1) the indigent owner makes a "good faith" claim and is already represented by court-appointed counsel in the related criminal case, and (2) the subject of the forfeiture is the indigent's primary residence. Additionally, nonindigent claimants may be entitled to court and litigation costs provided they "substantially prevail" in the civil forfeiture action. Finally, before CAFRA, the government was generally exempt from claims stemming from seizure and possession of an owner's property in civil forfeiture actions. CAFRA now provides for compensation to victims of forfeiture where their property was seized and they were not convicted of a crime giving rise to that forfeiture.

Third, innocent owners could lose their property when someone else used it without their permission or knowledge to commit a drug crime. In the case of *Calero-Toledo* v. *Pearson Yacht Leasing Company* (1974), for example, law enforcement officers found a marijuana cigarette onboard a yacht rented by the Pearson Yacht Leasing Company. The yacht was forfeited to the government because it was used to transport a controlled substance. The U.S. Supreme Court upheld the forfeiture, establishing the principle that the government can seize an innocent owner's property in a civil proceeding. This seeming injustice was corrected somewhat in 1988, when Congress passed the Asset Forfeiture Amendments Act. The act created forfeiture exceptions for some, but not all, innocent owners and for violations involving the possession of personal-use quantities of drugs. However, innocent owners were not fully protected by the exception. For example, in 1999, a Wichita, Kansas, couple had their motel forfeited and sold because drugs had been sold on the property. The couple had tried to keep drug dealers off the property by installing floodlights and fences and calling the police, but their property was forfeited anyway. CAFRA created an innocent owner defense applicable to all civil asset forfeiture statutes.

Still, critics argue that the standard of proof in civil forfeiture cases is too low. Because probable cause is the standard of proof necessary to seize property that was used to facilitate a drug crime, little more than hearsay evidence is required. Another problem with probable cause as the standard of proof in civil asset forfeiture proceedings is exemplified by the sheriff of Volusia County, Florida (near Daytona Beach), who defined probable cause for purposes of asset forfeiture as having more than $100 in cash.

Finally, critics maintain that civil asset forfeiture policy undermines the integrity of the police and the criminal justice system. The proceeds that can be had from civil asset forfeitures are a corrupting influence for many law enforcement officers. Sometimes officers are more concerned with seizing assets than they are with getting drugs off the streets. In some cases, law enforcement officers simply extort money and property from innocent people. Civil asset forfeiture laws sometimes promote other illegal practices such as racial profiling (which is described in Chapter 4) Sometimes resources are diverted from more serious crimes to drug cases that promise asset forfeitures. In short, although civil asset forfeiture helps fuel the war on

Myth Fact

Myth

Illegal drug use causes crime.

Fact

Illegal drug use is not a significant cause of crime. Although the effects of some illegal drugs may cause a very small number of violent crimes, the vast majority of drug-related crimes are caused by the drug laws, which make the possession, distribution, cultivation, or manufacture of certain drugs a crime. The drug laws also cause crime by creating an illegal market in which drug prices are artificially and dramatically increased. This makes it necessary for some drug users, especially addicts, to steal or deal to get money to buy drugs. It also contributes to the violence of rival drug dealers seeking to monopolize a market. The illegality of desired drugs also puts otherwise law-abiding people in contact with members of the criminal underworld from whom they can learn criminal skills. Ironically, alcohol is the only drug that has been found to cause a significant amount of crime, and alcohol is legal for adults.

drugs and can reduce the profits from the illegal drug trade, there are many reasons to question its fairness and utility, despite the significant reforms of CAFRA. Its harshest critics contend that civil asset forfeiture should be eliminated altogether because criminal asset forfeiture is available and has procedures that better protect the innocent.

CRITICISMS OF THE WAR ON DRUGS In addition to the already mentioned problems with specific aspects of drug enforcement, the war on drugs itself has been severely criticized. First, critics contend that the government has exaggerated the dangers of illegal drug use to gain public support for the war on drugs and has generally ignored the harms caused by the drug laws themselves. For example, it has been estimated that about 3,600 people die each year from the consumption of all illegal drugs combined. While any death from illegal drug consumption is regrettable, the 3,600 deaths attributed to illegal drugs pale in comparison to the approximately 200,000 alcohol-related and 400,000 tobacco-related deaths each year. Moreover, rarely are drug-related deaths the result of abuse or misuse of the drugs. Instead, most of the drug-related deaths are directly attributable to the drug laws that prohibit their use. For example, most heroin overdoses occur because the heroin is adulterated (that is, the drug is "cut" or mixed with dangerous substances to increase the quantity of the drug available to sell or to produce a more readily ingestible form of the drug). The reason why the heroin is adulterated is because it is illegal and unregulated; there is no quality control in its production and distribution. Also, because it is illegal, heroin addicts share needles, which spreads disease and illness. It has been estimated that 25 percent of all AIDS cases in the United States are a direct result of the unsafe and unsanitary conditions in which illegal drugs are consumed. The same is true of cocaine. Because of the drug laws, the price of using powder cocaine is too high for many people so they substitute the more affordable and more dangerous crack cocaine. A person is more likely to die or suffer injury from smoking the drug than he or she is from snorting it. As for marijuana, no one has ever died from using marijuana. The greatest danger to marijuana smokers is in smoking the drug after it has been adulterated by government control programs, such as the spraying of herbicides on marijuana crops.

Another way the government has tried to rally support for the drug war has been to try to persuade the public of a direct connection between illegal drug use and crime. However, as described in the nearby Myth/Fact box, it is not drugs that cause crime, but rather the drug laws that cause crime.

Second, critics have argued that the drug war is racist. Of the approximately 1.7 million people arrested in 2004 for drug abuse violations, 66 percent were white and 33 percent were black. Yet, blacks are only about 14 percent of all drug users, and a National Institute on Drug Abuse (NIDA) survey showed that the prevalence of drug use is nearly the same among whites and blacks. Furthermore, in many jurisdictions the penalties are much more severe for possession of crack cocaine than they are for the possession of powder cocaine, although pharmacologically they are identical drugs. About 60 percent of people arrested for possession of powder cocaine are white, while about 90 percent of the people arrested for possession of crack cocaine are black. Ironically, relatively low-level crack cocaine dealers have received

About 60 percent of people arrested for possession of powder cocaine are white, while about 90 percent of people arrested for possession of crack cocaine are black. *Should law enforcement authorities distinguish between powder cocaine and crack cocaine when making arrests for possession? Why or why not?*

longer prison sentences than wholesale-level powder cocaine dealers from whom the crack dealer originally bought the powder to make the crack.

Third, as noted previously, critics point out that the war on drugs and the huge amount of money involved in the drug trade have corrupted many law enforcement personnel, who have been found guilty of drug dealing, providing protection for drug dealers, conspiracy, extortion, bribery, robbery, theft, and murder. Unfortunately, examples abound. A *New York Times* report disclosed that each year more than 100 law enforcement officers are prosecuted in state and federal courts on drug corruption charges.

Fourth, critics maintain that the war on drugs is hugely expensive, diverts resources from arguably more important projects, and has had little lasting effect on illegal drug use. Between 1980 and 2003, the United States spent more than $300 billion on federal, state, and local antidrug efforts. That was more than was spent on medical research into cancer, heart disease, or AIDS—to name just three worthwhile projects. Furthermore, despite the huge amount of money and effort spent on the drug war, the prices of many illegal drugs have not increased and in many cases have fallen, and the purity of illegal drugs and their availability have not decreased but in many cases have increased. If the drug war were successfully reducing supply or demand, one would expect prices to increase, and the purity and availability of illegal drugs to decline.

Although the measurement of illegal drug use is fraught with all sorts of reliability problems, according to the Substance Abuse and Mental Health Services Administration's annual *National Household Survey on Drug Abuse*, there was a significant decline in illegal drug use among both youths and adults between 1979 and 1992 (from 25 million past-month illegal drug users to 12 million past-month illegal drug users). However, the number of past-month illegal drug users increased unevenly between 1992 and 2004. The estimated number of past-month illegal drug users in the United States in 2004 was 19.1 million. The higher number is attributed to a much higher rate of use among youths, a small increase in the rate of use among adults, and a 10 percent increase in the size of the U.S. population. Critics are calling for an end to the drug war. Some critics want illegal drugs to be decriminalized or legalized. Other critics want the drug problem treated as a public health problem and not as a criminal justice problem. Perhaps it is time to seriously rethink America's strategy for dealing with illegal drug use.

Drug Offenders in Prison

In 2003, 55 percent of federal prisoners and, in 2004, 21 percent of state prisoners were incarcerated for drug offenses. That compares with 58 percent of federal prisoners and 21 percent of state prisoners who were incarcerated for drug offenses in 1998.

Source: Paige M. Harrison and Allen J. Beck, "Prisoners in 2004," *Bureau of Justice Statistics Bulletin* (Washington, DC: GPO, U.S. Department of Justice, October 2005), p. 9, Table 13, and p. 10, Table 14; Allen J. Beck, "Prisoners in 1999," *Bureau of Justice Statistics Bulletin* (Washington, DC: GPO, U.S. Department of Justice, August 2000), p. 10, Table 15, and p. 12, Table 21.

THINKING CRITICALLY

1. What do you think are the pros and cons of being an investigator/detective? Does this type of work sound attractive to you?

2. Do you think there are any ways to protect individuals and businesses from becoming victims of cybercrime? If so, what do you propose?

3. Do you think the United States should change its drug enforcement strategy? If so, in what ways? If not, why not?

Community Policing

For decades, police followed the professional model, which rested on three foundations: preventive patrol, quick response time, and follow-up investigation. Sensing that the professional model did not always operate as efficiently and effectively as it could, criminal justice researchers set out to review current procedures and evaluate alternative programs. One of the first and best-known of these studies was the Kansas City, Missouri, Preventive Patrol Experiment, discussed earlier in this chapter. That study's conclusion was that preventive patrol did not necessarily prevent crime or reassure citizens. Following the study, some police departments assigned police units to proactive patrol, giving them specific assignments rather than having them randomly cruise the streets.

Another study, again with the Kansas City Police Department, examined the effects of police response time. The study found that police response time was

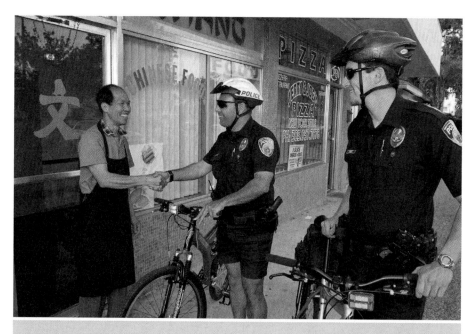

Community police officers visit with a citizen. *How does such activity contribute to crime-fighting?*

unrelated to the probability of making an arrest. Researchers discovered that the time it takes a citizen to report a crime—not the speed with which police respond—was the major determinant of whether an on-scene arrest took place or witnesses could be located. In 90 percent of crimes, citizens wait 5 to 10 minutes to call the police, precluding catching the criminal at the scene.

As preventive patrol and fast response time were being questioned, so too was follow-up investigation. A study by the Rand Corporation reviewed the criminal investigation process for effectiveness. The researchers concluded that the work of a criminal investigator alone rarely leads to an arrest and that the probability of arrest is determined largely by information that patrol officers obtain at the crime scene in their preliminary investigation.[29]

Criminal justice researchers continued their review of accepted police functions with the aim of making policing more effective by initiating new techniques and procedures. One of the interesting findings of the foot patrol research was that foot patrol officers were better able to deal with minor annoyances—such as rowdy youths, panhandlers, and abandoned cars—that irritate citizens.

In a theory called "broken windows," noted policing scholars James Q. Wilson and George Kelling proposed that those minor annoyances are "signs of crime" and cause a fear of crime and that if they are not dealt with early, more serious and more costly problems are likely to occur.[30] Wilson and Kelling concluded that to help solve both minor and major problems in a neighborhood and to reduce crime and fear of crime, police officers must be in close, regular contact with citizens. That is, police and citizens should work cooperatively to build a strong sense of community and should share responsibility in the neighborhood to improve the overall quality of life within the community.

Myth Fact

Myth

Shorter police response time contributes to more arrests.

Fact

For most crimes, police response time is irrelevant. Approximately two-thirds of crimes are "cold"; the offender is gone long before the crime is discovered. In cases where time counts, the critical delay often occurs in the time it takes the victim to call the police.

THE PHILOSOPHY AND COMPONENTS OF COMMUNITY POLICING

With community policing, citizens share responsibility for their community's safety. Citizens and the police work collectively to identify problems, propose solutions, implement action, and evaluate the results in the community. A community policing perspective differs in a number of ways from a traditional policing perspective. For example, in community policing, the police must share power with residents of a community, and critical decisions need to be made at the neighborhood level, not at a downtown police headquarters. Such decentralization of authority means that credit for bringing about a safer and more secure community must be shared with the people of the community, a tall order for any group of professionals to accept. Achieving the goals of community policing requires successful implementation of three essential and complementary components or operational strategies: community partnership, problem solving, and change management.[31]

COMMUNITY PARTNERSHIP Establishing and maintaining mutual trust between citizens of a community and the police is the main goal of the first component of community policing. Police have always recognized the need for cooperation with the community and have encouraged members of the community to come forward with crime-fighting information. In addition, police have spoken to neighborhood groups, worked with local organizations, and provided special-unit services. How are those cooperative efforts different from the community partnership of community policing?

In community policing, the police become an integral part of the community culture, and the community, in turn, helps the police define future crime prevention strategies and allocate community protection services. Establishing a community partnership means adopting a policing perspective that exceeds the standard law enforcement emphasis. The police no longer view the community as a passive presence connected to the police by an isolated incident or series of incidents. The community's concerns with crime and disorder become the target of efforts by the police and the community working together.

The Crime Act and COPS

The Violent Crime Control and Law Enforcement Act of 1994—popularly known as the Crime Act—authorized $8.8 billion over 6 years for grants to local policing agencies to add 100,000 officers and promote community policing in innovative ways. To implement the law, the Office of Community Oriented Policing Services (COPS) was created in the U.S. Department of Justice. COPS cuts red tape to make it easier for local police agencies to apply for and receive federal community policing grants.

A community police officer talks to a boy at the Puerto Rico Day Parade. *What, if anything, is the police officer trying to accomplish?*

For patrol officers, building police-community partnerships entails such activities as talking to local business owners to identify their concerns, visiting residents in their homes to offer advice on security, and helping to organize and support neighborhood watch groups and regular community meetings. It also involves ongoing communication with residents. For example, a patrol officer might canvass a neighborhood for information about a string of burglaries and then revisit those residents to inform them when the burglar is caught.

PROBLEM SOLVING Problem solving requires a lot more thought, energy, and action than traditional incident-based police responses to crime and disorder. In full partnership, the police and a community's residents and business owners identify core problems, propose solutions, and implement a solution. Thus, community members identify the concerns that they feel are most threatening to their safety and well-being. Those areas of concern then become priorities for joint police-community interventions.

For this problem-solving process to operate effectively, the police need to devote time and attention to discovering a community's concerns, and they need to recognize the validity of those concerns. Police and neighborhood groups may not always agree on the specific problems that deserve attention first. For example, the police may regard robberies as the biggest problem in a particular neighborhood, while residents find derelicts who sleep in doorways, break bottles on sidewalks, and pick through garbage cans the number one problem. In community policing, both problems should receive early attention from the police, other government agencies, and the community.

Some community policing advocates recommend a four-step problem-solving process referred to as SARA: *Scanning*—identifying problems; *Analysis*—understanding underlying conditions; *Response*—developing and implementing solutions; *Assessment*—determining the solutions' effect. One useful tool in working toward a solution is known as the *crime triangle*. The crime triangle is a view of crime and disorder as an interaction among three variables: a victim, an offender, and a location. Solutions can be developed that affect one or more of the three elements of the crime triangle. For example, suppose elderly residents are being jeopardized by speeding teenagers in automobiles as they walk across the streets of a suburban residential neighborhood. Using a crime triangle analysis might result in the following police-community solutions: using the juvenile court to alter the probation period of offending drivers (focus on the offender), installing speed bumps in the pavement or changing the cycles of traffic signals on opposite ends of the street so that motorists cannot build up speed (focus on the location), holding safety education classes at the senior center to educate elderly residents to use marked crosswalks (focus on the victim). More than likely, in community policing, a combination of those solutions would be used. Such a response to a community problem is much more thorough than merely having a squad car drive by the location when a citizen calls in a complaint.

CHANGE MANAGEMENT Forging community policing partnerships and implementing problem-solving strategies necessitate assigning new responsibilities and adopting a flexible style of management. Traditionally, patrol officers have been accorded lower status in police organizations and have been dominated by the agency's command structure. Community policing, in contrast, emphasizes the value of the patrol function and the patrol officer as an individual. It requires the shifting of initiative, decision making, and responsibility downward within the police organization. The neighborhood police officer or deputy sheriff becomes responsible for managing the delivery of police services to the community or area to which he or she is permanently assigned. Patrol officers are the most familiar with the needs and concerns of their

School Resource Officers

School resource officers use a community policing approach to provide a safe environment for students and staff. They respond to calls for service within the school and work with school administrators and staff to prevent crime and disorder by monitoring crime trends, problem areas, cultural conflicts, and other concerns. As of June 2003, local police departments had about 14,300 full-time sworn personnel serving as school resource officers.

SOURCE: Matthew J. Hickman and Brian A. Reaves, *Local Police Departments 2003* (Washington, DC: GPO, U.S. Department of Justice, Bureau of Justice Statistics, May 2006), p. iii.

Community police officers discussing neighborhood problems with residents. *In what ways can elderly citizens contribute to crime-fighting?*

communities and are in the best position to forge the close ties with the community that lead to effective solutions to local problems.

Under community policing, police management must guide, rather than dominate, the actions of the patrol officer and must ensure that patrol officers have the necessary resources to solve the problems in their communities. Management must determine the guiding principles to convert the philosophy of the agency to community policing and then to evaluate the effectiveness of the strategies implemented.

IMPLEMENTING COMMUNITY POLICING

Implementation plans for community policing vary from agency to agency and from community to community. The appropriate implementation strategy depends on conditions within the law enforcement agency and the community embarking on community policing. Successful implementation requires that the police and the members of the community understand the underlying philosophy of community policing and have a true commitment to the community policing strategy. Communication, cooperation, coordination, collaboration, and change are the keys to putting community policing into action. The community policing philosophy has become so popular and broadly implemented that it exists as the operating method of police departments in colleges and universities, transit systems, and even airports. At Dallas Love Field, City of Dallas police officers maintain a community police substation in the airport as part of the regular security force and receive specially marked federal funds and airport community police training. All this may be changing, however, because grant funding is being shifted from the federal Office of Community Oriented Policing Services (COPS) to the Department of Homeland Security. If, as some have argued, the philosophies of community policing and homeland security are incompatible, the era of community policing may be ending, as the era of homeland security policing begins.[32]

Community Policing

According to a recent survey, 14 percent of local police departments, employing 44 percent of all officers, maintained or created a written community policing plan during the 12-month period ending June 30, 2003. Nearly half (47 percent) of departments, employing 73 percent of all officers, had a mission statement that included some aspect of community policing. Fifty-eight percent of all departments, employing 82 percent of all officers, used full-time community policing officers in 2003; 54,800 local police officers were designated community policing officers in 2003. These numbers are down substantially from those reported in 2000.

SOURCE: Matthew J. Hickman and Brian A. Reaves, *Local Police Departments, 2003* (Washington, DC: GPO, U.S. Department of Justice, Bureau of Justice Statistics, May 2006), p. iii.

THINKING CRITICALLY

1. Can you think of ways to make community policing even more effective?

2. Do you think there is a certain operational style that is most appropriate for community policing? If so, which one?

Procedural Law and Policing

The police cannot legally enforce the criminal law any way they want. Among the constraints on their behavior are departmental policies and regulations, procedural law derived from U.S. Supreme Court decisions (case law), and the U.S. Constitution, especially the Fourth and Fifth Amendments. The latter two limitations are addressed in the following sections.

The Fourth Amendment (as well as other provisions of the Constitution) protects individual privacy against certain types of governmental interference. However, it does not provide a general constitutional "right to privacy," as many people wrongly believe. Nearly every governmental action interferes with personal privacy to some extent. Thus, the question in Fourth Amendment cases is limited to whether a governmental intrusion violates the Constitution.[33]

The procedural rights in the Fourth Amendment influence policing in the United States nearly every day. They concern the legality of searches and seizures and the question of what to do with evidence that is illegally obtained. **Searches** are explorations or inspections, by law enforcement officers, of homes, premises, vehicles, or persons, for the purpose of discovering evidence of crimes or persons who are accused of crimes. A search occurs "when an expectation of privacy that society is prepared to consider reasonable is infringed [by the government]."[34] **Seizures** are the taking of persons or property into custody in response to violations of the criminal law. A seizure of property occurs "when there is some meaningful interference [by the government] with an individual's possessory interests in that property."[35] For the seizure of a person, see *United States* v. *Mendenhall* (FYI on p. 99) and *California* v. *Hodari D.* (FYI on p. 102).

searches Exploration or inspections, by law enforcement officers, of homes, premises, vehicles, or persons, for the purpose of discovering evidence of crimes or persons who are accused of crimes.

seizures The taking of persons or property into custody in response to violations of the criminal law.

warrant A written order from a court directing law enforcement officers to conduct a search or to arrest a person.

arrest The seizing and detaining of a person by lawful authority.

According to the Supreme Court, the Fourth Amendment allows two kinds of searches and seizures: those made with a warrant and those made without a warrant. A **warrant** is a written order from a court directing law enforcement officers to conduct a search or to arrest a person. An **arrest** is the seizure of a person or the taking of a person into custody. An arrest can be either taking actual physical custody, as when a suspect is handcuffed by a police officer, or constructive custody, as when a person peacefully submits to a police officer's control. An arrest can occur without an officer's physically touching a suspect.

The Fourth Amendment requires only that searches and seizures not be "unreasonable." Searches and seizures conducted with a legal warrant are generally considered reasonable. However, what is "reasonable" in warrantless searches remained vague for more than 100 years after the ratification of the amendment. It was not until a series of cases beginning in the 1960s that the Supreme Court began to provide a more precise definition of the term. Because the law concerning warrantless searches and seizures is complex, only a relatively brief and simplified overview will be provided in that section.

Samar Kaukab sued the Illinois National Guard and O'Hare International Airport security officers for strip-searching her at the Chicago airport before a flight simply because she was wearing a hijab—a Muslim headscarf. *Were the security officers justified in conducting the strip search? Why or why not?*

SEARCHES AND SEIZURES WITH A WARRANT First, law enforcement officers must have *probable cause* before a judicial officer can legally issue a search or arrest warrant. Probable cause for a search warrant requires substantial and trustworthy evidence to support two conclusions: (1) that the specific objects to be searched for are connected with criminal activity and (2) that the objects will be found in the place to be searched. In nearly all jurisdictions, law enforcement officers seeking a search warrant must specify in a signed *affidavit,* a written and sworn declaration, the facts that establish probable cause. The facts in the affidavit are the basis for determining later whether there was probable cause to issue the warrant in the first place. Some jurisdictions allow sworn oral testimony to establish probable cause.

The Fourth Amendment requires that a search warrant contain a particular description of the place to be searched and the person or things to be seized. Thus, the warrant must be specific enough that a law enforcement officer executing it would know where to search and what objects to seize, even if the officer was not originally involved in the case. However, absolute technical accuracy in the description of the place to be searched is not necessary. It is required only that an officer executing a warrant can find, perhaps by asking questions of neighborhood residents, the place to be searched.

A warrant may also be issued for the search of a person or an automobile, rather than a place. A warrant to search a person should provide the person's name or at least a detailed description. A warrant to search an automobile should include either the car's license number or its make and the name of its owner.

Search warrants are required to be executed in a reasonable amount of time. For example, federal law requires that a search be conducted within 10 days after the warrant is issued. The federal government and nearly half of the states also have laws limiting the time of day during which search warrants may be executed. In those jurisdictions, searches may be conducted only during daytime hours unless there are special circumstances.

Generally, before law enforcement officers may enter a place to conduct a search, they must first announce that they are law enforcement officers, that they possess a warrant, and that they are there to execute it. The major exceptions to this requirement are situations in which it is likely that the evidence would be destroyed immediately on notification or in which notification would pose a threat to officers. However, if officers are refused entry after identifying themselves, they may then use force to gain entry, but only after they have given the occupant time to respond. In short, they cannot legally yell "police officers" and immediately kick down the door. The Supreme Court has held that under ordinary circumstances they must wait at least 15 to 20 seconds (see *United States* v. *Banks,* 2003). But even when the "knock-and-announce" rule is violated, the Supreme Court has recently declared that any incriminating evidence found does not require suppression and may be admissible (see *Hudson* v. *Michigan,* 2006). Finally, if in the course of conducting a legal search, law enforcement officers discover **contraband** (an illegal substance or object) or evidence of a crime not covered by the warrant, they may seize that contraband or evidence under the plain-view exception (discussed later) without getting a new warrant specifically covering it. Figure 3.3 shows a sample search and arrest warrant and the supporting affidavit.

ARRESTS WITH A WARRANT Most arrests are made without a warrant. Generally, an arrest warrant is legally required when law enforcement officers want to enter private premises to make an arrest unless there is consent or exigent circumstances (discussed later). An arrest warrant is issued only if substantial and trustworthy evidence supports these two conclusions: (1) a violation of the law has been committed and (2) the person to be arrested committed the violation.

SEARCHES AND SEIZURES WITHOUT A WARRANT In guaranteeing freedom from illegal searches and seizures, the Fourth Amendment protects a person's privacy. Under most circumstances, the amendment requires a warrant signed by a judge to authorize a search for and seizure of evidence of criminal activity. However, Supreme Court interpretations of the Fourth Amendment have permitted warrantless searches and seizures in some circumstances. A person is generally protected from searches and seizures without a warrant in places,

United States v. Mendenhall

In *United Sates* v. *Mendenhall* (1980), the Supreme Court created the following test for determining whether an encounter constitutes a Fourth Amendment seizure: "A person has been 'seized' within the meaning of the Fourth Amendment only if, in view of all the circumstances surrounding the incident, a reasonable person would have believed that he was not free to leave." The Court provided these examples of situations that might be construed as seizures, even if the person did not attempt to leave: (1) the threatening presence of several officers, (2) the display of a weapon by an officer, (3) some physical touching of the person, or (4) the use of language or a tone of voice that indicated that compliance with the officer's request might be compelled.

contraband An illegal substance or object.

FIGURE 3.3   Sample Search and Arrest Warrant

SEARCH AND ARREST WARRANT

THE STATE OF TEXAS § 155 E. Main Street
                    § Dallas, Dallas County, Texas
COUNTY OF DALLAS   §

THE STATE OF TEXAS to the Sheriff or any Peace Officer of Dallas County, Texas, or any Peace Officer of the State of Texas,

GREETINGS:

WHEREAS, the Affiant whose signature is affixed to the Affidavit appearing on the reverse hereof is a Peace Officer under the laws of Texas and did heretofore this day subscribed and swear to said Affidavit before me (which said affidavit is by this reference incorporated herein for all purposes), and whereas I find that the verified facts by Affiant in said Affidavit show that Affiant has probable cause for the belief he expresses therein and establishes the existence of proper grounds for the issuance of this Warrant:

NOW, THEREFORE, you are commanded to enter the suspecte described in said Affidavit and to there search for the per described in said Affidavit and to seize the same and brin And, you are commanded to arrest and bring before me ea and accused in said Affidavit. Herein fail not, but have yo this Warrant executed within three days, exclusive of the issuance and exclusive of the day of its execution with yo thereon, showing how you have executed the same.

ISSUED AT ___11:35___ o'clock ___A__ M., on this the ___23 of ___March___, 19_99___ to certify which witness day.

Sarah H. Solano
MAGISTRATE, DALLAS COUNTY, TE

RETURN AND INVENTORY

THE STATE OF TEXAS §
                    §
COUNTY OF DALLAS   §

The undersigned Affiant, being a Peace Officer under the and being duly sworn, on oath certifies that the foregoing Wa hand on the day it was issued and that it was executed on th of _____, 19_____, by making the search d therein and seizing during such search the following describe property:

_____
AFFIANT

SUBSCRIBED AND SWORN to before me, the undersigned the_____ day of_____, 19_____

_____
Notary Public in and for Dallas County, Te

AFFIDAVIT FOR SEARCH WARRANT AND ARREST WARRANT

THE STATE OF TEXAS § 155 E. Main Street
                    § City of Dallas, Dallas County, Texas
COUNTY OF DALLAS   §

The undersigned Affiant, being a Peace Officer under the laws of Texas and being duly sworn, on oath makes the following statements and accusations:

1. There is in Dallas County, Texas, a suspected place and premises described and located as follows: A one story family dwelling, which is white in color, with a grey composition roof. The location of this residence is 155 E. Main Street, located in the City of Dallas, Dallas County, Texas.

2. There is at said suspected place and premises personal property concealed and kept in violation of the laws of Texas and described as follows: A CONTROLLED SUBSTANCE: TO WIT: Cocaine

3. Said suspected place and premises are in charge of and controlled by each of the following persons: A white male approximately 25 years of age, 5'10 in height, 160 pounds, with a mustache, black hair and brown eyes and other person or persons whose names, ages, and descriptions are unknown to the affiant.

4. It is the belief of Affiant, and he hereby charges and accuses, that: The above listed white male described in paragraph number 3 was in possession of an amount of cocaine located in the residence at 155 E. Main Street, located in the City of Dallas, Dallas County, Texas.

5. Affiant has probable cause for said belief by reason of the following facts: Affiant, Officer Smith, is employed by the City of Dallas Police Department and is currently assigned to the Narcotics Bureau.

I , the affiant , personally purchased an amount of cocaine from the suspect described in paragraph number 3 out of the aforementioned address at 155 E. Main Street, and that the affiant has been inside the above described residence within the last 24 hours, and personally observed the above described white male and other person, persons, whose names, ages, and identities, and descriptions are unknown to the affiant, in possession of and selling cocaine. Detective Jones purchased 0.3g of cocaine from the above described suspect for twenty dollars U.S. Currency. The cocaine was field tested by the affiant who knows due to his experience as a narcotics officer, what cocaine looks like and how it is packaged for resale.

I , the affiant , observed this on March 22, 1999.

Wherefore, Affiant asks for issuance of a warrant that will authorize him to search said suspected place and premises for said personal property and seize the same and to arrest each said described and accused person.

James C. Smith
AFFIANT

Subscribed and sworn to before me by said Affiant on this the _23rd_ day of_____March_____, 19_99___.

Sarah H. Solano
MAGISTRATE, DALLAS COUNTY, TEXAS

such as home or office, where he or she has a legitimate right to privacy. That same protection, however, does not extend to all places where a person has a legitimate right to be. For example, the Supreme Court has permitted the stopping and searching of automobiles under certain circumstances and with probable cause. Several doctrines concerning search and seizure without a warrant have developed over time.

Before 1969, when law enforcement officers arrested a suspect, they could legally search, without a warrant, the entire premises surrounding the arrest. That kind of search is called a *search incident to arrest,* and like a search with a warrant, it required probable cause. Evidence obtained through a search incident to arrest was admissible as long as the arrest was legal.

In 1969, in the case of *Chimel* v. *California,* the Supreme Court limited the scope of *searches incident to an arrest.* The Court restricted the physical area in which officers could conduct a search to the area within the suspect's immediate control. The Court interpreted the area within the suspect's immediate control as an area near enough to the suspect to enable him or her to obtain a weapon or destroy evidence. The Court also ruled that it is permissible for officers, incident to an arrest, to protect themselves, to prevent a suspect's escape by searching the suspect for weapons, and to preserve evidence within the suspect's grabbing area.

The Supreme Court has continued to refine the scope of warrantless searches and seizures incident to an arrest. For example, in 1981, in *New York* v. *Belton,* the Court ruled that after police have made a lawful arrest of the occupant of an automobile, they may, incident to an arrest, search the automobile's entire passenger compartment, and the contents of any opened or closed containers found in the compartment. The police had long been able to legally search the automobile's trunk, providing there was probable cause (see *Carroll* v. *United States,* 1925). In *United States* v. *Ross* (1982) the Court held that when police "have probable cause to search an entire vehicle, they may conduct a warrantless search of every part of the vehicle [including the trunk] and its contents, including all containers and packages, that may conceal the object of the search." Then, in 1991, in the case of *California* v. *Acevedo,* the Court ruled that the police, "in a search extending only to a container within an automobile, may search the container without a warrant where they have probable cause to believe that it holds contraband or evidence." The Court will also allow the police, with probable cause, to search an automobile passenger's belongings, if he or she is capable of concealing the object of the search (see *Wyoming* v. *Houghton,* 1999).

Other Supreme Court decisions have established principles governing when private areas may be searched incident to an arrest. In 1968, for instance, in the case of *Harris* v. *United States,* the Court established the *plain-view doctrine.* Under this doctrine, the police may seize an item—evidence or contraband—without a warrant if they are lawfully in a position to view the item and if it is immediately apparent that the item is evidence or contraband. In 1990, the Court clarified its ruling in *Harris* by adding that the discovery of the item in plain view need not be "inadvertent." That is, the plain-view doctrine applies even when the police expect in advance to find the item in plain view (*Horton* v. *California*). Also, in 1990, in the case of *Maryland* v. *Buie,* the Court addressed the issue of *protective sweeps.* The Court held that when a warrantless arrest takes place in a suspect's home, officers, with reasonable suspicion, may make only a "cursory visual inspection" of areas that could harbor an accomplice or a person posing danger to them.

Even a warrantless search not incident to an arrest may be justified under the Supreme Court's *exigent circumstances* doctrine. It permits police to make warrantless searches in exigent, or emergency, situations. Such situations could include a need to prevent the imminent destruction of evidence, a need to prevent harm to individuals, or the hot pursuit of suspects.

E-mail and Privacy

E-mail does not have the same privacy protections as does "regular mail." Depending on where the e-mail is sent from and where it is sent to, privacy rights vary greatly. However, under no circumstances can e-mail messages ever be considered confidential. Both government employees (federal, state, and local) and employees in the private sector have few, if any, privacy rights in the e-mail messages they send or receive. Employers are free to examine all electronic communications stored on their systems. The e-mail messages of government employees may also be available to the public through a freedom of information request. In addition, commercial service providers (such as America Online) are permitted to disclose messages to law enforcement officials when they "inadvertently" come across messages containing references to illegal activity. Finally, regardless of the setting (work or home), e-mail can be subpoenaed, discovered, and intercepted under existing wiretap laws.

SOURCE: Erik C. Garcia, "E-mail and Privacy Rights," www.wings.buffalo.edu.

Meaning of Seizure

Supreme Court rulings often modify previous decisions. In *California* v. *Hodari D.* (1991), for example, the Court modified the plurality holding in *Mendenhall* (1980). In *Hodari D.*, the suspect ran from the police, and an officer pursued, thereby creating a circumstance in which a "reasonable person would have believed that she or he was not free to leave" or to disobey the officer's command to halt. There was no physical touching of the suspect. The Court held that in cases involving a "show of authority," as distinguished from physical touching, no "seizure" occurs unless and until the suspect yields or submits to the assertion of authority.

Frequently, law enforcement officers are not hampered by the warrant requirement, because suspects often consent to a search. In other words, law enforcement officers who do not have enough evidence to obtain a search warrant, or who either cannot or do not want to take the time and trouble to obtain one, may simply ask a suspect whether they may conduct a search. If the suspect consents voluntarily, the search can be made legally. Law enforcement officers call this strategy "knock and talk." In 1973, in the case of *Schenckloth* v. *Bustamonte,* the Supreme Court upheld the legality of *consent searches.* The Court also ruled that officers do not have to tell suspects that they have a right to withhold consent unless they ask.

It is not surprising that consent searches have become the most common type of searches performed by law enforcement officers. They are used frequently in traffic stops and drug interdiction efforts at airports and bus terminals. In the 1980s, as a new tool in the war on drugs, several police departments adopted programs in which officers boarded buses and asked passengers to consent to searches. The practice was challenged in a 1985 Florida case in which a bus passenger had consented to having his luggage searched. When the police found cocaine, the passenger was arrested and subsequently convicted. The Florida Supreme Court ruled that the search was unconstitutional. In 1991, the U.S. Supreme Court reversed the Florida Supreme Court (in *Florida* v. *Bostick*) and held that the search was not unconstitutional and that law enforcement officers may make such a search without a warrant or suspicion of a crime—as long as the passenger feels free to refuse the search.

Critics argue that, in most cases, consent searches cannot be truly voluntary, even when permission is granted, because most people are intimidated by the police and would have a hard time telling them no. Moreover, most people probably do not know that they may refuse a warrantless search except under the conditions described earlier.

Recently, in the case of *Georgia* v. *Randolph* (2006), the U.S. Supreme Court restricted consent searches of a home. In this case Randolph's estranged wife, concerned about his cocaine use, called the police and, when they arrived, told them they could find cocaine in their bedroom. The police asked her if they could conduct a search and she consented. Randolph, a lawyer, who was present at the time, objected to the search, but the police ignored him, entered the house, and found cocaine in the bedroom. Randolph was arrested and subsequently convicted of drug possession. On appeal, the U.S. Supreme Court, citing the Fourth Amendment's central value of "respect for the privacy of the home," ruled that warrantless searches of a home, even when a cohabitant consented to the search, are prohibited if the other cohabitant is physically present and objects to the search. As a result of the decision, the incriminating evidence was suppressed (that is, not admitted at the retrial). On the other hand, the consent of one co-occupant in the absence of another is generally considered sufficient to permit a home search by the police (see *United States* v. *Matlock,* 1974).

ARRESTS WITHOUT A WARRANT Officers may not enter a private home to make a warrantless arrest unless there is consent or the offense is a serious one and there are exigent circumstances, such as the likely destruction of evidence or the hot pursuit of a felony suspect. This is the same *exigent circumstances* doctrine that applies to warrantless searches and seizures.

A suspect who is arrested without a warrant and remains confined is entitled to have a judge determine whether there was probable cause for the arrest. Ordinarily, judges must make such a determination within 48 hours of arrest. The purpose of this proceeding is to ensure that the suspect's continuing custody is based on a judicial determination of probable cause and not merely on the police officer's judgment that probable cause supported an arrest.

THE EXCLUSIONARY RULE The **exclusionary rule** was created by the Supreme Court in 1914 in the case of *Weeks* v. *United States.* In *Weeks,* the Supreme

exclusionary rule The rule that illegally seized evidence must be excluded from trials in federal courts.

Court held that illegally seized evidence must be excluded from trials in federal courts. In 1961, the Warren Court extended the exclusionary rule to state courts in the case of *Mapp* v. *Ohio*. The exclusionary rule originally had three primary purposes: (1) to protect individual rights from police misconduct, (2) to prevent police misconduct, and (3) to maintain judicial integrity (for citizens to have faith in the administration of justice, courts should not admit evidence that is tainted by the illegal activities of other criminal justice officials). Today, however, the principal purpose of the exclusionary rule is to deter the police from violating people's Fourth Amendment rights.

In practice, when suspects want to claim that incriminating evidence was obtained through an illegal search and seizure, that a confession was obtained without the required warnings or was involuntary, that an identification was made as a result of an invalid police lineup, or that evidence was in some other way illegally obtained, they attempt, through their attorneys, to show at a suppression hearing that the search and seizure, for example, violated the Fourth Amendment. If they are successful in their claims, the evidence that was obtained as a result of the illegal search and seizure will not be admitted at trial.

By the late 1970s, public opinion polls showed that Americans were becoming increasingly alarmed about the problem of crime and especially about what they perceived as the practice of allowing a substantial number of criminals to escape punishment because of legal technicalities. One so-called legal technicality that received much of the public's scorn was the exclusionary rule. In 1984, responding at least in part to public opinion, the Supreme Court, under Chief Justice Warren Burger, decided three cases that had the practical effect of weakening the exclusionary rule.

Myth	Fact
Many criminals escape punishment because of the exclusionary rule.	Very few criminals escape punishment because of the exclusionary rule.

In two of the three cases, *United States* v. *Leon* and *Massachusetts* v. *Sheppard*, a *good faith exception* to the exclusionary rule was recognized. The Court ruled that as long as the police act in good faith when they request a warrant, the evidence they collect may be used in court, even if the warrant is illegal or defective. In the *Leon* case, the judge's determination of probable cause turned out to be wrong. Prior to *Leon*, such an error by a judge would have been recognized as a violation of the Fourth Amendment, and the evidence seized with the warrant would have been excluded at trial. The Court reasoned that it was unfair to penalize law enforcement officers who conduct searches in which incriminating evidence is found, when those officers conduct the search in good faith that they have a legal warrant. In the *Sheppard* case, the judge had used the wrong form for the warrant. As in *Leon*, the Court reasoned that it was unfair to penalize law enforcement officers, and the public, just because there was a flaw in the warrant, when the officers had conducted a search in good faith and found incriminating evidence.

The third case, *Nix* v. *Williams*, established an *inevitable-discovery exception* to the exclusionary rule. The *Nix* case involved a murderer whom police had tricked into leading them to the hidden body of his victim. In *Nix*, the Court held that evidence obtained in violation of a defendant's rights can be used at trial if the prosecution can show, by a preponderance of the evidence, that the information ultimately or inevitably would have been discovered by lawful means.

THE PATRIOT ACT Less than 2 months after the terrorist attacks of 9/11, and with little debate or scrutiny, Congress passed the "Uniting and Strengthening America by Providing Appropriate Tools Required to Intercept and Obstruct Terrorism Act of 2001," or the USA PATRIOT Act, for short.[36] Among a host of

Computer Errors

On March 1, 1995, in the case of *Arizona* v. *Evans*, the Supreme Court ruled that unlawful arrests based on computer errors do not always require the exclusion of evidence seized by police. In the *Arizona* case, the Court held that a good faith exception to the exclusionary rule could be made as long as the illegal seizure of evidence was caused by the errors of court employees and not the police. In that case, a Phoenix man who had been stopped for a traffic violation was arrested because a computer record showed an outstanding arrest warrant for some traffic violations. In fact, the warrant had been dropped 17 days earlier, but the action had not been entered into the computer. After the arrest, marijuana was seized from the man's car, and he was arrested for illegal possession.

provisions, the law gave broad new powers to the FBI, the CIA, and other U.S. foreign intelligence agencies to spy on American citizens. It also eliminated checks and balances on those powers such as judicial oversight, public accountability, and the ability to challenge government searches in court. For example, the law allowed the FBI to search private records (financial, medical, library, student—any recorded activity) *without a warrant and probable cause* and without having to reveal to anyone what it had done. Under the act, the FBI no longer needed probable cause to conduct wiretaps of criminal suspects when "a significant purpose" was gathering intelligence.

The act also created the new crime of "domestic terrorism." Under the act, members of controversial activist groups, such as Operation Rescue, Greenpeace, or the World Trade Organization protesters, could be charged with domestic terrorism if they committed acts "dangerous to human life" to "influence the policy of a government by intimidation or coercion." Even providing lodging or aid to such "terrorists" could initiate surveillance or prosecution. Another provision of the new law allowed the U.S. attorney general to detain noncitizens in the United States after certifying that there were "reasonable grounds to believe" that the noncitizen endangers national security. If a foreign country will not accept such noncitizens who are to be deported, they can be detained indefinitely without trial.

Ironically, as critics pointed out, most of the PATRIOT Act's changes to surveillance laws were part of a long-standing law enforcement wish list that Congress had repeatedly rejected. The events of 9/11 changed that. Critics also argued that the law was hurriedly passed without determining whether problems with existing surveillance laws contributed to the terrorist attacks and whether the new law would help prevent further attacks. Many of the law's provisions do not even deal with terrorism. Particularly troublesome to many critics was the law's elimination of the checks and balances placed on the government's surveillance powers. Most of those checks and balances were created after it was learned in the 1970s that the government had misused those powers. Among other things, the FBI and the CIA had illegally spied on more than half a million U.S. citizens during the McCarthy era and later. Perhaps the most notorious example of this clandestine activity was the illegal surveillance of Martin Luther King, Jr., during the 1960s.

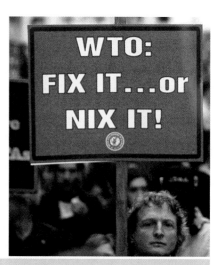

Under the PATRIOT Act, activist groups such as Operation Rescue, Greenpeace, or the World Trade Organization protesters could be charged with domestic terrorism if they committed acts "dangerous to human life" to "influence the policy of a government by intimidation or coercion." *Do you believe those groups engage in domestic terrorism? Why or why not?*

Critics took some comfort that several of the surveillance provisions of the PATRIOT Act were scheduled to expire on December 31, 2005. However, on March 9, 2006, President Bush signed into law the USA PATRIOT Act Improvement and Reauthorization Act of 2005 (after Congress had temporarily extended the original Act). The legislation made permanent 14 of the 16 USA PATRIOT Act provisions set to expire and placed four-year sunsets on the other two—the authority to conduct "roving" surveillance under the Foreign Intelligence Surveillance Act (FISA) and the authority to request production of business records under FISA. The new act also purportedly added dozens of additional safeguards to protect Americans' privacy and civil liberties. Critics contend the safeguards are inadequate. Among the provisions of the new legislation are the following:

- Authorized the attorney general to reorganize the Department of Justice by placing the department's primary national security elements under the leadership of a new assistant attorney general for national security. The new assistant attorney general will serve as the department's primary liaison to the new director of national intelligence, and the new division will gather expertise from across the department to create a focal point for providing advice on the numerous legal and policy issues raised by the department's national security missions.
- Provided tools to protect U.S. waterways and seaports from terrorists and thieves, including new or enhanced penalties for crimes such as smuggling goods into or out of the United States or bribing a public official to affect port security with the intent to commit international or domestic terrorism. Would-be terrorists will now face a U.S. Coast Guard empowered with new law enforcement tools for use at sea, including penalties for refusal to stop when ordered to do so and for transporting an explosive, biological agent, chemical weapon, or radioactive or nuclear materials knowing that the item is intended to be used to commit a terrorist act.
- Enhanced penalties for terrorism financing and closed a loophole in terrorist financing through *hawalas*, informal money transfer networks, rather than traditional financial institutions.
- The Combat Methamphetamine Act made certain drugs used in manufacturing "meth" "scheduled listed chemical products" harder to obtain in unlimited quantities and easier for law enforcement to track. It also enhanced penalties for the manufacture, smuggling, and selling of "meth."
- Eliminated confusion about the appropriate death penalty procedures for certain cases under the Controlled Substances Act and expanded on the authorities governing provision of counsel for death-penalty-eligible defendants who are unable to afford counsel.
- Provided clear intent standards and tough penalties for terrorist attacks and other violence targeted at U.S. rail systems and other mass transportation systems regardless of whether they operate on land, on water, or through the air.
- Continued to allow investigators to use so-called section 215 orders—court orders requiring production of business records or any "tangible things"—in all phases of national security investigations. Documents considered more sensitive, such as library, bookstore, medical, tax return, and gun sale records, require that applications to the FISA court for section 215 orders be signed by either the director or the deputy director of the FBI. Recipients of section 215 orders may seek judicial review and disclose receipt of the order to attorneys to obtain legal advice or assistance (something they were prohibited from doing under the original

FISA Court

Since its creation in 1978 a secretive federal court known as the Foreign Intelligence Surveillance Act Court, or FISA court, has approved thousands of Justice Department requests to conduct secret searches and surveillance of people in the United States who are suspected of having links to foreign agents or powers, often involving terrorism and espionage. The legislation that created the now 11-member FISA court also established a three-member Foreign Intelligence Surveillance Court of Review, which has never been used because the FISA court almost always grants the government's requests, and suspects are never notified that they are the target of a search or surveillance. The U.S. Supreme Court has the final authority to review cases from the Court of Review. The Supreme Court's chief justice appoints all members of both courts. The 11 FISA court judges are selected from among U.S. district court judges, and the three judges of the Court of Review are selected from the U.S. district courts or courts of appeals. Judges serve for a maximum of 7 years.

SOURCE: Federal Judicial Center, "Foreign Intelligence Surveillance Court," www.fjc. gov/public/home.nsf/hisc.

PATRIOT Act). Nevertheless, any employee who discloses a demand for such records, other than to the aforesaid attorney, can be imprisoned for five years under the new law.

- Amended the FISA court's authority to issue an electronic surveillance order that attaches to a particular target rather than particular phone or computer by increasing the level of detail needed to obtain an order and, in most cases, requiring the government to provide notice to the court within 10 days that surveillance had been directed at a new facility or place.
- To avoid adverse consequences such as endangering an individual's life or physical safety, allowed investigators to obtain court permission to delay giving notice that a search warrant had been executed for a presumptive limit of 30 days and extensions of 90 days.
- Limited the Patriot Act's broad definition of domestic terrorism to specific federal terrorism crimes, instead of any acts "dangerous to human life" to "influence the policy of a government by intimidation or coercion."[37]

Clearly, the catastrophic events of 9/11 have had a dramatic effect on American law enforcement and administration of justice. However, whether the changes that have been implemented and proposed in the wake of those events, such as the PATRIOT Act and the USA PATRIOT Act Improvement and Reauthorization Act of 2005, are desirable is a fair subject of debate in a free and democratic country.

Of all the due process guarantees in the Bill of Rights, those in the Fourth Amendment are the ones likely to require the most interpretation by the Supreme Court in the future. With advances in the technology of surveillance, the Court will have to determine the legality of increasingly more intrusive ways of gathering evidence. The star of a 1983 science fiction movie was a police helicopter named Blue Thunder. The helicopter was able to hover silently outside apartment buildings, record what was being said inside the apartments, and take pictures of what was being done. Although the movie was fictional, it will probably not be long before law enforcement has such equipment—if it does not have at least some of that equipment already. Will evidence obtained by means of the futuristic surveillance technology of Blue Thunder violate the Fourth Amendment prohibition against unreasonable searches and seizures?

The Supreme Court likely provided an answer to that question in *Kyllo* v. *United States* (2001). Danny Kyllo was convicted on a federal drug charge after federal agents, suspicious that Kyllo was growing marijuana in his home, used a thermal-imaging device to determine whether the heat coming from his house was consistent with the high-intensity lamps typically used in growing marijuana indoors. Based partly on the thermal imaging, a warrant was issued to search Kyllo's home, where agents found more than 100 marijuana plants growing. The Supreme Court, in a 5-4 ruling, held that the use of the thermal-imaging device before the warrant was issued was an impermissible search of Kyllo's home, violating the Fourth Amendment's prohibition of unreasonable searches and seizures. According to the Court, law enforcement agents must first obtain a search warrant before using high-tech devices to gather information from inside a home. At least for now, then, the use of futurist technology in the surveillance of a home, without a warrant, is legally prohibited. The use of a helicopter for visual aerial observation, however, probably is not (see *Florida* v. *Riley,* 1989).

self-incrimination Being a witness against oneself. If forced, it is a violation of the Fifth Amendment.

PROTECTION AGAINST COMPELLED SELF-INCRIMINATION Arguably, the most important procedural safeguard in the Fifth Amendment is the protection against compelled **self-incrimination.** The protection guarantees that in criminal cases, suspects or defendants cannot be forced to be witnesses against themselves. The protection is based on the belief that confessions may not be truthful if they are not made voluntarily. It also expresses an intolerance for certain methods used to extract confessions, even if the confessions ultimately prove to be reliable. A **confession** is an admission by a person accused of a crime that he or she committed the offense as charged. According to the Supreme Court's **doctrine of fundamental fairness,** confessions are inadmissible in criminal trials if they were obtained by means of either psychological manipulation or "third-degree" methods—for example, beatings, subjection to unreasonably long periods of questioning, or other physical tactics.

Although the Fifth Amendment protection against compelled self-incrimination has long been observed in federal trials, it was not until the 1960s, in the case of *Malloy* v. *Hogan* (1964), that the Fifth Amendment protection against compelled self-incrimination was extended to trials in state courts. In *Miranda* v. *Arizona* (1966), the Court broadened the protection against compelled self-incrimination to cover nearly all custodial police interrogations. (Custodial police interrogations essentially mean questionings that take place after an arrest or the functional equivalent of an arrest; they may or may not take place at the police station.) In *Miranda,* the Court added that confessions obtained without suspects' being notified of their specific rights could not be admitted as evidence. Perhaps even more important, it established specific procedural safeguards that had to be followed to avoid violation of the protection against compelled self-incrimination. The Court said:

> [P]rocedural safeguards must be employed to protect the privilege [against self-incrimination], and unless other fully effective means are adopted to notify the person of his right of silence and to assure that the exercise of the right will be scrupulously honored, the following measures are required. [The suspect] must be warned prior to any questioning (1) that he has the right to remain silent, (2) that anything he says can be used against him in a court of law, (3) that he has the right to the presence of an attorney, and (4) that if he cannot afford an attorney one will be appointed for him prior to any questioning if he so desires.

If suspects indicate, prior to or during questioning, that they wish to remain silent, the interrogation must cease; if they state that they want an attorney, the questioning must cease until an attorney is present. Where an interrogation is conducted without the presence of an attorney and a statement is taken, a heavy burden rests on the government to demonstrate that a suspect knowingly and intelligently waived his or her right to counsel. However, if an individual being questioned is not yet in custody, the *Miranda* warnings do not have to be given. Also, volunteered confessions do not violate *Miranda* or the Fifth Amendment.

The Fifth Amendment protection against compelled self-incrimination has been weakened recently by the Supreme Court. For example, in *New York* v. *Quarles* (1984), the Supreme Court created a public-safety exception to the Fifth Amendment protection. Also, in *Arizona* v. *Fulminante* (1991), the Court ruled that improper use of a coerced confession is a harmless trial error if other evidence is strong enough to convict the defendant. The burden of proof is on the state to show that a coerced confession is harmless error. The case involved a defendant who had been sentenced to death for killing his 11-year-old stepdaughter. While in prison, the defendant confessed to an FBI informant after the informant promised to protect the defendant from other inmates. Prior to *Fulminante,* such a conviction would most likely have been reversed on appeal because of the use of the coerced confession.

However, in *Dickerson* v. *United States* (2000), the Court reaffirmed the importance of *Miranda,* even when it inconveniences law enforcement officers.

confession An admission by a person accused of a crime that he or she committed the offense charged.

doctrine of fundamental fairness The rule that makes confessions inadmissible in criminal trials if they were obtained by means of either psychological manipulation or "third-degree" methods.

Coerced Confessions

The first time the Supreme Court held that a coerced confession, brutally beaten out of the suspect, was inadmissible in a state trial was in 1936, in the case of *Brown* v. *Mississippi.* However, in the *Brown* case, the Court did not find that the coerced confession violated the Fifth Amendment protection against self-incrimination. Rather, the Court found that it violated the Fourteenth Amendment right to due process.

Interrogation

In the case of *Rhode Island* v. *Innis* (1980), the Supreme Court stated: "[T]he term 'interrogation' under *Miranda* refers not only to express questioning, but also to any words or actions on the part of the police (other than those normally attendant to arrest and custody) that the police should know are reasonably likely to elicit an incriminating response from the suspect."

THINKING CRITICALLY

1. Do you think the provisions of the PATRIOT Act and the USA PATRIOT Act Improvement and Reauthorization Act of 2005 are necessary to effectively combat terrorism in the United States? Why or why not?

2. Do you think the use of torture to obtain information from terrorist suspects should be allowed? Why or why not?

In *Dickerson,* a bank robbery suspect asked the Court to throw out incriminating statements he made to FBI agents because he was not given *Miranda* warnings prior to questioning. Prosecutors argued that the suspect made voluntary statements, which were admissible under a law approved by Congress in 1968. The law gives federal judges authority to admit statements from suspects if the judges believe that the statements are voluntary. The Court disagreed and held that Congress did not have the authority to supersede the Supreme Court's interpretation of the Constitution. Therefore, the incriminating statements made by the bank robbery suspect were inadmissible.[38]

1. Identify characteristics of police work.

The role of the police officer is complex and requires a combination of special characteristics, which involve quick decision making, invisible work, "dirty work," and danger.

2. Distinguish among James Q. Wilson's three operational styles in policing.

Wilson's three operational styles in policing are legalistic, which emphasizes violations of the law and the use of arrests to resolve community disputes; watchman, which emphasizes informal means of resolving disputes and using arrest only as a last resort; and service, which emphasizes helping in the community over enforcing the law.

3. List the four major functions of police departments.

The four major functions of police departments in the United States are patrol, investigation, traffic, and drug enforcement.

4. List the drug enforcement strategies of local police agencies.

Although the particular drug enforcement strategies employed by individual agencies vary widely, the most common strategies are street-level enforcement, midlevel investigations, major investigations, crop eradication, smuggling interdiction, problem-oriented and community policing strategies, drug demand reduction, and asset forfeiture.

5. Explain the main components of community policing.

The three main components of community policing are community partnership, problem solving, and change management.

6. Identify four steps in a community policing approach to problem solving.

Community policing relies heavily on problem solving. The four steps in a community policing approach to problem solving are often referred to as SARA: Scanning—identifying problems, Analysis—understanding underlying conditions, Response—developing and implementing solutions, Assessment—determining the solutions' effect.

7. Describe the procedural rights in the Fourth Amendment.

The Fourth Amendment protects persons from unreasonable searches and seizures (including arrests). Under most circumstances, it requires that a judge issue a search warrant authorizing law officers to search for and seize evidence of criminal activity, but the warrant can be issued only when there is probable cause. In 1914, the Supreme Court adopted the exclusionary rule, which barred evidence seized illegally from being used in a criminal trial; in 1961, the rule was made applicable to the states. Subsequent Supreme Court decisions have narrowed the application of the exclusionary rule. The Fourth Amendment also protects persons from warrantless searches and seizures in places where they have a legitimate right to expect privacy. The protection, however, does not extend to every place where a person has a legitimate right to be. The Court has permitted stopping and searching an automobile when there is probable cause to believe the car is carrying something illegal.

8. Describe the procedural rights in the Fifth Amendment.

The Fifth Amendment provides many procedural protections, the most important of which is the protection against compelled self-incrimination. This protection was extended to most police custodial interrogations in the 1966 case of Miranda v. Arizona. *According to* Miranda, *police custody is threatening and confessions obtained during custody can be admitted into evidence only if suspects have been (1) advised of their constitutional right to remain silent, (2) warned that what they say can be used against them in a trial, (3) informed of the right to have an attorney, and (4) told that if they cannot afford an attorney, one will be appointed for them prior to questioning, if they so desire. Suspects may waive their* Miranda *rights, but only if the waiver is made knowingly, intelligently, and voluntarily. Other due process rights in the Fifth Amendment are the right to a grand jury indictment in felony cases (in federal court) and protection against double jeopardy.*

KEY TERMS

REVIEW QUESTIONS

1. What is a common source of role conflict for the police?

2. Distinguish among the three sets of operational styles identified by criminal justice scholars.

3. How are preventive patrol, directed patrol, and aggressive patrol different?

4. What are the major uses of GIS crime mapping in law enforcement?

5. What are some of the functions of a criminal investigator?

6. What are three distinct functions of DNA profiling?

7. What are two broad categories of cybercrime?

8. What are some of the more important functions of traffic units?

9. What are some of the problems with the use of civil asset forfeiture in drug enforcement?

10. What is the philosophy of community policing?

11. What are the three complementary operational strategies of community policing?

12. What are *searches* and *seizures*?

13. What is an *arrest*?

14. What two conclusions must be supported by substantial and trustworthy evidence before either a search warrant or an arrest warrant is issued? (The two conclusions are different for each type of warrant.)

15. In *Chimel* v. *California* (1969), what limitations did the U.S. Supreme Court place on searches incident to an arrest?

16. Today, what is the principal purpose of the exclusionary rule?

17. What are the major provisions of the PATRIOT Act?

IN THE FIELD

1. **SARA Approach** In groups of three or four, select a local crime or disorder problem. Using the first three components of the SARA approach to problem solving (scanning, analysis, and response) and considering the elements of the crime triangle, formulate some options to deal with the problem. Present your options to the class, and let the whole class vote to determine which option is the best to solve the problem. Do you agree with the class vote? Why or why not? What do the results of this vote say about attitudes toward crime-related problem solving?

2. **Law Enforcement Resources** Look through several police periodicals, such as *Law and Order*, *Police Chief*, or other professional police magazines. What do the advertised products tell you about law enforcement? What law enforcement issues are addressed in the articles? Write a brief summary of your findings.

1. **Cybercrime** Ask a local police officer what the needs of the police in combating cybercrime in your area are. Make a list of the types of cybercrimes that have actually occurred in your area. Compare and contrast that list with what experts on CNET (go to their Web page at www.CNET.com) and the material in your text describe as the important concerns in addressing cybercrime. Is there cause for concern? Why or why not?

2. **Drug Enforcement** To learn more about illegal drugs and drug control policy, visit the Web site of the Office of National Drug Control Policy at www.whitehousedrugpolicy.gov. Based on what you have learned, write an essay or prepare an oral presentation on whether national drug control policy has been or will be effective in reducing drug use and abuse among the American public.

1. **Police Patrol** Assume that you are the patrol commander in a southern city that has large numbers of African American and Hispanic residents. All shifts of your patrol division have embraced and supported a "broken windows" and "zero-tolerance" approach to patrol work. Your patrol division's style could clearly be called aggressive, but for the past 5 years the city's violent, property, and minor offense rates have been dropping steadily. Some citizens have complained each month about the aggressive and sometimes intrusive vehicle stops. Most of the complainants have been African Americans who live in neighborhoods where the recorded crime rate has dropped the most dramatically since the implementation of the aggressive patrol style. They accuse officers of racial profiling. Racial profiling is illegal and occurs when minority citizens are stopped in their cars and on the street for little or nothing more than their race as the cause. (Racial profiling is discussed in greater detail in the next chapter.) When applied to motorists, racial profiling has even acquired a popular name, "Driving While Black" or DWB or DWBB, "Driving While Black or Brown."
   a. What steps would you take as patrol commander to assure the chief of police, the city's leaders, and the public at large that neither racial profiling is occurring in your patrol division nor are infringements on citizens' liberties beyond what are legal and necessary?
   b. What impact would validated cases of "Driving While Black or Brown" (or racial profiling) in other cities have on your plan?

2. **Community Policing** You are a new community police officer assigned with seven other officers to a low-income, heterogeneous, high-turnover, high-crime neighborhood. How should you and your fellow officers address the following problems?
   a. Neighborhood residents, neighborhood business owners, and community leaders disagree about the most important problems of the neighborhood and what to do about them. What should you and your fellow officers do?
   b. You organize and heavily publicize a meeting to discuss neighborhood problems and their solutions. However, only about 10 to 20 percent of neighborhood residents attend and most of them are white and more affluent homeowners who live in the better parts of the neighborhood. Few minorities or renters attend. What should you and your fellow officers do?
   c. Your precinct captain disagrees with neighborhood residents about the most important problems in the neighborhood. Your precinct captain's top priority is abandoned cars used for drug dealing. The top priority of neighborhood residents is the overall appearance of the neighborhood. What should you and your fellow officers do?

To access more information and resources, including study questions, chapter summaries, and links, go to: www.mhhe.com/bohm1.

POLICING AMERICA: ISSUES AND ETHICS

CHAPTER OBJECTIVES

After completing this chapter, you should be able to:

1. Describe the general attitude of the public toward the police.

2. Summarize the steps in an effective police officer selection process.

3. Identify factors that affect the exercise of police discretion and methods of limiting discretion.

4. Describe two general ways that law enforcement agencies can reduce stress on the job.

5. Explain the circumstances under which police officers may be justified in using deadly force.

6. List some of the ways to control and reduce police corruption.

7. Define terrorism and identify different types of terrorism.

The Police and the Public

To carry out the duties of law enforcement, order maintenance, service, and information gathering successfully, the police must have the trust and cooperation of the public. The manner in which they carry out those functions, especially law enforcement and order maintenance, determines the community's respect for and trust in the police. Citizens who trust and respect the police are much more likely to help them carry out their duties; citizens who lack that trust and respect may rebel against the police in particular and government in general.

PUBLIC ATTITUDES TOWARD THE POLICE

What do people think of the police? The answer depends on what and whom you ask. It also depends on people's prior experience with the police. Research shows that citizens who have experienced positive contacts with the police generally have positive attitudes toward the police.[1] Figure 4.1 reveals that, overall, 27 percent of the public have "a great deal" of confidence in the police, 53 percent have "a fair amount" of confidence, 15 percent have "very little," and 2 percent have "no confidence at all." However, among blacks, only 14 percent have "a great deal" of confidence in the police, while 31 percent have "very little confidence" or "no confidence at all." What is it about the police that the public has or does not have confidence?

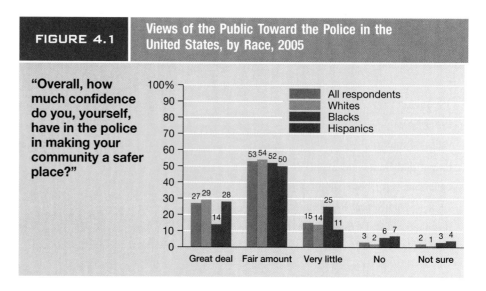

| FIGURE 4.1 | Views of the Public Toward the Police in the United States, by Race, 2005 |

"Overall, how much confidence do you, yourself, have in the police in making your community a safer place?"

All respondents
Whites
Blacks
Hispanics

Note: Percentages may not add up to 100% due to rounding.

Source: Harris Interactive® online survey conducted between September 6 and 12, 2005, among 2,242 U.S. adults aged 18 and older. Sampling error for the overall results is +/−2 percentage points. Data generously provided to author.

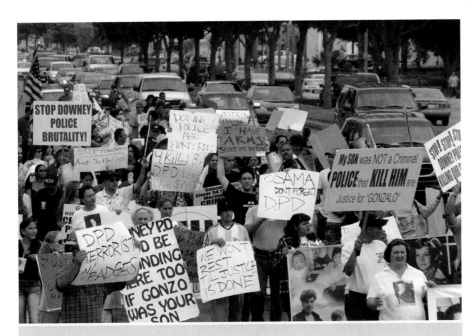

The level of respect and confidence the public has for the police is not particularly high, especially among minorities. *Why is this the case?*

To begin with, a majority or nearly a majority of the public rate the police "excellent" or "good" at being part of the community, responding quickly to calls for help and assistance, preventing crimes, solving crimes, being helpful and friendly, treating people fairly, not using excessive force, and preventing terrorist attacks. As shown in Figure 4.2, between 45 and 60 percent of the public rate the police "excellent" or "good" on the eight aforementioned issues. Between 30 and 40 percent rate the police "fair," and between 9 and 16 percent rate them "poor" or "terrible." A different poll shows that 60 percent of the public have "a great deal" or "quite a lot" of confidence in the police's ability to protect it from violent crime; 31 percent do "not [have] very much confidence"; 8 percent have "none at all"; and 1 percent have "no opinion." The public's confidence in the police's ability to protect it from violent crime has not changed much in more than two decades. In short, a majority of the public has at least some confidence in the ability of the police to do its job in a professional manner.

Among minorities, however, confidence in the police is much lower. On every measure of performance in Figure 4.2, blacks and Hispanics rate the police lower than whites. Other polls that measure other aspects of police performance reveal the same pattern:

- Only 43 percent of blacks and 41 percent of Hispanics, compared with 61 percent of whites, believe that "the police treat all races fairly."
- Eighty percent of blacks and 66 percent of Hispanics are much more likely to believe that "police brutality against minorities happens 'occasionally' (or more often) in their communities." Fifty-one percent of whites also agree with the statement.
- Thirty-two percent of blacks and 24 percent of Hispanics, compared with 6 percent of whites, believe that "police brutality against minorities in their communities happens 'often'."
- Forty-two percent of blacks and 39 percent of Hispanics, compared with 16 percent of whites, are sometimes "afraid that they will be arrested when they are completely innocent."[2]

About 50 percent of Americans rate the police as either good or excellent at solving crimes. *Why isn't the percentage higher?*

"How would you rate the police in your community on the following—excellent or good, fair, or poor or terrible?"

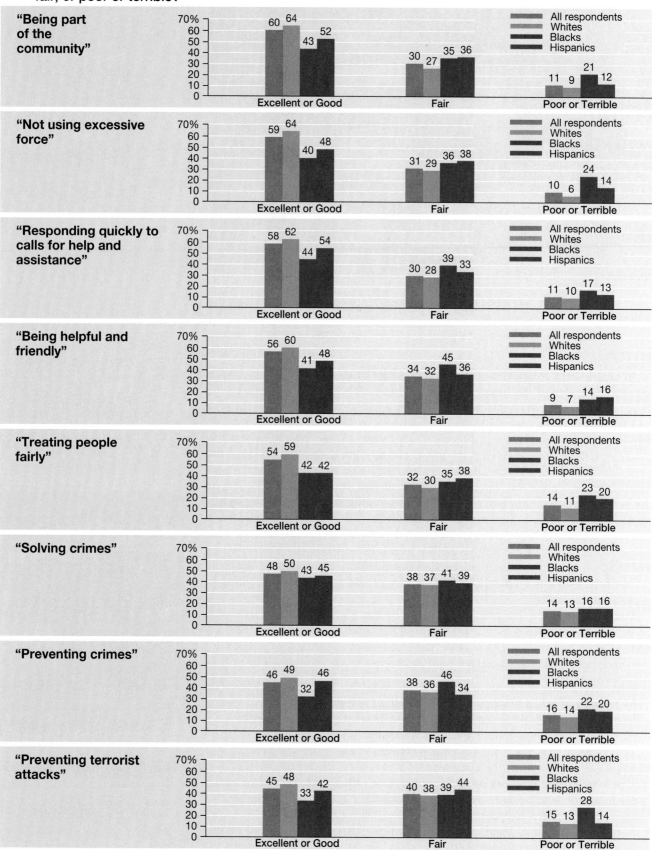

Note: Percentages may not add up to 100% due to rounding.

Source: Harris Interactive® online survey conducted between September 6 and 12, 2005, among 2,242 U.S. adults aged 18 and older. Sampling error for the overall results is +/−2 percentage points. Data generously provided to author.

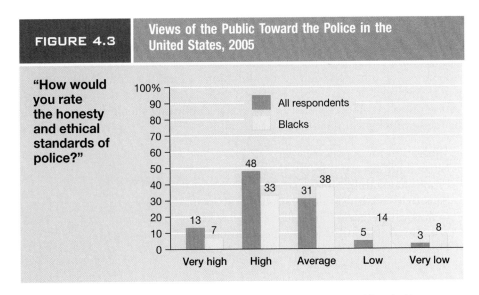

FIGURE 4.3

Views of the Public Toward the Police in the United States, 2005

"How would you rate the honesty and ethical standards of police?"

Source: Bureau of Justice Statistics, *Sourcebook of Criminal Justice Statistics Online*, www.albany.edu/sourcebook/pdf/t2212005.pdf.

When asked to rate the honesty and ethical standards of the police, 13 percent of the general public rate the police as "very high" on this measure, 48 percent rate them as "high," 31 percent rate them as "average," 5 percent rate them as "low," and 3 percent rate them as "very low." Blacks rate the honesty and ethical standards of police lower: Only 7 percent rate the police as "very high," 33 percent rate them as "high," 38 percent rate them as "average," 14 percent rate them as "low," and 8 percent rate them as "very low." (See Figure 4.3.)

In sum, these data clearly show that the public as a whole has more respect for the police and their honesty and ethical standards than it does for a variety of other occupations.[3] Yet, the level of respect and confidence is not particularly high, nor is it uniform across races. While most of the public believes that the police do a pretty good job, it also believes there is much room for improvement. One way to improve the police is to employ better police officers.

THINKING CRITICALLY

1. Why do you think that racial groups differ so greatly in their attitudes toward the police?

2. What do you think could be done to improve public attitudes toward the police?

3. How accurate do you think the public's perceptions of the police are?

4. How do the perceptions presented in this section compare with your own?

Police Recruitment and Selection

Deciding whom to employ should be simple: hire the type of police officer that the citizens of the community want. Of course, that approach assumes that the citizens of a community have some idea of what it takes to be a police officer. Then, there is the matter of which people to consult. Who should decide? The wealthy? The middle class? The poor? The politically conservative? The politically liberal? The young? The old? The business community? Community leaders? Crime victims? Those people most likely to be policed? Some consensus is needed on the type of police officer desired. Seeking that consensus in metropolitan communities is filled with conflict. Police administrators need to be very careful in choosing police officers, who may well be with the agency for 20 years or more. A police department will never reach its full potential without selecting the best available personnel. Selection decisions have momentous long-term implications for a police department.[4]

QUALITIES OF A SUCCESSFUL POLICE OFFICER

Given the complexity of the role of the police officer, it comes as no surprise that deciding what qualities the successful police officer needs is not easy. Indeed, police officers require a combination of qualities and abilities that is rare in any pool of applicants. Robert B. Mills, a pioneer in the psychological testing of police officers, believes that police applicants should possess the following psychological qualities:

- Motivation for a police career.
- Normal self-assertiveness.
- Emotional stability under stress.
- Sensitivity toward minority groups and social deviates.
- Collaborative leadership skills.
- A mature relationship with social authority.
- Flexibility.
- Integrity and honesty.
- An active and outgoing nature.[5]

The Berkeley, California, Police Department lists these qualities:

- Initiative.
- Ability to carry heavy responsibilities and handle emergencies alone.

CAREERS IN CRIMINAL JUSTICE

Police Officer

My name is Robert Bour. I really enjoy being a police officer in Tiffin, Ohio, a small city of about 20,000 people. My assignment is in the patrol section, but I also work as a bike patrol officer, a field training officer, and a member of the SWAT team. As a SWAT officer, I go out mainly on search warrant and drug raids and in cases where someone has barricaded him- or herself in and a life is in danger. In a small police department, you have the opportunity to be involved in a number of specialized assignments.

As a patrol officer, I have the opportunity to interact with the public a great deal. We have always done community policing here in one form or another. Small communities have to. You stop people on the street and say hello, chat with business owners, and meet as many residents as you can. People always have questions for you; often they are about traffic laws and enforcement.

I also have to respond to calls for services and these calls take precedence over everything else. I get one to three calls per hour on the evening and early morning shift, but there are rare times when I don't get any calls during the entire 10 hours of work.

My third area of activity involves self-initiated patrol activity. That includes traffic enforcement, of course, but also patrolling the alleys and streets around bars when

they are closing in order to protect inebriates who may have passed out outside the establishment. The patrol also includes guarding against people who may be driving under the influence of alcohol. Tiffin has two universities, so sometimes college students may get a little more disorderly than they should and we have to respond.

I graduated in 1992 from a police academy that was hosted by a local community college. Before becoming a police officer in Tiffin, I worked as a sheriff's deputy and a village police officer, both full- and part-time. The Tiffin police department now requires a 2-year college degree as the minimum to become employed. At the time I came on, it was not necessary, but I intend to go back to college and finish my degree anyway.

I can offer a few suggestions for anyone who wants to be a police officer. First, you should have a desire to work with people from diverse backgrounds because that is what police work is. Second, you must genuinely want to help people, keeping in mind that you are not always able to help everybody; sometimes that is frustrating. Finally, you must think about your family. They must support you in being a cop because there is some danger involved in the job. Still, police work is one of the best jobs a person can have.

What are the pros and cons of being a police officer?

- Social skills and ability to communicate effectively with persons of various cultural, economic, and ethnic backgrounds.
- Mental capacity to learn a wide variety of subjects quickly and correctly.
- Ability to adapt thinking to technological and social changes.
- Understanding of other human beings and the desire to help those in need.
- Emotional maturity to remain calm and objective and provide leadership in emotionally charged situations.
- Physical strength and endurance to perform these exacting duties.[6]

Three qualities seem to be of paramount importance. One commentator refers to them as the **three I's of police selection:** intelligence, integrity, and interaction skills. In short, police officers need to be bright enough to complete rigorous training. They should be honest enough to resist—and have a lifestyle that allows them to resist—the temptation of corrupting influences in law enforcement. They should also be able to communicate clearly and get along with people of diverse backgrounds.

Nearly as important as the three I's, however, are common sense and compassion. In resolving conflicts and solving problems they encounter, police officers must often choose a course of action without much time to think about it. Common sense is a key quality, for example, in locating a suspect who has just fled a crime scene on foot, or in deciding when to call off a high-speed vehicle pursuit that suddenly endangers innocent citizens and other police officers.

Police agencies also seek to employ officers with the core value of compassion. Without a genuine concern for serving one's fellow human beings, a police officer is not likely to sustain a high level of motivation over a long period of time. Many people the police meet on a daily basis simply need help, sometimes required by law, but more often these officers are spurred by a compassion for helping people no matter what their need.

Other qualities, such as physical strength, endurance, and appearance, seem less important. If you were the one who needed to be dragged from a burning automobile, however, the physical strength of the police officer might be important to you.

THE POLICE RECRUITMENT PROCESS

Few occupations have selection processes as elaborate as the ones used in choosing police officers in most departments of the nation. Before choices are made, a wide net must be cast in the recruiting effort to come up with enough potential applicants to fill the vacancies for an academy class. Police departments, often working with city personnel agencies, are generally guided in their selection decisions by civil service regulations. Those regulations are developed either locally or at the state level. They guarantee a merit employment system with equal opportunity for all.

Because employment qualifications are supposed to be based on perceived needs in policing, law enforcement agencies must be careful not to set unnecessary restrictions that have no bearing on an officer's ability to complete training and perform successfully on the job. The addition of just one seemingly minor qualification, such as requiring four pull-ups instead of three during physical ability testing, or making the eyesight requirement slightly more stringent, may eliminate thousands of men and women from the selection process in a large metropolitan area. It is difficult enough to find capable police candidates without needlessly eliminating them from the selection process.

three i's of police selection Three qualties of the American police officer that seem to be of paramount importance: intelligence, integrity, and interaction skills.

Police Salaries

In 2004, police and sheriff's patrol officers had median earnings of $45,210. The middle 50 percent earned between $34,410 and $56,360. The lowest 10 percent earned less than $26,910, and the highest 10 percent earned more than $68,880. Median annual earnings were $48,980 in state government, $45,010 in local government, and $44,750 in federal government.

SOURCE: U.S. Department of Labor, Bureau of Labor Statistics, *Occupational Outlook Handbook*, www.bls.gov/oco/ocos160.htm.

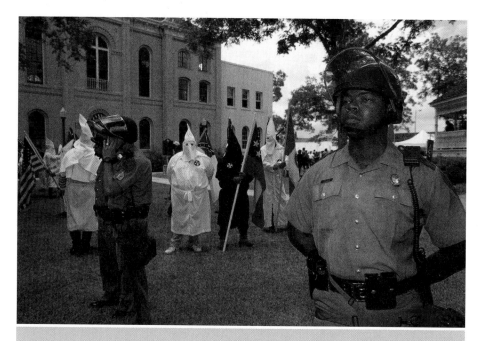

Police officers must have a variety of qualities to be successful on the job. *What qualities would you bring to the position?*

RECRUITMENT Most police agencies have finally realized that the kind of officers they desire will not gravitate naturally to the doors of the department. The search for top-notch applicants is very competitive, and many chiefs and sheriffs believe that they have to look at larger pools of applicants than in the past to find the same number of qualified officers. The reasons for the increased difficulty in finding good police candidates involve social maturity and lifestyle issues. Problems with drugs and alcohol, sexually transmitted

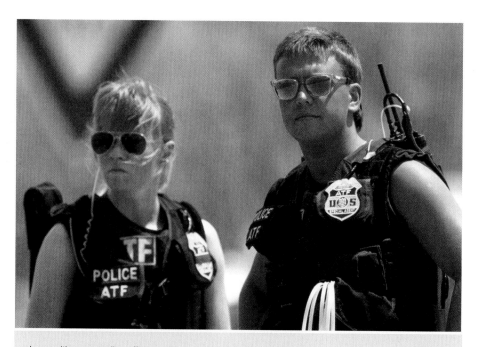

In recruiting new police officers, efforts are made to cast police work as an attractive and sustaining career. *What should people interested in becoming police officers be told about the job?*

TABLE 4.1	Average Base Annual Salary for Selected Positions in Local Police Departments, by Size of Population Served, 2003					
POPULATION SERVED	ENTRY-LEVEL OFFICER		SERGEANT OR EQUIVALENT		CHIEF	
	MINIMUM	MAXIMUM	MINIMUM	MAXIMUM	MINIMUM	MAXIMUM
All sizes	$28,200	$35,300	$36,600	$42,400	$48,800	$56,900
1,000,000 or more	$37,700	$57,800	$60,200	$73,500	$113,000	$157,100
500,000–999,999	36,600	54,900	58,000	69,600	109,700	143,200
250,000–499,999	38,300	53,500	54,600	66,900	94,400	129,200
100,000–249,999	39,600	54,000	56,000	68,000	95,000	123,100
50,000–99,999	37,400	51,200	54,500	65,300	85,500	106,900
25,000–49,999	35,900	48,600	53,400	62,400	77,700	94,500
10,000–24,999	33,000	45,000	47,400	55,200	65,900	77,800
2,500–9,999	29,000	36,200	37,400	43,600	48,900	56,200
Under 2,500	23,400	26,800	27,100	30,800	32,700	36,500

Note: Salary figures have been rounded to the nearest $100. Computation of average salary excludes departments with no full-time employee in that position.

Source: Matthew J. Hickman and Brian A. Reaves, *Local Police Departments, 2003* (Washington, DC: GPO, U.S. Department of Justice, Bureau of Justice Statistics, May 2006), p. 11, Table 20.

diseases, personal debt, and dependability have reduced the number of qualified police applicants.

The major goal of the recruiting effort is to cast police work as an attractive and sustaining career, even to those who might initially be turned off by it. Research supports the allure of policing for many people who view a career in law enforcement as financially rewarding and status enhancing. In addition, the work itself is intrinsically satisfying because it is nonroutine, exciting, generally outdoors, and people oriented.[7] Table 4.1 shows the average base annual salary for selected positions in local police departments, by size of population served in 2003. Many departments also offer the opportunity to earn special pay. Table 4.2 shows the percentage of local police

TABLE 4.2	Local Police Departments Authorizing Special Pay for Full-Time Sworn Personnel by Size of Population Served, 2003							
POPULATION SERVED	PERCENTAGE OF AGENCIES AUTHORIZING PAY FOR—							
	TUITION REIMBURSEMENT	EDUCATION INCENTIVE	MERIT	SHIFT DIFFERENTIAL	SPECIAL SKILLS	MILITARY DUTY	HAZARDOUS DUTY	BILINGUAL ABILITY
All sizes	35%	32%	21%	21%	13%	10%	5%	4%
1,000,000 or more	81%	75%	44%	81%	56%	19%	69%	50%
500,000–999,999	72	54	30	65	30	30	54	32
250,000–499,999	83	61	54	76	44	27	49	44
100,000–249,999	76	72	44	57	33	25	29	38
50,000–99,999	76	68	39	44	39	23	24	27
25,000–49,999	72	67	30	44	26	19	10	14
10,000–24,999	61	57	30	37	24	14	5	6
2,500–9,999	38	35	21	23	13	11	3	2
Under 2,500	13	11	14	6	3	4	3	—

Source: Matthew J. Hickman and Brian A. Reaves, *Local Police Departments, 2003* (Washington, DC: GPO, U.S. Department of Justice, Bureau of Justice Statistics, May 2006), p. 12, Table 21.

TABLE 4.3	Minority Representation in Local Police Departments in the United States, 2003

RACE/ETHNICITY	POLICE	POPULATION
Black	11.7%	12.2%
Hispanic	9.1	13.7
White	76.4	67.9
Other	2.8	6.2

Source: Matthew J. Hickman and Brian A. Reaves, *Local Police Departments, 2003* (Washington, DC: GPO, U.S. Department of Justice, Bureau of Justice Statistics, 2006), and U.S. Census Bureau.

Increase in Minority and Female Police Officers

From 1987 to 2003, the percentage of African American local police officers increased from 9.3 to 11.7; Hispanic officers from 4.5 to 9.1; other minority group members, such as Asians, Pacific Islanders, and American Indians, from 0.8 to 2.8; and female officers, from 7.6 to 11.3.

SOURCE: Matthew J. Hickman and Brian A. Reaves, *Local Police Departments, 2003* (Washington, DC: GPO, U.S. Department of Justice, Bureau of Justice Statistics, 2006), p. 7.

Women and Policing

The National Center for Women & Policing is a nationwide resource that seeks to increase the number of women in policing. You can visit its Web site at **www.womenandpolicing.org/ default.asp.** *What are some of the best ways to increase the number of women in policing?*

college academies Schools where students pursue a program that integrates an associate's degree curriculum in law enforcement or criminal justice with the state's required peace officer training.

departments, by size of population served, that authorize various types of special pay.

AFFIRMATIVE ACTION Since the passage of the Civil Rights Act of 1964 and the threat of court challenges to the fairness of the police selection process, police agencies have struggled to find the best-qualified applicants and yet achieve satisfactory race and gender representation within the ranks of the department. Failure to seriously pursue equitable representation has led to expensive lawsuits, consent decrees, and court-ordered quotas to achieve the desired diversity. Consequently, affirmative action has become a major concern in police selection and employment. Now affirmative action programs are being questioned on several legal grounds. That questioning may lead to more difficulty in trying to achieve race and gender balance in police departments.

How successful has affirmative action been in accomplishing the desired goal of race and gender balance in police departments? Affirmative action has been relatively successful in increasing the percentage of minority members in policing. It has been less successful in increasing the percentage of women. As noted previously, more than 70 percent of the sworn officers in the nation's police departments are white males. However, as shown in Table 4.3, the percentage of black and Hispanic officers in local departments is 11.7 and 9.1, respectively. Those figures closely approximate the percentage of blacks and Hispanics in the general population of the United States (12.7 percent for blacks and 10.9 percent for Hispanics). However, women, who compose over 50 percent of the United States population, represent only 11.3 percent of the police officers in local police departments.[8]

EDUCATION Given the amount of discretion that law enforcement officers have and the kinds of sociological problems with which they deal, selecting reasonably intelligent, college-educated officers seems a wise practice. Many police agencies in the country currently require some college background. As a result, the average level of education in policing today is nearly 2 years of college. Table 4.4 shows the minimum educational requirement for new officers in local departments, by size of population served. Among the advantages of hiring college-educated officers are the following:

1. Better written reports.
2. Enhanced communication with the public.
3. More effective job performance.
4. Fewer citizen complaints.
5. Wiser use of discretion.
6. Heightened sensitivity to racial and ethnic issues.
7. Fewer disciplinary actions.[9]

This list of advantages should impress police administrators and the public. Satisfied citizens, the savings of substantial amounts of money by avoiding lawsuits, and fewer disciplinary actions against officers are good reasons for law enforcement executives to search for police applicants with college backgrounds.

Recognition that college-educated police officers are generally better performers than officers without that level of education is long overdue. And the idea is catching on. Minnesota's Peace Officer Licensing Commission now requires a 4-year college degree for licensing. The Peace Officer Council in Ohio now has more than one dozen **college academies,** where

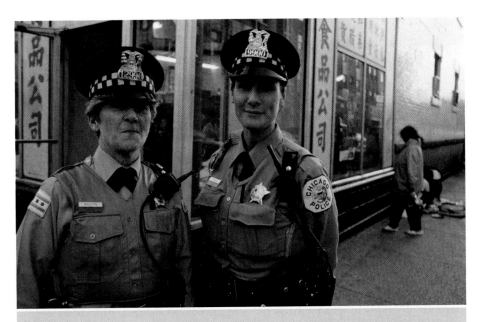

Increasing the number of female officers is a major concern in police selection and employment. *What are some of the advantages of having a greater number of female police officers?*

		PERCENTAGE OF AGENCIES REQUIRING A MINIMUM OF:			
POPULATION SERVED	**TOTAL WITH RE-QUIREMENT**	**HIGH SCHOOL DIPLOMA**	**SOME COLLEGE***	**2-YEAR COLLEGE DEGREE**	**4-YEAR COLLEGE DEGREE**
All sizes	98%	81%	8%	9%	1%
1,000,000 or more	98%	72%	18%	7%	1%
500,000–999,999	99	72	13	9	5
250,000–499,999	99	84	8	4	3
100,000–249,999	98	81	13	3	2
50,000–99,999	100	76	17	6	1
25,000–49,999	99	77	10	11	1
10,000–24,999	99	82	7	9	1
2,500–9,999	99	83	7	9	—
Under 2,500	97	82	6	9	0

TABLE 4.4 — Minimum Educational Requirement for New Officers in Local Police Departments, by Size of Population Served, 2003

Note: Detail may not add to total because of rounding.

*Nondegree requirements.

— Less than 0.5 percent.

Source: Matthew J. Hickman and Brian A. Reaves, *Local Police Departments, 2003* (Washington, DC: GPO, U.S. Department of Justice, Bureau of Justice Statistics, May 2006), p. 9, Table 16.

students pursue a program that integrates an associate's degree curriculum in law enforcement or criminal justice with the state's required peace officer training. Upon receipt of the associate's degree, students sit for the peace officer certification exam. If they receive a passing score on the exam, they are eligible to be hired by any police agency and to go to work without any additional academy training.

SUCCESSFUL RECRUITING PRACTICES

Where do you find the best-qualified police applicants? Some of the more successful recruiting practices have included going to colleges, neighborhood centers, and schools in minority communities; using television, radio, and newspaper advertisements; and working with local employment offices. Demystifying the nature of police work and the selection process and shortening the time from application to final selection have also helped to attract and retain qualified candidates.

public safety officers Police department employees who perform many police services but do not have arrest powers.

PUBLIC SAFETY OFFICERS Another promising recruitment strategy has been the employment of 18-year-olds as **public safety officers** (sometimes called community service officers or public service aides), who perform many police service functions but do not have arrest powers. By the time they are 21, the department has had an excellent opportunity to assess their qualifications and potential to be sworn officers.

police cadet program A program that combines a college education with agency work experience and academy training. Upon graduation, a cadet is promoted to police officer.

POLICE CADETS **Police cadet programs** have been around since the 1960s (Cincinnati Police), and as recently as the 1990s, the New York City Police launched a cadet program combining a college education with academy training and work experience in the police department. Upon graduation from the university, a cadet is promoted to police officer.

tech prep (technical preparation) A program in which area community colleges and high schools team up to offer 6 to 9 hours of college law enforcement courses in the eleventh and twelfth grades, as well as one or two training certifications, such as police dispatcher or local corrections officer. Students who graduate are eligible for police employment at age 18.

HIGH SCHOOL TECH PREP PROGRAMS Another program that is proving useful in attracting potentially capable police officers at an even earlier age is known as **tech prep,** or **technical preparation,** for a criminal justice career. Area community colleges and high schools team up to offer 6 to 9 hours of college law enforcement courses in the eleventh and twelfth grades,

Pictured here are police cadets searching a parking lot, where a woman was shot and killed by a sniper. *What are some of the advantages of police cadet programs?*

as well as one or two training certifications, such as police dispatcher or local corrections officer. Students who graduate are eligible for employment at age 18. They become interested in law enforcement work early and are ideal police applicants when they become old enough to apply. Accurate law enforcement career information can be passed on to high school students through a tech prep program because the teachers are required to either currently work in law enforcement or have police experience in their backgrounds.

POLICE CORPS The federal Police Corps program was created as part of the Violent Crime Control and Law Enforcement Act of 1994.[10] Its purposes are to (1) address violent crime by increasing the number of police with advanced education and training on community patrol and (2) provide educational assistance to law enforcement personnel and students who possess a sincere interest in public service in the form of law enforcement. Through its state-level affiliates, the program provides federal scholarships on a competitive basis to college students who agree to serve where needed on community patrol as police officers or sheriffs' deputies for at least 4 years. Students who are accepted into the Police Corps programs receive up to $3,750 a year to pay the expenses toward a bachelor's or graduate degree. A student may receive up to $15,000 under the program, including reasonable room and board. Undergraduate participants must be full-time students at an accredited public or nonprofit 4-year college or university. They may pursue a degree in any relevant field of study, including criminal justice or law enforcement. Shortly after graduation, participants begin their work as officers. Those who pursue a graduate degree complete their service in advance.

In addition to their college education, all Police Corps participants must satisfactorily complete a rigorous 16- to 24-week residential Police Corps basic law enforcement training program paid for by the federal government. The law enforcement agency with which the participant serves provides additional training as appropriate. If a Police Corps participant fails to complete his or her bachelor's degree, Police Corps training, and 4 years of required service with the assigned agency, he or she must repay all scholarships and reimbursements received through the program, plus 10 percent interest.

Police Corps participants are expected to work as community patrol officers in geographic areas that have a great need for additional officers and to be assigned to challenging beats where they can be most effective. The program encourages states, where feasible, to place participants in areas where they have community or family ties. Participants receive the same pay and benefits and have the same responsibilities as any other officer of similar rank and tenure.

THE POLICE SELECTION PROCESS

In many communities, selection of police officers takes place through a merit system. A **merit system** of employment is established when an independent civil service commission, in cooperation with the city personnel section and the police department, sets employment qualifications, performance standards, and discipline procedures. Officers employed under such a system are hired and tenured, in theory, only if they meet and maintain the employment qualifications and performance standards set by the civil service commission. Officers in such a system cannot be fired without cause.

To find the best possible recruits to fill department vacancies, police agencies use a selection process that includes some or all of the following steps.

merit system A system of employment whereby an independent civil service commission, in cooperation with the city personnel section and the police department, sets employment qualifications, performance standards, and discipline procedures.

Physical ability tests are common in police selection. *Why are they important?*

Screening New Police Recruits

In 2003, local police departments used the following methods to screen new recruits: criminal record checks (99 percent), background investigations (98 percent), personal interviews (98 percent), medical exams (85 percent), drug tests (73 percent), and psychological evaluations (67 percent).

SOURCE: Matthew J. Hickman and Brian A. Reaves, *Local Police Departments, 2003* (Washington, DC: GPO, U.S. Department of Justice, Bureau of Justice Statistics, 2006), p. 8.

SHORT APPLICATION This brief form registers the interest of the applicant and allows the agency to screen for such things as minimum age, level of education, residency, and other easily discernible qualifications.

DETAILED APPLICATION This document is a major source of information for the department and background investigators. The applicant is asked for complete education and work histories, military status, medical profile, references, a record of residence over many years, and other detailed information. Applicants are also asked to submit copies of credentials, military papers, and other certificates.

MEDICAL EXAMINATION This exam determines if applicants are free of disease, abnormalities, and any other medical problems that would disqualify them for police work. This information is critical because retiring a young officer on a medical disability shortly after employment could cost the public hundreds of thousands of dollars. Table 4.5 shows the percentage of local police departments by population served that use medical exams, as well as various interviews, tests, and other exams, in the selection of new officer recruits.

PHYSICAL ABILITY TEST Physical ability tests are common in police selection despite having been challenged in the courts as having an adverse effect on the hiring of female applicants. Physical ability tests were initially a direct response to the elimination of height and weight standards, which were also discriminatory against female applicants. The first tests required exceptional speed and strength, such as going over walls that were taller than any of the walls in the cities that had such tests. Those tests were struck down by the courts as not being job-related. Today, any physical ability tests must be based on a thorough analysis of the actual work of police officers. See Table 4.5 for the percentage of local police departments that use physical agility tests in the selection of new officer recruits.

WRITTEN EXAMINATION Police agencies once used intelligence tests in their selection process. Most agencies now use some type of aptitude, personality, general knowledge, reading comprehension, writing, or police skill exam. The courts have held that those tests must be true measures of the knowledge and abilities needed to perform police work successfully. Preemployment tests have been the subject of much controversy in the courts.

TABLE 4.5	Interviews, Tests, and Examinations Used in Selection of New Officer Recruits in Local Police Departments, by Size of Population Served, 2003

POPULATION SERVED	PERSONAL INTERVIEW	MEDICAL EXAM	DRUG TEST	PSYCHO- LOGICAL EVALUATION	PHYSICAL AGILITY TEST	WRITTEN APTITUDE TEST	PERSON- ALITY INVENTORY	POLY- GRAPH EXAM	VOICE STRESS ANALYZER	SECOND LANGUAGE ABILITY TEST
All sizes	98%	85%	73%	67%	50%	43%	26%	25%	4%	1%
1,000,000 or more	94%	100%	100%	100%	94%	81%	56%	81%	0%	0%
500,000–999,999	100	100	95	100	86	84	48	64	11	11
250,000–499,999	95	93	98	98	93	83	51	78	10	2
100,000–249,999	95	97	86	95	88	82	50	77	11	1
50,000–99,999	99	97	90	97	83	80	47	57	7	3
25,000–49,999	99	99	88	96	76	76	45	47	12	2
10,000–24,999	99	98	88	89	71	72	40	42	6	1
2,500–9,999	99	91	74	71	52	48	26	25	3	—
Under 2,500	98	73	63	47	31	20	16	11	2	—

Note: List of selection methods is not intended to be exhaustive.

—Less than 0.5%

Source: Matthew J. Hickman and Brian A. Reaves, *Local Police Departments, 2003* (Washington, DC: GPO, U.S. Department of Justice, Bureau of Justice Statistics, May 2006), p. 8, Table 14.

BACKGROUND INVESTIGATION Investigators in this process look for any factors in the backgrounds of applicants that would prevent them from performing successfully as police officers. Past drug use or excessive alcohol use, a poor driving record, employer problems, a bad credit history, criminal activity, and social immaturity are areas of concern in the background investigation. The investigator relies heavily on the detailed application, verifies its contents, explores any discrepancies, and develops additional leads to follow. Table 4.6 shows the percentage of local police departments by population served that use various types of background checks in the selection of new officer recruits.

TABLE 4.6	Background Checks Used in Selection of New Officer Recruits in Local Police Departments, by Size of Population Served, 2003

POPULATION SERVED	CRIMINAL RECORD CHECK	BACKGROUND INVESTIGATION	DRIVING RECORD CHECK	CREDIT HISTORY CHECK	VOLUNTEER SERVICE CHECK
All sizes	99%	98%	98%	55%	8%
1,000,000 or more	100%	100%	100%	81%	0%
500,000–999,999	100	100	100	89	19
250,000–499,999	100	100	98	88	7
100,000–249,999	100	99	98	88	12
50,000–99,999	99	100	99	87	8
25,000–49,999	100	100	99	83	11
10,000–24,999	99	99	99	76	8
2,500–9,999	99	98	99	55	9
Under 2,500	98	97	92	39	6

Note: List of selection methods is not intended to be exhaustive.

Source: Matthew J. Hickman and Brian A. Reaves, *Local Police Departments, 2003* (Washington, DC: GPO, U.S. Department of Justice, Bureau of Justice Statistics, May 2006), p. 8, Table 15.

PSYCHOLOGICAL TESTING Emotional stability and good mental health are critical to the ability to perform police work, which can be very stressful. Departments have been held liable for not screening their applicants for those psychological traits.[11]

Systematic psychological testing of police officers began in the 1950s. At first, the typical approach was to have the psychological evaluators look for disqualifying factors. The process included a pencil-and-paper test and a one-on-one interview with a psychologist. Today, the testing focus has generally shifted to a search for the positive psychological qualities required in police work. Current tests include multiple versions of both written and clinical evaluations.

The validity of psychological tests has been an issue for decades. Psychologists are often reluctant to rate with any specificity the police candidates they evaluate. Candidates considered "unacceptable" are sometimes classified as "uncertain" to avoid lawsuits. It is important to remember that understanding and predicting human behavior is an inexact art. So it is easy to appreciate the reluctance of psychologists to be more specific. See Table 4.5 for the percentage of local police departments by population served that use psychological tests and evaluation in the selection of new officer recruits.

ORAL INTERVIEW/ORAL BOARD This step is frequently the final one in the selection process. Members of the interview team have the results of the previous selection procedures, and they now have an opportunity to clear up inconsistencies and uncertainties that have been identified. The board normally restricts itself to evaluating the following qualities:

1. Appearance, poise, and bearing.
2. Ability to communicate orally and organize thoughts.
3. Attitude toward law enforcement and the job required of police officers.
4. Speech and the ability to articulate.
5. Attitude toward drug, narcotic, and alcohol use.
6. Sensitivity to racial and ethnic issues.[12]

See Table 4.5 for the percentage of local police departments by population served that use personal interviews in the selection of new officer recruits.

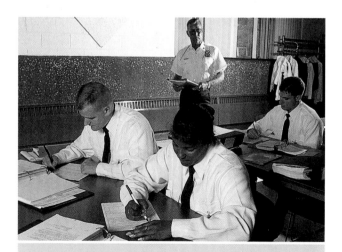

At the end of many police academy training programs, there is a state licensing or certification examination. *Do you believe those examinations are necessary? Why or why not?*

ACADEMY TRAINING The police academy is part of the selection process. Virtually every academy class in any sophisticated police department loses up to 10 percent of its students. Thus, to survive academy training, students must be committed to the process. Students undergo from 400 to more than 1,000 hours of academic, skill, and physical training and are tested virtually every week of the process. In 2003, for example, state-mandated field and academy training requirements for new officers averaged about 750 hours combined. Additional training beyond state requirements averaged about 200 hours (see Table 4.7). At the end of many academy training programs, students must take a state licensing or certification examination.

PROBATION Under local or state civil service requirements, employers may keep a new police officer on probation for 6 months to a year. The probation period gives the new police officer a chance to learn policing under the guidance of a well-qualified field training

| TABLE 4.7 | Training Requirements for New Officer Recruits in Local Police Departments, by Size of Population Served, 2003 |

	Average Number of Hours Required					
	Academy			**Field**		
Population Served	**Total**	**State-Mandated**	**Other Required**	**Total**	**State-Mandated**	**Other Required**
All sizes	628	588	40	326	147	179
1,000,000 or more	1,016	689	327	513	153	360
500,000–999,999	920	588	332	561	104	456
250,000–499,999	950	620	330	652	200	452
100,000–249,999	815	642	173	624	253	371
50,000–99,999	721	657	64	598	268	330
25,000–49,999	702	657	46	527	210	317
10,000–24,999	672	642	30	442	164	279
2,500–9,999	630	597	32	314	151	162
Under 2,500	577	542	35	199	106	93

Note: Average number of training hours excludes departments not requiring training.

Source: Matthew J. Hickman and Brian A. Reaves, *Local Police Departments, 2003* (Washington, DC: GPO, U.S. Department of Justice, Bureau of Justice Statistics, May 2006), p. 9, Table 17.

officer. Formal field training is a wise investment, and it ensures that new officers get as much knowledge and experience as possible before an agency commits to them for their careers.

A problem is that with police academy training now often extending 5 or 6 months, a 6-month probation period no longer seems logical. The agency is, in effect, offering the police officer tenure in a matter of weeks after graduation from the academy. This practice defeats the purpose of probation, which was designed to allow the employer to see whether the newly trained officer can successfully perform the job.

THE SELECTION OF A LAW ENFORCEMENT EXECUTIVE

No less important than the selection of operations-level officers is the choice of the chief executive of a police agency. This executive might be a chief of police, a sheriff, or the head of a state law enforcement organization. A crucial decision in the selection process is whether to allow people from outside the agency to apply. In some police agencies in the United States, civil service regulations prohibit the selection of outside candidates. The rationale for this rule is that there must be qualified internal candidates. In addition, it is discouraging to hardworking and talented police administrators to be denied a chance to lead the agency they have spent many years serving.

Actual hiring decisions are usually shared by members of a selection committee. Frequently, an executive search firm is also employed. The selection committee usually consists of representatives of the local government, the police department, the search firm, and the community. Applicants are put through a rigorous process that includes several visits to the city, written exams, interviews, and assessment center testing, in which candidates try to resolve real-world management problems. Once the interviews and testing have been completed, applicants are normally ranked, and the list is presented to the city manager, the mayor, or others so that a final selection can be made.

Executive Salaries

As of 2003, the average salary of police chiefs ranged from a low of $48,800 to a high of $56,900. However, salaries varied greatly depending on the city population size. For cities with populations of one million or more, the salary of police chiefs ranged from a low of $113,000 to a high of $157,100. On the other hand, in cities of fewer than 2,500 the salary of police chiefs ranged from a low of $32,700 to a high of $36,500. The same is true of county sheriffs. As of 2003, the average salary of county sheriffs ranged from a low of $54,500 to a high of $59,800. In counties with a population of one million or more, the salary range was $119,300 to $135,000. In counties with populations of fewer than 2,500 the salary range was $37,000 to $40,000.

SOURCE: Matthew J. Hickman and Brian A. Reaves, *Local Police Departments, 2003* (Washington, DC: GPO, U.S. Department of Justice, Bureau of Justice Statistics, May 2006), p. 11, Table 20: Matthew J. Hickman and Brian A. Reaves, *Sheriffs' Offices, 2003* (Washington, DC: GPO, U.S. Department of Justice, Bureau of Justice Statistics, May 2006), p. 11, Table 20.

The pursuit of a police chief's job is very competitive. Often several hundred candidates contend for a position even in a small suburban community. A typical police chief rarely serves longer than 10 years, and life in the chief's seat may not be very comfortable, particularly if a new chief intends to change things. Much of the political controversy and many of the social problems in major cities and counties end up at the door of the police department, so police chiefs must be politically savvy to survive. Many chiefs discover that they cannot please everybody, particularly if they are trying to change the department. Should police chiefs have protection under civil service? Most commentators say no, arguing that mayors and city managers ought to have the authority to pick the management teams that work immediately under their direction. A small number of cities give their police chiefs civil service protection to insulate them from unnecessary political interference.

The selection of a sheriff of one of the nation's counties is just as important as choosing a police chief. The difference in the two processes has to do with who does the selecting. In all but a few of the nation's counties, sheriffs are elected by the county's eligible voters. Not all sheriffs have a law enforcement background. In most states, they are not required to be licensed or certified peace officers as their deputies or municipal officers are. As a result, people from various occupations often succeed in being elected sheriff. To be elected, sheriffs must be good politicians. They often have a much better idea of the priorities of a community and wield more influence with prosecutors and in the legislature than chiefs of police. Sheriffs who do not exhibit this political acumen are not likely to be reelected.

THINKING CRITICALLY

1. What do you think are the most important qualities for police officers to have? Why?

2. How much formal education do you think police officers should have? Why?

Issues in Policing

The discussion of law enforcement thus far has made it clear that not all matters of policing in America are settled. In this final section of the chapter, some of the issues that continue to be major topics of debate in law enforcement and have significant impact on the quality of life in neighborhoods and communities across the nation will be highlighted.

DISCRETION

discretion The exercise of individual judgment, instead of formal rules, in making decisions.

Discretion is the exercise of individual judgment, instead of formal rules, in making decisions. No list of policies and procedures could possibly guide police officers in all of the situations in which they find themselves. Even the police officer writing a ticket for a parking meter violation exercises a considerable amount of discretion in deciding precisely what to do.[13] Police even have the discretion to ignore violations of the law when they deem it appropriate in the context of other priorities.

The issue of police discretion is very controversial. Some believe that the discretion of police officers should be reduced. The movement to limit the discretion of police officers is the result of abuses of that discretion, such as physical abuse of citizens or unequal application of the law in making arrests. Other people argue that we should acknowledge that officers operate with great discretion and not attempt to limit it. Advocates of this view believe that better education and training would help officers exercise their judgment more wisely.

PATROL OFFICER DISCRETION Patrol officers frequently find it necessary to exercise their discretion. Within the geographical limits of their beats, they have the discretion to decide precisely where they will patrol when they are not answering radio calls. They decide whom to stop and question. For example, they may tell some children playing ball in the street to move, while they ignore others. Patrol officers decide for themselves which traffic violators are worth chasing through busy traffic and which ones are not. They even have the right not to arrest for a minor violation when, for example, they are on the way to investigate a more serious matter.

Some of the more critical situations involve decisions about stopping, searching, and arresting criminal suspects. Many citizens have been inconvenienced and some have been abused because of a police officer's poor use of discretion in those areas.

Police officers cannot make an arrest for every violation of law that comes to their attention—that is, they cannot provide **full enforcement.** The police do not have the resources to enforce the law fully, nor can they be everywhere at once. And even if full enforcement were possible, it may not be desirable. For example, persons intoxicated in front of their own homes may not need to be arrested, but only to be told to go inside. Motorists slightly exceeding the speed limit need not be arrested if they are moving with the flow of traffic. Prostitution may be widely practiced in large metropolitan areas, but police officers have little to gain by searching hotels and motels to stamp it out, particularly when judges will turn the prostitutes right back out on the street. Generally, only when such an activity becomes a clear nuisance, is the subject of a public outcry, or threatens health and safety do the police department and its officers choose to take formal action.

The practice of relying on the judgment of the police leadership and rank-and-file officers to decide which laws to enforce is referred to as **selective enforcement.** The practice allows street police officers to decide important matters about peacekeeping and enforcement of the law. For most violations of the law, but not all felonies, a police officer can usually exercise a number of options:

1. Taking no action at all if the officer deems that appropriate for the situation.
2. Giving a verbal warning to stop the illegal action.

full enforcement A practice in which the police make an arrest for every violation of law that comes to their attention.

selective enforcement The practice of relying on the judgment of the police leadership and rank-and-file officers to decide which laws to enforce.

Police officers can exercise discretion in arrest situations. *Should police officers be allowed to use discretion in arrest situations? Why or why not?*

3. Issuing a written warning for the violation.
4. Issuing a citation to the perpetrator to appear in court.
5. Making a physical arrest in serious matters or in situations with repeat offenders.

FACTORS AFFECTING DISCRETION Dozens of studies have been conducted on the exercise of discretion by police patrol officers. A number of significant factors affect discretion:

- **The Nature of the Crime** The more serious the crime, the more likely it is that police officers will formally report it. In cases involving lesser felonies, misdemeanors, and petty offenses, police officers are more likely to handle the offenses informally. A minor squabble between over-the-fence neighbors is an example of a matter that would probably be handled informally.

- **Departmental Policies** If the leadership of a police department gives an order or issues a policy demanding that particular incidents be handled in a prescribed way, then an officer is not supposed to exercise discretion but is to do as the order or policy directs. Thus, if a city has had many complaints about dangerous jaywalking in a certain downtown area, the chief of police may insist that citations be issued to those found jaywalking, even though, in the past, citations had not been issued.

- **The Relationship Between the Victim and the Offender** Particularly for minor offenses, the closer the relationship between the victim of an alleged offense and the suspected perpetrator, the more discretion the officer is able to exercise. For example, police officers are not likely to deal formally with a petty theft between two lovers if they believe that the victim will not prosecute his or her partner.

- **The Amount of Evidence** If officers do not have enough evidence to substantiate an arrest or to gain a conviction in court, they are likely to handle the case in some way other than making an arrest.

- **The Preference of the Victim** Sometimes the victim of a crime may simply want to talk the matter over with someone, and the police are available on a 24-hour basis. Also, if the officer senses that the victim of a minor assault does not wish to prosecute the perpetrator of the offense, the patrol officer will not make a formal complaint, and the complainant will most likely never know that a report was not made.

- **The Demeanor of the Suspect** Suspects who are disrespectful and uncooperative may very well feel the full brunt of the law. Patrol officers often choose the most severe option possible in dealing with such suspects.

- **The Legitimacy of the Victim** Patrol officers are bound to pass some kind of judgment on the legitimacy of the victim. An assault victim who is belligerent and intoxicated, for instance, will not be viewed favorably by the investigating officer. Criminals victimized by other criminals are also seen as less than fully authentic victims, no matter what the offense.

- **Socioeconomic Status** The more affluent the complainant, the more likely a patrol officer is to use formal procedures to report and investigate a crime. Contrary to popular belief, the personal characteristics of an officer (such as race, gender, and education) do not seem to influence the exercise of discretion.

DISCRETION AND DOMESTIC VIOLENCE Police officers have intervened in domestic violence cases and other kinds of family disputes, sometimes off-duty, since the inception of public policing. For the longest period of time, these interventions were viewed as peace-keeping activities when, in fact, they should have been treated as criminal matters. Many women and some men were hurt, and some killed, as a result of the restrictions on the police in making arrests for assault misde-meanors not made in their presence and a view among the police that these calls were the private business of the family instead of real police matters. Traditionally, law enforcement has been less interested in arresting perpetrators of crimes when the victim and the perpe-trator have a close relationship.

Approximately one million women are victims of domestic violence each year. Even today, with every state requiring the police to have domestic violence interven-tion training, some commentators believe that the police are not the best qualified of available community helpers to intervene. On the other hand, if crimes are commit-ted in the form of physical abuse, the police are not only the best qualified to intervene but are also required by law to do so. Certainly, the availability of 24-hour serv-ice has always made the police the major responder to domestic violence calls.

Many states have mandatory arrest laws that require police officers to arrest any suspect who has battered a spouse or domestic partner. *Do you support mandatory arrest laws in domestic violence cases? Why or why not?*

The police in general do not relish the task of responding to domestic violence calls for several reasons. First, the calls can be dangerous, although generally no more dangerous than other disturbance calls. Nevertheless, officers are hurt each year by responding to domestic violence complaints. Second, police offi-cers know from experience that many of the tense and hostile dynamics that exist between quarreling spouses, couples, and other family members have a way of dissipating over time or at least subsiding for a while. Third, the police know that they have often conducted investigations, even arrested the sus-pected batterer, and the victim has later chosen to drop charges. Finally, the police know that responding to the minor assault cases in domestic violence calls is not always the best thing for the family because the arrest creates its own complications that may, in fact, exacerbate the family crisis to a state of irreparable harm.

Police have responded to domestic violence in three distinct ways: medi-ate the dispute, separate domestic partners in minor disputes, and arrest the perpetrator of the assault. Which of these ways is the most effective? This question was put to the test in a 3-year study in the city of Minneapolis. In minor domestic dispute cases, Minneapolis police officers gave up their dis-cretion in handling domestic violence calls. Instead of deciding for themselves the appropriate disposition for each call, they randomly chose either arrest, separation, or mediation. The results of the study showed that the arrested perpetrators were about half as likely to repeat their violence against the orig-inal victim.[14] This study may have been the impetus for many states to imple-ment a mandatory arrest domestic violence law. Subsequent studies, however, have not been able to clearly support the mandatory arrest disposition as the most effective way to handle the problem of domestic violence. Yet today nearly half of the states have a mandatory arrest law requiring the arrest of any suspect who has battered a spouse or domestic partner. While victim safety and welfare are indeed the major reasons for police intervention, more research is clearly needed to determine the best approaches to handling domestic violence calls.

racial profiling The stopping and/or detaining of individuals by law enforcement officers based solely on race.

Racial Profiling

According to a recent national survey, 53 percent of Americans think that the practice of stopping motorists because of their race or ethnicity is widespread among law enforcement officers. Sixty-seven percent of blacks and 63 percent of Hispanics believe the practice is widespread, while 50 percent of non-Hispanic whites believe it to be true. Only 31 percent of Americans believe the practice is justified: 23 percent of blacks, 30 percent of Hispanics, and 31 percent of non-Hispanic whites.

SOURCE: Darren K. Carlson, "Racial Profiling Seen as Pervasive, Unjust," The Gallup Organization, July 20, 2004.

ACLU
To learn more about what is being done to combat racial profiling, visit the American Civil Liberties Union (ACLU) Web site on racial profiling at **www.aclu.org/profiling.** *What can police departments do to prevent racial profiling?*

DISCRETION AND RACIAL PROFILING Racial profiling is of growing concern to law enforcement officials and the public. Just how frequently this illegal practice occurs is difficult to discern, particularly since the term *racial profiling* is seldom defined in the discussions found in the national media. Racial profiling is a law enforcement infringement on a citizen's liberty based solely on race. On freeways, highways, and streets throughout the nation blacks and other minorities are stopped for traffic violations and field interrogations in numbers disproportionate to their representation in the population. Many of these stops are pretext stops where the stop is justified by a minor equipment or moving traffic violation that might otherwise be ignored. Where the practice is widely experienced, it has been called "driving while black or brown" (DWBB). At the root of such a practice is racial stereotyping and prejudice.

Racial profiling is a hot topic in the U.S. Congress, state legislatures, county commissions, and city councils, as well as in the meeting rooms of civil rights and professional police organizations. The American Civil Liberties Union, for example, has started a national project to eliminate racial profiling and even provides citizens with a "Bust Card" that tells them how to respectfully interact with the police (acknowledging the difficulty of their job) even when falling victim to racial profiling.

Racial profiling to any degree is a blight on the record of professional law enforcement and democracy. Some of the methods that have been prescribed to stop racial profiling include racial and cultural diversity training for police personnel, strong discipline for errant officers, videotaping all traffic stops, collecting data on the race of stopped motorists and pedestrians and the disposition of the encounter, and having police officers distribute business cards to all motorists and pedestrians they stop.

The business card may reduce race-based stops because it would allow an officer to be easily identified at a later time. But city leaders throughout the United States are in a quandary as to precisely what to do to stop racial profiling. Thirty-six members of the National League of Cities' public safety committees met in Oklahoma City and determined that they oppose police profiling of suspects when it violates a person's civil rights, but they could not agree whether all profiling should be banned.[15]

FACTORS LIMITING DISCRETION Several methods are employed to control the amount of discretion exercised by police officers. One method is close supervision by a police agency's management. For example, a department may require that officers consult a sergeant before engaging in a particular kind of action. Department directives or policies also limit the options police officers have in particular situations. Decisions of the U.S. Supreme Court, such as one restricting the use of deadly force to stop a fleeing felon, limit the options available to officers on the street. Finally, the threat of civil liability suits has reduced the discretion an officer has, for example, in the use of deadly force or in the pursuit of fleeing suspects in an automobile.

The debate over how much control should be placed on the exercise of police discretion is ongoing. Few other professionals have experienced a comparable attack on their authority to make decisions for the good of the clients they serve. The continuing attempt to limit discretion also seems out of place at a time when community policing is being widely advocated. Remember that community policing decentralizes authority and places it in the hands of the local beat officers and their supervisors. Community policing is bound to fail if citizens see that the police they work with every day do not have the authority and discretion to make the decisions that will ultimately improve the quality of life in a community.

JOB STRESS

Stress in the workplace is common today. A recent survey revealed that 80 percent of responding workers reported at least some degree of stress.[16] Given the nature of police work, no one is surprised to discover that a law enforcement officer's job is stressful. Police officers intervene in life's personal emergencies and great tragedies. Working extended shifts, for example, at the scene of the bombing of the federal building in Oklahoma City or the World Trade Center disaster would tax the resources of even the most resourceful police officer. Who would deny the stress involved in working deep undercover on a narcotics investigation over a period of several months? Some officers are able to manage stress on the job better than others.

Job stress is defined as the harmful physical and emotional outcomes that occur when the requirements of a job do not match the capabilities, resources, or needs of the worker. Poor health and injury are possible results of prolonged job stress. Police work has long been identified as one of the most stressful of all occupations, and many police officers suffer each year from the deleterious effects of a job that tests their physical and emotional limits.

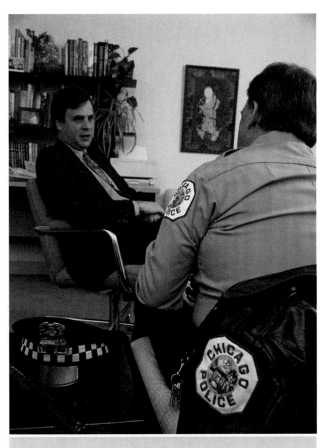

Police officers sometimes manage stress by seeking counseling. *Are there ways that you handle stress that you think would work particularly well in policing?*

SOURCES AND EFFECTS OF STRESS A number of conditions can lead to stress: (1) design of tasks—heavy lifting, long hours without breaks, and monotonous repetition of dangerous maneuvers; (2) management style—lack of participation by workers in decision making, poor communication, lack of family-friendly policies; (3) interpersonal relationships—poor social environment and lack of support from coworkers and supervisors; and (4) work roles—conflicting or uncertain job expectations, wearing too many hats, too much responsibility.[17] The signs that stress is becoming a problem with an officer are frequent headaches, difficulty in concentrating, short temper, upset stomach, job dissatisfaction, abuse of alcohol and drugs, and low morale. Individually and collectively these symptoms can have other origins, but job stress is often the source.

job stress The harmful physical and emotional outcomes that occur when the requirements of a job do not match the capabilities, resources, or needs of the worker.

COPICIDE As if the work of confronting dangerous suspects and preserving the peace were not stressful enough, "copicide" or "death by cop" has entered the worklife of some police officers. **Copicide** is a form of suicide in which a person gets fatally shot after intentionally provoking police officers.[18] A recent study of police shootings resulting in the death of a citizen in Los Angeles found that 10 percent could be attributed to copicide.[19] One commentator believes that "dozens of times each year during jittery hostage dramas and routine traffic stops, desperate people lure police officers into shooting them in a phenomenon known in law enforcement circles as 'suicide by cop'."[20] The truth is that no one knows exactly how many times copicide incidents occur each year. Most police officers require a lot of time to emotionally recover from a fatal shooting in circumstances where they were fully authorized to use deadly force. To later discover that they were provoked into killing people who simply used police as a tool in a suicide scheme creates an extra emotional burden to bear.

copicide A form of suicide in which a person gets fatally shot after intentionally provoking police officers.

STRESS MANAGEMENT AND REDUCTION Fortunately, there are ways to manage and reduce stress without leaving police work. The "fixes" for stress come in two general categories. Stress management now encompasses a variety of programs and procedures that include discussing stressful events with colleagues and mental health professionals, regular exercise, relaxation techniques such as structured visualization, a healthy diet that also eliminates caffeine and nicotine, enriched family support, religious support, prayer, meditation, and stress management classes that often involve spouses.

Organizational change can also reduce the potential for stress in the police work environment. Officers, for example, may be given more discretion in determining their work hours and shifts as long as the police agency is able to respond effectively to the workload requirements of the community. Flattening the organizational structure can help reduce stress by giving officers more discretion in carrying out the responsibilities of their job. Community policing is an effective paradigm for increasing officers' ability to control their work and perhaps minimize stress. Job redesign can assist assigning the right number and type of tasks to a police position when one job requires too much of an officer to maintain emotional stability and good health. Finally, excellent public safety equipment can minimize stress. Proper police weaponry, dependable vehicles, and the best of protective equipment such as high-grade body armor can not only protect officers but can also put their minds a little more at ease on those important concerns.[21]

USE OF FORCE

No issue in policing has caused as much controversy in recent decades as the use of force. In New York, Los Angeles, Detroit, Miami, and many other cities, excessive-force charges against police officers have been made and documented and have resulted in the loss of public confidence in the police. Although the vast majority of police officers of this country go to work every

| TABLE 4.8 | Types of Nonlethal Weapons Authorized for Personal Use by Sworn Personnel in Local Police Departments, by Size of Population Served, 2003 |

	PERCENTAGE OF AGENCIES AUTHORIZING							
	CHEMICAL AGENTS—PERSONAL USE				BATONS			
POPULATION SERVED	ANY TYPE IN SURVEY	PEPPER SPRAY	TEAR GAS	CS	ANY TYPE IN SURVEY	COLLAPSIBLE	TRADITIONAL	PR-24
All sizes	99%	98%	16%	14%	95%	88%	49%	42%
1,000,000 or more	94%	94%	19%	19%	100%	88%	56%	44%
500,000–999,999	97	97	19	22	100	89	60	38
250,000–499,999	98	95	24	22	100	83	54	44
100,000–249,999	99	99	22	24	99	93	56	44
50,000–99,999	99	97	25	27	99	92	45	39
25,000–49,999	100	100	24	21	99	93	44	39
10,000–24,999	99	98	22	17	97	91	47	45
2,500–9,999	98	98	13	14	94	88	47	41
Under 2,500	99	98	14	12	93	86	52	42

— Less than 0.5 percent.

Source: Matthew J. Hickman and Brian A. Reaves, *Local Police Departments, 2000* (Washington, DC: GPO, U.S. Department of Justice, Bureau of Justice Statistics, January 2003), p. 19, Table 39.

day with no intention of using excessive force, far too many instances of brutality still occur.

A precise definition of brutality is not possible. However, the use of excessive physical force is undoubtedly a factor in everyone's definition. For many people, particularly members of racial and ethnic minorities, brutality also includes verbal abuse, profanity, harassment, threats of force, and unnecessary stopping, questioning, and searching of pedestrians or those in vehicles.

EXCESSIVE FORCE Why do the police have to use force as frequently as they do? A major responsibility of police officers is to arrest suspects so that they can answer criminal charges. No criminal suspect wants his or her liberty taken away, so some of them resist arrest. Invariably, a few suspects are armed with some kind of weapon, and some are prepared to use that weapon against the police to foil the arrest. The police need to establish their authority to control such conflicts. They have a variety of nonlethal weapons at their disposal to accomplish that task (see Table 4.8). The disrespect and physical resistance that are frequently the result of encounters with suspects have caused the police on occasion to use **excessive force,** which is a measure of coercion beyond that necessary to control participants in a conflict.

excessive force A measure of coercion beyond that necessary to control participants in a conflict.

Not only is the persistent use of excessive force by the police against citizens unethical, civilly wrong, and criminally illegal, but it also creates a situation where nobody wins. Police may face criminal and civil prosecution in such cases, citizens build up layers of resentment against the police, and law enforcement agencies pay out millions of dollars in damages while losing respect in the eyes of the community. Disturbing events like the brutal beating and sexual assault of Abner Louima in 1997, and the shooting death of Amadou Diallo in 1999, by New York City police officers received nationwide media attention while causing great concern by citizens and law enforcement over the use of excessive force. There were also charges of racism by the police

TABLE 4.8	Types of Nonlethal Weapons Authorized for Personal Use by Sworn Personnel in Local Police Departments, by Size of Population Served, 2003 (concluded)

	PERCENTAGE OF AGENCIES AUTHORIZING					
			OTHER WEAPONS/ACTIONS			
POPULATION SERVED	SOFT PROJECTILE	ELECTRICAL DEVICES[a]	HOLDS/ NECK RESTRAINTS	RUBBER BULLET	BLACK- JACK	HIGH- INTENSITY LIGHT
All sizes	28%	23%	13%	8%	5%	1%
1,000,000 or more	69%	75%	31%	25%	6%	0%
500,000–999,999	48	43	16	16	3	0
250,000–499,999	59	56	39	22	7	2
100,000–249,999	66	50	36	22	2	2
50,000–99,999	72	46	30	22	3	2
25,000–49,999	57	39	12	19	3	1
10,000–24,999	42	31	12	10	3	—
2,500–9,999	28	21	9	6	4	0
Under 2,500	13	15	13	6	6	1

[a]Includes handheld direct contact devices (such as stun gun) and handheld stand-off devices (such as Taser).

There is much debate on how much control should be placed on the decisions of police officers in arrest situations. *How much control should be placed on them and why?*

Sidearms

In 2003, nearly all local police departments authorized patrol officers to carry one or more types of semiautomatic sidearms. This was up from 73 percent of departments in 1990. Among the semiautomatic firearms authorized in 2003 were the .40-caliber semiautomatic (authorized by 62 percent of departments), the 9 mm (34 percent), the .45-caliber (34 percent), the .357-caliber (16 percent), the 10 mm (10 percent), and the .380-caliber, (3 percent). Sixty-five percent of local departments, employing 81 percent of all officers, supplied regular field officers with their primary sidearm.

SOURCE: Matthew J. Hickman and Brian A. Reaves, *Local Police Departments, 2003* (Washington, DC: GPO, U.S. Department of Justice, Bureau of Justice Statistics, 2006), p. 25.

because both incidents involved the use of excessive force by white police officers against black men.

Abner Louima, a 30-year-old Haitian immigrant, was accused of assaulting a police officer outside a night-club in the city. Louima claimed that following his arrest and arrival at the station house, a white officer, Justin Volpe, savagely beat and sodomized him with a toilet plunger. In 1999, Volpe plead guilty to charges stemming from the beating. Charles Schwarz, another police officer accused of holding Louima down while Volpe attacked him, was convicted separately in a federal trial of violating Louima's rights. Three other NYPD officers said to be involved in the event were acquitted of all charges.

Amadou Diallo, a 22-year-old West African immigrant, was hit by 19 of the 41 bullets shot by police officers from the NYPD street crimes unit. Diallo died at the scene. The officers claimed that Diallo fit the description of a rape suspect for whom they had been searching. When the officers tried to stop Diallo, he reached for what police officers thought was a weapon; they then began to shoot. Apparently Diallo, who spoke little English, was reaching for his wallet. The officers involved in the shooting were charged with second-degree murder; however, a state jury found the officers innocent.

Although past and recent incidents of excessive force have been disturbing, research reveals that police brutality does not occur as often as some people might think. For example, in a study conducted in the state of Washington, only 4 percent of brutality complaints against the police could be substantiated, and most of the charges were of verbal abuse or insults.[22] Widespread media coverage of high-profile cases, such as the Los Angeles police officers' assault on Rodney King, can lead the public to believe that brutality is much more common than it really is. The Los Angeles police, however, had a higher rate of wounding and killing suspects than any other police department in the nation, according to the Christopher Commission, which investigated the assault on Rodney King.

DEADLY FORCE The greatest concern over the use of force by the police has to do with the infliction of death or serious injury on citizens and criminal suspects. Since the U.S. Supreme Court's 1985 decision in *Tennessee v. Garner*, the use of deadly force has been severely restricted, and police shootings of suspects and citizens have been reduced. In the *Garner* case, an unarmed teenage boy was shot as he fled a house burglary, failing to heed the warning to stop given by a Memphis police officer. The boy later died of a gunshot wound to the head. He was found with $10 in his pocket that he had stolen from the home. The Memphis officer was acting in compliance with his department's policy on the use of deadly force and with the law in Tennessee and in most other states in the nation.

Giving law enforcement officers the authority to use deadly force to stop a fleeing felon, even when they know the suspect is unarmed and not likely to be a danger to another person, derives from the common law in England and the United States, which permitted such a practice. At the time the rule developed, however, unlike today, dozens of crimes were capital offenses, and the fleeing suspect, if apprehended and convicted, would have been executed. The Garner decision, no doubt, was long overdue, and it included a rule that many police agencies in the nation had adopted years earlier. The perspective that professional law enforcement agencies had already begun to adopt on deadly force was from the Model Penal Code, Section 307(2)(B).

It reads:

The use of deadly force is not justifiable under this section unless:

1. The arrest is for a felony.
2. The person effecting the arrest is authorized to act as a peace officer or is assisting a person whom he believes to be authorized to act as a peace officer.
3. The actor believes that the force employed creates no substantial risk of injury to innocent persons.
4. The actor believes that: (a) The crime for which the arrest is made involved conduct including the use or threatened use of deadly force. (b) There is substantial risk that the person to be arrested will cause death or serious bodily harm if his on her apprehension is delayed.

Even with explicit guidelines, the decision to use deadly force is seldom clear-cut for police officers, because of the violent and occasionally ambiguous situations in which they find themselves. For example, consider the confrontation a Dallas, Texas, police officer had in the summer of 1993. As a plainclothes officer, he responded to a call at an apartment complex where it was reported that a man had fired shots. It was nighttime, and when he arrived at the parking lot of the complex, he saw a man perhaps 50 feet from him with the butt end of a pistol sticking out of the waistband of his trousers. The police officer told him to stop and put his hands in the air. Instead of doing what he was ordered to do, the man pulled the gun from his waistband and moved it toward the officer. The officer responded by firing his weapon several times at the man and killing him. Later, it was discovered that the man was a Mexican citizen who spoke no English.

Some members of the Hispanic community were enraged that the officer did not offer commands in Spanish, because Dallas officers were required to study 20 hours of the language in the police academy. After several months of investigation and the grand jury's ignoring the case, the officer was exonerated. However, the chief of police assured the community that new police recruits would study three times the previously required amount of Spanish and that annual in-service training would also require the study of Spanish. In addition, the chief stated that in situations such as the one in question, undercover and plainclothes officers would be required, if possible, to put on jackets that would readily identify them as police officers. Some people argue that the man with the gun in this situation not only did not understand English but also had no idea that the officer with a drawn gun was a police officer.

It should not be forgotten that citizens and criminal suspects also attack the police. Mentally ill persons, parties to a family dispute, and suspects trying to avoid arrest feloniously kill between 50 and 100 officers each year. More than 90 percent of officers are killed by assailants using firearms. In response, police officers exercise caution by wearing protective vests, they proactively use what they learn in courses on self-defense (unarmed and armed), and they attempt to defuse hostile situations through peaceful techniques they learn in training.

POLICE CORRUPTION

Almost from the beginning of formal policing in the United States, corruption of law enforcement officers has been a fact of life. Nothing is more distasteful to the public than a police officer or a whole department gone bad.

Use of Force Policies

In 2003, 95 percent of local police departments, employing 99 percent of all officers, had a written policy on the use of deadly force. Ninety percent of departments, employing 97 percent of all officers, had a written policy on the use of nonlethal force.

Source: Matthew J. Hickman and Brian A. Reaves, *Local Police Departments, 2003* (Washington, DC: GPO, U.S. Department of Justice, Bureau of Justice Statistics, 2006), p. 23.

Throughout history, police officers have bought their positions and promotions, sold protection, and ignored violations of the law for money.

Why is policing so susceptible to bribery and other forms of corruption? Perhaps it has to do with the combination of two critical features of the police role in society. On the one hand, the police have authority to enforce laws and to use power to make sure that those laws are obeyed. On the other hand, they also have the discretion not to enforce the law. The combination of those two features makes the police vulnerable to bribes and other forms of corruption. Other features of police work add to the potential for corruption: low pay in relation to important responsibilities, cynicism about the courts' soft handling of criminals that the police spend so much time trying to apprehend, society's ambivalence about vice (most citizens want the laws on the books, but many of them are willing participants), and the practice of recruiting officers from working-class and lower-class backgrounds, where skepticism about obeying the law might be more prevalent.

TYPES OF CORRUPTION In 1972, the Knapp Commission issued a report on corruption in the New York City Police Department. Two types of corrupt officers were identified: "grass eaters" and "meat eaters" **"Grass eaters"** were officers who occasionally engaged in illegal or unethical activities, such as accepting small favors, gifts, or money for ignoring violations of the law during the course of their duties. **"Meat eaters,"** on the other hand, actively sought ways to make money illegally while on duty. For example, they would solicit bribes, commit burglaries, or manufacture false evidence for a prosecution.[23]

More than 30 years ago, sociologist Ellwyn Stoddard identified a more complete list of types of police misconduct, with examples, in what he described as the "blue-coat code":

1. Bribery: accepting cash or gifts in exchange for nonenforcement of the law.
2. Chiseling: demanding discounts, free admission, and free food.
3. Extortion: the threat of enforcement and arrest if a bribe is not given.
4. Favoritism: giving breaks on law enforcement, such as for traffic violations committed by families and friends of the police.
5. Mooching: accepting free food, drinks, and admission to entertainment.
6. Perjury: lying for other officers apprehended in illegal activity.
7. Prejudice: unequal enforcement of the law with respect to racial and ethnic minorities.
8. Premeditated theft: planned burglaries and thefts.
9. Shakedown: taking items from the scene of a theft or a burglary the officer is investigating.
10. Shopping: taking small, inexpensive items from a crime scene or an unsecured business or home.[24]

CONTROLLING CORRUPTION Corruption in law enforcement strikes at the core of the profession and takes a heavy toll. All peace officer positions are positions of honor and trust, and agencies invest money and time in selecting officers with integrity. To see this investment lost is disheartening. But more than anything else, public confidence and trust plummet after a widely publicized corruption case, such as the police drug-trafficking episode in Miami. In the following list, some ways to control and reduce corruption in policing are described:

- **High Moral Standards** Selecting and maintaining officers with high moral standards is a step in the right direction. Some police agencies in

"grass eaters" Officers who occasionally engage in illegal and unethical activities, such as accepting small favors, gifts, or money for ignoring violations of the law during the course of their duties.

"meat eaters" Officers who actively seek ways to make money illegally while on duty.

"Collars for Dollars"

An 8-month investigation by the *Miami Herald* in 1997 documented a police scam involving hundreds of officers in thousands of cases in Dade County. Dubbed "collars for dollars," the scam works like this. Police officers list one another as witnesses in drunken-driving and misdemeanor cases even if they do little or no police work on the cases. They then go to court on over-time and receive pay they don't deserve. According to the newspaper report, "collars for dollars" happens often and costs Dade County taxpayers millions of dollars.

SOURCE: Jeff Leen, Gail Epstein, and Lisa Getter, "Dade Cops Like to Plan Collars for Dollars," *The Orlando Sentinel*, July 20, 1997, p. B-1.

the United States still hire convicted felons to do police work. In-depth academy and in-service training on ethical issues that officers are likely to face would prepare officers for the compromises they may be asked to make later in their careers.

- **Police Policies and Discipline** A police department should develop rigid policies that cover the wide range of activities that corruption comprises. Drug testing of officers, particularly those in narcotics-sensitive positions, may be necessary, although unpopular. Policies mean nothing unless they are enforced. Discipline should be imposed and prosecutions should go forward when officers are found guilty of violating established policies and laws.

- **Proactive Internal Affairs Unit** The **internal affairs investigations unit** of a police department should ferret out illegal and unethical activity. Any internal affairs unit that waits for complaints probably is not going to receive many of them. First-line supervisors should know whether their subordinates are engaging in unethical and illegal violations of department rules and state laws. They should also be held responsible for the actions of their subordinates.

- **Uniform Enforcement of the Law** If a police agency makes it clear that no group of citizens, no matter what their affiliation with the police department, is going to receive special treatment from the police department, the incentive for offering bribes and other forms of corruption will be minimized. This process starts with clear policies and procedures and must be backed up with discipline, when necessary.

- **Outside Review and Special Prosecutors** Heavily resisted by police leadership and police labor associations is any kind of outside review of their actions. However, both the Christopher Commission and the Knapp Commission are examples of outside reviews that brought about improvements in the agencies they investigated. Special prosecutors are recommended in serious cases to relieve the police and the government of any accusations of a whitewash.

- **Court Review and Oversight** Criminal prosecutions or civil liability suits deriving from police corruption cases can be very costly to a police agency. Such visible forms of oversight often result in adverse media coverage, civil liability awards, and higher insurance rates—all of which should encourage police agencies to control corruption.[25]

Policing is susceptible to bribery and other forms of corruption. Who is policing the police? Are controls adequate?

internal affairs investigations unit The police unit that ferrets out illegal and unethical activity engaged in by the police.

THINKING CRITICALLY

1. What do you think are the best ways for police officers to handle stress on the job?

2. What do you think are the best ways to reduce police corruption?

Terrorism and Homeland Security

Terrorism is one of the oldest forms of human conflict. Before societies began waging war against each other, individuals and small groups used acts of terror to achieve their goals, such as deposing existing leaders and frightening and repelling adversaries from territory they claimed for themselves.[26] Terrorism has been used by both right-wing and left-wing political organizations, by ethnic and nationalistic groups, by revolutionaries, and by the armies and secret police of established governments. However, according to the FBI, the modern era of terrorism did not begin until the late 1960s, and U.S. soil remained largely free from serious acts of international terrorism until the bombing of the World Trade Center in 1993.[27] Before then, the vast majority of deadly terrorist acts carried out in the United States were committed by domestic terrorists, such as Timothy McVeigh and Terry Nichols, who were responsible for the 1995 bombing of the Alfred P. Murrah Federal Building in Oklahoma City.[28] All that changed on September 11, 2001, when, according to Ambassador Francis X. Taylor, the then-U.S. Department of State's coordinator for counterterrorism, "the United States suffered its bloodiest day on American soil since the Civil War, and the world experienced the most devastating international terrorist attack in recorded history."[29]

On that infamous day in September, 19 hijackers belonging to the al Qaeda terrorist network commandeered four aircraft to commit the most audacious terrorist act in American history.

- Five terrorists hijacked American Airlines flight 11, which departed Boston for Los Angeles at 7:45 a.m. An hour later it was deliberately piloted into the North Tower of the World Trade Center in New York City.
- Five terrorists hijacked United Airlines flight 175, which departed Boston for Los Angeles at 7:58 A.M. At 9:05 the plane crashed into the South Tower of the World Trade Center. Both towers collapsed shortly thereafter, killing approximately 3,000 persons, including hundreds of firefighters and rescue personnel who were helping to evacuate the buildings.
- Four terrorists hijacked United Airlines flight 93, which departed Newark for San Francisco at 8:01 A.M. At 10:10 the plane crashed in Stony Creek Township, Pennsylvania, killing all 45 persons onboard. The intended target of this hijacked plane is not known, but it is believed that passengers overpowered the terrorists, thus preventing the aircraft from being used as a missile.
- Five terrorists hijacked American Airlines flight 77, which departed Washington Dulles Airport for Los Angeles at 8:10 A.M. At 9:39 the plane was flown directly into the Pentagon in Arlington, Virginia, near Washington, DC. A total of 189 persons were killed, including all who were onboard the plane.[30]

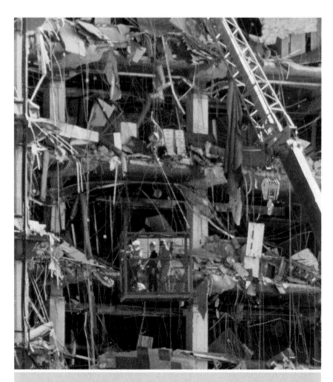

Prior to 9/11, the bombing of the Alfred P. Murrah Federal Building in Oklahoma City on April 19, 1995, by Timothy McVeigh was the worst incident of domestic terrorism in American history. *What are the similarities and differences between the bombing of the Murrah Federal Building by McVeigh and the 9/11 terrorist assaults on the World Trade Center and the Pentagon?*

DEFINITIONS AND TYPES OF TERRORISM

There is no single, universally accepted definition of terrorism, and types of terrorism can be distinguished by perpetrators, motives, methods, and targets. Whatever the definition, the key elements of terrorism are fear, panic, violence, and disruption.[31] The FBI defines

terrorism as "the systematic use of terror or unpredictable violence against governments, publics, or individuals to attain a political objective."[32] In the U.S. Code of Federal Regulations (28 C.F.R. Section 0.85), terrorism is defined as "the unlawful use of force and violence against persons or property to intimidate or coerce a government, the civilian population, or any segment thereof, in furtherance of political or social objectives."[33] Title 22 of the U.S. Code, Section 2656f(d), defines terrorism as "premeditated, politically motivated violence perpetrated against noncombatant targets by subnational groups or clandestine agents, usually intended to influence an audience."[34]

The FBI divides terrorism into two broad categories: domestic terrorism and international terrorism.

Domestic terrorism is the unlawful use, or threatened use, of force or violence by a group or individual based and operating entirely within the United States or its territories without foreign direction committed against persons or property to intimidate or coerce a government, the civilian population, or any segment thereof, in furtherance of political or social objectives.[35]

International terrorism involves violent acts dangerous to human life that are a violation of the criminal laws of the United States or any state, or that would be a criminal violation if committed within the jurisdiction of the United States or any state. These acts appear to be intended to intimidate or coerce a civilian population, influence the policy of a government by intimidation or coercion, or affect the conduct of a government by assassination or kidnapping. International terrorist acts occur outside the United States or transcend national boundaries in terms of the means by which they are accomplished, the persons they appear intended to coerce or intimidate, or the locale in which the perpetrators operate or seek asylum.[36]

The FBI further divides domestic terrorism into "right-wing terrorism," "left-wing terrorism," "special interest terrorism," and "individual terrorism." *Right-wing terrorist groups,* such as the Aryan Nations and the World Church of the Creator, generally oppose government in general and government regulation in particular. Members typically are virulent racists who believe in racial supremacy and conspiracy theories.[37] *Left-wing terrorist groups* generally believe in revolutionary socialist doctrine and seek radical change outside the established political process. They want to liberate people from the dehumanizing effects of capitalism and imperialism. With the collapse of the Soviet Union and the fall of communism in Eastern Europe in the 1980s, left-wing terrorist groups no longer pose much of a threat to the United States.[38] The goal of *special interest terrorist groups* is to change the attitudes of the public about specific issues that are important to the group rather than to bring about fundamental political change. These groups generally are fringe elements of antinuclear, environmental, pro-life, animal rights, and other movements.[39] As of this writing, the FBI considers the Animal Liberation Front (ALF) and the Earth Liberation Front (ELF) as two of the most active special interest terrorist groups. *Individual terrorist acts* are committed by "lone wolf" extremists who operate alone or in small groups and defy detection both as to their identities and their plans for destruction. Timothy McVeigh and Eric Robert Rudolph are examples of this category of terrorist.[40] Figure 4.4 classifies the type of perpetrators responsible for terrorist acts in the United States from 1980 through 2001.

The FBI estimates that about 20 to 30 percent of international terrorist incidents that occur annually in the United States and abroad are directed at U.S. interests.[41] These threats to U.S. interests are divided into three categories: state sponsors of international terrorism, formalized terrorist organizations,

terrorism The systematic use of terror or unpredictable violence against governments, publics, or individuals to attain a political objective; the unlawful use of force and violence against persons or property to intimidate or coerce a government, the civilian population, or any segment thereof, in furtherance of political or social objectives; or premeditated, politically motivated violence perpetrated against noncombatant targets by subnational groups or clandestine agents, usually intended to influence an audience.

domestic terrorism The unlawful use, or threatened use, of force or violence by a group or individual based and operating entirely within the United States or its territories without foreign direction committed against persons or property to intimidate or coerce a government, the civilian population, or any segment thereof, in furtherance of political or social objectives.

international terrorism Violent acts dangerous to human life that are a violation of the criminal laws of the United States or any state, or that would be a criminal violation if committed within the jurisdiction of the United States or any state. These acts appear to be intended to intimidate or coerce a civilian population, influence the policy of a government by intimidation or coercion, or affect the conduct of a government by assassination or kidnapping. International terrorist acts occur outside the United States or transcend national boundaries in terms of the means by which they are accomplished, the persons they appear intended to coerce or intimidate, or the locale in which the perpetrators operate or seek asylum.

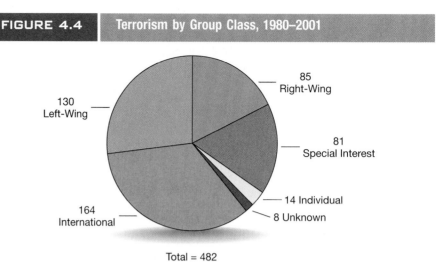

| FIGURE 4.4 | Terrorism by Group Class, 1980–2001 |

130 Left-Wing

85 Right-Wing

81 Special Interest

14 Individual

8 Unknown

164 International

Total = 482

Figure includes terrorist incidents, suspected terrorist incidents, and preventions.

Source: Federal Bureau of Investigation, *Terrorism 2000/2001*, p. 11, at www.fbi.gov/publications/terror/terroris.htm.

and loosely affiliated extremists and rogue international terrorists.[42] The principal *state sponsors of terrorism* are Cuba, Iran, Libya, North Korea, Sudan, and Syria. For these countries, terrorism is a tool of foreign policy.[43] *Formal terrorist organizations* are autonomous, generally transnational, and have their own personnel, infrastructures, financial arrangements, and training facilities. Examples are the Irish Republican Army, Palestinian Hamas, the Egyptian Al-Gama al-Islamiyya (IG), Lebanese Hezbollah, 17 November (based in Greece), and the Revolutionary Armed Forces of Columbia (FARC).[44] *Loosely affiliated extremists and rogue international terrorists* include the World Trade Center bombers and rogue terrorists such as Ramzi Yousef, Osama bin Laden, and members of al Qaeda.[45]

Another way of characterizing terrorism is by the methods terrorists use. The traditional method has involved a conventional bomb. However, today, the most-feared method involves weapons of mass destruction (WMDs), such as nuclear, radiological, and biological devices. Agroterrorism is another method and is an attack on a food source or the distribution of food supplies. Cyberterrorism, dubbed "information warfare," may take various forms including the hacking into or destroying of the nation's electronic infrastructure rendering mass communications via the Internet inoperable. High-energy radio frequency (HERF) and electromagnetic pulse weapons (EMPs) can shut down mass communication systems almost instantly.[46]

For purposes of this textbook, it is important to note that terrorists are criminals, according to the FBI's counterterrorism policy.[47] However, it is also important to remember that one person's terrorist is another person's freedom fighter. The British, for example, accused the American revolutionaries of being terrorists.[48]

THE LAW ENFORCEMENT RESPONSE TO TERRORISM

Terrorists' acts are often perpetrated by disaffected and angry individuals and groups who are far removed from the everyday American scene. Yet, through the media, American citizens are learning more about terrorism than ever before. Still, terrorism is a complex phenomenon. American law enforcement officers have no choice anymore. They must learn all they can to protect the nation and its people.

The FBI considers the Animal Liberation Front (ALF) and the Earth Liberation Front (ELF) as two of the most active special interest terrorist groups. *What do these two groups have in common with terrorist groups such as the Irish Republican Army, Palestinian Hamas, and the Revolutionary Armed Forces of Columbia (FARC)? How do they differ?*

Since the tragedy of September 11, 2001, terrorism has been at the top of the national agenda. People are frightened without knowing exactly what to do about it. Local, state, and federal law enforcement agencies have new responsibilities for the prevention of both domestic and international terrorism and for reducing America's fear. To guide them, especially at the national level, President George W. Bush has laid out four general policy principles:

1. Make no concessions to terrorists and strike no deals (even if U.S. citizens are held hostage).
2. Bring terrorists to justice for their crimes (no matter how long it takes).
3. Isolate and apply pressure on states that sponsor terrorism to force them to change their behavior.
4. Bolster the counterterrorist capabilities of those countries that work with the United States and require assistance.[49]

To prevent terrorism, billions of dollars are being committed and spent, and some civil liberties have been curtailed or severely restricted. The typical business or pleasure trip by airplane, for example, has become an even more taxing and intrusive experience. Even a simple trip to the library can make a person suspect should he or she select literary works that trigger the suspicion of a federal law enforcement agency. In a nation that was founded on the principles of freedom, openness, and anonymity for the most part, the new security, surveillance, and intelligence initiatives implemented since 9/11 have created concerns for many Americans.

Attempting to prevent terrorism is a daunting task. How can law enforcement officers protect every soft and hard target in America: all schools, all local water supplies, all food supply lines, all religious institutions, every public building in large and small communities, and all sources of energy? While Herculean does not adequately describe the charge, the protection of the American people and the nation's physical assets, as well as the reduction of fear from the threat of terrorism, is precisely what American law enforcement aims to do.

American law enforcement is now engaged in both defensive and offensive strategies to combat terrorism. However, in a free, open, and largely anonymous society, terrorists and potential terrorists know that the United States is fertile ground for terrorism. The police are faced with a dilemma. If the police are too aggressive trying to find and capture terrorists, American citizens are likely to become more fearful, anxious, and either resistant to or overly enthusiastic about repressive measures. If that occurs, terrorists win because fear, intimidation, disruption, and media attention to their cause are principal goals. On the other hand, if American law enforcement is not firm enough in its resolve and tactics to repress terrorism, terrorists will be able to again perpetrate a disaster on the public such as the events of 9/11, with loss of life, serious injury, fear, and anger. Such an event would likely encourage even tighter domestic security procedures, which would be resented by many members of the public, and the entire terror cycle would start over again. Law enforcement officers walk a fine line between preserving liberty and tranquility and providing security that may be perceived as excessive and repressive.

To illustrate, on June 17, 2003, President Bush issued guidelines barring federal agents from using race or ethnicity in routine investigations, but the policy permits exceptions in investigations involving terrorism and national security issues. Consequently, if law enforcement and intelligence officials receive information that terrorists of a certain ethnic group plan to hijack a plane in a particular state in the near future, officials are allowed to heighten security on men of that ethnicity that board planes in that area (also see the description of the PATRIOT Act in Chapter 3).[50]

HOW PREPARED IS THE UNITED STATES TO DEFEND AGAINST TERRORISM?

The answer to the preceding question depends on whom you ask, and there are many people and groups willing to give an answer. As noted in the last chapter, there already have been some successes. Terrorist acts have been prevented; terrorists have been captured and brought to justice; and the nation, as of October 2006, has avoided another tragedy of 9/11 proportions. Nevertheless, U.S. borders remain porous, and U.S. assets are still vulnerable.

In 2003, two reports critical of the nation's preparedness to respond to terrorist attacks were released. The independent and bipartisan Council on Foreign Relations concluded that the United States was "drastically underfunding local emergency responders and remains dangerously unprepared to handle another September 11 event."[51] The nonprofit Partnership for Public Service determined that the United States is likely to be overwhelmed in the event of a bioterrorism attack because of serious shortages in skilled medical and scientific personnel.[52] The conclusion, it seems, is that the United States has much more to do in its preparation to fight terrorism.

THINKING CRITICALLY

1. What type of terrorism do you think poses the greatest threat to the United States and why?

2. Which of America's assets do you think are most vulnerable to terrorist attacks, and what do you think can be done to better defend them?

1. Describe the general attitude of the public toward the police.

According to surveys, the American public is generally satisfied with the quality of the service the police provide. The level of confidence varies across racial and ethnic groups. As with most services, the public believes there is room for improvement.

2. Summarize the steps in an effective police officer selection process.

Police applicants go through several different kinds of testing to become law enforcement officers. Steps in an effective police officer selection process include: recruitment, short application, detailed application, medical examination, physical ability test, written examination, background investigation, psychological testing, oral interview/oral board, academy training, and a probationary employment period.

3. Identify factors that affect the exercise of police discretion and methods of limiting discretion.

Factors that affect the exercise of police discretion include the nature of the crime, departmental policies, the relationship between the victim and the offender, the amount of evidence, the preference of the victim, the demeanor of the suspect, the legitimacy of the victim, and the suspect's socioeconomic status. Methods of limiting police discretion are close supervision by a police agency's management, department directives and policies, U.S. Supreme Court decisions, and the threat of civil liability suits.

4. Describe two general ways that law enforcement agencies can reduce stress on the job

Two general ways that law enforcement agencies can reduce job stress for police officers are (1) to employ stress management strategies, such as discussing stressful events with colleagues and mental health professionals, regular exercise, relaxation techniques, healthy diet, religious support, enriched family support, prayer, meditation, and stress management classes that often involve spouses, and (2) to implement organizational change, such as allowing officers more discretion in determining work hours and shifts, flattening the organizational structure and giving officers more discretion in carrying out their responsibilities, job redesign that assigns unwanted or unnecessary tasks for a police offi-cer to another position, and having excellent public safety equipment such as weaponry, vehicles, and body armor.

5. Explain the circumstances under which police officers may be justified in using deadly force.

The use of deadly force by a police officer may be justifiable if (1) the arrest is for a felony; (2) the person effecting the arrest is authorized to act as a peace officer or is assisting a person whom he believes to be authorized to act as a peace officer; (3) the officer believes that the force employed creates no substantial risk of injury to innocent persons; (4) the officer believes that the crime for which the arrest is made involved conduct including the use or threatened use of deadly force; and (5) the officer believes there is substantial risk that the person to be arrested will cause death or serious bodily harm if his or her apprehension is delayed.

6. List some of the ways to control and reduce police corruption.

Ways to control and reduce police corruption include selecting and maintaining officers with high moral standards, developing rigid departmental policies that cover the wide range of activities that corruption comprises, disciplining and prosecuting officers who are guilty of violating established policies and laws, utilizing a proactive internal affairs investigations unit, holding first-line supervisors responsible for the actions of their subordinates, employing outside review and special prosecutors, and emphasizing to officers the costs to police agencies of criminal prosecutions and civil liability suits.

7. Define terrorism and identify different types of terrorism.

Terrorism has been defined as the systematic use of terror or unpredictable violence against governments, publics, or individuals to attain a political objective; the unlawful use of force and violence against persons or property to intimidate or coerce a government, the civilian population, or any segment thereof, in furtherance of political or social objectives; or premeditated, politically motivated violence perpetrated against noncombatant targets by subnational groups or clandestine agents, usually intended to influence an audience. Two broad categories of terrorism are domestic terrorism and international terrorism. Specific types of domestic terrorism are right-wing terrorism, left-wing terrorism, special interest terrorism, and individual terrorism. International terrorism is divided into state-sponsored terrorism, formalized terrorist organizations, and loosely affiliated extremists and rogue international terrorists.

KEY TERMS

three I's of police selection, p. 119
college academies, p. 122
public safety officers, p. 124
police cadet program, p. 124

tech prep (technical preparation), p. 124
merit system, p. 125
discretion, p. 130
full enforcement, p. 131
selective enforcement, p. 131
racial profiling, p. 134

job stress, p. 135
copicide, p. 135
excessive force, p. 137
"grass eaters," p. 140
"meat eaters," p. 140
internal affairs investigations unit, p. 141
terrorism, p. 143

domestic terrorism, p. 143
international terrorism, p. 143

REVIEW QUESTIONS

1. Explain how the three I's of police selection (intelligence, integrity, and interaction skills) relate to the success of a police officer.
2. What are some advantages of hiring college-educated police officers?
3. What are some arguments in favor of and opposing the reduction of police discretion?
4. Why do police generally not like to respond to domestic violence calls?
5. What is *racial profiling* in law enforcement, and what are some of the methods that have been prescribed to stop it?

6. What are some of the conditions that can lead to police job stress?
7. What is meant by *copicide*?
8. What is meant by *excessive force*?
9. What are some types of police misconduct?
10. What are President Bush's four general terrorism policy principles ?

IN THE FIELD

1. **Neighborhood Survey** Conduct a survey about the police in your neighborhood. Use the same survey questions and categories as in Figures 4.1, 4.2, and 4.3. Try to get respondents from as many races, genders, and age groups as possible. Compare the results of your survey with the results in Figures 4.1, 4.2, and 4.3. Note any gender, race, or age differences in responses.
2. **Police Recruiting** Contact your local police department, and find out what it does to

recruit police candidates. Does it run a police academy? Does it generally recruit officers from other jurisdictions? Compare your findings with those of others in the class and what you have learned from your textbook.

1. **Racial Profiling** Go to the Web site of the American Civil Liberties Union at www.aclu.org/RacialEquality/RacialEquality.cfm?ID=18163&c=133 and look at its report on "Driving While Black: Racial Profiling on Our Nation's Highways," by Professor David A. Harris from the University of Toledo College of Law. Read Professor Harris's report and his five recommendations for ending racial profiling. Which of the five recommendations do you agree with and why? Which do you disagree with and why? Discuss these findings in class and see if other students share your views.

2. **Job Qualifications** Go the Web sites of four large police departments (New York City at www.ci.nyc.ny.us/html/nypd/home.html; Los Angeles at www.lapdonline.org; Philadelphia at www.ppdonline.org; and Houston at www.houstontx.gov/police and identify the major qualifications to be a police officer that are listed there. What qualifications are the same or similar among the agencies you examined? What qualifications are unique among those listed by the four agencies? Which employment qualifications are the most difficult to meet? Do you agree that all of the qualifications most difficult to meet are necessary? Would you add any qualifications? If so, what would they be? What would be the impact of your new qualifications on the recruitment and selection of police officers?

1. **Police Academy** Recently, "Police Corps," a new military-style police academy, has opened in cities such as Jacksonville and Tampa, Florida. The cadets of the mentally exhausting 6-month program eat, sleep, and live together in rooms near the academy with no televisions and with the constant threat of surprise inspections. Their days involve marching in military formation with a platoon leader barking out cadences, weightlifting, and classes on self-defense as well as law and criminal procedure. Afternoons are spent at the firing range, where they train with pistols, MP-5 submachine guns, and AR-15 assault rifles. After ending their days at 10 P.M. with little or no time for themselves to relax or study, they are occasionally awakened at 2 A.M. as instructors push them for practice in high-speed driving and patrolling tactics. At some point in the course, the cadets are put through 24 to 72 hours of sleep deprivation to teach them the effects of stress and lack of sleep on their bodies. The punishment for not following orders correctly is push-ups.

   Supporters of the new academy maintain that the Navy SEAL–type training will help officers become more disciplined and community oriented. Critics contend that the program is too extreme and isn't necessary for a community police force, that it "isn't needed in our society unless we're in a warfare environment."

   a. What are the pros and cons of this new military-style police academy training?
   b. What effects, if any, are such training methods likely to have on police recruitment?
   c. Is such training needed in our society?

2. **Stress** You are the commander of the operations division of a medium-sized police department, in charge of the patrol, criminal investigation, and traffic sections.

   a. What would you do if several officers from each of the sections came to you and said that they believed that job stress was hindering officer performance and endangering the health of several officers in each of the units?
   b. How would you go about validating their claims of job stress in the work environment?
   c. If it were determined that stressors such as too frequent shift changes, poor communication among the various ranks, and a lack of sufficient safety equipment were present, what would be your plan to improve working conditions and reduce job stress?
   d. Provide a step-by-step summary of what you would do.

To access more information and resources, including study questions, chapter summaries, and links, go to: www.mhhe.com/bohm1.

PART THREE

THE COURTS

CHAPTER FIVE

THE ADMINISTRATION OF JUSTICE

CHAPTER OBJECTIVES

After completing this chapter, you should be able to:

1. Identify the type of court structure in the United States and describe its various components.

2. Summarize the purposes of courts.

3. Identify the most powerful actors in the administration of justice and explain what makes them so powerful.

4. Summarize the types of attorneys available to a person charged with a crime.

5. Describe the responsibilities of a judge.

6. Describe the purposes of an initial appearance.

7. Explain what bail is and describe the different methods of pretrial release.

8. Define what a grand jury is and explain its purposes.

9. Describe the purposes of the arraignment and the plea options of defendants.

10. Describe the interests served and not served by plea bargaining.

11. List and define the stages in a criminal trial.

12. Identify the trial rights of criminal defendants.

13. Describe some of the causes of wrongful convictions.

The American Court Structure

dual court system The court system in the United States, consisting of one system of state and local courts and another system of federal courts.

jurisdiction The authority of a court to hear and decide cases.

original jurisdiction The authority of a court to hear a case when it is first brought to court.

appellate jurisdiction The power of a court to review a case for errors of law.

general jurisdiction The power of a court to hear any type of case.

special jurisdiction The power of a court to hear only certain kinds of cases.

subject matter jurisdiction The power of a court to hear a particular type of case.

personal jurisdiction A court's authority over the parties to a lawsuit.

The United States has a **dual court system**—a separate judicial system for each of the states and a separate federal system. Figure 5.1 displays this dual court system and routes of appeal from the various courts. The only place where the two systems connect is in the U.S. Supreme Court.

The authority of a court to hear and decide cases is called the court's **jurisdiction.** It is set by law and is limited by territory and type of case. A court of **original jurisdiction** has the authority to hear a case when it is first brought to court. Courts having the power to review a case for errors of law are courts of **appellate jurisdiction.** Courts having the power to hear any type of case are said to exercise **general jurisdiction.** Those with the power to hear only certain types of cases have **special jurisdiction. Subject matter jurisdiction** is the court's power to hear a particular type of case. **Personal jurisdiction** is the court's authority over the parties to a lawsuit.

THE FEDERAL COURTS

The authority for the federal court system is the U.S. Constitution, Article III, Section 1, which states, "The judicial Power of the United States, shall be vested in one Supreme Court, and in such inferior courts as the Congress may from time to time ordain and establish." The federal court system includes the

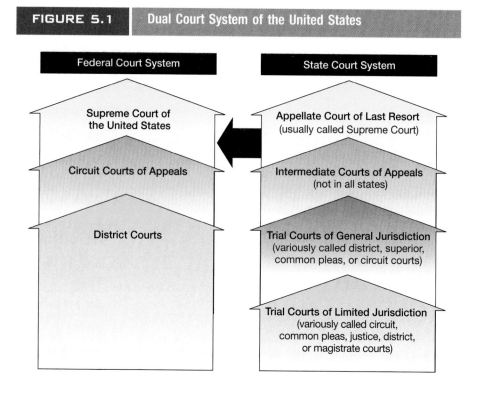

FIGURE 5.1   Dual Court System of the United States

| FIGURE 5.2 | The Federal Court Structure |

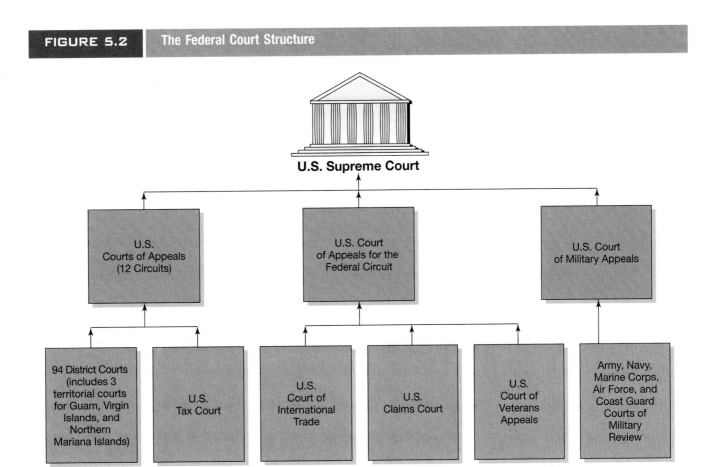

Supreme Court, the federal courts of appeals, and the federal district courts. The federal court system is shown in Figure 5.2.

U.S. DISTRICT COURTS Forming the base of the federal court structure are the U.S. district courts. These are courts of original jurisdiction, or courts where most violations of federal criminal and civil law are first adjudicated. Today, there are 94 district courts divided into 13 circuits, with at least one federal district court in each state, one each in the District of Columbia and the commonwealths of Puerto Rico and the Northern Mariana Islands, and one each in the U.S. territories of the Virgin Islands and Guam. In some states, the courts are divided into districts geographically. New York, for example, has northern, eastern, southern, and western district courts.

Two factors determine the jurisdiction of federal district courts: the subject matter of a case and the parties to a case. Federal district courts have subject matter jurisdiction over cases that involve federal laws, treaties with foreign nations, or interpretations of the Constitution. Cases involving admiralty or maritime law—the law of the sea, including ships, their crews, and disputes over actions and rights at sea—also come under federal district court jurisdiction.

Federal district courts have personal jurisdiction in cases if certain parties or persons are involved. These include (1) ambassadors and other representatives of foreign governments, (2) two or more state governments, (3) the U.S. government or one of its offices or agencies, (4) citizens of different states, (5) a state and a citizen of a different state, (6) citizens of the same state claiming lands under grants of different states, and (7) a state or its citizens and a foreign country or its citizens.

U.S. district courts are presided over by district court judges who are appointed by the president, are confirmed by the Senate, and, except for the territorial judges who serve 10-year terms, serve for life (if they choose, do not resign, or are not impeached and convicted by Congress). In 2006, there were 667 authorized federal district judgeships (including 11 temporary judgeships). Several district courts, such as the district court of North Dakota had only two judges, while the southern-district court of New York in New York City had the most with 28. The annual salary of a U.S. district court judge is $165,200 (as of January 1, 2006).[1] Usually a single federal judge presides over a trial, and trial by jury is allowed if requested by a defendant. Some complex civil cases are heard by a special panel of three judges. The bulk of the workload of the U.S. district courts is devoted to civil cases, the number of which has risen dramatically in recent years, to 253,273 in 2005. Federal criminal cases involve such crimes as bank robbery, counterfeiting, mail fraud, kidnapping, and civil rights abuses. Until 1980, the number of criminal cases in federal district courts remained relatively stable at about 30,000 a year. However, as a result of the federal government's war on drugs and an increase in illegal immigration cases, the number of criminal cases had more than doubled to 69,575 by the end of 2005. About 26 percent of the criminal cases filed in U.S district courts in 2005 were drug cases and about 25 percent were immigration cases.[2]

To ease the caseload of U.S. district court judges, Congress created the judicial office of federal magistrate in 1968. The title changed to magistrate judge in 1990. As their caseloads require and as funding from Congress permits, district judges may appoint magistrate judges to part-time or full-time positions. Magistrate judges handle civil consent cases, misdemeanor trials, preliminary hearings, pretrial motions and motion hearings, and conferences in felony cases.[3] The behavior of most United States judges is governed by a code of conduct, which is presented in Figure 5.3.

FIGURE 5.3	Code of Conduct for United States Judges
Canon 1	A Judge Should Uphold the Integrity and Independence of the Judiciary
Canon 2	A Judge Should Avoid Impropriety and the Appearance of Impropriety in All Activities
Canon 3	A Judge Should Perform the Duties of the Office Impartially and Diligently
Canon 4	A Judge May Engage in Extra-Judicial Activities To Improve the Law, the Legal System, and the Administration of Justice
Canon 5	A Judge Should Regulate Extra-Judicial Activities To Minimize the Risk of Conflict with Judicial Duties
Canon 6	A Judge Should Regularly File Reports of Compensation Received for Law-Related and Extra-Judicial Activities
Canon 7	A Judge Should Refrain from Political Activity

The Code of Conduct for United States Judges was initially adopted by the Judicial Conference on April 5, 1973, and was known as the "Code of Judicial Conduct for United States Judges." At its March 1987 session, the Judicial Conference deleted the word "Judicial" from the name of the Code. Substantial revisions to the Code were adopted by the Judicial Conference at its September 1992 session. This Code applies to United States Circuit Judges, District Judges, Court of International Trade Judges, Court of Federal Claims Judges, Bankruptcy Judges, and Magistrate Judges. Certain provisions of this Code apply to special masters and commissioners. In addition, the Tax Court, Court of Appeals for Veterans Claims, and Court of Appeals for the Armed Forces have adopted this Code. Persons to whom the Code applies must arrange their affairs as soon as reasonably possible to comply with the Code and should do so in any event within one year of appointment.

Source: Administrative Office of the U.S. Courts, Federal Judiciary Web site, "Judges and Judgeships" at www.uscourts.gov/guide/vol2/ch1.html.

CIRCUIT COURTS OF APPEALS A person or group that loses a case in district court may appeal to a federal circuit court of appeals or, in some instances, directly to the Supreme Court. Congress created the U.S. circuit courts of appeals in 1891 to reduce the case burden of the Supreme Court. The U.S. circuit courts of appeals have only appellate jurisdiction and review a case for errors of law, not of fact. Most appeals arise from the decisions of district courts, the U.S. Tax Court, and various territorial courts (see Figure 5.2). Federal courts of appeals also hear appeals of the rulings of regulatory agencies, such as the Federal Trade Commission. An appeal to the U.S. circuit court of appeals is a matter of right—the court cannot refuse to hear the case. However, unless appealed to the Supreme Court, decisions of the courts of appeals are final. U.S. courts of appeals heard more than 68,000 cases in 2005 (68,473); about 23 percent of those cases were criminal; another 25 percent were prisoner cases.[4]

There are currently 13 U.S. circuit courts of appeals (see Figure 5.4). Twelve of them have jurisdiction over cases from particular geographic areas. The Court of Appeals for the Federal Circuit, created in 1982, has national jurisdiction over specific types of cases, such as appeals from the U.S. Court of International Trade.[5] Like U.S. district judges, federal appellate judges are nominated by the president, are confirmed by the Senate, and may serve for life. Currently, 179 judges serve on the 13 U.S. circuit courts (167 on the 12 regional courts and 12 on the federal circuit). The yearly salary of a U.S. circuit court of appeals judge is $175,100 (as of January 1, 2006).[6] The number of judges assigned to each court of appeals ranges from 6 (the First Circuit) to 28 (the Ninth Circuit) and, normally, 3 judges sit as a panel.[7] Jury

Circuit Courts

The circuit courts are so named because early in the nation's history, federal judges traveled by horseback to each of the courts in a specified region, or "circuit," in a particular sequence. In short, they rode the circuit.

SOURCE: Howard Ball, "The Federal Court System," in R. J. Janosik (ed.), *Encyclopedia of the American Judicial System: Studies of the Principal Institutions and Processes of Law* (New York: Charles Scribner's Sons, 1987), p. 556.

| FIGURE 5.4 | The 13 U.S. Circuits |

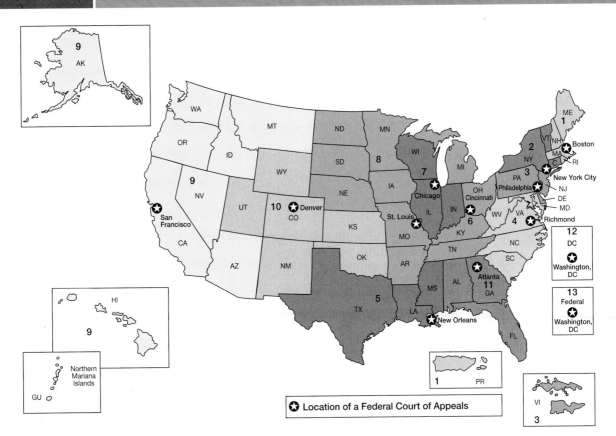

Location of a Federal Court of Appeals

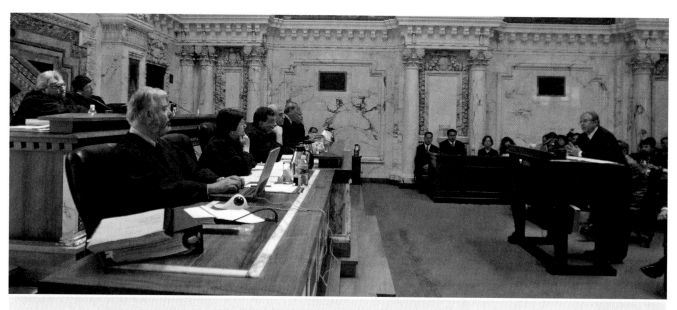

The 9th U.S. Circuit Court of Appeals in San Francisco, California (pictured here), has the most judges (28) of all the circuit courts of appeals. *What determines how many judges are selected to serve on a U.S. circuit court of appeals?*

The Judicial Conference of the United States

The Judicial Conference of the United States governs the federal court system. The conference is composed of 27 federal judges and is presided over by the chief justice of the U.S. Supreme Court. The conference meets twice a year to consider policies affecting the federal courts, to make recommendations to Congress on legislation affecting the judicial system, to propose amendments to the federal rules of practice and procedure, and to address administrative problems of the courts.

SOURCE: Administrative Office of the U.S. Courts, Federal Judiciary Web site at www.uscourts.gov/judconf.html.

trials are not allowed in these courts. In highly controversial cases, all of the judges in a circuit may sit together and hear a case. Those *en banc* hearings are rare; there probably are no more than 100 of them in all of the circuits in 1 year.

THE U.S. SUPREME COURT The U.S. Supreme Court is the court of last resort in all questions of federal law (see Figure 5.2). It has the final word in any case involving the Constitution, acts of Congress, and treaties with other nations. Under the Supreme Court's appellate jurisdiction, the Court hears cases appealed from federal courts of appeals, or it may hear appeals from federal district courts in certain circumstances in which an act of Congress has been held unconstitutional.

The Supreme Court may also hear cases that are appealed from the high court of a state, if claims under federal law or the Constitution are involved. In such cases, however, the Court has the authority to rule only on the federal issue involved, not on any issues of state law. For example, suppose a state tries a person charged with violating a state law. During the trial, the accused claims that the police violated Fourth Amendment rights with an illegal search at the time of the arrest. The defendant may appeal to the Supreme Court on the constitutional issue only. The Supreme Court generally has no jurisdiction to rule on the state issue (whether the accused actually violated state law). The Court would decide only whether Fourth Amendment rights were violated. Decisions of the Supreme Court are binding on all lower courts.

The Supreme Court is composed of a chief justice, officially known as the chief justice of the United States, and eight associate justices. They are appointed for life by the president with the consent of the Senate and, like other federal judges, can be removed from office against their will only by "impeachment for, and Conviction of, Treason, Bribery, or other high Crimes and Misdemeanors." The chief justice, who is specifically nominated by the president for the position, presides over the Court's public sessions and private conferences, assigns justices to write opinions (when the chief justice has voted with the majority), and supervises the entire federal judiciary. (When the chief justice has voted with the minority, the associate justice who has the greatest seniority, that is, has been on the Court the longest, assigns who writes the opinion.) The salary of the chief justice is $212,100; the salaries of the associate justices are $203,000 (as of January 1, 2006).[8]

For a case to be heard by the Supreme Court, at least four of the nine justices must vote to hear the case (the "rule of four"). When the required number of votes has been achieved, the Court issues a **writ of *certiorari*** to the lower court whose decision is being appealed, ordering it to send the records of the case forward for review. The Court is limited by law and custom in the types of cases for which it issues writs of *certiorari*. The Court will issue a "writ" only if the defendant in the case has exhausted all other avenues of appeal and the case involves a substantial federal question as defined by the appellate court. A substantial federal question, as noted, is one in which there is an alleged violation of either the U.S. Constitution or federal law.

When the Supreme Court decides a case it has accepted on appeal, it can do one of the following:

1. Affirm the verdict or decision of the lower court and "let it stand."
2. Modify the verdict or decision of the lower court, without totally reversing it.
3. Reverse the verdict or decision of the lower court, requiring no further court action.
4. Reverse the verdict or decision of the lower court and remand the case to the court of original jurisdiction, for either retrial or resentencing.

In some cases, the Supreme Court has ordered trial courts to resentence defendants whose original sentences violated the Eighth Amendment prohibition against cruel and unusual punishment. In other cases, prison authorities have been ordered to remedy unconstitutional conditions of imprisonment.

Appeals to the Supreme Court are heard at the discretion of the Court, in contrast to appeals to the U.S. circuit courts, which review cases as a matter of right. In 2004, for example, the Supreme Court heard and disposed of only 87 of the 7,496 cases filed for review.[9] In other words, in 2004, the Court opted not to review nearly 99 percent of the appealed cases—a figure typical of Court practice. Generally, the Supreme Court's refusal to hear a case ends the process of direct appeal. In certain circumstances, an imprisoned defendant whose appeal has been denied may still try to have the Supreme Court review his or her case on constitutional grounds by filing a **writ of *habeas corpus***. A writ of *habeas corpus*, which is guaranteed by Article I, Section 9, of the Constitution, the Federal Habeas Corpus Act, and state *habeas corpus* laws, is a court order directing a law officer to produce a prisoner in court to determine if the prisoner is being legally detained or imprisoned. The *habeas corpus* proceeding does not test whether the prisoner is guilty or innocent.

The Supreme Court also has original jurisdiction. However, Article III, Section 2.2, of the Constitution limits the Court's original jurisdiction to two types of cases: (1) cases involving representatives of foreign governments; and (2) certain cases in which a state is a party. Many cases have involved two states and the federal government. When Maryland and Virginia argued over oyster fishing rights, and when a dispute broke out between California and Arizona over the control of water from the Colorado River, the Supreme Court had original jurisdiction in the matters. Original jurisdiction cases are a very small part of the Court's yearly workload. Most of the cases the Court decides fall under its appellate jurisdiction.

Court Fees

The fee for filing an appeal with the U.S. Supreme Court is $300. Fees are waived for indigent defendants. Approximately 90 percent of the criminal proceedings appealed to the Supreme Court involve indigent defendants. The fees do not include the costs of printing various documents required under other court rules.

Source: Clerk of the Supreme Court; 28 U.S.C. § 1911.

Supreme Court Justices
The Supreme Court justices of the United States have varied biographical, legal, and educational backgrounds. Learn more about the current justices by going to the following Web site: **www.oyez.org/oyez/portlet/justices.** *What do the justices have in common? How do their backgrounds differ?*

writ of *certiorari* A written order, from the U.S. Supreme Court to a lower court whose decision is being appealed, to send the records of the case forward for review.

writ of *habeas corpus* An order from a court to an officer of the law to produce a prisoner in court to determine if the prisoner is being legally detained or imprisoned.

U.S. Supreme Court Justices. (L-R): Associate Justices Anthony Kennedy, Stephen Breyer, John Paul Stevens, Clarence Thomas, Chief Justice John Roberts, Associate Justices Ruth Bader Ginsburg, Antonin Scalia, Samuel Alito, and David Souter. Note that Chief Justice William Rehnquist died on September 3, 2005, and was replaced by Roberts, and Justice Sandra Day O'Connor retired in July 2005 and was replaced by Samuel Alito.

THE STATE COURTS

The state courts have general power to decide nearly every type of case, subject only to the limitations of the U.S. Constitution, their own state constitutions, and state law. State and local courts are the courts with which citizens most often have contact. These courts handle most criminal matters and the majority of day-to-day legal matters. The laws of each state determine the organization, function, and even the names of its courts. Thus, no two state court systems are exactly alike. For discussion purposes, it is useful to distinguish four levels of state courts: trial courts of limited jurisdiction, trial courts of general jurisdiction, intermediate appellate courts, and state courts of last resort.[10]

TRIAL COURTS OF LIMITED JURISDICTION At the base of the state court structure (see Figure 5.1) are the approximately 13,500 trial courts of limited jurisdiction, sometimes referred to generally as "inferior trial courts" or simply as "lower courts." Depending on the jurisdiction, those courts are called city courts, municipal courts, county courts, circuit courts, courts of common pleas, justice-of-the-peace courts, district courts, or magistrate courts. (Technically, most of the lower courts are not really part of the state judicial structure because they are the creation of, and funded by, either city or county governments.) In several states, judges of the lower courts are not required to have any formal legal training.

The lower courts typically deal with minor cases, such as ordinance and traffic violations, some misdemeanors, and—in many jurisdictions—civil cases involving less than $1,000. For those types of offenses, the lower courts in many states are allowed to conduct **summary** or **bench trials,** or trials without a jury. Typically, the greatest penalty that can be imposed is a fine of $1,000 and a maximum of 12 months in jail. Unlike trial courts of general jurisdiction,

Court TV

Over the past several years, there has been a growing interest in the inner workings of the American court system. This is evident in the popularity of the television network Court TV. Go to the Court TV Web site at **www.courttv.com**. Review the list of featured cases and the programming schedule for the network. *Why do you think that shows on Court TV are so popular?*

summary or **bench trials** Trials without a jury.

the lower courts are not courts of record, where detailed transcripts of the proceedings are made. Because they are not courts of record, an appeal from such a lower court requires a **trial *de novo*,** in which the entire case must be reheard by a trial court of general jurisdiction.

In addition to handling minor cases, the lower courts in most states hear the formal charges against persons accused of felonies, set bail, appoint counsel for indigent defendants, and conduct preliminary hearings for crimes that must be adjudicated at a higher level. The legal proceedings in these courts are typically less formal, and many cases are resolved without defense attorneys. Lower courts process and quickly dispose of large numbers of cases, approximately 90 million a year.

> **trial *de novo*** A trial in which an entire case is reheard by a trial court of general jurisdiction because there is an appeal and there is no written transcript of the earlier proceeding.

TRIAL COURTS OF GENERAL JURISDICTION Variously called district courts, superior courts, and circuit courts, depending on the jurisdiction, the more than 3,000 trial courts of general jurisdiction have the authority to try all civil and criminal cases and to hear appeals from lower courts. They are courts of record (formal transcripts of the proceedings are made), and judges and lawyers in those courts have formal legal training. Trial courts of general jurisdiction are funded by the state.

Augmenting trial courts of general jurisdiction are specialty courts that have been created during the past two decades to deal with increases in certain types of crimes or chronic social problems.[11] "Drug courts" were the first of these new "problem-solving" courts, the first of which was established in Dade County (Miami), Florida, in 1989. Within a decade, all but 10 states had at least one such court. Drug courts were created to (1) help handle the dramatic increase in drug cases resulting from the war on drugs that have been overwhelming the trial courts of general jurisdiction, and (2) use the court's authority to reduce crime by changing defendants' drug-using behavior. In exchange for the possibility of dismissed charges or reduced sentences, defendants accept diversion to drug treatment programs during the judicial process. Drug court judges preside over drug court proceedings, monitor the progress of defendants by means of frequent status hearings, and prescribe sanctions and rewards as appropriate, in collaboration with prosecutors, defense attorneys, treatment providers, and others.

Drug courts are popular. Research shows that active drug court participants, especially those who graduate from the program, are less likely to be rearrested than those in comparison groups; that recidivism reductions are maintained for substantial amounts of time after participants complete the drug court program; and that there is a positive cost/benefit ratio for drug court participants. In 1999, drug courts were officially endorsed by the National District Attorney's Association and the National Sheriff's Association. At the beginning of 2005, there were 1,621 drug courts—more than twice the number in December 2000. They were located in all 50 states, the District of Columbia, Guam, Northern Mariana Islands, Puerto Rico, the Virgin Islands, and a number of Native American Tribal Courts. New York had the most drug courts (165), followed by California (158) and Missouri (124).

Noelle Bush, daughter of Florida governor Jeb Bush, is shown with her brother George P. Bush in Orange County, Florida, drug court during her status hearing. Noelle was charged with contempt of court and spent 43 hours in jail for violating her court-ordered drug treatment plan. She was ordered to continue in the drug program. *Are drug courts a good idea? Why or why not?*

Drug courts are so popular and the need for them is perceived as so great that more specialized drug courts have been established. The first of these

Drug Courts

More than 70,000 drug court clients are being served at any given time throughout the United States and its territories.

Source: C. West Huddleston, III, Karen Freeman-Wilson, Douglas B. Marlowe, and Aaron Roussell, *Painting the Current Picture: A National Report Card on Drug Courts and Other Problem Solving Court Programs in the United States*, Vol. 1, No. 2 (Rockville, MD: National Drug Court Institute, May 2005), p. 7.

"subspecialty" drug courts was a women's drug court, which opened in Kalamazoo, Michigan, in 1992. That was followed in 1995 by the first juvenile drug court in Visalia, California, and the first family drug court in Reno, Nevada. Juvenile drug courts operate within juvenile courts and handle delinquency cases or status offenders who have alcohol and/or drug problems. Family drug courts deal with selected abuse, neglect, and dependency cases where parental substance abuse is a primary factor. Other specialized drug courts include adult drug courts (for nonviolent substance-abusing adult offenders), campus drug courts (for students with substance-abuse-related disciplinary cases that would otherwise result in expulsion from college), DWI (driving while intoxicated) drug courts (for alcohol/drug dependent offenders arrested for DWI), integrated-treatment courts (for juveniles and their families/guardians who need services to help juveniles make better choices about their lives and drug and alcohol abuse), reentry drug courts (for drug-involved offenders being released from local or state correctional facilities), and "tribal healing to wellness" drug courts (for Native American alcohol and/or drug-related offenders living in Native communities).

Drug courts have also provided the general model for the 2,558 (as of the start of 2005) other nondrug specialty courts. Missouri led the way with 179 of these other "problem-solving" courts; Florida was next with 150; and North Carolina was third with 129. These other "problem-solving" courts include child-support courts (for defendants with child-support issues), collections courts (for offenders, particularly probationers, who are having problems paying or are unwilling to pay court costs and restitution),[12] community courts (for low-level, nonviolent offenders who are required, as punishment for their crimes, to help in the restoring of distressed neighborhoods by cleaning streets and removing graffiti),[13] domestic-violence courts (for defendants facing domestic-violence charges and victims of domestic violence who need help), environmental courts (for defendants charged with housing, community health, solid waste, fire, building and zoning violations), gambling courts (for defendants suffering from a pathological or compulsive gambling disorder), gun courts (for defendants charged with illegal firearm possession), homeless courts (for homeless individuals with records of misdemeanor offenses, who, because of the records, are ineligible for government aid and, in some jurisdictions, such things as driver's licenses), mental health courts (for mentally ill or developmentally disabled individuals who have been charged with nonviolent misdemeanors and are in need of treatment),[14] teen courts (also called peer courts or youth courts; youths who commit minor offenses receive consequences for their behavior from a jury of their peers), and truancy courts (for children trying to overcome the underlying causes of truancy). All these specialty courts share three common characteristics: (1) they focus on one type of case; (2) court personnel receive specialized training for the particular type of case; and (3) judges closely monitor compliance with court dispositions.

INTERMEDIATE APPELLATE COURTS In some of the geographically smaller and less-populous states, there is only one appellate court, the state court of last resort, usually called the state supreme court. Many states, however, have created intermediate appellate courts to reduce the overwhelming case burden of the state supreme court. As of January 1, 2005, 40 states had intermediate courts of appeal.[15]

The intermediate appellate courts have no trial jurisdiction. They hear only appeals in both civil and criminal cases from the trial courts of general jurisdiction. An appeals court is charged with reviewing a case for errors of law and ensuring that legal procedures were followed. The decision rendered by the appeals court is based on a review of the trial court's official transcript and any other legally relevant information that may be submitted. Brief oral arguments by the attorneys for both sides are also allowed.

Like their federal counterparts, the intermediate appellate courts cannot refuse to hear any legally appealed case. The number of judges assigned to intermediate appellate courts ranges from 3 in some states to 105 in California.[16] Normally, three judges sit as a panel to decide cases.

STATE COURTS OF LAST RESORT   In most states, the state court of last resort is referred to as the state supreme court, although, as already noted, some states use different names. In Massachusetts and Maine, for example, the state court of last resort is called the supreme judicial court; in Maryland and New York, it is called the court of appeals. Oklahoma and Texas have two courts of last resort: the court of criminal appeals (for criminal appeals) and the supreme court (for civil cases). The court of last resort in 13 states or the chief justice of the court of last resort in 36 states is the designated head of a state's judicial branch. In one state, Utah, the Judicial Council is the designated head of the judicial branch.

As previously noted, the primary responsibility of state courts of last resort is to hear appeals from either trial courts of general jurisdiction (in those states without intermediate appellate courts) or intermediate appellate courts. In states with intermediate courts of appeal, the state court of last resort, like the U.S. Supreme Court, has discretion in which cases it will hear. And, like the U.S. Supreme Court, most state courts of last resort have original jurisdiction over a few types of cases.

Depending on the state, the number of judges who serve on the state court of last resort ranges from five to nine, though more than half the states have seven.[17] However, unlike judges of intermediate courts of appeal, judges of the state court of last resort are not divided into panels to hear cases. Instead, all the judges hear all of the cases; that is, they sit *en banc*. State courts of last resort have the final word on matters involving interpretation of state law. Although defendants dissatisfied with a verdict rendered in a state court of last resort may appeal the decision to the Supreme Court, the Supreme Court will hear the appeal only if it involves an alleged violation of the Constitution or federal law. In deciding cases, most state courts of last resort follow procedures similar to those employed by the Supreme Court.

THINKING CRITICALLY

1. What are some of the benefits of a dual court system?

2. Why is it difficult for a case to make it all the way to the Supreme Court? Should it be that difficult? Why or why not?

Purposes of Courts

Ted Rubin, former juvenile court judge and noted expert on juvenile justice, court, and rehabilitation issues, outlines 10 purposes of courts.[18] The first is to "do justice." However, whether justice is done usually depends on the interests and viewpoints of the parties involved in a dispute. Typically, the "winning" party believes that justice has been done, while the "loser" thinks otherwise.

A second purpose of courts is "to appear to do justice." Even when a decision rendered by a court seems unjust to some people, it is still important that the court appear to "do justice." The appearance of justice is accomplished primarily by providing due process of law. **Due process of law,** as noted in Chapter 4, refers to the procedures followed by courts to ensure that a defendant's constitutional rights are not violated.

due process of law The procedures followed by courts to ensure that a defendant's constitutional rights are not violated.

Courts provide a forum where disputes between people, such as the legendary feud between the Hatfields and McCoys (pictured here), can be resolved justly and peacefully. *How successful have the courts been in achieving this purpose? Defend your answer.*

A third purpose of courts is "to provide a forum where disputes between people can be resolved justly and peacefully." Until the creation of courts of law, disputes were often settled violently, through blood feuds and other acts of revenge. Aggrieved parties would gather their extended families and friends and make war against the families and friends of the person or persons who had presumably violated their rights. Sometimes those feuds would span generations, as did the legendary battles between the Hatfields and the McCoys. Courts were instituted, at least in part, to prevent those calamities. Thus, regardless of which side in a dispute "wins," what is important, from the standpoint of the court, is that the dispute be resolved justly and, perhaps more important, peacefully.

A fourth purpose of courts is "to censure wrongdoing." To *censure* means to condemn or to blame. In this context, it refers to condemning or blaming people who have violated the law.

Purposes five through eight involve specific outcomes that courts hope to achieve by their actions. They are **incapacitation,** or the removal or restriction of the freedom of those found to have violated criminal laws; **punishment,** or the imposition of a penalty for criminal wrongdoing; **rehabilitation,** or the attempt to "correct" the personality and behavior of convicted offenders through educational, vocational, or therapeutic treatment and to return them to society as law-abiding citizens; and **general deterrence,** or the attempt to prevent people in general from engaging in crime by punishing specific individuals and making examples of them. (Omitted from Rubin's list is special or specific deterrence.) These purposes are discussed at greater length in the next chapter under the goals of sentencing.

A ninth purpose of courts is to determine legal status. For example, courts determine marital status by dissolving marriages and granting divorces. Similarly, parental status is determined by approving adoptions.

A tenth and critically important purpose of courts is to protect individual citizens against arbitrary government action. Recourse through the courts is

incapacitation The removal or restriction of the freedom of those found to have violated criminal laws.

punishment The imposition of a penalty for criminal wrongdoing.

rehabilitation The attempt to "correct" the personality and behavior of convicted offenders through educational, vocational, or therapeutic treatment and to return them to society as law-abiding citizens.

general deterrence The attempt to prevent people in general from engaging in crime by punishing specific individuals and making examples of them.

available to citizens who have been abused by government agencies and agents. Examples of such abuses include illegal invasion of a person's privacy; interference with a person's First Amendment rights of religious choice, speech, press, and assembly; and denial of public employment because of race, gender, or age. In summary, by custom and law, courts have become an integral and seemingly indispensable part of modern life.

Key Actors in the Court Process

The three key actors in the court process are the prosecutor, the defense attorney, and the judge. In this section, the roles those three officers of the court play in the administration of justice are examined.[19]

THE PROSECUTOR

Because most crimes violate state laws, they fall under the authority, or jurisdiction, of the state court system and its prosecutors. The prosecutor is a community's chief law enforcement official and is responsible primarily for the protection of society.[20] Depending on the state, the prosecutor may be referred to as the district attorney, the prosecuting attorney, the county attorney, the state's attorney, the commonwealth's attorney, or the solicitor. In large cities, the day-to-day work of the prosecutor's office is performed by assistant district attorneys. Whatever the name, the prosecutor is the most powerful actor in the administration of justice. Not only do prosecutors conduct the final screening of each person arrested for a criminal offense, deciding whether there is enough evidence to support a conviction, but in most jurisdictions they also have unreviewable discretion in deciding whether to charge a person with a crime and whether to prosecute the case. In other words, regardless of the amount (or lack) of incriminating evidence, and without having to provide any reasons to anyone, prosecutors have the authority to charge or not charge a person with a crime and to prosecute or not prosecute the case. If they decide to prosecute, they also determine what the charge or charges will be. (The charge or charges may or may not be the same as the one or ones for which the person was arrested.) Prosecutors are not required to prosecute a person for all the charges that the evidence will support. However, the more charges they bring against a suspect, the more leverage prosecutors have in plea bargaining, which will be discussed later in this section. Regardless of the reason, when prosecutors elect not to prosecute, they enter a notation of **nolle prosequi (nol. pros.)** on the official record of the case and formally announce in court the decision to dismiss the charge or charges.

THE DECISION TO CHARGE AND PROSECUTE The exercise of prosecutorial discretion in charging contrasts sharply with the way prosecutors are supposed to behave in their professional capacities. Ideally, prosecutors are supposed to charge an offender with a crime and to prosecute the case if after full investigation three, and only three, conditions are met:

1. They find that a crime has been committed.
2. A perpetrator can be identified.
3. There is sufficient evidence to support a guilty verdict.

On the other hand, prosecutors are not supposed to charge suspects with more criminal charges or for more serious crimes than can be reasonably

U.S. Attorneys

Violations of federal laws are prosecuted by the U.S. Justice Department. The Justice Department is headed by the U.S. attorney general and staffed by 93 U.S. attorneys (Guam and the Northern Mariana Islands share one), each of whom is nominated to office by the president and confirmed by the Senate. One U.S. attorney is assigned to each of the federal district court jurisdictions. There were approximately 5,000 assistant U.S. attorneys in 2005.

SOURCE: United States Attorneys at www.usdoj.gov/usao/index.html and Executive Office for United States Attorneys, personal communication, July 26, 2005.

nolle prosequi (nol. pros.) The notation placed on the official record of a case when prosecutors elect not to prosecute.

supported by the evidence. They are not supposed to be deterred from prosecution because juries in their jurisdiction have frequently refused to convict persons of particular kinds of crimes. Conversely, they are not supposed to prosecute simply because an aroused public demands it. Prosecutors are not supposed to be influenced by the personal or political advantages or disadvantages that might be involved in prosecuting or not prosecuting a case. Nor, for that matter, are they supposed to be swayed by their desire to enhance their records of successful convictions. It would be naive, however, to believe that those factors do not have at least some influence on prosecutors' decisions to pursue or to drop criminal cases.

Prosecutors sometimes choose not to charge or prosecute criminal cases for any of the following nine additional reasons. The first is their belief that an offense did not cause sufficient harm. This decision is usually a practical one. Given limited time and resources, overworked and understaffed prosecutors often have to choose which cases go forward and which do not.

A second reason involves the relationship between the statutory punishment and the offender or the offense. In today's legal climate of increasingly harsh sentencing laws, a prosecutor may feel that the statutory punishment for a crime is too severe for a particular offender (for example, a first-time offender) or for a particular offense. In an effort to be fair, at least in their own minds, prosecutors in such cases impose their own sense of justice.

A third reason for not prosecuting, even when the three ideal conditions are met, is an improper motive on the part of a complainant. The prosecutor may feel that a criminal charge has been made for the wrong reasons. For example, if a prosecutor were convinced that a woman who caught her husband cheating had lied when charging her husband with beating her, the prosecutor might elect not to charge the husband with assault or some other crime.

A fourth reason prosecutors sometimes choose not to prosecute a case is that the particular law has been violated with impunity for a long time with few complaints by the public. In the case of "blue laws," for example, which may require stores to be closed on Sundays, prosecutors would occasionally get complaints from outraged churchgoers. In some cases, prosecutors simply ignored the complaints because the law, although on the books for decades, had not been enforced for years and few complaints had been received. In most states, incidentally, blue laws have been declared unconstitutional.

A fifth reason prosecutors often choose not to prosecute a case, even though, ideally, prosecution is required, is that a victim may refuse to testify. In rape cases, for example, prosecutors realize that it is nearly impossible to secure a conviction without the testimony of the victim. Thus, if the victim refuses to testify, the prosecutor may decide to drop the case, knowing that the chances of obtaining a conviction are reduced dramatically without the cooperation of the victim.

A sixth reason for not prosecuting has to do with humanitarian concerns for the welfare of the victim or the offender. In child sexual molestation cases, for example, conviction depends on the victim's testimony. Prosecutors may decline to prosecute because of the possible psychological injury to a child who is forced to testify. When offenders are suffering from mental illness, prosecutors may decide that diverting the offender to a mental health facility rather than prosecuting for a crime is in the best interests of all concerned.

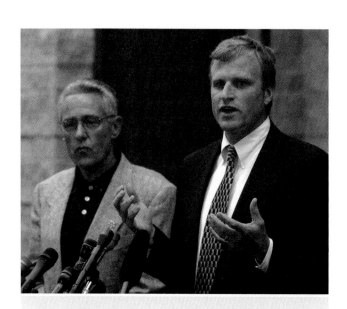

District Attorney Mark Hulbert, right, responds to questions about the arrest of Los Angeles Lakers' star Kobe Bryant during a news conference at the Eagle County Justice Center in Eagle, Colorado. Listening on the left is Sheriff Joseph Hoy. *Was it appropriate for DA Hulbert to hold a press conference about the case? Why or why not?*

Seventh, prosecutors sometimes do not prosecute a case otherwise worthy of prosecution because the accused person cooperates in the apprehension or conviction of other criminal offenders. In drug cases, for example, prosecutors often "cut deals" (make promises not to prosecute) with users or low-level dealers in order to identify "higher-ups" in the drug distribution network. Prosecutors make similar deals with low-level operatives in organized crime.

An eighth reason prosecutors sometimes choose not to prosecute is that the accused is wanted for prosecution of a more serious crime in another jurisdiction. Thus, there is little reason to expend resources prosecuting a case if an offender is likely to receive greater punishment for a crime committed elsewhere. It is easier and cheaper simply to extradite, or to deliver, the offender to the other jurisdiction.

Finally, if an offender is on parole when he or she commits a new crime, prosecutors may not prosecute the new crime because they consider it more cost-effective to simply have the parole revoked and send the offender back to prison.

THE DECISION TO PLEA-BARGAIN Unreviewable discretion in deciding whether to charge and prosecute citizens for their crimes is the principal reason the prosecutor is considered the most powerful figure in the administration of justice, but it is by no means the prosecutor's only source of power. Probably the most strategic source of power available to prosecutors is their authority to decide which cases to "plea-bargain." **Plea bargaining, or plea negotiating,** refers to the practice whereby the prosecutor, the defense attorney, the defendant, and—in many jurisdictions—the judge agree to a negotiated plea. For example, they may agree on a specific sentence to be imposed if the accused pleads guilty to an agreed-upon charge or charges instead of going to trial. It is the prosecutor alone, however, who chooses what lesser plea, if any, will be accepted instead of going to trial. Contrary to popular belief, justice in the United States is dispensed mostly

Not Prosecuting Cases

Insufficient evidence is the most frequent reason given by prosecutors for not prosecuting cases. In most cities, prosecutors refuse to formally charge a person in about one-half of all felony arrests.

plea bargaining or **plea negotiating** The practice whereby the prosecutor, the defense attorney, the defendant, and—in many jurisdictions—the judge agree on a specific sentence to be imposed if the accused pleads guilty to an agreed-upon charge or charges instead of going to trial.

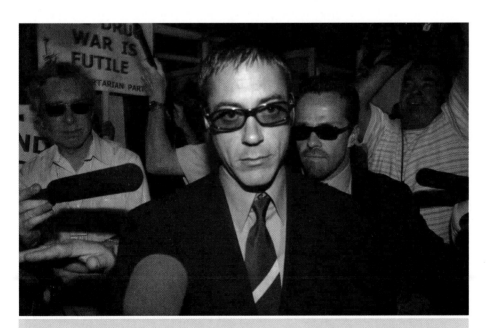

Actor Robert Downey Jr. departs Riverside County Superior Court after pleading no contest to a felony count for cocaine possession and a misdemeanor count for being under the influence of the drug in a plea bargain that allowed him to continue live-in drug treatment, rather than face jail time. *What factors might influence a prosecutor's plea-bargaining decision? Are all of those factors legitimate?*

Guilty Pleas

About 95 percent of all convictions in felony cases are the result of guilty pleas. Guilty pleas account for an even higher percentage of convictions in misdemeanor cases.

SOURCE: See, for example, Matthew R. Durose and Patrick A. Langan "Felony Sentences in State Courts, 2002," *Bureau of Justice Statistics Bulletin* (Washington, DC: GPO, U.S. Department of Justice, December 2004), p. 8, Table 9.

rules of discovery Rules that mandate that a prosecutor provide defense counsel with any exculpatory evidence (evidence favorable to the accused that has an effect on guilt or punishment) in the prosecutor's possession.

Running for Office

In most jurisdictions, prosecutors run for office on either the Democratic or Republican ticket, although in some jurisdictions, they are elected in nonpartisan races—that is, without party affiliation. Although prosecutors can be removed from office for criminal acts or for incompetence, removal is rare.

through plea bargaining. Criminal trials are relatively rare events; plea bargaining is routine. Plea bargaining and the different types of plea bargains will be discussed in more detail later in this chapter.

RECOMMENDING THE AMOUNT OF BAIL In addition to control over charging, prosecuting, and plea bargaining, another source of power for the prosecutor in many jurisdictions is the responsibility of recommending the amount of bail. Although the final decision on the amount or even the opportunity for bail rests with the judge, the prosecutor makes the initial recommendation. By recommending a very high bail amount, an amount that a suspect is unlikely to be able to raise, a prosecutor can pressure a suspect to accept a plea bargain. Bail will be discussed later in this chapter.

RULES OF DISCOVERY Perhaps the only weakness in a prosecutor's arsenal of weapons is the legal rules of discovery. The **rules of discovery** mandate that a prosecutor provide defense counsel with any exculpatory evidence in the prosecutor's possession. *Exculpatory evidence* is evidence favorable to the accused that has an effect on guilt or punishment. Examples of possible exculpatory evidence are physical evidence, evidentiary documents (such as a defendant's recorded statements to police, or reports of medical examinations or scientific tests), and lists of witnesses. A prosecutor's concealment or misrepresentation of evidence is grounds for an appellate court's reversal of a conviction. Defense attorneys, on the other hand, are under no constitutional obligation to provide prosecutors with incriminating evidence. However, most states and the federal system have by statute or by court rules given the prosecution some discovery rights (for example, the right to notice of the defense's intent to use an alibi or an insanity defense). The rationale for the rules of discovery is that, ideally, the prosecutor's job is to see that justice is done and not necessarily to win cases.

SELECTION AND CAREER PROSPECTS OF PROSECUTORS Given the power of prosecutors in the administration of justice, the public can only hope that prosecutors wield their power wisely and justly. We believe that many of them do. Unfortunately, political considerations and aspirations may be too enticing to some prosecutors, causing them to violate the canons of their position. The partisan political process through which the typical prosecutor is elected increases the chances that political influence will affect the prosecutor's decisions.

The potential for political influence is increased even further by prosecutors' frequent use of the position as a stepping-stone to higher political office (several mayors, governors, and presidents have been former prosecutors). There are very few career prosecutors. Those who are not elected to higher political office and those who choose not to seek it typically go into private law practice.

ASSISTANT DISTRICT ATTORNEYS The workhorses of the big-city prosecutor's office, as already noted, are the assistant district attorneys (or deputy district attorneys), who are hired by the prosecutor. Generally, assistant district attorneys are hired right out of law school or after a brief and usually unsuccessful stint in private practice. Most of them remain in the prosecutor's office for only 2 to 4 years and then go into, or back into, private law practice. Reasons for leaving the prosecutor's office include low pay, little chance for advancement, physical and psychological pressures, boredom, and disillusionment with the criminal adjudication process. Assistant district attorneys provide an important social service, and the job is a good way of gaining legal experience. Lawyers who occupy the position, however, usually do not consider it anything more than temporary employment before they go into private practice.

NATIONAL SURVEY OF PROSECUTORS The most recent government survey of prosecutors reported that 2,341 prosecutors' offices handled felony cases in 2001.[21] More than 79,000 attorneys, investigators, victim advocates, and support staff worked in those offices. The average number of employees across all prosecutor offices was 9, including the chief prosecutor. Full-time offices in large districts averaged staffs of 456, with an average of 151 assistant prosecutors, 21 supervisory attorneys (attorneys who also have managerial responsibilities), and 145 support staff. A prosecutorial district consists of one or more counties.

The total amount spent for prosecutorial services nationwide in 2001 was approximately $4.6 billion. The average budget was $2 million. Annual budgets ranged between $6,000 and $373 million. About one-third of the offices did not include in their budgets the costs of expert services, nearly half of the offices excluded investigators' services, about 60 percent of offices excluded DNA testing, and 85 percent of the budgets did not include the costs of social services. Most of the funding for prosecutors' offices came from county governments, although funding in some offices was also received from state governments, city governments, and grant funds.

CAREERS IN CRIMINAL JUSTICE

Assistant State Attorney

My name is Wilson Green and I am an assistant state attorney (prosecutor) in Orlando. I received a BA from Vanderbilt, an MDiv from Reformed Theological Seminary, and my JD from the University of Mississippi, with some navy time along the way. I interviewed for and began my current job about 20 years ago here at the State Attorney's Office.

I am in the homicide unit. Most of us deal either with misdemeanor or felony cases that are set for trial. Most cases are resolved by defendants pleading guilty (or no contest) and being sentenced by a judge, while others proceed to a jury trial. The prosecutor is assigned cases as they come to our office from law enforcement agencies and after the defendants have been formally charged by other attorneys in our office.

The first step is to "work up" each case—to review the entire file (police reports, witness statements, photos, tape recordings, lab reports, etc.) and to send out appropriate "discovery" to the defendant's attorney. Witnesses must be listed and subpoenaed for trial. Requests for further investigation may be needed as the prosecutor anticipates what the defense will probably be. Often the defense attorney will take depositions of state witnesses before trial, which we attend. There may also be pretrial hearings on legal issues, as well as plea negotiations.

Jury trials generally may last a day or so or up to a week or more. A prosecutor may have as many as a hundred cases pending at one time (spread over a period of a few months), with new ones coming in as fast as others are resolved. The stress level can be high at times, due to the caseload, problem cases, witness problems, cases being postponed at the last minute, not knowing which case will actually go to trial until the last minute, and having to make appropriate plea offers. On the plus side, prosecutors (who are to be "ministers of justice," not just "win" cases) have a beneficial role in society, have much discretion in handling their cases, are in the courtroom on a regular basis, and are in touch with the "real world" through their contact with police agencies, witnesses, victims, families of victims, judges, and juries. They can use both common sense and legal training. Each case seems to have something new.

Those considering becoming prosecutors might think about sampling criminal justice and prelaw undergraduate courses, taking advantage of internships with law enforcement agencies or prosecutors' offices, or simply observing court proceedings as a citizen. Use any employment opportunities as a way to gain common-sense experience that will help in a later career. Take advantage of any group or public speaking opportunities as well.

What do you think is the most challenging part of a prosecutor's job? Explain.

State law determines the number of chief prosecutors and whether they are elected or appointed. In 2001, all chief prosecutors were elected, except for those in Alaska, Connecticut, the District of Columbia, and New Jersey, where they were appointed. Nearly 90 percent of chief prosecutors were elected or appointed to 4-year terms. States with the largest number of chief prosecutors were Texas (155), Virginia (120), and Missouri (115).

Chief prosecutors served for an average of about 7 years. Nearly a third of the chief prosecutors had served 4 years or less, while one in five had served 15 years or more. The longest term of service reported in the survey was 40 years.

A chief prosecutor's annual salary depended primarily on whether the job was part-time or full-time and the size of the prosecutorial district. In 2001, 75 percent of chief prosecutors worked in districts with fewer than 100,000 residents, while only 5 percent served in districts with populations of 500,000 or more. Annual salaries of chief prosecutors in 2001 ranged from $10,500 to $189,000. Half of chief prosecutors earned $85,000 or more annually.

Nearly 27,000 assistant prosecutors, including supervisory attorneys, were employed in 2001. Entry-level annual salaries for half of the beginning assistant prosecutors were $35,000 or more. Full-time assistants with 5 years' experience earned $45,000 or more a year, and half of the supervisory attorneys made $60,000 or more a year. About a third of the offices had difficulties in recruiting or retaining staff attorneys. The primary reason for the problems was low salaries.

In 2000, prosecutors' offices closed more than 2.3 million felony cases and nearly seven million misdemeanor cases. That amounted to about 857 felony cases per 100,000 residents and approximately 87 felony cases per assistant prosecutor. As an indication of the importance of plea bargaining, the average number of felony jury trial verdicts per office was eight, while the average conviction rate for felony cases was about 90 percent.

The survey found an element of danger in the work of prosecutors. About 40 percent of prosecutors' offices reported a work-related threat or assault against a staff member in 2001. Approximately one-third of chief prosecutors and one-quarter of assistant prosecutors nationwide received a work-related threat or were assaulted. Consequently, various security measures were used for protection, such as electronic security systems, building guards, metal detectors, electronic surveillance, and police protection. About one in five chief prosecutors carried a firearm for personal security. Generally, the smaller the prosecutor's office, the more likely the chief prosecutor carried a firearm for protection.

THE DEFENSE ATTORNEY

The Sixth Amendment right to privately retained and paid-for counsel has existed in federal courts since the ratification of the Bill of Rights.[22] (The terms *counsel, attorney,* and *lawyer* are interchangeable.) Criminal defendants in state courts did not gain the right until 1954. In the case of *Chandler* v. *Fretag,* the Supreme Court held that the right to a privately retained lawyer is "unqualified"; that is, as long as a criminal defendant (or suspect) can afford to hire an attorney, he or she has the right to be represented by that attorney, not only at trial, but at any stage of the criminal justice process. But what if a criminal defendant were indigent, lacking the funds to hire an attorney? It was not until 1938, in the case of *Johnson* v. *Zerbst,* that the Supreme Court first extended the Sixth Amendment right to court-appointed counsel to indigent defendants facing felony charges in federal trials. Another 25 years passed before the right to court-appointed counsel was extended to indigent defendants facing felony charges in state courts. That right was granted in the

Right to Counsel

The Supreme Court extended the right to court-appointed counsel to indigents in death penalty cases in *Powell* v. *Alabama* (1932). The right, however, was extended only to indigents who were "incapable adequately of making [their] own defense because of ignorance, feeble-mindedness, illiteracy or the like." Moreover, the Court's decision in *Powell* was based on the Fourteenth Amendment right to due process and not on the Sixth Amendment right to counsel.

famous case of *Gideon* v. *Wainwright* (1963). In 1972, in the case of *Argersinger* v. *Hamlin,* the Court extended the Sixth Amendment right to court-appointed counsel to defendants in misdemeanor trials in which a sentence to jail might result. Thus, as a result of those decisions, no person may be imprisoned for any offense, whether classified as petty, misdemeanor, or felony, unless he or she is represented by counsel. If the person cannot afford to hire an attorney, then the court is required to appoint one. However, if there is no possibility of incarceration, then a defendant has no right to state-furnished counsel (see *Scott* v. *Illinois,* 1979). Later, in *Alabama* v. *Shelton* (2002), the Court added that indigents have a right to court-appointed counsel even when a defendant is given "a suspended sentence that may 'end up in the actual deprivation of a person's liberty'."

In other Supreme Court decisions, the Sixth Amendment right to counsel has been extended to indigents at additional *critical stages* and other circumstances in the administration of justice, "where substantial rights of the accused may be affected." Those include (by date of Supreme Court decision):

1. Arraignment, under most circumstances (*Hamilton* v. *Alabama,* 1961).
2. The plea bargaining process (*Carnley* v. *Cochran,* 1962).
3. Initial appearances where defendants may be compelled to make decisions that may later be formally used against them (*White* v. *Maryland,* 1963).
4. Interrogations after formal charges (*Massiah* v. *United States,* 1964).
5. Postcharge police lineups (*United States* v. *Wade,* 1967; *Gilbert* v. *California,* 1967).
6. Sentencing (*Mempa* v. *Rhay,* 1967).
7. Preliminary hearings (*Coleman* v. *Alabama,* 1970).
8. A psychiatric examination used by the prosecution to show that a murder defendant remains dangerous and should receive the death penalty (*Estelle* v. *Smith,* 1981).

To date, the Court has not extended the Sixth Amendment right to counsel to preindictment lineups, booking, grand jury investigations, or appeals after the first one. The Sixth Amendment not only guarantees the right to counsel in the areas to which it has been extended, it also guarantees the right to the "effective assistance of counsel" (see *McMann* v. *Richardson,* 1970). However, it was not until 1984, in the case of *Strickland* v. *Washington,* that the Supreme Court first established standards to define "ineffective assistance of counsel." The Court ruled that two facts must be proved to show that counsel was ineffective: (1) that counsel's performance was "deficient," meaning that counsel was not a "reasonably competent attorney" or that his or her performance was below the standard commonly expected, and (2) that the deficiencies in the attorney's performance were prejudicial to the defense, meaning that there is a "reasonable probability that, but for the counsel's unprofessional errors, the result of the proceeding would have been different." In other words, not only must it be shown that an attorney was incompetent, it must also be shown that there is a reasonable probability that the incompetence led to the final result. Thus, if the defendant were clearly guilty of the crime with which he or she was charged, it would most likely be impossible to win a claim of "ineffective assistance of counsel."

The right to counsel may be waived, but only if the waiver is made knowingly, intelligently, and voluntarily. Thus, the Sixth Amendment has also been interpreted to mean that defendants have the right to represent themselves, that is, to conduct the defense *pro se* (see *Faretta* v. *California,* 1975). However, if defendants choose to represent themselves, they cannot claim later, on appeal, that their defense suffered from ineffective assistance of counsel.

Determining Indigency

In some jurisdictions, indigency is determined by the examination of tax returns or the filing of affidavits documenting resources. Generally, defendants are deemed indigent if their resources place them below the government's official poverty level. In other jurisdictions, indigency is determined simply by defendants' response to the judge's question whether they can afford an attorney.

Source: See, for example, Steven K. Smith and Carol J. DeFrances, "Indigent Defense," *Bureau of Justice Statistics Selected Findings* (Washington, DC: GPO, U.S. Department of Justice, February 1996).

Public Opinion and Lawyers

In 2004, only 18 percent of Americans rated the honesty and ethical standards of lawyers "high" (14 percent) or "very high" (4 percent), 45 percent rated lawyers' honesty and ethical standards "average," 35 percent rated them "low" (24 percent) or "very low" (11 percent).

SOURCE: Roper Center at University of Connecticut, Public Opinion Online, www.web.lexis-nexis.com. ucfproxy.fcla.edu/universe/document?_m=f0222230acfb83883c8460ff9f1f216e&_docnum=8&wchp=dGLzVzz-zSkVA&_.

Lawyers are sometimes vilified by the media and the public for defending people unquestionably guilty of crimes. That lawyers sometimes succeed in getting guilty persons "off" by the skillful use of "legal technicalities" only makes matters worse. However, what some people fail to understand is that in the American system of justice, it is not the role of defense lawyers to decide their clients' guilt or innocence. Rather, the role of defense lawyers is to provide the best possible legal counsel and advocacy within the legal and ethical limits of the profession. Legal and ethical codes forbid lawyers, for example, to mislead the court by providing false information or by using perjured testimony (false testimony under oath). The American system of justice is based on the premise that a person is innocent until proven guilty. In the attempt to ensure, as far as possible, that innocent people are not found guilty of crimes, all persons charged with crimes are entitled to a rigorous defense. The constitutional right to counsel and our adversarial system of justice would be meaningless if lawyers refused to defend clients that they "knew" were guilty.

Not all lawyers are adequately trained to practice in the specialized field of criminal law. Law schools generally require only a one-semester course in criminal law and a one-semester course in criminal procedure, though additional courses may be taken as electives in a typical 6-semester or 3-year program. Many lawyers prefer to practice other, often more lucrative, areas of law, such as corporate, tax, or tort law. Compared with those other areas of legal practice, the practice of criminal law generally provides its practitioner less income, prestige, and status in the community.

For those reasons, criminal defendants in search of counsel are limited by practical considerations. They can choose a privately retained lawyer who specializes in criminal law, if they can afford one. Or, if they are indigent and cannot afford one, they will receive a court-appointed attorney (who may or may not be skilled in the practice of criminal law), a public defender, or a "contract" lawyer. In large cities, there is little problem in locating a criminal lawyer. They are listed in the Yellow Pages of the local telephone book. In rural areas, however, finding a lawyer who specializes in criminal law may be more difficult. Because of the lower volume of criminal cases in rural areas, attorneys who practice in those areas generally must practice all kinds of law to make a living; they cannot afford to specialize. Outside of large cities, then, a criminal defendant may have no better option than to rely on the services of a court-appointed attorney, a public defender, or a contract lawyer, whichever is provided in that particular jurisdiction. Court-appointed attorneys, public defenders, and contract lawyers will be discussed further later in this section.

CRIMINAL LAWYERS In discussing privately retained criminal lawyers, it is useful to think of a continuum. At one end are a very few nationally known, highly paid, and successful criminal lawyers, such as Gerry Spence, Thomas A. Mesereau Jr., and Alan Dershowitz. Those criminal lawyers generally take only three kinds of cases: (1) those that are sensational or highly publicized, (2) those that promise to make new law, or (3) those that involve large fees. A little further along the continuum is another small group of criminal lawyers, those who make a very comfortable living in the large cities of this country by defending professional criminals, such as organized crime members, gamblers, pornographers, and drug dealers. Toward the other end of the continuum are the vast majority of criminal lawyers who practice in the large cities of this country.

Most criminal lawyers must struggle to earn a decent living. They have to handle a large volume of cases to make even a reasonable salary. To attract clients, some criminal lawyers engage in the unethical practice of paying

From left to right, Thomas A. Mesereau Jr., Gerry Spence, and Alan Dershowitz are among the very few nationally known, highly paid, and successful criminal lawyers. *What do you think distinguishes these lawyers from all other lawyers?*

kickbacks to ambulance drivers, police officers, jailers, and bail bonds people for client referrals. Some criminal lawyers also engage in the unethical practice of soliciting new clients in courthouse hallways.

Although a few criminal lawyers are known for their criminal trial expertise, most relatively successful criminal lawyers gain their reputations from their ability to "fix" cases, that is, their ability to produce the best possible outcome for a client, given the circumstances of the case. Fixing cases usually involves plea bargaining but may also include the strategic use of motions for continuances and for changes in the judge assigned to the case. *Who* a lawyer knows is often more important than *what* the lawyer knows. In other words, a close personal relationship with the prosecutor or a hearing before the "right" judge is often far more important to the case's outcome (for example, a favorable plea bargain) than is an attorney's legal ability.

Besides legal expertise and good relationships with other actors in the adjudication process, the only other commodity criminal lawyers have to sell is their time. Thus, for the typical criminal lawyer, time is valuable. As a result, criminal lawyers try to avoid time-consuming court battles and are motivated to get their clients to plead guilty to reduced charges. Another reason most criminal lawyers prefer plea bargaining to trials is that they are more likely to receive a fee, however small, from their typically poor clients for arranging the plea. When cases go to trial and the legal fee has not been paid in advance, there is the possibility that the lawyer will receive no compensation or inadequate compensation from his or her client, especially if the case is lost.

To prevent nonpayment for services, criminal lawyers sometimes engage in unethical, if not illegal, behavior. Sometimes criminal lawyers plea-bargain cases that they know they can win at trial. They do this because they know that their clients do not have the money to compensate them for the time they would put into a trial. If clients have only a few hundred dollars, some unscrupulous criminal lawyers reason that those clients can afford only "bargain" justice. Another unethical tactic some criminal lawyers use to secure a fee from their clients is

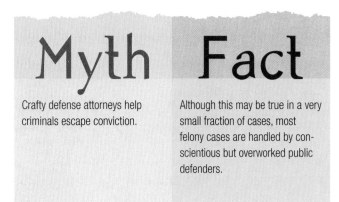

to seek delays in a case and allow their clients to remain in jail until they have been paid for services yet to be performed. Getting a client to pay a legal fee is not a legitimate basis for seeking a court delay.

Criminal lawyers often spend more time at the county jail and the courthouse, where their clients are, than in their offices, which generally are spartan compared with the plush offices of their corporate counterparts. They are sometimes told by their clients about grisly crimes that have been committed or will be committed in the future. Because of attorney-client privilege, the lawyer in possession of this information cannot reveal it, under penalty of disbarment (the revocation of his or her license to practice law). In short, many criminal lawyers are considered somewhat less than respectable by their professional colleagues and much of the general public because their clients are "criminals," they deal with some of the more unsavory aspects of human existence, and a few may engage in unethical behavior to earn a living.

THE COURT-APPOINTED LAWYER In some jurisdictions, criminal suspects or defendants who cannot afford to hire an attorney are provided with court-appointed lawyers. The court-appointed lawyer is usually selected in one of two ways. In some jurisdictions, lawyers volunteer to represent indigent offenders and are appointed by judges on a rotating basis from a list or from lawyers present in the courtroom. In other jurisdictions, lawyers are appointed by a judge from a list of attorneys who are members of the county bar association.

In the past, appointed lawyers frequently represented indigent clients *pro bono* (without pay). Today, however, the vast majority of appointed lawyers are paid by the jurisdiction. Hourly fees are usually much less than would be charged by privately retained counsel. Seldom is money available to hire investigators or to secure the services of expert witnesses, the lack of which weakens the defense that can be provided a client.

In addition, although appointed attorneys may be experts in some areas of law, they may not be familiar with the intricacies of a criminal defense. They may have never before represented a client charged with a crime. Nevertheless, many lawyers view their appointments as a public service and do their best to represent their clients in a professional manner. Some, however, take cases grudgingly (they can refuse an appointment only for very good reasons) and regard an appointment as a financially unrewarding and unpleasant experience. They perform well enough only to escape charges of malpractice. In many cases, an appointed attorney first meets his or her client in the courtroom, where they have a brief conference before a guilty plea is arranged.

THE PUBLIC DEFENDER In many jurisdictions today, people who are charged with crimes and cannot afford an attorney are provided with public defenders. Public defenders are paid a fixed salary by a jurisdiction (city, county, state, or federal) to defend indigents charged with crimes. Frequently, public defenders are assigned to courtrooms instead of to specific clients. They defend all of the indigent clients who appear in their courtrooms. As a result, a defendant may have a different public defender at different stages in the process (for example, preliminary hearing, arraignment, and trial). Public defenders commonly spend only 5 to 10 minutes with their clients. In addition, this bureaucratic arrangement makes the public defender a part of a courtroom work group that includes the judge, the prosecutor, and the other

Wrongful Convictions

An estimated 35,000 people are convicted wrongfully in American courts every year.

SOURCE: Based on figures provided in C. Ronald Huff, Arye Rattner, and Edward Sagarin, "Guilty Until Proven Innocent: Wrongful Conviction and Public Policy," *Crime and Delinquency* 32 (1986), pp. 518–44, and U.S. Department of Justice, Federal Bureau of Investigation, *Crime in the United States*, 2004 at www.fbi.gov/ucr/cius_04/persons_arrested/index.html.

courtroom actors with whom the public defender interacts daily. This work group, in turn, may be more interested in processing cases efficiently and maintaining cooperative relationships with each other than in pursuing adversarial justice. Nevertheless, despite the method of assignment, the impersonal nature of the defense, and the potential conflict of interest, most indigent clients in criminal cases prefer public defenders to court-appointed attorneys because public defenders practice criminal law full-time.

Like prosecutors, many public defenders regard their position not as a career, but as a valuable learning experience that will eventually lead to private law practice.

CAREERS IN CRIMINAL JUSTICE

Public Defender

My name is Junior A. Barrett and I am an assistant public defender in the Major Crimes Unit of the Public Defender Office in the Ninth Judicial Circuit (Orange and Osceola Counties in Florida). I have a bachelor of science degree in Criminal Justice Administration and Planning from John Jay College of Criminal Justice, City University of New York. I also have a juris doctor degree from Union University, Albany Law School, Albany, New York.

My decision to represent indigent clients was made before I even started college. I wanted to do something that was not only challenging, but where I felt I could help the poor. Growing up on the island of Jamaica and in Brooklyn, New York, I saw what can happen to people who don't receive proper legal representation. I knew people who were railroaded by the criminal justice system and by lawyers who did not really care, but instead saw what they did as just a job.

I started working for the Public Defender's Office in July of 1991 doing misdemeanor and traffic-related offenses. About six years ago, I was promoted to the Major Crimes Unit where I represent clients charged with capital sexual battery and first-degree murder.

My days are never typical. Sometimes they start with a trip to the Orange County Jail to talk to a client about his case and what we will need to do to prepare for court. Another day might begin with me sitting down with an investigator to talk about locating witnesses.

A large portion of my day is spent trying to reconstruct my client's life and reviewing evidence. Reconstructing my client's life involves contacting family and friends of my client. It also involves my spending a lot of time contacting different agencies in order to get copies of my client's school records, medical records, mental health records, military records, job records, and even records of

time the client spent in jail or prison. This information is then used to try and convince a jury that my client should not be executed.

Ultimately, everything I do is in preparation for trying the case. A first-degree murder trial usually takes about a week to try. If the death penalty is involved, it can take two weeks. Often, the case does not end at a trial. There are appeals, rehearings, and sometimes even retrials. It is hard to say what I like best and least about my job. Sometimes it is seeing the tears of joy running down the cheeks of my client as a jury says not guilty. Sometimes it is knowing that the State of Florida will not be able to execute my client. Other times it is the camaraderie that I find in the Public Defender's Office. On the flip side, one of the things I enjoy least about my job is a verdict of guilty in spite of the evidence. I also dislike the fact that even after a verdict of not guilty, my client's life is ruined forever. I have had clients who have lost many months of their lives because they were in jail awaiting a final disposition of their case. There is no way to give back to an innocent client the months he sat in jail waiting to be tried by a jury.

The job of an assistant public defender is a morally rewarding one. You deal with real-life situations that are often interesting, challenging, and fast paced. You put in long hours for little pay. You have to deal with assistant state attorneys who think your clients are scum, judges who care little for your clients' rights, and clients who sometimes verbally abuse you. If you can handle all that, at the end of the day you will feel that you have truly helped another human being. You have to be prepared to fight the good fight.

Would you choose to defend indigent clients? Why or why not?

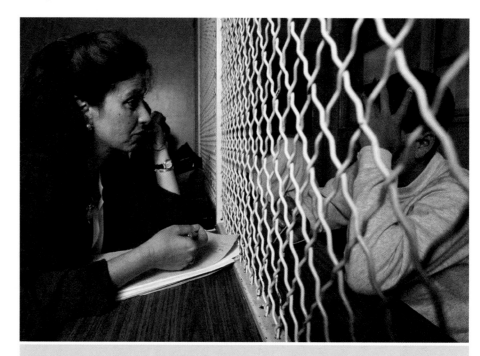

Defense lawyers spend much of their time at the local jail. *Do you think that the jail setting influences a lawyer's opinion of his or her client?*

Female Lawyers

In 1971, just 3 percent of all lawyers in the United States were women. By 1980, the percentage of female lawyers had increased to 8 percent, and by 2005, about 29 percent of all lawyers were women. In 1961, only 4 percent of the 16,489 first-year law students were women. In 2005, nearly half of the 48,239 first-year law students were women. Still, women comprise only about 17 percent of the partners in the nation's approximately 50,000 major law firms. The percentage of associates is much higher (about 43 percent). In 1981, Sandra Day O'Connor became the first female justice of the U.S. Supreme Court. Ruth Bader Ginsburg became the second in 1993. Also in 1993, Janet Reno became the first female attorney general of the United States.

SOURCE: American Bar Association, Commission on Women in the Profession, "A Current Glance at Women in the Law 2005" at www.abanet.org/women/womenstatistics.html; "Despite Gains, Women Lawyers Still Face Bias," *The Orlando Sentinel*, August 18, 1996, p. A20; "Where My Girls At? Women Are Finally Catching Up to Men in Law School Enrollment," *The Princeton Review* at www.princetonreview.com/law/research/articles/decide/gender.asp.

THE CONTRACT LAWYER A relatively new and increasingly popular way of providing for indigent defense is the contract system. In this system, private attorneys, law firms, and bar associations bid for the right to represent a jurisdiction's indigent defendants. Terms of contracts differ, but in the typical contract, counsel agrees to represent either all or a specified number of indigent defendants in a jurisdiction during a certain period of time, in exchange for a fixed dollar amount. Contracts are awarded on the basis of costs to the jurisdiction, qualifications of bidders, and other factors.

In certain situations, some jurisdictions employ a combination of indigent defense systems. For example, jurisdictions that regularly use public defenders sometimes contract out the defense of cases where there is a conflict of interest (for example, multiple-defendant cases) or cases that require special expertise (such as some death penalty cases).

COMPARING INDIGENT DEFENSE SYSTEMS At the end of the twentieth century, 90 percent of the nation's 100 most populous counties had public defender programs, 89 percent had assigned counsel programs, and 42 percent had contract programs.[23] More than $1 billion were spent on indigent defense in the most populous counties in 1999: approximately 73 percent on public defender programs, 21 percent on assigned counsel programs, and 6 percent on awarded contracts. County governments provided 60 percent of the funding, and state governments provided 25 percent of the funding.

The 100 most populous counties provided indigent defense in more than four million cases in 1999. More than 80 percent of the cases were handled by public defenders, 15 percent were handled by court-appointed private attorneys, and 3 percent by contract attorneys. Conviction rates for indigent defendants in federal and state courts were about the same as they were for defendants with privately retained counsel. However, incarceration rates were higher for defendants with publicly financed attorneys than for those with privately retained counsel: in the federal courts, 88 percent to 77 percent, and in the state courts,

71 percent to 54 percent. Ironically, the length of jail or prison sentence was shorter for defendants with publicly financed attorneys. Those defendants with publicly financed attorneys received sentences in federal courts that averaged just less than 5 years; those with privately retained counsel averaged sentences of a little more than 5 years. In the state courts, defendants with publicly financed attorneys received sentences that averaged about 2.5 years, while those with privately retained counsel received sentences that averaged about 3 years.

Nearly 70 percent of state prison inmates had attorneys appointed by the court. However, among minorities the percentage was higher: 77 percent of black inmates and 73 percent of Hispanic inmates. Among federal prison inmates, 65 percent of blacks, 57 percent of whites, and 56 percent of Hispanics had publicly financed attorneys.

THE JUDGE

For most people, black-robed judges are the embodiment of justice, and although they are generally associated with trials, judges actually have a variety of responsibilities in the criminal justice process.[24] Among their non-trial duties are determining probable cause, signing warrants, informing suspects of their rights, setting and revoking bail, arraigning defendants, and accepting guilty pleas. Judges spend much of the workday in their chambers (offices), negotiating procedures and dispositions with prosecutors and defense attorneys. The principal responsibility of judges in all their duties is to ensure that suspects and defendants are treated fairly and in accordance with due process of law.

Furthermore, in jurisdictions without professional court administrators, judges are responsible for the management of their own courtrooms and staff. Judges in some jurisdictions are also responsible for the entire courthouse and its personnel, with the added duties of supervising building maintenance, budgeting, and labor relations.

In jury trials, judges are responsible for allowing the jury a fair chance to reach a verdict on the evidence presented. Judges must ensure that their behavior does not improperly affect the outcome of the case. Before juries retire to deliberate and reach a verdict, judges instruct them on the relevant law. This involves interpreting legal precedents and applying them to the unique circumstances of the case. Those jury instructions are reviewable by an appellate court.

CHARACTERISTICS OF JUDGES In the United States, judges are overwhelmingly white and male. They generally come from upper-middle-class backgrounds, are Protestant, are better educated than most citizens, and average over 50 years of age. A majority of them were in private legal practice before becoming judges. Most were born in the communities in which they preside and attended college and law school in that state.

SELECTION OF JUDGES States vary in the ways they select judges. The two most common selection methods are election and merit selection. Other, less common ways of selecting judges are gubernatorial appointment and legislative election.

Like prosecutors, many state judges are elected to their positions in either partisan (with political party designation) or nonpartisan elections. This selection process exposes judges, like prosecutors, to potential charges of political influence. It may also discourage some of the best lawyers from becoming judges. Successful lawyers with lucrative practices may not want to interrupt their careers to take the chance of becoming a judge, only to lose the position in the next election. Besides, successful lawyers generally earn much more money than judges.

In an attempt to reduce the appearance of possible political influence, several states have adopted merit selection, sometimes referred to as the "Missouri

Judicial History

According to the Bible, the idea of judges was first suggested to Moses by his father-in-law, Jethro. Following their exodus from Egypt, the Hebrews, having been slaves, had no formal government. Because Moses was the only one among them with evident authority, he served as arbiter of domestic controversies—a time-consuming and exhausting job. Jethro recognized the problem with this arrangement and suggested to Moses that he create a kind of theocracy. Moses would be the supreme judge and would represent the people before God. He would also teach the people laws governing everyday behavior. The actual administration of the laws, which came from God through Moses, was to be handled "by able men, . . . such as fear God, men who are trustworthy and who hate a bribe." These "judges" were to be established in a hierarchical order, so that the highest would be rulers over thousands of people; beneath them would be, successively, rulers of hundreds, fifties, and tens.

SOURCE: Elisha P. Douglass, "Judges Were Suggested by Jethro," *The Anniston* (Alabama) *Star,* June 9, 1983.

Judges spend much of their workday in their chambers (offices). *How does this differ from what the public generally believes about judges?*

Plan," as their method of selecting judges. First used in Missouri in 1940, merit selection is a process in which the governor appoints judges from a list of qualified lawyers compiled by a nonpartisan nominating commission composed of both lawyers and other citizens. After serving a short term on the bench, usually 1 year, the appointed judges face the voters in an uncontested election. Voters are instructed to vote yes or no on whether the judge should be retained in office. If a majority vote yes, the judge remains in office for a full term (usually 6 years; the range is 4 years to life). In Illinois, a judge must receive at least 60 percent of the votes. Toward the end of the term, the judge must face the voters again in the same kind of election. The merit plan does not entirely eliminate political influence from the selection process, but it seems to have less potential for influence than the direct popular election of judges.

- As of June 2004, states used the following methods for initially selecting their highest *appellate court judges:*

  Merit selection—24 states (and the District of Columbia)
  Nonpartisan election—15 states
  Partisan election—6 states
  Appointment by the governor—4 states
  Appointment by the legislature—1 state

- As of the same date, states used the following methods for initially selecting their *general-jurisdiction court judges:*

  Nonpartisan election—18 states
  Merit selection—17 states (and the District of Columbia)
  Partisan election—9 states
  Appointment by the governor—3 states
  Election by the legislature—1 state

In California, local voters can choose either nonpartisan elections or gubernatorial appointment of general-jurisdiction court judges. In Kansas, in 17 of 31 districts, merit selection is used; the remaining 14 employ partisan elections.[25]

QUALIFICATIONS AND TRAINING   Although in most jurisdictions lower-court judges are not required to be lawyers or to possess any special educational or professional training, nearly all states require judges who sit on the benches of appellate courts and trial courts of general jurisdiction to be licensed attorneys and members of the state bar association. However, being a lawyer is not the same as being a judge. Many judges come to the bench without any practical experience with criminal law or procedure. Consequently, many states now require new appellate court and trial court judges to attend state-sponsored judicial training seminars. In addition, more than 1,500 judges a year take 1- to 4-week summer courses offered by the National Judicial College, founded in 1963 and located at the University of Nevada, Reno. Despite those efforts, most judges still learn the intricacies of their profession "on the job."

Pretrial Stages

Probably fewer than one-half of the crimes committed each year are reported to the police, and, of those, only a fraction are officially recorded. Of the crimes that are recorded by the police, only about 20 percent are "cleared by arrest." Still, an arrest by no means guarantees prosecution and conviction. As a result of initial prosecutorial screening, for example, about 25 percent of all arrests are rejected, diverted, or referred to other jurisdictions. Another 20 percent or so of all people arrested are released later for various reasons during one of the pretrial stages. Thus a powerful "funneling" or screening process in the administration of justice eliminates about one-half of all persons arrested. Figures 5.5 and 5.6 illustrate this funneling or screening process.

FIGURE 5.5	Funneling Effect

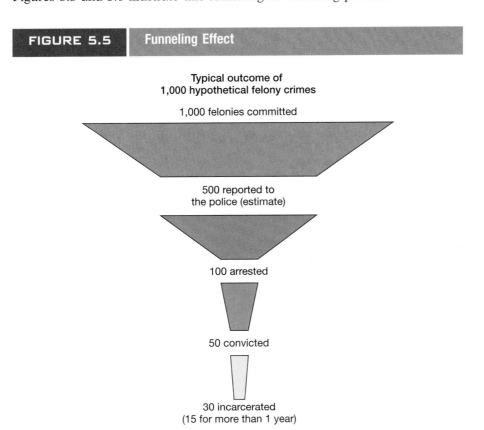

Typical outcome of
1,000 hypothetical felony crimes

1,000 felonies committed

500 reported to
the police (estimate)

100 arrested

50 convicted

30 incarcerated
(15 for more than 1 year)

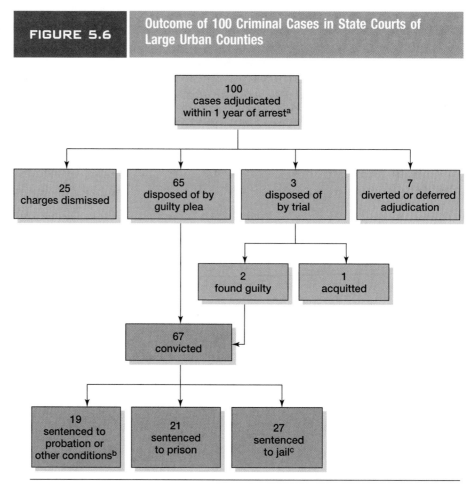

FIGURE 5.6 Outcome of 100 Criminal Cases in State Courts of Large Urban Counties

[a] From May 2002–May 2003.
[b] Other conditions include fines, community service, and treatment.
[c] Includes split sentences (jail and probation).

Source: Adapted from Thomas H. Cohen and Brian A. Reaves, *Felony Defendants in Large Urban Counties, 2002* (Washington, DC: GPO, U.S. Department of Justice, Bureau of Justice Statistics, February 2006).

The pretrial stages do not have the same names or order in every jurisdiction. So what follows should be considered only a general overview. States are required to provide only a prompt, neutral review of the evidence to determine whether there is probable cause that the suspect/defendant committed the crime or crimes with which he or she is charged. *Probable cause,* which was described in more detail in Chapter 1, is an abstract term that basically means that a law enforcement officer or a judge has trustworthy evidence that would make a reasonable person believe that, more likely than not, the proposed action, such as an arrest, is justified. Figure 1.1 in Chapter 1 provides a simplified view of the caseflow through the criminal justice process, highlighting pretrial stages.[26] The pretrial stages typical of many jurisdictions are described following a brief consideration of caseflow management.

CASEFLOW MANAGEMENT

Increasingly large caseloads in the state and federal courts are requiring new management skills that enable the courts to process a huge volume of civil and criminal cases as efficiently as possible. In a recent book on the subject, caseflow management was called "the conceptual heart of judicial administration in the new millennium."[27] Today's court administrators (see the nearby Careers in Criminal Justice box entitled Trial Court Administrator) are being influenced by basic business principles. Among the subjects being learned about managing jury trials, for example, are "How to Relieve Juror Boredom," "Routine Use of Anonymous Juries," "Juror Questions to Witnesses," and "Post-verdict Debriefings with the Trial Judge."[28] There is even a manual entitled *Managing Notorious Cases.*[29]

FROM ARREST THROUGH INITIAL APPEARANCE

Soon after most suspects are arrested, they are taken to the police station to be "booked." **Booking** is the process in which suspects' names, the charges for which they were arrested, and perhaps their fingerprints or photographs are entered on the police blotter. Following booking, a prosecutor is asked to review the facts of the case and, considering the available evidence, to decide whether a suspect should be charged with a crime or crimes (sometimes

booking The administrative recording of an arrest. Typically, the suspect's name, the charge, and perhaps the suspect's fingerprints or photographs are entered in the police blotter.

CAREERS IN CRIMINAL JUSTICE

Trial Court Administrator

My name is Todd Nuccio. I am the trial court administrator for the 26th Judicial District in North Carolina. The district encompasses Charlotte and greater Mecklenburg County. It is the largest jurisdiction in the state serving approximately 700,000 people.

I have a BA in political science from Northern Illinois University and an MS in judicial administration from the University of Denver, College of Law. I recently received another BA in psychology from the University of North Carolina at Charlotte because I have come to learn that 90 percent of successfully managing an organization depends upon one's ability to understand and motivate people.

During my final undergraduate semester, a constitutional law professor told me about a program that combined aspects of public administration and law.

Since graduation, I have held the position of assistant court administrator in the 7th Judicial District of Iowa, the trial court administrator position in the 12th Judicial District in North Carolina, and my current position here in Charlotte.

The responsibilities of a trial court administrator are similar to the more commonly known position of hospital administrator. The only difference is that the hospital administrator manages operations for doctors, whereas the trial court administrator manages operations for lawyers serving in the capacity of judges.

Court administration involves everything that goes into making a court system good or bad. The court manager's mission is to improve the administration of justice by: (1) working with other court officials to facilitate change, (2) initiating and coordinating discussions that form the basis of consensus, and (3) identifying problems and recommending solutions that lead to a more accessible, accountable, effective, and efficient court system.

My primary responsibilities include developing local rules and administrative policies to facilitate calendaring and administrative activities, research, strategic planning, case-flow and jury management, budgeting, personnel oversight, facilities management, grant procurement, program development, project management, coordination of alternative dispute-resolution programs, and oversight of the drug treatment and family court operations and collections department.

What I like best about my job is the variety. There are always new programs to develop and projects to manage.

What do you think are the pros and cons of being a trial court administrator?

prosecutors review a case prior to the arrest). As a result of the review, the prosecutor may tell the police that they do not have a case or that the case is weak, requiring further investigation and additional evidence.

However, if the prosecutor decides that a suspect is "chargeable," the prosecutor prepares a charging document. The crime or crimes with which the suspect is charged may or may not be the same crime or crimes for which the suspect was originally arrested.

There are three primary kinds of charging documents: (1) a complaint, (2) an information, and (3) a grand jury indictment. If the offense is either a misdemeanor or an ordinance violation, then the prosecutor in many jurisdictions prepares a complaint. A **complaint** is a charge that an offense has been committed by a person or persons named or described. Complaints must be supported by the oath or affirmation of either the arresting officer or the victim. If the offense is a felony, an information is used in those states that do not rely on a grand jury indictment. An **information** outlines the formal charge or charges, the law or laws that have been violated, and the evidence to support the charge or charges. A **grand jury indictment,** on the other hand, is a written accusation by a grand jury charging that one or more persons have committed a crime. Informations and grand juries are described later in this section.

On rare occasions, the police obtain an arrest warrant from a lower-court judge prior to making an arrest. An **arrest warrant** is a written order directing law enforcement officers to arrest a person. The charge or charges against a suspect are specified on the warrant. An example of an arrest warrant is provided in Chapter 3, Figure 3.3. Police officers more frequently make an arrest and then apply for an arrest warrant. Some jurisdictions have created joint police-prosecution teams so that decisions about arrest and chargeability can be coordinated and can be made early on. If no charges are filed, the suspect must be released.

After the charge or charges have been filed, suspects, who are now *defendants,* are brought before a lower-court judge for an initial appearance, where they are given formal notice of the charges against them and advised of their constitutional rights (for example, the right to counsel). The right to notice and a hearing is the very core of what is meant by due process. In *Twining* v. *New Jersey* (1908), for example, the Supreme Court held that "due process requires . . . that there shall be notice and opportunity for hearing given the parties. . . . [T]hese two fundamental conditions . . . seem to be universally prescribed in all systems of law established by civilized countries." Later, in *In re Oliver* (1948), the Court opined, "A person's right to reasonable notice of a charge against him, and an opportunity to be heard in his defense—a right to his day in court—are basic in our system of jurisprudence." The reason for the right is to prevent the practice, common in some countries, of holding suspects indefinitely without telling them why they are being held.

For misdemeanors or ordinance violations, a summary trial may be held at the initial appearance. About 75 percent of misdemeanants and ordinance violators plead guilty at the initial appearance and are sentenced on the spot. For felonies, a hearing is held to determine whether the suspect should be released or whether there is probable cause to hold the suspect for a preliminary hearing. If the suspect is to be held for a preliminary hearing, bail may be set if the judge believes release on bail is appropriate.

One of the critical questions about the initial appearance is how long suspects may be held in jail before being brought before a judge. In some countries the answer to the question is "indefinitely," but in the United States there is a limit so that innocent persons are not left in jail too long. If suspects are freed after having posted station-house bail (based on a bail fee

complaint A charging document specifying that an offense has been committed by a person or persons named or described; usually used for misdemeanors and ordinance violations.

information A document that outlines the formal charge or charges, the law or laws that have been violated, and the evidence to support the charge or charges.

grand jury indictment A written accusation by a grand jury charging that one or more persons have committed a crime.

arrest warrant A written order directing law enforcement officers to arrest a person. The charge or charges against a suspect are specified on the warrant.

schedule for minor offenses posted at the police station), then the initial appearance may be several days after the arrest. However, if suspects remain in custody (the usual scenario), they must be brought for an initial appearance "without unnecessary delay." In 1975, in *Gerstein* v. *Pugh,* the Supreme Court held that a "prompt" judicial hearing is required in a warrantless arrest to determine whether the officer had probable cause to make the arrest. The vast majority of arrests are warrantless. If suspects are not brought before a judge promptly, then they are to be released. The one exception to this requirement is suspects arrested on a Friday night and not brought before a judge until Monday morning.

A problem with the Supreme Court's promptness requirement is that the Court did not define *prompt.* The norm in most jurisdictions was between 24 and 72 hours. Even after the ruling, however, some jurisdictions held suspects much longer than that. For example, in 1975, a district court judge in Birmingham, Alabama, ruled that because of abusive holding practices in that city, suspects arrested on a felony charge could not be held longer than 24 hours. In 1984, the same judge set a new limit of 8 hours for holding suspects, because his previous order had been ignored. The judge added, however, that in certain cases a limited time extension could be obtained. In 1991, in *County of Riverside* v. *McLaughlin,* the Supreme Court finally clarified the situation by ruling that anyone arrested without a warrant may be held no longer than 48 hours before a judge decides whether the arrest was justified.

BAIL AND OTHER METHODS OF PRETRIAL RELEASE

A **bail bond** or **bail** is usually a monetary guarantee deposited with the court that is supposed to ensure that the suspect or defendant will appear at a later stage in the criminal justice process. In other words, it allows suspects or defendants to remain free while awaiting the next stage in the adjudication process. It is *not* a fine or a penalty; it is only an incentive to appear. Opportunities for bail follow arrest, initial appearance, preliminary hearing, arraignment, and conviction.

Although bail-setting practices vary widely by jurisdiction, the amount of bail, assuming that bail is granted, generally depends on the likelihood that the suspect or defendant will appear in court as required. If the suspect or defendant has strong ties to the community—for example, a house, a family, or a job—then the amount of bail will be relatively low (depending on the seriousness of the offense and other factors). However, if the suspect or defendant has few or no ties to the community, the amount of bail will be relatively high, or the judge may refuse to grant bail.

Next to likelihood of appearance, the most important factor in a judge's determination of the amount of bail—and, perhaps, whether bail is granted at all—is the seriousness of the crime. Generally, the more serious the crime, the higher the bail amount. A third influence on the amount of bail is prior criminal record. A prior criminal record usually increases the amount of bail. Jail conditions are a fourth influencing factor—at least on whether bail is set. If the jail is overcrowded, as are many of the jails in the United States, judges are more likely to grant bail, particularly in borderline cases.

In rare cases, when a judge believes that a suspect or defendant would pose a threat to the community if released, the judge can refuse to set bail. Holding suspects or defendants in jail without giving them an opportunity to post bail, because of the threat they pose to society, is called **preventive detention.** Preventive detention is used most often in cases involving violent crimes, drug crimes, and immigration offenses. However, in *U.S.* v. *Salerno* (1987), the Supreme Court made clear that before a judge can legally deny bail for reasons

bail bond/bail Usually a monetary guarantee deposited with the court to ensure that suspects or defendants will appear at a later stage in the criminal justice process.

Bail

The granting of bail and pretrial release to criminal suspects was common practice in England by the twelfth century. It was officially recognized and legally regulated by the Statute of Westminster in 1275.

Source: No author, "Bail: An Ancient Practice Reexamined," *Yale Law Journal* 70 (1961), pp. 966–77.

preventive detention Holding suspects or defendants in jail without giving them an opportunity to post bail, because of the threat they pose to society.

Myth   Fact

Preventive detention will reduce violent crime.

Preventive detention is not new and has always been used by judges in the United States, even though it was not referred to by that name. Judges simply set bail at a level beyond the financial means of a person suspected of violent crime.

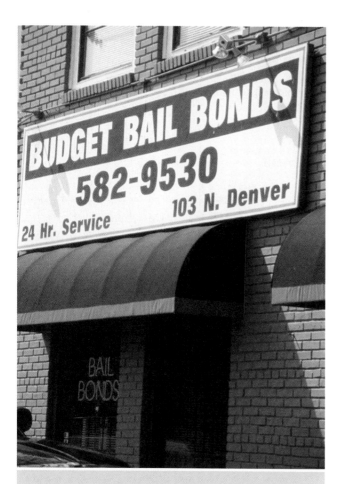

Without the cooperation of the bail bond industry, jail populations would be unmanageable. *Is that reason enough to allow the bail bond industry to exist?*

of preventive detention, a suspect or defendant must have the opportunity for a hearing on the decision. At the hearing, the individual circumstances of the suspect or defendant (such as community ties, convictions, and past dangerous tendencies) must be considered. About 60 percent of all states and the federal jurisdiction have enacted laws that provide for some form of preventive detention, although the laws, at least at the state level, are rarely implemented. The reason is that they are unnecessary. Judges have traditionally imposed high bail amounts on dangerous suspects or defendants. Preventive detention has been employed more frequently at the federal level.

For suspects or defendants who cannot afford to post bail, professional bonds people, who are private entrepreneurs, are available to post it for them for a nonrefundable fee. The fee is typically 10 percent of the required amount. Thus, a bonds person would collect $500 for posting a $5,000 bond. If a suspect or a defendant is considered a greater than average risk, then the bonds person can require collateral—something of value like money or property—in addition to the fee.

Bail bonds people are under no obligation to post a surety bond if they believe that a suspect or a defendant is a bad risk. If bonds people believe that a client might flee and not appear as required, they have the right to revoke the bond without refunding the fee. Bail bonds people or their agents (modern-day bounty hunters known as "skip tracers") are also allowed, without a warrant, to track down clients who fail to appear and to return them forcibly, if necessary, to the jurisdiction from which they fled. If the client crosses state lines, the bonds person does not have to seek extradition, as would a law enforcement official, to bring the client back. Clients sign extradition waivers as a condition of receiving bail.

In practice, most bail bonds people assume little risk. Many of them use part of their fee (generally 30 percent) to secure a surety bond from a major insurance company, which then assumes financial liability if the bail is forfeited. However, even this practice is unnecessary in many jurisdictions because the courts do not collect forfeited bonds. Judges are able to use their discretion to simply vacate outstanding bonds and, by doing so, relieve the bail bonds person or the insurance company of any financial obligation. Judges vacate bonds because they realize that without the cooperation of bail bonds people, the courts would be faced with an unmanageably large jail population and prohibitively high pretrial detention costs. If the bond is not vacated, the bonds person will generally stop looking for the fugitive after 2 years because, by then, there is little chance that the bonds person will get his or her money back.[30]

Suspects or defendants who post their own bail ("full cash bond," 100 percent of the amount required), or have family members or friends do it for them, get it all back after they appear. Sometimes the court will accept property instead of cash. If the suspect or defendant does not appear, the bail is forfeited and the judge issues a **bench warrant** or *capias* authorizing the suspect's or defendant's arrest. It is estimated that about 10,000 criminal defendants skip bail each year, costing local governments tens of millions of dollars. Part of the problem is that overburdened courts are not pursuing many criminal defendants on bond that fail to appear. Another problem is that new companies are writing bonds for more high-risk defendants. However, not all bail skippers flee. Some are just irresponsible and do not come to court until someone drags them in. Others change their address so often they do not receive the notices to appear. Still others do not appear because they are in jail or prison in other counties or states.[31] Once arrested, the absconder must be brought before the judge who issued the warrant and cannot be released on bail again. Failure to appear also constitutes a new offense, "bond jumping," that carries criminal penalties.

Courts in Illinois, Kentucky, and Pennsylvania, as well as the federal courts, allow defendants to post 10 percent of the required bond (*deposit bond*) directly with the court, thereby circumventing the need for bail bonds people. When a defendant makes all required court appearances, 90 percent of the amount posted is refunded (the remaining 10 percent covers administrative costs). Defendants who fail to appear are still liable for the entire bail amount.

The Eighth Amendment to the Constitution does not require that bail be granted to all suspects or defendants. It requires only that the amount of bail, when granted, not be excessive. What constitutes excessive bail is determined by several factors, including the nature and circumstances of the offense, the weight of evidence against the suspect/defendant, the character of the suspect/defendant, and the ability of the suspect/defendant to provide bail. The Eighth Amendment protection against excessive bail (and fines) is one of two Bill of Rights guarantees dealing directly with criminal justice that has not been extended to the states. (The other is the Fifth Amendment right to a grand jury indictment in felony cases. See *Hurtado* v. *California*, 1884.) However, there is a good possibility that the protection against excessive bail will be incorporated and made applicable to state-level criminal cases when the issue is finally brought before the Supreme Court.

The bail system has been criticized for unfairly discriminating against the poor, who are the least likely to have the assets for their own bail and are least able to pay the fee to a bail bonds person. In most jurisdictions, defendants held in jail because they are unable to post bail (about one-half of the jail population nationwide) are mixed with the rest of the jail population, that is, convicted offenders. They are also treated in the same way as the rest of the jail population. One of the tragedies of this practice is the occasional brutalization (for example, rape) of the jailed indigent defendant whose case is later dismissed for lack of evidence or who is found not guilty at trial. Although brutalization of any prisoner is horrible and reprehensible, it is particularly so when the prisoner is an innocent person.

Jailed indigent defendants are also likely to lose their jobs and have their personal lives disrupted in other ways as a result of their detention. Studies consistently show that jailed defendants, who are frequently brought into court in jail clothes and handcuffs, are more likely to be indicted and convicted and are sentenced more severely than defendants who have been released pending the next stage in the process. However, it is not clear whether those disparities are the result of pretrial detention or of the selection process

bench warrant or *capias* A document that authorizes a suspect's or defendant's arrest for not appearing in court as required.

Myth
The most dangerous defendants released on bail are the ones least likely to appear as required.

Fact
Defendants accused of minor offenses and released on bail have the highest rates of failure to appear.

FYI

Release on Bail

About 85 percent of all suspects or defendants are released prior to the final disposition of their cases but, in some jurisdictions, as many as 90 percent of them are held in jail because they are unable to afford bail.

release on own recognizance (ROR) A release secured by a suspect's written promise to appear in court.

conditional release A form of release that requires that a suspect/defendant maintain contact with a pretrial release program or undergo regular drug monitoring or treatment.

unsecured bond An arrangement in which bail is set but no money is paid to the court.

preliminary hearing In a felony case, a pretrial stage at which a judge determines whether there is probable cause to support the charge or charges imposed by the prosecutor.

in which suspects or defendants charged with more serious crimes and with prior criminal records are more likely to be denied bail.

When the crime is minor and suspects or defendants have ties to the community, they are generally released on their own recognizance. **Release on own recognizance (ROR)** is simply a release secured by a suspect's written promise to appear in court. Another nonfinancial means of release, more restrictive than ROR, is **conditional release.** This form of release (sometimes called *supervised release*) usually requires that a suspect/defendant maintain contact with a pretrial release program or undergo regular drug monitoring or treatment. Some conditional release programs also require a third-party custody agreement (that is, a promise by a reputable person to monitor the person released). Another way that suspects or defendants are released without a financial requirement is by **unsecured bond.** Under this arrangement, bail is set, but no money is paid to the court. Suspects or defendants are liable for the full amount of bail if they do not appear as required.

INFORMATION

If the decision is made to prosecute a defendant, in states that do not use grand juries, the prosecutor drafts a document called an *information.* The information outlines the formal charge or charges, the law or laws that have been violated, and the evidence to support the charge or charges. The information is generally filed with the court at the preliminary hearing or, if the preliminary hearing is waived, at the arraignment.

PRELIMINARY HEARING

The purpose of the **preliminary hearing,** used in about one-half of all states, is for a judge to determine whether there is probable cause to support the charge or charges imposed by the prosecutor. Preliminary hearings are used only in felony cases, and defendants may waive the right to the hearing. A preliminary hearing is similar to a criminal trial in two ways but also differs from a criminal trial in two ways. It is similar in that defendants can be represented by legal counsel and can call witnesses on their behalf. It differs in that the judge must determine only that there is probable cause that the defendant committed the crime or crimes with which he or she is charged. At criminal trials, guilt must be determined "beyond a reasonable doubt." Also, at preliminary hearings, unlike criminal trials, defendants have no right to be heard by a jury.

If the judge determines that there is probable cause that a defendant committed the crime or crimes with which he or she is charged, then the defendant is bound over for possible indictment in states with grand juries or for arraignment on an information in states without grand juries. In grand jury states, even if the judge at the preliminary hearing rules that there is insufficient evidence to proceed, the case is not necessarily dropped. The prosecutor could take the case directly to the grand jury. If the case is not dropped for lack of evidence, then the judge may set bail again or may continue the previous bail to ensure that the defendant appears at the next stage in the process.

Although judges at preliminary hearings are supposed to examine the facts of the case before making a probable cause determination, in practice they seldom do. In big cities, judges do not generally have the time to inquire into the facts of a case. Consequently, at most preliminary hearings, judges simply assume that if a police officer made an arrest and a prosecutor charged the defendant with a crime or crimes, then there must be probable cause that the defendant, in fact, committed the crime or crimes. Few cases are dismissed for lack of probable cause at preliminary hearings.

Preliminary Hearings

In some jurisdictions, preliminary hearings are frequently waived by defendants. Perhaps the best example is the federal courts, where the majority of criminal cases begin with a grand jury indictment rather than with an arrest.

GRAND JURY

A **grand jury** is generally a group of 12 to 23 citizens who, for a specific period of time (generally 3 months), meet in closed sessions to investigate charges coming from preliminary hearings or to engage in other responsibilities. Thus a primary purpose of the grand jury is to determine whether there is probable cause to believe that the accused is guilty of the charge or charges brought by the prosecutor. Grand juries do not convene every day. Many federal grand juries meet only once a week, and some may meet only twice a month. State practice varies, but a state grand jury may meet only twice a month, or even only once a month. Sometimes a grand jury does not convene unless it is asked to do so by a prosecutor with cases to hear. Grand juries are involved in felony prosecutions in about half the states and in the federal system. The alternative to the grand jury is the filing of an information.

Before appearing before a grand jury, the prosecutor drafts an **indictment,** a document that outlines the charge or charges against a defendant. Because the grand jury has to determine only whether there is probable cause that a defendant committed the crime or crimes with which he or she is charged, only the prosecution's evidence and witnesses are heard. In most jurisdictions, neither the defendant nor the defendant's counsel has a right to be present during the proceedings. Furthermore, in grand jury proceedings, unlike criminal trials, prosecutors are allowed to present *hearsay* evidence (information learned from someone other than the witness who is testifying). They may also use illegally obtained evidence because the exclusionary rule does not apply to grand jury proceedings. Prosecutors can subpoena witnesses to testify. A **subpoena** is a written order to testify issued by a court officer. A witness who refuses to testify can be held in contempt and can be jailed until he or she provides the requested information. In practice, however, a witness jailed for contempt is generally held only as long as the grand jury is in session and no longer than 18 months in the federal jurisdiction.

After hearing the prosecutor's evidence and witnesses, the grand jury makes its probable cause determination and, usually on a majority vote, either indicts (issues a *true bill*) or fails to indict (issues *no bill*). If the grand jury fails to indict, then in most jurisdictions, the prosecution must be dropped. However, in some jurisdictions, the case can be brought before another grand jury.

In practice, the grand jury system is criticized for merely providing a rubber stamp for whatever the prosecutor wants to do. In other words, in cases where the prosecutor wants an indictment, the grand jury is likely to indict. Likewise, in cases where the prosecutor does not want to indict, the grand jury tends to fail to indict. The reason that prosecutors are so successful with grand juries is that they manage the entire proceedings (remember, only the prosecution's evidence and witnesses are heard). So it should not be surprising that suspects waive the right to a grand jury hearing in about 80 percent of cases. Defendants may also waive the right to a grand jury hearing to speed up their trial date.

You might be wondering why prosecutors would want a grand jury to fail to indict after they have gone to the trouble of bringing a case to the grand jury in the first place. The reason is political. To avoid losing marginal cases or looking cowardly by dropping charges, prosecutors can bring a case to the grand jury, have the grand jury fail to indict, and then blame the grand jury for its failure. The strategy deflects criticism from the prosecutor to the anonymous members of the grand jury. Sometimes prosecutors delay preliminary hearings to await a grand jury action to avoid disclosing evidence in open court that might help defense attorneys at trial. Because of the way the grand jury is used today, some critics of the system suggest that it ought to be abolished.

grand jury Generally a group of 12 to 23 citizens who meet in closed sessions to investigate charges coming from preliminary hearings or to engage in other responsibilities. A primary purpose of the grand jury is to determine whether there is probable cause to believe that the accused committed the crime or crimes.

indictment A document that outlines the charge or charges against a defendant.

subpoena A written order to testify issued by a court officer.

Grand Jury Indictments

All but two states and the District of Columbia use grand juries to indict. Twenty-three states plus the District of Columbia require that indictments be used to charge certain crimes, generally serious crimes. Twenty-five states make the use of indictments optional. Connecticut and Pennsylvania have abolished the use of grand juries to return indictments, but they have retained them to investigate crimes and the conduct of public affairs. The most common civil matter they investigate is the operation and condition of local jails and other confinement facilities. In the federal system, a grand jury indictment is required in all felony prosecutions, unless the defendant waives that right.

Source: "Federal Grand Jury" at www.udayton.edu/~grandjur/index.htm.

ARRAIGNMENT

arraignment A pretrial stage to hear the information or indictment and to allow the defendant to enter a plea.

nolo contendere Latin for "no contest." When defendants plead *nolo*, they do not admit guilt but are willing to accept punishment.

The primary purpose of an **arraignment** is to hear the formal information or indictment and to allow the defendant to enter a plea. The two most common pleas are "guilty" and "not guilty." "Not guilty" is the most common plea at arraignments. However, some states and the federal courts allow defendants to plead *nolo contendere* to the charges against them. ***Nolo contendere*** is Latin for "no contest." When defendants plead "*nolo*," they do not admit guilt but are willing to accept punishment anyway. The *nolo* plea is used for strategic purposes. If a defendant does not admit guilt in a criminal trial, admission of guilt cannot be the basis for a subsequent civil lawsuit. If there is a subsequent civil lawsuit, the lack of an admission of guilt in a criminal trial may allow the defendant to avoid a penalty of treble, or triple, damages. Furthermore, in some states, defendants can stand mute or can plead "not guilty by reason of insanity." Standing mute at arraignment is interpreted as pleading "not guilty." In states that do not accept a plea of "not guilty by reason of insanity," defendants plead "not guilty" and assume the burden of proving insanity at trial.

If a defendant pleads guilty, the judge must determine whether the plea was made voluntarily and whether the defendant is fully aware of the consequences of his or her action. If the judge doubts either of those conditions, then the judge can refuse to accept the guilty plea and can enter in the record a plea of "not guilty" for the defendant.

At arraignment, the judge also determines whether a defendant is competent to stand trial. Defendants can seek a delay before trial to consult further with their attorneys. A defendant who does not already have an attorney can ask for one to be appointed. Finally, defendants sometimes attempt to have their cases dismissed at arraignment. For example, they may assert that the state lacks sufficient evidence or that improper arrest procedures were used.

THINKING CRITICALLY

Do you agree with the criticism that the poor are unfairly discriminated against because they are the least able to pay their own bail and the least able to pay the fee to a bail bonds person? Why or why not?

Plea Bargaining

As noted earlier in this chapter, justice in the United States is dispensed mostly through plea bargaining.[32] About 90 percent of all convictions in felony cases are the result of guilty pleas; criminal trials are relatively rare. We already saw in Figure 5.6 the typical outcome of 100 felony arrests and the prevalence of plea bargaining.

There are three basic types of plea bargains. First, the defendant may be allowed to plead guilty to a lesser offense. For example, a defendant may be allowed to plead guilty to manslaughter rather than to first-degree murder. Second, at the request of the prosecutor, a defendant who pleads guilty may receive a lighter sentence than would typically be given for the crime. Note, however, that the prosecutor can only recommend the sentence; the judge does not have to grant it. Third, a defendant may plead guilty to one charge in return for the prosecutor's promise to drop other charges that could be brought.

The bargain a prosecutor will strike generally depends on three factors. The most important factor is the seriousness of the offense. Generally, the more serious the crime, the more difficult it is to win concessions from the prosecutor. A second factor is the defendant's

All guilty pleas are the result of plea bargaining.

Although the vast majority of guilty pleas probably are a product of plea bargaining—we do not know for sure—some defendants simply plead guilty to the original charges and do not bargain.

criminal record. Defendants with criminal records usually receive fewer concessions from prosecutors. The final factor is the strength of the prosecutor's case. The stronger the case, the stronger is the position of the prosecutor in plea negotiations.

Surprisingly, there is neither a constitutional basis nor a statutory basis for plea bargaining. It is a custom that developed because of the mutual interests it serves. The custom received formal recognition from the Supreme Court in 1970 in the case of *Brady* v. *United States.* In that case, the Court upheld the use of plea bargaining because of the "mutuality of advantage" it provided the defendant and the state. In two later cases, the Court provided safeguards for the bargaining process. In the 1971 case of *Santobello* v. *New York,* the Court held that the "deal" offered by a prosecutor in a plea negotiation must be kept. In 1976, in the case of *Henderson* v. *Morgan,* the Court held that to be valid, a guilty plea must be based on full knowledge of its implications and must be made voluntarily. However, prosecutors are under no obligation to plea-bargain. Once defendants plead guilty and are sentenced, they are almost always stuck with the bargain, even if they have a change of heart. Nevertheless, in most jurisdictions, defendants are allowed to withdraw their guilty pleas before sentencing.

As just noted, the reason justice in the United States is administered primarily through plea bargaining is that the process seemingly serves the interests of all the court participants by, among other things, reducing uncertainty. Uncertainty is a characteristic of all criminal trials because neither the duration of the trial, which may be a matter of minutes or of months, nor the outcome of the trial can ever be predicted with any degree of accuracy. Plea bargaining eliminates those two areas of uncertainty by eliminating the need for a trial.

Plea bargaining also serves the interests of the individual participants in the administration of justice. Prosecutors, for example, are guaranteed high conviction rates. For prosecutors and, apparently, the general public, a conviction is a conviction, whether it is obtained through plea bargaining or as the result of a trial. A prosecutor's conviction rate is one of the principal indicators of job performance, and job performance certainly helps determine whether the prosecutor will fulfill his or her aspirations for higher political office.

Plea bargaining also serves the interests of judges by reducing their court caseloads, allowing more time to be spent on more difficult cases. In addition, if a large proportion of the approximately 90 percent of felony cases that are handled each year by plea bargaining were to go to trial instead, the administration of justice in the United States would be even slower than it already is.

Federal judges and the judges in seven states are legally prohibited from participating in plea negotiations. In other states, their role in the process is limited by law.

Plea bargaining serves the interests of criminal defense attorneys by allowing them to spend less time on each case. It also allows them to avoid trials. Trials are relatively expensive events. Because most criminal defendants are poor, they are usually unable to pay a large legal fee. Thus, when criminal defense attorneys go to trial, they are frequently unable to recoup all of their expenses. Plea bargaining provides many criminal defense attorneys with the more profitable option of charging smaller fees for lesser services and handling a larger volume of cases.

Even most criminal defendants are served by plea bargaining. A guilty plea generally results in either no prison sentence or a lesser prison sentence than the

Plea Bargaining

Plea bargaining became a common practice in state courts shortly after the Civil War. The practice was instituted at the federal level during Prohibition, in the 1930s, as a result of the tremendous number of liquor law violations.

Sources: Albert W. Alschuler, "Plea Bargaining and Its History," *Law and Society Review* 13 (1979), pp. 211–45; John F. Padgett, "Plea Bargaining and Prohibition in the Federal Courts, 1908–1934," *Law and Society Review* 24 (1990), pp. 413–50.

Myth   Fact

| Abolishing plea bargaining would reduce the level of serious crime. | Despite the administrative nightmare it would cause, the abolition of plea bargaining would probably only shift discretion to another area. It would be unlikely to have any effect on crime. |

Three Strikes Law

Although habitual-offender statutes have existed in many jurisdictions for decades, the first state to enact a "three strikes and you're out" law was Washington, in 1993. The Washington law, called the Persistent Offender Accountability Act, allows three-time felons to be imprisoned for life without parole. In August 1996, the Washington Supreme Court upheld the law as constitutional. In 2004, 26 states and the federal government had three-strike laws on their books.

Source: "Washington Court Deems '3 Strikes' Constitutional," *The Orlando Sentinel*, August 9, 1996, p. A-12; "Three strikes law" at www.en.wikipedia.org/wiki/Three_strikes_law.

THINKING CRITICALLY

1. Do you think that the plea-bargaining process is beneficial? Why or why not?

2. Why is murder the crime least likely by far to be resolved through a guilty plea (see Table 5.1)?

3. How could the plea-bargaining process be improved?

defendant might receive if found guilty at trial. Plea bargaining also often allows defendants to escape conviction of socially stigmatizing crimes, such as child abuse. By "copping" a plea to assault rather than to statutory rape, for example, a defendant can avoid the embarrassing publicity of a trial and the wrath of fellow inmates or of society in general.

Two types of criminal defendants are not served by the practice of plea bargaining. The first are innocent, indigent, highly visible defendants who fear being found guilty of crimes they did not commit and receiving harsh sentences. Such defendants are sometimes pressured by unscrupulous defense attorneys into waiving their constitutional right to trial. The second type is the habitual offender. In this context, a habitual offender is a person who has been convicted under a state's habitual-offender statute (sometimes called a "three strikes and you're out" law). Most such statutes provide that upon conviction of a third felony, a defendant must receive life imprisonment. Although habitual-offender statutes would seem to imprison offenders for life, they actually are used mostly as bargaining chips by prosecutors in plea negotiations and not as they were intended.

A problem with those statutes is illustrated by the Supreme Court case of *Bordenkircher* v. *Hayes* (1978). The defendant, who had previously been convicted of two minor felonies, was arrested and charged with forging an $88 check. The prosecutor in the case told the defendant that if he did not plead guilty to the charge and accept a 5-year prison sentence, which on its face seemed very harsh, then the prosecutor would invoke the state's habitual-offender statute. The statute required the judge to impose a sentence of life imprisonment if the defendant were found guilty at trial. The defendant elected to play "you bet your life" and turned down the prosecutor's plea offer. At trial, the defendant was found guilty of forging the check and was sentenced to life imprisonment. Clearly, the defendant in this case was not served by plea bargaining or, perhaps, was not served by refusing the prosecutor's offer. In either case, with the possible exception of habitual offenders and innocent people, plea bargaining serves the interests of all the actors in the administration of justice. It does so by allowing cases to be disposed of predictably, quickly, and with little of the adversarial conflict associated with criminal trials.

The Criminal Trial

One of the distinctive features of criminal justice in the United States is trial by a jury of one's peers.[33] The principal purpose of jury trials—and of criminal trials without juries—is to discover the truth of whether defendants are guilty or innocent of the crimes with which they are charged. The process by which truth is sought is an adversarial one regulated by very specific procedures and rules. The adversaries in a criminal trial are the state (represented by the prosecutor) and the defendant (usually represented by defense counsel). The burden of proof is on the prosecution to show, beyond a reasonable doubt, that the defendant is guilty. The goal of defense counsel is to discredit the prosecution's case and to create reasonable doubt about the defendant's guilt. It is the responsibility of the jury (in jury trials) or the judge (in trials without juries) to determine and assign guilt.

Myth Fact

Myth	Fact
Criminal justice in the United States is dispensed primarily through jury trials.	Jury trials are relatively rare. Approximately 90 percent of all criminal cases are resolved through guilty pleas. Only about 10 percent are decided by bench or jury trials.

TABLE 5.1	Distribution of Types of Felony Convictions in State Courts, by Offense, 2002

		PERCENTAGE OF FELONS CONVICTED BY—			
MOST SERIOUS CONVICTION OFFENSE	TOTAL	TRIAL			GUILTY PLEA
		TOTAL	JURY	BENCH	
All offenses	100%	5%	2%	3%	95%
Violent offenses	100%	10%	7%	3%	90%
Murder[a]	100	32	27	5	68
Sexual assault[b]	100	10	8	2	90
Rape	100	16	12	4	84
Other sexual assault	100	6	5	1	94
Robbery	100	9	6	3	91
Aggravated assault	100	8	4	4	92
Other violent[c]	100	8	4	4	92
Property offenses	100%	4%	1%	3%	96%
Burglary	100	4	2	2	96
Larceny[d]	100	4	1	3	96
Motor vehicle theft	100	3	2	1	97
Fraud[e]	100	3	1	2	97
Drug offenses	100%	4%	2%	2%	96%
Possession	100	2	1	1	98
Trafficking	100	5	2	3	95
Weapon offenses	100%	7%	3%	4%	93%
Other offenses[f]	100%	3%	1%	2%	97%

Note: This table is based on an estimated 492,848 cases. However, figures are adjusted for cases missing a designation of conviction type.
[a]Includes nonnegligent manslaughter.
[b]Includes rape.
[c]Includes offenses such as negligent manslaughter and kidnapping.
[d]Includes motor vehicle theft.
[e]Includes forgery and embezzlement.
[f]Composed of nonviolent offenses such as receiving stolen property and vandalism.

Source: Matthew R. Durose and Patrick A. Langan, "Felony Sentences in State Courts, 2002," *Bureau of Justice Statistics Bulletin* (Washington, DC: GPO, U.S. Department of Justice, December 2004), p. 8, Table 9.

Although all criminal defendants have a constitutional right to a jury trial (when imprisonment for 6 months or more is a possible outcome), only about 5 percent of all criminal cases are disposed of in this way. Approximately 90 percent of cases are resolved through a guilty plea, and the remaining cases are decided by a judge in a *bench trial* (without a jury). In most jurisdictions, defendants may choose whether they want to exercise their right to a jury trial or whether they prefer a bench trial. Table 5.1 shows the type of conviction of felony defendants in 2002, by type of offense. The principal reason that so few criminal cases are decided by criminal trials is undoubtedly the advantages associated with plea bargaining.

THE JURY

Trial by an impartial jury of one's peers is an exalted American tradition and a Sixth Amendment right.[34] Its principal purposes are:

1. To protect citizens against arbitrary law enforcement.
2. To prevent government oppression.
3. To protect citizens from overzealous or corrupt prosecutors and from eccentric or biased judges.

Trial by Jury

Trial by a jury of one's peers originated in England as a way of limiting the power of the king. When the Magna Carta was signed in 1215, it contained the following provision: No freeman shall be taken, or imprisoned, or disseized, or outlawed, or exited, or in any way harmed—nor will we go upon or send upon him—save by the lawful judgment of his peers or by the law of the land.

SOURCE: "Magna Carta" at www.britannia.com/history/magna2.html.

venire The pool from which jurors are selected.

As interpreted by the Supreme Court, defendants have the right to a jury trial only if they are charged with felonies or with misdemeanors punishable by more than 6 months' imprisonment. The right was extended to the states in 1968, in the case of *Duncan* v. *Louisiana*. Most states also allow defendants to be tried by a jury for less serious misdemeanors, but states are not constitutionally required to do so.

For practical purposes, the right to an impartial jury is achieved by providing a representative jury, that is, a jury randomly selected from a fair cross section of the community. However, whether members of such a jury will be impartial in a particular case is a question that defies an easy answer. Also, as noted previously, jury trials in the United States are relatively rare. So on those rare occasions when defendants are tried by a jury, seldom is the jury composed of their peers. Until the mid-twentieth century, many states excluded women and people of color from jury service. Even today, class, gender, and racial biases enter into the jury selection process.

In many jurisdictions, jury pools are selected from voter registration lists. About 30 percent of eligible voters do not register; in some jurisdictions, the rate is as high as 60 percent. People not registered to vote are excluded from jury service. Studies show that the poor, the poorly educated, the young, and people of color are least likely to register to vote and, as a result, are least likely to be called for jury service. To remedy this problem, some jurisdictions now use multiple-source lists for obtaining jurors. In addition to voter registration lists, their sources include lists of licensed drivers, lists of utility users, and names listed in the telephone directory. Appellate courts have ruled that master jury lists must reflect an impartial and representative cross section of the population. People of color and women cannot be excluded systematically from juries solely because of race, ethnicity, or gender. But this does not mean that people of color and women must be included on all juries, only that they cannot be denied the opportunity of being chosen for jury service.

From the master list of all eligible jurors (sometimes called the *master wheel* or the *jury wheel*), a sufficient number of people are randomly chosen to make up the jury pool, or **venire.** Those chosen are summoned for service by the sheriff. However, not all those summoned will actually serve on the venire. Potential jurors must generally be U.S. citizens, residents of the locality of the trial, of a certain minimum age, and able to understand English. Convicted felons and insane persons are almost always excluded. Most jurisdictions also require that jurors be of "good character" and be "well informed," which eliminates other potential jurors.

In addition, members of other groups often escape jury service. Professionals such as doctors, lawyers, and teachers; some elected officials; military personnel on active duty; and law enforcement personnel frequently are not called for jury duty because their professional services are considered indispensable or because they are connected to the criminal justice process. Many jurisdictions allow citizens to be excused from jury service if it would cause them physical or economic difficulties. Compensation for jury service is minimal, currently averaging $15 a day nationwide. The most generous state in 2003 was West Virginia, which paid its jurors $40.00 a day. The federal government also paid $40.00 a day. Other states, as well as the federal government, raised their pay to a maximum of $50.00 a day after a certain number of days of service. Some states do not pay jurors for the first day or first 3 days of jury service.[35] Not all employers pay for time lost from work. Consequently, only about 15 percent of adult Americans have ever served on juries. The result is that juries are composed disproportionately of retired persons, the unemployed, and homemakers with grown children—those people least likely to be inconvenienced by the requirement of many states for jurors to serve for 30 days.

From the venire, as many as 30 people (in felony prosecutions that mandate 12 jurors) are randomly selected by the court clerk for the jury panel from which the actual trial jury is selected. To ensure a fair trial, potential trial jurors go through ***voir dire,*** a process in which persons who might be biased or unable to render a fair verdict are screened out. During *voir dire,* which means "to speak the truth," the defense, the prosecution, and the judge question jurors about their backgrounds and knowledge of the case and the defendant. If it appears that a juror might be biased or unable to render a fair verdict, the juror can be challenged "for cause" by either the defense or the prosecution. If the judge agrees, the juror is dismissed from jury service. In death penalty trials, for example, death penalty opponents can be excluded from juries for cause if they are opposed to the death penalty under any circumstances (*Lockhart* v. *McCree,* 1986). Generally, there is no limit to the number of jurors that can be eliminated for cause. In practice, however, few potential jurors are eliminated for cause, except in high-profile trials, such as the O.J. Simpson murder trial in 1995.

Another way that either the defense or the prosecution can eliminate potential jurors from jury service is by the use of *peremptory challenges,* which allow either prosecutors or defense attorneys to excuse jurors without having to provide a reason. Peremptory challenges are frequently used to eliminate jurors whose characteristics place them in a group likely to be unfavorable to the case of either the prosecution or the defense. For example, in death penalty cases, prosecutors often use their peremptory challenges to eliminate people of color and women from the juries because, statistically, people of color and women are less likely to favor capital punishment. However, prosecutors must be careful in their use of peremptory challenges for such purposes because the Supreme Court has forbidden the use of peremptory challenges to exclude potential jurors solely on account of their race (*Batson* v. *Kentucky,* 1989) or gender (*J.E.B.* v. *Alabama,* 1994). The number of peremptory challenges is limited by statute. In most jurisdictions, the prosecution is allowed from 6 to 8 peremptory challenges and the defense from 8 to 10. *Voir dire* continues until the required number of jurors have been selected. The *voir dire* process may take an hour or two or, in rare cases, months.

Traditionally, a jury in a criminal trial, sometimes called a *petit jury* to distinguish it from a grand jury, consists of 12 citizens plus one or two alternates, who will replace any jurors unable to continue because of illness, accident, or personal emergency. Recently, however, primarily to reduce expenses, some states have gone to six-, seven-, and eight-member juries in noncapital criminal cases. The Supreme Court will not allow criminal trial juries with five or fewer members, and 12-member juries are still required in all states in capital (death penalty) cases.

Recently, attempts have been made to reduce the burden of jury service. In many jurisdictions, jurors can now call a number to find out whether they will be needed on a particular day during their term of service. Some jurisdictions have instituted "1 day/1 trial" jury systems, which require jurors to serve either for 1 day or for the duration of one trial. Once they have served, they are exempt from jury service for 1 or 2 years. Each year in the United States, approximately 2 million jurors serve in about 200,000 criminal and civil trials.

THE TRIAL PROCESS

Before a criminal trial formally begins, attorneys in about 10 percent of felony cases file pretrial motions. A motion is an application to a court, requesting a judge to order a particular action. Motions can also be made

voir dire The process in which potential jurors who might be biased or unable to render a fair verdict are screened out.

SmartJURY

Software, called SmartJURY, has been developed that can evaluate the demographic profile and verbal and nonverbal clues given by potential jurors to calculate with precision whether they will acquit or convict a criminal defendant. The cost of the software is $995 a year.

SOURCE: Amie K. Streater, "High-Tech, Cheap Way Found to Pick a Jury," *The Orlando Sentinel,* January 5, 2003, p. B5.

McVeigh's Jury Pool

The jury pool in Timothy McVeigh's trial for the Oklahoma City bombing favored the prosecution. Most members of the jury pool were white and well educated, had close ties to the military, and believed in God, family, and the justice system. All of them had vivid memories of the Oklahoma City bombing, and nearly every one of them said they could look McVeigh in the eye and sentence him to death. According to a former U.S. attorney for Colorado, Bob Miller, "As a prosecutor, I would feel pretty comfortable. And I wouldn't feel so comfortable if I was a defense attorney."

SOURCE: "McVeigh's Jury Pool: Educated, Patriotic," *The Orlando Sentinel,* April 20, 1997, p. A-5.

FIGURE 5.7 | **Stages in a Criminal Trial**

Go to Trials → Discovery Proceedings → Motions Filed → Trial

Defendant's Case ← Presentation of Evidence ← Government's (Prosecutor's) Case ← Opening Statements

Government's Rebuttal Case → Closing Arguments → Jury Instructions → Deliberations

VERDICT

during and after a trial. Common pretrial motions are to obtain discovery of the prosecution's evidence and to have some of the prosecution's evidence suppressed (for example, to have a confession ruled inadmissible because of *Miranda* violations).

The following is a general description of the stages in a criminal trial.[36] Figure 5.7 shows that process and includes some pretrial stages as well (not all stages occur in every trial). After the jury has been sworn in (if the case is tried before a jury) and the court clerk has read the criminal complaint, the prosecution begins the trial with an opening statement, outlining its case. Next is the opening statement by the defense. However, the defense is not required to make an opening statement. In some jurisdictions, the defense is allowed to defer its opening statement until after the prosecution has presented its case. Opening statements are rarely made in bench trials.

The prosecution then submits its evidence and questions its witnesses. The prosecution must establish beyond a reasonable doubt each element of the crime. The elements of a crime vary by offense and jurisdiction. In other words, two jurisdictions (for example, two states) may have different elements for the same crime. The specific elements of each crime are provided in state and federal statutes. Some of the elements common to most crimes are *actus reus* (criminal conduct—specifically, intentional or criminally negligent or reckless action that causes harm), *mens rea* (criminal intent; guilty state of mind), and concurrence (the *actus reus* and *mens rea* must occur together).

If the defense believes that the prosecution has failed to make its case, then the defense may choose to *rest*, that is, not to defend against the charge or charges. At this point, the defense in most states is allowed to request a *directed verdict* or to make a motion for dismissal. If the judge agrees with the defense that the prosecution's evidence is insufficient for conviction, then the judge can either direct the jury to acquit the defendant or "take the case from the jury" and grant the motion for dismissal.

If the defense does not seek a dismissal or a dismissal is not granted, the defense follows the prosecution with its witnesses and any contrary evidence. Then the prosecution and the defense take turns offering rebuttals to the other side's evidence, cross-examining witnesses, and reexamining their own witnesses. Following the rebuttal period, the prosecution summarizes its case.

Attorneys from opposing sides in a trial sometimes confer with the judge. *Why does this happen and what do you think is discussed?*

The defense then summarizes its case and makes its closing statement. The closing statement by the prosecution ends the adversarial portion of the trial.

Normally, after the closing statement by the prosecution, the judge instructs, or *charges,* the jury concerning the principles of law the jurors are to utilize in determining guilt or innocence. The judge also explains to the jury the charges, the rules of evidence, and the possible verdicts. In some jurisdictions, the judge summarizes the evidence presented from notes taken during the trial. The jury then retires to deliberate until it reaches a verdict. In a room where it has complete privacy, the jury elects from its members a foreperson to preside over the subsequent deliberations. Jurors are not allowed to discuss the case with anyone other than another juror. In some cases, a jury is sequestered at night in a hotel or motel to prevent any chance of outside influence.

To find a defendant guilty as charged, the jury must be convinced "beyond a reasonable doubt" that the defendant has committed the crime. Some juries reach a verdict in a matter of minutes; some juries have taken weeks or more. If the jury finds the defendant guilty as charged, as it does in two-thirds of criminal cases, the judge begins to consider a sentence. In some jurisdictions, the jury participates to varying degrees in the sentencing process. If the jury finds the defendant not guilty, the defendant is released from the jurisdiction of the court and is a free person. After the verdict has been read in the courtroom, either the defense or the prosecution may ask that the jury be polled individually, with each juror stating publicly how he or she voted.

In the federal courts and in nearly every state, a unanimous verdict is required. If, after serious deliberation, even one juror cannot agree with the others on a verdict, the result is a **hung jury.** In that case, the judge declares a mistrial, and the prosecutor must decide whether to retry the case. Recent data show that in the small number of jury trials (less than 3 percent of all criminal case dispositions), hung juries occur infrequently: only in about 6 percent of state court criminal jury trials and in fewer than

THINKING CRITICALLY

1. What are some of the benefits of having a trial by jury?
2. How could the jury system be improved so that there is a more diverse mix of people?

hung jury The result when jurors cannot agree on a verdict. The judge declares a mistrial. The prosecutor must decide whether to retry the case.

3 percent of federal court criminal jury trials. The percentage of hung juries in the state courts ranged from 0 percent to nearly 19 percent. In state court criminal trials that end in hung juries, possible outcomes include case dismissal, guilty plea, another jury trial, or a bench trial. The average percentage of hung juries in criminal trials has not varied much in the past 40 years.[37]

TRIAL RIGHTS

The Fifth and Sixth Amendments of the United States Constitution provide defendants at trial with several important rights. This section examines those rights.

RIGHT TO A SPEEDY AND PUBLIC TRIAL The Sixth Amendment right to a speedy and public trial applies directly to trials in federal courts. It was extended to trials in state courts in 1967, in the case of *Klopfer* v. *North Carolina* (right to a speedy trial), and in 1948, in the case of *In re Oliver* (right to a public trial). Delays in a trial can severely hamper a defendant's case if favorable witnesses have died, have moved and cannot be found, or have forgotten what they saw. Delays can also adversely affect defendants by forcing them to remain in jail for long periods of time while awaiting trial. A long wait in jail can be a very stressful and sometimes dangerous experience.

In *United States* v. *Marion* (1971), the Supreme Court held that the right to a speedy trial "is activated only when a criminal prosecution has begun and extends only to those persons who have been 'accused' in the course of that prosecution." It added that "invocation of the right need not await indictment, information, or other formal charge but begins with the actual restraints imposed by arrest if those restraints precede the formal preferring of charges." In determining what constitutes a speedy trial, the Supreme Court has created a balancing test that weighs both the defendant's and the prosecution's behavior (see *Barker* v. *Wingo*, 1972). Thus, the reason for the delay in a trial is critical. For example, a search for a missing witness would probably be considered an acceptable reason for delay. Court congestion, on the other hand, typically would not.

The acceptable length of delay in a trial also depends partly on the nature of the charge. In *Barker*, the Court held that "the delay that can be tolerated for an ordinary street crime is considerably less than for a serious, complex conspiracy charge." There has been great variation in the length of delay tolerated by specific courts.

The Sixth Amendment right to a public trial means that a trial must be open to the public, but it need not be open to all who want to attend. Obviously, the number of people who can attend a trial depends on the size of the courtroom. The right would be violated only if the trial were held, for example, in a prison or in a closed judge's chambers against a defendant's wishes. Defendants have no right to a private trial.

A trial may be closed to the public if the defendant's right to a public trial is outweighed by "a compelling state interest." However, before a trial is closed, "the party seeking to close the hearing must advance an overriding interest that is likely to be prejudiced, the closure must be no broader than necessary to protect that interest, the trial court must consider reasonable alternatives to closing the proceeding, and it must make findings adequate to support the closure" (*Waller* v. *Georgia*, 1984). In some cases, parts of a trial may be closed—for example, to protect the identity of an undercover informant during his or her testimony.

RIGHT TO BE TRIED IN THE STATE AND DISTRICT WHEREIN THE CRIME SHALL HAVE BEEN COMMITTED The Sixth Amendment guarantees the specific **venue,** or the place of trial. (Venue is also mentioned in the Constitution in

The Speedy Trial Act

Federal courts are now regulated by the Speedy Trial Act of 1974, which specifies two separate time limits: one for the period between arrest and charging, and the other for the period between charging and trial. The act stipulates that, generally, a delay between arrest and charging (that is, the filing of an indictment or information) may be no more than 30 days, and a delay between charging and trial may be no more than 70 days. The act also specifies periods of delay that do not count—for example, delay due to the unavailability of an essential witness or continuances (that is, postponements) that serve "the ends of justice." If the delay, excluding periods of delay that do not count, is longer than the number of days allowed, the court must dismiss the charges. A dismissal with prejudice, which is given when there are no good reasons for the delay, prevents the reprosecution of the case. A dismissal without prejudice gives the prosecutor the option of prosecuting the case again.

venue The place of the trial.

Article 3, Section 2: "Trial shall be held in the State where the said Crimes shall have been committed. . . .") The venue of a trial must be geographically appropriate. Generally, a crime must be tried in the jurisdiction—the politically defined geographical area—in which it was committed. However, if a defense attorney believes that a client cannot get a fair trial in the appropriate venue because of adverse publicity or for some other reason, the attorney can ask the court for a change of venue. If the change of venue is granted, the trial will be moved to another location (within the state in cases of state law violations), where, presumably, the adverse publicity or other factors are not as great.

RIGHT TO CONFRONT OPPOSING WITNESSES The Sixth Amendment right to confront opposing witnesses was extended to trials in state courts in 1965, in the case of *Pointer* v. *Texas*. In essence, it means that defendants have a right to be present during their trials (otherwise, they could not confront opposing witnesses) and to cross-examine witnesses against them. However, the right to be present during the trial may be forfeited by a defendant's disruptive behavior. Thus, if a defendant continues to scream, use profanity, or refuse to sit quietly after being warned by the judge, the judge may have the defendant removed from the trial (see *Illinois* v. *Allen,* 1970).

RIGHT TO COMPULSORY PROCESS FOR OBTAINING FAVORABLE WITNESSES This right ensures a defendant the use of the subpoena power of the court to compel the testimony of any witnesses who may have information useful to the defense. A *subpoena,* as noted preveiously, is a written order issued by a court that requires a person to appear at a certain time and place to give testimony. It can also require that documents and objects be made available for examination by the court. Even though the right to compulsory process for obtaining favorable witnesses was already applicable in many states because of its inclusion in state constitutions and laws, the Supreme Court officially extended it to state trials in 1967, in the case of *Washington* v. *Texas.*

PROTECTION AGAINST DOUBLE JEOPARDY The Fifth Amendment protection against **double jeopardy** provides that no person shall "be subject for the same offence to be twice put in jeopardy of life or limb." This right was extended to trials in state courts in the case of *Benton* v. *Maryland,* 1969.

When most people think of double jeopardy, they probably think of the classic case in which a defendant cannot be retried for the same crime or a related crime after he or she has been acquitted or convicted by a jury. However, the protection against double jeopardy can apply even without an acquittal or conviction. Technically, it does not apply until jeopardy has attached. If a trial ends before jeopardy has attached, the prosecution has the right to retry the defendant for the same charge in a new trial. But when does jeopardy attach? In jury trials, jeopardy attaches when the entire jury has been selected and sworn in. In a bench trial (a trial before a judge without a jury), jeopardy attaches when the first witness has been sworn in. In cases that are resolved through a guilty plea, jeopardy attaches when the court unconditionally accepts the defendant's plea. Even after jeopardy has attached, however, the prosecution is generally not barred from retrying a defendant when a mistrial has been declared or when a defendant appeals and is granted a new trial.

The theoretical rationale behind the protection against double jeopardy is that the state should have one and only one chance to convict a defendant charged with a crime. Otherwise, the state could endlessly harass its citizens, as sometimes happens in countries without this protection.

Jury Flexibility

In 1994, the state of Florida passed a law allowing a jury selected in one county to hear a trial in another county. Before the law, trials—not juries—were moved, often causing hardship to victims' families.

Stun Belts

In about 30 states, potentially disruptive defendants may have a stun belt strapped to their waist instead of being shackled. If they become violent or try to escape during court proceedings, a deputy can push a remote-control button that will deliver an 8-second charge of 50,000 volts and 4 milliamps of electricity to the defendants' kidneys. The jolt of electricity will likely knock them to the floor, incapacitate them, and cause them to writhe in pain. They may also lose control of their bladders and bowels. Apparently, the fear of being shocked is enough to keep defendants in line. Nationally, between about 1991 and 2002, the belt was strapped on 62,000 defendants and was activated only 34 times.

SOURCE: Susan Clary, "Stunning: Remote-Control Belts Keep Peace in Courts," *The Orlando Sentinel,* December 1, 2001, p. H6.

double jeopardy The trying of a defendant a second time for the same offense when jeopardy attached in the first trial and a mistrial was not declared.

Miscarriages of Justice

The legal system of the United States is unique in the world in the number of procedural rights that it provides people suspected or accused of crimes. The primary reason for procedural rights is to protect innocent people, as much as possible, from being arrested, charged, convicted, or punished for crimes they did not commit. One of the basic tenets of our legal system is that a person is considered innocent until proven guilty. However, even with arguably the most highly developed system of due-process rights in the world, people continue to be victims of miscarriages of justice. For example, attorney Barry Scheck and his colleagues report, "Of the first eighteen thousand results [of DNA tests] at the FBI and other crime laboratories, at least five thousand prime suspects were excluded *before* their cases were tried." In other words, more than 25 percent of the prime suspects were wrongly accused. Scheck is a co-founder of the Innocence Project at the Cardoza School of Law in New York City.[38]

CAREERS IN CRIMINAL JUSTICE

Paralegal

My name is Renée Daniel and I have an associate of applied science degree in paralegal studies from State Technical Institute at Memphis, now called Southwest Tennessee Community College. Currently I am a senior pursuing a bachelor of arts degree in criminology and criminal justice from the University of Memphis. After graduating from State Tech, I was chosen by the chairperson and associate professors of the Paralegal Studies Department to be the recipient of a scholarship to pursue my bachelor's degree and also work as a paralegal in the Shelby County Jail Law Library.

Prior to graduating from State Tech, I interned as a paralegal for the Shelby County Division of Corrections. As a paralegal intern I had the opportunity to learn the various duties and responsibilities a paralegal encounters. During my internship I was able to review and answer inmate disciplinary appeals, draft documents, review discovery for litigation, and research case law and brief cases.

As a paralegal in the County Jail I assist inmates/pre-trial detainees with legal research. Inmates are scheduled to report to the law library through program services in groups. My job involves assisting them in locating case law, statutes, sentencing guidelines, information pertaining to criminal procedure, pretrial motions, and petitions. I act as a liaison between the inmates and the courts by verifying all outgoing legal calls. I have contacted attorneys, probation officers, parole officers, court clerks, and, on some occasions, Immigration and Naturalization Services. My duties as a paralegal not only involve assisting inmates with preparation for trial/appeal but also managing and organizing the law library. I log and inventory all legal material that comes to the library and supervise the

placement and rotation of books and supplements. In order to adequately assist the inmates with significant research, the legal material must be monitored at all times. I consult frequently with practicing attorneys regarding relevant substantive and procedural legal material that would help those who are preparing for trial or filing motions. If we do not already have the material, I submit a request to the director of programs to order necessary items.

The aspect I like most about my job is the opportunity I have to utilize the skills I have learned in the Paralegal Studies and Criminology and Criminal Justice programs. I enjoy legal research and applying legal principles to substantive criminal law. My job allows me to see firsthand how the criminal justice system works from arrest to sentencing and appeal. What I like least about my job are the imperfections that exist in the criminal justice system. I often see several inmates who have been detained in the jail for a year or more before they are indicted. There have been cases where inmates have served their entire sentences in the jail by the time they go to trial. Another aspect about my job that I like least is the destructive behavior that some inmates display by destroying legal books. Once these books are destroyed it is difficult to have them replaced.

Paralegals work in several areas of the legal system with knowledge of substantive and procedural law. A paralegal has the opportunity to work in numerous areas of the law. I would advise paralegal students to intern first to gain insight and experience in the area of law in which they wish to work.

What type of growth opportunities would you expect as a paralegal?

Unfortunately, there is no official record of miscarriages of justice, so it is impossible to determine precisely how many actually occur each year. Nevertheless, in an effort to provide some idea of the extent of the problem, a study was conducted of wrongful convictions—miscarriages of justice at just one of the stages in the administration of justice.[39] In the study, *wrongful convictions* were defined as

> cases in which a person [is] convicted of a felony but later . . . found innocent beyond a reasonable doubt, generally due to a confession by the actual offender, evidence that had been available but was not sufficiently used at the time of conviction, new evidence that was not previously available, and other factors.

The conclusions of the study were based on the findings of a survey. All attorneys general in the United States and its territories were surveyed, and in Ohio, all presiding judges of common pleas courts, all county prosecutors, all county public defenders, all county sheriffs, and the chiefs of police of seven major cities were also surveyed. The authors of the study conservatively estimated that approximately 0.5 percent of all felony convictions are in error. In other words, of every 1,000 persons convicted of felonies in the United States, about 5 are probably innocent. The authors believe that the frequency of error is probably higher in less serious felony and misdemeanor cases.

Although an error rate of 0.5 percent may not seem high, consider that in 2004, a typical year, approximately 14 million people were arrested in the United States.[40] Assuming conservatively that 50 percent of all people arrested are convicted[41]—about 7 million convictions in 2004—then approximately 35,000 people were probably wrongfully convicted!

Eyewitness misidentification is the most important factor contributing to wrongful convictions. For example, a study of DNA exonerations by the Innocence Project found that more than 80 percent of wrongful convictions could be attributed, at least in part, to eyewitness or victim misidentification.[42] The second and third most important contributing factors are police and prosecutorial

Death Row Reversals

From 1973 through July 2006, 123 inmates in 25 states have been freed from death row because of evidence of their innocence. Common reasons for these reversals include (1) key witnesses lied or recanted their testimony, (2) police overlooked or withheld important evidence, (3) DNA testing showed someone else committed the crime, (4) the defense lawyer was incompetent or negligent, and (5) prosecutors withheld exculpatory evidence from the defense.

SOURCE: The Death Penalty Information Center, www.deathpenaltyinfo.org; Jonathan Alter, "The Death Penalty on Trial," *Newsweek*, June 12, 2000.

Roberto Miranda is one of more than 100 inmates since 1973 who has been released from death row because of evidence of his innocence. Mr. Miranda spent 14 years on Nevada's death row. *What, if anything, does the state of Nevada owe Mr. Miranda?*

errors, respectively. They accounted for nearly 65 percent of the DNA exonerations in the Innocence Project study.[43] Overzealous police officers and prosecutors, convinced that a suspect or defendant is guilty, may prompt witnesses, suggest to witnesses what may have occurred at the time of the crime, conceal or fabricate evidence, or even commit perjury. Another factor contributing to wrongful convictions is guilty pleas made "voluntarily" by innocent defendants. Innocent defendants are more likely to plead guilty to crimes they did not commit when they are faced with multiple charges and when the probability of severe punishment is great. They are also more likely to plead guilty to crimes they did not commit when they are mentally incompetent.

When the charge is a less serious one, innocent people who are unable to post bail sometimes admit guilt to be released from jail immediately. For many people, release from jail is more important than a minor criminal record. Besides, it is often difficult to prove one's innocence. (Remember that in the United States the prosecution is required to prove, beyond a reasonable doubt, that defendants are guilty. Defendants are not required to prove their innocence.) Problems faced by innocent people wrongly accused of crimes include inability to establish an alibi; misidentification by witnesses who swear they saw the defendant commit the crime; a lawyer who lacks the skill, time, or resources to mount a good defense; and a lawyer who is unconvinced of the defendant's innocence. Inadequate legal representation is one of the most important factors in wrongful convictions in death penalty cases.[44] It accounted for nearly a third of the wrongful convictions discovered in the Innocence Project study.[45]

Other factors contributing to wrongful convictions are community pressures, especially in interracial and rape cases; false accusations; knowledge of a defendant's prior criminal record; judicial errors, bias, or neglect of duty; errors made by medical examiners and forensic experts; and errors in criminal record keeping and computerized information systems.[46] In short, numerous factors can cause wrongful convictions. And remember, the foregoing discussion addresses only wrongful convictions; it does not consider wrongful arrests or other miscarriages of justice.

Despite such miscarriages of justice, many people still resent the provision of procedural safeguards to criminal suspects. The accusation is frequently made that procedural rights protect criminals and penalize victims—that many criminals escape conviction and punishment because of procedural technicalities. For example, a driving force behind the good faith and inevitable-discovery exceptions was the belief that a substantial number of criminal offenders escaped punishment because of the exclusionary rule. The available evidence, however, does not support the belief. One of the most thorough studies of the effect of the exclusionary rule was conducted by the National Institute of Justice (NIJ).[47] The NIJ study examined felony cases in California between 1976 and 1979—a period during which the American public was becoming increasingly alarmed about the problem of crime and especially about what was perceived as the practice of allowing a substantial number of criminals to escape punishment because of legal technicalities. The study found that only a tiny fraction (fewer than 0.5 percent) of the felony cases reaching the courts were dismissed because of the exclusionary rule. It is important to emphasize that the study examined only the cases that reached the courts. It excluded cases that prosecutors elected not to pursue to trial because they assumed that the exclusionary rule would make the cases impossible to win. However, studies show that although there is some variation between jurisdictions, fewer than 1 percent of cases overall are dropped by prosecutors before trial because of search and seizure problems.[48] Interestingly, 71.5 percent of the California cases affected by the exclusionary rule involved drug charges. The problem in

NIJ

Learn more about the National Institute of Justice and its various research findings by accessing their Web site at **www.ojp.usdoj.gov/nij.** *Why is it important to have research organizations like the NIJ?*

most of the drug cases was that in the absence of complaining witnesses, overaggressive law enforcement officers had to engage in illegal behavior to obtain evidence.

A study of the effect of the exclusionary rule at the federal level was conducted by the General Accounting Office (GAO).[49] The GAO examined 2,804 cases handled by 38 different U.S. attorneys in July and August of 1978. The GAO found results similar to those found by the NIJ in California. In only 1.3 percent of the nearly 3,000 cases was evidence excluded in the federal courts. Again, it is important to emphasize that the study included only cases that went to trial. However, as noted earlier, evidence shows that, overall, fewer than 1 percent of cases are dropped by prosecutors before trial because of search and seizure problems. It is important to understand, moreover, that having evidence excluded from trial does not necessarily mean that a case is impossible to win and that the defendant will escape punishment. A defendant may still be convicted on the basis of evidence that was not illegally obtained.

The *Miranda* mandates, like the exclusionary rule, are also viewed by many people as legal technicalities that allow guilty criminals to escape punishment. That view is fortified by Supreme Court Justice Byron White's dissent in *Miranda:* "In some unknown number of cases the rule will return a killer, a rapist or other criminal to the streets." No doubt, Justice White's warning is true, but the evidence suggests that only a very small percentage of cases are lost as a result of illegal confessions. In one large survey, for example, fewer than 1 percent of all cases were thrown out because of confessions illegally obtained.[50]

In another study of decisions made by the Indiana Court of Appeals or the Indiana Supreme Court from November 6, 1980, through August 1, 1986, the researchers found that in only 12 of 2,354 cases (0.51 percent) was a conviction overturned because of the failure of the police to correctly implement the *Miranda* safeguards.[51] In only 213 of the 2,354 cases (9 percent) was a claim even made about improper interrogation procedures by the police, and in 201 of those 213 cases, the conviction was affirmed by the appellate court, resulting in a reversal rate of 5.6 percent for the cases raising a *Miranda* question.

The authors of that study speculated on possible reasons for the low rate of successful appeals. One was that the police routinely comply with the *Miranda* decision. In fact, most police support *Miranda* and the other reforms because it makes them appear more professional. The second possible reason was that the police are able to solve most cases without having to question suspects. Studies show that the *Miranda* warnings rarely stop suspects from confessing anyway. Nearly 80 percent of suspects waive their *Miranda* rights. As many as 75 percent of suspects attempt to clear themselves in the eyes of the police and end up incriminating themselves instead; other suspects simply do not understand that they have a right to remain silent.[52] Third, the police are able to evade *Miranda* by using more-sophisticated strategies, such as skillfully suggesting that suspects volunteer confessions or casually talking with suspects in the back of squad cars.[53] And, fourth, prosecutors, knowing that they cannot win cases involving illegal interrogations, screen them out before trial or settle them through alternative means, such as plea bargaining. However, as with the exclusionary rule, fewer than 1 percent of cases overall are dismissed or handled in other ways by prosecutors because of *Miranda*.[54] In short, the available evidence suggests that the effects of both *Miranda* and the exclusionary rule in Fourth and Fifth Amendment contexts have been minor.[55]

Myth / Fact

Myth	Fact
Many criminals escape punishment because of the Supreme Court's decision in *Miranda* v. *Arizona*.	Very few criminals escape punishment because of that decision.

FYI

Reforming the Criminal Justice System

The authors of *Actual Innocence* suggest the following reforms: *DNA testing:* Allow postconviction DNA testing nationwide. Test DNA on unsolved crimes where evidence exists. *Witness IDs:* Independent, trained examiner who does not know the suspect should conduct lineups and photo IDs to ensure investigators don't influence witnesses. Videotape lineups, photo spreads, and other identification processes to ensure neutrality. *Confessions:* Videotape all interrogations. *Informants:* Committee of prosecutors should screen all informant testimony before permission to use at trial. All deals between prosecutors and informants must be in writing. *Forensics:* Crime labs should function and be funded separately from police, prosecution, or defense. Strengthen accreditation programs for labs, establish postgraduate forensic programs at universities. *Police, prosecutors:* Establish disciplinary committees to deal with legal misconduct by police and prosecution. *Defense attorneys:* Increase fees to attract competent lawyers. Public defenders' pay should equal prosecutors' pay. *Wrongful convictions:* Establish innocence commissions to investigate wrongful convictions. Create and fund innocence projects at law schools to represent clients. Provide compensation to those who were clearly wrongly convicted. Moratorium on death penalty.

SOURCE: Jim Dwyer, Peter Neufeld, and Barry Scheck, *Actual Innocence: Five Days to Execution and Other Dispatches from the Wrongly Convicted* (New York: Doubleday, 2000).

1. **Identify the type of court structure in the United States and describe its various components.**

   The United States has a dual court system—a separate judicial system for each of the states and a separate federal system. The only place where the two systems "connect" is in the U.S. Supreme Court. The federal court system is composed of U.S. district courts, U.S. circuit courts of appeals, and the U.S. Supreme Court. The state court system consists of trial courts of limited jurisdiction, trial courts of general jurisdiction, intermediate appellate courts (in most states), and state courts of last resort.

2. **Summarize the purposes of courts.**

   The purposes of courts are (1) to do justice, (2) to appear to do justice, (3) to provide a forum where disputes between people can be resolved justly and peacefully, (4) to censure wrongdoing, (5) to incapacitate criminal offenders, (6) to punish offenders, (7) to rehabilitate offenders, (8) to deter people from committing crimes, (9) to determine legal status, and (10) to protect individual citizens against arbitrary government action.

3. **Identify the most powerful actors in the administration of justice and explain what makes them so powerful.**

   Prosecutors are the most powerful actors in the administration of justice because they conduct the final screening of all persons arrested for criminal offenses, deciding whether there is enough evidence to support a conviction, and because, in most jurisdictions, they have unreviewable discretion in deciding whether to charge a person with a crime and prosecute the case.

4. **Summarize the types of attorneys available to a person charged with a crime.**

   People charged with crimes may have privately retained counsel, or if indigent, they may have court-appointed attorneys, public defenders, or "contract" lawyers, depending on which is provided by the jurisdiction.

5. **Describe the responsibilities of a judge.**

   Judges have a variety of responsibilities in the criminal justice process. Among their nontrial duties are determining probable cause, signing warrants, informing suspects of their rights, setting and revoking bail, arraigning defendants, and accepting guilty pleas. Judges spend much of the workday in their chambers, negotiating procedures and dispositions with prosecutors and defense attorneys. The principal responsibility of judges in all of those duties is to ensure that suspects and defendants are treated fairly and in accordance with due process of law. In jury trials, judges are responsible for allowing the jury a fair chance to reach a verdict on the evidence presented. A judge must ensure that his or her behavior does not improperly affect the outcome of the case. Before juries retire to deliberate and reach a verdict, judges instruct them on the relevant law. Additionally, in jurisdictions without professional court administrators, each judge is responsible for the management of his or her own courthouse and its personnel, with the added duties of supervising building maintenance, budgets, and labor relations.

6. **Describe the purposes of an initial appearance.**

   At the initial appearance—the first pretrial stage—defendants are given formal notice of the charges against them and are advised of their constitutional rights. For a misdemeanor or an ordinance violation, a summary trial may be held. For a felony, a hearing is held to determine whether the suspect should be released or whether the suspect should be held for a preliminary hearing.

7. **Explain what bail is and describe the different methods of pretrial release.**

   Bail is usually a monetary guarantee deposited with the court that is supposed to ensure that the suspect or defendant will appear at a subsequent stage in the criminal justice process. Different pretrial release options include station-house bail, surety bonds, full cash bonds, deposit bonds, release on own recognizance (ROR), conditional release, and unsecured bonds.

8. **Define what a grand jury is and explain its purposes.**

   A grand jury is a group of generally 12 to 23 citizens who, for a specific period of time, meet in closed sessions to investigate charges coming from preliminary hearings or to engage in other responsibilities. A primary purpose of the grand jury is to determine whether there is probable cause to believe that the accused committed the crime or crimes with which he or she is charged by the prosecutor. Other purposes of a grand jury are to protect citizens from unfounded charges and to consider the misconduct of government officials.

9. Describe the purposes of the arraignment and the plea options of defendants.

The primary purpose of arraignment is to hear the formal information or grand jury indictment and to allow defendants to enter a plea. Plea options include "guilty," "not guilty," and in some states and the federal courts, "nolo contendere." In some states, defendants can also stand mute or can plead "not guilty by reason of insanity."

10. Describe the interests served and not served by plea bargaining.

Plea bargaining seemingly serves the interests of all the court participants by, among other things, reducing uncertainty about the length or outcome of trials. Plea bargains serve prosecutors by guaranteeing them high conviction rates; judges by reducing court caseloads; defense attorneys by allowing them to avoid trials and spend less time on each case; and even some criminal offenders by enabling them to escape a prison sentence altogether, to receive a lesser sentence than they might have received if convicted at trial, or to escape conviction of socially stigmatizing crimes. Two types of criminal offenders are not served by plea bargaining: (1) innocent, indigent defendants who fear being found guilty of crimes they did not commit and receiving harsh sentences, and (2) habitual offenders.

11. List and define the stages in a criminal trial.

The stages in a criminal trial are as follows: (1) selection and swearing in of the jury, in jury trials; (2) opening statements by the prosecution and the defense; (3) presentation of the prosecution's case; (4) presentation of the defense's case;

(5) rebuttals, cross-examination, and reexamination of witnesses; (6) closing arguments by the defense and the prosecution; (7) the judge's instructing, or charging, the jury; and (8) deliberation and verdict.

12. Identify the trial rights of criminal defendants.

Among the trial rights of criminal defendants are (1) the right to a speedy and public trial; (2) the right to be tried in the state and district wherein the crime shall have been committed; (3) the right to confront opposing witnesses; (4) the right to compulsory process for obtaining favorable witnesses; and (5) protection against double jeopardy.

13. Describe some of the causes of wrongful convictions.

Some of the causes of wrongful convictions are as follows: (1) eyewitness misidentification, which is the most important factor contributing to wrongful convictions; (2) police and prosecutorial errors, such as prompting witnesses, suggesting to witnesses what may have occurred at the time of the crime, concealing or fabricating evidence, and committing perjury; (3) guilty pleas made voluntarily by innocent defendants faced with multiple charges or severe punishment or because they are mentally incompetent; (4) inadequate legal representation; (5) community pressures, especially in interracial and rape cases; (6) false accusations; (7) knowledge of a defendant's prior criminal record; (8) judicial errors, bias, or neglect of duty; (9) errors made by medical examiners and forensic experts; and (10) errors in criminal record keeping and computerized information systems.

KEY TERMS

1. What is the difference between *original* and *appellate jurisdiction*? Between *general* and *special jurisdiction*? Between *subject matter* and *personal jurisdiction*?

2. Under what circumstances will the U.S. Supreme Court issue a writ of *certiorari*?

3. What are "specialty" courts?

4. Ideally, what are the three conditions that must be met before a prosecutor charges a person with a crime and prosecutes the case?

5. Why do prosecutors sometimes choose not to prosecute criminal cases?

6. In general, when does an individual accused of a crime have the right to counsel?

7. By what methods are judges selected?

8. What is the "funneling" or screening process in the administration of justice?

9. When do suspects officially become defendants?

10. How long may suspects arrested without a warrant be held in jail before being brought before a judge for an initial appearance?

11. In what two ways are preliminary hearings similar to criminal trials, and in what two ways do preliminary hearings differ from criminal trials?

12. What is the primary purpose of a grand jury?

13. What are three basic types of plea bargains?

14. What are three principal purposes of jury trials?

15. What is *voir dire*, and what is its purpose?

16. What are the stages of a criminal trial?

17. What does it mean to say that a defendant has the right to a "speedy" and "public" trial?

18. What is a subpoena?

1. **Bail Bonds** Visit the office of a local bail bonds person. It is generally near the courthouse and well marked. Ask the bonds person to describe the job. Ask about major problems with the business and satisfactions of the job. Specific questions could be: (1) For what type of offender is it most risky to provide bail? (2) How does a bail transaction work? (3) Do bonds people actually have to give money to the court when they put up bail?

2. **Court Proceedings** Visit several different types of courts, such as a lower court, a trial court, an appellate court, state courts, and federal courts. Observe the proceedings and describe how they differ from or are similar to those described in this chapter and to one another.

3. **Report on a Criminal Trial** Scan a local newspaper for a story of a criminal trial. Write a report that includes information about (1) the type of court in which the trial is being held and why it has jurisdiction, (2) the type of case being tried (misdemeanor or felony), and (3) the outcome of the case.

1. **District Courts** Go to the Federal Judiciary Web site at www.uscourts.gov and find the directory of district courts. Look up the number of districts your state is divided into, where the courts for the districts are located, and how many judgeships are authorized for each district. Report the results to your class or instructor.

2. **State Courts** Go to the National Center for State Courts Web site at www.ncsconline.org/D_Research/Ct_Struct/Index.html, click on your state, and with the information you find write a report about your state court system. Be sure to describe how your state court system compares with the general state court system described in your textbook.

1. **What Would You Do?** As a defense attorney, what would you do under the following circumstances?

   a. Your client tells you that he committed the crime or crimes for which he is being prosecuted.

   b. Your client tells you about a serious crime that will be committed sometime next week.

   c. Your client tells you that if you lose the case, his friends will harm your family.

   d. You learn that your client, who has paid you nothing so far for your services, will not be able to pay your fee.

   e. Your client insists on testifying, even though you believe that it is not in his best interests to do so.

2. **Jury Nullification** In John Grisham's 1992 novel, *A Time to Kill*, the defendant, a black man whose young daughter was viciously raped by two white men, is on trial for gunning down the two men on the courthouse steps in full view of many bystanders. Even though it was obvious to all that the defendant had killed the two men, the jury in the case returned a not-guilty verdict, and the defendant was allowed to walk free. This is an example of jury nullification, the power of a jury in a criminal case to acquit a defendant despite overwhelming evidence. The jury can acquit for any reason or for no reason at all, and the decision of the jury cannot be appealed. Jury nullification is one of the problems cited by critics who call for the abolition of the present American jury system. Another complaint about the jury system is the inability of some jurors in some trials to understand legal arguments, the evidence presented, or the instructions of the judge. Critics of the jury system suggest replacing jury trials with bench trials or with trials before a panel of judges or substituting professionally trained jurors for the current "amateur" jurors.

   a. Should the American jury system be abolished? Why or why not?

   b. Do you believe that any of the alternatives suggested by jury critics would produce a better or more just system? Defend your answer.

To access more information and resources, including study questions, chapter summaries, and links, go to: www.mhhe.com/bohm1.

CHAPTER SIX

Sentencing, Appeals, and the Death Penalty

CHAPTER OUTLINE

CHAPTER OBJECTIVES

After completing this chapter, you should be able to:

1. Identify the general factors that influence a judge's sentencing decisions.

2. Describe how judges tailor sentences to fit the crime and the offender.

3. Distinguish between indeterminate and determinate sentences.

4. Explain the three basic types of determinate sentences.

5. List five rationales or justifications for criminal punishment.

6. Explain the purposes of presentence investigation reports.

7. List the legal bases for appeal.

8. Identify the type of crime for which death may be a punishment.

9. Summarize the three major procedural reforms the U.S. Supreme Court approved for death penalty cases in the *Gregg* decision.

Sentencing

If a criminal defendant pleads guilty or is found guilty by a judge or jury, then the judge must impose a sentence.[1] In a few jurisdictions, sentencing is the responsibility of the jury for certain types of offenses (for example, capital crimes). Table 6.1 displays, by offense, the amount of time between conviction and sentencing for defendants in state courts in 2002. As Table 6.1 shows, for most offenses a majority of defendants are sentenced either on the day of conviction or the next day.

Sentencing is arguably a judge's most difficult responsibility. Judges cannot impose just any sentence. They are limited by the U.S. Constitution's Eighth

TABLE 6.1	Time between Felony Conviction and Sentencing in State Courts, by Offense, 2002			
		PERCENTAGE OF FELONS SENTENCED WITHIN:		
MOST SERIOUS CONVICTION OFFENSE	TOTAL	0–1 DAY	2–60 DAYS	61 DAYS OR MORE
TOTAL				
All offenses	100%	68%	17%	15%
VIOLENT OFFENSES	100%	60%	22%	17%
Murder[a]	100	52	27	21
Sexual assault[b]	100	59	21	20
Robbery	100	54	27	19
Aggravated assault	100	64	20	16
Other violent[c]	100	58	24	17
PROPERTY OFFENSES	100%	71%	16%	14%
Burglary	100	66	18	16
Larceny[d]	100	73	15	12
Fraud[e]	100	72	14	14
DRUG OFFENSES	100%	69%	16%	15%
Possession	100	74	15	11
Trafficking	100	65	17	18
WEAPON OFFENSES	100%	69%	21%	11%
OTHER OFFENSES[f]	100%	69%	17%	15%

Note: "Total" includes all cases, whether or not conviction type was known, and is based on an estimated 523,747 cases in 126 counties.
Detail may not add to the total because of rounding.
[a]Includes nonnegligent manslaughter.
[b]Includes rape.
[c]Includes offenses such as negligent manslaughter and kidnapping.
[d]Includes motor vehicle theft.
[e]Includes forgery and embezzlement.
[f]Composed of nonviolent offenses such as receiving stolen property and vandalism.

Source: Matthew R. Durose and Patrick A. Langan, *State Court Sentencing of Convicted Felons, 2002* (May 2005), www.ojp.usdoj.gov/bjs/abstract/scsc02st.htm, Table 4.10.

Amendment and statutory provisions; guided by prevailing philosophical rationales, organizational considerations, and presentence investigation reports; and influenced by their own personal characteristics.

THE U.S. CONSTITUTION'S EIGHTH AMENDMENT

The Eighth Amendment prohibits excessive fines and cruel and unusual punishments.

EXCESSIVE FINES What is excessive depends on the seriousness of the crime. For example, in a conviction for illegal possession of a small amount of marijuana, a defendant's having to forfeit his or her home might be considered an excessive fine. Along with excessive bail, this protection has not been extended to the states.

PROTECTION AGAINST CRUEL AND UNUSUAL PUNISHMENTS The prohibition of "cruel and unusual punishments" was extended to trials in state courts in 1962, in *Robinson* v. *California*. Generally, discussions of this issue involve the practice of capital punishment, or the death penalty, which will be discussed later in this chapter. Here only a brief history of the definition of cruel and unusual punishments is provided.

For approximately 120 years after the adoption of the Bill of Rights, the Supreme Court employed a fixed, historical meaning for "cruel and unusual punishments." In other words, the Court interpreted the concept's meaning in light of the practices that were authorized and were in use at the time the Eighth Amendment was adopted (1791). Thus, only the most barbarous punishments and tortures were prohibited. Capital punishment itself was not prohibited, because there was explicit reference to it in the Fifth Amendment and it was in use when the Eighth Amendment was adopted.

The Court, in *Wilkerson* v. *Utah* (1878), provided examples of punishments that were prohibited by the Eighth Amendment because they involved "torture" or "unnecessary cruelty." They included punishments in which the criminal "was emboweled alive, beheaded, and quartered." In another case, *In re Kemmler* (1890), the Court expanded the meaning of cruel and unusual punishments to include punishments that "involve torture or lingering death . . . something more than the mere extinguishment of life." The Court also provided some examples of punishments that would be prohibited under that standard: "burning at the stake, crucifixion, breaking on the wheel, or the like."

In 1910, in the noncapital case of *Weems* v. *United States*, the Supreme Court abandoned its fixed, historical definition of cruel and unusual punishments and created a new one. Weems was a U.S. government official in the Philippines who was convicted of making two false accounting entries, amounting to 612 pesos (about $56 in 2005 dollars).[2] He was sentenced to 15 years of hard labor and was forced to wear chains on his ankles and wrists. After completing his sentence, he was to be under surveillance for life, and he was to lose his voting rights as well. Weems argued that his punishment was disproportionate to his crime, and, therefore, cruel and unusual.

The Court agreed with Weems and, breaking with tradition, held "(1) that the meaning of the Eighth Amendment is not restricted to the intent of the Framers, (2) that the Eighth Amendment bars punishments that are excessive, and (3) that what is excessive is not fixed in time but changes with evolving social conditions." Thus, the Court no longer interpreted the concept of cruel and unusual punishments in the context of punishments in use when the Eighth Amendment was adopted. Instead, it chose to interpret the concept in the context of "evolving social conditions."

The Court further clarified its position nearly 50 years later, in another noncapital case, *Trop* v. *Dulles* (1958). As punishment for desertion during World War II, Trop was stripped of his U.S. citizenship. In reviewing the case on appeal, the Court ruled that the punishment was cruel and unusual because it was an affront to basic human dignity. Noting that the "dignity of man" was "the basic concept underlying the Eighth Amendment," the Court held that Trop's punishment exceeded "the limits of civilized standards." Referring to the earlier *Weems* case, the Court emphasized that "the limits of civilized standards . . . draws its meaning from the evolving standards of decency that mark the progress of a maturing society." Those "evolving standards of decency" are, in turn, determined by "objective indicators, such as the enactments of legislatures as expressions of 'the will of the people,' the decisions of juries, and the subjective moral judgments of members of the Supreme Court itself." In short, it appears that a punishment enacted by a legislature and imposed by a judge or jury will not be considered cruel and unusual, as long as the U.S. Supreme Court determines that (1) it is not grossly disproportionate to the magnitude of the crime, (2) it has been imposed for the same offense in other jurisdictions, and (3) it has been imposed for other offenses in the same jurisdiction (see *Solem* v. *Helm*, 1983; *Harmelin* v. *Michigan*, 1991; *Ewing* v. *California*, 2003; *Lockyer* v. *Andrade*, 2003).

STATUTORY PROVISIONS

State and federal legislative bodies enact penal codes that specify appropriate punishments for each statutory offense or class of offense, such as a class B felony or class C felony. Currently, five general types of punishment are in use in the United States: fines, probation, intermediate punishments (various punishments that are more restrictive than probation but less restrictive and costly than imprisonment), imprisonment, and death. As long as judges impose one or a combination of those five punishments, and the sentence type and length are within statutory limits, judges are free to set any sentence they want.

Thus, within limits, judges are free to tailor the punishment to fit the crime and the offender. As noted, judges can impose a combination sentence of, for example, imprisonment, probation, and a fine. They can suspend the imprisonment portion of a combination sentence, or they can suspend the entire sentence if the offender stays out of trouble, makes **restitution** (pays money or provides services to victims, their survivors, or the community to make up for the injury inflicted), or seeks medical treatment. If the offender has already spent weeks, months, or sometimes even years in jail awaiting trial, judges can give the offender credit for jail time and deduct that time from any prison sentence. When jail time is not deducted from the sentence, it is called "dead time." In some cases, the sentence that a judge intends to impose closely matches the time an offender has already spent in jail awaiting trial. In such cases, the judge may impose a sentence of "time served" and release the offender. When an offender is convicted of two or more crimes, judges can order the prison sentences to run concurrently (together) or consecutively (one after the other). Judges can also delay sentencing and retain the right to impose a sentence at a later date if conditions warrant. Table 6.2 shows, by offense, the types of felony sentences imposed by state courts in 2002. Note that 69 percent of all offenders were incarcerated; only 31 percent received probation. The largest percentage of offenders incarcerated were violent offenders (77 percent).

The sentence of death is generally limited to offenders convicted of "aggravated" murder, and because most criminal offenders are poor, fines are

The Longest Sentences

The longest prison sentence in the United States is believed to be a 10,000-year sentence imposed on Dudley Wayne Kyzer, 40, on December 4, 1981, in Tuscaloosa, Alabama, for a triple murder committed in 1976. The longest federal prison sentence is presumably the 845-year sentence imposed on Sholam Weiss, 47, in absentia, on February 15, 2000, in Orlando, Florida, for his role in the largest insurance company fraud in American history.

SOURCE: George E. Rush, *The Dictionary of Criminal Justice*, 5th ed. (Sluice Dock, Guilford, CT: Dushkin/McGraw-Hill, 2000), p. 295; Susan Clary, "Almost 3 Years Later, Weiss Shows in Court," *The Orlando Sentinel*, June 11, 2002, p. C1.

restitution Money paid or services provided by a convicted offender to victims, their survivors, or the community to make up for the injury inflicted.

| TABLE 6.2 | Distribution of Types of Felony Sentences Imposed in State Courts, by Offense, 2002 |

| | | PERCENTAGE OF FELONS SENTENCED TO— | | | |
| | | INCARCERATION | | | |
MOST SERIOUS CONVICTION OFFENSE	TOTAL	TOTAL	PRISON	JAIL	PROBATION
ALL OFFENSES	100%	69%	41%	28%	31%
VIOLENT OFFENSES	100%	77%	52%	25%	23%
Murder[a]	100	95	91	4	5
Sexual assault[b]	100	82	59	23	18
Rape	100	89	67	22	11
Other sexual assault	100	78	55	23	22
Robbery	100	86	71	15	14
Aggravated assault	100	71	42	29	29
Other violent[c]	100	77	42	35	23
PROPERTY OFFENSES	100%	66%	38%	28%	34%
Burglary	100	72	46	26	28
Larceny[d]	100	67	36	31	33
Motor vehicle theft	100	76	37	39	24
Fraud[e]	100	59	31	28	41
DRUG OFFENSES	100%	66%	39%	27%	34%
Possession	100	62	34	28	38
Trafficking	100	68	42	26	32
WEAPON OFFENSES	100%	73%	45%	28%	27%
OTHER OFFENSES[f]	100%	70%	35%	35%	30%

Note: For persons receiving a combination of sentences, the sentence designation came from the most severe penalty imposed—prison being the most severe, followed by jail, then probation. Prison includes death sentences. Felons receiving a sentence other than incarceration or probation are classified under "probation." This table is based on an estimated 919,387 cases.
[a]Includes nonnegligent manslaughter.
[b]Includes rape.
[c]Includes offenses such as negligent manslaughter and kidnapping.
[d]Includes motor vehicle theft.
[e]Includes forgery and embezzlement.
[f]Composed of nonviolent offenses such as receiving stolen property and vandalism.

Source: Matthew R. Durose and Patrick A. Langan, *State Court Sentencing of Convicted Felons, 2002* (May 2005), www.ojp.usdoj.gov/bjs/abstract/scsc02st.htm, Table 1.2.

seldom imposed for serious crimes. (When they are, it is generally for symbolic reasons.) Thus, in practice, judges have three sentencing options—probation, intermediate punishments, and imprisonment. Later chapters in this text will cover those options. The death penalty will be discussed at the end of this chapter.

The type of sentence imposed on an offender can be a highly volatile issue. Also controversial is the length of the sentence imposed. Judges in states that have indeterminate sentencing statutes generally have more discretion in sentencing than do judges in states with determinate sentencing laws. An **indeterminate sentence** has a fixed minimum and maximum term of incarceration, rather than a set period. Sentences of 10 to 20 years in prison or of not less than 5 years and not more than 25 years in prison are examples of indeterminate sentences. The amount of the term that is actually served is determined by a parole board. In 2002, about 25 percent of prison releases were determined by a parole board decision.[3]

Indeterminate sentences have been a principal tool in the effort to rehabilitate offenders for much of the past 80 years. They are based on the idea that correctional personnel must be given the flexibility necessary to successfully treat offenders and return them to society as law-abiding members. The rationale underlying indeterminate sentencing is that the time needed for

indeterminate sentence A sentence with a fixed minimum and maximum term of incarceration, rather than a set period.

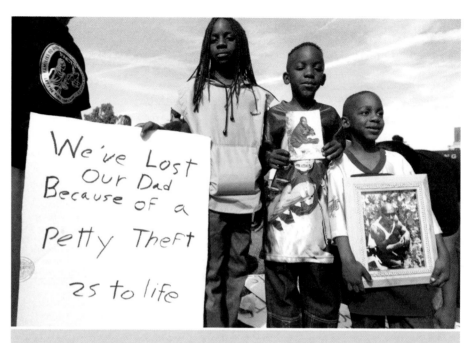

"Three strikes and you're out" laws have been used against offenders whose third felony was a relatively minor offense. *Are "three strikes" laws good laws? Why or why not?*

Sentencing

In 1975, Maine became the first state to replace indeterminate sentencing with determinate sentencing. It abolished parole at the same time.

SOURCE: Robert Carter, "Determinate Sentences," pp. 147–49, in M. D. McShane and F. P. Williams III (eds.), *Encyclopedia of American Prisons* (New York: Garland, 1996), p. 148.

determinate sentence A sentence with a fixed period of incarceration, which eliminates the decision-making responsibility of parole boards.

flat-time sentencing Sentencing in which judges may choose between probation and imprisonment but have little discretion in setting the length of a prison sentence. Once an offender is imprisoned, there is no possibility of reduction in the length of the sentence.

good time The number of days deducted from an inmate's sentence by prison authorities for good behavior or for other reasons.

mandatory sentencing Sentencing in which a specified number of years of imprisonment (usually within a range) is provided for particular crimes.

"correcting" different offenders varies so greatly that a range in sentence length provides a better opportunity to achieve successful rehabilitation.

Beginning in the early 1970s, social scientists and politicians began to question whether the rehabilitation of most criminal offenders was even possible. Skepticism about rehabilitation of offenders, a public outcry to do something about crime, and a general distrust of decisions made by parole boards continued to grow. By the mid-1970s, several state legislatures had abandoned or at least de-emphasized the goal of rehabilitation and had begun to replace indeterminate sentencing with determinate sentencing.

A **determinate sentence** has a fixed period of incarceration, which eliminates the decision-making responsibility of parole boards. The hope of determinate sentencing is that it will at least get criminals off the street for longer periods of time. Some people also consider a determinate sentence more humane because prisoners know exactly when they will be released, something that they do not know with an indeterminate sentence. Several states and the federal government have developed guidelines for determinate sentencing; other states have established sentencing commissions to do so.

There are three basic types of determinate sentences: flat-time, mandatory, and presumptive. With **flat-time sentencing,** judges may choose between probation and imprisonment but have little discretion in setting the length of a prison sentence. Once an offender is imprisoned, there is no possibility of a reduction in the length of the sentence. Thus, parole and **good time** (the number of days deducted from a sentence by prison authorities for good behavior or for other reasons) are not options under flat-time sentencing. Before New York imposed the first indeterminate sentence in the United States in 1924, nearly all sentences to prison in the United States were flat-time sentences. Flat-time sentences are rarely imposed today.

With **mandatory sentencing,** the second type of determinate sentencing, a specified number of years of imprisonment, usually within a range, is provided for particular crimes. Mandatory sentencing usually allows credit for good time but does not allow release on parole. Beginning in the 1980s, two principal variations of mandatory sentencing emerged. The first was mandatory minimum sentences, which require that offenders serve a specified amount of prison time. Mandatory minimum sentences are most frequently imposed on offenders who commit certain types of offenses such as drug offenses, offenses committed with weapons, and offenses committed by repeat or habitual ("three strikes and you're out") offenders. All states and the federal government have one or more mandatory minimum sentencing laws.

Similar to mandatory minimum sentences are sentences based on truth-in-sentencing laws. First enacted in the state of Washington in 1984, truth-in-sentencing laws require offenders to serve a substantial portion of their prison sentence, usually 85 percent of it. Most truth-in-sentencing laws target violent offenders and restrict or eliminate parole eligibility and good-time credits. Probably because of incentive grants authorized by Congress in 1994 to build or expand correctional facilities, nearly all states and the District of Columbia have enacted truth-in-sentencing laws modeled after the federal government's, which requires that for certain offenses 85 percent of a prison sentence must be served.

The third type of determinate sentencing is presumptive sentencing. **Presumptive sentencing** allows a judge to retain some sentencing discretion, subject to appellate review. In presumptive sentencing, the legislature determines a sentence range for each crime usually based on the seriousness of the crime and the criminal history of the offender. The judge is expected to impose the typical sentence, specified by statute, unless mitigating or aggravating circumstances justify a sentence below or above the range set by the legislature. A **mitigating circumstance** (for example, the defendant has no significant history of prior criminal activity) reduces the degree of an offender's blameworthiness for a criminal act, while an **aggravating circumstance** (for example, the crime was especially heinous, atrocious, or cruel) increases the degree of an offender's blameworthiness for a criminal act. Any sentence that deviates from the norm must be explained in writing and is subject to appellate review. Generally, with presumptive sentencing, credit is given for good time, but there is no opportunity for parole. Presumptive sentencing is a compromise between legislatively mandated determinate sentences and their indeterminate counterparts. Figure 6.1 displays Minnesota's presumptive sentencing guidelines grid.

Presumptive sentences may also be based on sentencing guidelines developed, not by legislatures, but by sentencing commissions composed of both criminal justice professionals and private citizens. Sentencing guidelines are a different way of restricting the sentencing discretion of judges. In 1984, Congress created the nine-member U.S. Sentencing Commission, which is charged with creating and amending federal sentencing guidelines.

In today's "law and order" climate, state legislatures, as noted, are increasingly replacing indeterminate sentences with determinate ones. This trend, however, has not escaped criticism. For example, it has been argued that the consequences of determinate sentencing include longer prison sentences and overcrowded prisons. Whether it is the result of a shift in sentencing philosophy

Myth Fact

Myth Determinate sentencing, especially mandatory sentencing, has a significant impact on serious crime.

Fact In practice, this myth has at least two problems. First, "mandatory" aspects of the laws are easy to evade. Second, the basic assumption on which the myth rests is wrong: that "soft" judges release too many dangerous offenders on probation. A recent study shows that 69 percent of all felons convicted in state courts were sentenced to either prison or jail; only 31 percent received probation. Seventy-seven percent of violent offenders and 66 percent of drug offenders were incarcerated. In the federal courts, 83 percent of felons were sentenced to incarceration.

SOURCE: Matthew R. Durose and Patrick A. Langan, "Felony Sentences in State Courts, 2002," *Bureau of Justice Statistics Bulletin* (Washington, DC: GPO, U.S. Department of Justice, December 2004), p. 2, Table 2 and p. 3.

presumptive sentencing Sentencing that allows a judge to retain some sentencing discretion, subject to appellate review. The legislature determines a sentence range for each crime.

mitigating circumstance A factor (for example, the defendant has no significant history of prior criminal activity) that reduces the degree of an offender's blameworthiness for a criminal act.

aggravating circumstance A factor (for example, the crime was especially heinous, atrocious, or cruel) that increases the degree of an offender's blameworthiness for a criminal act.

FIGURE 6.1 | Sample Sentencing Guidelines

MINNESOTA SENTENCING GUIDELINES GRID

Presumptive Prison Sentence Lengths in Months

LESS SERIOUS ⟵————————⟶ MORE SERIOUS

SEVERITY OF OFFENSE (Illustrative Offenses)	CRIMINAL HISTORY SCORE						
	0	1	2	3	4	5	6 or more
Sale of simulated controlled substance	12*	12*	12*	13	15	17	19 *18-20*
Theft Related Crimes ($2500 or less) Check Forgery ($200–$2500)	12*	12*	13	15	17	19	21 *20-22*
Theft Crimes ($2500 or less)	12*	13	15	17	19 *18-20*	22 *20-22*	23 *22-24*
Nonresidential Burglary Theft Crimes (over $2500)	12*	15	18	21	24 *23-25*	27 *26-28*	30 *29-31*
Residential Burglary Simple Robbery	18	23	28	33 *31-35*	38 *36-40*	43 *41-45*	48 *46-50*
Criminal Sexual Conduct 2nd Degree	21	27	33	39 *37-41*	45 *43-47*	51 *49-53*	57 *55-59*
Aggravated Robbery, 1st Degree Criminal Sexual Conduct, 2nd Degree	48 *44-52*	58 *54-62*	68 *64-72*	78 *74-82*	88 *84-92*	98 *94-102*	108 *104-112*
Criminal Sexual Conduct, 1st Degree Assault, 1st Degree	86 *81-91*	98 *93-103*	110 *105-115*	122 *117-127*	134 *129-139*	146 *141-151*	158 *153-163*
Murder, 3rd Degree Murder, 2nd Degree (felony murder)	150 *144-156*	165 *159-171*	180 *174-186*	195 *189-201*	210 *204-216*	225 *219-231*	240 *234-246*
Murder, 2nd Degree (with intent)	306 *299-313*	326 *319-333*	346 *339-353*	366 *359-373*	386 *379-393*	406 *399-413*	426 *419-433*

▨ At the discretion of the judge, up to a year in jail and/or other non-jail sanctions can be imposed instead of prison sentences as conditions of probation for most of these offenses. If prison is imposed, the presumptive sentence is the number of months shown.

☐ Presumptive commitment to state prison for all offenses.

Notes: 1. Criminal history score is based on offender's prior record and seriousness of prior offenses. 2. Numbers in italics represent the range of months within which a judge may sentence without the sentence being deemed a departure from the guidelines. 3. First degree murder is excluded from the guidelines by law and carries a mandatory life sentence.

*One year and one day

Source: Minnesota Sentencing Guidelines Commission. Effective August 1, 2004, www.msgc.state.mn.us/sentencing_guidelines.htm

or some other factor or factors, there is no question that the United States has been experiencing a dramatic increase in the number of people sentenced to prison and in the length of terms of incarceration. A result has been a crisis of prison overcrowding. In recent years, the United States has had one of the highest imprisonment rates in the world. Furthermore, as of 2005, the entire adult correctional departments of 10 states (Alabama, Colorado, Connecticut, Maryland, Michigan, Mississippi, Missouri, New Jersey, New York, and West Virginia) were under court orders to reduce overcrowding or improve other conditions of confinement. In another 8 states (Delaware, Florida, Georgia, Illinois, Indiana, Ohio, Wisconsin, and Wyoming) and the Federal Bureau of Prisons, one or more institutions were under court orders to reduce overcrowding or improve other conditions of confinement. (No information was available for Nevada, New Mexico, South Carolina, Tennessee, and Virginia.)[4]

A related criticism of determinate sentencing is that it produces an unusually harsh prison system. For example, because of prison overcrowding, many states have all but abandoned even the pretense of rehabilitating offenders. Prisons are increasingly becoming places where offenders are simply "warehoused." In addition, because of the abolition of good time and parole under some determinate sentencing schemes, prison authorities are having a more difficult time maintaining discipline and control of their institutions. Eliminating good time and parole removed two of the most important incentives that prison authorities use to get inmates to behave and to follow prison rules. Also, because of the perceived harshness of some of the determinate sentencing schemes, some judges simply ignore the guidelines. Other judges have ignored sentencing guidelines because they believe they are too lenient. In short, many judges resent sentencing guidelines and refer to their use as "justice by computer."

A third criticism of determinate sentencing is that it merely shifts sentencing discretion from judges to legislatures and prosecutors (through plea bargaining). Whether this shift in sentencing responsibility is desirable is a matter of debate. On one hand, prosecutors generally exercise their discretion in secret, whereas judges exercise discretion in the open. Also, prosecutors and legislators are generally subject to more political influence than are judges.

Yet, on the other hand, one of the major criticisms of indeterminate sentencing and a principal reason for the adoption of determinate sentencing schemes by some states is judicial disparity in sentencing. Judges vary widely in the sentences they impose for similar crimes and offenders. For example, in one study, 41 New York state judges were asked to review files of actual cases and to indicate the sentences they would impose. Sentences for the same crime were quite different. In one case, a heroin addict robbed an elderly man at gunpoint. The assailant was unemployed, lived with his pregnant wife, and had a minor criminal record. He was convicted of first-degree robbery, and under New York's indeterminate sentencing statute, the actual sentence was between 0 and 5 years. When the 41 judges were asked what sentence they would impose in the case, 22 percent of them chose the actual sentence (between 0 and 5 years), 29 percent chose a sentence of 5 to 10 years, another 29 percent selected a sentence of 10 to 15 years, 12 percent opted for a

Truth in Sentencing

Violent offenders sentenced to prison in 2002 were sentenced to serve an average of 84 months in prison. It is estimated that they will serve 62 percent of their prison sentences or 52 months prior to release. Under a truth-in-sentencing law requiring 85 percent of the sentence to be served, violent offenders would be expected to serve an estimated 19 months longer.

SOURCE: Calculated from Matthew R. Durose and Patrick A. Langan, "Felony Sentences in State Courts, 2002," *Bureau of Justice Statistics Bulletin* (Washington, DC: U.S. Department of Justice, 2004), p. 5, Table 4.

Myth Fact

Myth Judges are "soft" on crime, allowing many dangerous criminals to escape imprisonment.

Fact Whether an offender is imprisoned usually depends on the facts of the case. In cases of robbery and burglary, for example, judges are generally "hard" on robberies involving strangers and relatively "soft" on prior-relationship burglaries. According to a 2002 public opinion poll, 67 percent of Americans think that the courts are not harsh enough with criminals. In general, however, the "softness" or "hardness" of a judge's sentence depends on the seriousness of the offense, and only about 10 percent of all felonies reported to the police are violent.

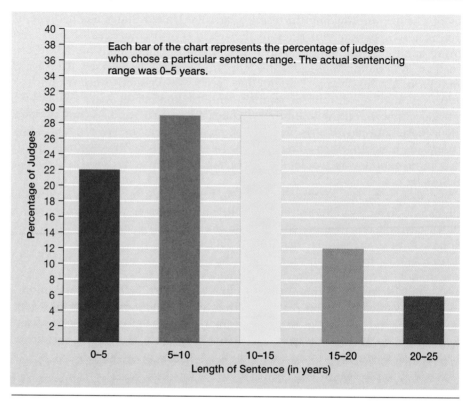

FIGURE 6.2   **Sentencing Choices of 41 New York State Judges**

Each bar of the chart represents the percentage of judges who chose a particular sentence range. The actual sentencing range was 0–5 years.

Source: Adapted from "Sentence Disparity in New York: The Response of Forty-One Judges," *The New York Times,* March 30, 1979, p. B3.

Public Opinion and Sentencing

Only 38 percent of Americans think that mandatory sentences are a good idea; 45 percent think that judges should be able to decide.

SOURCE: Peter D. Hart Research Associates, Inc., "Changing Public Attitudes toward the Criminal Justice System: Summary of Finding" (February 2002), p. 5, www.soros.org/initiatives/justice/articles_publications/publications/hartpoll_20020201.

CJ ONLINE

U.S. Sentencing Commission
To learn more about the U.S. Sentencing Commission, visit its Web site at **www.ussc.gov.** *Why do you think sentencing commissions are necessary?*

sentence of 15 to 20 years, and 7 percent of them chose a sentence of 20 to 25 years.[5] Figure 6.2 displays the judges' choices. Table 6.3 provides a comparison of the outcomes of felony convictions in state and federal courts in 2002. Obviously, different judges view the same circumstances very differently. Critics have charged that disparity in sentencing has resulted in discrimination against people of color and the poor.

A fourth, related criticism of determinate sentencing in those jurisdictions that retain good time is that sentencing discretion, at least to some degree, actually shifts from legislators and prosecutors to correctional personnel. By charging inmates with violations of prison rules, correctional personnel can reduce (if the charges are upheld) the amount of good time earned by inmates and, by doing so, increase an inmate's time served.

A fifth criticism of determinate sentencing is that it is virtually impossible for legislatures or sentencing commissions to define in advance all the factors that ought to be considered in determining a criminal sentence.

PHILOSOPHICAL RATIONALES

The goals of criminal justice in the United States are the prevention and the control of crime. Those are also the goals of criminal sanctions or criminal punishment—the penalties that are imposed for violating the criminal law. What has always been at issue, however, is how best to achieve those goals. This decision is the main problem faced by legislators who determine what the criminal sanctions will be in general and by judges who make sentencing decisions in individual cases. Historically, four major rationales or justifications

| TABLE 6.3 | Comparison of the Outcomes of Felony Convictions in State and Federal Courts, 2002 | | | | | | | |

Most Serious Conviction Offense	Felony Convictions			Federal Felony Convictions as Percent of Total	Percentage of Felons Sentenced to Incarceration (Prison or Jail)		Mean Sentence Length (in Months) for Felons Sentenced to Incarceration (Prison or Jail)	
	Total	State	Federal		State	Federal	State	Federal
ALL OFFENSES	1,114,217	1,051,000	63,217	5.7%	69%	83%	36 mo	58 mo
VIOLENT OFFENSES	199,607	197,030	2,577	1.3%	77%	93%	62 mo	89 mo
Murder	9,264	8,990	274	3.0	95	93	217	109
Sexual assault	35,813	35,500	313	0.9	82	90	78	96
Rape	11,040	10,980	60	0.5	89	88	104	154
Other sexual assault	24,773	24,520	253	1.0	78	91	65	83
Robbery	40,021	38,430	1,591	4.0	86	97	79	91
Aggravated assault	95,871	95,600	271	0.3	71	79	37	38
Other violent	18,638	18,510	128	0.7	77	90	33	91
PROPERTY OFFENSES	337,886	325,200	12,686	3.8%	66%	59%	28 mo	24 mo
Burglary	100,689	100,640	49	—	72	74	36	33
Larceny	125,850	124,320	1,530	1.2	67	50	22	29
Motor vehicle theft	18,629	18,530	99	0.5	76	73	18	31
Other theft	107,221	105,790	1,431	1.3	65	48	22	29
Fraud	111,347	100,240	11,107	10.0	59	60	24	23
Fraud	57,299	47,610	9,689	16.9	56	60	22	24
Forgery	54,048	52,630	1,418	2.6	61	60	26	21
DRUG OFFENSES	366,564	340,330	26,234	7.2%	66%	91%	32 mo	76 mo
Possession	129,590	127,530	2,060	1.6	62	90	22	79
Trafficking	236,984	212,810	24,174	10.2	68	91	38	76
WEAPON OFFENSES	38,033	32,470	5,563	14.6%	73%	92%	28 mo	84 mo
OTHER OFFENSES	172,127	155,970	16,157	9.4%	70%	82%	23 mo	31 mo

— Less than 0.05%.

The vast majority of all felony convictions in the United States occur in State courts. Overall, Federal courts account for a relatively small number.

- In 2002, federal courts convicted 63,217 persons of a violent, property, drug, or other felony. State courts convicted an estimated 1,051,000, bringing the combined U.S. total to 1,114,217 felons convicted. Federal courts accounted for 6% of the national total.
- Violent offenses comprised 4% of felony convictions in federal courts but 19% of those in state courts.
- In 2002, 83% of felons convicted in federal courts were sentenced to incarceration. The remaining 17% received probation. State courts sentenced 69% of felons to incarceration (prison or jail) and 31% to straight probation.
- The average federal incarceration sentence was just under 5 years in 2002. By contrast, state incarceration sentences (prison or jail) had an average of 3 years.
- Federal drug offenders received incarceration terms that were more than twice the length of drug offenders in state courts (6 years and 4 months versus 2 years and 8 months).
- In 2002, federal offenders released from prison served an average of 91% of their prison term before release. Felons convicted in state courts served a significantly smaller proportion of their total incarceration sentence. For instance, state prisoners (not including felons sentenced to jail) served about 51% of their total prison sentence in 2002.

Source of federal data: Federal statistics shown in the above table are from the same database that was used to create Tables 5.1. and 5.2 of the BJS publication *Compendium of Federal Statistics, 2002* (NCJ 205368). Tables 5.1 and 5.2 figures differ from the above figures because of offense definitions.

Source: Matthew R. Durose and Patrick A. Langan, "Felony Sentences in State Courts, 2002" *Bureau of Justice Statistics Bulletin* (Washington, DC: GPO, U.S. Department of Justice, 2004, p. 3).

have been given for the punishment imposed by the criminal courts: retribution, incapacitation, deterrence, and rehabilitation. A fifth rationale, restoration, has also been receiving greater attention.

Frequently, judges impose sentences for all five reasons, but at certain times in history, one or more of the reasons have been seen as less important than the others. Today, for example, punishment is imposed less for rehabilitative

Appropriate Sentencing

Most Americans (76 percent) think that the courts do not sentence offenders appropriately. Nearly all of those people (67 percent) feel that criminals are not treated harshly enough.

SOURCE: Kathleen Maguire and Ann L. Pastore (eds.), *Sourcebook of Criminal Justice Statistics 2001* (Online), p. 137, Table 2.54 at www.albany.edu/sourcebook; Kathleen Maguire and Ann L. Pastore (eds.), *Sourcebook of Criminal Justice Statistics 2003* (Online), pp. 140–41, Table 2.47 at www.albany.edu/sourcebook.

In response to overcrowding, some states erected tents on prison grounds, as in this Huntsville, Texas, facility. *Do you think that the use of tents to deal with prison overcrowding is acceptable? Why or why not?*

retribution A justification for punishment that implies repayment for an offense committed.

revenge The punishment rationale expressed by the biblical phrase, "An eye for an eye, and a tooth for a tooth." People who seek revenge want to pay back offenders by making them suffer for what they have done.

just deserts The punishment rationale based on the idea that offenders should be punished automatically, simply because they have committed a crime—they "deserve" it—and the idea that the punishment should fit the crime.

purposes than it once was because of the prevalent view that we do not know how to change the behavior of criminal offenders. Each of the rationales for criminal punishment now will be examined.

RETRIBUTION From biblical times through the eighteenth century, **retribution** was the dominant justification for punishment. It implies repayment for an offense committed. Although it has probably always played some role in sentencing decisions, it is now increasingly popular with the public as a rationale for punishment. However, retribution is an imprecise term that has been defined in many ways.[6] Nevertheless, when people say that criminal punishment should be imposed for retribution, what most of them want is probably either revenge or just deserts. **Revenge** is the justification for punishment expressed by the biblical phrase, "An eye for an eye, and a tooth for a tooth." People who seek revenge want to pay back offenders by making them suffer for what they have done. The concept of **just deserts** is another justification in which punishment is seen as a payback, one that is based on something more than vindictive revenge. It supposedly does not contain the emotional element of vengeance. Just deserts draws part of its meaning from the idea, attributed to the German philosopher Immanuel Kant (1724–1804), that offenders should be punished automatically, simply because they have committed a crime—they "deserve" it. Another aspect of just deserts is proportionality of punishment. That is, a punishment should fit the crime and should not be more nor less than the offender deserves.

Based on the assumption that the desire for revenge is a basic human emotion, retributivists generally believe that state-authorized punishment greatly reduces the likelihood that individual citizens will take it upon themselves to pay back offenders for what they have done. Vigilante justice is thereby avoided. Retributivists also believe that if offenders are not punished for their crimes, then other people will lose respect for the criminal law and will not obey it.

Finally, retribution is the only rationale for criminal punishment that specifically addresses what has happened in the past; that is, to pay back offenders for their crimes. All the other rationales focus on the future and seek to influence it; for example, to restrain or prevent an offender from committing future crimes.

INCAPACITATION **Incapacitation** is the removal or restriction of the freedom of those found to have violated criminal laws. Incapacitation makes it virtually impossible for offenders to commit crimes during the period of restraint. Banishment or exile was once used to achieve incapacitation. Even today, foreign nationals are deported after conviction of certain crimes. Currently, incapacitation is achieved primarily through imprisonment, which keeps inmates from committing further crimes (at least outside the prison). Some states, as noted previously, have habitual-offender statutes or "three strikes and you're out" laws that are intended to incapacitate repeat felons for life. Capital punishment is the ultimate means of incapacitation. An executed offender can never commit a crime again.

incapacitation The removal or restriction of the freedom of those found to have violated criminal laws.

DETERRENCE There are two forms of deterrence. **Special** or **specific deterrence** is the prevention of individuals from committing crime again by punishing them. **General deterrence** is the prevention of people in general from engaging in crime by punishing specific individuals and making examples of them.

One of the problems with general deterrence as a rationale for punishment is that even though it makes intuitive sense, social science is unable to measure its effects. Only those people who have not been deterred come to the attention of social scientists and criminal justice personnel.

special or **specific deterrence** The prevention of individuals from committing crimes again by punishing them.

general deterrence The prevention of people in general from engaging in crime by punishing specific individuals and making examples of them.

REHABILITATION For nearly 100 years, between the 1870s and 1970s, the primary rationale for punishing criminal offenders was **rehabilitation,** which

rehabilitation The attempt to "correct" the personality and behavior of convicted offenders through educational, vocational, or therapeutic treatment and to return them to society as law-abiding citizens.

Historically, many people have believed that public executions have a general deterrent effect. *Do you agree? Why or why not?*

Rehabilitation

In 2003, 72 percent of Americans either completely agreed (29 percent) or mostly agreed (43 percent) that the criminal justice system should try to rehabilitate criminals and not just punish them; only 25 percent either mostly disagreed (14 percent) or completely disagreed (11 percent).

Source: *Sourcebook of Criminal Justice Statistics Online*, www.albany.edu/sourcebook/pdf/t20012.pdf (Table 2.0012).

Victim Assistance
The U.S. Department of Justice established the Office for Victims of Crime (OVC) in 1983. OVC provides federal funding for victim assistance and compensation programs throughout the country. It also develops policies and works with criminal justice professionals in order to support crime victims. Visit the OVC Web site at **www.ojp.usdoj. gov/ovc.** *Do you think that enough is being done to support crime victims?*

is the attempt to "correct" the personality and behavior of convicted offenders through educational, vocational, or therapeutic treatment. The goal was to return them to society as law-abiding citizens. However, the goal of rehabilitating offenders was challenged on the grounds that we simply do not know how to correct or cure criminal offenders because the causes of crime are not fully understood. Beginning in the mid-1970s, the goal of rehabilitation was abandoned altogether in some states, or at least de-emphasized in favor of the goals of retribution and incapacitation. In other states, attempts at rehabilitation continue in an institutional context that seems to favor retribution and incapacitation (as it probably always has). Some critics have suggested that punishment and rehabilitation are incompatible ways of preventing and controlling crime and that rehabilitation generally cannot be achieved in a prison setting. This criticism, however, has apparently not influenced judges, who continue to send criminal offenders to prison to rehabilitate them.

RESTORATION AND VICTIMS' RIGHTS Until recently, victims of crime and their survivors have generally been forgotten or neglected in criminal justice. They have not been important or respected participants in the adjudication process except, perhaps, as witnesses to their own or their loved ones' victimization. Beginning in the 1980s, however, because of increased scholarly attention to their plight and a fledgling victims' rights movement, attempts have been made to change the situation. Today, at least in some jurisdictions, a greater effort is being made to do something for victims and their survivors—to restore them, as much as possible, to their previous state and to make them "whole" again.

In the early 1980s, only four states had laws that protected the basic rights of crime victims in the criminal justice system. Now, every state has such laws. In fact, there has been an explosion of activity in this area over the last 25 years. States have enacted more than 30,000 crime-victim-related statutes, at least 32 state victims' rights constitutional amendments have been passed, and the federal government has passed legislation providing basic rights and services to federal crime victims, such as victim assistance and victim compensation programs.[7]

The federal government, through its Crime Victims Fund, has also made millions of dollars available for state crime victim compensation, local victim assistance programs, and national training and technical assistance. The Crime Victims Fund is derived from fines, forfeited bonds, and penalties paid by federal criminal offenders, as well as gifts, bequests, and donations. Since the fund was established in 1984 and through 2004, about $6.7 billion have been awarded, and 2 to 4 million victims have been helped each year.[8]

Among the rights now granted crime victims in at least some jurisdictions are:

- The right to notice of victims' rights.
- The right to be treated with fairness, dignity, and respect.
- The right to be informed, present, and heard at important criminal justice proceedings.
- The right to confer with the prosecutor.
- The right of sexual assault victims to be paid for forensic exams.
- The right to HIV testing of sex offenders and notification of the results.
- The right to reasonable protection from the accused.
- The right to privacy (including a prohibition against compelling testimony about personal information in open court, exclusion or limited disclosure of victim-identifying information in criminal justice records, and protection from release of addresses and phone numbers provided for notice purposes).

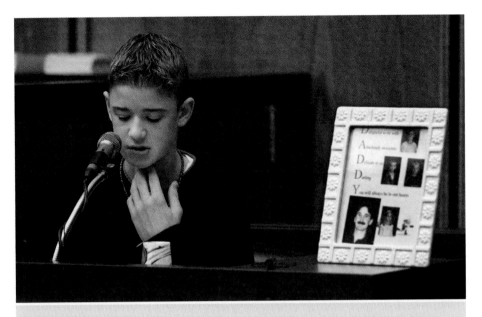

Brendan Costin, the 14-year-old son of hockey dad victim Michael Costin, becomes emotional as he delivers a victim impact statement about his deceased father while sitting next to a framed memorial the family set up on the witness stand at the sentencing hearing of hockey dad Thomas Junta. *Should victim-impact statements be allowed at sentencing hearings? Why or why not?*

- The right to a speedy resolution of the case.
- The right to a prompt return of the victim's property.
- The right to notice of the offender's release.
- The right to restitution from the offender or compensation from the state.[9]

In the sentencing process, the U.S. Supreme Court ruled in 1991 in *Payne* v. *Tennessee* that judges and juries may consider *victim-impact statements* in their sentencing decisions. **Victim-impact statements** are descriptions of the harm and suffering that a crime has caused victims and their survivors. Before the Court's 1991 decision, victim-impact statements were considered irrelevant and potentially inflammatory and were not allowed.

Despite the many rights that have been granted crime victims in the United States, there are many problems with the victims' rights laws and their implementation. Victims' rights vary greatly among states and at the federal level. Even in states that have constitutional rights for victims, those rights often are ignored, suffer from arbitrary implementation, or depend on the whims of criminal justice officials. Victims from other cultures and those with disabilities frequently are not informed of their rights or given the opportunity to participate in criminal and juvenile justice proceedings. There are also gaps in the laws. For example, many states do not provide comprehensive rights for the victims of crimes committed by juveniles. Victims' rights in tribal, military, and administrative proceedings are generally nonexistent.[10]

Another effort at restoration places equal emphasis on victims' rights and needs and the successful reintegration (and, in some cases, initial integration) of offenders into the community. Unlike retribution, which focuses almost entirely on offenders and their punishments, restorative justice seeks to restore the health of the community, repair the harm done, meet victims' needs, and require the offender to contribute to those repairs. In restorative justice the criminal act is condemned, offenders are held accountable,

victim-impact statements Descriptions of the harm and suffering that a crime has caused victims and their survivors.

1984 Crime Control Act

The 1984 Federal Comprehensive Crime Control Act requires that when offenders convicted of federal violations are sentenced to probation, they must pay a fine, make restitution, perform community service, or do all three.

participants are involved, and repentant offenders are encouraged to earn their way back into society.[11]

Restitution and community service are two examples of restorative practices (they are used for other purposes as well). Restitution is a court requirement that a victims' convicted offender pay money or provide services to victims, survivors, or the community that has been victimized. Typically, laws specify that restitution may be ordered to cover medical expenses, lost wages, counseling expenses, lost or damaged property, funeral expenses, and other direct out-of-pocket expenses. In more than one-third of all states, courts are required by law to order restitution unless there are compelling or extraordinary circumstances.[12] Unfortunately, a problem with restitution is that most offenders have neither the financial means nor the abilities to provide adequate restitution.

CAREERS IN CRIMINAL JUSTICE

Victim Advocate

My name is Dori DeJong and I am a victim advocate with the Denver District Attorney's Office in Denver, Colorado. I have a bachelor's degree in education from the University of Northern Colorado, a master's degree in social work and a Juris Doctor from the University of Denver. Prior to working in the district attorney's office, I worked as a counselor at a children's psychiatric hospital, as a children's counselor at a battered women's shelter, and as a legal advocate for a community agency that provided assistance to victims of domestic violence. I decided to become a victim advocate because it was a great way to combine my educational background in both social work and law.

A typical day as a victim advocate includes contacting the victims of crimes (domestic violence, stranger assault, sex assault, child abuse, etc.) and explaining the criminal justice system to them; providing details about their specific case; giving notification of their rights as a victim; referring victims to various outside assistance agencies; and obtaining their input as to the best possible outcome of the case in which they are involved. Additionally, I coordinate and participate in the meetings between the victims and the assistant district attorneys to assist in the preparation of the victims for trial, and to answer any questions they have about the process. I accompany the victims in the courthouse on the day of the trial to provide encouragement, support, and understanding of the process in order for them to get through a very difficult experience. I also send update letters and victim impact statements to victims, notify other agencies and jurisdictions of active cases, run criminal background checks on defendants to identify habitual offenders, and maintain statistics on

domestic violence cases. I have regular contact and communication with police officers, detectives, district attorneys, investigators, and other victim advocates. I also communicate with staff from outside assistance agencies to help sustain continuing support for the victim.

The most positive aspect of the job is the ability to help people and feel that you are really making a difference in someone's life. It is so encouraging when you have a client call you months or even years after you've assisted them, to thank you and tell you what a difference you've made in their lives and their children's lives. It is also rewarding to be a part of the prosecution team that holds criminals responsible and accountable for their behavior. Being a victim advocate can sometimes be difficult and frustrating because you work with people that are in crisis, and often are not appreciative of your involvement in their lives. Sometimes their anger about the incident is misdirected at the victim advocate and the system, which is trying to provide justice.

The job of a victim advocate is interesting, challenging, often fast paced, and can be very rewarding. However, the job can also be overwhelming since it frequently involves dealing with offensive criminal defendants and their actions, and the sometimes inequitable system of justice. If you are considering a job as a victim advocate, I would encourage you to volunteer or do an internship in an agency that works with victims. This invaluable experience will provide you with the knowledge to determine if this career suits you.

Do you have any characteristics and/or abilities that you think would make you particularly suited to be a victim's advocate? If so, what?

ORGANIZATIONAL CONSIDERATIONS

A judge's sentence is also guided by organizational considerations. The practice of plea bargaining has already been discussed at some length, where it was shown that without it the judicial process could not function. For practical reasons, judges almost always impose the sentence agreed upon during plea negotiations. If they did not, plea bargaining would not work. That is, if defendants could not be sure that judges would impose the agreed-upon sentence, there would be no reason for them to plead guilty. They might as well take their chances at trial.

Another organizational consideration is the capacity of the system. As already noted, many of the prisons in this country and some entire state prison systems are overcrowded and are under federal court order to reduce the problem. Judges in jurisdictions with overcrowded prisons are generally less inclined to sentence offenders to prison.

A third organizational consideration is the cost-benefit question. Every sentence involves some monetary and social cost. Judges must be sensitive to this issue and must balance the costs of the sentence they impose with the benefits that might be derived from it.

A judge's sentencing is the result of a complex set of factors. *Which factors do you consider to be the most important and the least important? Why?*

PRESENTENCE INVESTIGATION REPORTS

A purpose of **presentence investigation reports** (PSIs or PSIRs), used in the federal system and by the majority of states, is to help judges determine the appropriate sentence for particular defendants. They are also used in classifying probationers, parolees, and prisoners according to their treatment needs and security risk. Generally, a PSI is prepared by a probation officer, who conducts as thorough a background check as possible on a defendant. In some jurisdictions, probation officers recommend a sentence based on the information in the PSI. In other jurisdictions, they simply write the report and do not make a sentencing recommendation. Studies show that judges follow the sentencing recommendations in PSIs most of the time, although they are not required to do so.

In most jurisdictions, after the PSI has been submitted to the judge, a sentencing hearing is held at which the convicted defendant has the right to address the court before the sentence is imposed. This procedure is called **allocution.** During allocution, a defendant is identified as the person found guilty and has a right to deny or explain information contained in the PSI if his or her sentence is based on it. The defendant also has the opportunity to plead for a **pardon** (a "forgiveness" for the crime committed that stops further criminal processing). He or she may also attempt to have the sentencing process stopped or may explain why a sentence should not be pronounced. However, defendants are not entitled to argue during allocution about whether they are guilty. Among the claims that a convicted offender can make at allocution are the following:

1. That he or she is not the person who was found guilty at trial.
2. That a pardon has been granted for the crime in question.
3. That he or she has gone insane since the verdict was rendered. Rules of due process prohibit the sentencing of convicted offenders if they do not understand why they are being punished. Punishment must be deferred until they are no longer insane.
4. That she is pregnant. The sentence of a pregnant offender must be deferred or adjusted, especially in a capital case.

presentence investigation reports Reports, often called PSIs or PSIRs, that are used in the federal system and the majority of states to help judges determine the appropriate sentence. They are also used in classifying probationers, parolees, and prisoners according to their treatment needs and security risk.

allocution The procedure at a sentencing hearing in which the convicted defendant has the right to address the court before the sentence is imposed. During allocution, a defendant is identified as the person found guilty and has a right to deny or explain information contained in the PSI if his or her sentence is based on it.

pardon A "forgiveness" for the crime committed that stops further criminal processing.

PERSONAL CHARACTERISTICS OF JUDGES

Although extralegal factors are not supposed to influence a judge's sentencing decision, studies show that they invariably do. Judges, after all, are human beings with all of the human frailties and prejudices of other human beings. Among the personal characteristics of judges that have been found to affect their sentencing decisions are the following:

1. Their socioeconomic backgrounds.
2. The law schools they attended.
3. Their prior experiences both in and out of the courtroom.
4. The number of offenders they defended earlier in their careers.
5. Their biases concerning various crimes.
6. Their emotional reactions and prejudices toward the defendants.
7. Their own personalities.
8. Their marital and sexual relations.

In summary, a judge's sentencing decision is the result of the complex interplay of several different factors. Those factors include the U.S. Constitution's Eighth Amendment, statutory provisions, philosophical rationales,

CAREERS IN CRIMINAL JUSTICE

Court Reporter

My name is Debora Randolph, and I am an official court reporter with the Johnson County, Kansas District Court. I have an associate of applied science degree in court reporting and also an associate's degree in specialized business.

I began thinking about a career in court reporting when I was in high school. At the time, Kansas City Business College was the only school that had a court reporting program but it was being phased out. I then enrolled in another program and received my specialized business degree. I worked as a secretary at first. Still having a desire to be a court reporter, I opened the phonebook hoping to find a school that offered such a program and came across Brown Mackie College. I enrolled in the evening program and attended school for 2 years while working a full-time job as an administrative assistant. I successfully completed the program and received an AA degree. I then took and passed the required state certification test and was hired by the state of Kansas. I subsequently received my national certification. I have also taught court reporting courses.

As an official court reporter for the state of Kansas, my job entails recording verbatim reports of judicial trials, conferences, and hearings. Notes are taken at a high rate of speed through the use of a stenotype machine. As an officer of the court, it is my responsibility to prepare a complete and accurate report of proceedings, which may involve highly technical terminology used in a number of different fields. Although the proceedings may not be transcribed until some time later, I also provide "real-time" or instant-text translation feed to the attorneys and judges. Text is displayed on computer monitors for attorneys and judges to view during the proceedings. Additionally, I provide input to the judge and administrative assistant regarding docket management.

One of the things I like best about my job is I am constantly learning because of the varied cases I take. I also get to listen to some very interesting life experiences. Court reporting is an interesting, challenging, and rewarding career; however, because of the long hours involved, it can be overwhelming. I often work evenings and weekends producing transcripts. I would advise anyone who is thinking of court reporting as a career to be prepared to dedicate a considerable amount of time to the profession. Many aspiring court reporters do not make it past the first year of school. Training requires much practice time to learn to "write" up to 25 words per minute in addition to the other core requirements.

Which aspect of this job would you find the most rewarding?

organizational considerations, presentence investigation reports, results of the allocution, and personal characteristics of the judge.

Appeals

As described previously, defendants can appeal their convictions either on legal grounds (for example, defects in jury selection, improper admission of evidence at trial, mistaken interpretations of law) or on constitutional grounds (for instance, illegal search and seizure, improper questioning of the defendant by the police, identification of the defendant through a defective police lineup, incompetent assistance of counsel). However, they are not entitled to present new evidence or testimony on appeal if that evidence or testimony could have been presented at trial. If new evidence is discovered that was unknown or unknowable to the defense at trial, then an appeal can sometimes be made on the basis of that new evidence. Still, in *Herrera* v. *Collins*, 1993, a death penalty case, the Supreme Court ruled that, absent constitutional grounds, new evidence of innocence is no reason for a federal court to order a new state trial. In any event, because the defendant has already been found guilty, the presumption of innocence no longer applies during the appellate process, and the burden of showing why the conviction should be overturned shifts to the defendant.

Generally, notice of intent to appeal must be filed within 30 to 90 days after conviction. Also, within a specified period of time, an *affidavit of errors* specifying the alleged defects in the trial or pretrial proceedings must be submitted. If those two steps are followed, the appellate court must review the case. Nevertheless, very few appeals are successful. Nearly 80 percent of state trial court decisions are affirmed on appeal. (See Chapter 5 for more on the appellate courts.)

THINKING CRITICALLY

1. What do you think are some of the most important issues to consider when sentencing a convicted criminal?
2. Do you think that victims should play more or less of a role in sentencing?

THINKING CRITICALLY

Why do you think so few appeals are successful? Do you think the appeals process works effectively? Why or why not?

The Death Penalty

Before concluding this chapter, we will examine in some detail the death penalty in the United States, because, as the Supreme Court has acknowledged, "death is different."[13] Other sentencing options are discussed in later chapters of this book. As a punishment for the most heinous of crimes, the death penalty, or capital punishment, differs from all other criminal sanctions, not only in the nature of the penalty itself (the termination of life), but also in the legal procedures that lead to it. However, before describing the unique way in which capital punishment is administered in the United States, some background about the penalty is provided.

A BRIEF HISTORY OF THE DEATH PENALTY IN THE UNITED STATES

When the first European settlers arrived in America, they brought with them the legal systems from their native countries, which included the penalty of death for a variety of offenses. For example, the English Penal Code at the time, which was adopted by the British colonies, listed more than 50 capital

For a century after the ratification of the Eighth Amendment, hanging was the only legally authorized method of execution in the United States. The one exception was that spies, traitors, and deserters convicted under federal statutes could be shot. Hanging is no longer authorized as the sole or principal method of execution in any executing jurisdiction. *Why was hanging as a method of execution abandoned?*

Women Executed

Of the 3,373 people on death rows in the United States, as of January 1, 2006, only about 1.6 percent were women. As of January 1, 2006, only 11 women have been executed in the United States since 1962. The first was Velma Barfield, who was executed in North Carolina on October 2, 1984.

SOURCE: Death Penalty Information Center at www.deathpenaltyinfo.org.

offenses, but actual practice varied from colony to colony. In the Massachusetts Bay Colony, 12 crimes carried the death penalty:

- Idolatry.
- Witchcraft.
- Blasphemy.
- Rape.
- Statutory rape.
- Perjury in a trial involving a possible death sentence.
- Rebellion.
- Murder.
- Assault in sudden anger.
- Adultery.
- Buggery (sodomy).
- Kidnapping.

In the statute, each crime was accompanied by an appropriate biblical quotation justifying the capital punishment. Later the colony added arson, treason, and grand larceny to the list of capital offenses. In contrast, the Quakers adopted much milder laws. The Royal Charter for South Jersey (1646), for example, did not permit capital punishment for any crime, and in Pennsylvania, William Penn's Great Act of 1682 limited the death penalty to treason and murder. Most colonies, however, followed the much harsher British Code.

The earliest recorded lawful execution in America was in 1608 in the colony of Virginia. Captain George Kendall, a councillor for the colony, was executed for being a spy for Spain. Since Kendall about 19,000 legal executions have been performed in the United States under civil authority. However, only about 3 percent of those people executed since 1608 have been women. Ninety percent of the women executed were executed under local, as opposed to state, authority, and the majority (87 percent) were executed before 1866. The first woman executed was Jane Champion in the Virginia colony in 1632. She was hanged for murdering and concealing the death of her child, who was fathered by a man other than her husband.

In addition, about 2 percent of those executed in the United States since 1608 have been juveniles, those whose offenses were committed prior to their eighteenth birthdays. The first juvenile executed in America was Thomas Graunger in the Plymouth Colony in 1642, for the crime of bestiality. Between 1990 and 2005, the United States was one of only seven countries that had executed anyone under 18 years of age at the time of the crime; the others were the Democratic Republic of Congo, Iran, Nigeria, Pakistan, Saudi Arabia, and Yemen. Pakistan, Yemen, and the United States (as of March 1, 2005) no longer execute juveniles. The United States had executed 22 juveniles since 1976.[14]

ENTER THE SUPREME COURT

For more than 150 years, the United States Supreme Court ("the Court") has exercised its responsibility to regulate capital punishment in the United States and its territories. Among the principal issues the Supreme Court considered in relation to capital punishment before 1968 concerned the means of administering the death penalty. The Court upheld the constitutionality of shooting (*Wilkerson* v. *Utah*, 1878), electrocution (*In re Kemmler*, 1890), and a second electrocution after the first attempt had failed to kill the offender (*Louisiana ex rel. Francis* v. *Resweber*, 1947). Currently, there are five methods of execution authorized: lethal injection, electrocution, lethal gas, hanging, and firing squad. Lethal injection is the primary method of execution used by all executing states, except Nebraska. Table 6.4 lists the states that employ each method of execution.

TABLE 6.4	Method of Execution, by Jurisdiction, May 2006				
LETHAL INJECTION	**LETHAL INJECTION (CONTINUED)**	**ELECTROCUTION**	**LETHAL GAS**	**HANGING**	**FIRING SQUAD**
Alabama[1,2]	New Hampshire[11]	Alabama[1,2]	Arizona[1,3]	New Hampshire[11]	Idaho[7]
Arizona[1,3]	New Jersey	Arkansas[1,4]	California[1,5]	Washington[1]	Oklahoma[12]
Arkansas[1,4]	New Mexico	Florida[1,6]	Maryland[1,10]		Utah[1]
California[1,5]	New York	Illinois[1,8]	Missouri[1]		
Colorado	North Carolina	Kentucky[1,8]	Wyoming[14]		
Connecticut	Ohio	Nebraska			
Delaware	Oklahoma[12]	Oklahoma[12]			
Florida[1,6]	Oregon	South Carolina[1]			
Georgia	Pennsylvania	Tennessee[13]			
Idaho[1,7]	South Carolina[1]	Virginia[1]			
Illinois[1,8]	South Dakota				
Indiana	Tennessee[1,13]				
Kansas	Texas				
Kentucky[1,9]	Utah[1]				
Louisiana	Virginia[1]				
Maryland[1,10]	Washington[1]				
Mississippi	Wyoming[14]				
Missouri[1]	U.S. Government				
Montana	U.S. Military				
Nevada					

1. Authorizes two methods of execution.
2. Effective July 1, 2002, Alabama authorizes lethal injection unless the inmate requests electrocution.
3. Arizona authorizes lethal injection for persons sentenced after November 15, 1992; those sentenced before that date may select lethal injection or lethal gas.
4. Arkansas authorizes lethal injection for persons committing a capital offense after July 4, 1983; those who committed the offense before that date may select lethal injection or electrocution.
5. California authorizes lethal injection unless the inmate requests lethal gas.
6. Florida allows inmates to choose either lethal injection or electrocution.
7. Idaho authorizes firing squad only if lethal injection is "impractical."
8. Illinois authorizes electrocution if lethal injection is ever held to be unconstitutional.
9. Kentucky authorizes lethal injection for those convicted after March 31, 1998; those who committed the offense before that date may select lethal injection or electrocution.
10. Maryland authorizes lethal injection for those whose capital offenses occurred on or after March 25, 1994; those who committed the offense before that date may select lethal injection or lethal gas.
11. New Hampshire authorizes hanging only if lethal injection cannot be given.
12. Oklahoma authorizes electrocution if lethal injection is ever held to be unconstitutional and firing squad if both lethal injection and electrocution are held unconstitutional.
13. Tennessee authorizes lethal injection for those sentenced after January 1, 1999, and those currently on death row will choose between the electric chair and lethal injection.
14. Wyoming authorizes lethal gas if lethal injection is ever held to be unconstitutional.

The method of execution of federal prisoners for offenses under the Violent Crime Control and Law Enforcement Act of 1994 is that of the state in which the conviction took place. If the state has no death penalty, the judge may choose the method of another state. For offenses under the 1988 Drug Kingpin law, the method of executions is lethal injection.

Source: The Death Penalty Information Center, www.deathpenaltyinfo.org, May 16, 2006.

Between 1968 and 1972, a series of lawsuits challenged various aspects of capital punishment as well as the constitutionality of the punishment itself. During this period, an informal moratorium on executions was observed, pending the outcome of the litigation, and no death row inmates were executed. Some of the suits were successful, and some of them were not. Finally, on June 29, 1972, the Supreme Court set aside death sentences for the first time in its history. In its decisions in *Furman* v. *Georgia, Jackson* v. *Georgia,* and *Branch* v. *Texas* (hereafter referred to as the *Furman* decision), the Court held that the capital punishment statutes in those three cases were unconstitutional because they gave the jury complete discretion to decide whether to impose the death penalty or a lesser punishment in capital cases. Although nine separate opinions were written—a very rare occurrence—the majority of five justices (Douglas, Brennan, Stewart, White,

Heckler v. Chaney

In the 1985 case of *Heckler v. Chaney,* the Supreme Court upheld the constitutionality of lethal injection as an execution method.

During the twentieth century, more people were executed by electrocution than by any other method. Today, Nebraska is the only state that still uses electrocution as the sole method of execution. *Why have states abandoned electrocution as an execution method?*

and Marshall) pointed out that the death penalty had been imposed arbitrarily, infrequently, and often selectively against people of color. According to the majority, those statutes constituted "cruel and unusual punishment" under the Eighth and Fourteenth Amendments. (The four dissenters were Chief Justice Burger and Justices Blackmun, Powell, and Rehnquist.) It is important to emphasize that the Supreme Court did not rule that the death penalty itself was unconstitutional, only the way in which it was being administered.

The practical effect of the *Furman* decision was that the Supreme Court voided the death penalty laws of some 35 states, and more than 600 men and women had their death sentences vacated and commuted to a term of imprisonment. Although opponents of capital punishment were elated that the United States had finally joined all the other Western industrialized nations in abolishing capital punishment either in fact or in practice, the joy was short-lived. By the fall of 1974, 30 states had enacted new death penalty statutes that were designed to meet the Court's objections.

The new death penalty laws took two forms. Some states removed all discretion from the process by mandating capital punishment upon conviction for certain crimes (mandatory statutes). Other states provided specific guidelines that judges and juries were to use in deciding if death was the appropriate sentence in a particular case (guided-discretion statutes).

The constitutionality of the new death penalty statutes was quickly challenged, and on July 2, 1976, the Supreme Court announced its rulings in five test cases. In *Woodson* v. *North Carolina* and *Roberts* v. *Louisiana*, the Court rejected "mandatory" statutes that automatically imposed death sentences for defined capital offenses. However, in *Gregg* v. *Georgia*, *Jurek* v. *Texas*, and *Proffitt* v. *Florida* (hereafter referred to together as the *Gregg* decision), the Court approved several different forms of guided-discretion statutes. Those statutes, the Court wrote, struck a reasonable balance between giving the jury some guidance and allowing it to consider the background and character of the defendant and the circumstances of the crime.

The most dramatic effect of the *Gregg* decision was the resumption of executions on January 17, 1977, when the State of Utah executed Gary Gilmore (at his own request) by firing squad. Since then 1,022 people have been executed in 33 states and by the federal government, which has executed three (as of May 5, 2006).[15] More than half of the 1,022 executions have taken place in just three states—Texas (363), Virginia (95), and Oklahoma (80). Figure 6.3 shows the states in which executions have taken place. Note that Texas alone accounts for more than one-third of all post-*Furman* executions. Texas has executed more than three times as many offenders as any other state.

Table 6.5 shows the race or ethnicity and gender of both the defendants executed and their victims, as well as defendant-victim racial or ethnic combinations.

Myth   Fact

There is no gender discrimination in the administration of capital punishment.

Although women commit approximately 20 percent of all criminal homicides, only 10 women— about 1 percent of all executions since 1977—have been executed since executions resumed in 1977.

| FIGURE 6.3 | State-by-State Count of Inmates Executed in 33 States Since Executions Resumed in 1977 |

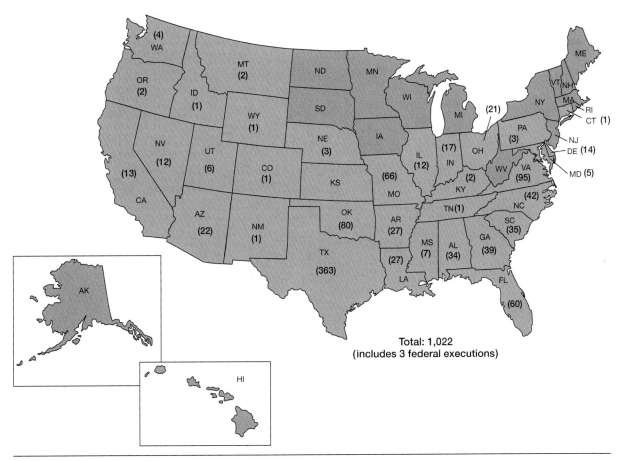

Total: 1,022
(includes 3 federal executions)

Source: Adapted from Death Penalty Information Center at www.deathpenaltyinfo.org, May 2006.

As shown, nearly all of the people executed since Gilmore's execution in 1977 have been male, while the gender of the victims is divided nearly evenly between males and females. As for race, nearly 58 percent of all people executed under post-*Furman* statutes have been white; about 34 percent have been black. Thus, the percentage of blacks who have been executed far exceeds their proportion of the general population (about 13 percent). Particularly interesting is that more than 80 percent of the victims of those executed have been white. What makes this finding interesting is that murders, including capital murders (all post-*Furman* executions have been for capital murders; see the following discussion), tend to be intraracial crimes. However, the death penalty is imposed primarily on the killers of white people, regardless of the race or ethnicity of the offender. The figures on defendant-victim racial or ethnic combinations (see Table 6.5) further support this conclusion. Note that about 54 percent of executions have involved white killers of white victims, and about 21 percent of executions have involved black killers of white victims. On the other hand, only about 11 percent of executions have been of black killers of black victims, and there have been only 12 executions of white killers of black persons (about 1 percent).

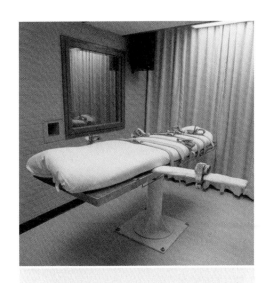

Lethal injection has become the sole or principal method of execution in all but one executing jurisdiction in the United States (the exception is Nebraska). Why?

TABLE 6.5	Race or Ethnicity and Sex of Defendants Executed and Their Victims and Defendant-Victim Racial or Ethnic Combinations

GENDER OF DEFENDANTS EXECUTED			GENDER OF VICTIMS		
Total Number 1004			Total Number 1501		
Female	11	(1.10%)	Female	741	(49.37%)
Male	993	(98.90%)	Male	760	(50.63%)

RACE OF DEFENDANTS EXECUTED			RACE OF VICTIMS		
White	580	(57.77%)	White	1199	(79.88%)
Black	340	(33.86%)	Black	208	(13.86%)
Latino/a	63	(6.27%)	Latino/a	63	(4.20%)
Native American	14	(1.39%)	Native American	5	(0.33%)
Asian	7	(0.70%)	Asian	26	(1.73%)

DEFENDANT-VICTIM RACIAL COMBINATIONS					
White Defendant and			Asian Defendant and		
White Victim	546	(54.38%)	White Victim	2	(0.20%)
Black Victim	12	(1.20%)	Black Victim	0	(0.00%)
Latino/a Victim	10	(1.00%)	Latino/a Victim	0	(0.00%)
Asian Victim	3	(0.30%)	Asian Victim	5	(0.50%)
Native American Victim	0	(0.00%)	Native American Victim	0	(0.00%)
Black Defendant and			Native American and		
White Victim	207	(20.62%)	White Victim	12	(1.20%)
Black Victim	107	(10.66%)	Black Victim	0	(0.00%)
Latino/a Victim	13	(1.29%)	Latino/a Victim	0	(0.00%)
Asian Victim	7	(0.70%)	Asian Victim	0	(0.00%)
Native American Victim	0	(0.00%)	Native American Victim	2	(0.20%)
Latino/a Defendant and			TOTAL		
White Victim	32	(3.19%)	White Victim	799	(79.85%)
Black Victim	2	(0.20%)	Black Victim	121	(12.05%)
Latino/a Victim	25	(2.49%)	Latino/a Victim	48	(4.78%)
Asian Victim	1	(0.10%)	Asian Victim	16	(1.59%)
Native American Victim	0	(0.00%)	Native American Victim	2	(0.20%)

Note: In addition, there were 18 defendants executed for the murders of multiple victims of different races. Of those, 10 defendants were white, 5 black, and 3 Latino. (1.79%)

Source: *Death Row, U.S.A.*, NAACP Legal Defense and Educational Fund (January 1, 2006).

Currently (as of July, 2006), 39 jurisdictions have capital punishment statutes; 14 jurisdictions do not have capital punishment statutes. (In 2004, the death penalty statutes of New York and Kansas were declared unconstitutional. In June 2006, the U.S. Supreme Court overruled the Kansas Supreme Court and held that Kansas's death penalty statute was constitutionally valid.) Figure 6.4 shows the jurisdictions with and without capital punishment statutes.

In decisions since *Gregg*, the Supreme Court has limited the crimes for which death is considered appropriate and has further refined death penalty jurisprudence. In 1977, in the cases of *Coker* v. *Georgia* and *Eberheart* v. *Georgia*, the Court held that rape of an adult female (in *Coker*) and kidnapping (in *Eberheart*), where the victim was not killed, do not warrant death. Those two decisions effectively limited the death penalty to those offenders convicted of capital, or aggravated, murder.

In 1986, in *Ford* v. *Wainwright*, the Court barred states from executing inmates who have developed mental illness while on death row, and, in 2002, in *Atkins* v. *Virginia*, the Court held that it is cruel and unusual punishment to

FIGURE 6.4 | Jurisdictions With and Without Capital Punishment Statutes

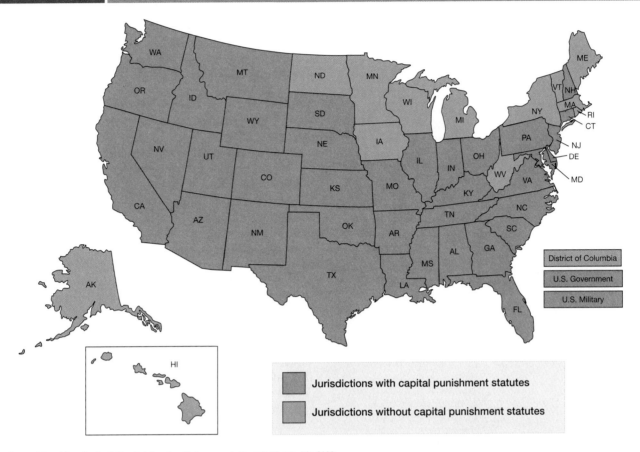

District of Columbia

U.S. Government

U.S. Military

Jurisdictions with capital punishment statutes

Jurisdictions without capital punishment statutes

Source: Adapted from the Death Penalty Information Center, www.deathpenaltyinfo.org, July, 2006.

The most celebrated recent execution by firing squad was the January 17, 1977, execution of Gary Gilmore in Utah. It no longer is authorized as the sole or principal method of execution in any executing jurisdiction. *Does execution by firing squad have any advantages over other methods of execution? If so, what are they?*

execute the mentally retarded. In the 2005 case of *Roper* v. *Simmons,* the Court, again referring to "evolving standards of decency," effectively limited capital punishment to offenders who are 18 years of age or older at the time of their offenses. Another death penalty decision of the Supreme Court is the 1987 case of *McCleskey* v. *Kemp,* in which the Court held that state death penalty statutes are constitutional even when statistics indicate that they have been applied in racially biased ways. The Court ruled that racial discrimination must be shown in individual cases. The *McCleskey* decision was particularly disheartening to opponents of capital punishment because, for them, the case was the last best chance of having the Supreme Court declare the death penalty unconstitutional once and for all.

The 1994 federal crime bill (the Violent Crime Control and Law Enforcement Act) expanded the number of federal crimes punishable by death to about 50. (Estimates vary depending on whether statutes or offenses are counted, and how offenses are counted.) All but four of the federal crimes involve murder. The four exceptions are treason; espionage; drug trafficking in large quantities; and attempting, authorizing, or advising the killing of any public officer, juror, or witness in a case involving a continuing criminal enterprise—regardless of whether such a killing actually occurs. In addition, the bill reinstated the death penalty for federal crimes for which previous death penalty provisions could not pass constitutional muster. The new law brought the earlier statutes into compliance with guidelines established by the Supreme Court. The U.S. government executed Timothy

Myth

Capital punishment is no longer administered in a way that is racially discriminatory and legally impermissible.

Fact

Dozens of scientific studies clearly show that the death penalty continues to be administered in a legally impermissible and discriminatory fashion against blacks and the killers of whites.

SOURCE: For a summary of those studies, see David C. Baldus and George Woodworth, "Race Discrimination and the Death Penalty: An Empirical and Legal," in J. R. Acker, R. M. Bohm, and C. S. Lanier (eds.), *America's Experiment with Capital Punishment: Reflections on the Past, Present, and Future of the Ultimate Penal Sanction*, 2nd ed. (Durhan, NC: Carolina Academic Press, 2003), pp. 501–51; United States General Accounting Office, *Death Penalty Sentencing: Research Indicates Pattern of Racial Disparities, Report to the Senate and House Committees on the Judiciary* (Washington: GPO, 1990). For the view that the evidence does not show racial discrimination, see William Wilbanks, *The Myth of a Racist Criminal Justice System* (Monterey, CA: Brooks/Cole, 1987).

bifurcated trial A two-stage trial (unlike the one-stage trial in other felony cases) consisting of a guilt phase and a separate penalty phase.

McVeigh and Juan Raul Garza in 2001, and Louis Jones, Jr., in 2003. They were the first federal executions in nearly 40 years. Prior to those three, the last execution by the U.S. government was on March 15, 1963, when Victor H. Feguer was hanged at Iowa State Penitentiary.

THE PROCEDURAL REFORMS APPROVED IN *GREGG*

It is important to emphasize that the Supreme Court approved the new death penalty statutes in *Gregg* "on their face." That is, the Court assumed, without any evidence, that the new guided-discretion statutes would eliminate the arbitrariness and discrimination that the Court found objectionable in its *Furman* decision. The Court was particularly optimistic about the following procedural reforms: bifurcated trials, guidelines for judges and juries, and automatic appellate review.

BIFURCATED TRIALS A **bifurcated trial** is a two-stage trial—unlike the one-stage trial in other felony cases—consisting of a guilt phase and a separate penalty phase. If, in the guilt phase, the defendant is found guilty as charged, then at the penalty phase, the jury must determine whether the sentence will be death or life in prison (there are no other choices except, in most death penalty states, life imprisonment without opportunity for parole).

Some states require the selection of two separate juries in capital trials, one for the guilt phase and one for the penalty phase. During *voir dire* in capital cases, each side is generally allowed more peremptory challenges, necessitating a larger panel from which to select the jury. California, for example, allows 26 peremptory challenges in capital cases and only 10 in noncapital cases. During both phases of a bifurcated capital trial, evidence may be introduced and witnesses may be called to testify. In short, all of the procedures of due process apply to both phases of the bifurcated trial.

GUIDELINES FOR JUDGES AND JURIES What the Court found especially appealing about the guided-discretion statutes approved in *Gregg* is that judges and juries are provided with standards that presumably restrict, but do not eliminate, their sentencing discretion. Specifically, judges and juries, in most states, are provided with lists of aggravating and, at least in some states, mitigating factors. The Court has since ruled (in *Lockett* v. *Ohio*, 1978; *Bell* v. *Ohio*, 1978; and *Hitchcock* v. *Dugger*, 1987) that judges and juries must consider any mitigating circumstance offered by the defense, whether it is listed in the statute or not. Table 6.6 lists the aggravating and mitigating factors in Florida's current death penalty statute. The factors are typical of most states that provide them.

Under Florida's death penalty statute, which is an "aggravating-versus-mitigating" type, at least one aggravating factor must be found before death may be considered as a penalty. If one or more aggravating factors is found, it is weighed against any mitigating factors. If the aggravating factors outweigh the mitigating factors, the sentence is death. However, if the mitigating factors outweigh the aggravating factors, the sentence is life imprisonment without opportunity for parole. Currently, in Florida (and Alabama) the jury's

TABLE 6.6	Aggravating and Mitigating Factors in Florida's Death Penalty Statute

AGGRAVATING FACTORS

1. The capital felony was committed by a person previously convicted of a felony and under sentence of imprisonment or placed on community control or on felony probation.

2. The defendant was previously convicted of another capital felony or of a felony involving the use or threat of violence to the person.

3. The defendant knowingly created a great risk of death to many persons.

4. The capital felony was committed while the defendant was engaged, or was an accomplice, in the commission of, or an attempt to commit, or flight after committing or attempting to commit, any: robbery; sexual battery; aggravated child abuse; abuse of an elderly person or disabled adult resulting in great bodily harm, permanent disability, or permanent disfigurement; arson; burglary; kidnapping; aircraft piracy; or unlawful throwing, placing, or discharging of a destructive device or bomb.

5. The capital felony was committed for the purpose of avoiding or preventing a lawful arrest or effecting an escape from custody.

6. The capital felony was committed for pecuniary gain.

7. The capital felony was committed to disrupt or hinder the lawful exercise of any governmental function or the enforcement of laws.

8. The capital felony was especially heinous, atrocious, or cruel.

9. The capital felony was a homicide and was committed in a cold, calculated and premeditated manner without any pretense of moral or legal justification.

10. The victim of the capital felony was a law enforcement officer engaged in the performance of his or her official duties.

11. The victim of the capital felony was an elected or appointed public official engaged in the performance of his or her official duties if the motive for the capital felony was related, in whole or in part, to the victim's official capacity.

12. The victim of the capital felony was a person less than 12 years of age.

13. The victim of the capital felony was particularly vulnerable due to advanced age or disability, or because the defendant stood in a position of familial or custodial authority over the victim.

14. The capital felony was committed by a criminal street gang member, as defined in § 874.03.

15. The capital felony was committed by a person designated as a sexual predator pursuait to s.775.21 or a person previously designated as a sexual predator who had the sexual predator designation removed.

MITIGATING FACTORS

1. The defendant has no significant history of prior criminal activity.

2. The capital felony was committed while the defendant was under the influence of extreme mental or emotional disturbance.

3. The victim was a participant in the defendant's conduct or consented to the act.

4. The defendant was an accomplice in the capital felony committed by another person and his or her participation was relatively minor.

5. The defendant acted under extreme duress or under the substantial domination of another person.

6. The capacity of the defendant to appreciate the criminality of his or her conduct or to conform his or her conduct to the requirements of law was substantially impaired.

7. The age of the defendant at the time of the crime.

8. The existence of any other factors in the defendant's background that would mitigate against imposition of the death penalty.

Source: Online Sunshine View Statutes (2006) "The 2006 Florida Statutes." http://www.leg.state.fl.us/statutes/index.cfm?mode=View%20Statutes&SubMenu=1&App_mode=Display_Statutes&Search_String=aggravating+circumstances&URL=CH0921/Sec141.HTM

recommendation is only advisory to the judge. That is, in those states, the judge may impose death even if the jury recommends life, or may impose life even if the jury recommends death. This override provision may not survive constitutional challenge because in *Ring* v. *Arizona* (2002) the U.S. Supreme Court ruled that juries and not judges must determine whether death is the appropriate penalty in a capital case.

Another type of guided-discretion statute is Georgia's "aggravating-only" statute. In Georgia, if a jury finds at least one statutory aggravating factor, then it may, but need not, recommend death. The jury may also consider any mitigating factors, although mitigating factors are not listed in the statute, as they are in some states. The judge must follow the jury's recommendation.

A third type of guided-discretion statute is Texas's "structured-discretion" statute. In Texas, aggravating or mitigating factors are not listed in the statute. Instead, during the sentencing phase of the trial, the state and the defendant or the defendant's counsel may present evidence about any matter that the court deems relevant to sentence, that is, any aggravating or mitigating factors. On conclusion of the presentation of the evidence, the court submits the following issues to the jury:

1. Whether the defendant would possibly commit criminal acts of violence that would constitute a continuing threat to society.
2. Whether the defendant actually caused the death of the deceased or did not actually cause the death of the deceased but intended to kill the deceased or another or anticipated that a human life would be taken (if raised by the evidence).

During penalty deliberations, juries in Texas must consider all evidence admitted at the guilt and penalty phases. Then, they must consider the two aforementioned issues. To answer yes to the issues, all jurors must answer yes; to answer no to the issues, 10 or more jurors must answer no. If the two issues are answered in the affirmative, jurors are then asked if there is a sufficient mitigating factor or factors to warrant that a sentence of life imprisonment rather than a death sentence be imposed. To answer no to this issue, all jurors must answer no; to answer yes, 10 or more jurors must agree. If the jury returns an affirmative finding on the first two issues and a negative finding on the third issue, then the court must sentence the defendant to death. On the other hand, if the jury returns a negative finding on either of the first two issues or an affirmative finding on the third issue, then the court must sentence the defendant to life imprisonment.

AUTOMATIC APPELLATE REVIEW The third procedural feature of most of the new death penalty statutes is automatic appellate review. Currently, 37 of the 38 states with death penalty statutes provide for automatic appellate review of all death sentences, regardless of the defendant's wishes. South Carolina allows the defendant to waive sentence review if the defendant is deemed competent by the court; also, the federal jurisdiction does not provide for automatic appellate review.) Most of the 37 states automatically review both the conviction and the sentence (Idaho, Montana, Oklahoma, South Dakota, and Tennessee review only the sentence).[16] Generally, the automatic review is conducted by the state's highest appellate court. If either the conviction or the sentence is overturned, then the case is sent back to the trial court for additional proceedings or for retrial. It is possible that the death sentence may be reimposed as a result of this process.

Some states are very specific in defining the review function of the appellate courts, while other states are not. Although the Supreme Court does not require it

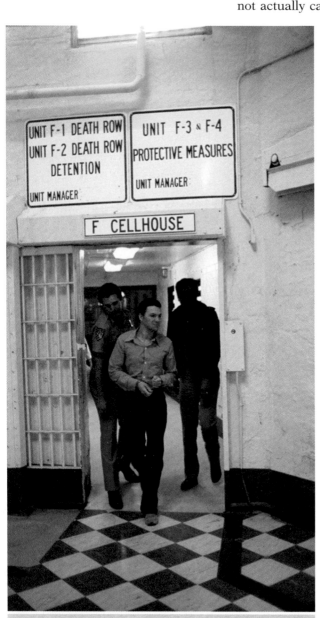

The death row population in the United States has remained relatively stable in recent years. *What factors have kept it from growing faster?*

TABLE 6.7	The Appellate Process in Capital Cases

STAGE 1

Step 1: Trial and Sentence in State Court

Step 2: Direct Appeal to the State Appeals Court

Step 3: U.S. Supreme Court for Writ of *Certiorari*

STAGE 2

Step 1: State Post Conviction

Step 2: State Court of Appeals

Step 3: U.S. Supreme Court for Writ of *Certiorari*

STAGE 3

Step 1: Petition for Writ of *Habeas Corpus* in Federal District Court

Step 2: Certificate of Probable Cause and Request for Stay of Execution

Step 3: U.S. Court of Appeals

Step 4: U.S. Supreme Court for Writ of *Certiorari*

Step 5: Request for a Stay of Execution

Source: Raymond Paternoster, *Capital Punishment in America* (New York: Lexington, 1991), p. 203. Reprinted by permission of Raymond Paternoster.

(*Pulley* v. *Harris,* 1984), some states have provided a proportionality review. In a **proportionality review,** the appellate court compares the sentence in the case it is reviewing with penalties imposed in similar cases in the state. The object of proportionality review is to reduce, as much as possible, disparity in death penalty sentencing.

In addition to the automatic appellate review, there is a dual system of collateral review for capital defendants. In other words, capital defendants may appeal their convictions and sentences through both the state and the federal appellate systems. Table 6.7 shows the general appeals process in death penalty cases.

Some death row inmates whose appeals have been denied by the U.S. Supreme Court may still try to have the Supreme Court review their cases on constitutional grounds by filing a writ of *habeas corpus.* Recall that a writ of *habeas corpus* is a court order directing a law officer to produce a prisoner in court to determine whether the prisoner is being legally detained or imprisoned. Critics maintain that abuse of the writ has contributed to the long delays in executions (currently averaging more than 10 years after conviction) and to the high costs associated with capital punishment.

Congress passed the Antiterrorism and Effective Death Penalty Act of 1996, in part to speed up the process and reduce costs. President Clinton signed it into law on April 24, 1996. The law requires that second or subsequent *habeas* petitions be dismissed when the claim had already been made in a previous petition. It also requires that new claims be dismissed, unless the Supreme Court hands down a new rule of constitutional law and makes it retroactive to cases on collateral review. Under the act, the only other way the Supreme Court will hear a claim made for the first time is when the claim is based on new evidence not previously available. Even then, the new evidence must be of sufficient weight, by a clear and convincing standard of proof, to convince a judge or jury that the capital defendant was not guilty of the crime or crimes for which he or she was convicted.

The act also made the federal appellate courts "gatekeepers" for second or subsequent *habeas corpus* petitions. Thus, to file a second or subsequent claim under the new law, a capital defendant must first file a motion in the appropriate appellate court announcing his or her intention. A panel of three judges

proportionality review A review in which the apellate court compares the sentence in the case it is reviewing with penalties inposed in similar cases in the state. The object is to reduce, as much as possible, disparity in death penalty sentencing.

must then hear the motion within 30 days. The judges must decide whether the petitioner has a legitimate claim under the new act. If the claim is denied, the new law prohibits any review of the panel's decision, either by a rehearing or writ of *certiorari* to the Supreme Court. So far, the Supreme Court has upheld the constitutionality of the law.

Some people argue that the appellate reviews are unnecessary delaying tactics (at least those beyond the automatic review). However, the outcomes of the reviews suggest otherwise. Nationally, between 1973 and 2004, one-third of the initial convictions or sentences in capital cases were overturned on appeal,[17] and, contrary to popular belief, those reversals were generally not the result of so-called legal technicalities. They were the product of "such fundamental constitutional errors" as denial of the right to an impartial jury, problems of tainted evidence and coerced confessions, ineffective assistance of counsel, and prosecutors' references to defendants who refuse to testify.[18]

The number of persons currently on death rows in the United States is 3,373 (as of January 1, 2006). Figure 6.5 shows the race, ethnic, and gender distributions of the death row population. Because there are so few executions each year (the largest number since 1977 was 98, in 1999), and the number of new death sentences has been declining in the past few years (168 in 2002, 152 in 2003, and 125 in 2004),[19] the size of the death row population in the United States does not change very much. What keeps the death row population from growing much larger is that about three of every four inmates have been removed from death row by having their convictions or sentences reversed (about 2,500 as of the beginning of 2004). In addition, since January 1, 1973, 335 death row inmates have received commutations (reductions in sentences, granted by a state's governor), and 279 have died of natural causes or have been killed.[20]

PROSPECTS FOR THE FUTURE

These are interesting times when it comes to the death penalty in the United States. It appears that capital punishment is receiving more attention than usual. Although less than half of the world's nations still have a death penalty,

---

FIGURE 6.5   **The Total Number of Death Row Inmates, by Race and Gender**

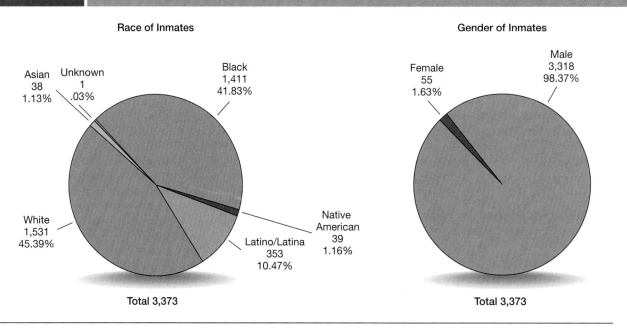

Race of Inmates

Asian 38 1.13% Unknown 1 .03% Black 1,411 41.83% White 1,531 45.39% Latino/Latina 353 10.47% Native American 39 1.16%

Total 3,373

Gender of Inmates

Female 55 1.63% Male 3,318 98.37%

Total 3,373

Source: Adapted from *Death Row, U.S.A.*, NAACP Legal Defense and Educational Fund (Winter 2006). Data depicted are as of January 1, 2006.

those that do have one seldom use it. Among Western, industrialized nations, the United States stands alone as the only nation to employ capital punishment. However, even within the United States, 14 jurisdictions do not have a death penalty, and among the 39 jurisdictions that do have one, only a handful of them use it more than occasionally, and almost all of them are located geographically in the South.

Consider the distribution of the 1,022 executions conducted in the United States between January 17, 1977, and May 5, 2006:[21]

- The 1,022 executions have occurred in 33 of the 38 death penalty jurisdictions.
- Five jurisdictions with death penalty statutes (including the U.S. military) have not had a single execution.
- Fifteen jurisdictions, including the District of Columbia, do not have death penalty statutes.
- Fifteen of the 33 "executing" states (45 percent) have held fewer than 10 executions.
- Only 18 "executing" states (55 percent) have conducted 10 or more executions.
- Sixty-five percent of all executions have taken place in just five states— Texas, Virginia, Oklahoma, Missouri, and Florida.
- Fifty-three percent of all executions have taken place in just three states—Texas, Virginia, and Oklahoma.
- Texas, alone, accounts for more than a third of all the executions.
- Of the states that have conducted 10 or more executions, 11 (about 60 percent) are southern or border states.
- More than 70 percent of all executions have occurred in the South.[22]

Thus, for all intents and purposes, the death penalty today is a criminal sanction that is used more than occasionally in only a few non-Western countries and a few states in the American South. This is an important point because it raises the question of why those death penalty—or more precisely, executing— jurisdictions in the world need the death penalty, while all other jurisdictions in the world—the vast majority—do not.

There are several other reasons to believe that the death penalty in the United States may be a waning institution. First, although abstract support for the death penalty remains relatively high—it was 64 percent in 2005—it was the lowest level recorded by Gallup since 1978. When respondents are provided an alternative, such as life imprisonment with absolutely no possibility of parole (LWOP), support for the death penalty falls to about 50 percent (56 percent in 2005). In a 2005 CBS News poll, support for the death penalty was only 39 percent when respondents were provided with alternatives: 39 percent chose life with no parole, 6 percent picked a long sentence with parole, and 13 percent volunteered the answer "depends." The level of interest in both the death penalty and LWOP was lower in the CBS News poll primarily because of the percentage of the public that responded "depends."[23]

Second, the American public continues to express some concern about the way the death penalty is being administered. For example, the 2005 Gallup poll found that 35 percent of the American public did not believe that the death penalty is applied fairly. However, the 73 percent of Americans in 2003 that believed an innocent

Myth

Innocent people are never executed in error.

Fact

As many as 25 people (and likely more) may have been executed in error in the United States since 1976.

Source: Talia Roitberg Harmon and William S. Lofquist, "Too Late for Luck: A Comparison of Post-*Furman* Exonerations and Executions of the Innocent," *Crime and Delinquency* 51 (2005), pp. 498–520; Patrick Lehner, "Abolition Now!!!" at www.abolition-now.com/; The Death Penalty Information Center, www.deathpenaltyinfo.org/innocothers.html#executed.

person had been executed in the last 5 years dropped to 59 percent in 2005. Most people believe that the execution of innocent people is a rare occurrence. For example, 57 percent of respondents believed that the execution of an innocent person happened no more than 5 percent of the time. Only about 11 percent of respondents believed that more than 20 percent of executions involved innocent people.[24] Although concern about the death penalty's administration has waned somewhat from the level of concern expressed in 2000, it remains higher than it was prior to revelations about the quality of justice in capital murder trials, the overturning of several convictions as a result of DNA tests, and the resulting moratorium on executions in Illinois and elsewhere.

A third factor is the positions taken by respected organizations within the United States, such as the American Bar Association (ABA) and organized religions. In 1997, the ABA adopted a resolution that requested death penalty jurisdictions to refrain from using the sanction until greater fairness and due process could be assured. In July 2000, the ABA's president, Martha Barnett, a "reluctant supporter" of the death penalty, reiterated the call for a moratorium on executions. Besides inadequate counsel and a lack of due process, she cited racial bias, racial profiling, and the execution of the mentally retarded and juveniles as problems with the death penalty's administration.[25] The leaders of most organized religions in the United States—whether Catholic, Protestant, or Jewish—openly oppose capital punishment. The only religious organizations that support capital punishment are (1) the Southern Baptist Convention, (2) Jehovah's Witnesses, (3) Seventh Day Adventists, (4) the Church of Jesus Christ of Latter Day Saints (Mormons), and (5) certain conservative and orthodox Jewish groups.[26]

Myth

Most defendants facing the death penalty receive competent legal representation.

Fact

According to a *National Law Journal* study, criminal defendants in six southern states—Alabama, Florida, Georgia, Louisiana, Mississippi, and Texas (states that account for more than one-half of all post-*Furman* executions)—often wind up on death row after being represented by inexperienced, unskilled, or unprepared court-appointed lawyers. Many poor defendants sentenced to death had lawyers who had never handled a capital trial before, or lawyers who had been reprimanded or disciplined or were subsequently disbarred.

Source: Marcia Coyle, Fred Strasser, and Marianne Lavelle, "Fatal Defense," *The National Law Journal* 12 (June 11, 1990), pp. 29–44.

A fourth factor is world opinion. All of our major allies except Japan have abolished the death penalty. In Europe the death penalty is viewed as a violation of human rights.[27] Demonstrations protesting against the U.S. death penalty have been held in France, Spain, and Norway.[28] A condition for admittance into the European Union (EU) is the abolition of the death penalty. That is why Turkey recently abolished its death penalty. Admittance into the 40-nation Council of Europe also requires the renouncing of the death penalty. Georgia, a former republic of the Soviet Union, effectively abolished its death penalty in 1997 so that it could join the Council. Russia has promised to end its death penalty so that it, too, can secure membership in the Council. Figure 6.6 lists the principal executing countries of the world in 2005. The United Nations Commission on Human Rights has repeatedly condemned the death penalty in the United States, urging the U.S. government to stop all executions until it brings states into compliance with international standards and laws. Of particular importance, some foreign businesses may make economic decisions based on a state's use of the death penalty. In a 1998 letter to then Texas governor George W. Bush, a European Parliament official wrote, "Many companies, under pressure from shareholders and public opinion to apply ethical business practices, are beginning to consider the possibility of restricting the investment in the U.S. to states that do not apply the death penalty."

| FIGURE 6.6 | The Principal Executing Countries in the World Ranked by Number of Executions in 2005 |

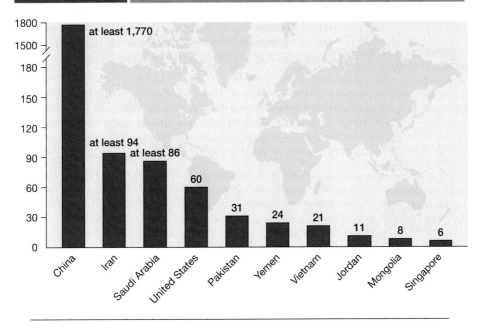

Note: These figures include only cases known to Amnesty International; the true figures were certainly higher.

Source: The Death Penalty Information Center, "The Death Penalty: An International Perspective," www.deathpenaltyinfo.org/article.php?did=127&scid=30#interexec (accessed May 16, 2006).

On the other hand, capital punishment in some states has proven stubbornly resilient. There are reasons to believe that in those U.S. states the death penalty will remain a legal sanction for the foreseeable future. One reason is that death penalty support among the American public, at least according to the major opinion polls, remains relatively strong. It is unlikely that the practice of capital punishment could be sustained if a majority of American citizens were to oppose it. In no year for which polls are available has a majority of Americans opposed the death penalty (the first national death penalty opinion poll was conducted in December 1936).[29]

Although life imprisonment without opportunity for parole (LWOP) seems to be a popular alternative to the death penalty in polls, a problem with the LWOP alternative is that the public is very skeptical about the ability of correctional authorities to keep capital murderers imprisoned for life. In a national survey, only 11 percent of registered voters believed that an offender sentenced to LWOP would never be released from prison.[30] Thus, although half of the public may say that it prefers LWOP to capital punishment, in practice, the public probably does not want to make the substitution because it fears that the alternative might not adequately protect it from the future actions of convicted capital offenders.

The abiding faith of death penalty proponents in the ability of legislatures and courts to fix any problems with the administration of capital punishment is another reason for its continued use in some places. However, the three-decade record of "fine-tuning" the death penalty process remains ongoing. Legislatures and courts are having a difficult time "getting it right," despite spending inordinate amounts of their resources trying.

As for the positions against capital punishment taken by respected organizations in the United States, "true believers" in the death penalty could care less what others think, especially in the case of organizations such as the American

Justice Blackmun and the Death Penalty

For more than 20 years, Justice Harry A. Blackmun supported the administration of capital punishment in the United States. However, on February 22, 1994, in a dissent from the Court's refusal to hear the appeal of a Texas inmate scheduled to be executed the next day, Blackmun asserted that he had come to the conclusion that "the death penalty experiment has failed" and that it was time for the Court to abandon the "delusion" that capital punishment could be administered in a way that was consistent with the Constitution. He noted that "from this day forward, I no longer shall tinker with the machinery of death."

SOURCE: *Callins* v. *Collins*, 114 S. Ct. 1127 (1994).

Myth

The monetary costs of capital punishment are less than the monetary costs of life imprisonment without opportunity for parole.

Fact

The monetary costs of capital punishment (that is, the entire legal process) currently average between $2.5 million and $5 million per execution. The monetary costs of life imprisonment without opportunity for parole are unlikely to cost much more—and may cost much less—than $1 million per offender. It reportedly cost the state of Florida $10 million to execute serial killer Ted Bundy in 1989. The federal government spent more than $100 million to execute mass murderer Timothy McVeigh in 2001.

Source: Robert M. Bohm, *Deathquest II: An Introduction to the Theory and Practice of Capital Punishment in the United States*, 2nd ed. (Cincinnati: Andersen, 2003), p. 135.

Bar Association. This holds true for world opinion as well. In the case of organized religions, the situation is probably more complex. Although most people who consider themselves religious and are affiliated with religions whose leadership opposes capital punishment probably respect the views of their leaders, they obviously live their daily lives and hold beliefs about capital punishment (and other issues such as abortion) based on other values.

Another sign of the death penalty's staying power in the United States is that no jurisdiction that adopted new death penalty statutes in the wake of *Furman* has abolished the penalty, including those jurisdictions that have never used it. If there were a serious threat to the retention of capital punishment—indeed, if it were abolished in some jurisdictions—then the effort to retain or reinstate it would likely begin in earnest. Currently, there is no need for such an effort.

Some death penalty opponents believe that a principal reason for the continuing support of capital punishment is that most people know very little about the subject and what they think they know is based almost entirely on myth. It is assumed that if people were educated about capital punishment, most of them would oppose it. Unfortunately, research suggests that educating the public about the death penalty may not have the effect abolitionists desire.[31] Although information about the death penalty can reduce support for the sanction—sometimes significantly—rarely is the support reduced to less than a majority, and the reduction in support may be only temporary.

What else, then, sustains the public's death penalty support? There are at least three more major factors:

1. The desire for vindictive revenge.
2. The incapacitative power of the penalty.
3. The symbolic value it has for politicians and law enforcement officials.

In a recent Gallup poll on the subject, 50 percent of all respondents who favored the death penalty selected "An eye for an eye/convicted deserve to be executed" as a reason.[32] The reasons selected second most often (by only 11 percent) were "Save taxpayers money/Cost associated with prison and deterrence." No other reasons were selected by more than 10 percent of the death penalty proponents.

The choice of "An eye for an eye/convicted deserve to be executed" indicates support of the penal purpose of retribution. Those who chose this reason want to repay the offender for what he or she has done. This response, moreover, at least the "eye for an eye" part, has a strong emotional component and thus has been called "vindictive revenge."[33] That the public may support the death penalty primarily for vindictive revenge raises two important questions. First, is the satisfaction of the desire for vindictive revenge a legitimate penal purpose? And second, does pandering to or legitimizing this desire for vindictive revenge contribute to the violence in our nation?

Another factor that sustains death penalty support is the unquestionable incapacitative power of the penalty: Once a capital offender has been executed, he or she can never kill again. Although this seems persuasive, it is not a reason often given by the public. Only 7 percent of Gallup-polled death penalty proponents chose it.

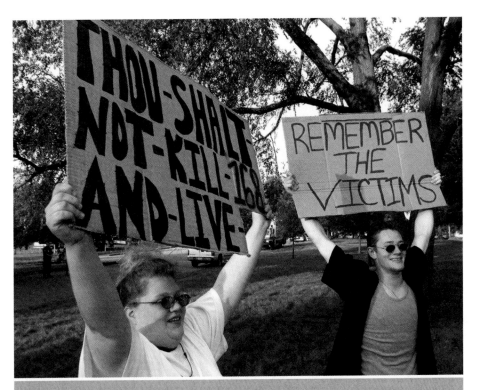

According to public opinion polls, a majority of Americans support the death penalty. *Why?*

Nevertheless, research confirms that a small percentage of capital offenders released from prison have killed again. The execution of all convicted capital offenders would have prevented those killings. However, a problem with simply executing all convicted capital offenders is that, inevitably, innocent people are executed. The possibility of executing an innocent person does not seem to be a crucial problem for a majority of Supreme Court justices, given the Court's recent ruling in this area (see the FYI on *Herrera* v. *Collins*, 1993). It might, however, be a problem for many Americans. In any event, to prevent capital offenders from killing again, doesn't it make sense simply to keep them imprisoned? At least then, if errors are made, they can be rectified to some degree.

A final factor that sustains death penalty support is the symbolic value it has for politicians and criminal justice officials. Politicians use support for the death penalty as a symbol of their toughness on crime. Opposition to capital punishment is invariably interpreted as symbolic of softness on crime. Criminal justice officials and much of the public often equate support for capital punishment with support for law enforcement in general. It is ironic that although capital punishment has virtually no effect on crime, the death penalty continues to be a favored political silver bullet—a simplistic solution to the crime problem used by aspiring politicians and law enforcement officials.

Herrera v. *Collins*

In *Herrera* v. *Collins* (1993) the Supreme Court held that in the absence of constitutional grounds, new evidence of innocence is no reason for the Court to order a new trial. According to the majority opinion: "Where a defendant has been afforded a fair trial and convicted of the offense for which he was charged, the constitutional presumption of innocence disappears. . . . Thus, claims of actual innocence based on newly discovered evidence [are not] grounds for . . . relief absent an independent constitutional violation occurring in the course of the underlying state criminal proceedings." For some, the decision is a reasonable response to the Court's need to limit its jurisdiction in *habeas corpus* cases.

THINKING CRITICALLY

1. Do you think the death penalty helps to prevent crime in the United States? Why or why not?

2. Do you think the death penalty should continue to be legal in this country? Why or why not?

1. Identify the general factors that influence a judge's sentencing decisions.

In sentencing, judges are limited by the U.S. Constitution's Eighth Amendment and statutory provisions; guided by prevailing philosophical rationales, organizational considerations, and presentence investigation reports; and influenced by their own personal characteristics.

2. Describe how judges tailor sentences to fit the crime and the offender.

Judges have several ways to tailor sentences to fit the crime and the offender. They can impose a combination sentence of imprisonment, probation, and a fine. They can suspend the imprisonment portion of a combination sentence, or they can suspend the entire sentence if the offender stays out of trouble, makes restitution to the victim, or seeks medical treatment. Judges can give offenders credit for time spent in jail while awaiting trial, deducting that time from any prison sentence. A judge may even impose a sentence of "time served" and release the offender. When an offender is convicted of two or more crimes, a judge can order the prison sentences to run concurrently or consecutively. Judges can also delay sentencing and retain the right to impose a sentence at a later date if conditions warrant it.

3. Distinguish between indeterminate and determinate sentences.

An indeterminate sentence has a fixed minimum and maximum term of incarceration, rather than a set period. A determinate sentence, on the other hand, has a fixed period of incarceration and eliminates the decision-making responsibility of parole boards.

4. Explain the three basic types of determinate sentences.

There are three basic types of determinate sentences: flat-time, mandatory, and presumptive. With flat-time sentencing, judges may choose between probation and imprisonment but have little discretion in setting the length of a prison sentence. With mandatory sentencing, a specified number of years of imprisonment (usually within a range) is provided for particular crimes. Mandatory sentencing generally allows credit for

good time but does not allow release on parole. Presumptive sentencing allows a judge to retain some sentencing discretion (subject to appellate review). It requires a judge to impose the normal sentence, specified by statute, on a "normal" offender who has committed a "normal" crime. However, if the crime or the offender is not normal—if there are mitigating or aggravating circumstances—then the judge is allowed to deviate from the presumptive sentence.

5. List five rationales or justifications for criminal punishment.

Five rationales or justifications for criminal punishment are retribution, incapacitation, deterrence, rehabilitation, and restoration.

6. Explain the purposes of presentence investigation reports.

Presentence investigation reports (PSIs) help judges determine the appropriate sentences for particular defendants. PSIs are also used in the classification of probationers, parolees, and prisoners according to their treatment needs and their security risks.

7. List the legal bases for appeal.

Defendants can appeal their convictions either on legal grounds (such as defects in jury selection, improper admission of evidence at trial, mistaken interpretations of law) or on constitutional grounds (such as illegal search and seizure, improper questioning of the defendant by the police, identification of the defendant through a defective police lineup, and incompetent assistance of counsel).

8. Identify the type of crime for which death may be a punishment.

In the United States, death is the ultimate punishment. At the state level, death can be imposed only for the crime of aggravated murder and a few other seldom-committed offenses.

9. Summarize the three major procedural reforms the U.S. Supreme Court approved for death penalty cases in the *Gregg* decision.

The three major procedural reforms the Court approved in Gregg were bifurcated trials, guidelines for judges and juries to follow, and automatic appellate review.

restitution, p. 210
indeterminate
  sentence, p. 211
determinate sentence,
  p. 212
flat-time sentencing,
  p. 212
good time, p. 212
mandatory sentencing,
  p. 212

presumptive sentenc-
  ing, p. 213
mitigating circum-
  stance, p. 213
aggravating circum-
  stance, p. 213
retribution, p. 218
revenge, p. 218
just deserts, p. 218
incapacitation, p. 219

special or specific
  deterrence, p. 219
general deterrence,
  p. 219
rehabilitation, p. 219
victim-impact state-
  ments, p. 221
presentence investiga-
  tion reports, p. 223
allocution, p. 223

pardon, p. 223
bifurcated trial,
  p. 232
proportionality review,
  p. 235

REVIEW QUESTIONS

1. What constitutes "cruel and unusual punish-ment" according to several Supreme Court decisions?

2. What are five general types of punishment currently being used in the United States?

3. What are some criticisms of determinate sentencing?

4. Which rationale for criminal punishment is the only one that specifically addresses what has happened in the past, and what are its two major forms?

5. What are three organizational considerations that may influence a judge's sentencing decision?

6. What is *allocution*?

7. What two steps must be taken before an appellate court will hear an appeal?

8. What was the landmark 1972 decision in which the Supreme Court set aside death sentences for the first (and only) time in its history?

9. What are the five methods of execution currently available in the United States?

IN THE FIELD

1. **Sentencing** Select a criminal case that is currently receiving publicity in your community. Conduct an informal survey, asking respondents what sentence they believe would be appropriate in the case. Ask them why they chose the sentence. Determine whether respondents tended to agree with one another. If they did not tend to agree, speculate on the reasons for the disagreement.

2. **Death Penalty Opinion** With family members or friends, discuss the death penalty. Ask them why they hold their particular positions (in favor, opposed, undecided). Also, ask them under what circumstances they would change their positions. Would any of the mitigating circumstances listed in Table 6.6 cause any of them to change their positions?

1. **Death Penalty** Access the Death Penalty Information Center Web site at www. deathpenaltyinfo.org and the "Pro Death Penalty pages" at www. prodeathpenalty.com. Choose the same topic included in both sources, and review the information provided. Write a brief summary of the information you discovered and how it affected your view of capital punishment.

2. **Mandatory Minimums** Access the Web site of Families Against Mandatory Minimums at www.famm.org. After studying information provided at the site, write an essay or prepare an oral presentation critiquing mandatory minimum sentences.

TICAL THINKING EXERCISES

1. **The Three Strikes Law** In March 1995, a 27-year-old man who had stolen a slice of pizza from a group of children sitting outside a pizza parlor became the first person to be sentenced to 25 years to life in prison under California's "three strikes and you're out" law. Enacted March 7, 1995, the law was reinforced November 8, 1995, by a constitutional amendment supported by 72 percent of California voters. The "three strikes" law is triggered by two past felony convictions. In this case, the defendant was convicted of "petty theft with a prior felony conviction." He had already been convicted of robbery, attempted robbery, drug possession, and riding a stolen motorcycle.
   a. It will cost the taxpayers of California about $26,000 a year to incarcerate the man. Is it worth it? Is it a wise expenditure of tax dollars?
   b. Is the punishment proportional to the crime or crimes? Should it be?
   c. Do you think "petty theft with a prior conviction" is a legitimate trigger of a "three strikes" law?
   d. There is no question that the offender was a criminal. He had a reputation for being a bully. Nevertheless, are "three strikes and you're out" laws an ethically defensible way of dealing with such criminals? Why or why not?

2. **Sentencing** You are a juror in a death penalty case. The defendant in the case has already been found guilty of capital murder during the guilt phase of the trial. During the penalty phase, you have to determine whether the defendant is to be sentenced to death or to life imprisonment without opportunity for parole (LWOP). The judge has instructed you (and the rest of the jury) to consider the aggravating and mitigating circumstances of the case. If the aggravating circumstances outweigh the mitigating circumstances, you are expected to vote for death. On the other hand, if the mitigating circumstances outweigh the aggravating circumstances, you are expected to vote for LWOP. The lone aggravating circumstance in the case is that the defendant committed the capital murder during the commission of a robbery. Though they are not aggravating circumstances, the defendant also has two prior convictions for robbery and one prior conviction for the sale of illegal drugs. Under which of the following mitigating circumstances would you vote for LWOP or death in this case? Explain the reasons for your decision.
   a. The defendant has no significant history of prior criminal activity.
   b. The defendant is a female with children.
   c. The defendant acted under extreme duress or under the substantial domination of another person.
   d. The defendant was seriously abused, both mentally and physically, as a child.
   e. The capacity of the defendant to appreciate the criminality of his or her conduct or to conform his or her conduct to the requirements of law was substantially impaired.

To access more information and resources, including study questions, chapter summaries, and links, go to: www.mhhe.com/bohm1.

CORRECTIONS

CHAPTER SEVEN

INSTITUTIONAL CORRECTIONS

CHAPTER OUTLINE

Historical Overview of Institutional Corrections

European Background

Developments in the United States

The Incarceration Boom

Recent Trends

Prison Inmate Characteristics

Incarceration Facilities

Organization and Administration by Government

Classification and Other Special Facilities

Men's Prisons

Women's Prisons and Cocorrectional Facilities

Jails and Lockups

Institutional Security, Services, and Programs

Security and Inmate Discipline

Services and Programs

CHAPTER OBJECTIVES

After completing this chapter, you should be able to:

1. Summarize the purposes of confinement in Europe before it became a major way of punishing criminals.

2. Describe how offenders were punished before the large-scale use of confinement.

3. Explain why confinement began to be used as a major way of punishing offenders in Europe.

4. Describe the recent trends in the use of incarceration in the United States.

5. List some of the characteristics of the incarcerated population in the United States.

6. Describe how incarceration facilities are structured, organized, and administered by the government in the United States.

7. Name some of the common types of correctional facilities in the United States.

8. Identify some of the procedures that institutions employ to maintain security and order.

9. List the services and programs that are commonly available to inmates.

Historical Overview of Institutional Corrections

Students often wonder why they must learn about the history of institutional corrections. One reason is that it is impossible to fully understand (and improve) the present state of affairs without knowledge of the past; the present developed out of the past. People who fail to remember the past are destined to repeat its mistakes. Another reason is that nothing helps us see how institutional corrections is linked to our larger society and culture better than the study of history. Try to keep those two points in mind when studying history.

EUROPEAN BACKGROUND

In Europe, institutional confinement did not become a major punishment for criminals until the 1600s and 1700s. (In the United States, institutional confinement was not used extensively as a punishment until the 1800s.) As a practice, though, institutional confinement has existed since ancient times. Before the 1600s, however, it usually served functions other than punishment for criminal behavior. For example, confinement was used to:

1. Detain people before trial.
2. Hold prisoners awaiting other sanctions, such as death and corporal punishment.
3. Coerce payment of debts and fines.
4. Hold and punish slaves.
5. Achieve religious indoctrination and spiritual reformation (as during the Inquisition).
6. Quarantine disease (as during the bubonic plague).[1]

FORERUNNERS OF MODERN INCARCERATION Unlike modern incarceration, which strives to change the offender's character and is carried out away from public view, popular early punishments for crime, which predated the large-scale use of imprisonment, were directed more at the offender's body and property; one basic goal was to inflict pain.[2] Furthermore, those punishments were commonly carried out in public to humiliate the offender and to deter onlookers from crime. Examples of such early punishments are fines, confiscation of property, and diverse methods of corporal and capital punishment. Some popular methods of corporal and capital punishment were beheading, stoning, hanging, crucifixion, boiling and burning, flogging, branding, or placement in the stocks or pillory.[3] As this brief list illustrates, the eventual shift to incarceration reduced the severity and violence of punishment.

Myth   Fact

Myth	Fact
Throughout history, imprisonment has been the primary sentence for lawbreakers, and it still is today.	Viewed historically, imprisonment is a relatively recent sentence for lawbreaking. Even today in the United States, the number of people in prison is small compared with the number on probation or under other types of supervision in the community.

Two additional forerunners of modern incarceration were banishment and transportation. In essence, they were alternatives to the more severe corporal punishments or capital punishment. Originating in ancient times, banishment required offenders to leave the community and live elsewhere, commonly in the wilderness. The modern version of banishment is long-term incarceration (for example, life imprisonment without opportunity for parole). As population and urban growth displaced frontiers across Europe and as demands for cheap labor increased with the rise of Western capitalism, transportation of offenders from their home nation to one of that nation's colonies gradually replaced banishment. England, for instance, was transporting hundreds of convicts a year to North America by the early 1600s.[4] Transportation fell into disuse as European colonies gained independence.

The closest European forerunners of the modern U.S. prison were known as **workhouses** or *houses of correction*. Offenders were sent to them to learn discipline and regular work habits. The fruits of inmate labor were also expected to pay for facility upkeep and even to yield a profit. One of the first and most famous workhouses, the London Bridewell, opened in the 1550s, and workhouses spread through other parts of Europe thereafter. Such facilities were used extensively throughout the next three centuries, coexisting with such responses to crime as transportation, corporal punishment, and capital punishment. In fact, crowding in workhouses was a major impetus for the development of transportation as a punishment.

REFORM INITIATIVES The Enlightenment thinkers and reformers of the 1700s and 1800s described the penal system of their day with such terms as *excessive, disorderly, inefficient, arbitrary, capricious, discriminatory* (against the poor), and *unjust*. Three reformers who were important to initiatives in corrections were Cesare Beccaria (1738–1794), John Howard (1726–1790), and Jeremy Bentham (1748–1832).

Mamertine Prison

Although it surely did not resemble today's prisons, one of the earliest known prisons was the Mamertine Prison, built around 64 B.C. under the sewers of Rome.

SOURCE: Robert Johnson, *Hard Time: Understanding and Reforming the Prison*, 3rd ed. (Belmont, CA: Wadsworth, 2002), p. 19.

workhouses European forerunners of the modern U.S. prison, where offenders were sent to learn discipline and regular work habits.

Besides being painful, placement in the stocks or pillory was intended to humiliate and shame offenders. *Is a greater emphasis on the shame of punishment needed today? If so, how should it be accomplished?*

Criminologists Graeme Newman and Pietro Marongiu contend that Milanese philosopher Cesare Beccaria's famous book, *On Crimes and Punishments* (1764), though often acclaimed for its originality, actually brought together the reformist principles espoused by other thinkers of the era, such as Montesquieu and Voltaire.[5] One of those principles concerned replacing the discretionary and arbitrary administration of justice with a system of detailed written laws describing the behaviors that constitute crime and the associated punishments. People need to know, Beccaria believed, exactly what punishments are prescribed for various offenses if the law is to deter criminal behavior. As part of his quest to deter crime, Beccaria declared that the punishment should fit the crime in two senses. First, the severity of punishment should parallel the severity of harm resulting from the crime. Second, the punishment should be severe enough to outweigh the pleasure obtainable from the crime. Furthermore, to deter crime, he believed, punishment needed to be certain and swift. Certainty implies that the likelihood of getting caught and punished is perceived as high. Swiftness implies that punishment will not be delayed after commission of the crime.

Myth

The reason punishment fails to adequately deter crime in the United States is that it is not severe enough.

Fact

The United States has a higher rate of imprisonment and longer sentences than virtually any other nation. It is also one of the few advanced, industrialized nations to have retained the death penalty. It is hard indeed to support the argument that our punishment is not severe enough. Certainty and swiftness, however, are lacking, and that is the failure to which Beccaria would probably point.

Beccaria did not ground his thinking firmly in empirical observations and did little to actively campaign for the reforms he advocated.[6] The work of John Howard, an English sheriff and social activist, presents an interesting contrast in that regard. Howard's 1777 book, *The State of the Prisons in England and Wales,* was based on his visits to penal institutions in various parts of Europe. Howard was appalled by the crowding, overall poor living conditions, and disorderly and abusive practices he observed in those facilities. He advocated that penal environments be made safe, humane, and orderly. Howard's opinion was that incarceration should do more than punish—that it should also instill discipline and reform inmates. Toward that end, he proposed an orderly institutional routine of religious teaching, hard work, and solitary confinement to promote introspection and penance.[7] Howard's work inspired the growing popularity of the term *penitentiary* to refer to penal confinement facilities.

In **penology,** the study of prison management and the treatment of offenders, English philosopher Jeremy Bentham is perhaps best remembered for his idea that order and reform could be achieved in a prison through architectural design. His **panopticon** ("all-seeing" or "inspection-house") prison design consisted of a round building with tiers of cells lining the circumference and facing a central inspection tower so that prisoners could be watched by staff from the tower. Although no facilities completely true to Bentham's panopticon plan were ever constructed, structures similar in design were erected at Illinois's Stateville Penitentiary (now Stateville Correctional Center), which opened in 1925.

In sum, the historical roots of the modern prison lie in Europe. It was in America, however, that the penitentiary concept was first put into wide practice.

penology The study of prison management and the treatment of offenders.

panopticon A prison design consisting of a round building with tiers of cells lining the inner circumference and facing a central inspection tower.

DEVELOPMENTS IN THE UNITED STATES

In colonial America, penal practice was loose, decentralized, and unsystematic, combining private retaliation against wrongdoing with fines, banishment, harsh corporal punishments, and capital punishment. Local jails were scattered about the colonies, but they were used primarily for temporary holding rather than for punishment.[8] Some people, such as William Penn, the famous Quaker and founder of Pennsylvania, promoted incarceration as a humane alternative to the physically brutal punishments that were common. However, that idea was largely ignored because there was no stable central governmental authority to coordinate and finance (through tax revenue) the large-scale confinement of offenders.

THE PENITENTIARY MOVEMENT In the aftermath of the American Revolution, it rapidly became apparent that the colonial system of justice would not suffice. Economic chaos and civil disorder followed the war. Combined with population growth and the transition from an agricultural society to an industrial one, they created the need for a strong, centralized government to achieve political and economic stability. The rise of the penitentiary occurred in that context.[9] Philosophically, it was guided by Enlightenment principles. In 1790, the Walnut Street Jail in Philadelphia was converted from a simple holding facility to a prison to which offenders could be sentenced for their crimes. It is commonly regarded as the nation's first state prison. In a system consistent with Howard's plan, its inmates labored in solitary cells and received large doses of religious teaching. Later in the 1790s, New York opened Newgate Prison. Other states quickly followed suit, and the penitentiary movement was born. By 1830, Pennsylvania and New York had constructed additional prisons to supplement their original ones.

Stateville Correctional Center in Illinois is similar in design to Bentham's panopticon plan. *Why wasn't this prison design used more widely in the United States?*

Pennsylvania and New York pioneered the penitentiary movement by developing two competing systems of confinement.[10] The **Pennsylvania system,** sometimes called the *separate system,* required that inmates be kept in solitary cells so that they could study religious writings, reflect on their misdeeds, and perform handicraft work. In the New York system, or the **Auburn system** (named after Auburn Penitentiary and also referred to as the *congregate* or *silent system*), inmates worked and ate together in silence during the day and were returned to solitary cells for the evening. Ultimately, the Auburn system prevailed over the Pennsylvania system as the model followed by other states. It avoided the harmful psychological effects of total solitary confinement and allowed more inmates to be housed in less space because cells could be smaller. In addition, the Auburn system's congregate work principle was more congruent with the system of factory production emerging in wider society than was the outdated craft principle of the separate system. If prison labor was to be profitable, it seemed that the Auburn plan was the one to use.

It is interesting that although penitentiary construction flourished and the United States became the model nation in penology during the first half of the nineteenth century, there was serious discontent with the penitentiary by the end of the Civil War. There were few signs penitentiaries were deterring crime, reforming offenders, or turning great profits from inmate labor. In fact, prisons were becoming increasingly expensive to run, and opposition was growing to selling prisoner-made goods on the open market. With faith in the penitentiary declining, the stage was set for a new movement—a movement that, rather than challenging the fundamental value of incarceration as a punishment, sought to improve the method of incarceration.

THE REFORMATORY MOVEMENT The reformatory movement got its start at the 1870 meeting of the National Prison Association, in Cincinnati. The principles adopted there were championed by such leaders in the field as Enoch Wines (1806–1879) and Zebulon Brockway (1827–1920).[11] A new type of institution, the reformatory, was designed for younger, less hardened offenders, between 16 and

Pennsylvania system An early system of U.S. penology in which inmates were kept in solitary cells so that they could study religious writings, reflect on their misdeeds, and perform handicraft work.

Auburn system An early system of penology, originating at Auburn Penitentiary in New York, in which inmates worked and ate together in silence during the day and were placed in solitary cells for the evening.

The Elmira Reformatory, which opened in 1876 in Elmira, New York, was the first institution for men that was based on reformatory principles. *What caused the change in penal philosophy?*

30 years of age. Based on a military model of regimentation, it emphasized academic and vocational training in addition to work. A classification system was introduced, in which inmates' progress toward reformation was rated. The sentences for determinate periods of time (for example, 5 years) were replaced with indeterminate terms, in which inmates served sentences within given ranges (for example, between 2 and 8 years). Parole or early release could be granted for favorable progress in reformation.

It has been observed that indeterminate sentences and the possibility of parole facilitate greater control over inmates than do determinate sentences. Many inmates are interested, above all else, in gaining their freedom. The message conveyed by indeterminate sentences and the possibility of parole is this: "Conform to institutional expectations or do more time."

INSTITUTIONS FOR WOMEN Until the reformatory era, there was little effort to establish separate facilities for women. Women prisoners were usually confined in segregated areas of male prisons and generally received inferior treatment. The reformatory movement, reflecting its assumptions about differences between categories of inmates and its emphasis on classification, helped feminize punishment.[12] The first women's prison organized according to the reformatory model opened in Indiana in 1873. By the 1930s, several other women's reformatories were in operation, mainly in the Northeast and the Midwest. Most employed cottages or a campus and a family-style living plan, not the cell-block plan of men's prisons. Most concentrated on molding inmates to fulfill stereotypical domestic roles, such as cleaning and cooking, upon release.

TWENTIETH-CENTURY PRISONS Criminologist John Irwin has provided a useful typology for summarizing imprisonment in the last century.[13] According to Irwin, three types of institutions have been dominant. Each has dominated a different part of the century. The dominant type for about the first three decades was the "big house." In Irwin's words:

> The Big House was a walled prison with large cell blocks that contained stacks of three or more tiers of one- or two-man cells. On the average, it held 2,500 men. Sometimes a single cell block housed over 1,000 prisoners in six tiers of cells. Most of these prisons were built over many decades and had a mixture of old and new cell blocks. Some of the older cell blocks were quite primitive.[14]

It is important to realize that big houses were not new prisons, distinct from earlier penitentiaries and reformatories. They were the old penitentiaries and reformatories, expanded in size to accommodate larger inmate populations. Originally, big-house prisons exploited inmate labor through various links to the free market. Industrial prisons predominated in the North, while plantation prisons characterized much of the South. With the rise of organized labor and the coming of the Great Depression, free-market inmate labor systems fell into demise during the 1920s and 1930s. Big houses became warehouses oriented toward custody and repression of inmates.

What Irwin calls the "correctional institution" arose during the 1940s and became the dominant type of prison in the 1950s. Correctional institutions generally were smaller and more modern in appearance than big houses. However, correctional institutions did not replace big houses; they simply supplemented them, though correctional-institution principles spread to many big houses. Correctional institutions emerged as penologists turned to the field of medicine as a model for their work. During that phase of corrections, a so-called **medical model** came to be used, as crime was seen as symptomatic of personal illness in need of treatment. Under the medical model, shortly after being sentenced to prison, inmates were subjected to psychological assessment and diagnosis during classification processes. Assessment and diagnosis were followed by treatment designed to address the offender's supposed illness. The main kinds of treatment, according to Irwin, were academic and vocational education and therapeutic counseling. After institutional treatment came parole, which amounted to follow-up treatment in the community. Importantly, the ways of achieving control over inmate behavior shifted from the custodial repression typical of the big house to more subtle methods of indirect coercion: inmates knew that failure to participate in treatment and exhibit "progress" in prison meant that parole would be delayed.

Big-house prisons, which consisted of large cellblocks containing stacks of cells, were the dominant prison design of the early twentieth century. *What are some problems with the big-house prison design?*

During the 1960s and 1970s, both the effectiveness and the fairness of coerced prison rehabilitation programming began to be challenged,[15] and the correctional institution's dominance began to wane. In Irwin's view, the third type of prison, the "contemporary violent prison," arose by default as the correctional institution faded. Gone were many of the treatment-program control mechanisms of the correctional institution. Further, many of the repressive measures used to control inmates in the big house became illegal after the rise of the inmates' rights movement during the 1960s (to be discussed later). In essence, what emerged in many prisons was a power vacuum that was filled with inmate gang violence and interracial hatred.

medical model A theory of institutional corrections, popular during the 1940s and 1950s, in which crime was seen as symptomatic of personal illness in need of treatment.

PRIVATIZATION AND SHOCK INCARCERATION As will be readily apparent in the next section of this chapter, the last three decades are likely to be remembered for the largest incarceration boom to date and for desperate attempts to deal with prison crowding by developing alternatives to traditional incarceration.

One alternative to traditional confinement is the move toward **privatization,** the involvement of the private sector in the construction and operation of confinement facilities. The private sector has a long tradition in institutional corrections. For instance, such diverse services as food, legal aid, medical and psychiatric care, and education have long been provided through private vendors. There is a rich history of private labor contracting in the operation of prisons, and it is now witnessing something of a revival in certain jurisdictions. Also, the private sector has operated juvenile institutions for many years. But mounting prison populations, combined with space and budget limitations, have helped give privatization new twists. One of those twists entails having the private sector finance construction of institutions under what amounts to a lease-purchase agreement. The Potosi Correctional Center in Missouri was constructed under such a strategy. In another twist, the state contracts with private companies like U.S. Corrections Corporation to have them operate prisons. One of the earliest privately operated state prisons for adult felons, Kentucky's minimum-security Marion Adjustment Center, was opened in January 1986.

privatization The involvement of the private sector in the construction and the operation of confinement facilities.

The Convict Lease System

One of the darkest chapters in the history of American corrections involves the convict lease system that was adopted by many southern states following the Civil War. It perpetuated slavery in the states that embraced it. Counties and states leased thousands of prisoners (mostly black) to private individuals and companies to work (and die) in cotton fields, mines, and forests of the Deep South. Governments made millions of dollars in lease payments, and those who leased prisoners and brutally exploited them made millions more. The practice did not end until the 1930s.

Source: Fletcher M. Green, "Some Aspects of the Convict Lease System in the Southern States," *Essays in Southern History,* vol. 31 (Durham: University of North Carolina Press), 1949.

shock incarceration The placement of offenders in facilities patterned after military boot camps.

At the end of 2001, 27 states, the District of Columbia, Puerto Rico, the Federal Bureau of Prisons, the Immigration and Naturalization Service, and the U.S. Marshals Service had contracts in force with 1 or more of 13 private companies to house prisoners in 154 privately managed, secure adult correctional facilities (jails or prisons).[16] About 40 percent of those facilities were located in Texas (with 42) and California (with 22). No other jurisdiction had more than eight private adult correctional institutions; most jurisdictions had only one facility.[17] Together, those institutions had the capacity to hold approximately 6 percent of all local, state, and federal inmates.[18] Two companies—Corrections Corporation of America (with a 52 percent market share) and Wackenhut Corrections Corporation (with a 22 percent market share)—dominate the industry.[19]

Proponents of states' contracting to have the private sector finance construction and operate prisons often point to efficiency, flexibility, and cost-effectiveness. Opponents frequently worry about liability issues, about creating a profit motive for incarcerating people, and about the incentive to trim inmate services and programs to maximize profits.

Research shows the following about private correctional facilities:

- Private facilities can be constructed and opened more quickly. Following contract awards, private facilities can be constructed within 12 to 18 months; similar facilities constructed by governments usually take 36 to 48 months to be brought "on line."
- Construction cost savings of 25 percent or more and operating cost savings of 10 to 15 percent are common for private facilities. However, other research shows that these cost savings can be illusory, that there are wide variations among facilities. For example, a survey of private correctional management companies found that the average savings from privatization was only about 1 percent, achieved mostly through reduced labor costs. It is also unclear whether any cost savings can be sustained over time.
- The quality of services and programs in private facilities is frequently superior to that in publicly operated facilities.
- Private contractors can frequently deliver correctional services more cost-effectively than public employees.
- Privatization can substantially reduce legal liability costs of operating prisons and jails.
- Necessary changes in the nature and scope of prisoner programs can be made quicker and easier in private facilities.
- The existence of private facilities in a jurisdiction sometimes encourages improvements in the public facilities in that jurisdiction.
- Prisoners in private facilities have a broader array of legal remedies when challenging conditions of confinement than prisoners in public facilities.[20]

Despite this list of advantages, the future of correctional privatization may depend on the answer to a philosophical question: To what degree should governments cede their correctional responsibilities to the private sector?

A second confinement alternative to traditional incarceration is **shock incarceration,** the placement of offenders in facilities patterned after military boot camps. Such facilities are ordinarily designed for young, nonviolent offenders without extensive criminal records. Instead of being given traditional prison sentences, those offenders are sentenced to shock incarceration facilities (for example, "boot camps") for relatively short periods (for instance, 90 days). There, they are subjected to a

The incarceration boom of the past three decades has required the construction of dozens of new prisons. *Was this construction boom necessary? Why or why not?*

strict, military-style program of work, physical conditioning, and discipline. Boot camps vary considerably in their emphasis on treatment. After completing the program, inmates are released into the community on probation or parole. Shock incarceration is appealing to those who wish to convey a "tough on crime" message to the general public. However, as criminologists Doris Layton MacKenzie and James Shaw observe, the "studies examining the recidivism of boot camp releasees have been disappointing for those who expect the programs to affect offenders' activities after release."[21]

The popularity of boot-camp programs has probably peaked. In 1997, the California state legislature ended the state's boot-camp program after 5 years of operation. A California Department of Corrections evaluation found that the program reduced neither recidivism nor costs to the state.[22] Boot-camp prisons are considered an intermediate sanction, which will be discussed in Chapter 9 ("Community Corrections").

CYCLES IN HISTORY The history of institutional corrections has evolved in cycles of accumulation. Developments viewed as innovative replacements for old practices almost always contain vestiges of the old practices, and the old practices seldom disappear when "new" ones are introduced. The new is implemented alongside the old and contains elements of the old. Penitentiaries were not torn down when reformatories were introduced, nor were big houses abolished when correctional institutions arose. Similarly, many jurisdictions have recently moved away from indeterminate sentences toward determinate ones. Those determinate sentences, although often seen as innovative, are hard to distinguish from the fixed sentences that preceded the move to indeterminate sentencing. Likewise, the modern trend toward boot camps revives the quasi-military organization that was present at Elmira Reformatory. An interesting question is whether penological history represents progress or the coming back around of what went around before.

Chain gangs are another recent example of the "what goes around comes around" phenomenon. In 1995, Alabama became the first state to reintroduce the chain gang. Arizona, Oklahoma, and Wisconsin (which used stun belts instead of chains) soon followed. Arizona is also the first state to allow female prisoners to work on chain gangs.[23] These states (except Wisconsin) put shackled prisoners to work along the roadside, cutting high weeds, picking up trash, and clearing muddy ditches. Arizona's female chain gang members also dig graves and bury indigents who have died, paint curbs, and remove graffiti. Prisoners are supervised by gun-toting guards. Alabama's experiment with chain gangs lasted less than 4 years. Among problems blamed for its demise were escape attempts, inmate fights, lack of productivity (people chained together move slowly), and the need for more guards inside prisons. Oklahoma and Wisconsin also no longer employ chain gangs. As of this writing, Arizona was still using chain gangs but participation was voluntary. In addition, unlike in Alabama where inmates were chained together, in Arizona, inmates are chained individually. Widespread use of chain gangs ended between the Depression and World War II, though it was not until the late 1970s that Alabama abolished the practice.

FYI

Prison Growth

Several states in the United States now have as many prisons in operation as some entire Western nations—or more. As of January 1, 2005, the states and the federal government, combined, operated more than 1,000 adult prisons.

SOURCE: *American Correctional Association 2005 Directory: Adult and Juvenile Correctional Departments, Institutions, Agencies and Probation and Parole Authorities* (Lanham, MD: American Correctional Association, 2005), calculated from data on p. 30.

THINKING CRITICALLY

1. Do you think any of the early forerunners to modern corrections (such as banishment, etc.) could be used today? Why or why not?

2. Do you think that shock incarceration has any merit? Why or why not?

The Incarceration Boom

For most of the past 65 years, the incarceration rate was fairly steady. Only since 1973 has there been a continuing increase, with each year showing a new high.

Federal versus State Prisons

Only about 12 percent of all inmates at midyear 2005 were in federal prisons. The remaining 88 percent were in state prisons.

Source: Paige M. Harrison and Allen J. Beck, "Prison and Jail Inmates at Midyear 2005," *Bureau of Justice Statistics Bulletin* (Washington, DC: U.S. Department of Justice, May 2006).

RECENT TRENDS

There were 329,821 inmates in state and federal prisons at the end of 1980 (305,458 state prison inmates and 24,363 federal prison inmates). By mid-decade, the total number of prison inmates had increased 52 percent, to 502,752 inmates, and by the end of the 1980s, there were a total of 712,967 inmates, an increase of 116 percent over 1980.[24] That represents an average increase of about 9 percent per year.

About a decade and a half later, at midyear 2005, the adult prison population stood at 1,431,468 (1,255,514 state prison inmates and 175,954 federal prison inmates), an increase of 100 percent over the beginning of 1990 and an increase of 334 percent over 1980. The total number of prison inmates at midyear 2005 was 2 percent more than the record high of 1,404,032 inmates at year-end 2001. (Between 1980 and midyear 2005, the state prison population increased 311 percent and the federal prison population increased 622 percent.) In other words, between 1980 and midyear 2005, the adult prison population (both state and federal) had more than quadrupled.[25]

However, the growth of the prison population slowed somewhat in the 1990s to an average of about 6.5 percent per year (from approximately 9 percent per year during the 1980s). In 1999, the prison population grew 3.4 percent—the smallest yearly increase since 1988. Between year-end 2003 and year-end 2004, the prison population grew 1.9 percent (the state prison population increased only 1.6 percent, while the federal prison population increased 4.2 percent). The level of growth (1.1 percent) in the state and federal prison population in 2001 was the lowest annual rate recorded since 1972 and is entirely attributable to the slower growth in the state prison population. The overall growth of the state (but not federal) prison population has been slowing since 1995.[26] Table 7.1 shows the jurisdictions with the largest and smallest numbers of prison inmates and the highest and lowest incarceration rates per 100,000 residents at midyear 2005. (Incarceration rates are discussed later in this section.)

TABLE 7.1	Jurisdictions with the Largest and Smallest Numbers of Prison Inmates and Incarceration Rates per 100,000 Residents at Midyear 2005		
PRISON POPULATION	NUMBER OF INMATES		RATE PER 100,000 STATE RESIDENTS[a]
5 LARGEST:			
Federal	184,484	Louisiana	824
Texas	171,338	Texas	703
California	166,532	Mississippi	682
Florida	87,545	Oklahoma	655
New York	62,963	Alabama	587
5 SMALLEST:			
North Dakota	1,338	Maine	153
Vermont	1,975	Minnesota	179
Wyoming	2,026	Rhode Island	179
Maine	2,084	New Hampshire	196
New Hampshire	2,561	North Dakota	199

[a]The number of prisoners with a sentence of more than 1 year per 100,000 residents in the state population.

Source: Paige M. Harrison and Allen J. Beck, "Prison and Jail Inmates at Midyear 2005," *Bureau of Justice Statistics Bulletin* (Washington, DC: GPO, U.S. Department of Justice, May 2006), pp. 1 and 3, Table 2.

The approximately 1.4 million state and federal prison inmates incarcerated in the United States at midyear 2005 do not include 101,228 prisoners held in privately operated facilities (as of June 30, 2005) and 74,718 state and federal prisoners held in local jails or other facilities operated by county or local authorities (as of year-end 2004). It also does not include the 747,529 local jail inmates (as of June 30, 2005; more about the jail population later); the 15,757 inmates held in territorial and commonwealth prisons (as of June 30, 2004); the 9,788 inmates held in facilities operated by or exclusively for the Bureau of Immigration and Customs Enforcement (formerly the U.S. Immigration and Naturalization Service) (as of June 30, 2004); the 2,177 inmates in military facilities (as of June 30, 2004); the 1,826 inmates in jails in Indian country (as of midyear 2003); or the 96,655 inmates (as of October 2003) in juvenile facilities (discussed in Chapter 10). Overall, the United States had approximately 2.5 million people incarcerated at midyear 2005.[27]

Similar, though somewhat less drastic, trends are evident when local jails are examined. Between 1982 and 1990, the number of jail inmates increased nearly 89 percent, from 209,582 to 395,553. On June 30, 2005, the local jail population stood at a record high of 747,529 inmates, an increase of about 90 percent over the beginning of 1990 and 260 percent over 1982.[28] If the additional 71,905 persons being supervised outside a jail facility (in community service programs, weekender programs, by electronic monitoring, etc.) at midyear 2005 are added to the 747,529 confined inmates, the total number of people under the supervision of local jails increases to 819,434, an increase of about 4 percent over the previous year.[29] Table 7.2 lists the 10 largest local jail jurisdictions in the United States, along with their average daily populations at midyear 2004 (the latest year for which data were available).

We must be cautious about looking exclusively at changes in the sheer number of people incarcerated, because such changes do not take into consideration changes in the size of the general population. We might wonder whether big increases in the number of people incarcerated simply reflect growth in the U.S. population. Researchers typically convert a raw figure to an **incarceration rate** to deal with that problem. The incarceration rate is calculated by dividing the number of people incarcerated by the population of the area and multiplying the result by 100,000:

Incarceration rate = number incarcerated/population × 100,000

Figure 7.1 is a display of the incarceration boom of recent years with shifts in the size of the general population taken into account. As shown in the figure, the U.S. adult prison incarceration rate was comparatively stable from the period before 1930 until the mid-1970s, at which time the dramatic upward climb began. Between 1980 and midyear 2005, the prison incarceration rate rose approximately 250 percent, from 139 to 488 prisoners per 100,000 residents.[30] Likewise, between 1982 and midyear 2005, the jail incarceration rate rose from 90 to 252 per 100,000 residents, or approximately 180 percent.[31]

Incarceration rates also differ significantly among nations. The data in Figure 7.2 show the prison population rates for 25 selected nations as of the most recent year available. Note that the United States has the highest rate of incarceration in the world.

TABLE 7.2	The 10 Largest Local Jail Jurisdictions with Their Average Daily Populations at Midyear 2004	
JURISDICTION	**AVERAGE DAILY POPULATION**	
Los Angeles County, CA	18,512	
New York City, NY	13,751	
Cook County, IL	10,535	
Maricopa County, AZ	8,657	
Harris County, TX	8,200	
Philadelphia City, PA	7,376	
Dallas County, TX	7,090	
Dade County, FL	6,619	
Orleans Parish, LA	5,923	
Orange County, CA	5,569	

Source: Adapted from Paige M. Harrison and Allen J. Beck, "Prison and Jail Inmates at Midyear 2004," *Bureau of Justice Statistics Bulletin* (Washington, DC: U.S. Department of Justice, April 2005).

incarceration rate A figure derived by dividing the number of people incarcerated by the population of the area and multiplying the result by 100,000; used to compare incarceration levels of units with different population sizes.

Incarceration Rates

Males are far more prone to crime and incarceration than females. At midyear 2005, the rate for men was 925 per 100,000 men, compared with 64 per 100,000 for women.

Source: Paige M. Harrison and Allen J. Beck, "Prison and Jail Inmates at Midyear 2005," *Bureau of Justice Statistics Bulletin* (Washington, DC: U.S. Department of Justice, May 2006), p. 5.

Corrections

| FIGURE 7.1 | Sentenced Prisoners in State and Federal Institutions |

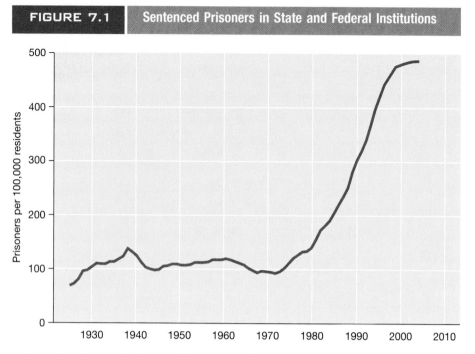

Source: Kathleen Maguire and Ann L. Pastore (eds.), *Sourcebook of Criminal Justice Statistics 1996* (Washington, DC: GPO, U.S. Department of Justice, Bureau of Justice Statistics, 1997), p. 517, Table 6.4 and p. 518, Table 6.21; Paige M. Harrison and Allen J. Beck, "Prisoners in 2004," *Bureau of Justice Statistics Bulletin* (Washington, DC: GPO, U.S. Department of Justice, October 2005).

| FIGURE 7.2 | Incarceration Rates for Selected Nations |

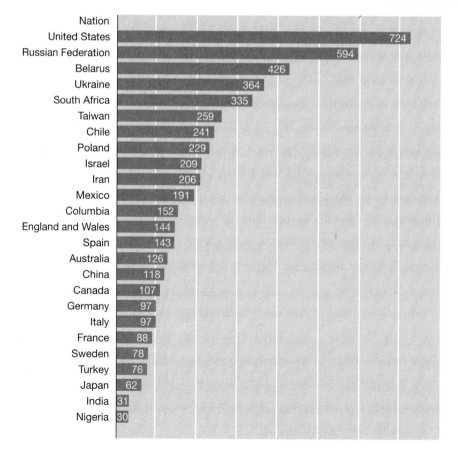

Source: Kings College London: International Centre for Prison Studies, www.kcl.ac.uk/depsta/rel/icps/worldbrief/highest_to_lowest_rates.php.

Incarceration Rates
For the incarceration rates of 213 nations, access the International Centre for Prison Studies at **www.kcl.ac.uk/depsta/rel/icps/worldbrief/highest_to_lowest_rates.php.** *Why do you think incarceration rates vary so greatly among different nations?*

Annual incarceration rates such as those depicted in Figure 7.2 and discussed earlier reflect the numbers of people admitted to institutions, the lengths of time those people serve, and (for purposes of international comparisons) the nations' levels of crime. Nations with higher levels of crime, with more people admitted to prison, and with prisoners serving longer terms can be expected to have higher annual rates of incarceration. Thus, James Lynch argues that the type of international comparisons depicted in Figure 7.2 may be misleading because the United States has a more serious crime problem than most other nations.[32] Lynch contends that if the analysis is controlled for nations' levels of crime, the differences between the United States and other nations in the use of imprisonment are smaller.

THE CROWDING ISSUE Crowding has always been a problem in American prisons, but it has become especially troublesome over the past three decades. The increase in prison construction across the nation of late, while staggering, has failed to keep pace with the increase in prison populations, produced partly by the war on drugs. Eighteen states now have at least one institution under court order to rectify crowded conditions, and many state prisoners are being held in local jails because of insufficient prison space. Furthermore, crowded prisons are often volatile prisons, and efforts to address problems related to crowding frequently end up diverting resources from inmate services and programs. How did we arrive at this state of affairs?

The most obvious explanation is that a massive outbreak of crime in the United States has fueled the growth of the prison population. But as criminologist Nils Christie and a number of other observers have pointed out, that explanation is simply not supported by the data, which show relatively stable, and in some cases even declining, rates of crime for much of the period of the incarceration boom.[33] Likewise, there has not been an increase in the proportion of young adults, who constitute the most prison-prone age group, in the general population.

Law professor Franklin Zimring offers an interesting public opinion explanation.[34] Zimring claims that members of the public will think punishment for crime is too soft and will demand more imprisonment as long as they think crime is too high. The problem is that prisons generally do an unsatisfactory job of controlling crime, so the public continues to perceive crime as high, despite increases in the prison population. The inability of prisons to control crime fuels the public demand for still more punishment (such as more imprisonment). Zimring uses the analogy of a person who finds that the medicine he or she has been taking for a headache is not helping and decides to increase the dose of the same medication.

We can expand a bit on Zimring's perspective. Over the last 200 years, Americans have developed a tradition of strong reliance on the prison to control crime. It has never done very well. As Zimring observes, the typical response to high crime and high recidivism is to conclude that criminals are not being punished enough and to gradually increase the use of imprisonment. In pursuing that strategy, we get caught in a loop. We are continually forced to direct the greatest

Prison Costs

In 1995, for the first time ever, more money was spent building new prisons than new university structures in the United States—$2.5 billion for construction in higher education and $2.6 billion for prison construction. From 1987 to 1995, state prison expenditures rose 30 percent while higher-education funding fell 18 percent.

SOURCE: "More Spent on Prisons Than Universities in 1995," *The Orlando Sentinel*, February 25, 1997, p. A-6.

Myth / Fact

Myth Six percent of America's criminals commit 70 percent of all violent crimes. Thus, crime control could be improved dramatically if only those 6 percent were imprisoned.

Fact This well-publicized statistic comes from a misinterpretation of two studies focusing on criminal activity by boys born in Philadelphia. Dr. Marvin Wolfgang of the University of Pennsylvania discovered that 6 percent of the boys born in Philadelphia in 1945 were responsible for more than half of the serious crimes committed by the entire group. Of those born in 1958, 7.5 percent committed 69 percent of the serious crimes. Those who cite these outdated studies focus erroneously on 6 percent of "criminals"—as if future high-rate offenders could be predicted—instead of 6 percent of all male children born in a given year, whose future criminal behavior is also not predictable.

SOURCE: William M. DiMascio, *Seeking Justice: Crime and Punishment in America* (New York: Edna McConnell Clark Foundation, 1997), p. 12.

Prison Resources

About two-thirds of all money spent on corrections is used to finance institutions. Roughly a quarter of all persons under correctional supervision are incarcerated. Therefore, about three-quarters of the correctional population must be accommodated with one-third of the resources.

Myth Fact

Prisons have a revolving door, and inmates are now serving far shorter prison terms than in the past.

Since 1923 the average prison term served by inmates in the United States has remained constant at about 2 years. State prisoners are still serving sentences that average 2 years. Federal inmates, however, have been serving slightly longer sentences since the passage of the Sentencing Reform Act of 1984 and the adoption of mandatory sentencing laws. The act introduced truth in sentencing in federal courts, which mandates that offenders serve a minimum of 85 percent of their sentences.

SOURCE: William M. DiMascio, *Seeking Justice: Crime and Punishment in America* (New York: Edna McConnell Clark Foundation, 1997), p. 16; *Sourcebook of Criminal Justice Statistics Online*, Table 6.55; Matthew R. Durose and Patrick A. Langan, "Felony Sentences in State Courts, 2002," *Bureau of Justice Statistics Bulletin* (Washington, DC: GPO, U.S. Department of Justice, December 2004), p. 5, Table 4.

portions of our overall correctional budgets toward imprisonment. Relatively few resources are left to develop effective programs in community corrections and crime prevention programs that might reduce reliance on imprisonment. The lack of resources devoted to community corrections and crime prevention helps ensure that programs in those areas will fail to control crime. So there will always be an abundant supply of offenders to feed the prison population and escalate the cost of maintaining that population. The irony is clear and substantial. While crowding in correctional institutions suggests the need for effective alternatives in community corrections and crime prevention, that same crowding and the resources it consumes preclude such alternatives. Ineffectiveness in community corrections and crime prevention simply makes the crowding worse, thereby consuming even more resources.

PRISON INMATE CHARACTERISTICS

Who are the people in prison, and why are they there? First, we must distinguish between federal and state prisoners. At midyear 2005, 88 percent of all prisoners in the United States were state prisoners, while only 12 percent were federal prisoners.[35] Because most prisoners are state prisoners, we will focus on them. At the end of this section, however, we will indicate some important differences between state and federal prisoners. One last point before we begin: The characteristics of both state and federal prisoners are remarkably stable over time; that is, they do not change much from one year to the next.

From Figure 7.3 it is evident that the largest proportion of state prisoners are male and black. In addition, a large proportion had not completed high school or did not have a GED, were under 35 years of age and never married, were employed full-time prior to arrest, and had relatively low monthly incomes. Three things about these data bear mention. First, even though there is actually a greater percentage of females than males in the U.S. population, males make up about 93 percent of the state and federal prison population; that is what is meant by saying that men are disproportionately represented in prison. Second, although 68 percent of the prisoners were employed in the month preceding their arrests, the monthly income figures reveal the low-paying jobs they held. More than half of all inmates had monthly incomes under $1,000 in the month prior to their current arrest. (However, only about 10 percent of state inmates were homeless—living on the street or in a shelter—in the year prior to their incarceration.) Third, blacks are disproportionately represented in state prisons. While blacks make up approximately 13 percent of the general U.S. population, they account for nearly half of the state prison population. Further, the vast majority of blacks in prison are male, and black males constitute somewhere around half of all black persons in the United States. The overrepresentation of blacks in prison is a very heated issue in criminal justice today, and research has not established a consensus on the reasons for that overrepresentation. Currently,

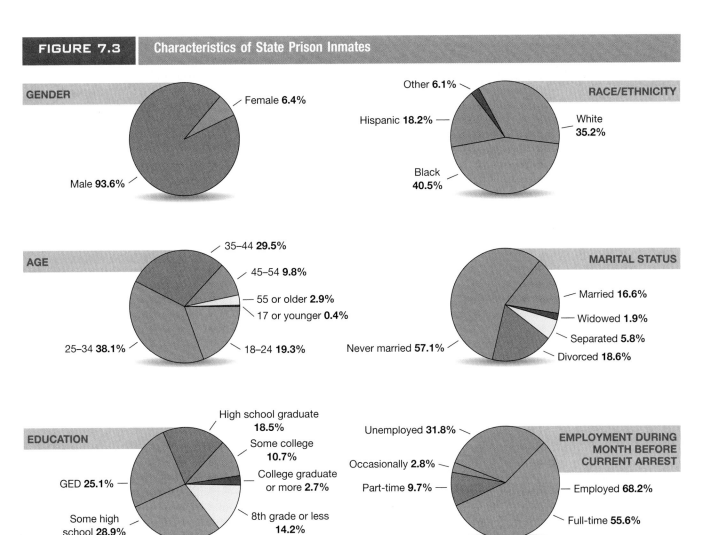

FIGURE 7.3   **Characteristics of State Prison Inmates**

Source: Estimates for gender and race/ethnicity from Paige M. Harrison and Allen J. Beck, "Prisoners in 2004," *Bureau of Justice Statistics Bulletin* (Washington, DC: U.S. Department of Justice, October 2005), p. 9, Table 12. Disaggregated estimates for age graciously provided by Allen Beck from "Prison and Jail Inmates at Midyear 2002," U.S. Department of Justice, Bureau of Justice Statistics; data for the other characteristics are from published and unpublished data from 1997 surveys of state and federal inmates that were graciously provided by Allen Beck and Christopher Mumola, U.S. Department of Justice, Bureau of Justice Statistics (November 9, 2000).

however, the weight of the evidence suggests that offense seriousness and prior criminal record generally exert a stronger impact on decisions to imprison than do extralegal factors such as race.[36]

In 2002, about half of state prison inmates were serving sentences for violent offenses, about 20 percent were serving sentences for property offenses, approximately 21 percent were serving terms for drug offenses, and most of the remainder were doing time for public order offenses. A more detailed breakdown for the violent and property offense categories is shown in Table 7.3.

The overall profile of inmate characteristics does not change drastically when we shift our attention to the federal prison population. However, there are some noteworthy differences. For example, in 2005, about 56 percent of the federal prison population were white, about 32 percent were Hispanic, and about 40 percent were black. Federal inmates are, on average, somewhat older (average age = 37) and possess higher education levels than state inmates. Also, about 53 percent of federal inmates were serving time for drug offenses.[37]

Incarcerated Parents

In 2004, nearly 1.9 million children had at least one parent in state or federal prison (up from less than 1.5 million in 1999).

Source: Center for Children of Incarcerated Parents: CCIP Data Sheet 3a, www. e-ccip.org/publication.html; Christopher J. Mumola, "Incarcerated Parents and Their Children," *Bureau of Justice Special Report* (Washington, DC: GPO, U.S. Department of Justice, August 2000).

TABLE 7.3	Most Serious Offenses for Which State Inmates Were Serving Sentences in 2002				
OFFENSE	**PERCENTAGE OF INMATES**	**OFFENSE**	**PERCENTAGE OF INMATES**	**OFFENSE**	**PERCENTAGE OF INMATES**
VIOLENT OFFENSES	50.5	**PROPERTY OFFENSES**	20.4	**DRUG OFFENSES**	21.4
Murder[a]	12.0	Burglary	10.6	Public Order Offenses[b]	7.1
Manslaughter	1.4	Larceny	3.9	Other/Unspecified Offenses[c]	0.6
Rape	4.9	Motor Vehicle Theft	1.5		
Other Sexual Assault	6.6	Fraud	2.5		
Robbery	13.8	Other Property Offenses	2.0		
Assault	9.4				
Other Violent Offenses	2.4				

Note: Data are for inmates with a sentence of more than 1 year under the jurisdiction of state correctional authorities.
[a]Includes nonnegligent manslaughter.
[b]Includes weapons, drunk driving, court offenses, commercialized vice, morals and decency charges, liquor law violations, and other public-order offenses.
[c]Includes juvenile offenses and unspecified felonies.

Source: Paige M. Harrison and Allen J. Beck, "Prisoners in 2004," *Bureau of Justice Statistics Bulletin* (Washington, DC: GPO, U.S. Department of Justice, October 2005), p. 9, Table 13.

Incarceration Facilities

In the United States, the organizational and administrative structure of institutional corrections is diffuse and decentralized. Primary administrative responsibility for facilities lies with the executive branch of government, but the legislative and judicial branches are also involved. For example, the legislative branch appropriates resources and passes statutes that affect sentence length. The judicial branch sentences offenders to facilities and oversees the legality of institutional practices.

THINKING CRITICALLY

What do the characteristics of prison inmates say about American society as a whole?

CJ ONLINE

U.S. Corrections
To learn more about a variety of issues that affect corrections in the United States, go to **www.corrections.com**. *What does this tell you about the state of corrections in the United States?*

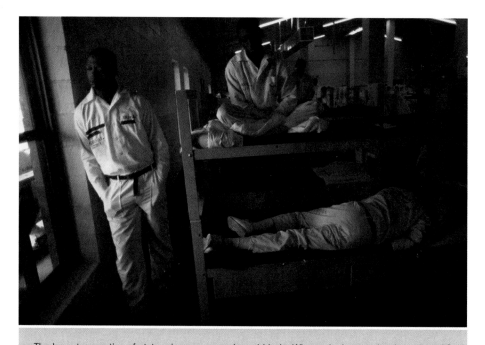

The largest proportion of state prisoners are male and black. *Why, and what can be done about it?*

ORGANIZATION AND ADMINISTRATION BY GOVERNMENT

Incarceration facilities exist at all three levels of government (federal, state, and local), and power and decision-making responsibility are widely distributed both among and within levels. Within broad guidelines, the federal level and the various state and local (county and city) jurisdictions have much autonomy to organize and carry out incarceration practices. As a general rule, the federal government operates its own prison system, each state operates its own prison system, and local jurisdictions operate their own jail systems. Decentralization and autonomy notwithstanding, there are interrelationships between levels. For example, federal requirements affect the operation of state prisons, and local jails are affected by both federal and state regulations.

Federal institutions are administered by the Federal Bureau of Prisons (BOP), which was established within the U.S. Justice Department in 1930 under the Hoover administration. Before the BOP was created, there were seven federal prisons, each separately funded and each operated under policies and procedures established by its warden. The BOP's mission is "to protect society by confining offenders in the controlled environments of prison and community-based facilities that are safe, humane, and appropriately secure, and that provide work and other self-improvement opportunities to assist offenders in becoming law-abiding citizens."[38] The bureau's central office is in Washington, DC, and there are six regional offices, in Philadelphia; Annapolis Junction, Maryland (near Baltimore); Atlanta; Dallas; Kansas City, Kansas; and Dublin, California (near San Francisco). The bureau also has two staff training centers and 28 community corrections offices. As of May 2006, the BOP operated more than 106 institutions (see Figure 7.4). The bureau's facilities hold inmates convicted of violating the U.S. Penal Code. In 2001, the BOP assumed the added responsibility of incarcerating the District of Columbia's sentenced felons because of federal legislation passed in 1997.[39] The administrative organization of the bureau is shown in Figure 7.5. The bureau has come to serve as a source of innovation and professionalization in the field of institutional corrections.

Although states vary in the way they organize institutional corrections, each state has a department of corrections or a similar administrative body to coordinate the various adult prisons in the state. Whether federal or state, correctional institutions are formal, bureaucratic organizations characterized by agency goals, rules and regulations, a staff chain of command, a staff division of labor, and similar features. Most adult prisons employ a quasi-military model of administration and management. Figure 7.6 displays the organizational chart for the California Department of Corrections.

CLASSIFICATION AND OTHER SPECIAL FACILITIES

When offenders are sentenced to the custody of the department of corrections in most states, they are transported

The Largest Prison System

By midyear 2002, the federal prison system, with 161,681 inmates, for the first time in U.S. history had more inmates than any state system. By June 30, 2005, the federal prison population stood at 184,484 inmates and was still the largest. (Texas was second with 171,338 inmates.)

SOURCE: Paige M. Harrison and Jennifer C. Karberg, "Prison and Jail Inmates at Midyear 2002," *Bureau of Justice Statistics Bulletin* (Washington, DC: U.S. Department of Justice, April 2003); Paige M. Harrison and Allen J. Beck, "Prison and Jail Inmates at Midyear 2005," *Bureau of Justice Statistics Bulletin* (Washington, DC: U.S. Department of Justice, May 2006), p. 3, Table 2.

Harley G. Lappin, Director, Federal Bureau of Prisons. *What do you suppose are the major challenges for the director of the BOP?*

FIGURE 7.4 Locations of Institutions in Federal Bureau of Prisons

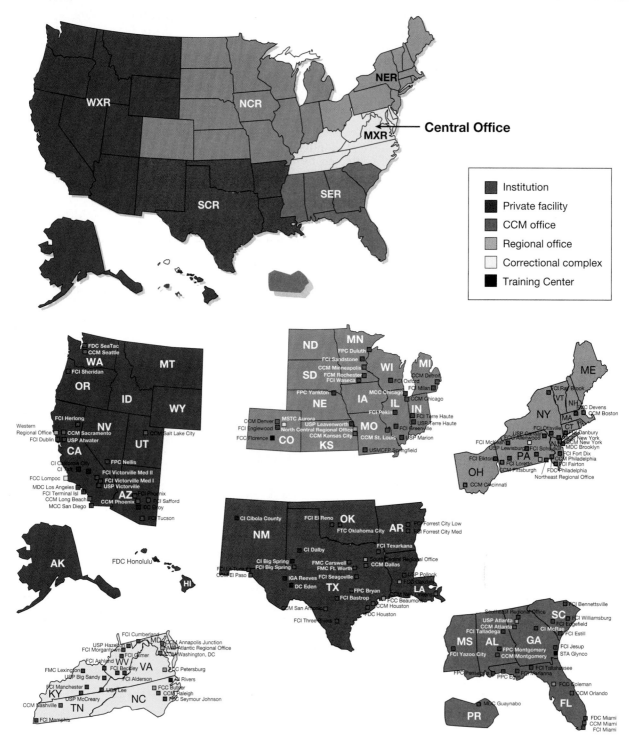

Source: Adopted from the Federal Bureau of Prisons at www.bop.gov, May 2006. Some locations have more than one institution.

FIGURE 7.5   Organization of Federal Bureau of Persons

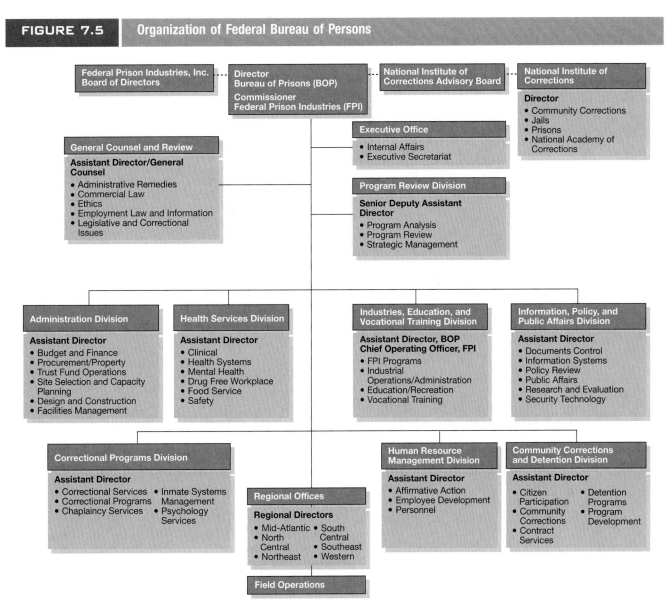

initially to a **classification facility** (sometimes referred to as an assessment, reception, or diagnostic center). Stays at classification facilities are ordinarily short (for example, 60 days). The process of classification entails assessing an offender's security risk and determining which program services (for instance, counseling and education) the offender needs. Assessment information is used in deciding to which institution in the jurisdiction an offender will go to begin his or her term and which problems (such as alcohol dependency) the offender must address while imprisoned. A variety of other factors influence those decisions, including the nature of the offense; the offender's prior record (if any), propensity toward violence and escape, and vulnerability to victimization by other inmates; and the programs offered at the state's various institutions, as well as the levels of crowding at those institutions. The idea is to place inmates in facilities that can accommodate their risk-and-needs profiles.

Classification is not a onetime process; it occurs periodically throughout an inmate's sentence. Inmates are routinely monitored and reclassified to preserve institutional security and for purposes of transfer, programming, and release decisions.

Classification centers are not the only short-term-stay facilities. For example, the Federal Bureau of Prisons administers a number of medical institutions

classification facility A facility to which newly sentenced offenders are taken so that their security risks and needs can be assessed and they can be assigned to a permanent institution.

FIGURE 7.6   **Organization of the California Department of Corrections**

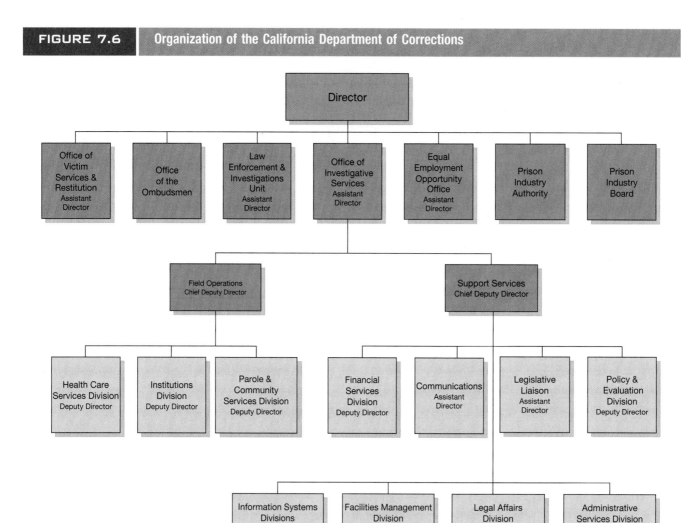

For full content go to www.cdc.state.ca.us/CDC/div_prog.asp.

that receive inmates with health problems and provide them with health care services. If an inmate's condition improves, he or she is returned to the institution of origin or sent to another institution to complete the sentence. Other short-term facilities in various jurisdictions provide services for offenders with mental disorders.

MEN'S PRISONS

security level A designation applied to a facility to describe the measures taken, both inside and outside, to preserve security and custody.

Men's prisons, the most common general type of prison in the nation, are often distinguished from one another by **security level.** An institution's security level is determined by two related factors: (1) the degree of external or perimeter security surrounding the prison and (2) the measures taken to preserve internal security within the institution. The simplest security level categorization is maximum, medium, and minimum. Of the more than 1.1 million male state prison inmates incarcerated on September 30, 2004, 9.4 percent were in maximum-security facilities, 37.1 percent were in medium-security facilities, 34.4 percent were in minimum-security facilities, and 6.5 percent were unclassified or in other facilities, such as multilevel-security facilities, reception and diagnostic facilities, admissions and orientation facilities, and community (low-security) facilities such as prerelease facilities. In addition, 12.1 percent of the inmates were in correctional facilities designated as "high/close," a security level between maximum and medium, and 0.5 percent were in supermaximum-security facilities.[40] Jurisdictions vary in the security categorizations they use.

MAXIMUM-SECURITY FACILITIES Maximum-security facilities (the BOP refers to them as high-security institutions or United States Penitentiaries) are characterized by very tight external and internal security. A high wall or razor-wire fencing, with armed-guard towers, electronic detectors, or both, usually surrounds the prison. External armed patrol is also common. Some maximum-security institutions have a wide, open buffer zone between the outer wall or fence and the free community. Most maximum-security prison designs follow the radial plan or the telephone pole plan. Pottsville Prison is based on the radial plan, and the Oregon State Correctional Institution displays the telephone pole design. Internal security consists of such features as cell-block living, restrictions on inmate movement, and the capability of closing off areas of the institution to contain riots and disruptions.

"SUPERMAX" FACILITIES A recent development is the construction of "ultramaximum-security" or "supermaximum-security" prisons intended to house notorious offenders and problem inmates from other institutions. These prisons utilize total isolation of inmates and constant lockdowns, during which inmates are not permitted to leave their cells. The Federal Bureau of Prisons opened one of the first of these types of prisons in November 1994 in Florence, Colorado. The $60 million state-of-the-art prison (a modern-day Alcatraz) was custom-built to hold the 400 most predatory convicts in the federal system. The new prison is divided into nine units. Security is controlled by means of 1,400 electronically controlled gates and doors and 168 television monitors. Each unit is self-contained and includes separate sick-call rooms, law libraries, and barber chairs. Inmates do not leave their cells for more than an hour a day. When they must leave their cells, they do so only with leg irons, handcuffs, and an escort of two or three guards per inmate. Each cell has a double-entry door, with the classic barred cage door backed up by a windowed steel door that minimizes voice contact among prisoners. After 3 years of this type of confinement, a successful inmate can gradually regain social contact by being allowed to go to the recreation yard or the cafeteria.[41] Currently, more than 40 states and the federal government are operating either one or more "supermax" units within existing maximum-security facilities or entire "supermax" facilities.[42] Pelican Bay State Prison in northern California and Red Onion State Prison in Virginia are examples of the ultramaximum- or supermaximum-security prison.

Prison Misconduct

Ten federal prison guards at the super-maximum-security prison at Florence were indicted for 52 acts of abuse against at least 20 inmates from 1995 to 1997. The renegade group of guards, called "The Cowboys," was charged with kicking inmates, smashing their heads into walls, and mixing human waste into their food. In some cases, the guards injured themselves so they could claim the inmates had attacked them first. Some of the guards told prosecutors that they had a "green light" from prison authorities to "take care of business."

SOURCE: "Guards Charged with Abusing Prisoners," *The Orlando Sentinel*, November 4, 2000, p. A10.

Pottsville Prison in Pennsylvania (left) is an example of the radial prison design, and the Oregon State Correctional Institution (right) is an example of the telephone pole prison design. *What are advantages and disadvantages of each of these prison designs?*

Detention Camp Six

A new prison building at Camp Delta called Detention Camp Six is scheduled to open in July 2006. The 220-bed building is designed to be safer for long-term detainees and their guards. It will also require less manpower to operate.

Source: "Halliburton Subsidiary to Build New Gitmo Prison," *The Orlando Sentinel*, June 18, 2005, p. A12.

CAMP DELTA: A SPECIAL SUPERMAXIMUM FACILITY The war on terrorism has given rise to a new, special kind of supermaximum-security prison, Camp Delta, at the Guantanamo Bay Naval Base in Cuba.[43] The prison is composed of several camps and holds about 450 of what Pentagon officials call the "worst of the worst enemies in the war on terror." The first prisoners arrived from Afghanistan in January 2002. They are to be held until they no longer have useful intelligence to provide, are cleared of criminal wrongdoing, and no longer pose a threat to the United States. They may be held until the war on terror is over, whenever that might be.

Camp Delta, on a bluff overlooking the Caribbean Sea, is surrounded by chain-link fence, lined with green nylon windscreen, and topped with spirals of razor wire. Troops patrol the perimeter on foot, in machine-gun-mounted Humvees, and aboard Piranha boats. Military Police guards watch rows of cellblocks from covered wooden watchtowers. A cellblock consists of a long hallway with 7-by-8-foot green steel-grate cells on either side. Each cell holds one prisoner, and most prisoners remain in their cells 23.5 hours a day. Prisoners can see and talk to one another from their cells. Each cell has a sink with running water and a floor toilet. At the end of the cellblock is a 30-by-30-foot enclosed and covered gravel exercise area that the best-behaved prisoners may use for up to 30 minutes a day. There are also individual outdoor showers.

Each prisoner receives a Quran, oils, beads, and a prayer mat. An arrow stenciled on each steel bed points east to Mecca. Prisoners may receive and write letters to family. Censors read all letters. Personnel from the military, CIA, FBI, and other agencies interrogate prisoners regularly. There have been no escape attempts. Most prisoners are well behaved, although a few of them throw water and sometimes urine on the guards, yell insults and obscenities, refuse to return eating utensils after meals, and, recently, have gone on a hunger strike. Camp officials claim that many of the prisoners arrived with mental-heath problems. Mental-health professionals are on staff to serve them.

Camp Delta, the supermaximum-security prison in Cuba, holds what Pentagon officials call the "worst of the worst enemies in the war on terror." *Should Camp Delta be run like other supermaximum-security prisons, or should special procedures be employed because of the unique inmate population? It special procedures should be employed, what should they be?*

Some prisoners were receiving psychotherapy, antidepressants, and antipsychotic drugs. Since Camp Delta opened 3 prisoners have committed suicide (as of June 2006), and at least 34 prisoners have attempted suicide (though the number is likely higher). Most have tried to hang themselves with bed sheets or clothes. The three successful suicides occurred at night; bed sheets were used. Consequently, guards now give bed sheets to prisoners only when they go to bed and remove them after they wake up in the morning. Troublemakers are moved to solid-steel-walled cells that impede communication with other prisoners and are allowed to shower only twice a week. Cooperative prisoners may be moved to Camp Four, a medium-security section of Camp Delta. In Camp Four, prisoners live in open bays of 10 bunks and may gather and eat in open common areas.

Critics contend that not all of the prisoners are terrorists or have meaningful connections to the Taliban or al Qaeda. Prisoners are from 42 countries. Most of them are from the Middle East and Central Asia, but some of them are citizens of Great Britain, Canada, Australia, China, and Russia. Unfortunately, for them, there is no way to challenge their detention. The Pentagon will not hold the Geneva Convention hearings that would officially classify them as either prisoners of war or terror suspects, and the federal courts have determined that they do not have jurisdiction over the prisoners. As of June 2006, three prisoners had been charged with crimes and 300 prisoners had been released or transferred. No new prisoners have been incarcerated since September 2004 (as of June 2006). The status of the remaining detainees is reviewed every year by military administrative review boards, which recommend whether a prisoner should be released or detained further.

MEDIUM-SECURITY FACILITIES Compared with maximum-security prisons, medium-security institutions place fewer restrictions on inmate movement inside the facility. Cellblocks often coexist with dormitory- or barracks-type living quarters, and in some medium-security prisons, cells are relatively few. Typically, there is no wall for external security. Fences and towers exist but are less forbidding in appearance; razor wire may be replaced with less expensive barbed wire.

LOW-SECURITY FACILITIES The BOP operates low-security facilities, a classification between medium- and minimum-security. Low-security facilities have double-fenced perimeters, mostly dormitory or cubicle housing, and strong work and program components.

MINIMUM-SECURITY FACILITIES Compared with prisons at the other security levels, minimum-security prisons are smaller and more open. Inmates are frequently transferred to such prisons from more secure facilities after they have established records of good behavior or when they are nearing release. Dorm or barracks living quarters predominate, and often there are no fences. Some inmates may be permitted to leave the institution during the day to work (under *work release*) or study (under *study release*) in the community. Likewise, some inmates may be granted furloughs so that they can reestablish ties with family members, make living arrangements for their upcoming release, or establish employment contacts.

CUSTODY LEVEL VERSUS SECURITY LEVEL *Custody level* should be distinguished from *security level*. Whereas institutions are classified by security level, individual inmates are classified by custody level. An inmate's **custody level** indicates the degree of precaution that needs to be taken when working with that inmate. Confusion arises because custody levels are sometimes designated by the same terms used to designate institutional security levels (maximum,

custody level The classification assigned to an inmate to indicate the degree of precaution that needs to be taken when working with that inmate.

medium, and minimum). However, the two levels are independent of each other. For example, some inmates with medium or minimum custody levels may be housed in maximum-security prisons.

WOMEN'S PRISONS AND COCORRECTIONAL FACILITIES

As pointed out earlier, women make up about 7 percent of the population of both state and federal prisons. In recent years, however, incarceration rates for females in the United States have grown faster than incarceration rates for males. For example, between 1995 and 2005 the annual rate of growth of the female inmate population has averaged 4.8 percent, compared with a 3.1 percent average increase in the male inmate population. While the total number of male inmates has grown nearly 32 percent between 1995 and 2005, the number of female inmates has increased 53 percent. Nevertheless, at year-end 2004 there were 64 sentenced female inmates per 100,000 women in the United States, compared to 920 sentenced male inmates per 100,000 men.[44] One difference between male and female state prisoners is that a somewhat greater proportion of women than men are serving sentences for property offenses (28.7 percent female vs. 19.9 percent male) and drug offenses (31.5 percent female vs. 20.7 percent male), while a greater proportion of men are serving time for violent crimes (51.7 percent male vs. 33 percent female).[45] Other differences are that female inmates are more likely than male inmates to have dependent children and to be serving their first prison term. Figure 7.7 shows the percentage of the adult state prison population by security level and gender.

In 2004, 89 percent of all state adult prisons in the nation were for men only, 9 percent were for women only, and 2 percent were for both men and women.[46] Many states operate only one major prison for women. In general, prisons exclusively for women are smaller and house fewer inmates than institutions exclusively for men. Dorm and cottage plans are much more common than cell-block plans in institutions for women.

Cocorrectional facilities, which house both male and female inmates, have been in operation (in contemporary form) since the 1970s. The goal of cocorrections is to normalize the prison environment by integrating the daytime activities of the sexes. In 2004, 22 cocorrectional prisons were in operation in the United States in addition to several other cocorrectional facilities and centers.[47] Cocorrectional prisons are usually small, and security is typically

cocorrectional facilities Usually small, minimum-security institutions that house both men and women with the goal of normalizing the prison environment by integrating the daytime activities of the sexes.

| FIGURE 7.7 | Percentage of Adult State Prison Inmate Population by Security Level and Gender, September 2004 |

Source: *American Correctional Association 2005 Directory: Adult and Juvenile Correctional Departments, Institutions, Agencies and Probation and Parole Authorities* (Lanham, MD: American Correctional Association, 2005), calculated from data on p. 56.

minimum. A comprehensive review of the effect of cocorrections on women prisoners paints a bleak picture: "[C]ocorrections offers women prisoners few, if any, economic, educational, vocational, and social advantages. Cocorrections benefits male prisoners and system maintenance."[48]

JAILS AND LOCKUPS

A **lockup** is a very short-term (for instance, 24- to 48-hour) holding facility that is frequently located in or very near an urban police agency so that suspects can be held pending further inquiry into their cases by the police or the court. If there is cause, a suspect may be transferred from the lockup to the jail.

A **jail** is a facility that holds convicted offenders and unconvicted persons for relatively short periods. The modern term "jail" comes from the English term "gaol" (the pronunciation is identical), and English gaols have a history that dates to the 1100s. In contrast to prisons, most jails are administered at the county or city level of government. Excluding lockups, there are more jails (between 3,000 and 4,000) than any other kind of confinement facility in the United States. Although most jails in the United States are small (about half of them hold fewer than 50 people), some, such as those in Los Angeles and New York City, are very large (refer to Table 7.2).

JAIL FUNCTIONS Most people think of jails primarily as short-term holding facilities where suspects or defendants are detained pending further court processing, such as arraignment, trial, conviction, or sentencing. In practice, though, jails serve a catchall function in criminal justice and corrections. For example, jails also do the following:

- Receive individuals pending arraignment and hold them awaiting trial, conviction and sentencing.
- Readmit probation, parole, and bail-bond violators and absconders.
- Temporarily detain juveniles pending transfer to juvenile authorities.
- Hold mentally ill persons pending their movement to appropriate health facilities.
- Hold individuals for the military.
- Hold individuals for protective custody.
- Hold individuals for contempt (contempt refers to conduct that defies the authority or dignity of a court or legislature).
- Hold witnesses for the courts (witnesses are sometimes held in jails for their safety or if they are unlikely to appear in court when requested).
- Release convicted inmates to the community upon completion of sentence.
- Transfer inmates to federal, state, or other authorities.
- House inmates for federal, state, or other authorities because of crowding of their facilities.
- Sometimes operate community-based programs as alternatives to incarceration (those programs are described in Chapter 9).
- Hold inmates sentenced to short terms (generally 1 year or less).[49]

Because jails must be able to hold all types of people, including those who pose grave threats to the security and safety of others, the limited funds available through local taxes are directed primarily toward custody and security. Accommodations, services, and programs for inmates often suffer as a consequence.

JAIL POPULATIONS The number of people being held in local jails has risen dramatically in recent years. The U.S. local jail population increased from 209,582 in 1982 to 747,529 at midyear 2005, an increase of about 257 percent (see Figure 7.8). The jail incarceration rate was 96 inmates per 100,000 U.S.

lockup A very short-term holding facility that is frequently located in or very near an urban police agency so that suspects can be held pending further inquiry.

jail A facility, usually operated at the local level, that holds convicted offenders and unconvicted persons for relatively short periods.

Jail Statistics
To obtain the most recent jail statistics, go to the Bureau of Justice Statistics at **www.ojp.usdoj.gov/bjs/jails.htm.** *How has the jail population changed between 1990 and midyear 2005?*

FIGURE 7.8	Growth in Local Jail Population, 1982–Midyear 2005

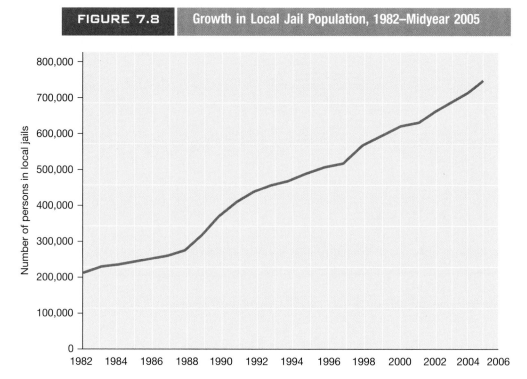

Source: Adapted from Darrell K. Gilliard and Allen J. Beck, "Prison and Jail Inmates at Midyear 1997," *Bureau of Justice Statistics Bulletin* (Washington, DC: U.S. Department of Justice, January 1998); Craig A. Perkins, James J. Stephan, and Allen J. Beck, "Jails and Jail Inmates 1993–1994," *Bureau of Justice Statistics Bulletin* (Washington, DC: U.S. Department of Justice, April 1995); Allen J. Beck, "Prison and Jail Inmates at Midyear 1999," *Bureau of Justice Statistics Bulletin* (Washington, DC: U.S. Department of Justice, April 2000); Paige M. Harrison and Jennifer C. Karberg, "Prison and Jail Inmates at Midyear 2002," *Bureau of Justice Statistics Bulletin* (Washington, DC: U.S. Department of Justice, April 2003); Paige M. Harrison and Allen J. Beck, "Prison and Jail Inmates at Midyear 2004," *Bureau of Justice Statistics Bulletin* (Washington, DC: U.S. Department of Justice, April 2005); Paige M. Harrison and Allen J. Beck, "Prison and Jail Inmates at Midyear 2005," *Bureau of Justice Statistics Bulletin* (Washington, DC: U.S. Department of Justice, May 2006).

residents in 1983; by June 30, 2005, that number had climbed to 252 per 100,000, an increase of 163 percent.[50] Although just 1 percent of the jail population consisted of juveniles, that percentage amounts to 6,759 juveniles. The practice of holding juveniles in adult jails, where they are vulnerable to influence and victimization by adult criminals, is most common in rural areas, where there are no separate juvenile detention centers. That practice has been the target of much criticism and many policy initiatives for more than two decades. Nevertheless, the number of juveniles held in adult jails had been on the rise in recent years until lately; the number decreased by 15 percent between midyear 1995 and midyear 2005 (from 7,800 to 6,759).[51] Table 7.4, which displays selected characteristics of the jail population, also shows that the greatest proportions of jail inmates were male and racial or ethnic minorities in 2005. Less than half of the jail population had been convicted of criminal activity. The remainder were unconvicted persons (usually awaiting trial or other case disposition).

In a classic study of jails,[52] criminologist John Irwin found that, although members of the public tend to believe that jails are heavily populated with dangerous criminals, jails actually hold few such people. Jails are populated disproportionately with members of what Irwin calls the "rabble" class. The rabble class consists of people who are poor, undereducated, alienated from mainstream society, disreputable, and more likely than the general population to belong to an ethnic minority. Most of them have not committed serious offenses. In short, Irwin argues that the main function of the jail is to manage or control marginal members of our society and that as an unintended

TABLE 7.4	Selected Characteristics of Jail Inmates, Midyear 2005				
INMATE CHARACTERISTIC	PERCENTAGE OF INMATES (TOTAL = 747,529)	INMATE CHARACTERISTIC	PERCENTAGE OF INMATES (TOTAL = 747,529)	INCARCERATION RATE PER 100,000 Residents IN EACH GROUP	
AGE		RACE/HISPANIC ORIGIN		White, Non-Hispanic	166
Juvenile	1.0	White, non-Hispanic	44.3	Black, Non-Hispanic	800
Adult	99.0	Black, non-Hispanic	38.9	Hispanic	268
GENDER		Hispanic	15.0	Other	88
Male	87.3	Other	1.7		
Female	12.7				
		LEGAL STATUS (ADULTS ONLY)			
		Convicted	38.0		
		Unconvicted	62.0		

Source: Paige M. Harrison and Allen J. Beck, "Prison and Jail Inmates at Midyear 2005," *Bureau of Justice Statistics Bulletin* (Washington, DC: U.S. Department of Justice, May 2006).

result of that process, the degradation those people experience in jail makes them even more marginal.

However, another study of jail bookings challenges Irwin's conclusion that jails tend to house mostly "rabble." By analyzing the characteristics of persons booked into two jails (one urban, one rural), researchers found that nearly 47 percent had been charged with felonies, and more than 90 percent had been booked for a felony or a class A misdemeanor. Moreover, in 1-day counts of those jails, the researchers discovered that 82.5 percent of those held had been either charged with or convicted of a felony offense. As the authors of the study observe, "These data do not appear to support Irwin's claims about detached and disreputable persons whose real problem is offensiveness, not serious criminality."[53]

JAIL ARCHITECTURE AND MANAGEMENT PHILOSOPHIES Jails have traditionally represented, and continue to represent, one of the most problematic aspects of criminal justice. Many jails in the nation are old buildings plagued by overcrowding, a lack of services and programs for inmates, inadequate staffing, and unsanitary and hazardous living conditions. Some of the interrelated reasons for those problems are (1) the limited and unstable nature of local taxes to fund and staff jails, (2) a general lack of public support for jail reform, (3) rapid rates of inmate turnover, which make it difficult to coordinate programs, and (4) the sheer diversity of the risks and needs of the inmates. Also, in many areas, the chief jail administrator is the local sheriff, an elected or appointed political official. Because jails are usually under local administration, they are sometimes affected by the erratic and corrupt elements that often characterize local politics.

With increasing pressure from the courts to reform jail conditions and management practices,[54] efforts at jail reform continue. Historically, jails have progressed through three general overlapping stages of architectural design. Each design reflects a different philosophy about how to operate a jail.[55] The earliest jails, which date back to the eighteenth century, were built in a linear design. These *first-generation jails* have inmates live together in cells, dormitories, or "tanks." The cells line corridors, which make the supervision of inmates difficult (see Figure 7.9). Guards (they did not become "correctional officers" until the late 1960s or early 1970s, see the nearby FYI) at regular intervals walk up and down the corridors and observe inmates in their cells. To observe the inmates in the dormitories or tanks, guards periodically walk through the dormitories or along a perimeter

Largest Jail Population

During 2004, the average daily population of the nine jails in Los Angeles County, California, the largest jail system in the nation, was 18,512 inmates.

SOURCE: Paige M. Harrison and Allen J. Beck, "Prison and Jail Inmates at Midyear 2004," *Bureau of Justice Statistics Bulletin* (Washington, DC: U.S. Department of Justice, April 2005).

FIGURE 7.9 | A Typical First-Generation Jail Design

Linear/Intermittent
Surveillance

Typical
housing
unit

In first-generation jails, correctional officers cannot observe all inmate housing areas from one location, so they can only provide intermittent surveillance. *What are the advantages and disadvantages of working in this type of jail?*

Source (of diagram): *Podular, Direct Supervision Jails: Information Packet*, U.S. Department of Justice, National Institute of Corrections, Jails Division, January 1993, at www.nicic.org/resources/topics/DirectSupervisionJails.aspx.

First-Generation Jails

The first-generation jail in which Robert Bohm (author of this textbook) worked in the early 1970s was located on the eleventh to fifteenth floors of the Jackson County Courthouse in Kansas City, Missouri. When Bohm was hired as a guard, the official title of the jail was the Jackson County Jail. During the time he worked there, the official title of the jail was changed to the Jackson County Department of Corrections, and Bohm became a "correctional officer." Physically, the jail remained the same, and Bohm's work duties did not change.

SOURCE: Personal experience.

catwalk, which separates them from the inmates by bars. (This type of supervision is referred to as "intermittent surveillance.") A "48-man tank," for example, is a large cage that might have six inner cells, each with eight bunks, that open into a "dayroom" or "bullpen" equipped with two long metal picniclike tables attached to the floor and, perhaps, one television for the entire tank. In the cells, beds, sinks, and toilets are made of reinforced metal and are bolted to the floor or wall. There is little direct contact between the guards and inmates, unless the guards have to respond to an incident, such as a fight or medical emergency. The first-generation jail is often a separate building or set of buildings surrounded by walls of reinforced concrete topped with razor wire (but see the nearby FYI). Many first-generation jails resemble early prisons.

Second-generation jails began to emerge in the 1960s. In these jails, correctional officers constantly supervise inmates from secure control booths that overlook inmate living areas, called "pods" or "modules." (This type of supervision is referred to as "indirect supervision" or "remote surveillance.") Cells

FIGURE 7.10 | A Typical Second-Generation Jail Design

In second-generation jails, correctional officers continuously observe inmates from a secure control booth that overlooks inmate living areas, called "pods" or "modules." They provide indirect or remote supervision. *What are the advantages and disadvantages of working in this type of jail?*

Source (of diagram): *Podular, Direct Supervision Jails: Information Packet*, U.S. Department of Justice, National Institute of Corrections, Jails Division, January 1993, at www.nicic.org/resources/topics/DirectSupervisionJails.aspx.

become rooms and are clustered around dayrooms or common living areas, where inmates can congregate for activities (see Figure 7.10). Inmate rooms have reinforced metal doors with unbreakable windows instead of bars and generally house only one or two inmates. Beds, sinks, toilets, desks, and tables (in the dayrooms) are made of concrete or reinforced metal bolted to the floor or wall. There is very little direct interaction between inmates and correctional officers. Officers generally communicate with inmates by using a public address or intercom system. When trouble occurs inside the living area, a

FIGURE 7.11   A Typical Third-Generation Jail Design

Podular/Direct Supervision

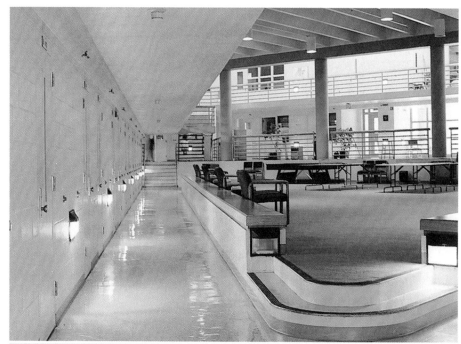

Third-generation jails employ a "podular" or "modular" design, but unlike in second-generation jails, correctional officers are stationed inside the housing unit where they directly supervise and interact with inmates. *What are the advantages and disadvantages of working in this type of jail?*

Source (of diagram): *Podular, Direct Supervision Jails: Information Packet*, U.S. Department of Justice, National Institute of Corrections, Jails Division, January 1993, at www.nicic.org/resources/topics/DirectSupervisionJails.aspx.

Video Visitation

To reduce costly and potentially dangerous inmate transport and to stop contraband from entering the institution, some new-generation jails are employing new technology for visitation. They are installing state-of-the-art video screens and phones in cubicles or carrels in inmate living areas and in remote video visitation centers for family members and friends. Attorneys, chaplains, or others visiting inmates for professional reasons, however, still are allowed to visit in person.

SOURCE: Doris Bloodsworth, "Jail Ready to Debut Visitation by Video," *The Orlando Sentinel*, January 5, 2003, p. B1.

response team is called to intervene. The facility's perimeter walls continue to be made of reinforced concrete topped with razor wire or, in some cases, fences secured by razor wire.

Third-generation, new-generation, or *direct-supervision jails* emerged in the late 1970s. They use a "podular" or "modular" design similar to the one employed in second-generation jails in which inmates' rooms are arranged around a common area or dayroom. A third-generation jail may have one or more pods, with a pod typically containing 48 to 60 beds. However, in third-generation jails, there is no secure control booth for correctional officers, and there are no physical barriers between correctional officers and inmates (see Figure 7.11). Officers may have a desk or table for paperwork, but it is in the open dayroom area. Many new-generation jails have added amenities in inmate living areas, such as carpeting, upholstered furnishings, individual shower stalls, several television sets and viewing areas, collect-call telephones, game tables, and exercise equipment. Third-generation jails generally have strong perimeter security.

The pods in third-generation jails are self-contained to reduce costly and potentially dangerous inmate transport. Consider visitation, for example. In older jails, including many second-generation jails, inmates are moved from secure housing units to a visitation area. In many new-generation jails, visitors are taken to the housing unit by way of a nonsecure corridor and visit through a high-security glass barrier. The inmate stays securely in the housing unit and the visitor stays in the nonsecure corridor. This arrangement also stops contraband from entering the institution by way of visitors. To reduce inmate transport, many new-generation jails also have their own courtroom, which is used primarily for arraignments and other pretrial proceedings.

The major difference between second- and third-generation jails is that third-generation jails are based on a different philosophy or management strategy called *direct supervision*. In this strategy, correctional officers continue to constantly supervise inmates, but rather than isolate themselves from the inmates, they are stationed inside the pod to give the inmates the opportunity to directly and regularly interact with them. (Direct supervision is also employed in some prisons.) In the new-generation jail, each congregate living area is a staff post, usually with one correctional officer in direct control of 40 to 50 inmates.

Correctional officers in direct-supervision jails are more than just "turnkeys"; they are professionals who need skills in interpersonal communication, crisis intervention, and counseling. Perhaps that is why research has found that female officers do at least as well as male officers while working in male units. Officers are taught to view the pods as space that they control, to be leaders and mentors in their pods, and to encourage inmates to change their destructive behaviors and ways of thinking. Correctional officers are more independent in direct-supervision jails and have the primary responsibility for daily decision making in the pods. Supervisors evaluate officer performance based on some of the following objectives:

- Being in daily contact with inmates in pods.
- Refraining from doing or saying anything that would belittle or degrade an inmate.
- Reporting promptly critical information to superior officers (for example, inmate escape plans).
- Engaging in continual visual observation of inmates.
- Investigating activity appearing out of the ordinary.[56]

Research suggests that direct-supervision jails provide a less-stressful, more positive, and safer environment for inmates and staff, may enhance supervision by reducing the number of unsupervised areas, and reduce inmate violations for contraband possession, destruction of property, escapes, disrespecting officers and staff, suicides, and violence, including sexual assaults.[57] In 2001, there were approximately 293 direct-supervision jails in all 50 states, the District of Columbia, and Puerto Rico.[58] Figure 7.12 shows the American Jail Association's Code of Ethics for Jail Officers. It reflects the professionalism expected of correctional officers who work in today's jails.

Prison Watchtowers Being Replaced

In a recent national trend, prison watchtowers staffed with prison guards are being replaced with electronic security systems. Under the new system, the interior fence is outfitted with one device that detects movements such as the fence being shaken or cut and then sounds an alarm. Razor wire is then unrolled between the interior and exterior fences. Motion detectors that sound alarms when triggered also monitor that space. Once an alarm sounds, officers in the main control room can radio officers inside the prison and those circling the prison in vehicles. The electronic system is cheaper, too. It costs $175,000 to install the system, which should last 8 to 10 years. It costs about $800,000 to staff the watchtowers.

SOURCE: "Prisons Favoring Electronic Security," *The Orlando Sentinel*, February 4, 2002, p. C3.

THINKING CRITICALLY

1. What, if any, impact does a jail's architectural design have on inmates?

2. Do you agree that one of a jail's functions is to manage marginal members of society? Why or why not?

As an officer employed in a detention/correctional capacity, I swear (or affirm) to be a good citizen and a credit to my community, state, and nation at all times. I will abstain from questionable behavior which might bring disrepute to the agency for which I work, my family, my community, and my associates. My lifestyle will be above and beyond reproach and I will constantly strive to set an example of a professional who performs his/her duties according to the laws of our country, state, and community and the policies, procedures, written and verbal orders, and regulations of the agency for which I work.

On the Job I promise to:

KEEP — The institution secure so as to safeguard my community and the lives of the staff, inmates, and visitors on the premises.

WORK — With each individual firmly and fairly without regard to rank, status, or condition.

MAINTAIN — A positive demeanor when confronted with stressful situations of scorn, ridicule, danger, and/or chaos.

REPORT — Either in writing or by word of mouth to the proper authorities those things which should be reported, and keep silent about matters which are to remain confidential according to the laws and rules of the agency and government.

MANAGE — And supervise the inmates in an evenhanded and courteous manner.

REFRAIN — At all times from becoming personally involved in the lives of the inmates and their families.

TREAT — All visitors to the jail with politeness and respect and do my utmost to ensure that they observe the jail regulations.

TAKE — Advantage of all education and training opportunities designed to assist me to become a more competent officer.

COMMUNICATE — With people in or outside of the jail, whether by phone, written word, or word of mouth, in such a way so as not to reflect in a negative manner upon my agency.

CONTRIBUTE — To a jail environment which will keep the inmate involved in activities designed to improve his/her attitude and character.

SUPPORT — All activities of a professional nature through membership and participation that will continue to elevate the status of those who operate our nation's jails. Do my best through word and deed to present an image to the public at large of a jail professional, committed to progress for an improved and enlightened criminal justice system.

The American Jail Association's Board of Directors has approved the AJA Code of Ethics as part of an integral program to achieve a high standard of professional conduct among those officers employed in our nation's jails. Adopted by the American Jail Association Board of Directors on November 10, 1991. Revised May 19, 1993.

Institutional Security, Services, and Programs

In many ways, an incarceration facility is like a miniature society within the larger society. Institutions have many of the same features as the wider society, such as security procedures for maintaining order and preserving the safety of inhabitants, as well as a variety of services and programs meant to provide for inmate needs and encourage inmates to better themselves.

SECURITY AND INMATE DISCIPLINE

An orderly and safe environment is the foundation for all else that happens in an institution. When the environment is not stable, everything else tends to become secondary. For that reason, security procedures strongly affect the daily activities of both staff and inmates.

In any prison or jail, special security precautions are directed toward certain locations because of the importance of those locations to the institution's capacity for maintaining order. Examples of such locations include:

1. The front entry to the facility, through which all persons coming and going must pass.
2. The control room, which is usually located close to the front entry and is the heart of the institution's communication system.
3. The cellblocks or other quarters where the inmates live.
4. The dining area.
5. The area where the institution's confidential records and documents are maintained.
6. The indoor recreation areas and the outdoor recreation area or yard.
7. The sites where inmates work.

Handmade weapons such as those shown here are contraband and make prisons and jails dangerous places. *Where do inmates get the materials for these weapons?*

CAREERS IN CRIMINAL JUSTICE

Visitation Coordinator

My name is Pat Bryant and I am an administrative coordinator with the Central Visitation Center (CVC) for the South Carolina Department of Corrections (SCDC), Charleston, South Carolina. I have a bachelor of science degree in criminal justice from Benedict College, Columbia, South Carolina. I have held several positions with the South Carolina Department of Corrections during the course of my career, including administrative assistant, project developer, and business manager, to name a few. I have found these positions to be very rewarding.

The inmate visitation program is recognized by SCDC as an integral component of the rehabilitation process as it encourages inmates to have the opportunity to visit with family members and friends. The Central Visitation Center became operational in the fall of 1996 at which time I became the administrative coordinator.

A typical day as administrative coordinator for CVC involves communicating directly with family and friends of inmates in person, by telephone, or written correspondence and explaining to the prospective visitor the reason he/she may have been disapproved as a visitor, and providing guidance and technical assistance as it relates to inmate visitation to the 31 correctional institutions within the SCDC and other law enforcement agencies as requested. One of the most significant aspects of this job is ensuring that all Requests for Visiting Privileges forms are reviewed and approved (if deemed appropriate) and an automated record is created for the prospective visitor. The CVC processes approximately 500–600 visitation applications per day. Some other aspects of this job include coordinating and conducting training for employees involved in the inmate visitation process and conducting semiannual visits to each institution to ensure visitation procedures are being implemented according to policy.

While the job of administrative coordinator is certainly an interesting one, it can also be a challenge. The reward is knowing that you have assisted someone who may not have had a clear understanding of the visitation process and being a part of the solution.

What do you think are the greatest challenges for a visitation coordinator?

Family visitation is extremely important to inmate morale. *What are other advantages and disadvantages of family visitation?*

Conjugal Visits

In 1918, James Parchmann, the warden at Mississippi State Penitentiary, introduced conjugal visits as an incentive for inmates to work harder. Today, conjugal visitation only survives in 6 states: California, Connecticut, Mississippi, New Mexico, New York, and Washington.

SOURCE: Patrick Rodgers, "Conjugal Visits: Preserving family bonds behind bars" at www.legalzoom.com/articles/article_content/article12959.html (accessed August 3, 2006).

conjugal visits An arrangement whereby inmates are permitted to visit in private with their spouses or significant others to maintain their personal relationship.

snitch system A system in which staff learn from inmate informants about the presence of contraband, the potential for disruptions, and other threats to security.

All institutions routinely employ a range of security procedures to maintain control over inmates. The classification of inmates by custody levels, mentioned earlier, is one such method. An inmate's custody level indicates the degree of precaution to be used when working with that inmate. In some facilities, certain inmates are given special custody designations that distinguish them from members of the general inmate population. Those inmates are not permitted to live among the general population of the facility. For example, inmates who are vulnerable to assault by other inmates may be designated for protective custody, meaning that they are to be kept segregated for their own safety. In contrast, inmates who represent a danger to other inmates or staff may be designated for administrative segregation, indicating that they must be kept in secure isolation so that they cannot harm others. Inmates who display signs of serious mental disorders may be segregated in a similar fashion.

As a basis for security procedures, institutions publish written rules that regulate the daily activities of inmates and staff alike. During the course of daily activities, staff routinely count inmates to detect escapes, and inmate whereabouts are constantly monitored within the facility. There are standard procedures for staff to follow when transporting certain inmates within the facility or from the facility to an outside location, such as to another prison, to court, or to a hospital in the community. Much effort goes into controlling the property of the institution—for example, firearms, medicine, keys, tools, and basic commodities like clothes and food. In many prisons and jails, searches of inmates' clothing and bodies and shakedowns (usually random and warrantless searches) of their cells are commonplace in an effort to control the flow of contraband, especially handmade knives and other weapons. There are special procedures and even special staff units for responding to riots, escapes, and other disturbances.

The mail and phone conversations of inmates may be monitored if there is sufficient security justification. Inmates may visit with relatives and friends only at designated times and may visit only those people the institution has approved. Although a small number of prisons permit **conjugal visits**—in which an inmate and his or her spouse or significant other visit in private to maintain their personal relationship—routine visits usually occur in large, open rooms with other inmates, their visitors, and staff present. Visits are supervised closely because of the potential for contraband to enter the prison (but see the discussion of visitation in new-generation jails in the previous section).

It is important to emphasize that written rules and regulations are not the exclusive basis for institutional security. Written rules and regulations are part of an institution's formal bureaucratic structure, which was discussed earlier in this chapter. Within that formal structure, there develops an unwritten, informal structure of norms and relations that is vital to the operation of the facility. For example, most institutions have an elaborate **snitch system** in which staff learn from inmate informants about the presence of contraband, the potential for disruptions, and other threats to security. Informants often receive special concessions and protection in exchange for snitching on other inmates. Such arrangements can be very elaborate, as illustrated by the research of criminologists James Marquart and Ben Crouch. In their study of a Texas prison, Marquart and Crouch found that certain elite inmates, known as *building tenders,* actually functioned as extensions of the uniformed guard force to achieve control of the institution.[59] The use of inmates (building tenders or trustees) to discipline other inmates was formally outlawed in 1984.

Inmates who violate formal institutional regulations may be subjected to disciplinary measures. Staff members typically have broad discretion when they detect rule violations. They may simply overlook the infraction or may issue an informal warning. Alternatively, they may file a disciplinary report so that formal sanctions can be considered. The report usually leads to a disciplinary hearing, during which the charges and supporting evidence are presented to the institution's disciplinary committee or hearing officer. If the report is found to be valid, a number of sanctions are possible. For example, the inmate may have some of his or her privileges temporarily restricted (for instance, no commissary or store privileges for 30 days), may be placed in solitary confinement or "the hole" for a specified number of days, may forfeit some of the time that has been deducted from his or her sentence for good behavior, or may even be transferred to another facility. Because institutions have many rules governing the behavior of inmates, it should come as no surprise that rule infractions and disciplinary measures occur frequently.[60]

SERVICES AND PROGRAMS

Many of the human services and programs found in the free society are duplicated within institutions. At a minimum, inmates must be fed, clothed, and provided with such basic shelter requirements as warmth, electricity, and plumbing, and their health care needs must be addressed.

Food services are an important part of an institution's operation. Waste and inefficiency must be avoided to control expense, but inmate demand and dietary standards must be met.

Prisons and jails are buildings that, like all buildings, require maintenance and repair. A large portion of the maintenance and repair work is performed by inmates as part of their job assignments.

Courts have held that inmates are entitled to medical and dental services. Prisons normally have an infirmary where less serious ailments can be treated. More serious problems necessitate transfer to either a prison with more extensive medical services or a hospital in the local community.

Institutions make an array of services available to inmates for their leisure time. We have already mentioned mail, phone, and visitation services. In addition, institutions operate commissaries where inmates can purchase such items as food, tobacco, radios, reading materials, and arts and crafts supplies. A number of recreational facilities are also provided, such as weight-lifting equipment, softball fields, basketball courts, game tables, and television viewing areas. In addition, legal resources and religious services are available. They will be discussed in more detail in the next chapter. Although most prisons still offer a substantial number of services to prisoners, there has been a movement to reduce services over the past two decades.

INMATES WITH SPECIAL NEEDS All institutions have special-needs populations. Although those populations generally consist of far fewer inmates than the general prison population, it is still necessary to provide services for them. For example, elderly inmates frequently need more medical attention than younger inmates. The number of elderly prison inmates is increasing. In 1991, 3.6 percent (or about 25,650) of state and federal prisoners were 55 or older. In 2004, 5 percent (or about 67,200) were 55 or older—an increase of 39 percent in the percentage of inmates 55 or older and an increase of 162 percent in the number of inmates 55 or older. In the federal prison system, each inmate 55 or older costs the government about $69,000 a year in maintenance costs, two or three times as much as is spent on inmates younger than 55. Most of the added expense is related to health costs. One health-related problem that

Prison Security

A recent national survey revealed that 67 percent of the American public think that prisons do an excellent (18 percent) or good (49 percent) job of "maintaining high security to keep prisoners from escaping"; 23 percent think that they do only a fair job, and 8 percent think they do a poor job (2 percent had no opinion). As for "maintaining a safe environment for inmates in prison," 30 percent of the public think that the prisons are excellent (5 percent) or good (25 percent), 37 percent think they are only fair, and 26 percent think they are poor (7 percent had no opinion).

SOURCE: *Sourcebook of Criminal Justice Statistics 2001*, p. 112, Table 2.20, at www.albany.edu/sourcebook.

Aging Inmates

Correctional officials generally consider 50-year-old inmates geriatrics because their lives have probably been filled with violence, drug, alcohol and tobacco abuse, poor diets, and inadequate medical care.

SOURCE: "Virginia Opens Special Prison for Aging Inmates," *The Dallas Morning News*, July 3, 1999, www.dallasnews.com/national/ 0703nat4prison.html, December 21, 2000.

has not been adequately addressed is the decreased mobility of older inmates—a problem that current prisons are rarely designed to accommodate.[61]

Another special-needs population is the mentally ill.[62] Since the deinstitutionalization of the mentally ill in the 1960s, in favor of treating them in the community, prisons and especially jails have become surrogate public mental hospitals. According to recent research, at least 16 percent of the total jail and prison population, or approximately 300,000 inmates, have a serious mental illness. The costs of incarcerating the mentally ill are huge. The Justice Department estimates that it costs at least $15 billion a year to house inmates with psychiatric disorders (about $50,000 per inmate per year). Such inmates may require segregated housing for their own protection and the protection of other inmates, frequent consultation with psychologists and psychiatrists, efforts to ensure that they take prescribed medication, and special safety precautions (for example, for a suicidal inmate, the use of paper sheets rather than cloth to prevent hanging).

The problem is particularly acute in jails. Mentally ill people are frequently held in jails even though they have not been charged with a crime. Many of them are held under state laws that permit emergency detentions of people suspected of being mentally ill. They are typically incarcerated pending a psychiatric evaluation or until they can be transported to a psychiatric hospital.

Most mentally ill inmates who are arrested are charged with misdemeanors such as trespassing or disorderly conduct. They are also frequently charged with drug- or alcohol-related offenses. Inmates with more serious psychiatric problems, such as paranoid schizophrenia, are sometimes arrested for assault because they mistakenly believe that someone was following them or trying to hurt them. Police also arrest people with severe psychiatric problems (so-called mercy bookings) to protect them from harm. This is especially true of women on the streets who are easily victimized, including being raped. Family members sometimes have mentally ill relatives arrested because it is the easiest and most effective way to get the mentally ill relative needed treatment. Sometimes being incarcerated is the only way for mentally ill people to get needed treatment.

Unfortunately, for the mentally ill, most jails do not provide adequate mental health services. More than 20 percent of jails provide no mental health services at all. Correctional officers in the vast majority of jails receive either no training or less than 3 hours of training in dealing with the special needs of inmates with severe mental illness. Prisons generally do a better job of accommodating the needs of mentally ill inmates. For example, at midyear 2000, nearly 90 percent of state public and private adult prisons provided mental health services to their inmates. About 12.5 percent of state prisoners were receiving some mental health therapy or counseling. About 10 percent of state prisoners were receiving psychotropic medications.[63] Still, jails and prisons are often brutal places for mentally ill inmates, where they are vulnerable to assault, rape, and exposure to infectious diseases. Because many of them are unable to describe their symptoms to correctional officers, their needs, even in facilities equipped to deal with them, are often ignored.

Much controversy surrounds the presence of the human immunodeficiency virus (HIV) and acquired immune deficiency syndrome (AIDS) among institutional populations. As of year-end 2003, 2 percent of

Myth Fact

Myth: The high cost of incarceration is a product of amenities provided to inmates, such as cable television, law libraries, and weight-lifting equipment. Eliminating these "country club" add-ons will make prison costs more reasonable.

Fact: Actually, 4 out of every 5 dollars of prison operating costs are for employee salaries and facility maintenance. In addition, debt service to finance prison construction triples the original cost of construction. A maximum security prison in New York State, for example, costs about $100,000 per bed to build, but financing costs add another $200,000 per bed. Finally, costs have grown substantially as a result of the health care needs of an increasingly older and AIDS-afflicted inmate population.

SOURCE: William M. DiMascio, *Seeking Justice: Crime and Punishment in America* (New York: Edna McConnell Clark Foundation, 1997), p. 9.

state prison inmates (22,028) and 1.1 percent of federal prison inmates (1,631) were reported by prison officials to be HIV-positive.[64] About 21 percent of the HIV-infected inmates were held in New York prisons. Of the HIV-positive inmates, 25 percent (5,944) had confirmed cases of AIDS. This was a small increase from the 5,528 confirmed cases of AIDS in 2000, which was the first decrease in confirmed AIDS cases since data were first collected in 1991. In 2003, 268 state prison inmates and 14 federal prison inmates died from AIDS-related causes. In 2000, the 174 state prison inmates to die from AIDS-related causes were the fewest in 10 years and less than a fifth of the number (1,010) recorded in 1995—the peak year. In 2003, 8 percent of state prison inmate deaths were attributed to AIDS, down from 32 percent in 1995. At the end of 2002, the rate of confirmed AIDS cases in state and federal prisons was more than 3 times the rate in the total U.S. population. Intravenous drug use is the key risk factor for AIDS among inmates.

At year-end 2000, 20 states and the federal government tested all inmates for HIV at some point during their sentences, a controversial practice known as *mass screening*. New York, Oregon, Virginia, and the Federal Bureau of Prisons (BOP) test inmates chosen randomly. Most jurisdictions test inmates if they have HIV-related symptoms, or if inmates request a test. The BOP and 41 states test inmates if they have been involved in an incident, and 15 states test "high-risk" inmates. Alabama, Missouri, Nevada, and the BOP test inmates before their release. The testing policies of each jurisdiction have not changed much since 1991. In addition to mass mandatory screening, other debated issues are whether HIV-positive inmates should be segregated and the degree to which HIV-positive test results should be kept confidential by attending medical staff. At present, the trend seems to be away from blanket segregation and toward confidentiality.

INMATE REHABILITATION PROGRAMS Inmates hoping to better themselves during their incarceration normally have the opportunity to participate in a number of rehabilitation programs. The particular programs offered vary across jurisdictions and institutions. Examples are:

1. Self-improvement programs offered by religious and civic groups (Alcoholics Anonymous, the Jaycees, a Bible club).
2. Work programs.
3. Education and vocational training.
4. Counseling and therapy.

Work Programs Since the creation of the first houses of correction in Europe, there has been one constant: the belief that the imprisonment experience should improve inmates' work habits. Today, however, there is tremendous variation among institutions regarding work programs. In some institutions, all inmates who are physically able are required to work. In other institutions, the inmates who work are those who choose to do so. Likewise, there is great variation in the types of work inmates perform. Some inmates are employed to help the daily running of the institution and work in such areas as food services, maintenance and repair, laundry, health care, and clerical services. Other inmates work in factories at industrial tasks, such as wood or metal manufacturing. Still other inmates perform agricultural work.

As of January 1, 2001 (the latest year for which data are available), the average daily wage earned by prison inmates working in agency-operated industries ranged

Myth Fact

Myth: The services and programs available to inmates make prisons seem like country clubs. Therefore, services and programs should be severely cut back or eliminated so that inmates receive punishment while incarcerated.

Fact: First, the services and programs available to inmates are sometimes of inferior quality when compared with those available in the free community. Second, programs and services perform a vital time management function. Institutions would be much more volatile and disorderly than they currently are without programs and services to fill time.

from $3.03 to $8.14, compared to $2.17 to $8.94 in 1999. The average workday was slightly down to 6.78 hours per day from 7 hours. The average daily wage earned by prison inmates working in nonindustry jobs ranged from $0.93 to $4.73, down from $1.42 to $5.09 in 1999. The average workday was about the same as in 1999. Some states, such as Georgia and Texas, do not pay inmates for their work. The state of Nevada pays its inmates the most, $31.41 a day, for work in agency-operated industries (Hawaii paid its inmates $49.88 in 1999); the state of Washington pays its inmates the most, $30.45 a day, for work in nonindustry jobs (it paid its inmates $29.75 in 1999). Inmates who work in privately operated industries generally earn more.[65]

Institutions also vary in the degree to which the private sector is involved in work programming. Although the early history of the prison in the United States was characterized by extensive ties between inmate labor and the free market, those ties diminished during the first half of the 1900s. That change was due to concern by organized labor about unemployment among free citizens, concern by businesses that did not employ convict labor about their ability to compete on the open market, and concern by prison reformers about exploitation of inmates. Because of a series of laws restricting the private use of inmate labor, the state-use system became—and still is—the predominant way of arranging inmate work programs. Under that system, inmates are allowed to produce goods and services for the government. For example, in the main work program operated by the Federal Bureau of Prisons, known as UNICOR, inmates make a variety of products used by agencies of the federal government. Recently, however, legal restrictions on the private use of prison labor have been loosened, and the practice is witnessing somewhat of a resurgence in certain jurisdictions.

Education and Vocational Training It has long been assumed that rehabilitation can be facilitated by improving inmates' academic skills and providing them with job skills. Many offenders enter prison with deficits in their education. It is not at all uncommon to encounter adult inmates who are reading, writing, and performing math operations at an elementary school level. Therefore, much prison education amounts to remedial schooling designed to prepare inmates to obtain their GEDs. College courses are made available in

Research shows that inmates exposed to education programs have lower recidivism rates than nonparticipants. *Why do only 25–50 percent of inmates take part in some form of education?*

some prisons through correspondence or study release arrangements or by bringing college instructors to the prison to offer courses. However, low educational levels render college courses inappropriate for many inmates.

A recent study found that two-thirds of prison inmates have such poor reading and arithmetic skills that they are unable to write a brief letter explaining a billing error or to interpret a bar graph. Only about half of all prisoners have completed high school or its equivalent, but even inmates who have a high school diploma demonstrate lower basic skills than do members of the general public with a high school diploma. Yet, over the past few years, while the prison population has expanded dramatically, more than half the states have cut back their educational and training budgets. The percentage of inmates enrolled in educational programs ranges from a high of 86 percent in Kentucky to a low of 7 percent in Nebraska. In most states, only 25–50 percent of inmates take part in some form of education, even though several studies show that inmates exposed to education programs have lower recidivism rates than nonparticipants.[66]

Some prison vocational programs operate as part of job assignments (on-the-job training), and others are separate from job assignments. Either way, the goal is to provide inmates with job skills that will improve their marketability upon release. Most prison vocational training is geared toward traditional blue-collar employment, such as welding and auto mechanics. Vocational programs offered in women's prisons have often been criticized for concentrating excessively on stereotypical women's jobs, such as cosmetology.

Counseling and Therapy A wide range of counseling techniques and therapy modalities are used in prisons across the nation. The description of specific techniques and modalities, however, is beyond the scope of this chapter.[67] Suffice it to say that the techniques and modalities used at a given institution ordinarily reflect the training and professional orientation of the treatment staff—caseworkers, religious counselors, social workers, psychologists, and psychiatrists.

A distinction is usually drawn between individual counseling, which involves one-on-one interaction between the counselor and the inmate, and group counseling, which involves the interaction of the counselor with a small group of inmates. Those categories of treatment may overlap, because an inmate receiving individual counseling may also be in group counseling, and many of the techniques and principles used in individual counseling are also applied to group settings. Still, the distinction has merit, because individual counseling is more appropriate for some inmates (for example, those with deep-seated problems who will require long-term help), and group counseling is more appropriate for other inmates (for example, those who are defensive, manipulative, and prone to denying their problems).

Group counseling is more popular than individual counseling in institutional settings, primarily because it is more economical and because there are large numbers of inmates who share similar backgrounds and problems. In fact, the members of a group are frequently selected on the basis of their common backgrounds and problem behavior patterns. For example, a group may consist of persons who have substance abuse problems or those who are sex offenders. Some institutions employ a variant of group therapy known as **milieu therapy** (also called a *therapeutic community*). Rather than having inmates attend periodic group sessions (one or two hourly sessions per week), milieu therapy encompasses the total living environment of inmates so that the environment continually encourages positive behavioral change. In effect, the entire inmate population becomes the group, and inmates have active roles in helping other inmates change.

Most counselors and therapists who work in prison spend a considerable portion of their time performing **crisis intervention.** Crisis intervention consists of a counselor's efforts to address some crisis that has erupted in an inmate's

milieu therapy A variant of group therapy that encompasses the total living environment so that the environment continually encourages positive behavioral change.

crisis intervention A counselor's efforts to address some crisis in an inmate's life and to calm the inmate.

Rehabilitating Inmates

A recent national survey shows that only 14 percent of the American public think that prisons are doing an excellent (2 percent) or good (12 percent) job "rehabilitating inmates so they are less likely to commit crimes in the future"; 34 percent think they do only a fair job, and 48 percent think they do a poor job. The rest had no opinion.

SOURCE: *Sourcebook of Criminal Justice Statistics 2001* (online), p. 112, Table 2.20.

less-eligibility principle The position that prisoners should receive no service or program superior to the services and programs available to free citizens without charge.

life (for example, suicidal thoughts, rejection by the spouse, a mental breakdown, or a conflict between inmates). Institutions are stressful living environments, so inmate crises are common. The counselor's task is to assist inmates in restoring a state of emotional calm and greater stability so that problems can be addressed rationally before inmates harm themselves or others.

Programs in Perspective We usually think of rehabilitation programs as serving one main objective: to help inmates better themselves. In practice, however, programs serve other, more subtle functions as well. Programs give inmates a way to occupy themselves; they help inmates manage time. They also help the institution achieve control over inmates. For example, inmates who are in counseling for displaying too much aggression toward other inmates may realize that unless they demonstrate "progress" in reducing their aggression, the counselor will not recommend them to the parole board for early release (in states where parole is available). Although such progress may be achieved quickly in prison, it may be short-lived upon release. Similarly, from the standpoint of inmates, the most desirable work assignments are those that give inmates access to valued resources (for instance, a kitchen job provides greater access to food). More desirable work assignments are routinely held out by the staff as privileges to be earned through good behavior.

Institutional programs are also plagued by a variety of problems that hinder their ability to effect rehabilitation. For example, prison work assignments frequently do not parallel work in the free world. In prison, workdays are often short and interrupted. In many cases, there is little concern for the quantity and quality of work. Furthermore, some of the jobs lack any real counterpart in the free world. The classic example is license plate manufacturing. In many prisons, educational programs suffer from a lack of funding. Vocational training focuses primarily on traditional blue-collar jobs and thus prepares inmates to enter jobs for which there is already abundant competition. A dilemma is created by the argument that inmates should not receive highly technical or professional training (such as training in computer programming) because many members of the free, law-abiding community cannot afford such training. That argument is based on the **less-eligibility principle,** the position that prisoners should receive no service or program superior to the services and programs available to free citizens without charge. Moreover, prison education and vocational programs can do little to create jobs. If an inmate returns to a community with a poor economy and high unemployment, the education and training received in prison may do little more than raise the inmate's expectations to unrealistic levels.

For their part, counseling and therapy programs must operate against the harsh realities of the prison environment, where custody and security ordinarily take priority over rehabilitation. Despite those obstacles, some programs are able to bring about positive changes in offenders' attitudes and behavior. Psychologist Ted Palmer has observed that although no single type of treatment can be identified as the most effective, one feature that seems to characterize programs that consistently reduce offender recidivism is the quality of the program's implementation. Thus, when the integrity of treatment efforts is allowed to take priority over institutional concerns for security and custody, offending can be reduced.[68] Also, as criminologist Robert Johnson points out, many counseling programs place nearly exclusive emphasis on inmates' pasts and futures, with insufficient attention given to present coping patterns. Johnson recommends that programs begin teaching inmates to cope maturely and constructively with their present environment so that they will be better able to cope with life after release.[69]

THINKING CRITICALLY

1. Do you think inmate rehabilitation programs can truly make a difference? Why or why not?

2. Do you think inmates should earn money for the work they do while in prison? Why or why not?

SUMMARY

1. **Summarize the purposes of confinement in Europe before it became a major way of punishing criminals.**

   Confinement became a major way of punishing criminals in Europe in the 1600s and 1700s. Before that, it was used to (1) detain people before trial, (2) hold prisoners awaiting other sanctions, such as death and corporal punishment, (3) coerce payment of debts and fines, (4) hold and punish slaves, (5) achieve religious indoctrination and spiritual reformation (as during the Inquisition), and (6) quarantine disease (as during the bubonic plague).

2. **Describe how offenders were punished before the large-scale use of confinement.**

   Before the large-scale use of confinement, punishments were directed more at the offender's body and property. One basic goal was to inflict pain. Those punishments were commonly carried out in public to humiliate the offender and to deter onlookers from crime. Examples of such punishments are fines, confiscation of property, and diverse methods of corporal and capital punishment.

3. **Explain why confinement began to be used as a major way of punishing offenders in Europe.**

   Enlightenment-era reforms led to an emphasis on deterring and reforming criminals through confinement. Confinement was also advocated as a humane alternative to older punishments. In addition, during the 1500s and 1600s, workhouses were established as places where offenders could be sent to learn discipline and productive work habits.

4. **Describe the recent trends in the use of incarceration in the United States.**

   There has been a dramatic increase since the mid-1970s in the number of people incarcerated in the United States, partly due to the war on drugs. That increase has been accompanied by much concern over rising costs and institutional crowding. In response to those problems, confinement alternatives to traditional incarceration have been developed. Two of those alternatives are contracts with the private sector for the construction or operation of some confinement facilities and the use of shock incarceration, or "boot camp" prisons, for young, nonviolent offenders without extensive prior criminal records.

5. **List some of the characteristics of the incarcerated population in the United States.**

   The incarcerated population in the United States is disproportionately male, black, young, single, undereducated, and poor. More than half of state prison inmates are serving time for violent offenses, whereas 53 percent of federal prison inmates are serving sentences for drug offenses. More than half of jail inmates are unconvicted, usually awaiting trial or other case disposition.

6. **Describe how incarceration facilities are structured, organized, and administered by the government in the United States.**

   Incarceration facilities in the United States are administered primarily by the executive branch of government. They exist at all three levels of government. Prisons are administered at the federal level and state levels, while jails tend to be locally administered. Despite this diversification, all the institutions have somewhat similar administrative structures, ranging from the warden or superintendent at the top to the correctional (line) officers at the bottom.

7. **Name some of the common types of correctional facilities in the United States.**

   Common types of adult correctional facilities in the United States include (1) classification and special facilities, (2) supermaximum-, maximum-, medium-, and minimum-security men's prisons, (3) women's and cocorrectional facilities, and (4) jails and lockups.

8. **Identify some of the procedures that institutions employ to maintain security and order.**

   To maintain security and order, correctional institutions employ a number of procedures. Among them are the use of custody designations for inmates, inmate counts, property control, searches of inmates and their living quarters, and restrictions on inmate communication (mail, phone calls, and visits) with outsiders. Also, institutions commonly rely on inmate-informant, or snitch, systems to maintain security. Inmates found guilty of violating institutional rules may be subjected to a variety of disciplinary sanctions (such as loss of good time, restriction of privileges, and solitary confinement) to deter future rule infractions.

9. **List the services and programs that are commonly available to inmates.**

   Some of the services and programs available to inmates are subsistence services (food, clothing, and shelter), health care services, legal services, recreation, and religious services. There are also a number of programs designed to improve inmates' lives. They include low-paying work, education and vocational training, and group and individual counseling.

KEY TERMS

workhouses, p. 249
penology, p. 250
panopticon, p. 250
Pennsylvania system, p. 251
Auburn system, p. 251
medical model, p. 253

privatization, p. 253
shock incarceration, p. 254
incarceration rate, p. 257
classification facility, p. 265

security level, p. 266
custody level, p. 269
cocorrectional facilities, p. 270
lockup, p. 271
jail, p. 271
conjugal visits, p. 280

snitch system, p. 280
milieu therapy, p. 285
crisis intervention, p. 285
less-eligibility principle, p. 286

REVIEW QUESTIONS

1. What did Cesare Beccaria, the Enlightenment thinker, mean when he said that a punishment should fit the crime?

2. What reforms in penal institutions did John Howard advocate in his book *The State of the Prisons in England and Wales* (1777)?

3. What is generally considered the first state prison in the United States, and of what did the daily routine of inmates in this prison consist?

4. How did the Pennsylvania system of confinement differ from the Auburn system of confinement, and which system became the model followed by other states?

5. What were the main features of the reformatory?

6. According to John Irwin, what three types of penal institutions dominated different parts of the last century?

7. What is an incarceration rate, and why is it used?

8. How does the incarceration rate of the United States compare with the incarceration rates of other countries?

9. How does the author of this textbook explain the prison overcrowding crisis in the United States?

10. What are some major differences between the federal prison and state prison populations?

11. What is the official mission of the Federal Bureau of Prisons?

12. What are the purposes of inmate classification?

13. What are prison security and custody levels, and how do they differ?

14. What are the purposes of a jail?

15. Why do jails represent one of the most problematic aspects of criminal justice?

16. What are some objectives of inmate rehabilitation programs?

17. What is the less-eligibility principle, as applied to corrections?

IN THE FIELD

1. **Prison Tour** Many prisons and jails conduct tours for students in criminal justice courses. Arrange to visit one or more prisons and jails in your area. Compare and contrast what you see during your visit(s) with the material in this chapter. Also, if you tour both a prison and a jail, describe similarities and differences between the two institu-tions. Either present your findings orally in class or put them in writing for your instructor.

2. **Create a Prison** Design a prison conceptually and, perhaps, three-dimensionally. Decide what type of inmates the prison is to hold (men, women, or both; prisoners requiring maximum security, minimum security, etc.) and what the security level will be. Consider location, architectural design, bureaucratic structure, security and discipline procedures, and inmate services and programs.

1. **Federal Bureau of Prisons** Go to the Federal Bureau of Prisons at www.bop.gov. Access "Public Info" and then "Quick Facts and Statistics" from the topic list. Use the data provided to construct a current profile of inmates. Then access the "Weekly Population Report," and search for data about any federal prisons in your state. Write a brief report on what you find.

2. **Incarceration Worldwide** Review the document, "Comparative International Rates of Incarceration: An Examination of Causes and Trends," at The Sentencing Project at www.sentencingproject.org/june/usccr-incarceration.pdf. Write a brief essay explaining why rates of incarceration vary so greatly among countries of the world.

1. **Prison Research** A Florida prison has recently been transformed into a combination hospital and prison where most inmates have HIV. They participate in tests of some of the newest HIV drugs being developed and have access to some of the nation's leading AIDS researchers. Only about 120 of the 3,000 or so state inmates who are known to be HIV positive are able to participate. Some inmates are due to be released in a few weeks or months; others are serving life sentences. On the street, the treatment would cost about $1,400 a month; participating inmates get it for free.

   The program is controversial. Although it has been praised as a model for the rest of the country's prisons to copy, it has also been criticized for conducting drug trials or medical studies on inmates. Because inmates are a captive audience, a major question is whether they can truly give informed consent to participate in the voluntary program. Before they are allowed to participate, inmates must sign a five-page consent form that lists the possible benefits and side effects of the drugs. The state also has no relationship with the drug companies and accepts no money from them.
   a. Should the program continue and be spread to other prisons? Why or why not?
   b. Address these questions: Can inmates give informed consent? Does it matter? If inmates are allowed to participate, how should they be chosen from among all those who volunteer?

2. **The Ex-Convict** To the average citizen, the ex-convict is an individual of questionable character. This image is reinforced by the fact that the only thing that is usually newsworthy about ex-convicts is bad news, such as when they are rearrested. Few citizens know a rehabilitated offender for obvious reasons. Yet, the rehabilitated ex-convict faces a variety of civil disabilities. Not the least among those is the difficulty of getting a "good" job. On virtually every job application, there is the question: "Have you ever been convicted of a felony or misdemeanor or denied bond in any state?" In addition, prospective employers generally ask applicants to reveal their former substance abuse, which is a problem that most former offenders had. An affirmative answer to either question almost always eliminates a person's chance for employment.
   a. How can ex-offenders shed the ex-convict status? Should they be allowed to shed it? Why or why not?
   b. Does your answer to (a) change depending upon the ex-convict's conviction offense?

To access more information and resources, including study questions, chapter summaries, and links, go to: www.mhhe.com/bohm1.

CHAPTER EIGHT

PRISON LIFE, INMATE RIGHTS, RELEASE, AND RECIDIVISM

CHAPTER OUTLINE

Living in Prison

    Inmate Society

    Life in Women's Prisons

Correctional Officers

Inmate Rights and Prison Reform

    Access to the Courts and Legal Services

    Procedural Due Process in Prison

    First Amendment Rights

    Eighth Amendment Rights

    Fourteenth Amendment Rights

    The Limits of Litigation

Release and Recidivism

CHAPTER OBJECTIVES

After completing this chapter, you should be able to:

1. Distinguish between the deprivation and importation models of inmate society.

2. Explain how today's inmate society differs from those of the past.

3. Identify some of the special features of life in women's prisons.

4. Describe the profile of correctional officers and explain some of the issues that they face.

5. Identify prisoners' rights and relate how they were achieved.

6. List the two most common ways that inmates are released from prison and compare those two ways in frequency of use.

7. Summarize what recidivism research reveals about the success of the prison in achieving deterrence and rehabilitation.

Living in Prison

When people think of prisons, they usually imagine the big-house, maximum-security prison for men. Indeed, the majority of scholarly research on prison life has focused on this type of institution. In this chapter, we survey some of that research. However, we caution the reader to be careful about generalizing findings from studies of the big house to all institutions. As we have already seen, institutions are quite diverse.

INMATE SOCIETY

total institution An institutional setting in which persons sharing some characteristics are cut off from the wider society and expected to live according to institutional rules and procedures.

In his classic book *Asylums*, sociologist Erving Goffman described prisons as **total institutions.** Goffman defined a total institution as "a place of residence and work where a large number of like-situated individuals, cut off from the wider society for an appreciable period of time, together lead an enclosed, formally administered round of life."[1] As already pointed out and as further implied by Goffman's definition, a prison represents a miniature, self-contained society.

Although prisons are certainly influenced by the outside world,[2] they are also separated and closed off from that world. A society of prisoners, like any society, possesses distinctive cultural features (values, norms, and roles), and because prisoners do not serve their time completely isolated from other inmates, the features of the inmate society influence the way prisoners adjust to prison life.

convict code A constellation of values, norms, and roles that regulate the way inmates interact with one another and with prison staff.

Central to the inmate society of traditional men's prisons in the United States is the convict code. The **convict code** is a constellation of values, norms, and roles that regulate the way inmates interact with one another and with prison staff. For example, a principle of the convict code is that individual inmates should mind their own affairs and do their own time. Other principles are that inmates should not inform the staff about the illicit activities of other prisoners and that inmates' overall attitude and behavior should be indifferent to the staff and loyal to other convicts. "Conning" and manipulation skills are highly valued under the code, as is the ability to show strength, courage, and toughness.

deprivation model A theory that the inmate society arises as a response to the prison environment and the painful conditions of confinement.

Two major theories of the origins of the inmate society have been advanced: the deprivation model and the importation model. Advocates of the **deprivation model** (sometimes called the "indigenous origins model") contend that the inmate society arises in response to the prison environment and the painful conditions of confinement.[3] Specifically, imprisonment deprives inmates of such things as material possessions, social acceptance, heterosexual relations, personal security, and liberty. This environment of shared deprivation gives inmates a basis for solidarity. The inmate society and its convict code represent a functional, collective adaptation of inmates to this environment. When an inmate enters prison for the first time, the inmate is socialized into the customs and principles of the inmate society, a process former correctional officer Donald Clemmer termed **prisonization.**[4] Clemmer believed that the longer inmates stayed in prison, the more "prisonized" they became and the more likely they were to return to crime after their release from prison.

prisonization The process by which an inmate becomes socialized into the customs and principles of the inmate society.

importation model A theory that the inmate society is shaped by the attributes inmates bring with them when they enter prison.

An alternative to the deprivation model is the **importation model,** which holds that the inmate society is shaped by factors external to the prison

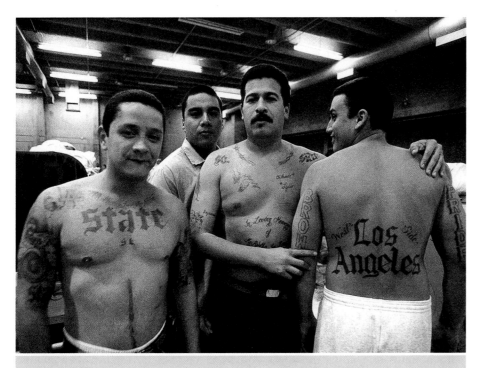

Conflict builds when inmates form competing gangs along ethnic, racial, and geographic lines. *Why do inmates form gangs in prison?*

environment—specifically, the preprison experiences and socialization patterns that inmates bring with them when they enter prison.[5] For example, inmates who were thieves and persistently associated with other thieves before going to prison bring the norms and values of thieves into the prison. They will remain more loyal to those norms and values than to the staff while incarcerated. On the other hand, if an inmate primarily conformed to the law before entering prison, the inmate will probably exhibit greater loyalty to staff norms once in prison. In short, the deprivation model assumes that new inmates are socialized into the existing inmate society, which arises in response to the prison environment; the importation model suggests that the inmate society is the product of the socialization inmates experience before entering prison.

The deprivation and importation models were developed from studies of prisons of the pre-1960s era. Some scholars believe that the image of a fairly unified inmate society with an overarching convict code fails to characterize many of today's crowded and violent prisons. According to those scholars, several factors have rendered the inmate society fragmented, disorganized, and unstable:

1. Increasing racial heterogeneity.
2. The racial polarization of modern prisoners.
3. Court litigation.
4. The rise and fall of rehabilitation.
5. The increased politicalization of inmates.

The order and stability provided by the old inmate subculture have been replaced by an atmosphere of conflict and tension, in which inmates align themselves into competing gangs (such as the Aryan Brotherhood, the Mexican Mafia, and the Black Guerrilla Family) and other inmate organizations (such as the Lifer's Club and the Muslims).[6]

VIOLENCE AND VICTIMIZATION It is generally agreed that there is more physical violence by inmates in today's men's prisons than there was in earlier

Attica Prison Riot

The deadliest prison riot in the nation's history occurred at the Attica Correctional Facility in upstate New York in September 1971. The uprising began when inmates took over one of the prison yards, and held 49 guards hostage, demanding better living conditions within the facility. It ended 4 days later after state troopers, under orders from then governor Nelson Rocke-feller, raided the prison, sparking violence that left 11 guards and 32 prisoners dead and more than 80 others wounded. On February 15, 2000, a U.S. district court judge approved a settlement under which New York State, without admitting wrong-doing or liability, would pay $8 million to 1,280 inmates who were abused by law enforcement officials during the riot. The agreement concluded a long-stalled $2.8 billion class action lawsuit originally filed against prison and state officials in 1974.

SOURCE: "$8 Million Award Ends Attica Prison Suit," *Facts on File: World News Digest with Index*, no. 3097 (April 13, 2000), p. 248.

periods. In recent years, thousands of inmates and staff have been assaulted. In 2004, for example, 51 inmates were killed in state prisons.[7] There is also consensus that staff violence against inmates is less common today. However, the number of inmates killed by staff in the last few years is unknown.

Commonly cited reasons for high rates of prison violence include improper management and classification practices by staff, high levels of crowding and competition over resources, the young age of most inmates in many prisons, and increases in racial tensions and prison gang activity. Although gang and racial conflicts surely play a role, it seems unlikely that the bulk of prison violence is extensively planned or gang-orchestrated. One reason is that many prisons across the United States lack well-developed gang structures and serious gang problems, but they are still plagued by violence. Furthermore, what we know about violent crime in general suggests that much prison violence is probably spontaneous, motivated by particular circumstances. Some common perpetrator motives for physical violence in prison are to (1) demonstrate power and dominance over others; (2) retaliate against a perceived wrong, such as the failure of another inmate to pay a gambling debt; and (3) prevent the perpetrator from being victimized (for example, raped) in the future.

A good deal of prison violence—but not all—has sexual overtones. It is important to realize that not all instances of sex in prison are violent, that not all instances are homosexual in nature, and that sexual encounters can involve both inmates and staff. Instances of prison sex can be further divided into three basic categories: (1) consensual sex for gratification, (2) prostitution, and (3) sexual assault. The third category obviously involves violence, and the first two sometimes have indirect links to violence. For example, a consensual sexual relationship between two inmates may have started out as a forced one. Likewise, an inmate who is vulnerable to sexual assault may perform sexual favors for an aggressive, well-respected prisoner in exchange for protection from other inmates. In the language of the prison, such vulnerable inmates are known as "punks." Prison sexual encounters can be intraracial or interracial; however, sexual assaults are more often interracial than intraracial.

Prison violence and disorder generally result spontaneously from particular circumstances. *What are some of those circumstances?*

Physical victimization is not the only or even the most frequent kind of victimization that takes place in prison. Sociologist Lee Bowker identifies three other kinds: economic, psychological, and social.[8] As with physical victimization, these three kinds may be perpetrated by inmates against other inmates, by inmates against staff, or by staff against inmates. In addition, the four kinds of victimization are interrelated: Combinations can occur, and one can lead to another.

All societies have an economy, and most have a black-market component. The inmate society is no exception. The **sub-rosa** (secret or underground) **economy** of an institution consists of the exchange of goods and services that, though often illicit, are in high demand among inmates. Examples of such goods and services include food, clothes, alcohol and other drugs, pornography, weapons, loan services, protection, sex, and gambling. Engaging in illicit economic exchanges is commonly referred to as "playing the rackets" or "hustling." Cigarettes often serve as the medium of exchange because currency is typically contraband. The money inmates earn from prison work is usually maintained in accounts from which they may deduct only specified amounts for specified purposes. Hence, packs and cartons of cigarettes assume the symbolic value of money in the sub-rosa economy. However, currency may also be used. Like any kind of contraband (drugs, for example), currency can enter the institution via mail, visits, or staff. The sub-rosa economy sets the stage for various types of economic victimization, including theft, robbery, fraud, extortion, loan-sharking, and price-fixing by gangs and cliques.

Prostitution is part of prison culture in many institutions. *Why do some prisoners prostitute themselves?*

sub-rosa economy The secret exchange of goods and services among inmates; the black market of the prison.

Psychological victimization consists of subtle manipulation tactics and mind games that occur frequently in prison. For example, a staff member may obtain sensitive confidential information from an inmate's file and proceed to "mess" with the inmate's mind by threatening to convey the information to other inmates. Likewise, an inmate may threaten to convey to superiors some instance of a staff member's corruption or failure to follow procedure. Examples of psychological victimization are numerous. Combined with the crowded and noisy living conditions, separation from the outside world, and the threats to physical safety, psychological victimization contributes significantly to the stress of the prison environment. It is small wonder that many prisoners suffer from a host of psychological maladaptations, such as fear, paranoia, excess anxiety, depression, anger, and lack of trust in others.

Social victimization involves prejudice or discrimination against a person because of some social characteristic that person has. The social characteristic may be race, age, class background, religious preference, political position, or another factor. For example, racial segregation and discrimination against minorities was official policy in many prisons until the 1960s. Following the desegregation movement in the wider society, prisons, too, have become more racially integrated. Today, the segregation that remains is typically voluntary on the part of inmates.

INMATE COPING AND ADJUSTMENT Living in prison is fundamentally different from living in the free community. In prison, for example, deprivation of personal freedom and material goods is much more pronounced. There is less

Inmates develop a variety of coping mechanisms in prison. *If you were in prison, how would you cope?*

Drug Use in Federal Prisons

The Justice Department's Inspector General reported on January 22, 2003, that more than 2,800 federal inmates (about 2 percent of the federal prison population) had tested positive for illegal drugs each year from 1997 to 2001. Fifty inmates had died of drug overdoses since 1997, and drugs had been confiscated in more than 1,100 separate incidents since 2000. Narcotics typically entered the prison system through visitors, prison staff, and the mail.

SOURCE: *Facts on File World Digest* 63, no. 3245 (February 20, 2003), p. 108.

privacy, there is more competition for scarce resources, and life is typified by greater insecurity, stress, and unpredictability. Moreover, prison life may encourage qualities counter to those required for functioning effectively in the free community. Criminologist Ann Cordilia, expanding on the work of Erving Goffman, argues that prisons "desocialize" and alienate inmates by discouraging personal responsibility and independence, creating excessive dependency on authority, and diminishing personal control over life events.[9] One result is what Goffman called "self-mortification," a subduing or deadening of self-identity and self-determination.[10]

Therefore, a person coming from the free community into prison must learn to cope with and adjust to the institutional environment. Building on the ideas of criminologist Hans Toch,[11] criminologist Robert Johnson identifies two broad ways that inmates cope with imprisonment.[12] Some inmates enter what Johnson describes as the public domain of prison culture. Predatory, violent convicts, many of whom have lengthy prior records of incarceration (that is, are "state-raised youths") dominate this domain. Those convicts seek power and status in the prison world by dominating and victimizing others. Johnson claims that most inmates do not enter the public domain and live by its norms. Instead, most enter the prison's private culture. To understand this method of coping and adjustment, we must realize that each inmate brings a unique combination of personal needs into prison. That is, inmates vary in their needs for such things as privacy, environmental stimulation, safety, and emotional feedback. Entering the private culture of the prison means finding in the diverse environment of the institution a niche that will accommodate the inmate's unique combination of needs. For example, an inmate who has strong needs for privacy, safety, and intellectual stimulation may arrange to have a job in the prison library. The library becomes the inmate's niche. The private domain of prison culture consists of many diverse niches.

From another perspective, criminologist John Irwin suggests that in coping and adjusting to prison, an inmate will develop a prison career or lifestyle.[13]

Three such lifestyles are "doing time," "jailing," and "gleaning." Inmates who adopt the "doing time" lifestyle are primarily concerned with getting out of prison as soon as possible and avoiding hard time in the process. Avoiding hard time means maximizing comfort and minimizing discomfort in a way that does not threaten to extend the sentence or place the inmate in danger. The "jailing" lifestyle is often embraced by people with lengthy prior records of incarceration, who are more accustomed to life *in* an institution than life *outside* one. Those inmates are concerned with achieving positions of influence in the inmate society; prison is their world. "Gleaning" entails trying to take advantage of the resources available for personal betterment, such as obtaining marketable vocational skills. The idea is to prepare for life after release. Relatively few inmates adopt the gleaning lifestyle.

LIFE IN WOMEN'S PRISONS

Life in women's prisons is similar to life in men's prisons in some respects, but there are also important differences. For example, both female and male inmates must cope with the deprivations, stress, depersonalization, and authoritarian atmosphere of prison life. However, women's prisons are usually not characterized by the levels of violence, interpersonal conflict, and interracial tension found in men's institutions. Nor is the antistaff mentality of male prisoners as common among female inmates. Consequently, the environments of women's institutions are often less oppressive.

Those observations should not be taken to mean that female inmates generally do easier time than male inmates. Indeed, it has been suggested that women experience imprisonment more negatively than men.[14] A major reason for this is separation from friends and family.[15] Female inmates are more likely than male inmates to have children and to have been living with those children immediately before incarceration. In recent years, for example, about 65 percent of female state prisoners had children under 18 years old, and about the same percentage of those women lived with their children before incarceration.[16]

Procedures for determining the custodial relationship between a female inmate and her child vary widely. In some cases, very young children of

Female inmates are an increasing part of the nation's prison population. *Why?*

incarcerated women may live with their mothers in prison for a temporary period. In other cases, maternal custody might be terminated. The procedure depends on the jurisdiction and the particular circumstances. A common arrangement is for children to reside with their fathers, grandparents, or other relatives or friends during the period of incarceration. Visitation is often irregular or nonexistent, and the amount of visitation is dictated by institutional rules and the geographic distance between children and their mothers.[17]

PSEUDOFAMILIES AND HOMOSEXUALITY A distinguishing feature of the inmate society in many women's prisons is the presence of make-believe families, known as pseudofamilies. Studies have discovered that some female inmates adopt family roles, such as mother, daughter, sister, husband, and father to form kinship networks.[18] The number of inmates who adopt masculine roles, known as "butches," appears to be small in comparison with the number who take on feminine roles.[19] Furthermore, kinship ties may cut across racial lines, reflecting that race is not the divisive factor in women's prisons that it is in men's institutions. Pseudofamily structures are central to inmate society in women's prisons, providing social interaction and emotional support. Sociologist Rose Giallombardo suggests that pseudofamilies provide imprisoned women with the family affiliation and bonding that they have been socialized to desire but have been deprived of by incarceration.[20]

Family activity and homosexual activity appear to be relatively independent of each other. A female prisoner who is involved in homosexuality may or may not be

Myth

Virtually all female prisoners are lesbians.

Fact

Although there are no totally reliable data on the proportion of female inmates who engage in homosexuality while incarcerated, a reasonable estimate (based on the literature) is approximately half. This proportion is comparable to the proportion of male prisoners who do so.

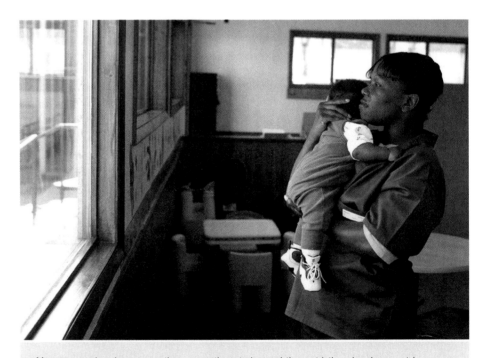

Many women in prison are mothers or mothers-to-be, and the restrictions imprisonment imposes on them as they try to maintain relationships with their children affect their physical and emotional well-being. *How could the stress of a prison mother's parent/child relationship be reduced?*

part of a family. Likewise, a female prisoner who is part of a make-believe family may or may not be involved in homosexuality. If she is, she may be having homosexual relations with someone who is part of the family or with someone who is not. The number of female prisoners who take part in family activities probably exceeds the number who participate in homosexuality. In addition, the majority of female inmates who participate in homosexuality are what sociologists David Ward and Gene Kassebaum call "turnouts," those who were heterosexual before incarceration and will return to heterosexuality upon release.[21] As in men's prisons, interracial homosexuality is quite common, but in contrast to men's prisons, the overwhelming majority of homosexual activity in women's institutions is consensual and is rooted in affection and attachment instead of dominance motives.

INMATE ROLES Social scientist Esther Heffernan identified three roles that women commonly adopt when adjusting to prison. Heffernan's roles are very similar to roles identified by sociologist Clarence Schrag in his work on male inmates.[22] The "square" role is adopted by women who were primarily non-criminals before coming to prison, and those women tend toward conventional behavior in prison. The square role discussed by Heffernan corresponds to the "square john" role identified by Schrag. Heffernan's "life" role is analogous to Schrag's "right guy" role. Inmates who assume the life role were habitual offenders before coming to prison, and they continue to adhere to antisocial and antiauthority norms in prison. The "cool" role, or what Schrag referred to as the "con politician," is occupied by sophisticated professional criminals. They try to do easy time by manipulating other inmates and the staff to their own advantage.

> ## THINKING CRITICALLY
>
> 1. In comparison to male prisons, why do you think that there is less violence, interpersonal conflict, and interracial tension in women's prisons?
>
> 2. Should very young children of incarcerated women be allowed to temporarily live with their mothers in prison? Why or why not?

Correctional Officers

In 1976, criminologist Gordon Hawkins wrote, "It is in fact remarkable how little serious attention has been paid to prison officers in the quite extensive literature on prisons and imprisonment."[23] Although it has increased steadily since, research on prison staff remains sparse compared with research on inmates. Most studies of prison staff have concentrated on guards or correctional officers, and there is good reason for this. Correctional officers represent the majority of staff members in a prison, are responsible for the security of the institution, and have the most frequent and closest contact with inmates. Yet correctional officers should not be thought of as existing in isolation from the larger structure of the prison bureaucracy discussed in the last chapter.

As of September 30, 2004, there were about 439,000 employees of adult correctional agencies in the United States, an increase of about 0.3 percent from the same date in 2003.[24] Of those 439,000 employees, about 281,500 (about 64 percent) were uniformed staff, an increase of more than 7 percent over the previous year. Uniformed staff consists of all correctional security staff, including majors, captains, lieutenants, sergeants, and officers. Most of the uniformed staff were correctional officers. In 2004, the turnover rate for correctional security staff in state facilities was 15.5 percent; the rate for correctional security staff in federal facilities was 4.6 percent. About 95 percent of both uniformed staff and correctional officers were employed by state agencies. About 75 percent of uniformed staff, including correctional officers,

Correctional Officer Salaries

Starting salaries for entry-level state correctional officers ranged from $18,360 in Louisiana to $41,834 in New Jersey as of August 2005. The starting salary for entry-level federal correctional officers in 2005 was $30,438 plus a locality supplement for some areas. Salaries were subject to increases after completion of preservice training and a probationary period.

SOURCE: Louisiana Department of Public Safety and Corrections, Corrections Services, www.corrections.state.la.us/Employment/employment.htm; New Jersey Department of Corrections, Careers in Corrections, www.state.nj.us/corrections/careers.html; Federal Bureau of Prisons, personal communication (August 5, 2005).

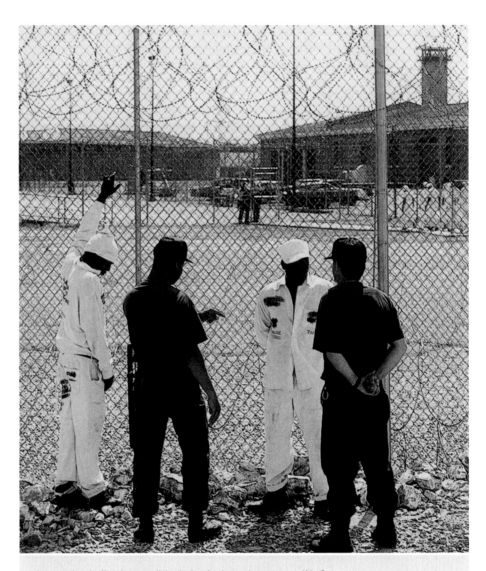

A correctional officer's custodial role is of primary importance. *Why?*

Inmate Assaults

Although rates of inmate assaults on prison staff have been increasing, the likelihood of an individual staff member's being the victim of an inmate assault, especially a lethal assault, remains fairly low. The assault of staff by inmates is a serious problem and is always a threat in prison, but the risks should not be exaggerated.

were male, about 67 percent were white, 24 percent were black, 7 percent were Hispanic, and 2 percent were other. The average ratio of correctional officers to inmates across the states in 2004 was one officer for every 6.96 inmates (up from 5.95 the previous year), and the average ratio in federal prisons was one correctional officer for every 10 inmates (the same as the previous year).

Correctional officers face a number of conflicts in their work. Criminologists Richard Hawkins and Geoffrey Alpert observe that the job is characterized by both boredom and stimulus overload; officers assigned to the towers may experience the former, whereas officers assigned to work the cell blocks may experience the latter.[25] Much also has been written about the role ambiguity and role strain resulting from conflict between custody and treatment objectives. How does an officer supervise and discipline inmates and at the same time attempt to counsel and help them? Traditionally, the role of guards was clearer and less ambiguous; they were responsible for custody. With the advent of rehabilitation, guards became correctional officers, and the custodial role grew clouded with treatment considerations. In addition, a series of court decisions has given many officers the perception that they have lost power while inmates have gained it.[26] Officers generally have considerable discretion in discharging their duties within the constraints of rules, regulations, and policies. Yet, because they lack clear and specific guidelines on how to exercise their discretion, they feel vulnerable to second-guessing by their superiors and the courts.

A popular misconception has been that officers manage inmates with an iron fist and are therefore corrupted by the power they have over inmates. However, as sociologist Greshan Sykes realized, the limits on an officer's power may be the real source of corruption.[27] Although their formal role places them in a superior position over inmates, officers must still obtain a measure of voluntary compliance from inmates. In the modern prison, it is impossible to rely exclusively on force to gain compliance if bureaucratic inefficiency, mass inmate rebellion, and court litigation are to be avoided. Moreover, because of the nature of the prison environment, officers do not have many incentives they can use to solicit compliance, and they do not directly control many of the main rewards, such as release date. Still, officers' performance is often judged by how smoothly the officers interact with inmates and get inmates to go along with their wishes. Consequently, many officers seek inmate compliance through informal negotiation and exchange, and this practice can promote corruption. For example, an officer may gain compliance by becoming friendly with particular inmates, by granting inmates concessions in exchange for their cooperation, and by overlooking certain rule infractions in exchange for compliance with other rules. A study of a federal prison by criminologist John Hewitt and his colleagues found that inmates reported committing, and officers reported observing, far more prison rule infractions than were documented in the institution's official disciplinary files.[28]

How do correctional officers respond to their roles and their work conditions? According to Hawkins and Alpert, some officers become alienated and cynical and withdraw from their work. Withdrawal can be figurative: An officer may minimize his or her commitment to the job and may establish a safe and comfortable niche in the prison, such as prolonged tower duty. Withdrawal can also be literal: Turnover and absenteeism are high in many prison systems. Other officers become overly authoritarian and confrontational in a quest to control inmates by intimidation. Those officers put up a tough facade similar to that displayed by some inmates. Still other officers respond by becoming corrupt (for example, selling drugs to inmates in response to a low salary).[29] Finally, a number of officers respond by adopting a human-services orientation toward their work.[30] Those officers seek to make prison a constructive place for themselves and for inmates. They try to deliver goods and services to inmates in a regular and responsive manner, to advocate and make referrals on behalf of inmates when appropriate, and to assist inmates in coping with prison by providing protection and counseling.

Efforts are under way to transform prison work from a mere job into a profession, but a number of problems and issues surround those efforts. First, factors such as low pay, the nature and prestige of the work, and the remote location of many prisons make recruitment of new officers difficult in some jurisdictions. Some people take prison work simply because they believe that nothing better is currently available, with the intent of leaving as soon as a better job opens. Second, the general lack of competition for prison jobs in many jurisdictions makes it difficult to impose restrictive criteria for choosing among applicants. Most states require that applicants be of a certain age (18 or 21) and have completed high school or the GED. Some states have additional requirements, such as no prior felony convictions, related work experience, and the passing of certain tests. Third, in some jurisdictions, a backlash

Turnover Rates

In 2004, the average turnover rate for correctional officers in state prisons was 15.5 percent, up from 13.7 percent in 2003. South Carolina had the highest turnover rate (37.5 percent), while Georgia had the lowest (1.3 percent). The turnover rate for correctional officers in the federal system was 4.6 percent, down from 4.9 percent in 2003.

Source: *American Correctional Association 2005 Directory: Adult and Juvenile Correctional Departments, Institutions, Agencies and Probation and Parole Authorities* (Lanham, MD: American Correctional Association, 2005), p. 48; *American Correctional Association 2004 Directory: Adult and Juvenile Correctional Departments, Institutions, Agencies and Probation and Parole Authorities* (Lanham, MD: American Correctional Association, 2004), p. 48.

Female Correctional Officers

In 1978, Linda Allen became the first female correctional officer to work at a high-security institution (the U.S. penitentiary at McNeil Island, Washington, now a Washington State correctional facility). Today it is commonplace for female correctional officers to work in federal and state high-security institutions.

Source: Harry E. Allen and Clifford E. Simonsen, *Corrections in America: An Introduction,* 8th ed. (Upper Saddle River, NJ: Prentice Hall, 1998), p. 539.

against affirmative action—which has increased female and minority representation among correctional officers—has resulted in tensions between the genders and races[31] and resentment by some white male officers. In jurisdictions where this backlash has occurred, efforts toward professionalization have been hampered. Fourth, once officers have been recruited and hired, they need to be trained, and the move toward professionalization has been accompanied by increased attention to training. Officers are usually trained at the outset of their jobs and then receive annual training thereafter. At present, however, training standards are not uniform across or even within jurisdictions. For example, more than 60 percent of agencies require at least 200 hours of coursework during initial training sessions; Florida, New Hampshire, and Utah require more than 500 hours; and California and Michigan require 640 hours.[32] (See Table 8.1 for the program components of correctional training programs.) Still, when turnover rates are high, training costs are high, and training may start to be viewed as a waste of money and time. Fifth, professionalization has been accompanied by increased unionism among officers. At the end of 2002, only Arkansas, Georgia, Missouri, Nevada, New Mexico, North Carolina, North Dakota, South Dakota, Tennessee, Texas, Vermont, and Wyoming reported that unions were not part of their correctional systems.[33] Although guard unions can help improve pay levels, job benefits, and work conditions, unions can also divide the superior and subordinate ranks. In addition, most guard unions have a very limited ability to engage in collective bargaining because strikes are commonly illegal.

THINKING CRITICALLY

1. What do you think could be done to further professionalize corrections work?

2. What are some ways you can think of to add selectivity to correctional worker recruitment?

CAREERS IN CRIMINAL JUSTICE

Correctional Sergeant

My name is Pietro DeSantis II and I am a correctional sergeant employed by the California Department of Corrections, assigned to the California Correctional Center (CCC) in Susanville, California. I have an associate of science degree from Lassen Community College in Susanville. I began my career as a correctional officer with the department in November of 1986 and was promoted to sergeant in February of 1996. During my tenure with corrections I have also been chapter president and board member of the California Correctional Peace Officer Association and commissioner and curriculum review committee chair of the Correctional Peace Officer Standards and Training (CPOST) Commission.

A normal workday starts as soon as you arrive on grounds and start talking to staff who are either beginning or ending their shift. Normal shifts at CCC are first watch (2200–0600 hours), second watch (0600–1400 hours), and third watch (1400–2200 hours). A normal day on all three watches starts with a security check of our safety equipment and security locks. First watch staff normally read the incoming and outgoing mail, count the inmate population three times, and ensure workers for the culinary service are awakened and report to work. Second watch staff normally feed breakfast and lunch to the inmates and supervise the inmate workers who clean the living quarters, inner perimeter yard areas, and the outside grounds. Third watch staff normally deliver the mail, count the inmates twice, feed them dinner, and house new arrivals from the transportation buses. As a sergeant, I could be assigned to supervise an office or unit with between zero and forty correctional officers.

Before entering into a career within corrections, I strongly suggest you do everything possible to become an effective communicator.

Why do you think it is important for a correctional officer to be an effective communicator?

TABLE 8.1	Percentage of Correctional Training Programs with Particular Program Components			
Administration	78%		Inmate manipulation	100%
Chemical agents	87		Inmate mental health	83
Communicable diseases	93		Inmate programs	85
Communications	98		Race relations	91
CPR	96		Report writing	100
Crisis management	98		Security devices	96
Ethics	98		Self-defense	100
Firearms	87		Spanish	15
Fire/safety	96		Special populations	89
First aid	98		Stress reduction	91
Hostages	93		Substance abuse	89
Inmate classification	98		Suicide prevention	93
Inmate gangs	91		Transportation	89
Inmate health care	78		Use of force	98
Inmate management	89		Workplace violence	63

Source: American Correctional Association, *Corrections Compendium* (Lanham, MD: American Correctional Association, February 2003), p. 11.

Inmate Rights and Prison Reform

Over the past four decades, the major means of reforming prisons has been court intervention. Until the middle of the twentieth century, the courts followed a **hands-off philosophy** toward prison matters. Under this hands-off philosophy, court officials were reluctant to hear prisoners' claims regarding their rights while they were incarcerated. Among other considerations, court officials questioned whether they had the necessary expertise in evaluating prison administration, and judges did not want to undermine the power of prison authorities. As a consequence of this inaction, prisoners, for all practical purposes, had no civil rights. (Remember that civil rights are those rights an individual possesses as a member of the state, especially those guaranteed against encroachment by the government.) This situation began to change as progress was made in civil rights in the wider society. Inmates were first granted rights of access to the courts, and the courts subsequently turned their attention to other rights.

hands-off philosophy A philosophy under which courts are reluctant to hear prisoners' claims regarding their rights while incarcerated.

ACCESS TO THE COURTS AND LEGAL SERVICES

Ordinarily, prisoners want to get their cases into the federal courts because they perceive those courts as more receptive to their claims than state courts. In its 1941 landmark ruling in *Ex parte Hull,* the U.S. Supreme Court granted inmates the right of unrestricted access to the federal courts. Just 3 years later (in *Coffin* v. *Reichard,* 6th Cir., 1944), a federal circuit court held that prisoners may challenge in federal court not only the fact of their confinement but also the conditions under which they are confined. But the most important U.S. Supreme Court ruling in this area (*Cooper* v. *Pate*) did not occur until 1964, when Thomas Cooper, a Stateville inmate, first successfully used Section 1983 of the Federal Civil Rights Act of 1871 to challenge the conditions of confinement. Prior to the ruling in *Cooper,* inmates had relied primarily on *habeas corpus* petitions to obtain access to the federal courts. **Habeas corpus** is a court order requiring that a confined person be brought to court so that

habeas corpus A court order requiring that a confined person be brought to court so that his or her claims can be heard.

Petitions Filed by Prison Inmates

In 2004, state and federal prison inmates filed 47,018 petitions in federal district courts seeking release from prison (*habeas corpus;* 50 percent) alleging civil rights violations (33 percent), or complaining of prison conditions (17 percent).

SOURCE: *Sourcebook of Criminal Justice Statistics Online,* Table 5.65.

his or her claims can be heard. For various technical reasons, it has normally been easier for prisoners to win federal cases under Section 1983 than under *habeas corpus*. In effect, then, the *Cooper* decision launched the prisoners' rights movement by opening the door to a flood of Section 1983 claims from prisoners. Calling *Cooper* v. *Pate* "the Supreme Court's first modern prisoners' rights case," law professor James Jacobs writes:

> But for the prisoners' movement it was not the breadth of the decision that mattered but the Supreme Court's determination that prisoners have constitutional rights; prison officials were not free to do with prisoners as they pleased. And the federal courts were permitted, indeed obligated, to provide a forum where prisoners could challenge and confront prison officials. Whatever the outcome of such confrontations, they spelled the end of the authoritarian regime in America penology.[34]

However, by the 1990s, Congress had become exasperated with the flood of claims by prisoners challenging their conditions of confinement in the federal courts. In response, it passed the Prison Litigation Reform Act (PLRA) of 1995.[35] The intent of the legislation was to restrict and discourage litigation by prison inmates. The PLRA mandates that prisoners must exhaust all available prison administrative remedies, that is, prison grievance procedures, before they can bring lawsuits in federal court challenging prison conditions. If all administrative remedies are not exhausted, that is, pursued to their conclusion, then the federal courts are obligated to dismiss the lawsuits. The PLRA applies to civil actions arising under federal law that challenge conditions of confinement or the effects of actions by government officials on the lives of prison inmates. It does not apply to *habeas corpus* proceedings that challenge the fact or duration of prison confinement. The act also restricts the relief that courts may grant in successful lawsuits. Relief to correct the violation cannot extend any further than the particular plaintiff or plaintiffs that filed the lawsuit. Any relief that is granted must be narrowly drawn, extending no further than necessary to correct the violation of the federal right. It must also be the least intrusive means necessary to correct the violation. In granting

Inmates are entitled to adequate law library facilities. *Why do inmates have this right and should they?*

relief, the court must give substantial weight to any adverse impact on public safety or the operation of a criminal justice system the relief may cause. The court is not authorized, in exercising its remedial powers, to order the construction of prisons or the raising of taxes.

To get their cases to court, prisoners need access to legal materials, and many of them need legal assistance from persons skilled in law. The U.S. Supreme Court has recognized those facts. In *Johnson* v. *Avery* (1969), the Court held that inmates skilled in legal matters (so-called **jailhouse lawyers**) must be permitted to assist other inmates in preparing cases unless the government provides a reasonable alternative. Furthermore, in *Bounds* v. *Smith* (1977), the U.S. Supreme Court ruled that inmates are entitled to either an adequate law library or adequate legal assistance. So if a correctional institution does not wish to allow a jailhouse-lawyer system and does not wish to provide adequate library facilities for inmates, the implication is that the correctional institution should allow inmates to consult with licensed attorneys to obtain legal assistance.

jailhouse lawyers Inmates skilled in legal matters.

PROCEDURAL DUE PROCESS IN PRISON

In the last chapter, we noted that inmates can face disciplinary action for breaking prison rules. The U.S. Supreme Court has moved to ensure that inmates receive minimal elements of due process during the disciplinary process. Probably the most important case in this area is *Wolff* v. *McDonnell* (1974). In *Wolff*, the Court held that although inmates facing a loss of good time for a rule infraction are not entitled to the same due process protections as in a criminal trial, such inmates are entitled to (1) a disciplinary hearing by an impartial body, (2) 24 hours' written notice of the charges, (3) a written statement of the evidence relied on and the reasons for the disciplinary action, and (4) an opportunity to call witnesses and present documentary evidence, provided that this does not jeopardize institutional security. The Court ruled that inmates are not entitled to confront and cross-examine people who testify against them or to have legal counsel.

FIRST AMENDMENT RIGHTS

The First Amendment to the Constitution guarantees freedom of speech, press, assembly, petition, and religion. The U.S. Supreme Court has rendered numerous decisions affecting prisoners' rights to freedom of speech and expression and freedom of religion.

FREE SPEECH The significant case of *Procunier* v. *Martinez* (1974) dealt with censorship of prisoners' outgoing mail but is generally regarded as applicable to other aspects of correspondence and expression. In *Procunier*, the Supreme Court ruled that censorship is legal only if it furthers one or more of the following substantial government interests: security, order, and rehabilitation. Moreover, the degree of censorship can be no greater than that required to preserve the government interest in question.

RELIGIOUS FREEDOM With the demise of the hands-off policy, the first substantive right won by inmates was freedom of religion, which was awarded to Black Muslims in *Cooper* v. *Pate*. As a rule, inmates are free to practice either conventional or unconventional religions in prison, and prison officials are obligated to provide accommodations. However, restrictions may be imposed, for example, where prison officials can demonstrate convincingly that religious practices compromise security or are unreasonably expensive. Granting special religious privileges can also be denied on the grounds that they will cause other groups to make similar demands. In general, the reasons given for restricting religious freedom must be compelling, and the restrictions imposed must be no more limiting than necessary.

The Fortune Society
The Fortune Society is a not-for-profit community-based organization staffed mostly by ex-offenders. The organization is dedicated to educating the public about prisons and prison life, criminal justice issues, and the root causes of crime. You can visit the Web site for the Fortune Society at **www.fortunesociety.org.**
Do you think organizations such as this one are necessary? Why or why not?

EIGHTH AMENDMENT RIGHTS

As described in Chapter 6, the Eighth Amendment outlaws the imposition of cruel and unusual punishment. The courts have considered a number of issues under the umbrella of cruel and unusual punishment.

CAREERS IN CRIMINAL JUSTICE

Commissioner of Corrections

My name is Christopher B. Epps and I am a commissioner of corrections. Appointed Commissioner of Corrections for the Mississippi Department of Corrections by Mississippi Governor Ronnie Musgrove in August of 2002, I was confirmed by the State Senate in April of 2003.

As a 20-year practitioner of corrections, I eagerly accepted the governor's invitation to head the state's prison system. I joined the Mississippi Department of Corrections in 1982 as a correctional officer at the Mississippi State Penitentiary and, throughout the course of my career, held a wide range of responsible positions, including disciplinary hearing officer; case manager; case manager supervisor; director of treatment; deputy superintendent/chief of security; director of offender services; director of records; chief of staff; deputy commissioner of community services; deputy commissioner of institutions; and, currently, commissioner of corrections.

My statutory responsibilities as the agency's chief executive, administrative, and fiscal officer are to

- Implement and administer laws and policy relating to corrections and coordinate the efforts of the department with those of the federal government and other state departments and agencies, county governments, municipal governments, and private agencies concerned with providing offender services.
- Establish standards, in cooperation with other state agencies having responsibility as provided by law, provide technical assistance, and exercise the requisite supervision as it relates to correctional programs over all state-supported adult correctional facilities and community-based programs.
- Promulgate and publish such rules, regulations, and policies of the department as are needed for the efficient governance and maintenance of all facilities and programs in accord insofar as possible with currently accepted standards of adult offender care and treatment.
- Provide the parole board with suitable and sufficient office space and support resources and staff necessary to conducting parole board business under the guidance of the chairman of the parole board.

- Make an annual report to the governor and the legislature reflecting the activities of the department and make recommendations for improvement of the services to be performed by the department.
- Cooperate fully with periodic independent internal investigations of the department and to file the report with the governor and the legislature.
- Perform such other duties necessary to effectively and efficiently carry out the purposes of the department as may be directed by the governor.

The overall responsibilities of the commissioner are many and varied. Chief among those is to provide and promote public safety by overseeing the management of the state prison system, which currently includes over 40,000 convicted felons divided evenly between those in the state's facilities for incarceration and those under the jurisdiction of the state while living among the general population. My office is responsible for assuring that the offenders' custody, care, control, and treatment are consistent with sound correctional principles and constitutional practices; and that the prison system is managed efficiently and effectively within the restraints of limited state budgets and resources, staff shortages, and rising costs.

The role of the commissioner requires strong leadership and problem-solving skills comparable to those of a city's mayor. With a confined population of inmates, the commissioner is on 24-hour call to respond to emergencies and to ensure that utility services are uninterrupted, educational programs are appropriate and responsive, food resources and medical services are available, sanitation requirements are satisfied, and security is not compromised.

In general, the commissioner of corrections must have all the qualities of a good statesman to conduct government business and policy and to carry out the mandates of multiple authorities including the governor, legislature, and state and federal courts.

What personality characteristics do you think it would take to be the manager of a state prison?

MEDICAL CARE In 1976, the Supreme Court decided *Estelle* v. *Gamble.* The Court ruled that inmates, under the Eighth Amendment, have a right to adequate medical care, but that inmates claiming Eighth Amendment violations on medical grounds must demonstrate that prison officials have shown deliberate indifference to serious medical problems. Under these conservative and subjective criteria, medical services and circumstances usually have to be really bad—even extreme—for inmates to win cases. Furthermore, the deliberate-indifference standard formulated in *Estelle* now applies to Eighth Amendment challenges to any condition of confinement, medical or otherwise.[36]

STAFF BRUTALITY Ironically, the Eighth Amendment has done little to protect inmates from staff brutality because brutality is normally construed as a tort rather than a constitutional issue.[37] (Recall that a tort is the breach of a duty to an individual that results in damage to him or her. It involves only duties owed to an individual as a matter of law.) However, whipping and related forms of corporal punishment have been prohibited under this amendment. Also, in *Hudson* v. *McMillian* (1992), the Supreme Court found that staff use of force against an inmate need not cause a significant physical injury to violate the Eighth Amendment.

TOTAL PRISON CONDITIONS Totality-of-conditions cases involve claims that some combination of prison practices and conditions (crowding, lack of services and programs, widespread brutality, and labor exploitation, for example) makes the prison, as a whole, unconstitutional under the Eighth Amendment. It is primarily in this area that the Eighth Amendment has been used. For example, in the famous case of *Holt* v. *Sarver* (1971), the entire Arkansas prison system was declared unconstitutional on grounds of totality of conditions and was ordered to implement a variety of changes. Totality-of-conditions rulings were later handed down against prisons in Alabama (*Pugh* v. *Locke,* 1976) and Texas (*Ruiz* v. *Estelle,* 1982).

As a rule, inmates are free to practice their religion in prison. Religious symbols and practices that interfere with institutional security can be restricted. *Should religious practices be allowed in prisons? Why or why not?*

Brubaker

In *Holt* v. *Sarver* (1971), the Supreme Court ordered the reform of the Arkansas prison system. The movie *Brubaker*, starring Robert Redford, is a fictionalized account of the real story of Tom Murton, warden of Arkansas's Tucker & Cummins prison in 1967–68. Murton's evidence was instrumental in the Supreme Court's decision. The U.S. district court characterized the Arkansas prison as "a dark and evil world completely alien to the free world."

Prisons have long had the right to provide only the minimal conditions necessary for human survival. Such conditions include the necessary food, shelter, clothing, and medical care to sustain life. Whether institutional crowding violates the Eighth Amendment is typically determined in relation to total prison conditions. Instead of being treated as a separate issue, crowding is viewed as part of the totality of conditions. The Supreme Court has been reluctant to side with inmates in their challenges to crowding. In both *Bell* v. *Wolfish* (1979) and *Rhodes* v. *Chapman* (1981), the Court refused to prohibit the placing of two inmates in cells designed for one person ("double-bunking") as a response to crowding.

OTHER PRISON CONDITIONS FOUND TO VIOLATE THE EIGHTH AMENDMENT
Federal courts have found all of the following prison conditions to be in violation of the Eighth Amendment's prohibition of cruel and unusual punishments:

- Inadequate ventilation.
- Excessive heat.
- Excessive cold.
- Lack of drinkable water (also lack of cold water where prison yard temperatures reached 100 degrees).
- Toxic or noxious fumes (pesticides sprayed into housing units; inadequate ventilation of toxic fumes in inmate workplaces).
- Exposure to sewage (exposure to flooding and human waste).
- Exposure to secondhand tobacco smoke (cellmate smoked five packs of cigarettes a day).
- Excessive noise.
- Sleep deprivation.
- Sleeping on the floor (failure to provide inmates with a mattress and bed or bunk).
- Lack of fire safety.
- Risk of injury or death in the event of an earthquake.
- Inadequate food or unsanitary food service.
- Inadequate lighting or constant lighting.
- Exposure to insects, rodents, and other vermin.
- Defective plumbing.
- Deprivation of basic sanitation.
- Denial of adequate toilet facilities.
- Exposure to asbestos (exposure to "moderate levels of asbestos" did not violate the Eighth Amendment).
- Exposure to the extreme behavior of severely mentally ill prisoners (exposure to constant screaming and feces-smearing of mentally ill prisoners "contributes to the problems of uncleanliness and sleep deprivation, and by extension mental health problems, for other inmates").
- Miscellaneous unhealthy or dangerous conditions (unsafe conditions for prisoners performing electrical work; prisoner injured in vehicle accident after transport officers refused to fasten his seat belt).[38]

FOURTEENTH AMENDMENT RIGHTS

The Fourteenth Amendment guarantees U.S. citizens due process of law and equal protection under law. The due process clause inspired the Supreme Court's decision in the previously discussed case of *Wolff* v. *McDonnell*, for example. Likewise, the equal-protection clause has led the Supreme Court to forbid racial discrimination (*Lee* v. *Washington*, 1968) and has led state courts to target gender discrimination (*Glover* v. *Johnson*, ED Mich., 1979). Compared with the rights of male inmates, however, the rights of female prisoners remain

In 1981, the U.S. Supreme Court refused to hold that double-bunking in prison cells was cruel and unusual punishment. *Should double-bunking be allowed in prisons? Why or why not?*

underdeveloped. The inmates' rights movement has been primarily a male phenomenon, and the rights of female prisoners deserve more attention from the courts in the future.

THE LIMITS OF LITIGATION

The progress toward prison reform resulting from the inmates' rights movement should not be underestimated. Nevertheless, one can question on a number of grounds the almost exclusive reliance, during the past four decades, on court intervention to reform the nation's prisons. Perhaps the most basic and compelling argument is that the monies being spent by prison systems to defend against inmate lawsuits and to comply with court orders (when inmate suits are successful) could have been spent better to reform the unacceptable practices that sparked the suits in the first place. Meanwhile, those prison systems are unable to address problems that help generate further inmate lawsuits precisely because they are defending against new suits and trying to comply with past court orders. The result is that even more money must be spent for legal defense and compliance with court orders. This cycle is difficult to break.

Court litigation is not just an expensive way to reform prisons; it is also a very slow and piecemeal way. A high percentage of lawsuits filed by inmates are judged frivolous and are therefore dismissed. If an inmate's suit is not judged frivolous, the inmate must still win the case in court, and many lose in the process. Even when inmates win a case, their success usually does not lead to wide-scale reforms. Successful, large-scale, class-action suits that have far-reaching impact on the prison system are relatively uncommon and will become more so under the Prison Litigation Reform Act of 1995. Moreover, winning a case and then getting the desired changes implemented can take many years. Prison systems do not comply automatically with court decrees. Achieving compliance with court orders often requires sustained monitoring

THINKING CRITICALLY

1. What do you think are legitimate complaints from prisoners?
2. What constitutional rights do you think should be extended to prisoners? Or do you think prisoners already have too many rights? Why?

by court-appointed officials as well as considerable negotiation and compromise by all parties involved to agree on a timetable and the specific nature of reforms. Finally, the transformation of traditional, ingrained practices in a prison system can render the prison environment chaotic and unstable, at least in the short run.

Release and Recidivism

Most inmates (approximately 93 percent) will eventually be released from prison. The 7 percent of inmates who will not be released are serving death or life sentences and likely will die in prison. Figure 8.1 shows the causes of death of the 3,137 inmates who died in prison in 2004. Eighty percent died of natural causes.

Depending on the jurisdiction and the specific case, inmates may be released from prison in a number of ways. Examples include expiration of the maximum sentence allowed by law (known as "maxing out"); **commutation,** or reduction of the original sentence by executive authority; release at the discretion of a parole authority; and mandatory release. Of those ways, the two most common are release at the discretion of a parole authority and mandatory release.

The term **parole** has two basic meanings. It can refer to a way of being released from prison before the entire sentence has been served, or it can refer to a period of community supervision following early release. We are concerned here with the former meaning. In jurisdictions that permit parole release, inmates must establish eligibility for parole. Eligibility normally requires that inmates have served a given portion of their terms minus time served in jail prior to imprisonment and minus good time. **Good time** is time subtracted from the sentence for good behavior and other meritorious activity in prison. Once eligible, an inmate submits a parole plan stipulating such things as where he or she plans to live and work upon release. The parole authority, which may consist of a board, members of the board, or a representative of the board, then considers the inmate's plan. The parole authority also considers reports from institutional staff who have worked with the inmate. The decision to grant or deny parole is announced at a parole-grant hearing. Parole will be discussed more fully in the next chapter.

commutation Reduction of the original sentence given by executive authority, usually a state's governor.

parole The conditional release of prisoners before they have served their full sentences.

good time The number of days deducted from an inmate's sentence by prison authorities for good behavior or for other reasons.

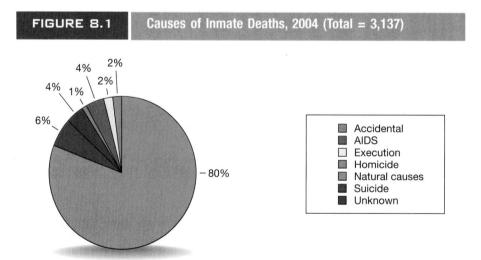

| FIGURE 8.1 | Causes of Inmate Deaths, 2004 (Total = 3,137) |

Source: *American Correctional Association 2005 Directory: Adult and Juvenile Correctional Departments, Institutions, Agencies and Probation and Parole Authorities* (Lanham, MD: American Correctional Association, 2005). Note: Cause of death was reported for only 2,496 of the 3,137 inmate deaths. Percentages were calculated based on the 2,496 figure. Data were not reported for California and Vermont. Reprinted with permission.

Most parole decisions are made by administrative boards whose members are appointed by state governors. An inmate's eligibility for release on parole depends on requirements set by law and on the sentence imposed by the court. *Should parole be abolished? Why or why not? If not, how could the decision-making process be improved?*

Mandatory release is release under the provisions of law, not at the discretion of a parole board. The inmate is released after serving his or her sentence or a legally required portion of the sentence, minus good-time credits. Mandatory release is similar to parole in that persons let out under either arrangement ordinarily receive a period of community supervision by a parole officer or the equivalent. Their freedom from prison is conditioned on following the rules of their community supervision (for example, obeying curfew, abstaining from drug use, and maintaining gainful employment) and on avoiding criminal activity.

In 1977, approximately 72 percent of inmates released from state prisons were released at the discretion of parole boards; only about 6 percent left prison under mandatory release that year. By contrast, in 2003, 22 percent were released by parole boards, compared with approximately 52 percent in 2004, who received mandatory release.[39] This shifting pattern indicates the strong emphasis placed on determinate sentencing during the 1980s and 1990s and the use of statistical guidelines to structure early-release decisions.

When inmates are released from correctional institutions, the hope is that as a result of deterrence or rehabilitation (discussed in Chapter 6), they will not return to criminal activity. Hence, we will conclude this chapter by considering **recidivism**—the return to illegal activity after release. Measuring recidivism and attributing the lack of recidivism to the influence of correctional programs are complicated by scientific methodological problems. Nevertheless, numerous studies conducted during the past couple of decades in several different jurisdictions reveal that recidivism rates, when recidivism is defined in a similar way, have remained remarkably stable.

At this writing, the most recent national study of recidivism among state prisoners found that 67.5 percent of nearly 300,000 former inmates released from prisons in 1994 were rearrested for a new offense within 3 years of their release.[40] A similar study of inmates released in 1983 showed that 62.5 percent of them were rearrested within 3 years of their release.[41] Inmates in the

mandatory release A method of prison release under which an inmate is released after serving a legally required portion of his or her sentence, minus good-time credits.

recidivism The return to illegal activity after release from incarceration.

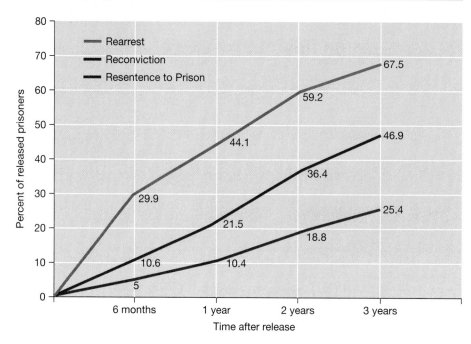

| FIGURE 8.2 | Recidivism Rates of Prisoners Released in 1994 from Prisons in 15 States, by Time After Release |

Source: Patrick A. Langan and David J. Levin, "Recidivism of Prisoners Released in 1994," *Bureau of Justice Statistics Special Report* (Washington, DC: GPO, U.S. Department of Justice, June 2002), p. 3.

Early Release

Most offenders who receive lengthy prison terms (for example, 25 years) do not serve the entire term, and many do not even come close to doing so. The reason is the availability of parole, good time, and other mechanisms for reducing time served. Some opponents of those reductions in terms fail to understand that the mechanisms are essential to the operation of many current prison systems. Without them, many systems would be rendered dysfunctional by crowding. Additionally, without early release incentives for inmates, it would be extremely difficult to maintain order in prisons.

more recent study were from Arizona, California, Delaware, Florida, Illinois, Maryland, Michigan, Minnesota, New Jersey, New York, North Carolina, Ohio, Oregon, Texas, and Virginia. The average prison sentence was about 5 years. On average, the inmates were released after serving 35 percent of their sentences, or about 20 months.

The study used four measures of recidivism: rearrest, reconviction, resentence to prison, and return to prison with or without a new sentence. In addition to the 67.5 percent of prisoners rearrested for a new offense (almost exclusively a felony or a serious misdemeanor), 46.9 percent were reconvicted for a new crime, 25.4 percent were resentenced to prison for a new crime, and 51.8 percent were returned to prison for a new crime (25.4 percent) or for a technical violation of release conditions (26.4 percent), such as failing a drug test or missing an appointment with their parole officer (see Figure 8.2). Not all reconvicted prisoners were sentenced to another prison term for their new offenses. Some were sentenced to confinement in a local jail or probation.

Released prisoners with the highest rearrest rates were motor vehicle thieves (78.8 percent), those in prison for possessing or selling stolen property (77.4 percent), larcenists (74.6 percent), burglars (74 percent), robbers (70.2 percent), and those in prison for possessing, using, or selling illegal weapons (70.2 percent). Released prisoners with the lowest rearrest rates were those in prison for homicide (40.7 percent), nonrape sexual assault (41.4 percent), rape (46 percent), and driving under the influence (51.5 percent). Rearrests of the released prisoners accounted for about 5 percent of all arrests for serious crime from 1994 to 1997. Among other notable findings:

- Men were more likely than women to be rearrested (68.4 percent vs. 57.6 percent), reconvicted (47.6 percent vs. 39.9 percent), resentenced to prison for a new crime (26.2 percent vs. 17.3 percent), and returned to prison with or without a new prison sentence (53 percent vs. 39.4 percent).

- Blacks were more likely than whites to be rearrested (72.9 percent vs. 62.7 percent), reconvicted (51.1 percent vs. 43.3 percent), resentenced to prison for a new crime (28.5 percent vs. 22.6 percent), and returned to prison with or without a new prison sentence (54.2 percent vs. 49.9 percent).
- Non-Hispanics were more likely than Hispanics to be rearrested (71.4 percent vs. 64.6 percent), reconvicted (50.7 percent vs. 43.9 percent), and returned to prison with or without a new prison sentence (57.3 percent vs. 51.9 percent). The difference between non-Hispanics and Hispanics in being resentenced to prison for a new crime was not significant.
- Younger persons were more likely to be rearrested than older persons. For example, more than 80 percent of those under age 18 were rearrested, while only 45.3 percent of those 45 or older were rearrested.

Nearly 70 percent of the inmates released in 1994 had a record of violence. Seventy percent of the released inmates had five or more prior arrests (not counting the arrest that brought them to prison). Half of the inmates had two or more prior convictions (not including the conviction that resulted in their prison sentence). For 56 percent of the released inmates, the prison sentence they were serving when released was their first-ever sentence to prison; the other 44 percent had previously served time in prison.

The nearly 300,000 inmates released in 1994 had amassed 4.1 million arrest charges before their most recent imprisonment and an additional 744,000 charges within 3 years of release. A small percentage of offenders was responsible for a large number of the arrests. An estimated 6.4 percent of the inmates were each charged with 45 or more crimes before and after their release in 1994. About 7.6 percent of all released prisoners were rearrested for a new crime in a state other than the one that released them. They were charged with committing 55,760 such crimes. There was no evidence that spending more time in prison raised the recidivism rate. The evidence was mixed with regard to whether serving more time reduced recidivism. A good predictor of whether an inmate will continue to commit crimes following release is the number of times the inmate has been arrested in the past. Prisoners with longer prior records were more likely to be rearrested than prisoners with shorter prior records. As other recidivism research has shown, the first year of release is the most critical one. Nearly two-thirds of all the recidivism of the first 3 years occurred in the first year (see Figure 8.2).

Obviously, those research findings are not good news for people who believe that imprisonment can achieve large-scale deterrence of crime and rehabilitation of criminals. More bad news for deterrence advocates comes from the research of sociologist Ben Crouch, who found that newly incarcerated offenders frequently express a preference for prison over probation sentences. Crouch explains:

> A fundamental irony emerges in our justice system. That is, the lawbreakers whom middle-class citizens are most likely to fear and want most to be locked away . . . tend to be the very offenders who view prison terms of even two or three years as easier than probation and as preferable. To the extent that these views among offenders are widespread, the contemporary demand for extensive incarceration (but often for limited terms) may foster two unwanted outcomes: less deterrence and more prisoners.[42]

Similar research by criminologist Kenneth Tunnell shows that most repeat property offenders are not threatened by the prospects of imprisonment.[43]

Unfavorable news for advocates of rehabilitation began trickling in even before the release, in 1974, of the famous Martinson report, which cast grave

Civil Disabilities of Convicted Felons

Depending on the jurisdiction, convicted felons lose a variety of civil rights. Among the most common rights forfeited are the rights to vote, hold public office, serve on a grand or petit jury, practice a profession that requires an occupational or professional license, be a parent (termination of parental rights), and carry or possess firearms. In many states, women convicted of drug offenses may be denied welfare benefits. If convicted of a federal felony, a person is ineligible for enlistment in any of the armed services, may have public housing benefits restricted under certain circumstances, and, depending on the crime, may lose veteran benefits, including pensions and disability. A majority of jurisdictions provide a means for restoring lost rights. Some rights are restored automatically. Other rights are restored by executive or judicial proceedings that are often based on the ex-offender's demonstration that he or she has been rehabilitated. Some rights are lost permanently.

Source: "Civil Disabilities of Convicted Felons: A State-by-State Survey," U.S. Department of Justice, Office of the Pardon Attorney, October 1996, at www.usdoj.gov/pardon/readingroom.htm; Kevin G. Buckler and Lawrence F. Travis III, "Reanalyzing the Prevalence and Social Context of Collateral Consequence Statutes," *Journal of Criminal Justice* 31 (2003), pp. 435–453.

doubts on the ability of prisons to reform offenders.[44] In a later study, criminologist Lynne Goodstein demonstrated that the inmates who adjusted most successfully to prison had the most difficulty adjusting to life in the free community upon release. About her research, Goodstein writes:

> These findings provide a picture of the correctional institution as a place which reinforces the wrong kinds of behaviors if its goal is the successful future adjustment of its inmates. In the process of rewarding acquiescent and compliant behavior, the prison may, in fact, be reinforcing institutional dependence.[45]

Of course, some people are deterred from crime by the threat of imprisonment, and the prison experience does benefit some inmates in the way rehabilitation advocates envision. Criminologists Frank Cullen and Paul Gendreau recently completed a comprehensive review of research that evaluated the effects of correctional interventions on recidivism rates.[46] They found that across studies, the correctional interventions reduced recidivism rates, on average, 10 percent. The most successful interventions reduced recidivism 25 percent. They used cognitive-behavioral treatments, targeted known predictors of crime for change, and intervened mainly with high-risk offenders. Cognitive-behavioral treatments emphasize the important role of thinking in how people feel and behave. Therapists help offenders identify the thinking that is causing their problematic feelings and behavior and then teach them how to replace those thoughts with thoughts that will lead to more desirable feelings and actions. Cullen and Gendreau also reported that punishment-oriented, correctional interventions generally had no effect on offender criminality.

We must be careful not to hold unrealistic expectations about what imprisonment can accomplish in our society. Traditionally, we have placed undue confidence in the ability of imprisonment to control crime. But imprisonment is a reactive (versus proactive) response to the social problem of crime, and crime is interwoven with other social problems, such as poverty, inequality, and racism, in our wider society. We should not expect imprisonment to resolve or control those problems.

THINKING CRITICALLY

1. Do you think anything could be done to lower recidivism rates among offenders? If so, what?

2. In your opinion, should prisoners be allowed to reduce their time in prison through parole or good time? Why or why not?

SUMMARY

1. Distinguish between the deprivation and importation models of inmate society.

   The deprivation model of inmate society empha-sizes the role of the prison environment in shap-ing the inmate society. The importation model of inmate society emphasizes attributes inmates bring with them when they enter prison.

2. Explain how today's inmate society differs from those of the past.

   Compared with prisons of the past, the inmate society in today's prisons is much more frag-mented and conflict-ridden. Physical, psychologi-cal, economic, and social victimization are facts of life in many contemporary institutions. Inmates must learn to cope with this state of affairs. Some do so by becoming part of the prison's violent public culture. Others carve out niches and meet their needs in the prison's pri-vate culture.

3. Identify some of the special features of life in women's prisons.

   Life in women's prisons is somewhat different from life in men's prisons. In particular, women's prisons often have less stringent secu-rity measures, are less violent, and are character-ized by pseudofamily structures that help the inmates cope.

4. Describe the profile of correctional officers and explain some of the issues that they face.

   The growing number of correctional officers who staff prisons are predominantly white and male. Correctional officers face a number of problems in their work, including low pay, work-related conflicts, and a potential for corruption. They are also subject to role conflict because of their dual objectives of custody and treatment. Some officers respond to those problems more con-structively than others. Efforts are ongoing to transform prison work into a profession, and issues surrounding those efforts include

   recruitment and selection, the backlash against affirmative action and other hiring practices, training, and unionism.

5. Identify prisoners' rights and relate how they were achieved.

   The main way that prisoners have gained rights during the past four decades is through interven-tion by the courts. Until the 1960s, inmates had minimal rights. As the hands-off policy was lifted, prisoners gained a number of important rights: greater access to the courts, easier access to legal services in prison, and improved prison disciplinary procedures. They also gained certain rights under the First, Eighth, and Fourteenth Amendments.

6. List the two most common ways that inmates are released from prison and compare those two ways in frequency of use.

   Most inmates are released from prison at the discretion of a parole authority or under mandatory release laws. Mandatory release, a method of prison release under which an inmate is released after serving a legally required portion of his or her sentence minus good-time credits, has begun to rival parole release in frequency of use.

7. Summarize what recidivism research reveals about the success of the prison in achieving deterrence and rehabilitation.

   When inmates are released from prison, it is hoped that they will not return to crime. Stud-ies show, however, that the rate of return to crime, or recidivism, is high. Studies also show that recidivism rates have remained fairly con-stant for a long time. Those studies call the deterrence and rehabilitation rationales into question. As a society, our expectations of what incarceration can accomplish are proba-bly unrealistic.

KEY TERMS

total institution, p. 292
convict code, p. 292
deprivation model, p. 292
prisonization, p. 292

importation model, p. 292
sub-rosa economy, p. 295
hands-off philoso-phy, p. 303

habeas corpus, p. 303
jailhouse lawyer, p. 305
commutation, p. 310

parole, p. 310
good time, p. 310
mandatory release, p. 311
recidivism, p. 311

REVIEW QUESTIONS

1. What did Erving Goffman mean when he wrote that prisons are *total institutions*?
2. What is the *convict code*, and why is it central to inmate society in traditional men's prisons?
3. What is *prisonization*?
4. What factors have rendered contemporary inmate society fragmented, disorganized, and unstable?
5. What are some of the reasons for high rates of prison violence?
6. What are four types of victimization that take place in prisons?
7. What are some of the general ways that inmates cope and adjust to the institutional environment, according to Johnson, Irwin, and Heffernan?
8. According to Hawkins and Alpert, what are four ways that correctional officers respond to their roles and their work conditions?
9. In *Wolff* v. *McDonnell* (1974), what rights were given to inmates facing disciplinary actions, and what rights were not extended?
10. How has court intervention limited prison reform?

IN THE FIELD

1. **Rehabilitation Programs** Contact a local prison or jail, and arrange to investigate one or more rehabilitation programs. Obtain pertinent written material, and observe the program in operation as much as possible. Assess how successful the program is in achieving its goals. Consider these specific issues:
   (1) What are the goals of the program?
   (2) Are the goals of the program clearly defined in some document?
   (3) Is the program administered in an effective way?
   (4) Is instruction adequate?
   (5) Is there adequate equipment (if applicable)?
   (6) Will the skills learned in the program be important to inmates upon release?
   (7) How likely are inmates to successfully complete the program?
   (8) Does the program have an evaluation component that would allow officials to determine the program's success or failure?
   (9) On what basis is the program's success or failure judged? After assessing the program, explain what changes, if any, you would recommend.

2. **Prison Films** Watch a video or movie about prison life. Good choices are *Murder in the First* with Kevin Bacon and Christian Slater, *The Shawshank Redemption* with Tim Robbins and Morgan Freeman, *Birdman of Alcatraz* with Burt Lancaster, *Brubaker* with Robert Redford, and *Cool Hand Luke* with Paul Newman. From what you have learned in this chapter, determine how realistic the portrayals are. Note common themes.

ON THE NET

1. **Life in Prison** Visit the Web site of the North Carolina Department of Corrections at www.doc.state.nc.us/dop/CPtour/index.htm. Access "A Tour of Central Prison." Pretend you are an inmate and write an essay describing your experiences in the prison.

2. **Virtual Prison Tour** Access the Florida Department of Corrections Web site at www.dc.state.fl.us and take the virtual prison tour through Florida prisons. In either an oral or written presentation describe your impressions of the prison. What surprised you? What, if anything, disturbed you? What changes, if any, should be made? As an option include North Carolina's Central Prison in your description—see On the Net exercise 1.

1. **Right to Vote** As of August 2005, more than 4 million Americans were denied the right to vote because they were felons or ex-felons. In 48 states and the District of Columbia, incarcerated felons were denied the right to vote (only Maine and Vermont permitted prison inmates to vote); 35 states disenfranchised felony probationers or parolees (or both); and 13 states additionally disenfranchised some or all ex-felons who completed their sentences. Regarding the latter category, Alabama, Florida, Iowa, Kentucky, Mississippi, Nevada, Virginia, and Wyoming denied the right to vote to all ex-offenders who completed their sentences; Arizona and Maryland disenfranchised recidivists; Tennessee disenfranchised ex-felons convicted prior to 1986; Washington disenfranchised ex-felons convicted prior to 1984; and Delaware disenfranchised some ex-offenders for 5 years following their release from prison.

   Each state has developed its own process of restoring voting rights to ex-offenders, but most of those processes are so cumbersome that few ex-offenders are able to take advantage of them. As a result, in the 2000 presidential election, for example, an estimated 4.7 million people (2.3 percent of the voting-age population) were disenfranchised by virtue of having a felony conviction on their record. Of those people disenfranchised, 13 percent were black men. In seven states, 25 percent of the black men were disenfranchised.

   A recent national opinion poll found that 80 percent of the public favors restoring voting rights to ex-felons, generally, while a low of 52 percent even favors restoring voting rights to sex offenders. Sixty percent support enfranchising felony parolees, and 66 percent favor enfranchising ex-felons convicted of a violent crime who have served their entire sentence.

   a. Should incarcerated felons have the right to vote? What about felony probationers or parolees? What about ex-felons who have completed their sentences? What about sex offenders who have completed their sentences? What about felons who were convicted of a violent crime and have completed their sentences? Justify your answers.

   b. If you believe that voting rights should be restored, should there be conditions? If so, what should they be?

   c. Currently, some states restore voting rights automatically; other states do so by executive or judicial action. If you believe that voting rights should be restored, what should the process entail?

2. **Inmate Organ Transplants** On January 3, 2003, a California prison inmate received a donor heart. He had suffered congestive heart failure the month before. The inmate was serving a 14-year sentence for robbery, and the transplant and treatment for his illness cost California taxpayers about $1 million. Medical professionals defended the transplant, saying the recipient met medical criteria. Prison officials cited a 1976 Supreme Court decision and a 1997 California ruling by the Ninth U.S. Circuit Court of Appeals requiring them to meet inmate medical needs. Critics point out that, among other things, at the time of the surgery, more than 4,000 Americans were on a waiting list for heart transplants, and 700 would die that year waiting for one. The prison inmate died about a year after receiving the transplant. Prison authorities noted that he had failed to maintain rigorous medical routines following the transplant.

   a. Should prison inmates be eligible for organ transplants?

   b. Does it matter whether they can pay for them?

   c. What does the law require prison officials to do about organ transplants?

   d. Should the "less eligibility" principle apply to organ transplants? Why or why not?

   e. Should there be limits to the medical services provided to prison inmates and, if so, what should the limits be?

To access more information and resources, including study questions, chapter summaries, and links, go to: www.mhhe.com/bohm1.

CHAPTER NINE

COMMUNITY CORRECTIONS

CHAPTER OUTLINE

CHAPTER OBJECTIVES

After completing this chapter, you should be able to:

1. Define community corrections and identify the goals and responsibilities of community corrections agencies and their staffs.

2. Define probation and summarize the research findings on recidivism rates.

3. Distinguish parole from probation.

4. Explain the functions of a parole board.

5. Describe how intermediate sanctions differ from traditional community corrections programs.

6. Explain two major concerns about intensive-supervision probation and parole (ISP).

7. Explain what day reporting centers and structured fines are.

8. Explain what home confinement and electronic monitoring are.

9. Identify the goal of halfway houses and compare them with other community corrections programs.

10. Summarize the purposes and outcomes of temporary-release programs.

Community Corrections: Definition and Scope

community corrections The subfield of corrections in which offenders are supervised and provided services outside jail or prison.

Community corrections can be broadly defined as the subfield of corrections consisting of programs in which offenders are supervised and provided services outside jail or prison. For this reason, community corrections is sometimes referred to as *noninstitutional corrections*. Community corrections includes such programs as diversion, restitution, probation, parole, halfway houses, and various provisions for temporary release from prison or jail. Those programs are the subject of this chapter.

It is important to realize that community corrections is a generic term. Federal, state, and local jurisdictions differ widely in the way they organize and administer community corrections and in the specific procedures they use. Criminologist David Duffee's delineation of three varieties of community corrections illustrates this diversity.[1] Community-run correctional programs are controlled by local governments, with minimal connection to state and federal authorities. In effect, local officials determine how such programs will be run within the broad guidelines of state and federal laws. In community-placed programs, as in community-run ones, offenders are handled by agencies within the local district, but agencies in community-placed programs are connected to central state or federal authorities, or both. Consequently, central authority affects program operation, and community-placed programs tend to be more isolated from local affairs than are community-run programs. Community-based correctional programs are a combination of the other two types. Connection to central authority for resources and other support services (a feature of community-placed programs) is combined with strong links between the program and the surrounding locality (a feature of community-run programs).

Myth Fact

Myth

Modern community correctional programs are invariably "soft on crime." They focus too much on rehabilitation, to the exclusion of punishment, deterrence, and incapacitation.

Fact

Major prison crowding in the past 15 years or so has made it necessary to channel into the community, under supervision, many felons who formerly would have gone to (or stayed in) prison. The priorities and operations of community agencies have shifted to meet this challenge. Many community programs—especially the newer "intermediate sanctions," such as electronic monitoring—emphasize punishment, deterrence, and incapacitation as much as, if not more than, rehabilitation.

GOALS AND STAFF ROLES

As described in Chapter 6, the goals of sentencing, which also are the goals of corrections, include punishment, deterrence, incapacitation, and rehabilitation. Yet, as a subfield of corrections, community corrections has traditionally emphasized rehabilitation. Although community programs are concerned with supervising and controlling offenders and ensuring that they follow the rules of their sentences, there is frequently great emphasis on assisting offenders with personal problems and needs. Another emphasis is establishing stronger ties

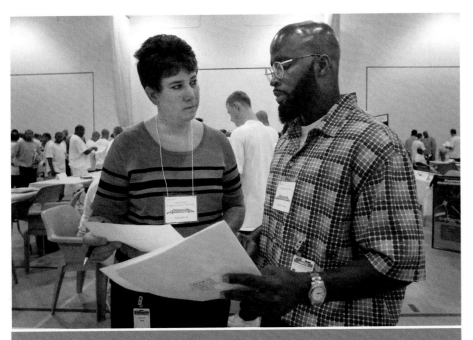

One aspect of probation and parole is client counseling. *What kinds of counseling problems are probation or parole officers likely to encounter?*

Reform versus Punishment

According to a public opinion poll, 90 percent of Americans support the development of local programs to keep more nonviolent and first-time offenders active and working in the community. Yet, only 8 percent of Americans favor shortening sentences.

SOURCE: Timothy J. Flanagan, "Reform or Punish: Americans' Views of the Correctional System," in T. J. Flanagan and D. R. Longmire (eds.), *Americans View Crime and Justice: A National Public Opinion Survey* (Thousand Oaks, CA: Sage, 1996), p. 87.

between the offender and the community, by helping the offender get and keep a job, for example. However, the traditional preoccupation of community corrections with rehabilitation has given way in recent years to concern with the other goals.

The staff of community correctional programs have two potentially competing roles that reflect different goals. The first amounts to a law enforcement role: seeing that offenders comply with the orders of community sentences. This means that staff must supervise offenders, investigate possible rule infractions, and take action to address any serious or repeated rule violations.

The other role of staff is to help offenders identify and address their problems and needs. This role has three aspects. The first is the direct provision of services, such as counseling, to offenders. The second is commonly described as the "resource broker" role. In this role, staff identify particular problems and needs and refer offenders to various community agencies for help. An important advantage of community corrections is that correctional agencies can draw on the services of other agencies in the locality. For example, a probation officer may refer a client to a local mental health center for counseling. The third aspect of the helping role is advocacy. A community may not offer services that a significant number of offenders require, for example, opportunities for vocational training. It is the responsibility of staff to advocate greater availability for services that are lacking and to work with community leaders to develop those services.

Many people believe that community correctional staff *should* occupy the dual roles of enforcing the law and helping clients. Those people maintain that supervision and control are necessary to facilitate rehabilitation and that rehabilitation enhances supervision and control. Opponents of that position point to the potential for conflict between roles. They argue that such conflict creates undue stress for staff and makes it difficult to accomplish anything of value.

Funding Corrections

Of all adults under some type of correctional supervision in the United States, approximately 30 percent are confined in prisons or jails. Approximately 70 percent are serving community sentences. Approximately 80 percent of all funds allocated to corrections in the United States are spent to build and run institutions, and about 20 percent are spent on community corrections. Thus, 80 percent of the funds are spent on 30 percent of the correctional population, and 20 percent of the funds are left to accommodate 70 percent of that population.

SOURCE: Lauren E. Glaze and Seri Palla, "Probation and Parole in the United States, 2004," *Bureau of Justice Statistics Bulletin* (Washington, DC: GPO, U.S. Department of Justice, November 2005), p. 2; *Sourcebook of Criminal Justice Statistics Online*, www.albany.edu/sourcebook/, p. 13, Table 1.10.

A study of the attitudes of community correctional staff toward their work found that staff attitudes have been shifting away from the helping role and toward the law enforcement role. The findings of this study indicate the declining emphasis on rehabilitation in community corrections and suggest that the potential for role conflict may lessen as well.[2]

THE IMPORTANCE OF COMMUNITY CORRECTIONS

A discussion of the definition and scope of community corrections would not be complete without stressing how other components of criminal justice depend on community programs. It is not feasible to send all convicted persons—or even all felons—to jail or prison; resources are simply too limited. Were it

CAREERS IN CRIMINAL JUSTICE

U.S. Probation Officer

My name is Steve E. Whisenant and I am an officer with the Federal Corrections and Supervision Division of the U.S. Courts, better known as the U.S. Pretrial and Probation Office. I supervise the Hickory and Statesville, North Carolina, offices, two of the five U.S. Pretrial and Probation Offices that serve the Western District of North Carolina.

My interest in criminal justice was initiated because law enforcement offered a challenging and exciting work environment. At age 20, I began employment with the Burke County, North Carolina, Sheriff's Office. While working as a deputy sheriff, I enrolled in a criminal justice program at Western Piedmont Community College in Morgantown, North Carolina. After receiving a police science associate degree, I transferred to an evening program to earn a bachelor of science degree in social science/criminal justice from Gardner-Webb University in Boiling Springs, North Carolina.

During my service with the sheriff's office as a patrol officer, detective, and captain of law enforcement operations, I met the U.S. probation officer who worked in Burke County. After 9 rewarding years as a sheriff's deputy, the lure of a more stable work schedule and the absence of an election every 4 years made a position with the U.S. Probation Office appealing.

My career as a U.S. probation officer began in 1986. I worked in all three of our major units: (1) pretrial; (2) presentence writing; and (3) supervision. Each of these units offers unique and rewarding challenges. The pretrial unit completes background investigations, prepares written reports, and recommends release conditions for the magistrate's court. This unit also supervises defendants released under various bond conditions including electronic monitoring. Following a defendant's plea or verdict of guilty, the presentence unit conducts investigations and prepares detailed reports with sentencing recommendations for the district court. Its duties include contact with offenders, various law enforcement officers, U.S. attorneys, defense attorneys, and judges. The supervision unit supervises offenders who receive probation or who are released from imprisonment on parole or supervised release. They have contact with a number of persons including local law enforcement agencies, treatment providers, and offenders' employers, families, and acquaintances.

Some challenges faced by probation and pretrial staff include having little control over their workload numbers. Cases are generated by other federal agencies' arrests, releases from prison, and violations generated by the supervised offenders. Additionally, changes in the types of offenders and crimes committed, coupled with society's changing needs and expectations for supervising offenders require a successful organization to be flexible and innovative.

Our district's leadership solicits input from every employee in how to best accomplish the organization's mission. Opportunities to work on various committees and projects abound. Employees are encouraged to promote our organization's national vision statement to exemplify the highest standards in community corrections.

As a supervisor, I support a very competent and highly professional organization. My recommendation for anyone seeking a career within this organization is to excel in fields like criminal justice, psychology, sociology, or human relations.

What do you think are the most important abilities that one must have to be a successful probation officer?

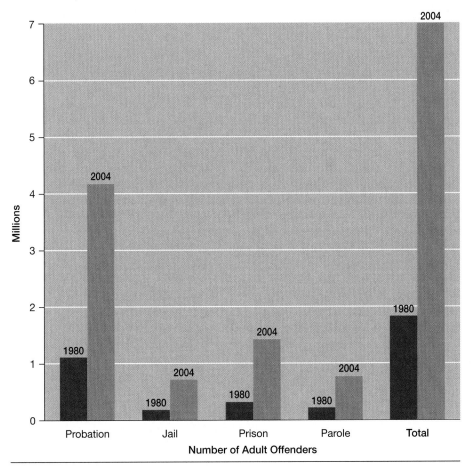

FIGURE 9.1   **Corrections Populations in the United States**

Number of Adult Offenders

Source: Lauren E. Glaze and Seri Palla, "Probation and Parole in the United States, 2004," *Bureau of Justice Statistics Bulletin* (Washington, DC: GPO, U.S. Department of Justice, November 2005), p. 1. Figures for 1980 are from Ann L. Pastore and Kathleen Maguire (eds.), *Sourcebook of Criminal Justice Statistics 1999* (Washington, DC: GPO, U.S. Department of Justice, Bureau of Justice Statistics, 2000), p. 484, Table 6. 1.

Increases in the Criminal Justice System

The percentage of adult citizens under control of the criminal justice system increased substantially over the last two and a half decades. It increased from a little more than 1 percent of the adult population in 1980 to more than 3 percent of all adults in 2004.

Source: Justice department statistician Allen J. Beck, quoted in "Parolees, Probationers Hit Record 4.5 million," *The Orlando Sentinel*, July 24, 2000, p. A10. Lauren E. Glaze and Seri Palla, "Probation and Parole in the United States, 2004," *Bureau of Justice Statistics Bulletin* (Washington, DC: GPO, U.S. Department of Justice, November 2005), p. 1.

not for the availability of community programs, the courts and institutional corrections would be overwhelmed by the sheer number of cases.

To illustrate, examine Figure 9.1, which presents data on the number of adults under the supervision of state and federal corrections agencies at the end of 1980, compared with the end of 2004. Note that at the end of 2004, the number of offenders in jail and prison combined is considerably smaller than the number serving community sentences on probation and parole. Approximately 5 million adults were on probation or parole at the end of 2004, compared with about 2 million in jail or prison.

Figure 9.1 also shows that large increases in the prison and jail populations have been accompanied by large increases in the probation and parole populations. Between 1980 and 2005, the probation population increased by 271 percent, and the parole population by 247 percent. The comparable increases in the prison and jail populations were 345 percent and 292 percent, respectively.

THINKING CRITICALLY

Which do you think is more beneficial to society: community corrections or prison? *Why?*

Probation

probation A sentence in which the offender, rather than being incarcerated, is retained in the community under the supervision of a probation agency and required to abide by certain rules and conditions to avoid incarceration.

Probation can be defined as a sentence imposed by the courts on offenders who have either pleaded guilty or been found guilty. Instead of being incarcerated, an offender placed on probation is retained in the community under the supervision of a probation agency. The offender is provided with supervision and services. Continuation of probation (that is, avoidance of incarceration) depends on the offender's compliance with the rules and conditions of the probation sentence. Probation is the most frequently imposed criminal sentence in the United States. Table 9.1 shows the states with the largest probation populations and the highest and lowest rates of persons under probation supervision per 100,000 adult U.S. residents at year-end 2004.

Probation should be distinguished from diversion, although, in broad terms, probation can be thought of as a type of posttrial diversion from incarceration. **Diversion** refers to organized and systematic efforts to remove people from the criminal justice process by placing them in programs that offer alternatives to the next, more restrictive stage of processing. Although diversion is commonly associated with juvenile justice, it is also used in adult criminal justice. Diversion can occur at any point from the initial police contact up to, and even in conjunction with, formal sentencing. For example, the police may divert a domestic violence case by making a referral to a family-in-crisis center instead of making an arrest. Instead of filing charges against an arrestee who is an alcoholic, a prosecutor may divert the case to a detoxification and counseling agency. Those are examples of *pretrial* diversion. *Posttrial* diversion—for example, probation—occurs when an offender who has pleaded guilty or been found guilty is placed in a program that is an alternative to a more restrictive sentence, such as incarceration.

diversion Organized, systematic efforts to remove individuals from further processing in criminal justice by placing them in alternative programs; diversion may be pretrial or posttrial.

There are five types of probation:

1. *Straight probation* occurs when an offender is sentenced only to probation, with no incarceration or other form of residential placement.
2. In *suspended-sentence probation,* the judge pronounces a jail or prison sentence but suspends the sentence on the condition that the offender performs well on probation.

TABLE 9.1	States with the Largest Probation Populations and the Highest and Lowest Rates of Persons Under Probation Supervision per 100,000 Adult U.S. Residents at Year-End 2004				
STATES WITH THE LARGEST PROBATION POPULATIONS	**NUMBER SUPERVISED**	**STATES WITH THE HIGHEST RATES OF SUPERVISION, 2004**	**PERSONS SUPERVISED PER 100,000 ADULT U.S. RESIDENTS***	**STATES WITH THE LOWEST RATES OF SUPERVISION, 2004**	**PERSONS SUPERVISED PER 100,000 ADULT U.S. RESIDENTS***
Texas	428,773	Massachusetts	3,301	New Hampshire	431
California	384,852	Rhode Island	3,117	West Virginia	488
Florida	281,170	Minnesota	2,959	Utah	621
Ohio	227,891	Delaware	2,940	Kansas	697
Michigan	176,083	Washington	2,654	Nevada	723
Pennsylvania	167,180	Texas	2,643	North Dakota	744
Massachusetts	163,471	Ohio	2,626	Virginia	769
Illinois	143,871	Indiana	2,511	New York	833
New Jersey	143,315	Michigan	2,323	Maine	901
Washington	125,222	Hawaii	2,224	South Dakota	926

Note: This table excludes the District of Columbia, a wholly urban jurisdiction, Georgia probation counts, which included case-based counts for private agencies, and Idaho probation counts in which estimates for misdemeanors were based on admissions.*Rates are computed using the U.S. adult resident population on July 1, 2004.

Source: Lauren E. Glaze and Seri Palla, "Probation and Parole in the United States, 2004," *Bureau of Justice Statistics Bulletin* (Washington, DC: GPO, U.S. Department of Justice, November 2005), p. 3, Table 1.

Alcoholics Anonymous and Al-Anon are frequently used as diversion programs for offenders who otherwise would be incarcerated. *Should some offenders be diverted from jail or prison? Why or why not?*

3. With a *split sentence,* the judge divides a single sentence into a relatively short jail term followed by probation supervision (for example, a 5-year probation sentence with the first 6 months to be served in jail).
4. *Shock probation* usually involves two sentences. The offender is initially sentenced to prison but is soon (perhaps after 120 days) recalled to court and placed on probation.
5. *Residential probation* involves placement of the probationer in a structured, but generally open, living environment, such as a halfway house. When residential probation is used, it is common for the probationer to spend the early part of the sentence in the residential facility and then, upon successful discharge, to complete the probation sentence living in the free community.

At year-end 2004, 56 percent of adults on probation in the United States were sentenced to straight probation, 24 percent were sentenced to suspended-sentence probation, 8 percent were sentenced to split-sentence probation, and the remainder were sentenced to other types of probation.[3]

A probation agency has three fundamental objectives. The first is to assist the court in matters pertaining to sentencing. This is accomplished by conducting inquiries and furnishing the court with information about offenders' backgrounds and current situations. The second objective is to promote community protection by supervising and monitoring the activities of persons sentenced to probation. The third objective is to promote the betterment of offenders by ensuring that they receive appropriate rehabilitation services. Thus, probation agencies work closely with the courts to assist offenders and, when possible, help them avoid incarceration without compromising the safety and security of the community.

HISTORICAL CONTEXT

Probation developed out of various practices used under English common law. One such practice, known as benefit of clergy, allowed certain accused individuals to appeal to the court for leniency in sentencing by reading from the Bible. Another practice was judicial reprieve, whereby a convicted offender could ask the judge to suspend the sentence on the condition that the offender display good future behavior. Those and other practices were important forerunners of modern probation.

The more immediate origins of modern probation lie in the efforts of John Augustus (1785–1859), a Boston shoemaker, who is considered the "father" of probation. Starting in the early 1840s, Augustus volunteered to stand bail and assume custody for select, less serious offenders in exchange for the judge's deferring the sentence. Augustus was responsible for monitoring offenders' activities and later reporting to the judge on their performance in the community. If the judge was satisfied with community performance, charges were dropped; if not, sentencing proceeded.

Influenced by the efforts of Augustus, Massachusetts passed the first formal probation law in 1878. By 1920, a majority of the states allowed probation. However, it was not until 1957 that all states had probation statutes. The federal probation system was established in 1925.[4] In more than 160 years, probation has grown from the efforts of a volunteer in Boston into the most frequently used sentence in criminal justice.

ADMINISTRATION

As mentioned earlier in the chapter, probation is administered in many different ways across the nation. The federal government administers its own probation system under the Administrative Office of the Courts, and each state has responsibility for determining how to administer probation. In some states, such as Kentucky, probation is administered at the state level as part of a department of corrections or other state agency. In other states, such as California and Indiana, probation administration is a local function. Still other states combine state and local administration. Under *probation subsidy*, which became popular in the 1960s, states agree to financially support locally administered probation services in exchange for the localities' not sentencing all their offenders to the state prison system. The goal is to give localities a financial incentive to retain offenders in their communities when possible.

There are other variations in the way probation is administered. Depending on the jurisdiction, administrative responsibility may lie with the executive branch, the judicial branch, or both. Adult and juvenile probation services can be administered separately or jointly, as can misdemeanor and felony services. Finally, probation administration can be combined with parole administration, or the two may be separate.

PROCESS AND PROCEDURES

A probation sentence can be viewed as a process with an identifiable beginning and end. The process consists of three basic stages:

1. Placement of an offender on probation by a judge.
2. Supervision and service delivery for the probationer by probation officers.
3. Termination of the probation.

Before and during the process, probation agency staff employ a number of important procedures, which will be examined in the following subsections.

PLACEMENT ON PROBATION In deciding whether an offender should be sentenced to probation, a judge usually considers a host of factors, such as statutes outlining eligibility for probation, structured sentencing guidelines (in jurisdictions where they are used), recommendations from the prosecuting

John Augustus

John Augustus, the prosperous Boston shoemaker who initiated the concept of probation, received no pay for his 18 years of court work. He used his own money and voluntary contributions from others to finance his efforts.

SOURCE: John Augustus, *A Report of the Labors of John Augustus, For the Last Ten Years, In Aid of the Unfortunate* (Boston: Wright and Hasty, 1852); reprinted as John Augustus, *First Probation Officer* (New York: National Probation Association, 1939).

Federal Probation Officers

As of June 2004, the Administrative Office of the U.S. Courts employed 4,593 probation officers. They supervise offenders placed on probation and supervised release and conduct presentence investigations to assess the risk to the community of future criminal behavior, the harm caused by the offense, the need for restitution, and the defendant's ability to pay restitution.

SOURCE: Brian A. Reaves, "Federal Law Enforcement Officers, 2004," *Bureau of Justice Statistics Bulletin* (Washington, DC: GPO, U.S. Department of Justice, July 2006), p. 3.

and defense attorneys, the offender's freedom or detention in jail before and during trial, the presentence investigation report prepared by the probation agency, and characteristics of the offender and offense. Judges ordinarily give great consideration to the seriousness of the current offense and the prior legal record of the offender. Cases involving more serious offenses or offenders with more extensive prior records are less likely to receive probation.

The Presentence Investigation The **presentence investigation (PSI)** is conducted by the probation agency at the request of the judge, usually during the period between the finding or plea of guilt and sentencing. In performing a PSI, a probation officer conducts an inquiry into the offender's past and current social and psychological functioning as well as the offender's prior criminal record. The main task of the inquiry is to estimate the risk the offender presents to the community and to determine the offender's treatment needs. The probation officer obtains the necessary information by interviewing the offender and others who know the offender, such as an employer, family members, and victims. The officer also reviews relevant documents and reports. The information is assembled into a PSI report, which is submitted to the court.

A sample PSI checklist appears in Table 9.2. There are no universally accepted standards for PSI report format and content. However, reports typically contain the following basic elements:

1. A face sheet of identifying demographic data.
2. A discussion of the instant or current offense as perceived by the police, the victim, and the offender.
3. A summary of the offender's prior legal record.
4. An overview of the offender's past and present social and psychological functioning.
5. The probation officer's evaluation of the offender and the officer's recommendation for an appropriate sentence.

The probation officer must convey the essential information in a concise and objective manner that supports the sentencing recommendation being offered.

Once prepared, the PSI report serves a variety of functions. It is useful in formulating supervision and treatment plans for persons who are given probation sentences. It also serves as the baseline for progress reports on probationers. When an offender is sent to prison, the report helps prison officials learn about and make decisions about the offender. However, the most well-known and immediate function of the PSI report is to assist judges in arriving at a proper sentence.

In most cases, there is a high degree of consistency between the sentencing recommendation in the PSI report and the actual sentence handed down by the judge. As shown in the accompanying Myth/Fact box, however, this does not mean that judges are always strongly influenced by probation officers' sentencing recommendations. In some cases, probation officers recommend sentences that they believe are consistent with judicial expectations.

TABLE 9.2	Checklist for Completing a Presentence Investigation Report

Face sheet of identifying demographic information:
   Name, aliases, and address
   Physical description
   Social security number
   Date and place of birth
   School history, occupation, marital status, family members

Instant offense:
   Offense and docket number
   Name(s) of codefendants, if any
   Prosecutor and defense attorney (names and addresses)
   Means of conviction (trial, plea agreement, etc.)
   Sentencing date

Presentence investigation:
   Defendant's version of events relating to offense
   Victim impact, restitution needs
   Jail time served in connection with offense
   Previous record
   Social history (family, friends, self-image)
   Educational history
   Marital history
   Employment history
   Economic situation
   Religious association
   Outside interests
   Health (including drug and alcohol use)
   Present attitudes of defendant
   Plea agreement (if any)
   Fiscal impact of sentencing option(s) to victim and state
   Psychiatric insights
   Statement of probation officer

Sentencing recommendation:

Probation plan:
   Length of probationary period
   Probationer reporting requirements
   Job placement
   Postemployment education training needs
   Community service requirements
   Other probation requirements

presentence investigation (PSI) An investigation conducted by a probation agency or other designated authority at the request of a court into the past behavior, family circumstances, and personality of an adult who has been convicted of a crime, to assist the court in determining the most appropriate sentence.

As part of a presentence investigation, a probation officer interviews an offender to obtain background information for the court. *What kinds of background information, if any, should influence the length and type of sentence? Why?*

Presentence Investigation Reports

Probation personnel wrote about 460,000 presentence investigation reports during 2000. Personnel in more than 70 percent of the agencies also supervised probationers. In 2000, probation staff in New York wrote the most PSIs (118,446), while staff in Maine wrote the fewest (92).

SOURCE: Camille Graham Camp and George M. Camp, *The 2001 Corrections Yearbook: Adult Systems* (Middletown, CT: Criminal Justice Institute, 2002), p. 221.

In addition to questions about the actual effect of PSI reports on sentencing decisions, another issue is whether courts should use PSIs conducted by private individuals and agencies rather than by probation agencies. Private PSIs became popular in the 1960s. Private individuals and agencies may conduct PSIs under contract with the defense or the court. Advocates of privately prepared PSIs argue that privatization reduces probation agency workloads and saves tax dollars (when such PSIs are commissioned by the defendant). Opponents argue that improper sentences may be recommended, that private PSIs can discriminate against the poor, and that the PSIs can reduce the credibility and funding of probation agencies.

The PSI report is usually the property of the court for which it is prepared. Once the report is submitted to the court, a copy is often provided to the defendant, defense counsel, and the prosecuting attorney. Both parties have the opportunity to review the report for accuracy and to bring any concerns to the court's attention. This process is known as "disclosure," and there has been controversy about it. Those who oppose the practice of disclosure maintain that people with important information may not make it available if the offender will see it and know who provided it. Those who support disclosure, on the other hand, argue that it is a matter of fairness that the offender be able to see the information on which the sentence is based, to ensure that it is accurate.

The Probation Order When an offender is sentenced to probation, the court files the appropriate documents indicating the length and conditions of the probation sentence (see Figure 9.2).

Although the length of probation sentences varies between jurisdictions and between cases, it is common for adults placed on probation for misdemeanor offenses to receive 1- to 2-year terms. Those convicted of felonies and sentenced to probation generally receive longer terms (for example, 5 years). Some states allow sentences of lifetime probation. In some cases, the court

FIGURE 9.2   Sample Probation Order

State of New Jersey

STANDARD CONDITIONS
of
ADULT PROBATION

PROBATIONER:

CASE FILE # /DOCKET #

COUNTY

The Court, believing that you are capable of living a useful and law-abiding life in the community, has sentenced you to probation for a period of _____ , beginning _____ _____ . While on probation, you will be under the supervision of a probation officer. You are required to comply with the conditions of probation listed below.

If there is probable cause to believ
probation, the Court may commit you t
probation, it may impose on you any se
nally convicted, up to and including the

1. You shall obey all federal, state, and
   officer if you are arrested or issued a

2. You shall report to your probation o

3. You shall answer truthfully all inquir

4. You shall permit your officer to visit

5. You shall submit at any time to a sea
   person, place of residence, vehicle, o

6. You shall promptly report any chang
   obtain permission from your probati
   may not leave the state of New Jersey
   tion officer.

7. You shall cooperate in any medical a
   probation officer recommends.

8. You shall submit to drug or alcohol t

9. You shall support your dependents a

10. You shall seek and maintain gainful
    your place of employment or find yo

11. You shall not have in your possessio
    2C: 39 et seq. If you possess a firear
    bation officer. In addition, if you pre
    your local police department or to a
    officer.

12. You shall make payments on any fine, penalty assessment, restitution or other financial obligation as provided by Court order. Failure to comply may result in further Court action, pursuant to *N.J.S.A.* 2C:46-2b; including attachment of your wages, filing of a civil judgment, and/or extension of your probation term.

| VCCB $_____ | DEDR $_____ | Fine $_____ |
| FLF $_____ | Restitution $_____ | Other $_____ |

Total Amount Ordered $_____ . This will be paid at the rate of $_____ per _____ . If no payment schedule is established, the total is due forthwith. If the offense occurred on or after February 1, 1993, a transaction fee of up to $1.00 is to be paid on each occasion when a payment or installment payment is made (*N.J.S.A.* 2C:46-1d.).

Special Conditions

You must also comply with the following special conditions of probation imposed by the Court in accordance with *N.J.S.A.* 2C: 45-1 et seq.:

☐ ___ Hours of Community Service
☐ ___ Days in the County Jail
☐ Driver's License Suspended for _____
☐ Obtain a General Equivalency Diploma (GED)
☐ Complete Court Ordered Treatment Program

☐ _____
☐ _____
☐ _____
☐ _____
☐ _____

Specify Program

I have received a copy of the rules and conditions of probation which have been read and explained to me. I understand the above rules and conditions of probation and that they apply to me, and I further understand that failure to comply on my part constitutes a violation of probation and will cause my return to Court. If I am arrested or detained in any other state or jurisdiction within the United States while I am on this term of probation, my signature below shall be deemed to be a waiver of extradition.

PROBATIONER   DATE

PROBATION OFFICER   DATE

ADDRESS: _____
_____

Telephone: _____

DOB: ___/___/___   SS#: _____

Driver's License #: _____

Myth | Fact

Myth	Fact
An essential function of the PSI report is to individualize justice by helping judges structure their sentencing decisions around the offender's unique circumstances.	In an important study, criminologist John Rosecrance found that experienced probation officers try to recommend sentences that are consistent with judicial expectations, given the seriousness of the offense and the offender's prior criminal record. Rosecrance found that officers selectively structure information in the report to support the recommendations they have already decided on. Information that is inconsistent with those recommendations is minimized in the report. Rosecrance's research implies that the PSI report merely gives the sentencing process a guise of individualized justice.

SOURCE: John Rosecrance, "Maintaining the Myth of Individualized Justice: Probation Presentence Reports," *Justice Quarterly* 5 (1988), pp. 235–56.

probation conditions Rules that specify what an offender is and is not to do during the course of a probation sentence.

restitution Money paid or services provided to victims, their survivors, or the community by a convicted offender to make up for the injury inflicted.

has the authority to grant early discharge from probation for commendable performance or to extend the term of probation.

Probation conditions are rules that specify what an offender is and is not to do during the course of a probation sentence. They are of crucial significance because the success or failure of the probationer is evaluated with respect to those rules. There are two types of conditions. *Standard* or *general conditions* apply to all persons placed on probation and pertain primarily to control and supervision of the offender. *Special conditions* are imposed at the discretion of the judge and probation officials and are designed to address the offender's particular situation. Special conditions frequently deal with treatment matters. For example, an offender may be ordered to participate in drug abuse counseling. Special conditions can be creative. For example, in Massachusetts, Connecticut, Texas, and a few other states, a special condition of probation for some offenders is participation in a reading program called "Changing Lives Through Literature." Eligible offenders agree to attend a class on a college campus each week for 10 or 12 weeks. They read and discuss such books as *The Old Man and the Sea, Deliverance, The Sea Wolf, Of Mice and Men,* and *One Flew Over the Cuckoo's Nest.* If they complete the program, their probation is reduced, usually by 3 months. An evaluation of the first four classes in Massachusetts found that only 18 percent of the men who completed the class committed crimes again, compared with 43 percent in a comparable group of offenders.[5]

In recent years it has become increasingly common for jurisdictions to include restitution orders as part of probation, as either a standard condition or a special condition. (See standard condition 12 in Figure 9.2.) **Restitution,** you may recall, usually means that the offender provides either the victim or the community with money or work service.

In some areas, the court may later amend or modify conditions outlined in the initial probation order. The conditions can be made more or less restrictive, depending on the probationer's behavior. However, to be legal, it is necessary for all conditions, regardless of when they are imposed, to be clear, reasonable, permitted by the Constitution, and related to the rehabilitation of the offender or the protection of society, or both.[6]

SUPERVISION AND SERVICE DELIVERY Once offenders have been placed on probation, the probation agency must shift attention to supervision and service delivery. At this point, probationers must be assigned to probation officers. In making assignments, it is important to match officer and probationer characteristics. For example, a manipulative probationer who poses a risk to community security might be assigned to an officer with a law enforcement orientation. An offender who poses little risk but has pressing treatment needs might be assigned to an officer with more of a helping background.

Because not all persons placed on probation require the same amounts and types of supervision and services, an important task is to determine what is appropriate for each client. In recent years, this task has been facilitated by the development of risk-and-needs-assessment instruments such as the one shown in Figure 9.3. The probation agency can more objectively determine

FIGURE 9.3   **Sample Risk and Needs Assessment Instrument**

DEPARTMENT OF CORRECTIONS
DIVISION OF PROBATION & PAROLE

Client No. _____   Client Name: _____   Officer No. _____

CLIENT RISK ASSESSMENT

Instructions: Enter numerical rating in box at right.

1. TOTAL NUMBER OF PRIOR FELONY CONVICTIONS:
   (include juvenile adjudications, if known)
   a. None .... Enter 0
   b. One .... Enter 2
   c. Two or more .... Enter 4

2. PRIOR NUMBER OF PROBATION/PAROLE SUPERVISION PERIODS:
   (include juvenile, if known)
   a. None .... Enter 0
   b. One or more .... Enter 4

3. PRIOR PROBATION/PAROLE REVOCATIONS:
   (adult only)
   a. None .... Enter 0
   b. One or more .... Enter 4

4. AGE AT FIRST KNOWN CONVICTION OR ADJUDICATION:
   (include juvenile, if known)
   a. 24 years or older .... Enter 0
   b. 20 through 23 years .... Enter 2
   c. 19 years or younger .... Enter 4

5. HISTORY OF ALCOHOL ABUSE:
   a. No history of abuse .... Enter 0
   b. Occasional or prior abuse .... Enter 2
   c. Frequent current abuse .... Enter 4

6. HISTORY OF OTHER SUBSTANCE ABUSE:
   (prior to incarceration for parolees)
   a. No history of abuse .... Enter 0
   b. Occasional or prior abuse .... Enter 1
   c. Frequent current abuse .... Enter 2

7. AMOUNT OF TIME EMPLOYED IN LAST 12 MONTHS:
   (prior to incarceration for parolees, based on 35 hr. week)
   a. 7 months or more .... Enter 0
   b. 4 months through 6 months .... Enter 1
   c. Less than 4 months .... Enter 2
   d. Not applicable .... Enter 0

8. AGENT IMPRESSION OF OFFENDER'S ATTITUDE:
   a. Motivated to change, receptive to assistance .... Enter 0
   b. Dependent or unwilling to accept responsibility .... Enter 3
   c. Rationalizes behavior, negative, not motivated to change ..... Enter 5

9. RECORD OF CONVICTION FOR SELECTED OFFENSES:
   (include current offense, add categories and enter total)
   a. None of the following ....Enter 0
   b. Burglary, Theft, Auto Theft, Robbery .... Add 2
   c. Forgery, Deceptive Practices (Fraud, Bad Check, Drugs) ...... Add 3

10. ASSAULTIVE OFFENSES:
    a. Crimes against persons which include use of weapon, physical force, threat of force, all sex crimes, and vehicular homicide
       ☐ Yes ☐ No

Total Score ☐☐
(Range 0-34)

CLIENT NEED ASSESSMENT

Instructions: Enter numerical rating in box at right.

1. ACADEMIC/VOCATIONAL SKILLS:
   a. High school or above skill level .... Enter 0
   b. Has vocational training, additional not needed/desired .... Enter 1
   c. Has some skills; additional needed/desired .... Enter 3
   d. No skills, training needed .... Enter 5

2. EMPLOYMENT:
   a. Satisfactory employment for 1 year or longer .... Enter 0
   b. Employed, no difficulties reported, or homemaker, student, retired, or disabled and unable to work .... Enter 1
   c. Part-time, seasonal, unstable employment or needs additional employment; unemployed, but has a skill .... Enter 4
   d. Unemployed & virtually unemployable; needs training ...... Enter 7

3. FINANCIAL STATUS:
   a. Longstanding pattern of self-sufficiency .... Enter 0
   b. No current difficulties .... Enter 1
   c. Situational or minor difficulties .... Enter 4
   d. Severe difficulties .... Enter 6

4. LIVING ARRANGEMENTS (Within last six months):
   a. Stable and supportive relationships with family or others in living group .... Enter 0
   b. Client lives alone or independently within another household . . Enter 1
   c. Client experiencing occasional, moderate interpersonal problems within living group ....Enter 4
   d. Client experiencing frequent and serious interpersonal problems within living group ....Enter 6

5. EMOTIONAL STABILITY:
   a. No symptoms of instability .... Enter 1
   b. Symptoms limit, but do not prohibit adequate functioning ...Enter 5
   c. Symptoms prohibit adequate functioning .... Enter 8

6. ALCOHOL USAGE (Current):
   a. No interference with functioning .... Enter 1
   b. Occasional abuse, some disruption of functioning, may need treatment .... Enter 4
   c. Frequent abuse, serious disruption, needs treatment......... Enter 7

7. OTHER SUBSTANCE USAGE (Current):
   a. No interference with functioning .... Enter 1
   b. Occasional substance abuse, some disruption of functioning, may need treatment .... Enter 4
   c. Frequent substance abuse, serious disruption, needs treatment .Enter 6

8. REASONING/INTELLECTUAL ABILITY:
   a. Able to function independently .... Enter 1
   b. Some need for assistance, potential for adequate adjustment . . Enter 4
   c. Deficiencies suggest limited ability to function independently . . Enter 7

9. HEALTH:
   a. Sound physical health, seldom ill .... Enter 1
   b. Handicap or illness interferes with functioning on a recurring basis .... Enter 2
   c. Serious handicap or chronic illness, needs frequent medical care .... Enter 3

10. AGENT'S IMPRESSION OF CLIENT'S NEEDS:
    a. None .... Enter 0
    b. Low .... Enter 1
    c. Moderate .... Enter 4
    d. High .... Enter 6

Total Score ☐☐
(Range 5-61)

SCORING AND OVERRIDE

Instruction: Check appropriate block
SCORE BASED SUPERVISION LEVEL ☐ Maximum ☐ Medium ☐ Minimum
Check if there is an override ☐ Override Explanation _____

FINAL CATEGORY OF SUPERVISION ☐ Maximum ☐ Medium ☐ Minimum

Date Supervision Level Assigned
MONTH   DAY   YEAR
☐☐ ☐☐ ☐☐☐☐

APPROVED (Supervisor Signature and Date) _____   Agent

the amount and type of supervision a probationer requires by examining the risk score. For instance, a probationer with a risk score in the maximum range might receive weekly contacts from the probation officer, whereas a probationer with a minimum-range risk score might receive monthly contacts. Likewise, the amount and kind of services are directed by the needs score. The point is to ensure that the highest levels of supervision are reserved for probationers who present the greatest risk to the community and that the highest levels of treatment services are reserved for those who present the greatest needs.

Once risk-and-needs assessment has been completed, the probation agency can formulate supervision and treatment plans for its clients. In effect, those plans further specify the conditions of probation and describe what is expected of probationers. Some of the requirements might include weekly contacts with the probation officer, random drug tests, weekly Alcoholics Anonymous meetings, or obtainment of a GED. Once supervision and treatment plans are set, the monitoring of probationers and the periodic filing of progress reports for the court can begin.

TERMINATION OF PROBATION Ultimately, the probation agency must make recommendations to the court about how probation is to be terminated. Clients who have generally fulfilled the conditions of their sentences and have served their terms are recommended for successful discharges. If a client has violated the conditions of probation, the probation agency may recommend **revocation,** which entails repealing the probation sentence and substituting a more restrictive sentence, such as a jail or prison term.

Revocation can be recommended for two general categories of violations. One category involves commission of new offenses. The second category, known as **technical violations,** involves failure to abide by the technical rules of the sentence. For example, a probationer might fail to report regularly to the probation officer or might leave the jurisdiction without the officer's consent. A recommendation of revocation is not automatic in the event of a violation, even if the violation is a new crime. Probation agents have considerable discretion on this matter. If the violation is a serious crime, a recommendation of revocation is very likely. On the other hand, a less serious offense or a technical violation may result in a warning, a tightening of probation conditions (perhaps the addition of a nightly curfew), or a brief jail term. Many probation agencies tend to let technical violations and petty offenses accumulate, with warnings and condition modifications along the way. However, repeated and excessive violations of this nature usually result in revocation recommendations.

If the probation agency asks the court to consider revocation of probation, the court must work within the guidelines of case law established by the U.S. Supreme Court. Two landmark cases are *Morrissey* v. *Brewer* and *Gagnon* v. *Scarpelli.* The Court's 1972 ruling in *Morrissey* v. *Brewer* dealt with parole revocation, but by virtue of the 1973 ruling in *Gagnon* v. *Scarpelli,* it also applies to probation revocation. *Morrissey* established that revocation is to be a two-stage process. In the first stage, there must be an informal, preliminary inquiry to establish probable cause that a violation has occurred. If probable cause is established, then in the second stage, there must be a formal court hearing to determine whether the violation warrants revocation. Offenders have certain rights at both stages. They include the right to notice of the hearing and charges, the right to be present at the hearing and to present evidence and witnesses, and the right to a detached and neutral hearing body.

revocation The repeal of a probation sentence or parole, and substitution of a more restrictive sentence, because of violation of probation or parole conditions.

technical violations Failure to abide by the technical rules or conditions of probation or parole (for example, not reporting regularly to the probation officer), as distinct from commission of a new criminal act.

Revocation

If probation is revoked, the judge can impose any sentence, including incarceration that was authorized for the offense for which the offender was originally placed on probation. Furthermore, the time already spent on probation, even though it may be several years, does not count as credit against the new sentence.

SOURCE: www.defgen.state.vt.us/lawbook/ch38.htm.

The *Gagnon* decision extended the requirements of *Morrissey* to include probationers and also addressed the issue of right to counsel, which the *Morrissey* decision did not address. In *Gagnon,* the Court ruled that there is no absolute right to counsel at revocation proceedings. Whether the offender is provided with counsel is determined on a case-by-case basis, and if there is no compelling reason for providing counsel, counsel is unnecessary. However, the Court added that in probation revocation hearings, counsel should be provided when probationers present a timely claim that (1) they did not commit the violation, or (2) there are mitigating circumstances making revocation inappropriate. In other situations, attorneys are allowed at revocation hearings as long as defendants provide their own, at no cost to the state.

ISSUES IN PROBATION

Probation is an evolving, changing field with many controversial issues. Several such issues have already been considered in this chapter. We now turn our attention to some additional issues.

PROBATION FEES Increases in the probation population have been accompanied by increases in the financial costs of probation. Consequently, a trend has emerged toward having probationers pay fees (for example, $30 per month) to help offset the cost of their supervision and treatment. Probation fees—or supervision fees, as they are sometimes called—are distinct from fines, court costs, and restitution.

Advocates of probation fees argue that fees can help contain the increasingly high costs of probation. Advocates further contend that because the majority of probationers can afford reasonable monthly fees, it is only fair that those probationers be held responsible for supporting at least part of the services they receive. On the other hand, critics charge that fees are unfair for indigent offenders and that offenders should not have to pay for services they are mandated to receive. Critics also claim that the administrative costs associated with collecting fees can exceed the amount of money collected. Given the skyrocketing number of persons on probation and the high cost of supervision and treatment, it seems unlikely that the trend toward probation fees will decrease in the near future.

LEGAL ISSUES: CONFIDENTIALITY AND PRIVACY Counseling is often an aspect of probation. It can be argued that to protect the counseling relationship, the information a probationer shares with a counselor should not be divulged to outside parties. However, it can also be argued that the counselor, who could be the offender's probation officer or a counselor to whom the probation officer has referred the offender, has a duty to divulge information about certain activities, particularly new crimes and technical violations, to appropriate authorities, such as police officers and judges. To what degree, then, should confidentiality govern the relationship between probation officer and probationer? In *Minnesota* v. *Murphy* (1984), the U.S. Supreme Court held that this relationship is not governed by the same degree of confidentiality as that between attorney and client or between physician and patient. Counselors

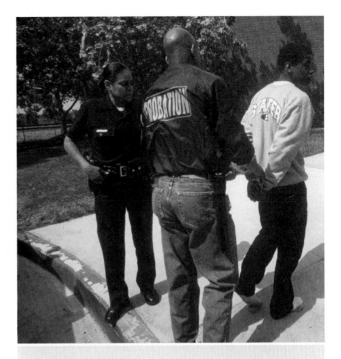

Committing a new crime or violating the conditions of probation may lead to revocation of probation. *How serious should a new crime or violation of probation conditions be before probation is revoked?*

Probation Fees

In 1929, Michigan became the first jurisdiction in the United States to impose probation supervision fees.

SOURCE: www.appa-net.org.

Probation Failures

During 2004, 15 percent of probationers who were discharged from supervision were incarcerated because of a rule violation or new offense. Another 4 percent of those discharged had absconded, and 10 percent were unsuccessful for other reasons.

Source: Lauren E. Glaze and Seri Palla, "Probation and Parole in the United States, 2004," *Bureau of Justice Statistics Bulletin* (Washington, DC: GPO, U.S. Department of Justice, November 2005), p. 6.

taking probationer referrals can reveal information about a probationer's illegal activities to the probation officer, and the probation officer can notify the police.

Another issue is the conditions under which a probation officer may search a probationer's home for evidence. In its decision in *Griffin* v. *Wisconsin* (1987), the Supreme Court held that a search warrant based on probable cause is unnecessary for a probation officer to search a probationer's home; reasonable grounds is a sufficient basis for the search. This decision and the *Murphy* decision show that probationers are generally entitled to fewer due process protections than free citizens who are not on probation. Whether this is just and fair is open to debate.

CASELOAD AND RECIDIVISM With the probation population growing each year, it is not unusual for probation officers in larger urban jurisdictions to have as many as 200 offenders in their caseloads. Large caseloads, in turn, have been criticized for contributing to recidivism (the return of probationers to crime during or after probation). Clearly, it is difficult for probation officers with large caseloads to give each case individual attention and to provide proper supervision and services for all their clients.

Interestingly, however, research has generally failed to confirm that smaller caseloads, such as 25 cases per officer, are associated with decreased recidivism. In the words of criminologist Jay S. Albanese and his colleagues, "It appears from many studies that the simple expedient of reducing caseloads will not of itself assure a reduction of recidivism."[7] In fact, it is reasonable to suppose that caseload reduction may sometimes be associated with an increase in recidivism detected by probation officers, because officers with smaller caseloads are able to scrutinize each probationer's activities more closely. There is some support for this supposition.[8] However, to the extent that (1) large caseloads promote recidivism because of the inability of probation officers to provide sufficient supervision and services and (2) smaller caseloads inflate recidivism numbers because of greater scrutiny of probationers' activities, probation agencies are in a no-win situation with respect to the issue of optimal caseload.

How effective is probation in controlling recidivism? First, it should be noted that researchers attempting to address this question confront a variety of difficulties. One difficulty is deciding whether to define probationer recidivism in terms of technical violations, arrests for new crimes, new convictions, or revocations. The definition employed affects the amount of recidivism uncovered. Another important difficulty lies in accurately determining whether it is the probation experience or some additional factor that is responsible for the recidivism observed among a group of probationers. A simple finding that recidivism is low among a group of probationers does not necessarily mean that probation is containing recidivism. Other factors, such as improvements in the local economy or the selection of low-risk offenders for probation, may be responsible. To date, many studies of probation effectiveness have not been designed well enough to rule out the role of factors other than the probation experience. Difficulties like these must be kept in mind when reviewing studies on probation recidivism.

Research suggests that probation is less effective than many people would like in curtailing rearrests of felony offenders. In a well-known California study by criminologist Joan Petersilia and her colleagues, approximately 1,700 felony offenders placed on probation were tracked for a period of 40 months. During this period, about two-thirds of the probationers were rearrested, more than half were reconvicted, and about one-third were sent to jail or prison.[9] In a similar but larger-scale study by the U.S. Justice Department, 79,000 felons sentenced to probation in 1986 by state courts in 17 states were followed for 3 years. By 1989, 43 percent of those felons had been arrested for new felonies: 8.5 percent were rearrested for violent offenses, 14.8 percent for property crimes, 14.1 percent for drug offenses, and the remainder for other crimes.[10]

In general, the recidivism figures associated with probation do not seem substantially higher or lower than those associated with incarceration. (See Chapter 8 for data on recidivism following incarceration.) Accordingly, it can be argued that when feasible, probation should be the preferred sentence because probation costs less than imprisonment. Of course, this logic holds true only if probation does not culminate in revocation followed by incarceration. If revocation and subsequent incarceration do occur, the combined costs of probation followed by incarceration may well exceed the cost of incarceration alone.

THINKING CRITICALLY

1. What do you think makes an offender an ideal candidate for probation?

2. What are the benefits and drawbacks of probation versus traditional jail time?

Parole

Recall that probation refers to the court-imposed sentence in which the offender, rather than being imprisoned, stays in the local community under the supervision of a probation officer. Two basic differences between probation and **parole** are that (1) parole is not a court-imposed sentence, and (2) parole is used with persons leaving prison. For purposes of definition, parole can be divided into two components. *Parole release* is one mechanism for releasing persons from prison. It involves releasing the inmate from prison, at the discretion of a parole board or similar paroling authority, before his or her sentence expires. *Parole supervision*, the aspect of parole that is often confused with probation, occurs after parole release. Essentially, parole supervision is a community-based continuation of the prison sentence. It involves supervision of the released offender in the community, often for a period roughly equal to the time remaining in the prison sentence.

Probation and parole supervision have similar features, which is why the two are sometimes confused. For example, both involve specific rules and conditions that offenders must follow to avoid revocation, and both entail providing offenders with supervision and services. In some instances, one officer may supervise both probationers and parolees. However, *probationer* and *parolee* are two distinct legal statuses. It is not uncommon for parole rules and conditions to be somewhat stricter and for officers to be less tolerant of violations committed by parolees; revocation of parole may be sought quickly, even for a technical parole violation. In addition, parolees often face greater adjustment problems because of the stigma attached to their prison records and because of the time they have spent away from the free community.

Just as there are different types of probation (suspended-sentence probation, split-sentence probation, etc.), there are two general types of parole. In *straight parole,* offenders are released from prison directly into the community under the supervision of the parole agency. In *residential parole,* offenders serve part of the parole term in a community residential facility or halfway house. There are two variants of residential parole. In the first variant, offenders are released from prison into the residential facility, where they spend a temporary, transitional period before returning home. The idea is to make the release process a gradual one. In the second variant, a person who violates the conditions of parole is kept on parole and is placed in the residential

parole A method of prison release whereby inmates are released at the discretion of a board or other authority before having completed their entire sentences; can also refer to the community supervision received upon release.

facility for a period of structured living, rather than having parole revoked and being returned to prison.

There are four fundamental objectives of parole. Two of these are also objectives of probation and were discussed earlier in this chapter. As with probation, parole is meant to provide community safety and to promote offender betterment and reintegration into society. The other two objectives of parole are more subtle, often unstated, but no less important. They are to (1) relieve and contain prison crowding and (2) control the behavior of prison inmates.

Since its inception parole has functioned as a "safety valve" for institutional corrections; crowding levels can be better contained if more inmates are

CAREERS IN CRIMINAL JUSTICE

Parole Agent

My name is Arthur J. Ramirez and I am a Parole Agent III (PA III) for the California State Department of Corrections (CDC) Parole and Community Services Division (P&CSD). Since 1983 I have also taught undergraduate and graduate criminal justice courses at California State University, Long Beach. I hold a bachelor of science degree in criminal justice, two master's degrees (community clinical psychology and criminal justice), as well as a doctorate degree in criminology. I chose to work with ex-felons in order to be in a unique position to improve the quality of life in our society.

As a PA III, I provide supervisory direction with respect to the philosophies, policies, and procedures of the CDC for the Long Beach I Parole Unit. I also complete a number of adjunct assignments for the department. A typical day includes reviewing my management formation system to ensure that the operations of the parole unit run smoothly. I hold case conferences with parole agents and/or review reports, written by them, related to the progress of parolees or parole violations committed by them. I review each case in order to determine the appropriate action. The actions may include reviewing cases for discharge from parole, referring parolees to community programs that are in line with their needs, approving funds to assist parolees, and reviewing activity reports to continue parolees on parole as a disposition after a parole violation. This allows the parolee to remain in the community and is often accompanied with a referral to a social program. I also make decisions to return parolees back into custody for parole violations. This includes reviewing the violation reports prior to submitting them to the Board of Prison Terms. Additionally, I review reports to initiate warrants for the arrest of

parolees when they abscond from parole. Another typical day may also include traveling to Sacramento to attend a Commission on Correctional Peace Officer Standards and Training (CPOST) Curriculum Review Committee meeting. In this capacity, I review lesson plans submitted by youth and adult corrections agencies statewide and health care services to ensure that they are in line with the professional training standards established and approved by CPOST.

It is very rewarding to see parolees making a positive adjustment in their reintegration into society from imprisonment. It is also frustrating to see them being returned to prison for parole violations despite effective casework by a parole agent. Our society is currently faced with the challenge to provide the highest quality criminal justice services in order to respond to our criminal justice problems. I enjoy being a part of this process at the local and state levels. The field of criminal justice provides many career position opportunities for students. I fully believe that students today need to plan for their future careers systematically. Students interested in working in the field of criminal justice need to contact practicing professionals in the community in order to find out more about the position opportunities available in the field. I also recommend that students interested in working in parole should volunteer or enroll in an internship program with an agency that works with parolees or offenders. This will assist them in deciding whether a career in parole is for them.

Compare the information above with the career box on probation officers. Which position would you be more attracted to? Why?

granted early release. One of the clearest manifestations of this objective is the growing popularity of emergency release laws that permit executive authorities (usually governors) to accelerate parole eligibility for selected inmates when prison crowding reaches a particular level. Parole also gives prison officials some control over the behavior of inmates. The prospect of early release gives inmates an incentive to cooperate with prison officials and to avoid infractions of prison rules.

HISTORICAL CONTEXT

As with probation, parole emerged from earlier practices. One of those is the *tickets-of-leave* concept pioneered around the mid-1800s by Captain Alexander Machonochie off the coast of Australia and by Sir Walter Crofton in Ireland. Under this concept, inmates, after serving a portion of their sentences and exhibiting good performance in prison, could be granted tickets of leave, whereby they were released into the community under supervision. Release was made conditional on continuation of good behavior, so the practice was also known as conditional pardon.

The idea of releasing some prisoners early to community supervision and making release contingent on good conduct found its way to the United States. The idea was initially implemented, along with indeterminate sentencing, in the 1870s by Zebulon Brockway at Elmira Reformatory in New York. Brockway's system allowed prison officials to grant parole release to inmates they perceived as ready for release. Parole spread rapidly after its inception at Elmira. By the turn of the century, 20 states had provisions for parole, and by 1920, the majority of states had adopted such provisions.[11]

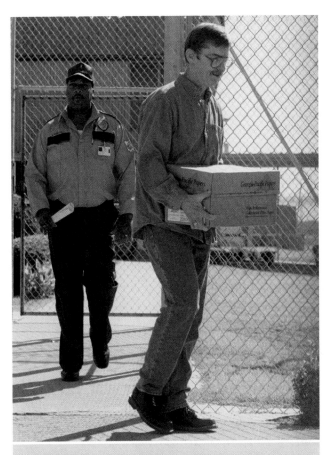

Some offenders are released on parole before the end of their sentences, on the condition that they remain law-abiding and follow the rules designed to control their movement and to help them adjust to society. *Should parole be abolished? Why or why not?*

ADMINISTRATION

It is helpful to divide parole administration into two areas. The first area is the parole board, or a similar paroling authority, which makes parole release decisions. The second is the parole field service agency, which provides parole supervision in the community after release.

Parole administration, like probation administration, exhibits much variation across the nation. At the federal level, the paroling authority is the United States Parole Commission, and field services are administered by the Administrative Office of the Courts. Each state is responsible for administering its own parole system. Parole at the state level is generally an executive branch function, and each state has its own paroling authority. In most states, parole boards and field service agencies are administratively separate, although in some states, the board administers field services.[12] Whether probation and parole field services are jointly administered by the same government agency varies among the states. It has become quite common, however, for states to combine probation and parole administration. In Kentucky, for example, the same unit of the department of corrections administers both.

Federal Parole

Anyone who has committed a federal crime after November 1, 1987, is no longer eligible for federal parole. (It has been abolished.) Such persons now must serve their entire sentences, less a maximum of 54 days a year good time, if granted. Those people sentenced or under supervision before November 1, 1987, are still eligible for federal parole supervision.

SOURCE: United States Parole Commission at www.usdoj.gov/uspc/mission.html.

Another area of difference between states is whether the paroling authority or board is (1) administratively autonomous and independent of prison officials or (2) administratively consolidated with the department of corrections. Most parole boards are autonomous.[13]

In many ways the parole board is the centerpiece of parole administration; the board is very influential in establishing a jurisdiction's parole policies. A national survey of parole boards found that in most states, the governor, subject to legislative confirmation, appoints parole board members. Appointment terms in most states are 4 to 6 years, and the vast majority of states use renewable appointments. The professional qualifications required for appointment differ across states. Interestingly, law in many jurisdictions requires no minimum professional qualifications. The number of parole board members also varies by state, with five and seven members being common. A minority of states employ part-time parole board members. Most of the nations' board members are white, approximately one-quarter are female, and the average age of board members is about 50.[14]

PROCESS AND PROCEDURES

Besides helping establish the jurisdiction's parole policies, the parole board is generally responsible for managing parole release processes and making decisions to terminate parole supervision.

THE PAROLE BOARD—RELEASE AND TERMINATION Prior to appearing before the parole authority for a parole-grant hearing, a prisoner must first become eligible for parole and complete a parole plan describing such things as where he or she plans to live and work after release. In addition, prison staff usually prepare a preparole report for the parole board. The report summarizes the characteristics of the inmate and his or her offense, reviews the inmate's adjustment to prison and his or her progress toward rehabilitation, and presents the inmate's parole plan. Reports sometimes contain a recommendation about whether the inmate should be paroled.

Depending on the jurisdiction and the particular case, the actual parole-grant hearing can be conducted by the full parole board, a partial board, or representatives of the board known as examiners or hearing officers. Roughly half of the states rely on hearing officers.[15] Other concerned parties, such as prison staff, prosecuting attorneys, and victims, may also be present. Parole hearings are typically quite short and routine. Parole authorities review relevant documents, such as the inmate's parole plan, the preparole report, and victim statements, and often interview the inmate. Authorities then vote on whether to grant or to deny parole release. In more than half of the states, the inmate is notified of the outcome of voting at the hearing or immediately thereafter. In the remaining states, notification time frames range from 1 week to more than 30 days.[16] If parole is denied, the inmate is automatically eligible for a future hearing.

Increasingly, parole authorities are using structured instruments called **parole guidelines** to estimate the probability of recidivism and to direct their release decisions. Those guidelines are similar to the sentencing guidelines used by judges and the risk-and-needs-assessment instruments used in probation work. Only about half the jurisdictions employ parole guidelines, and even in those jurisdictions, parole authorities often have the discretion to override guideline recommendations.[17] A sample parole guideline instrument, developed by the United States Parole Commission, is presented in Figure 9.4.

Parole authorities consider a variety of factors in determining whether to grant or to deny an inmate parole. Furthermore, those factors tend to be

Charles Manson

In April 2002, Charles Manson, then 67, was denied parole for the tenth time. He was sentenced to death in 1970 for his role in the 1969 Tate-LaBianca murders. When the Supreme Court declared capital punishment unconstitutional in 1972, his death sentence was automatically commuted to life imprisonment with opportunity for parole. His next parole hearing is scheduled for 2007.

SOURCE: "Charles Manson Denied 10th Parole Bid," CBSNEWS.com at www.cbsnews.com/stories/2002/04/25/national/main507237.shtml.

parole guidelines Structured instruments used to estimate the probability of parole recidivism and to direct the release decisions of parole boards.

| FIGURE 9.4 | Parole Guideline Instrument |

Item A.   PRIOR CONVICTIONS/ADJUDICATIONS
(ADULT OR JUVENILE) .... ❑
None .... = 3
One .... = 2
Two or three .... = 1
Four or more .... = 0

Item B.   PRIOR COMMITMENT(S) OF MORE THAN
THIRTY DAYS (ADULT OR JUVENILE) .... ❑
None .... = 3
One .... = 2
Three or more .... = 0

Item C.   AGE AT CURRENT OFFENSE/PRIOR
COMMITMENTS .... ❑
Age at commencement of the current offense:
26 years of age or more .... = 2*
20–25 years of age .... = 1*
19 years of age or less .... = 0
*EXCEPTION: If five or more prior commitments of
more than thirty days (adult or juvenile), place an "x"
here___ and score this item .... = 0

Item D.   RECENT COMMITMENT-FREE PERIOD
(THREE YEARS) .... ❑
No prior commitment of more than thirty days (adult
or juvenile) or released to the community from last
such commitment at least three years prior to the
commencement of the current offense .... = 1
Otherwise .... = 0

Item E.   PROBATION/PAROLE/CONFINEMENT/ESCAPE
STATUS VIOLATOR THIS TIME .... ❑
Neither on probation, parole, confinement, or
escape status at the time of the current offense, nor
committed as a probation, parole, confinement, or
escape status violator this time .... = 1
Otherwise .... = 0

Item F.   HEROIN/OPIATE DEPENDENCE .... ❑
No history of heroin/opiate dependency ... = 1
Otherwise .... = 0

TOTAL SCORE .... ❑

Source: Paul F. Cromwell and George C. Hellinger, *Community-Based Corrections*, 3rd ed. (St. Paul, MN: West, 1994), p. 232

assigned different levels of importance. A recent analysis of national data found that the four most important factors, in order, are as follows:

1. Seriousness of the current offense.
2. History of prior violent behavior.
3. Prior felony convictions.
4. Use of a firearm in committing the current offense.

Other relevant factors include the number of prior incarcerations, prior adjustment on parole, prison disciplinary record, psychological reports, and victim input.[18]

Due process in parole release decisions was addressed by the U.S. Supreme Court in *Greenholtz* v. *Inmates of the Nebraska Penal and Correctional Complex* (1979). Noting that parole release is an act of grace, the Court held that release on parole is distinct from parole revocation. Thus, the Court declined to apply the provisions outlined in *Morrissey* v. *Brewer*, discussed earlier in this chapter, to parole release. Consequently, what constitutes acceptable due process in release decision making is largely case-specific. Jurisdictions vary considerably in their due process provisions for parole hearings. Most of the jurisdictions allow inmates to be represented by attorneys.[19]

Once inmates receive parole release, they begin the period of parole supervision, discussed later, which continues until it is terminated. In addition to its responsibility for release decisions, the parole board is responsible for parole termination decisions. In most jurisdictions, the board can discharge individuals from parole supervision; this is commonly done upon the recommendation of the parole supervision agency. Alternatively, if no board action is taken, the individual is discharged from parole upon expiration of the legal sentence.

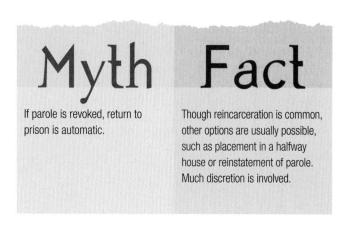

Myth If parole is revoked, return to prison is automatic.

Fact Though reincarceration is common, other options are usually possible, such as placement in a halfway house or reinstatement of parole. Much discretion is involved.

Parole revocation is also the responsibility of the parole board and can occur in response to new crimes or technical violations. Parole revocation is quite similar to probation revocation and is governed by the same case law (*Morrissey* v. *Brewer* and *Gagnon* v. *Scarpelli*). As is true in the field of probation, parole officers enjoy considerable discretion when deciding whether to recommend revocation for violations. If revocation is sought, the two-stage hearing process required under *Morrissey* becomes applicable. Although parole authorities consider various factors in determining whether to revoke parole, research indicates that the two most important factors are the seriousness of the violation and the recommendation of the supervising parole officer.[20]

FIELD SERVICES—SUPERVISION AND SERVICE DELIVERY Traditionally, most parole supervision or field service agencies were administered by parole boards. This situation has changed dramatically since the 1960s. Currently, most field service agencies are administratively separate from the parole board.[21] In most of those jurisdictions, parole supervision is administered by the department of corrections. Nevertheless, the basic task of field service agencies has remained constant through the years—to provide control and assistance for persons reentering the community from prison.

Virtually everything that was stated earlier in this chapter about probation supervision and service delivery applies to parole supervision and service delivery. The subtle differences between the two are overshadowed by the many similarities. However, one difference warrants mention. Specialization is more common in parole than in probation supervision. Under specialization, offenders who pose a similar threat to public safety or those who share similar treatment needs are grouped together and assigned to the same officers. Specialization by parole officers is used in slightly more than half the jurisdictions. The two most common areas for specialization are with sex offenders and substance-abusing offenders.[22]

Social scientist Richard McCleary conducted what is considered a classic sociological study of a parole supervision agency.[23] In his book *Dangerous Men*, McCleary observes that parole officers are very concerned with avoiding "trouble" from parolees. Trouble is defined broadly as anything that runs counter to the status quo of the parole agency. Trouble can threaten the agency's public image, thus bringing the agency pressure—and possibly increased structure—from political officials. The likelihood of trouble is reduced to the extent that officers can anticipate what clients might do in response to threats of various punishments and rewards from officers. "Dangerous men" are parolees who do not respond predictably to officers' threats and promises. Dangerous men are not necessarily prone to violent behavior; they are merely unpredictable. Because unpredictability implies possible trouble, officers try to identify dangerous men as soon as possible in the supervision process. The dangerous-man label is used sparingly because it means greater supervision and more documentation and paperwork for officers. However, the label can protect the supervising officer and the agency from subsequent criticism because, early on, it conveys that problems may be expected from a particular parolee. Concerned parties in the parole bureaucracy are alerted to what might happen, and the potential for "surprises" is reduced. Once parolees have acquired the dangerous-man label, the agency is quick to seek reasons to revoke their paroles. McCleary's research underscores the crucial significance of agency bureaucratic dynamics in shaping supervision practices.

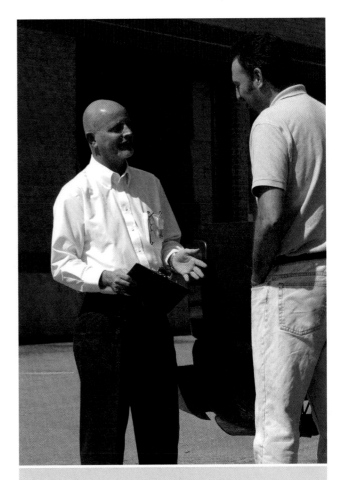

Parole officers frequently meet their clients at the clients' workplaces. *What problems, if any, might be created by this practice?*

PAROLE ISSUES

Since the 1970s discretionary parole release has been among the most controversial issues in criminal justice. Proponents of parole release argue, for example, that early release provisions are essential for controlling prisoners' behavior and for containing institutional crowding. However, several criticisms have been directed at parole release. Some critics claim that parole undermines both retribution and deterrence because offenders are permitted to leave prison early, sometimes many years before finishing their maximum sentences. Similarly, critics argue that because prisons generally fail to reform offenders and it is impossible for parole boards to accurately predict which offenders will commit new crimes, parole does not sufficiently guarantee public safety. Other critics believe that parole is unfair to offenders. Those opponents charge that parole leads to significant disparities in time served in prison for offenders who should be serving equal amounts of time. For example, two offenders in the same jurisdiction with very similar prior legal backgrounds may be convicted of committing armed robbery under very similar circumstances. One offender may serve 5 years in prison and receive parole, whereas

Public Opinion

According to a public opinion poll, nearly two-thirds of all Americans support allowing prisoners to earn early release through good behavior and participation in educational and work programs. However, only 21 percent of Americans are willing to give parole boards more authority to release offenders early, and 75 percent of Americans do not want to parole prisoners who have been paroled before for a serious crime.

Source: Timothy J. Flanagan, "Reform or Punish: Americans' Views of the Correctional System," in T. J. Flanagan and D. R. Longmire (eds.), *Americans View Crime and Justice: A National Public Opinion Survey* (Thousand Oaks, CA: Sage, 1996), p. 87.

the other may serve twice as long before release. Another contention of critics is that linking the degree of participation in prison treatment programs to the possibility of early parole amounts to subtly coercing inmates into programs that are often of questionable effectiveness.

Those and other criticisms helped persuade a number of jurisdictions to curtail discretionary parole release. Instead, they moved from indeterminate sentencing to determinate sentencing, decreased reliance on parole release and increased reliance on mandatory release, and devised both sentencing and parole guidelines. There were even forceful calls and some initiatives undertaken to completely abolish parole release, although the movement to abolish parole seems to have peaked.[24] Currently, 18 states (Arizona, 1994; Arkansas, 1994; California, 1976 [but see below]; Delaware, 1990; Florida, 1983; Illinois, 1978; Indiana, 1977; Kansas, 1993; Maine, 1975; Minnesota, 1980; Mississippi, 1995; North Carolina, 1994; Ohio, 1996; Oregon, 1989; South Dakota, 1996; Virginia, 1995; Washington, 1984; and Wisconsin, 1999) and the federal government have abolished early release by discretion of a parole board for all offenders. However, parole boards still have discretion over inmates who were sentenced for crimes committed prior to the effective date of the law that eliminated parole board release. A few other states have abolished parole release for certain violent or felony offenders (Alaska, Georgia, Louisiana, Massachusetts, Maryland, Missouri, New Jersey, New York, Oklahoma, South Carolina, and Tennessee). California allows discretionary release by a parole board only for offenders with indeterminate life sentences.[25] It is important to note that while discretionary release from prison by a parole board has been eliminated by some states, postrelease supervision still exists and is generally referred to as community or supervised release. Parole boards, in various forms, have the responsibility to set conditions of release for offenders under community or supervised release, the authority to return an offender to prison for violating the conditions of supervised release, and the power to grant parole for medical reasons.[26]

Besides the issue of whether parole release should exist, there are a number of other pressing concerns surrounding parole. They include legal issues, strained parole resources, and parolee adjustment and recidivism.

Legal Issues There are two general categories of legal issues that relate to parole: (1) parolees' civil rights and (2) the liabilities of parole officials.

Individuals forfeit a variety of civil rights when they are convicted of a felony. Some of those include the right to hold public office and certain other jobs, the right to jury service, and the right to obtain some types of licenses and insurance. Although the specific rights forfeited vary by jurisdiction, in many instances parolees must seek court action to restore their rights following release from incarceration. Only a few jurisdictions grant their parole boards authority to restore ex-offenders' rights.[27]

People who support denying released inmates certain rights argue that the practice is necessary to preserve public safety and maintain high moral standards in society. Opponents argue that it is unfair to continue penalizing individuals who have "paid their debts." They point out that denial of civil liberties contributes to poor adjustment on parole. Given the current posture of the nation toward felons and ex-felons, it seems unlikely, at least in the foreseeable future, that the majority of persons coming out of prison will have their rights fully restored.

Can parole board officials and field service agents be held legally liable if a parolee's actions cause harm to a victim or victims? The answer is a qualified yes. Even though the vast majority of paroling authorities enjoy some type of immunity from liability (through constitution, statute, or case law), such immunity has been eroding in recent years.

According to attorney and criminal justice professor John Watkins, Jr., three central elements must be proven to establish liability on the part of parole and probation officials:

1. The existence of a legal duty owed the public.
2. Evidence of a breach of the required standard of duty.
3. An injury or damage to a person or group proximately caused by the breach of duty.

Watkins further observes that as a general rule, tort liability applies to injuries, or damages, caused by the negligent or improper performance of ministerial functions, but not to injuries caused by unsatisfactory performance of discretionary functions. A *discretionary* function is one "that may involve a series of possible choices from a wide array of alternatives, none of which may be absolutely called for in a particular situation." A *ministerial* function is "one regarding which nothing is left to discretion—a simple and definite duty imposed by law, and arising under conditions admitted or proved to exist."[28] An example of a breach of a ministerial function would be if a parole board were to completely disregard parole guidelines that the board is legally bound to consider before releasing inmates. Thus, if parole and probation officials wish to minimize the likelihood of being held liable, those officials should determine what is legally required of them in their jurisdiction and make good faith efforts to abide by those requirements.

STRAINED PAROLE RESOURCES Parole supervision agencies across the nation are currently attempting to manage record numbers of parolees. On December 31, 2004, for example, 765,355 adults were under active parole supervision. This represents an increase of about 44 percent over the total number of parolees on December 31, 1990.[29] Table 9.3 shows the states with the largest parole populations and the highest and lowest rates of persons under parole supervision per 100,000 adult U.S. residents at year-end 2004. Moreover, an increasingly large proportion of parolees has been released from prison early because of pressures to relieve institutional crowding, rather than because those persons have been judged good candidates for parole. Such parolees often require above-average levels of supervision and services. Because most

Parole Officer Caseloads

The average parole officer caseload for 18 jurisdictions with separate probation and parole agencies during 2003 was 60. The range was from a low of 5 in Wyoming to a high of 117 in Hawaii. The average caseload in the 23 jurisdictions with combined probation and parole agencies was 92. The range was from 52 in West Virginia to 225 in Vermont. In jurisdictions with separate probation and parole agencies, probation caseloads are nearly always larger than parole caseloads—frequently much larger.

SOURCE: *American Correctional Association 2004 Directory: Adult and Juvenile Correctional Departments, Institutions, Agencies and Probation and Parole Authorities* (Lanham, MD: American Correctional Association, 2004), p. 75.

TABLE 9.3	States with the Largest Parole Populations and the Highest and Lowest Rates of Persons Under Parole Supervision per 100,000 Adult U.S. Residents at Year-End 2004				
STATES WITH THE LARGEST PAROLE POPULATIONS		**STATES WITH THE HIGHEST RATES OF SUPERVISION, 2004**	**PERSONS SUPERVISED PER 100,000 ADULT U.S. RESIDENTS***	**STATES WITH THE LOWEST RATES OF SUPERVISION, 2004**	**PERSONS SUPERVISED PER 100,000 ADULT U.S. RESIDENTS***
California	110,261	Pennsylvania	806	Washington	3
Texas	102,072	Oregon	761	Maine	3
Pennsylvania	77,175	Louisiana	728	Florida	36
New York	54,524	Arkansas	715	Rhode Island	44
Illinois	34,277	Texas	629	North Carolina	45
Louisiana	24,387	California	419	North Dakota	48
Georgia	23,344	Missouri	398	Nebraska	61
Michigan	20,924	South Dakota	382	Virginia	78
Oregon	20,858	New York	372	Massachusetts	78
Ohio	18,882	Illinois	362	Delaware	85

Note: This table excludes the District of Columbia.
*Rates are computed using the U.S. adult resident population on July 1, 2004.

Source: Lauren E. Glaze and Seri Palla, "Probation and Parole Populations in the United States, 2004," *Bureau of Justice Statistics Bulletin* (Washington, DC: GPO, U.S. Department of Justice, November 2005), p. 3, Table 1.

jurisdictions are facing pressure to expand prison space, it is not surprising that parole resources, such as budgets and staffing, have failed to keep pace with those developments.

The long-term implications of this predicament are often unappreciated. Parolee recidivism is normally quite high, partly because of the strained resources of parole agencies. The typical public and political response to high parolee recidivism is to demand a "get-tough" stance that culminates in the return of large numbers of parolees to prison. This exacerbates both prison crowding and the tendency to rely on parole release to relieve crowding. The result is further strain on parole resources and, consequently, further recidivism.

PAROLEE ADJUSTMENT AND RECIDIVISM A key to successful community adjustment for inmates leaving prison is **reintegration,** which means rebuilding former prosocial ties to the community and establishing new ties. An important part of reintegration is finding a satisfactory job and obtaining adequate subsistence funds through legal means.

The stigma of a prison record can result in grim employment prospects, especially without the assistance of the parole agency. Yet, research suggests that obtaining employment improves adjustment to community life. In a study of the effects of postrelease employment on the emotional well-being of a sample of ex-felons in Texas and Georgia, it was found that employment enhanced emotional well-being by providing wages and improving perceptions of self-worth. The research discovered that sustained unemployment caused emotional distress. This distress reduced the motivation of releasees to search for jobs. In the words of the study's author, "Unemployment fed on itself by creating psychological stress which in turn reduced effectiveness in finding work."[30] Related evidence suggests that providing newly released ex-inmates with temporary unemployment benefits can decrease the recidivism rate, although it is important that such benefits not create a work disincentive.[31]

Research spanning three decades shows that fewer than half of all state prison inmates released on parole successfully complete their term of supervision.[32] For example, during the 1990s, the percentage of successful parole discharges ranged from about 42 percent to about 49 percent. In 2004 (the latest year for which data were available), 46 percent of state parolees successfully completed their term of supervision, 39 percent were returned to prison or jail, 10 percent absconded, and the remainder failed to successfully meet the conditions of supervision but were discharged without incarceration.

States vary widely in their rates of success (see Table 9.4). For example, in 1999, both Massachusetts and Mississippi reported 83 percent success rates, while Utah (18.5 percent) and California (21 percent) had the lowest rates. Differences in success rates can be attributed to a number of factors such as variations in the parole populations (for example, age at release, criminal history, and most serious offense), the level of supervision, and parole agency policies on the revocation of technical violators.

The research shows that inmates released from prison on parole for the first time are more likely to succeed than re-releases. Re-releases are inmates who are being discharged from prison on parole who have served time for a previous violation of parole or conditional release or a new offense committed while under previous parole supervision. In 1999, for example, 63.5 percent of first releases were successful, compared to 21 percent of re-releases (see Table 9.5). However, the success rate for first-time releases declined the longer the inmate had been in prison. In 1999, 74 percent of first-time releases who had been in prison less than 12 months succeeded on parole, compared to 62 percent of first-time releases who had been in prison for 5 years or more (see Table 9.5).

---

reintegration The process of rebuilding former ties to the community and establishing new ties after release from prison.

Parole Violations

A 40 percent increase in the number of offenders returned to prison for parole violations is one of the reasons for the growth in the state prison population between 1990 and 2005. In 2004, 187,000 of the offenders entering state prison had violated the conditions of their parole, up from 133,870 in 1990. In 2004, 39 percent of the inmates had their paroles revoked because either of a rule violation or new offense. An additional 10 percent had absconded and the remainder had failed to successfully meet the conditions of supervision but were discharged without incarceration.

SOURCE: Lauren E. Glaze and Seri Palla, "Probation and Parole in the United States, 2004," *Bureau of Justice Statistics Bulletin* (Washington, DC: U.S. Department of Justice, November 2005), p. 9.

TABLE 9.4	**Percent Successful Among State Parole Discharges, by State, 1990, 1995, and 1999**

REGION AND JURISDICTION	PERCENT SUCCESSFUL OF ALL PAROLE DISCHARGES		
	1990	1995	1999
ALL STATES	44.6%	44.3%	41.9%
NORTHEAST			
Connecticut	55.0%	55.3%	57.7%
Maine	/	/	/
Massachusetts	75.8	71.3	82.9
New Hampshire	60.1	67.3	—
New Jersey	61.3	43.1	55.1
New York	48.9	51.9	54.9
Pennsylvania	79.2	70.3	/
Rhode Island	62.6	64.8	65.9
Vermont	38.2	48.6	65.8
MIDWEST			
Illinois	47.0%	66.3%	62.9%
Indiana	73.0	74.6	63.0
Iowa	69.8	68.0	60.9
Kansas	11.5	37.4	32.3
Michigan	52.7	60.0	51.9
Minnesota	73.3	66.6	55.7
Missouri	52.5	66.4	40.4
Nebraska	68.2	57.3	62.9
North Dakota	76.6	75.7	79.1
Ohio	52.4	50.0	43.6
South Dakota	66.8	70.6	62.6
Wisconsin	72.6	59.1	63.4
SOUTH			
Alabama	28.8%	/	72.1%
Arkansas	68.1	40.1%	39.6
Delaware	82.8	—	/
Dist. of Columbia	40.1	48.8	—
Florida	61.2	40.9	56.5
Georgia	62.2	60.2	63.4
Kentucky	22.6	31.6	33.7
Louisiana	61.5	47.8	46.9
Maryland	67.2	64.6	47.0
Mississippi	62.6	78.2	82.7
North Carolina	78.8	68.4	79.8
Oklahoma	69.2	67.0	75.4
South Carolina	54.7	55.9	65.3
Tennessee	35.9	25.8	42.3
Texas	35.1	41.0	54.9
Virginia	68.0	57.8	63.2
West Virginia	48.2	46.0	65.2
WEST			
Alaska	44.0%	39.5%	33.7%
Arizona	62.3	48.9	61.9
California	19.4	20.9	21.3
Colorado	58.2	48.9	36.3
Hawaii	13.1	40.5	32.4
Idaho	61.5	26.0	46.4
Montana	55.3	—	59.9
Nevada	70.4	74.6	66.8
New Mexico	37.8	28.9	28.5
Oregon	27.9	39.6	50.6
Utah	21.8	23.7	18.5
Washington	47.9	29.4	/
Wyoming	66.1	48.5	59.6

Note: Based on the *Annual Parole Survey.* Counts are for discharges between January 1 and December 31 of each year.
— Not reported.   / Not calculated.

Source: Timothy A. Hughes, Doris James Wilson, and Allen J. Beck, "Trends in State Parole, 1990–2000," *Bureau of Justice Statistics Special Report* (Washington, DC: GPO, U.S. Department of Justice, October 2001), p. 11, Table 15.

| TABLE 9.5 | Percent Successful Among State Parole Discharges, by Selected Characteristics, 1990 and 1999 |

	PERCENT SUCCESSFUL	
CHARACTERISTIC	1990	1999
GENDER		
Male	35.9%	39.3%
Female	37.1	47.7
RACE/HISPANIC ORIGIN		
White non-Hispanic	44.1%	40.9%
Black non-Hispanic	33.2	39.0
Hispanic	31.0	50.6
Other	33.6	42.2
AGE AT PAROLE DISCHARGE		
17 or younger	26.2%	42.9%
18–24	33.4	36.3
25–29	34.8	42.6
30–34	34.1	39.0
35–39	36.8	38.3
40–44	38.4	39.5
45–54	46.2	43.1
55 or older	56.6	54.5
METHOD OF RELEASE		
Discretionary parole	51.6%	54.1%
Mandatory parole	23.8	33.1
TYPE OF RELEASE		
First release	56.4%	63.5%
Re-release	14.6	21.1
MOST SERIOUS OFFENSE		
Violent	39.1%	41.0%
Property	33.8	36.5
Drug	33.7	40.9
Public-order	46.1	47.1
TIME SERVED IN PRISON*		
Less than 12 months	74.6%	74.0%
12–23 months	67.7	68.7
24–59 months	59.1	62.7
60 months or more	49.5	62.0

Note: Based on prisoners with a sentence of more than 1 year who were released from state prison. Data are from the *National Corrections Reporting Program.*
*First releases only.

Source: Timothy A. Hughes, Doris James Wilson, and Allen J. Beck, "Trends in State Parole, 1990–2000," *Bureau of Justice Statistics Special Report* (Washington, DC: GPO, U.S. Department of Justice, October 2001), p. 12, Table 18.

Success rates also vary by method of release. State inmates released by a parole board ("discretionary parole") almost always have a higher rate of success than inmates released through "mandatory parole" (that is, inmates who generally are sentenced under determinate sentencing statutes and are released from prison after serving a portion of their original sentence minus any good time earned). In 1999, for example, 54 percent of inmates released through discretionary parole were successful, while only 33 percent of inmates receiving mandatory parole were successful (see Table 9.5). However, there was an interesting interactive effect in 1999. Inmates released from prison for the first time were more likely to succeed on mandatory release than on discretionary release (79 percent vs. 61 percent), while re-releases were more likely to succeed on discretionary release than on mandatory release (37 percent vs. 17 percent).

There is also a temporal element to parole success or failure. The chances of failure are generally highest during the early stages of parole. The first year appears to be the most critical if a successful discharge from parole is going to occur. In 1999, parolees who succeeded served an average of 27 months under parole supervision, while parolees who failed served an average of 24 months under supervision. Among inmates released from prison for the first time, those who were released by a parole board and succeeded served, on average, 34 months under supervision. Those who failed served an average of 26 months under supervision. Inmates who were released from prison for the first time on mandatory parole and succeeded served, on average, 21 months under supervision, while those who failed served an average of 19 months under supervision.

Parole success and failure also vary by parolee gender, race or ethnicity, age, and most serious offense for which he or she was incarcerated. In 1999, 48 percent of female parolees were successfully discharged from supervision, while only 39 percent of males were successfully discharged. Between 1990 and 1999, the rate of success for female parolees increased about 11 percent; the rate of success for male parolees increased about 3 percent. As for race or ethnicity, in 1999, 51 percent of Hispanic parolees were successfully discharged (up from 31 percent in 1990); 41 percent of white, non-Hispanics were successfully discharged (down from 44 percent in 1990); 39 percent of black, non-Hispanics were successfully discharged (up from 33 percent in 1990); and 42 percent of parolees of other races or ethnicities were successfully discharged (up from 34 percent in 1990). Older parolees (those 45 or older) had the highest rates of successful parole completion in both 1990 and 1999. More than half of the parolees age 55 or older were successfully discharged in both years. Among parolees in other age groups, success rates varied between about 33 percent and 43 percent. Finally, in 1999, 47 percent of parolees whose most serious offense was a public-order crime were successfully discharged from supervision (up from 46 percent in 1990), followed by 41 percent of violent and drug offenders (up from 39 percent and 34 percent in 1999, respectively), and 36.5 percent of property offenders (up from 34 percent in 1990). (See Table 9.5.)

THINKING CRITICALLY

1. How much weight do victim impact statements get in the decision to grant parole?

2. Given what you have read, do you think there are ways to improve the parole process? If so, what can be done?

Intermediate Sanctions

Recent dramatic increases in prison, parole, and probation populations have fundamentally altered the field of community corrections. Community corrections has been forced to accommodate (1) growing numbers of the types of offenders the field has traditionally accommodated, plus (2) offenders who would have been sent to—or remained in—prison had sufficient space been available. At the same time, the field has witnessed a general decline in philosophical support for rehabilitation, coupled with a growing emphasis on punishing and controlling offenders. Since the 1980s the intermediate-sanction trend has grown within this context.

In restrictiveness and punitiveness, intermediate sanctions lie somewhere between traditional probation and traditional imprisonment or, alternatively, between imprisonment and traditional parole supervision (see Figure 9.5).

FIGURE 9.5   Relationship of Intermediate Sanctions to Traditional Sanctions

No Sanction	Traditional Probation	Intermediate Sanctions	Traditional Imprisonment	Intermediate Sanctions	Traditional Parole Supervision

Intermediate sanctions are designed to widen the range of incarceration alternatives and to calibrate that range according to the differential risks and needs of offenders.

As a rule, the newer intermediate sanctions are oriented less toward rehabilitation and more toward retribution, deterrence, and incapacitation than older community correctional programs. However, the distinction between intermediate sanctions and older, more traditional programs has become somewhat blurred because some traditional programs, such as restitution and halfway houses, have been incorporated into the intermediate-sanction category. The specific intermediate sanctions to be discussed in this section include intensive-supervision probation and parole, day reporting centers, structured fines (or day fines), home confinement and electronic monitoring, and halfway houses.

INTENSIVE-SUPERVISION PROBATION AND PAROLE (ISP)

intensive-supervision probation and parole (ISP) An alternative to incarceration that provides stricter conditions, closer supervision, and more treatment services than do traditional probation and parole.

Intensive-supervision probation and parole (ISP) provides stricter conditions, closer supervision, and more treatment services than do traditional probation and parole. Offenders are often selected for ISP on the basis of their scores on risk-and-needs-assessment instruments. Alternatively, they may be placed on ISP after violating regular probation or parole. Most ISP programs are for nonviolent felons.

The ISP programs in existence across the nation are diverse, and some programs come much closer than others to providing supervision and services that are genuinely intensive. In theory, ISP programs have the following features:

1. Specially trained intensive-supervision officers with small caseloads (for example, 25 cases per officer).
2. Inescapable supervision, such as multiple weekly contacts between officers and clients and frequent testing for drug use.
3. Mandatory curfews.
4. Mandatory employment or restitution requirements, or both.
5. Mandatory or voluntary participation in treatment.
6. Supervision fees to be paid by clients.

ISP usually lasts 6 months to 2 years. Typically, offenders must pass through a series of phases that become progressively less restrictive during the period of intensive supervision.

The majority of states have implemented ISP programs for adult probationers and parolees.[33] However, out of all persons placed on probation or parole, relatively few are placed under intensive supervision because of resource limitations and the small caseloads required by ISP. Although it is commonly argued that ISP costs less money than incarceration, provided it is not followed by incarceration due to revocation, ISP generally costs more than traditional probation or parole. For this reason, it is used rather sparingly.

ONLINE

American Probation and Parole Association
The American Probation and Parole Association explores issues relevant to the field of community corrections. You can visit its Web site at **www.appa-net.org/.**
Would a career in probation or parole be of interest to you? Why or why not?

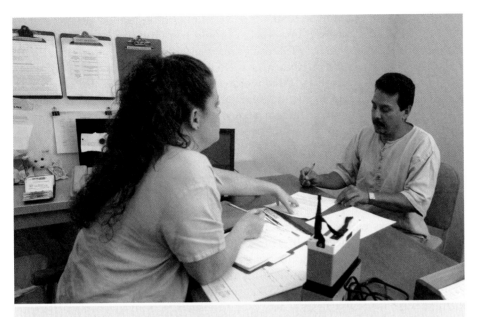

Intensive-supervision probation and parole (ISP) provides stricter conditions, closer supervision, and more treatment services than do traditional probation and parole. *Is ISP worth the extra expense? Why or why not?*

Although a number of concerns have been raised about ISP, two of the most important are (1) the potential for net widening and (2) the lack of demonstrated reduction of recidivism.

Net widening takes various forms and can plague virtually any type of community correctional program. Net widening occurs when the offenders placed in a novel program like ISP are not the offenders for whom the program was intended. The consequence is that those in the program receive more severe sanctions than they would have received had the new program remained unavailable. Suppose, for example, that a jurisdiction facing a prison crowding crisis establishes a new intensive probation program so that a substantial number of nonviolent offenders can be sentenced to ISP rather than prison. That is, the ISP target group consists of nonviolent felons who would have gone to prison had ISP not become available. If only persons who would formerly have gone to prison are placed on ISP, net widening has not taken place. However, if persons who would formerly have been placed on regular probation are now placed on ISP, net widening has occurred. To the degree that such net widening is the result, ISP becomes a costly addition to ordinary probation, instead of serving its intended function of providing a cost-efficient alternative to imprisonment.

Again, it is important to realize that almost all community correctional programs, especially those specifically designed to divert offenders from more severe sanctions, are vulnerable to net widening. Net widening can be avoided or minimized by establishing and following standard criteria for assigning offenders to programs. If the goal of an intensive probation program is to divert offenders from prison, then only prison-bound offenders should be placed in

Myth   Fact

Myth: Incarceration for technical violations prevents crime.

Fact: In the largest controlled experiment ever conducted nationwide on intensive-supervision probation and parole, researchers found that offenders who committed technical violations were no more likely to be arrested for new crimes than those who did not commit technical violations.

SOURCE: Joan Petersilia and Susan Turner, *Evaluating Intensive Supervision Probation/Parole: Results of a Nationwide Experiment* (Washington, DC: GPO, U.S. Department of Justice, National Institute of Justice, Research in Brief, 1993).

net widening A phenomenon that occurs when the offenders placed in a novel program are not the offenders for whom the program was designed. The consequence is that those in the program receive more severe sanctions than they would have received had the new program remained unavailable.

Intensive Probation and Parole

In 2003, the average caseloads for regular probation and parole supervision were 112 and 60, respectively. By contrast, the 2003 average caseloads for intensive probation and parole supervision were 26 and 24, respectively. The 2000 average costs per day for regular probation and parole supervision were $2.16 and $4.76, respectively, while the 2000 average costs per day for intensive probation and parole supervision were $9.94 and $12.42, respectively. It is important to note, however, that caseloads and amounts spent on the two types of probation and parole supervision varied greatly across the nation. The average daily cost per prison inmate in 2000 was $61.04.

SOURCE: *American Correctional Association 2004 Directory: Adult and Juvenile Correctional Departments, Institutions, Agencies and Probation and Parole Authorities* (Lanham, MD: American Correctional Association, 2004), p. 75; Camille Graham Camp and George M. Camp, *The 2001 Corrections Yearbook: Adult Systems* (Middletown, CT: Criminal Justice Institute, 2002), pp. 106, 195, and 206.

the program. Offenders who would have been placed on regular probation had the intensive program been unavailable should continue to be placed on regular probation. When modern ISP programs were introduced in the early 1980s, there was much optimism that a cost-efficient means of diverting offenders from prison and controlling their recidivism had been found. Writing about the Georgia ISP program, social scientists Billie Erwin and Lawrence Bennett stated that "the recidivism rates are considerably better . . . than for groups under regular probation and for those released from prison. [ISP] offenders commit fewer and less serious crimes."[34] Erwin and Bennett also estimated that Georgia saved $6,775 for each case diverted from prison into ISP.

Unfortunately, the initial optimism surrounding ISP has not been sustained according to subsequent, well-designed research by Joan Petersilia and her colleagues. In one study, criminologists Petersilia and Turner compared offenders who had been randomly assigned to either intensive or regular probation in three California counties. Efforts were made to ensure that only high-risk, serious offenders were included in the study, and offenders were followed for 6 months after program placement. Across counties, an average of 30 percent of the ISP cases had technical violations, and about 20 percent had new arrests. In two counties, ISP clients were significantly more likely than regular probationers to incur technical violations, but neither more nor less likely to incur new arrests. In the other county, ISP cases and regular probationers did not differ significantly in technical violations or new arrests. Petersilia and Turner observe that in the first two counties, the increased supervision of ISP may simply have increased awareness of clients' technical violations. That is, regular probationers may have committed just as many technical violations, but more of the violations may have escaped detection because of less supervision. More important, Petersilia and Turner point out that if ISP simply increases awareness of technical violations and if the official response to such violations is swift revocation of ISP followed by incarceration, two things may occur. First, because offenders are no longer at risk of recidivism in the community once they are incarcerated, the artificial impression may be created that ISP is associated with low arrest rates. Second, ISP will fuel the prison crowding problem it is intended to relieve.[35]

In another study, Petersilia and Turner evaluated a national ISP demonstration project in 14 jurisdictions across nine states.[36] The 14 programs were implemented between 1986 and 1991 and involved approximately 2,000 offenders. In each program, offenders were assigned randomly to either ISP or an alternative sanction, such as regular probation, prison, or regular parole. They were then followed for 1 year. The average results across jurisdictions are summarized in Table 9.6. ISP was associated with a substantially higher percentage of technical violations than the alternative sanctions. Again it appears that ISP may have increased detection of technical violations and thereby inflated incarceration rates. The data suggest that if ISP is to relieve

TABLE 9.6	Offender Recidivism Averages in Petersilia and Turner's Study of ISP in 14 Jurisdictions		
SANCTION	PERCENTAGE ARRESTED	PERCENTAGE WITH TECHNICAL VIOLATIONS	PERCENTAGE RETURNED TO PRISON
ISP	37	65	24
Alternative	33	38	15

Source: Joan Petersilia and Susan Turner, *Evaluating Intensive Supervision Probation/Parole: Results of a Nationwide Experiment* (Washington, DC: GPO, U.S. Department of Justice, National Institute of Justice, Research in Brief, 1993).

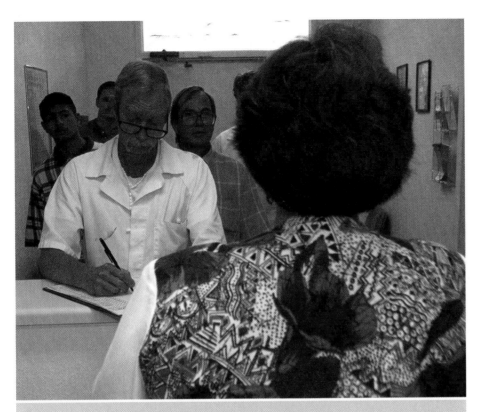

Day reporting centers, which may be publicly or privately operated, are corrections centers where offenders must report regularly to comply with a sentence. Most day center programs include employment, counseling, education, and community service components. *Should the use of day reporting centers be expanded? Why or why not?*

prison crowding in any meaningful way, officials will have to become more reluctant to revoke ISP and impose incarceration for technical violations.

DAY REPORTING CENTERS

Day reporting centers, a relatively new facet of the intermediate-sanction movement, emerged in Great Britain in the 1970s and were pioneered in the United States in Massachusetts in 1986. The centers can be administered publicly or privately and are designed primarily for offenders who would otherwise be in jail or prison. This includes offenders such as those on ISP and those awaiting trial who did not receive release on recognizance or bail. Offenders are permitted to live at home but must report to the center regularly to confer with center staff about supervision and treatment matters. Program components commonly focus on work, education, counseling, and community service.[37] The program objectives devised for offenders by the Metropolitan Day Reporting Center in Boston are illustrated in Figure 9.6. In June 2005, 4,747 offenders nationwide were being supervised by personnel of day reporting centers instead of being confined in jails (down from 6,627 in June 2004). The 2005 figure represents about 7 percent of offenders being supervised outside a jail facility.[38]

day reporting centers Facilities that are designed for offenders who would otherwise be in prison or jail and that require offenders to report regularly to confer with staff about supervision and treatment matters.

STRUCTURED FINES, OR DAY FINES

Another relatively new intermediate sanction, at least in the United States, is structured fines, or day fines.[39] **Structured fines,** or **day fines,** differ

structured fines, or day fines Fines that are based on defendants' ability to pay.

FIGURE 9.6 | **Metropolitan Day Reporting Center Participant Program Objectives**

I _____, agree to participate in
the activities and to adhere to the schedule of this contract. I understand that
this contract may be modified during my participation in the Day Reporting
Center and I agree to those modifications as determined by my participation.

Objectives   *Time frame*

Reporting: I will report in to the Center at the times designated by my case
               manager and as noted on my daily itinerary.

               I will call in to the Center at the times designated by my ca[se]
               manager and as noted on my daily itinerary.

Supervision: I will be available for phone calls or house checks by Day
               Reporting Center staff at the locations listed on my daily itine[rary]

Employment: Employer: _____
               Address: _____
                        _____
               Contact Person: _____
               Telephone: _____
               Hours: _____
               Salary: _____
                        _____

Financial: I agree to submit my pay stub to the Center for verification [of]
               my employment. I further agree to work with my case
               manager on budgeting my money; including the payment of
               any court-ordered fines or other restitution.
               Details: _____
                        _____
                        _____

Substance Abuse Treatment: I agree to participate in the following program[s to]
               address my substance abuse problems: _____

Urinalysis: I agree to submit to urinalysis testing upon the request of Day
               Reporting Center staff. _____

Curfew: I understand that I am to be at my residence from the hours of
               _____ P.M. to _____ A.M., and that I may be contacted by
               Day Reporting Center staff during that time. _____

Other Objectives: _____
               _____
               _____
               _____
               _____
               _____
               _____
               _____
               _____
               _____
               _____

_____   _____
Client   *Date*

I agree to assist _____ to achieve the
listed objectives of this contract in my capacity as case manager.

_____   _____
Case Manager   *Date*

No Time for Fine

The U.S. Supreme Court has ruled that an offender cannot be imprisoned for failure to pay a fine unless the default is willful, if imprisonment is not an authorized penalty for the offense of which the defendant was convicted.

SOURCE: *Tate v. Short* (1971).

fundamentally from the fines (called *tariff fines*) more typically imposed by American criminal courts. Whereas tariff fines require a single fixed amount of money, or an amount of money within a narrow range, to be paid by all defendants convicted of a particular crime, *without regard to their financial circumstances,* structured fines are based on defendants' ability to pay. The basic premise of structured fines is that "punishment by a fine should be proportionate to the seriousness of the offense and should have roughly similar impact (in terms of economic sting) on persons with differing financial resources who are convicted of the same offense."

The creation of a structured fine is a two-part process. In the first part, the number of fine units for a crime is determined from a scale that ranks crimes according to their seriousness. In the second part, the dollar amount of the fine is determined by multiplying the number of fine units by a proportion of the defendant's net daily income (hence the term *day fine*), adjusted to account for dependents and special circumstances.

Structured fines were first introduced in the 1920s in Sweden and soon thereafter were adopted by other Scandinavian countries. West Germany began employing them in the early 1970s. The western European nations have made day fines the sanction of choice in a large proportion of criminal cases, including many involving serious offenses. For example, in Germany, day fines are used as the only sanction for three-fourths of all offenders convicted of property crimes and for two-thirds of all offenders convicted of assaults.

The first structured-fine program in the United States began in 1988 in Richmond County (Staten Island), New York, as a demonstration project. Other structured-fine demonstration projects have been established in Maricopa County (Phoenix), Arizona; Bridgeport, Connecticut; Polk County (Des Moines), Iowa; and four counties in Oregon (Marion, Malheur, Josephine, and Coos). An evaluation of the Richmond County project, sponsored by the National Institute of Justice, showed very promising results.

Among the presumed advantages of structured-fine or day-fine programs are the following:

1. Offender accountability—"The offender is, quite literally, made to pay his or her debt to society."
2. Deterrence—"Structured fines provide an economic disincentive for criminal behavior."
3. Fairness—Structured fines are fairer than tariff fines because tariff fines frequently are too low to be meaningful to wealthier offenders and too high for poorer offenders to pay.
4. Effective and efficient use of limited system resources—"Structured fines are relatively inexpensive to administer compared with most other types of intermediate sanctions."
5. Revenue—"Structured fines can be more effective than tariff fines in generating revenue."
6. Credibility for the court—Because offenders pay in full in a very large proportion of cases, the sanction has credibility with the offender and the community.

Among the problems with structured fines are the following:

1. Collection problems—"If judges are not convinced that such fines will be paid in a high proportion of cases, or if offenders assume that the fines need not be paid, the usefulness of the structured fine as a criminal sanction is seriously eroded."
2. The effect of other monetary penalties—In most U.S. jurisdictions, defendants convicted of crimes have a variety of monetary penalties to pay, for example, penalty assessment fees, crime victim compensation fees, indigent defense fees, and probation fees. Those monetary sanctions create a high cost to a defendant, even before a fine is imposed. A fine added to those costs may exceed the ability of poorer defendants to pay.

HOME CONFINEMENT AND ELECTRONIC MONITORING

In **home confinement** programs (also known as *home incarceration, home detention,* and *house arrest*), offenders are required by the court to remain in their homes except for preapproved periods of absence. For example, offenders may be permitted to leave home to go to work, school, or church or to run errands. Home confinement is usually considered more punitive than ISP but is often used in conjunction with ISP. For example, home confinement may be required during the initial phase of intensive probation or may be

Structured Fines

Regarding the use of structured fines, or day fines, in the United States, criminologists Norval Morris and Michael Tonry make this interesting observation: "It is paradoxical that a society that relies so heavily on the financial incentive in its social philosophy and economic practice should be so reluctant to use the financial disincentive as a punishment of crime."

Source: Norval Morris and Michael Tonry (eds.), *Between Prisons and Probation: Intermediate Punishments in a Rational Sentencing System* (New York: Oxford University Press, 1990), p. 111.

home confinement A program that requires offenders to remain in their homes except for approved periods of absence; commonly used in combination with electronic monitoring.

electronic monitoring An arrangement that allows an offender's whereabouts to be gauged through the use of computer technology.

ordered if an offender violates probation or parole. Home confinement can also serve as an alternative to pretrial detention in jail.

House arrest has traditionally been employed in the military and has a long history of limited use in criminal justice. However, home confinement programs did not gain wide popularity until **electronic monitoring** equipment became readily available during the 1980s. Electronic monitoring allows an offender's whereabouts to be gauged through the use of computer technology. Before the use of electronic monitoring, it was time-consuming and expensive for officials to ensure that offenders were complying with home confinement orders. Electronic monitoring rendered home confinement more practical and cost-effective because officials did not have to rely on personal phone calls and home visits to assess compliance with home detention orders. Today, it is very common for home confinement programs to have electronic monitoring components. In June 2005, for example, 12,900 offenders nationwide who otherwise would have been confined in a jail facility were being supervised in a home detention program (about the same number as in June 2004). That represents about 18 percent of offenders being supervised outside a jail facility. Of those offenders participating in a home detention program, nearly 90 percent were being electronically monitored.[40]

Electronic monitoring devices are used to verify, either through phone lines or radio signals, that offenders are at their designated locations at particular times. The two most popular electronic monitoring devices are the continuously signaling and programmed contact systems. In the continuously signaling system, an offender wears a small transmitter, usually on the ankle, that sends encoded signals to a nearby receiver at regular intervals. In essence, the receiver communicates with the monitoring agency's computer, which contains the offender's schedule, so staff can determine whether the offender is in the designated location at the required time. Under the programmed contact arrangement, the agency's computer generates either random or scheduled phone calls to the designated location, and the offender must respond to the calls. The type of response required from the offender depends on the specific device. For example, some devices require the offender to insert a wristlet into a verifier box hooked on the phone. Others require the offender to speak for purposes of voice verification.

Home confinement and electronic monitoring have not yet been evaluated extensively. However, a national survey found that electronic monitoring has expanded rapidly since its inception. Furthermore, there appears to be a trend toward using electronic monitoring with offenders who have committed more serious crimes.

As might be expected, home confinement and electronic monitoring are controversial practices. This is particularly true of monitoring. Supporters argue that home confinement and monitoring are cost-effective alternatives to incarceration in jail or prison that allow offenders to receive more supervision and punishment than they would receive on traditional probation or parole. Another argument is that offenders are spared the potentially harmful effects of institutionalization, one of the most important of which is the breaking of family ties.

Critics counter with a variety of claims. One important criticism is that home confinement and monitoring

Home confinement requires offenders to remain in their homes except for preapproved periods of absence. Most programs use electronic monitoring equipment to verify that offenders are at their designated locations at particular times. *For what type of offenders are home confinement and electronic monitoring appropriate, and for what type of offenders are they not?*

encroach on the constitutional rights to privacy, protection against self-incrimination, and protection against unreasonable search and seizure. Critics maintain that not only the offender's rights are threatened, but also the rights of persons who share the offender's residence. However, it seems unlikely that the use of those sanctions will be severely restricted on constitutional grounds in the foreseeable future. As criminologists Rolando del Carmen and Joseph Vaughn observe, "A review of decided cases in probation and parole indicates that while the use of electronic devices raises constitutional issues, its constitutionality will most likely be upheld by the courts, primarily based on the concept of diminished rights [for offenders]."[41]

Some people worry that home confinement and electronic monitoring may discriminate against economically disadvantaged persons, who are less likely to have homes and telephone systems for the installation of monitoring devices. Others are concerned that offenders and manufacturers of monitoring equipment have become locked in a perpetual and costly battle to outwit one another. Manufacturers continually work to devise monitors that will resist offender tampering. Meanwhile, offenders seek ways to manipulate the latest monitoring innovations on the market. This situation, of course, is potentially lucrative for equipment vendors, but it is potentially costly for taxpayers and for offenders who must pay monitoring fees. A broader criticism is that a profit incentive is being created to subject more and more persons to government surveillance.

Some people object to monitoring on the grounds that it is impersonal, thus removing the human and helping elements from community corrections. Those critics suggest that by reducing the need for skill and professionalism on the part of probation and parole officers, monitoring may undermine rehabilitation. As criminologist John Conrad writes:

> Probation and parole were once intended to help men and women in the worst kind of trouble to find ways to lead law abiding lives. No more. Official services to offenders in the community have been transformed into a cat-and-mouse game in which surveillance, not service, has become the primary, if not the exclusive requisite. . . . Electronic surveillance is a recent and welcomed contribution of high technology to the community control of convicted offenders. We settle for temporary control in place of a serious program for changes in attitude, behavior and style of life.[42]

A recent investigation of Florida's house-arrest program provides empirical support for these criticisms. It also reveals some problems heretofore overlooked by house-arrest critics.[43] Florida's house-arrest program, which the Florida Department of Corrections manages and calls "community control," is the largest such program in the United States. In 2002, the state supervised about 10,000 active program participants a day—6 percent of whom were electronically monitored. Since its inception in 1983 and through 2002, more than 215,000 offenders have served time in the program.

A principal reason for the program's creation was the prospect of saving money by reducing the prison population. Whether the program has achieved that goal is a difficult question to answer. On the one hand, participation in house arrest is significantly cheaper than the costs of incarceration. In 2002, house-arrest program participants cost the state as little as $11.16 a day, while state prison inmates cost the state $49.75 a day. By that measure, the program has saved the state of Florida millions of dollars. On the other hand, if in the absence of the program, offenders would have been placed on regular probation, for which the average cost per probationer per day in 2000 was $3.85, then the program produced no cost savings and was just a more expensive alternative to regular probation.

Electronic Monitoring

Electronic monitoring has rapidly become one of the most widespread and controversial innovations in community corrections since the idea was first introduced, in the 1960s. The first statewide home confinement program without electronic monitoring was implemented in Florida in the early 1980s. St. Louis was one of the cities to pioneer such programming in the early 1970s. Among the first jurisdictions to implement an electronic monitoring program was Palm Beach County, Florida, in 1984.

SOURCE: J. R. Lilly and R. A. Ball, "A Brief History of House Arrest and Electronic Monitoring," *Northern Kentucky Law Review* 13, no. 3 (1987), pp. 343–74.

Some electronic monitoring devices use global positioning systems (GPS). *In what ways are GPS-equipped monitoring devices superior to conventional phone or radio signal devices?*

The house-arrest program may have reduced the prison population, but that is not entirely clear, either. From June 1983 through June 2003, Florida's prison population increased each year except from June 1983 to June 1984. During that period, it increased a total of 196 percent. Still, the program may have reduced the prison population by approximately 10,000 inmates per year—the number participating in the house-arrest program. However, if the program participants would have been sentenced to regular probation instead of prison in the absence of the program, then the program did not reduce the prison population.

In any event, Florida's house-arrest program has about a 40 percent success rate. That is, about two of every five program participants (each year between 1996 and 2001) completed a year in the program without being removed for committing new crimes or violating other program rules. The other "unsucc-essful" 60 percent of Florida's house-arrest participants were removed from the program and usually incarcerated during the first year for committing crimes or violating rules. About 45 percent of the participants removed from the program violated program rules such as testing positive for drugs, leaving home without authorization, failing to pay restitution, or possessing a firearm.

In addition, during the past two decades, program participants killed at least 234 people and committed at least 538 sex crimes. Approximately 2,000 to 3,000 violent offenders are sentenced to house arrest each year. Of that number, about 400 are placed in the program even though state law prohibits it. In Florida, offenders are not to be placed on house arrest if (1) they have been convicted of a crime that appears on a specific list of violent felonies, including robbery, kidnapping, and assault; and (2) they have a prior conviction from that same list. Judges who sentence such offenders to house arrest either don't know the law or ignore the law. Some judges claim that the law makes no sense. They argue that the law allows some violent offenders barred from house arrest to be placed on probation, where they get even less supervision.

Another problem is that between 2,500 and 3,000 house-arrest participants each year flee the program. Although most of them are caught, nearly 5,000 program participants—including 14 killers and 115 people convicted of sex crimes—have not been recaptured. The program is also understaffed. In 2002, for example, the average caseload was 39 even though the state legislature set a limit at 25 cases per officer. By law, officers are supposed to check on program participants three times a week. In practice, however, most participants are checked on only twice a week. For one of those checks, the participant reports to a Department of Corrections office.

House-arrest participants who wear electronic monitors are five times more likely to successfully complete their sentences and half as likely to flee the program. However, as noted previously, only about 6 percent of house-arrest participants are electronically monitored. The problem is money. In 2002, it cost $20.33 a day to monitor an offender by satellite and $13.91 a day to monitor an offender by radio frequency. By comparison, it cost $11.16 to supervise a house-arrest participant without electronic monitoring. Florida uses two types of electronic monitoring tracking systems. The newer and more expensive technology utilizes global positioning system (GPS) satellites that track an offender's whereabouts 24 hours a day. The other, older and less expensive technology sends signals over telephone lines. It is called "RF" monitoring for radio frequency. It cannot tell the agency where an offender is, but it can tell when the offender is home or not and alert the department. Both types of monitoring have their problems. For example, the GPS generates numerous false alarms—a monthly average of 29 false alarms each in 2001. The GPS signal also will not penetrate most buildings. Even so, it would seem that electronic monitoring of house-arrest participants would be a good investment, but the Department of Corrections prefers to use the bulk of its resources on prisons.

HALFWAY HOUSES

Halfway houses (sometimes referred to as *community correctional centers*) are community-based residential facilities that are an alternative to confinement in jail or prison. Although those facilities are an alternative to more secure and restrictive placements, they provide a much more controlled environment than is possible with traditional probation and parole, or even with ISP and home confinement. As the term *halfway* implies, the offender is midway between jail or prison and the free community.

The goal of halfway houses is to provide offenders with a temporary (for instance, 6-month) period of highly structured and supportive living so that they will be better prepared to function independently in the community upon discharge. To this end, most programs place a heavy emphasis on addressing offenders' educational and employment deficits. For example, persons who have not completed high school are encouraged to obtain the GED, individuals who have few marketable job skills are encouraged to complete vocational training, and those who lack employment are assisted in finding and keeping jobs.

Halfway houses have existed in the United States since the mid-1800s and, prior to the 1960s, were used primarily for persons coming out of prison and making the transition back into the community. During the 1960s, the number and functions of halfway house programs in the nation expanded. In addition to providing services for parolees and prereleasees (prisoners nearing their release dates), houses began to service probationers, pretrial detainees, and persons on furlough from prison. More recently, in the 1980s, halfway houses became an integral part of the intermediate-sanction

Costs of Electronic Monitoring

In 2000, the average costs per day for electronic monitoring of probationers and parolees were $4.99 and $23.02, respectively. This compares with average daily costs of $9.94 and $12.42 for intensive probation and parole supervision, $2.16 and $4.76 for regular probation and parole supervision, and $61.04 for prison incarceration.

SOURCE: Camille Graham Camp and George M. Camp, *The 2001 Corrections Yearbook: Adult Systems* (Middletown, CT: Criminal Justice Institute, 2002), pp. 106 and 206.

halfway houses Community-based residential facilities that are less secure and restrictive than prison or jail but provide a more controlled environment than other community correctional programs.

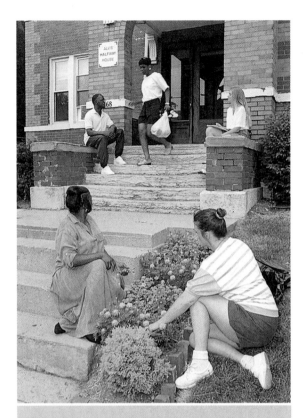

Halfway houses may be operated by private-for-profit or not-for-profit contractors or by public agencies. Some provide room, board, and help with employment. Others provide remedial education, individual or group counseling, and other types of life skills training. *Should halfway houses be restricted in the type of offender that is accepted? If yes, what types of offenders should be barred?*

ICCA

To learn more about halfway houses, visit the Web site of the International Community Corrections Association (ICCA), formerly the International Halfway House Association, at **www.iccaweb.org/.** *Does working in a halfway house appeal to you? Why or why not?*

movement. They are now sometimes used in conjunction with other intermediate sanctions. For example, as part of a probation sentence, an offender may complete a stay in a halfway house before being discharged to ISP, or a person who has violated a home confinement order may be placed in a halfway house program to give authorities added control.

Halfway houses are quite diverse. Not all houses are for offenders; some facilities serve other populations, such as those with mental disorders or drug addictions. Programs for offenders may serve a specific category of offenders, such as all probationers or all parolees, or some combination of offender groups. In addition, a halfway house's population may be all male, all female, or both male and female. Some houses rely heavily on referrals to other local agencies to ensure that offenders' treatment needs are met, whereas others provide extensive in-house treatment. Programs can be administered publicly or privately, but private administration is more common. Public programs may be administered at the federal, state, or local level of government.

PROCEDURES Halfway house programming involves five basic procedures:

1. Referral.
2. Administrative screening.
3. Intake and orientation.
4. Program participation.
5. Termination of the stay.

Referral of clients to a halfway house may be done by a correctional institution (as in the case of prereleasees), a court, or a probation or parole agency. The fundamental issue referral sources must confront is whether the offender will benefit from halfway house placement without compromising community safety. Thus, such factors as the offender's propensity for violence and degree of employment and educational deficits are generally given great weight in determining whether to make a referral.

When a referral is made, the next step is *administrative screening,* in which halfway house administrators examine the case and decide whether to accept the offender into the program. Some house administrators have more authority to reject referrals than others. Administrators of private houses often have more discretion to decline referrals than do administrators of public programs. An important point to note is that referral sources and house administrators are sometimes motivated by differing objectives. For instance, correctional institution staff may be motivated by the desire to reduce crowding in their facilities, whereas house administrators may wish to maximize the rate of successful discharge from their programs.

If administrative screening results in a decision to accept the referral, the focus shifts to *intake and orientation.* This entails assessing the new resident's risks and needs as well as orienting him or her to the rules, expectations, and routines of the program. An important aspect of intake and orientation is determining exactly what the resident should accomplish during the stay to improve his or her life and reduce the likelihood of recidivism. That determination is usually written as a treatment plan with specific goals and objectives.

With respect to *program participation*, many halfway houses have a series of levels, or phases, through which residents must pass to receive a successful discharge. Typically, each level is associated with progressively more demanding goals and responsibilities for the resident to meet and also with more privileges and freedoms. For example, a requirement for an offender to move from the entry level to the second level may be the successful completion of a job skills class. Upon promotion to level two, the offender may receive one weekend furlough per month to spend with family and friends. Promotion to level three may carry additional furlough time and require that the offender obtain a job and complete a class on job retention skills.

As noted previously, halfway houses usually provide a variety of treatment services, such as employment counseling and training, life skills training, substance abuse intervention, and remedial education. Those services are provided either directly by house staff or indirectly through referrals to community agencies. To allow control and supervision, houses have a number of rules that govern both the in-house behavior of residents and residents' activities away from the facility. Those rules cover such matters as interaction between residents, care of facility property, curfews, and the use of alcohol. Progress through program levels requires completion of the goals and responsibilities associated with a particular level, participation in relevant treatment components, and compliance with house rules. Failure to achieve goals, to complete treatment components, or to abide by rules can result in the resident's staying at a given level or being demoted to a lower level.

A resident's behavior must be monitored and periodically reviewed throughout the term of program participation because, ultimately, the house administration must decide the resident's *termination*, or discharge, status. Residents who have satisfactorily completed all of the required levels are discharged into the community, frequently under probation or parole supervision. If a resident fails to make satisfactory progress through levels in a reasonable time, compiles an excessive number of less serious rule violations, or commits a serious rule infraction (such as another felony), the resident can also be discharged from the facility. An unsuccessful discharge can be granted at any point in a resident's stay and is frequently followed by incarceration.

Issues Several issues surround the use of halfway houses. Two of the most critical issues are (1) the relations between a halfway house and the local community of which it is a part and (2) recidivism among persons who have been discharged from the house.

For a halfway house to be established in a community and to operate effectively, cooperative relations between the staff of the house and members of the community are essential. Halfway house staff often depend on the surrounding community for such things as resident health care, counseling services, educational programming, and job placements. Furthermore, unfavorable reactions from community members toward residents will simply reinforce the sense of marginalization and alienation that many offenders already experience. To the extent that community members feel threatened by residents or have poor relations with staff, the halfway house program is in jeopardy.

Virtually all halfway houses must confront the issue of community resistance, and some must confront outright hostility from community members. There are at least two keys to doing this effectively. First, halfway house officials must actively cultivate support and assistance from community members by engaging in open, honest communication with them from the earliest possible stage of the halfway house's existence. Many fears that community members have of residents are founded on inaccurate, media-fueled stereotypes and can be reduced with realistic, factual information.

Halfway Houses for White-Collar Offenders

The Justice Department is no longer allowing the U.S. Bureau of Prisons to assign first-time nonviolent white-collar offenders to federal halfway houses instead of prisons. Advocates of the nearly two-decade-old practice argue that it reduced prison crowding and encouraged rehabilitation of low-risk offenders. Critics claim that the practice allowed wealthy white-collar offenders to circumvent sentencing guidelines and escape prison.

Source: Dan Eggen, "Wealthy Criminals Will Head for Prison," *The Orlando Sentinel*, January 7, 2003, p. A5.

Myth

When an offender halfway house is established in a neighborhood, crime rates increase and property values fall.

Fact

Research on this subject has confirmed neither of those assumptions. Crime rates and property values tend to remain the same.

Second, it is very helpful if community members can see that the halfway house is contributing something of value to the community, rather than simply consuming resources. For example, house residents can be involved in well-publicized and highly visible community service projects that save tax dollars. Also, in houses where a high proportion of residents are employed, community residents should be frequently reminded that residents are contributing to the tax base instead of consuming public revenue as jail or prison inmates. If community members can be convinced that the halfway house has a positive, contributing side, they are likely to be more accepting of the house.

Just as there are ways to facilitate cooperative community relations, there also are ways to create unfavorable relations. One way to almost ensure poor relations is for the halfway house to be sprung on the community without any notice of the desire of officials to establish the house and without community input in the early planning process. Another common mistake is for halfway house officials to be content with a low-profile image once the house is established. Believing that adequate community relations will exist as long as offenders are controlled and unfavorable media exposure is avoided, officials may try to minimize exposure of house operations to the public. The typical result is an atmosphere of secrecy, suspicion, and distrust. When the inevitable negative incident occurs, such as a crime by a resident against a community member, public outcry against the house is likely.

How many persons placed in halfway houses successfully complete their stays, and how high is recidivism among former residents after discharge? Those questions were addressed in a study of 156 probationers admitted to a halfway house in Michigan.[44] The study found that nearly 60 percent of all probationers received unsuccessful discharges. However, other studies have discovered successful discharge figures as high as 60 percent.[45] The Michigan study tracked former halfway house residents for 7 years after their discharges. The researchers found that approximately 67 percent of the former residents were arrested at least once during the 7-year period for some type of criminal activity; about 60 percent were arrested at least once for felonies. However, persons who had successfully completed the halfway house program were significantly less likely to incur new arrests than the persons who had not done so. For instance, 44 percent of the persons who had received successful discharges were arrested for new felonies, compared with 68.8 percent of those who had received unsuccessful discharges.

In another study, the recidivism of offenders who had been placed in halfway house programs was compared with the recidivism of those placed on regular probation supervision. Using a 3-year follow-up period, the researchers found that 29.5 percent of the former halfway house residents and 30.7 percent of the regular probationers experienced new criminal convictions. Slightly more than 40 percent of the halfway house residents had failed to complete their programs successfully.[46]

Research clearly suggests that a large number of offenders placed in halfway houses do not successfully complete their programs. However, those who do receive successful discharges seem less likely to commit new crimes than those who do not. Yet, there is little reason to believe that halfway houses are associated with less recidivism than other types of community corrections programs.

THINKING CRITICALLY

1. Do you think people should have the right to reject the placement of a halfway house in their neighborhood? Why or why not?

2. What could be done to bring about good relations between a community and the halfway house located within the community?

Temporary-Release Programs

Temporary-release programs allow inmates in jail or prison to leave the facility for short periods to participate in approved community activities. Those programs are designed to permit inmates to establish or maintain community ties, thereby gradually preparing them for reentry into society. The programs also give institutional authorities a means of testing the readiness of inmates for release as well as a means of controlling institutional behavior. Not surprisingly, opportunities for temporary release create a major incentive for inmates to engage in the conduct desired by officials.

Three common temporary-release programs are work release, study release, and furloughs. The persons involved in such programs may be prison or jail inmates, or halfway house residents. As should be apparent from the previous section of this chapter, temporary release is an integral aspect of halfway houses. In prisons and jails, temporary release is reserved for inmates who have demonstrated that they are appropriate candidates to participate in community-based activities.

Organized temporary-release programs are not new in American corrections. Although the programs date to the early 1900s, they did not gain widespread popularity until the 1960s, when the emphasis on community corrections began to grow. Today, almost all states offer temporary release.[47]

In work-release programs, inmates leave the facility for certain hours each day to work for employers in the free community. Work-release inmates are paid prevailing wages, but they are usually required to submit their paychecks to corrections officials to deduct for such things as dependent support and restitution orders before placing the balance in inmates' accounts. Inmates may withdraw some money while in the facility but are usually required to save a certain amount for their ultimate release from incarceration. A limitation of such programs is that most inmates must settle for low-skilled and low-paying jobs. This limitation exists because:

1. A large proportion of inmates lack the educational and vocational backgrounds needed to secure higher-paying employment.
2. There is more competition for higher-paying jobs.
3. Many employers are reluctant to hire work-release inmates, especially for jobs that pay well and require skill and responsibility.

Study-release inmates can leave prison for high school equivalency classes, vocational training, or college coursework. A limitation of study release is that, unlike work release, it does not generate financial resources. If inmates cannot pay for their own educational programs or obtain financial aid, study release must be funded by the jurisdiction. Even in the unlikely event that a jurisdiction has resources to fund study release, there may still be reluctance to do so because of the argument that inmates are getting free education at taxpayers' expense.

In furlough programs, inmates are granted leaves of absence for brief periods (for example, 48 hours) to accomplish specific things. Inmates may be granted furloughs to spend time with family members, to attend funerals, or to search for employment and housing before release.

One commonly voiced fear about temporary-release programs is that inmates will flee or commit serious crimes while away from the facility. In fact, research shows that most inmates neither flee nor commit serious offenses. The most frequent problems are late returns and the use of alcohol and illegal drugs.

Temporary-release programs became a significant issue in the U.S. presidential election campaign of 1988. Massachusetts Governor Michael Dukakis, the Democratic presidential nominee, was heavily criticized by Vice President George Bush, the Republican nominee, for allowing temporary release of

temporary-release programs Programs that allow jail or prison inmates to leave the facility for short periods to participate in approved community activities.

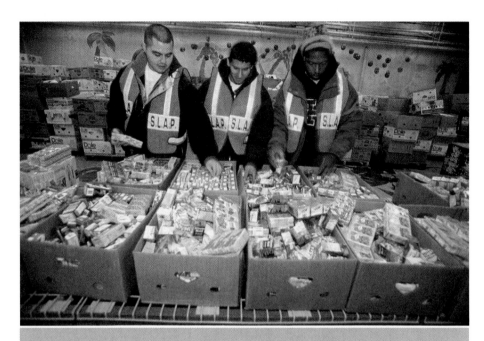

Temporary-release programs allow inmates in jail or prison to leave the facility for short periods to participate in approved community activities. *Should temporary release from jail or prison be allowed? Why or why not?*

inmates with records of violence. Willie Horton, a black man who had been serving a first-degree murder sentence at a Massachusetts institution, committed violent crimes against a white couple during his tenth furlough from the institution. Bush made much of the "liberal" prison release policies of Massachusetts in an attempt to discredit Dukakis.

Around the same time, an evaluation of temporary release in Massachusetts was being conducted. The evaluation was published in 1991.[48] The researchers studied persons released from Massachusetts facilities between 1973 and 1983. Offenders were tracked for 1 year after release, and recidivism was defined as return to prison. The recidivism of persons who participated in furloughs, prerelease-center (halfway house) programs, and both furloughs and prerelease centers was compared with the recidivism of persons who participated in neither. Using statistical controls for differences in offenders' backgrounds, researchers concluded that "prerelease programs following prison furloughs, and prison furloughs alone, appear to reduce dramatically the risks to public safety after release." This study implies that eliminating or significantly curtailing temporary-release programs is likely to result in a long-term decline in community safety and an increase in recidivism.

THINKING CRITICALLY

1. Do you think offenders should be allowed to take college courses, at taxpayers' expense, through study-release programs? Why or why not?

2. Do you think temporary-release programs help rehabilitate offenders? Why or why not?

SUMMARY

1. Define community corrections and identify the goals and responsibilities of community corrections agencies and their staffs.

Although community corrections programs are very diverse across the nation, the common feature of those programs is that they provide supervision and treatment services for offenders outside jails and prisons. The dual emphasis on supervision and treatment creates a potential role conflict for community corrections staff. There is some indication, however, that the traditional focus on treatment has been declining relative to the growing emphasis on supervision.

2. Define probation and summarize the research findings on recidivism rates.

The most commonly used type of community sentence is probation. Offenders placed on probation are supervised and provided with various services in the community instead of being incarcerated. In return, they are required to abide by the rules of the probation sentence. Overall, studies indicate that probation is about as effective as incarceration in controlling recidivism. Available data indicate that recidivism is quite high among felons sentenced to probation. Furthermore, research has not found a strong association between probation officers' caseloads and the likelihood of probationer recidivism. If anything, reduced caseloads seem to increase the probability that instances of recidivism will be detected.

3. Distinguish parole from probation.

Unlike probation, parole is not a court-imposed sentence. Parole is a mechanism of releasing persons from prison and a means of supervising them after release, instead of an alternative to an incarceration sentence. Parole supervision is often confused with probation because the two share many similarities. Four major objectives of parole agencies are to: (1) preserve community safety by supervising the behavior of parolees; (2) promote the betterment of parolees by responding to their treatment needs; (3) control prison crowding; and (4) control the behavior of prison inmates by providing early release opportunities in exchange for good prison conduct.

4. Explain the functions of a parole board.

In general, a parole board directs a jurisdiction's parole policies and manages the parole release and termination processes. Parole board members (or their representatives) conduct parole-grant hearings to determine which inmates should receive early release from prison. Boards also determine whether to revoke the parole of persons who have violated parole conditions. In most states, field service agencies are administratively independent of parole boards. A field service agency provides community supervision and treatment services for persons who have been granted parole release by the board and makes recommendations to the board concerning termination of parole.

5. Describe how intermediate sanctions differ from traditional community corrections programs.

Compared with traditional programs in community corrections, intermediate sanctions are oriented less toward rehabilitation and more toward retribution, deterrence, and incapacitation. They are more punitive and more restrictive. The recent popularity of intermediate sanctions is attributable largely to the record high levels of prison crowding that plague many jurisdictions and a corresponding need to devise acceptable alternatives to imprisonment.

6. Explain two major concerns about intensive-supervision probation and parole (ISP).

Two major concerns about ISP are (1) the potential for net-widening, and (2) the lack of demonstrated reduction of recidivism. Net-widening occurs when offenders placed in a novel program such as ISP are not the offenders for whom the program was intended. The consequence is that those in the program receive more severe sanctions than they would have received had the new program been unavailable. Studies show that ISP is associated with a substantially higher percentage of technical violations than alternative sanctions such as regular probation, prison, or regular parole.

7. Explain what day reporting centers and structured fines are.

Day reporting centers allow offenders to live at home but require them to report to the center regularly to confer with center staff about supervision and treatment matters. Program components commonly focus on work, education, counseling, and community service. Structured fines, or day fines, differ fundamentally from the fines (called tariff fines) more typically imposed by American criminal courts. Whereas tariff fines require a single fixed amount of money, or an amount within a narrow range, to be paid by all defendants convicted of a particular crime, without regard to their financial circumstances, structured fines, or day fines, are based on defendants' ability to pay. The basic premise of

*structured fines is that punishment by a fine
should be proportionate to the seriousness of
the offense and should have a roughly similar
economic impact on persons with differing
financial resources who are convicted of the
same offense.*

8. Explain what home confinement and electronic
monitoring are.

*In home confinement programs (also known
as home incarceration, home detention, and
house arrest), offenders are required by the
court to remain in their homes except for
preapproved periods of absence. Electronic
monitoring, which is generally coupled with
home confinement, allows an offender's
whereabouts to be gauged through the use of
computer technology.*

9. Identify the goal of halfway houses and compare them with other community corrections
programs.

*The goal of halfway houses is to provide
offenders with a temporary (for instance, 6-
month) period of highly structured and supportive living so that they will be better prepared to function independently in the
community upon discharge. To this end, most
programs place a heavy emphasis on addressing offenders' educational and employment
deficits. Research clearly suggests that a large*

*number of offenders placed in halfway houses
do not successfully complete their programs.
However, those who do receive successful discharges seem less likely to commit new crimes
than those who do not. Yet, there is little reason to believe that halfway houses are associated with less recidivism than other community corrections programs.*

10. Summarize the purposes and outcomes of
temporary-release programs.

*By allowing incarcerated persons to temporarily
leave their facilities to participate in approved
activities in the community, temporary-release
programs are intended to foster ties between
inmates and their communities, thus gradually
preparing inmates for return to society. These
programs also give officials a way to judge the
readiness of inmates for release, and since most
inmates want to participate in temporary release,
the programs give inmates an incentive to maintain good institutional behavior. Although fear
and other forms of resistance from community
members often plague the programs, there is
evidence that participation in temporary release
is associated with a decreased likelihood of
recidivism upon release from incarceration. Some
common types of temporary release include work
release, study release, and furlough.*

KEY TERMS

community corrections,
  p. 320
probation, p. 324
diversion, p. 324
presentence investiga-
  tion (PSI), p. 327
probation conditions,
  p. 330
restitution, p. 330

revocation,
  p. 332
technical violations,
  p. 332
parole, p. 335
parole guidelines,
  p. 338
reintegration,
  p. 344

intensive-supervision
  probation and parole
  (ISP), p. 348
net widening,
  p. 349
day reporting centers,
  p. 351
structured fines, or day
  fines, p. 351

home confinement,
  p. 353
electronic monitoring,
  p. 354
halfway houses,
  p. 357
temporary-release
  programs, p. 361

REVIEW QUESTIONS

1. What are David Duffee's three varieties of community corrections, and how do they differ?

2. What are three aspects of the helping role of
community corrections staff?

3. Why is community corrections important?

4. What are five types of probation?

5. What are three fundamental objectives of
probation agencies?

6. What is a probation subsidy, and what is its
goal?

7. What is the main task of the PSI?

8. What are two types of probation conditions, and how do they differ?

9. For what general types of violations can probation be revoked?

10. What two landmark Supreme Court cases define the procedural guidelines for revoking probation or parole?

11. What are two general types of parole, and what is their function?

12. According to a recent study, what are the four most important factors parole authorities consider before granting release on parole?

13. What are some criticisms of parole release?

14. What are two ways that halfway house officials might effectively confront community resistance?

IN THE FIELD

1. **Tour a Probation Agency** Take a guided tour of the probation or parole agency in your community. (1) Ask the guide to explain the various activities of the agency. Also ask to speak with various officers about their work. (2) Request sample copies of agency documents, such as

risk-and-needs-assessment instruments. (3) Write a short essay describing what the agency documents reveal about the work of the agency.

2. **Evaluate Halfway House Rules** Obtain a copy of the rules of behavior for a halfway house. (1) Evaluate the rules, and decide whether you think they are too strict, not strict enough, or on target. (2) Rewrite any rules that you think need changing.

ON THE NET

1. **Local Community Corrections** Visit the Sedgwick County, Kansas, Department of Corrections, Community Corrections Web site (www.sedgwickcounty.org/corrections/afs.html) or the North Carolina Department of Correction, Division of Community Corrections Web site (www.doc.state.nc.us/doc/index.htm). Choose from the topics provided, and write a brief summary of the information you find and how it is related to community corrections.

2. **U.S. Parole Commission** Visit the Web site of the United States Parole Commission at www.usdoj.gov/uspc and click on "Our History" to read a contextual history of the federal parole system. Then click on "Answering Your Questions" for the answers to many commonly asked questions about federal parole. Write a short essay explaining why you support or oppose the 1987 abolition of federal parole.

CRITICAL THINKING EXERCIS

1. **Probation/Parole Officer** You are a probation or parole officer. Your caseload averages 100 clients.
   a. A client tells you that her boss is treating her unfairly at work because of her criminal record and probation or parole status. Your client is afraid of being fired and having her probation or parole revoked. What do you do?
   b. You discover that a client is using marijuana. You like the client, and other than

the marijuana use, he has been doing well on probation or parole. What do you do?
   c. You have a problem client who is using drugs (marijuana and cocaine), hanging out with a "bad" group of people, and probably (though you have no hard evidence) committing petty thefts to support her drug habit. You have warned the client to stop this behavior, but she has ignored your warnings. Furthermore, the client has threatened to harm you and your family

should you revoke her probation or parole. What do you do?

    d. You have a client who, as a condition of his probation or parole, is required to earn his GED. Although the client has been attending classes regularly and seems to be trying very hard, his teacher informs you that the client just does not have the intellectual capacity to earn the GED. What do you do?

2. **Halfway House** As an employee of your state department of corrections, you have been asked to establish a halfway house for parolees, all of whom are former substance abuse offenders, in the nice, middle-class community where you live. Assuming that you take the job, how would you address the following questions?

    a. Would you communicate to the community your intention of establishing the halfway house? Why or why not?

    b. How would you address community resistance to the halfway house should it arise?

    c. Would you ask community residents to aid you in your efforts? Why or why not?

    d. Besides community resistance, what other problems might arise in your effort to establish the halfway house? How would you handle them?

    e. Would you be willing to remain a resident of the community after the halfway house is established (especially if you have a family with small children)? Why or why not?

To access more information and resources, including study questions, chapter summaries, and links, go to: www.mhhe.com/bohm1.

PART FIVE

JUVENILE JUSTICE

CHAPTER TEN

Juvenile Justice

CHAPTER OUTLINE

Historical Development of Juvenile Justice

The Development of Institutions for Youths

The Development of the Juvenile Court

The Processing of Juvenile Offenders

The Informal Juvenile Justice Process

The Formal Juvenile Justice Process

Correctional Programs for Juveniles

Community-Based Correctional Programs
for Juveniles

Institutional Programs for Juveniles

CHAPTER OBJECTIVES

After completing this chapter, you should be able to:

1. Describe some of the early institutions used to respond to wayward and criminal youths.

2. Explain the effects of some landmark U.S. Supreme Court cases on the juvenile justice system.

3. Identify and describe factors that influence the ways that police process juvenile cases.

4. Summarize the rationale for the use of diversion in juvenile justice.

5. Describe the adjudication hearing in juvenile justice.

6. Describe the disposition hearing and the types of dispositions available to the juvenile court.

7. Identify the types and describe the effectiveness of community-based correctional programs for juveniles.

8. Summarize recent trends in juvenile incarceration.

9. Identify the types and describe the effectiveness of institutional programs for juveniles.

Historical Development of Juvenile Justice

From a historical perspective, juvenile delinquency and a separate justice process for juveniles are recent concepts. So, too, are the ideas of childhood and adolescence. **Juvenile delinquency** is a special category of offense created for youths—that is, in most U.S. jurisdictions, persons between the ages of 7 and 18. Through most of recorded history, the young have not enjoyed the statuses of childhood and adolescence as special times during which the young need nurturing and guidance for their healthy development.

Before the sixteenth century, the young were viewed either as property or as miniature adults who, by the age of 5 or 6, were expected to assume the responsibilities of adults. They were also subject to the same criminal sanctions as adults. However, in the sixteenth and seventeenth centuries, a different view of the young emerged that recognized childhood as a distinct period of life, and children as corruptible but worth correcting.[1] Youths began to be viewed, not as miniature adults or as property, but rather as persons who required molding and guidance to become moral and productive members of the community. American colonists brought with them those new ideas about

juvenile delinquency A special category of offense created for youths who, in most U.S. jurisdictions, are persons between the ages of 7 and 18.

Description when liberated.	Age (on discharge)	*11*	Photograph of Prisoner.
	Height	*4 ft 1 3/4*	
	Hair	*Brown*	
	Eyes	*Brown*	
	Complexion	*Fresh*	
	Where born	*Middlesex*	
	Married or single	*Single*	
	Trade or occupation	*None*	
	Any other distinguishing mark	*Scar on*	
	forehead and on right shoulder		

Until the early 1900s, children were subject to the same punishments as adults. *Should children be punished in the same way as adults? Why or why not?*

childhood as well as European mechanisms for responding to violators of social and legal rules.

During the colonial period, the family was the basic unit of economic production and the primary mechanism through which social control was exerted. Survival depended on the family's ability to produce what it needed, rather than relying on the production of others. Consequently, a primary responsibility of the family was overseeing the moral training and discipline of the young. During this period, two age-old mechanisms were employed to teach children who were difficult to handle or needed supervision in a trade to allow them an opportunity to earn a livelihood. One of those mechanisms was the **apprenticeship system,** which served as a primary means for teaching skilled trades to the children of the middle and upper classes. The other tradition was the binding-out system, which was reserved for poor children. Under the **binding-out system,** children were bound over to masters for care. However, under this system, masters were not required to teach the youths a trade. As a result, boys were often given farming tasks, while girls were assigned to domestic duties.[2]

Religion, particularly in New England, was another powerful force that shaped social life in the colonies. Regular church attendance was expected, and religious beliefs dominated ideas about appropriate behavior. Present-day concerns about the separation of church and state were nonexistent. What was believed to be immoral was also unlawful and subject to punishment by the authorities. Punishments such as fines, whipping, branding, and the use of stocks and the pillory served as reminders to both young and old that violations of community norms would not go unpunished.[3]

By the early 1800s, the social organization of colonial life began to change as a result of economic and social developments. The family-based production unit that had characterized colonial social life was giving way to a factory-based system in the growing towns. As parents—particularly fathers—and children began to leave the home for work in a factory, fundamental changes occurred in the relationships between family members and in the role of the family in controlling the behavior of children. Further, as industry developed and as towns grew, communities became more diverse and experienced problems on a scale unheard of during earlier periods.

THE DEVELOPMENT OF INSTITUTIONS FOR YOUTHS

At the time of the American Revolution, Philadelphia had fewer than 20,000 residents, and other large towns, such as New York, Boston, Newport, and Charleston, had fewer than 15,000 inhabitants each. However, by 1820, the population of New York City was about 120,000 and was growing rapidly as a result of immigration. Immigration, in turn, was changing the composition of communities, which had been more homogeneous during colonial times.

THE HOUSES OF REFUGE Accompanying those changes in the social and economic life of the growing cities were a host of social problems, such as poverty, vagrancy, drunkenness, and crime, including crimes committed by children. In response to those conditions, the first correctional institutions specifically for youths developed. Those institutions were called **houses of refuge.** The first was established in New York City in 1825, and houses of refuge soon spread to other cities such as Boston and Philadelphia.[4]

A primary goal of the houses of refuge was to prevent pauperism and to respond to youths who were ignored by the courts. Houses of refuge were meant to be institutions where children could be reformed and turned into hardworking members of the community. To accomplish this mission, youths

apprenticeship system The method by which middle- and upper-class children were taught skilled trades by a master.

binding-out system Practice in which children were "bound over" to masters for care. However, under the binding-out system, masters were not required to teach youths a trade.

Juvenile Crime Wave

Each generation of Americans seems to believe that the country is experiencing a "juvenile crime wave."

SOURCE: Thomas J. Bernard, *The Cycle of Juvenile Justice* (New York: Oxford University Press, 1992).

houses of refuge The first specialized correctional institutions for youths in the United States.

Houses of refuge were the first correctional institutions specifically for youths. *Should houses of refuge be used again for delinquent youths? Why or why not?*

were placed in houses of refuge for indeterminate periods or until their 18th or 21st birthdays. Placement, moreover, did not require a court hearing. A child could be committed to a house of refuge by a constable, by a parent, or on the order of a city alderman.[5]

While there, children engaged in a daily regimen of hard work, military drills, and enforced silence, as well as religious and academic training. It was also common practice for outside contractors to operate shops within the houses of refuge. In those shops, children produced goods such as shoes or furniture, and in return, the houses of refuge were paid 10 to 15 cents per youth each day. This arrangement allowed houses of refuge to pay a substantial percentage of their daily operating expenses.[6] When the youthful inmates failed to meet production quotas, they were often punished. After "reformation," boys were frequently indentured to masters on farms or to tradesmen, and girls were placed in domestic service.[7]

PLACING OUT Soon after the establishment of houses of refuge, reformers began to recognize the inability of those institutions to accommodate the large numbers of children needing placement and to either reform or control youths. One early response to those problems was the development of placing out. **Placing out,** which involved the placing of children on farms in the West

placing out The practice of placing children on farms in the Midwest and West to remove them from the supposedly corrupting influences of their parents and the cities.

and Midwest, was believed to have several advantages over the houses of refuge. First, placing out was seen as a way of removing children from the supposedly corrupting influences of their parents, who frequently were immigrants, and especially of the cities, which reformers viewed as breeding grounds for idleness and crime. Second, many reformers recognized that the conditions in the houses of refuge were counterproductive to the goal of reform. Third, rural areas were assumed to be an ideal environment for instilling in children the values the reformers cherished—values that stressed discipline, hard work, and piety.

Agents hired by charitable organizations would take children west by train and place them with farm families. Although some children were placed in caring homes and were treated as members of the family, others were not so lucky. Many of the children who were placed out were required to work hard for their keep, were abused, were not accepted as members of the family, and never saw their own families again.

PROBATION Another effort to deal with troubled children was initiated by a Boston shoemaker, John Augustus. As described in Chapter 9, Augustus spent considerable time observing the court and became convinced that many minor offenders could be salvaged. As a result of his concern and his willingness to work with offenders, Augustus was permitted to provide bail for his first probation client in 1841.

Augustus's first client was a drunkard who showed remarkable improvement during the period in which he was supervised. The court was impressed with Augustus's work and permitted him to stand bail for other minor offenders, including children.

After Augustus died, the Boston Children's Aid Society and other volunteers carried on his work. Then, in 1869, the state of Massachusetts formalized the existing volunteer probation system by authorizing visiting probation agents, who were to work with both adult and child offenders who showed promise. Under this arrangement, youths were allowed to return home to their parents, provided they obeyed the law.[8] In 1878, an additional law was passed in Boston that provided for paid probation officers.[9] Subsequently, several other states authorized the appointment of probation officers. However, it was not until after the turn of the twentieth century and the development of the first juvenile court that probation gained widespread acceptance.[10]

REFORM SCHOOLS, INDUSTRIAL SCHOOLS, AND TRAINING SCHOOLS By the late 1800s, the failure of houses of refuge was well known. Dislocations produced by the Civil War placed tremendous strain on houses of refuge and the placing-out system. Perhaps most disappointing, the number of problem youths was growing. In response, state and city governments took over the administration of institutions for juvenile delinquents. Another response was the establishment of **reform, industrial, or training schools,** correctional facilities that focused on custody.[11] Those institutions were of two types: cottage reformatories and institutional reformatories.

Cottage reformatories were usually located in rural areas to avoid the negative influences of the urban environment. They were intended to closely parallel family life. Each cottage contained 20–40 youths, who were supervised by cottage parents charged with the task of overseeing residents' training and education.[12]

In addition to cottage reformatories, larger, more institutional reformatories were developed in many states. Like the cottage reformatories, the institutional reformatories were usually located in rural areas in an effort to remove youths from the negative influences of city life. However, the institutions were frequently large and overcrowded.

reform, industrial, or training schools Correctional facilities for youths, first developed in the late 1800s, that focused on custody. Today, those institutions are often called training schools and although they may place more emphasis on treatment, they still rely on custody and control.

cottage reformatories Correctional facilities for youths, first developed in the late 1800s, that were intended to closely parallel family life and remove children from the negative influences of the urban environment. Children in those facilities lived with surrogate parents, who were responsible for the youths' training and education.

Juveniles incarcerated at the turn of the twentieth century were put into job training programs that would help them when they were released. Typically, male offenders learned industrial trades; female offenders learned ironing, laundry work, and cooking. *Should these practices be revived? Why or why not?*

Another development, in the late 1800s, was the establishment of separate institutions for females. Previously, girls had been committed to the same institutions as boys, although there was strict gender segregation in those institutions. Moreover, girls were often committed by parents or relatives for moral, as opposed to criminal, offenses. Those moral offenses consisted of such actions as "vagrancy, beggary, stubbornness, deceitfulness, idle and vicious behavior, wanton and lewd conduct, and running away."[13] The expressed goal of those institutions was to prepare girls to be good housewives and mothers. Yet, the institutions, like those for boys, were little different from the prisons of that era.

The reform, industrial, and training schools placed more emphasis on formal education than did the houses of refuge, but in many other respects there was little difference. Indeed, those institutions confronted many of the same problems as the houses of refuge had. Moreover, the conditions in the reformatories were certainly no better than those in the houses of refuge, and in many cases they were worse.

THE DEVELOPMENT OF THE JUVENILE COURT

By the end of the 1800s, a variety of institutions and mechanisms had been developed in response to problem children. Still, the problems presented by children who were believed to be in need of correctional treatment—problems such as homelessness, neglect, abuse, waywardness, and criminal behavior—proved difficult to solve. Consequently, during the late 1800s a new group of reformers, the *child savers*, began to advocate a new institution to deal with youth problems. This new institution was the juvenile court.

THE SOCIAL CONTEXT OF THE JUVENILE COURT The period from 1880 to 1920, a period historians refer to as the Progressive Era, was a time of major change in the United States. Although industrialization and urbanization were well under way, and previous waves of immigrants had added to the population of the country, the pace of industrialization, urbanization, and immigration quickened.

In an effort to respond to the problem of youth crime and waywardness, reformers again sought to save children from the crime-inducing conditions of

The Progressive Era

The city of Chicago provides a good example of the changes experienced during the Progressive Era. Between 1890 and 1910, Chicago's population grew from one million to two million. Between 1880 and 1890, the number of factories nearly tripled. By 1889, nearly 70 percent of the inhabitants of the city were immigrants.

SOURCE: Harold Finestone, *Victims of Change* (Westport, CT: Greenwood Press, 1976).

the cities. Supported by important philanthropic and civic organizations, the child savers worked to improve jail and reformatory conditions. However, the primary outcome of the child-saving movement was the extension of governmental control over children's lives. The child savers argued for stricter supervision of children, and they improved legal mechanisms designed to regulate children's activities.[14] In short, the child savers felt that children needed to be protected and that the best institutions for protecting them were government agencies such as the police and the courts, as well as local charitable organizations.

THE LEGAL CONTEXT OF THE JUVENILE COURT By the late 1800s, legal mechanisms for treating children differently and separately from adults had existed for some time. For example, jurisdictions had set the minimum age at which a child could be considered legally responsible for criminal behavior. Minimum ages for placement in adult penitentiaries were also enacted during the first half of the 1800s.[15] Moreover, special institutions for dealing with youths had been in existence since 1825, when the first house of refuge was established in New York City. Yet, cases involving juveniles were still heard in criminal courts. Many of the child savers believed that criminal courts failed to respond adequately to many of the transgressions of the young.

The legal philosophy justifying state intervention in the lives of children, the doctrine of **parens patriae** (the state as parent), was given judicial endorsement in the case *Ex parte Crouse* (1838). Mary Ann Crouse had been committed to the Philadelphia House of Refuge by her mother against her father's wishes. Mary Ann's father contested his daughter's placement, arguing that she was being punished even though she had committed no criminal offense. However, the Pennsylvania Supreme Court ruled that Mary Ann's placement was legal because (1) the purpose of the Philadelphia House of Refuge was to reform youths, not to punish them, (2) formal due process protections provided to adults in criminal trials were unnecessary because Mary Ann was not being punished, and (3) when parents were unwilling or unable to protect their children, the state had a legal obligation to do so.[16]

However, the right of the state to intervene in the lives of children did not go unchallenged. In *People* v. *Turner* (1870), for example, the Illinois Supreme Court ruled that Daniel O'Connell, who was committed to the Chicago House of Refuge against both his parents' wishes, was being punished and not helped by his placement. The court also decided that because placement in the house of refuge actually was punishment, due process protections were necessary.[17] The ruling, together with increasing concern over the willingness or ability of the criminal courts to protect or control youths, led reformers in Chicago to consider other mechanisms by which their aims might be achieved. The mechanism they created was the first juvenile court, which was established in Chicago in 1899 by passage of the Juvenile Court Act in Illinois.[18] Some scholars argue that the Juvenile Court Act was a means for the child savers, intent on salvaging poor children—especially poor immigrant children—to get around the *Turner* decision's requirement of due process protections for youths.

THE OPERATION OF EARLY JUVENILE COURTS The Juvenile Court Act of 1899 gave the Chicago juvenile court broad jurisdiction over persons under the age of 16 who were delinquent, dependent, or neglected. In addition, the act required:

1. The court to be overseen by a special judge.
2. Hearings to be held in a separate courtroom.
3. Separate records to be kept of juvenile hearings.[19]

It also made probation a major component of the juvenile court's response to offenders and emphasized the use of informal procedures at each stage of the juvenile court process. Indeed, this informality has been a hallmark of the

parens patriae The legal philosophy justifying state intervention in the lives of children when their parents are unable or unwilling to protect them.

Daniel O'Connell

Like Mary Ann Crouse, who was committed by her mother against her father's wishes, Daniel O'Connell was institutionalized even though he had committed no criminal offense. He was placed in the house of refuge because he was perceived to be in danger of becoming a pauper or a criminal. However, Daniel's case differed from Mary Ann's because both his parents objected to his placement and, even more important, because the court ruled that Daniel's placement was harmful, not helpful.

juvenile court since its beginning, a key feature distinguishing it from criminal court proceedings. The major reason for this informality is that the juvenile court has traditionally focused not on the act, but on the *whole child.*

In practice, the informality of the juvenile court allowed complaints against children to be made by almost anyone in the community. It also allowed juvenile court hearings to be held in offices, instead of in traditional courtrooms, and to be closed to the public, unlike criminal trials, which were open to the public. In the typical juvenile court hearing, the only persons present were the judge, the parents, the child, and the probation officer, who met and discussed the case. Also, few (if any) records were kept of hearings, proof of guilt was not necessary for the court to intervene in children's lives, and little or no concern for due process existed. Finally, judges exercised wide discretion in how they dealt with children, ranging from a warning to placement in an institution.[20]

The idea of a juvenile court spread rapidly after the passage of the Juvenile Court Act. Within a decade, 10 states had established special courts for children, and by 1925 all but two states had juvenile courts.[21] Moreover, those juvenile courts followed closely the model developed in Chicago of an informal court intended to "serve the best interests of children."

Despite the growing popularity of the new courts, they did not go completely unchallenged. In the case *Commonwealth of Pennsylvania v. Fisher* (1905), for example, the Pennsylvania Supreme Court again examined the juvenile court's mission, the right to intervene, and the due process protections owed to children. In this case, Frank Fisher, a 14-year-old male, was indicted for larceny and committed to the house of refuge until his 21st birthday. Frank's father objected to his placement, claiming that Frank's 7-year sentence for a minor offense was more severe than he would have received in criminal court.[22]

In its ruling, the Pennsylvania Supreme Court upheld the idea of the juvenile court, and in many respects repeated the arguments it had made in the *Crouse* decision. The court found that the state may intervene in families when parents are unable or unwilling to prevent their children from engaging in crime and that Frank was being helped by his placement in the house of refuge. It further ruled that due process protections were unnecessary when the state acted under its *parens patriae* powers.[23]

The *Fisher* case set the legal tone for the juvenile court from its beginnings until the mid-1960s, when new legal challenges began to be mounted. Those legal challenges attempted primarily to expand juveniles' due process protections. Critics of the juvenile courts recognized that despite their expressed goal of "serving the best interests of children," the established institutions of juvenile justice often did the opposite.

THE LEGAL REFORM YEARS: THE JUVENILE COURT AFTER *GAULT* The 1960s and 1970s provided the social context for a more critical assessment of American institutions, including juvenile justice. Beginning in the mid-1960s and continuing though the mid-1970s, a number of cases decided by the U.S. Supreme Court altered the operation of the juvenile court. The most important of those cases was *In re Gault,* which expanded the number of due process protections afforded juveniles within the juvenile court. However, a number of other cases also helped define juveniles' rights within juvenile justice and contributed to the legal structure found in juvenile courts today. The first of those cases was *Kent* v. *United States* (1966).

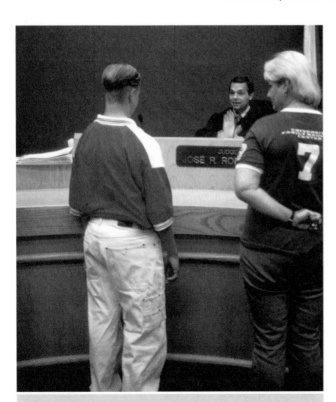

The use of informal procedures is characteristic of the juvenile court system. *Are the juvenile court's informal procedures desirable? Why or why not?*

Morris Kent was a 16-year-old juvenile on probation who was transferred to criminal court to stand trial on charges of robbery and rape. Although the juvenile court judge received several motions from Kent's attorney opposing the transfer, he made no ruling on them. Further, after indicating that a "full investigation" had been completed, the juvenile court judge transferred Kent to criminal court for trial.[24] Thus, an important decision had been made, the decision to try Kent as an adult, even though no hearing had been held. Kent's attorney had no opportunity to see or to question material that had been used to make the decision to transfer jurisdiction, and no reasons for the court's decision were given.

The *Kent* case is important for several reasons. It was the first major ruling by the U.S. Supreme Court that closely examined the operation of the juvenile courts. It also made clear the need for due process protections for juveniles who were being transferred to criminal court for trial. The Court noted that even though a hearing to consider transfer to criminal court is far less formal than a trial, juveniles are still entitled to some due process protections. Specifically, the Court ruled that before a juvenile court could transfer a case to criminal court, there must be a hearing to consider the transfer, the defendant must have the assistance of defense counsel if requested, defense counsel must have access to social records kept by the juvenile court, and the reasons for the juvenile court's decision to transfer must be stated.[25]

Having given notice that it would review the operations of the juvenile court, the Supreme Court, within a year of the *Kent* decision, heard another landmark case. This case, *In re Gault* (1967), went far beyond the ruling in *Kent* in its examination of juvenile court practices. The *Gault* case is important because it extended a variety of due process protections to juveniles. In addition, the facts of the case clearly demonstrate the potential for abuse in the informal practices of the traditional juvenile court.

Gerald Gault was 15 years old when he, along with a friend, was taken into custody by the Gila County, Arizona, sheriff's department for allegedly making an obscene phone call to a neighbor, Ms. Cook. At the time of his arrest, Gerald was on 6-months' probation as a result of his presence when another friend had stolen a wallet from a woman's purse. Without notifying his mother, a deputy took Gerald into custody on the oral complaint of Ms. Cook and transported him to the local detention unit.

When Ms. Gault heard Gerald was in custody, she went to the detention facility. The superintendent of the facility told her that a juvenile court hearing would be held the next day. On the following day, Gerald, his mother, and the deputy who had taken Gerald into custody appeared before the juvenile court judge in chambers. The deputy had filed a petition alleging that Gerald was delinquent. Ms. Cook, the complainant, was not present. Without being informed that he did not have to testify, Gerald was questioned by the judge about the telephone call and was sent back to detention. No record was made of this hearing, no one was sworn, and no specific charge was made, other than an allegation that Gerald was delinquent. At the end of the hearing, the judge said he would "think about it." Gerald was released a few days later, although no reasons were given for his detention or release.

On the day of Gerald's release, Ms. Gault received a letter indicating that another hearing would be held a few days later about Gerald's delinquency. The hearing was held and, again, the complainant was not present. Again, there was no transcript or recording of the proceedings, and what was said was later disputed by the parties. Neither Gerald nor his parent was advised of a right to remain silent, a right to be represented by counsel, or any other constitutional rights. At the conclusion of the hearing, Gerald was found delinquent and was committed to the state industrial school until he was 21 years old, unless released earlier by the court. This meant that Gerald received a sentence of up to 6 years for an offense that if committed by an adult, would

In re

The Latin phrase *in re* in the description of court cases (for example, *In re Gault*) means, literally, "in the matter of" or "concerning." It is used when a case does not involve adversarial parties.

Juvenile Justice by State
Go to **www.acf.dhhs.gov/programs/ cb/laws/pi/pi9902a7.htm** to access the Web site for the National Center for Juvenile Justice to find descriptive information and analyses of the various juvenile justice systems in the United States. Compare your state's juvenile justice system to that of another state. *How are the two states similar? Different?*

Due Process

Many states have required more due process protections for juveniles than have been mandated by the Supreme Court. For example, many state laws specify that juveniles have a right to trial (adjudication) by a jury. In fact, Texas requires that all adjudications be heard by a jury. Nevertheless, jury trials are rare in states that have this right, including Texas. This is because the right must be exercised or, as in Texas, the automatic right to a trial by jury can be waived. In practice, jury trials are often discouraged because they are time-consuming and costly.

In the 1967 landmark case of *In re Gault*, Supreme Court Justice Abe Fortas wrote, "Due process of law is the primary and indispensable foundation of individual freedom." *Do you agree with Justice Fortas? Why or why not?*

adjudication The juvenile court equivalent of a trial in criminal court, or the process of rendering a judicial decision regarding the truth of the facts alleged in a petition.

Juvenile Courts

Each state has at least one court with juvenile jurisdiction, but only in a few states is it called juvenile court. Other names include district, superior, circuit, county, family, or probate court. Regardless of the name, courts with juvenile jurisdiction are generally referred to as juvenile courts.

SOURCE: Melissa Sickmund, "Juveniles in Court," *Juvenile Offenders and Victims National Report Series Bulletin* (Washington, DC: GPO, U.S. Department of Justice, Office of Juvenile Justice and Delinquency Prevention, June 2003), p. 4.

have been punished by a maximum sentence of 2 months in jail and a $50 fine.

When the case finally reached the Supreme Court, the Court held that a youth has procedural rights in delinquency hearings where there is the possibility of confinement in a state institution. Specifically, the Court ruled that juveniles have a right against self-incrimination, a right to adequate notice of charges against them, a right to confront and to cross-examine their accusers, and a right to assistance of counsel. In addition, the Court's ruling implied that juveniles also have the rights to sworn testimony and appeal.

The landmark *Gault* decision was not the last Supreme Court decision to influence juvenile court procedures. The Supreme Court further expanded protections for juveniles 3 years after *Gault*. In a 1970 case, *In re Winship*, the Court ruled that delinquency charges must be proven beyond a reasonable doubt where there was a possibility that a youth could be confined in a locked facility. Until the *Winship* ruling, the standard of proof typically employed at the adjudication stage of the juvenile justice process was a preponderance of the evidence, the level of proof employed in civil proceedings. **Adjudication** is the juvenile court equivalent of a trial in criminal court, or the process of rendering a judicial decision regarding the truth of the facts alleged in a petition. Under the preponderance-of-the-evidence standard of proof, juveniles could be adjudicated delinquent (found guilty) if the weight of the evidence was slightly against them, a much lower standard of proof than the standard required in criminal courts.

It is important to note that both the *Gault* and *Winship* decisions not only increased procedural formality in juvenile court cases but also shifted the traditional focus from the "whole child" to the child's act. Once this shift occurred, it was only a short step to offense-based sentencing and the more punitive orientation that is characteristic of the juvenile justice system today.

The Supreme Court's extension of due process protections to juveniles slowed in the year following the *Winship* decision. In a 1971 ruling, *McKeiver v. Pennsylvania*, the Court held that juveniles were not entitled to a trial by jury. The Court cited several reasons for the decision:

1. The Court did not want to turn the juvenile court into a fully adversarial process.
2. The Court determined that bench trials could produce accurate determinations.
3. The Court felt that it was too early to completely abandon the philosophy of the juvenile court and its treatment mission.

To grant juveniles all of the protections accorded adults, the Court surmised, would make the juvenile court indistinguishable from the criminal court.

The continued informality of the juvenile court may explain why very few youths contest charges against them and why a surprising number of youths who are not adjudicated delinquent (found guilty) are placed on probation. Indeed, most youths who appear before the juvenile court admit to the charges against them.[26] Moreover, data collected by the National Center for Juvenile Justice indicate that in 2002 (the latest year for which data were available), about 8 percent of youths who were not adjudicated delinquent in juvenile courts were still placed on some form of probation (see also Figure 10.3 on page 388).[27]

Today, juveniles have been granted many, but not all, of the due process protections given adults in criminal trials. However, the daily operation of juvenile courts calls into question the extent to which court-mandated changes in juvenile justice procedures have influenced the traditional informality of the juvenile court. Juvenile court procedures are still characterized by an informality that most people would find unacceptable if it were applied to adults in criminal court.

The Processing of Juvenile Offenders

Juvenile delinquency in the United States is widespread, and people respond to it both formally and informally. Informal responses consist of actions taken by members of the public that do not rely on official agencies of juvenile justice. Formal responses, on the other hand, rely on official agencies of juvenile justice such as the police and juvenile court. Figure 10.1 depicts the stages in the formal juvenile justice process. Before providing a detailed examination of the formal juvenile justice process, however, we take a brief look at the informal juvenile justice process.

THE INFORMAL JUVENILE JUSTICE PROCESS

An examination of the juvenile justice process usually begins with the police, and the police do play a critical role in juvenile justice. However, any discussion of the juvenile justice process should really begin with the public, because police involvement with juveniles is typically the result of citizen complaints.

The informal actions taken by citizens to respond to delinquency constitute an **informal juvenile justice** process that operates outside the official agencies of juvenile justice. Many illegal behaviors by juveniles are handled informally by neighbors, business owners, teachers, and others who are not part of the formal juvenile justice apparatus. The informal processing of juveniles is important because it is one of the mechanisms that operates to control youths' behavior. The more citizens rely on informal control and the more effective it is, the less necessary the formal processing of juveniles becomes.

Although many delinquent actions are handled informally, in other instances members of the public decide to call the police or the juvenile court and to request action from the formal agencies of juvenile justice. Thus, most youths become involved in the formal juvenile justice process when the people who make up the informal process decide, in their discretion, to involve the police or the juvenile court. This means that some combination of the public and the police plays a major role in determining who the clientele of juvenile justice will be.

THE FORMAL JUVENILE JUSTICE PROCESS

The police represent the primary gatekeepers to the formal juvenile justice process. For example, in 2002 (the latest year for which data are available), 82 percent of delinquency cases referred to the juvenile courts came from police agencies.[28] This percentage has remained about the same for about two decades. In the case of status offenses, however, the percentage of cases referred from police agencies varies greatly by offense. In 2002, for example, 92 percent of status liquor law violation cases were referred by police agencies to the juvenile courts, while only 55 percent of cases of running away, 30 percent of ungovernability (being beyond the control of parents or guardians) cases, and 14 percent of truancy cases were referred from police agencies.[29] **Status offenses** are acts that are not crimes when committed by adults but are illegal for minors.

Illegal Behavior

Although few juveniles commit serious violent crimes, self-report studies show that most juveniles have engaged in some type of illegal behavior. For example, a 2004 national survey of high school seniors revealed that nearly 71 percent of them had consumed alcohol illegally during the last 12 months, and 48 percent of them had consumed alcohol illegally within the previous 30 days.

Source: U.S. Department of Justice, Bureau of Justice Statistics, "Drug Use," www.ojp.usdoj.gov/bjs/dcf/du.htm.

informal juvenile justice The actions taken by citizens to respond to juvenile offenders without involving the official agencies of juvenile justice.

status offenses Acts that are not crimes when committed by adults but are illegal for minors (for example, truancy or running away from home).

FIGURE 10.1 The Formal Juvenile Justice Process

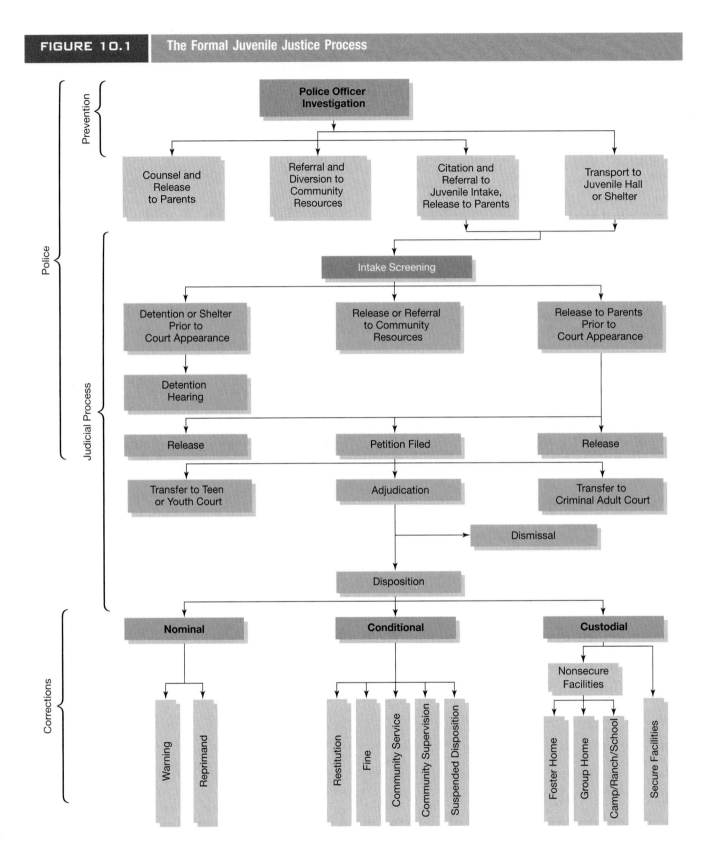

THE POLICE RESPONSE TO JUVENILES Like citizens, the police exercise discretion in handling juvenile cases. Typical responses that police officers may employ are to

1. Warn and release.
2. Refer to parents.
3. Refer to a diversionary program operated by the police or another community agency.
4. Refer to court.

In some communities, an officer may have a variety of options, while in other communities available options are more limited.

Describing the typical police response to juveniles in trouble is difficult because there is considerable variation in the ways individual officers approach juvenile offenders. A number of factors influence the ways police officers handle juvenile suspects. Among those factors are the following:

1. The seriousness of the offense.
2. The police organization.
3. The community.
4. The wishes of the complainant.
5. The demeanor of the youth.
6. The gender of the offender.
7. The race and social class of the offender.

Offense Seriousness The most important factor in the decision to arrest is the seriousness of the offense. Regardless of the subject's demeanor or other factors, as the seriousness of the offense increases, so does the likelihood of arrest. Most police-juvenile encounters involving felony offenses result in an arrest. However, most police-juvenile encounters involve minor offenses. When offenses are minor, a number of other factors have been found to influence police decision making.

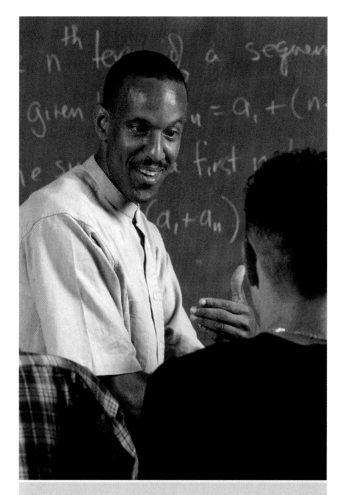

Teachers are an important part of the informal juvenile justice process. *What can teachers do to keep students from becoming delinquent?*

The Police Organization As described in Chapter 3, police departments develop their own particular styles of operation. Those styles, in turn, help structure the way officers respond to juvenile offenders. For example, in one study that categorized police departments by the extent to which they employed a legalistic style of policing, characterized by a high degree of professionalism and bureaucratic structure, it was discovered that officers in most legalistic departments were more likely to arrest juvenile suspects than were officers in less legalistic departments.[30] Thus, the ways that police department personnel respond to juvenile offenders is to some extent a product of the organizational characteristics and policies developed by their individual departments. However, police departments do not operate in a political and social vacuum. They are also influenced by the communities in which they operate.

The Community Communities influence policing in a variety of ways. Through their interactions with residents of a community, police develop assumptions about the communities they police, the people who live in those communities, and the ability and willingness of community residents to respond to crime and delinquency. Research suggests that police operate differently in lower-class communities than in wealthier communities. Police expect lower-class communities to have higher levels of crime and delinquency

Juveniles and Curfew

Juvenile arrests for curfew and loitering violations increased 35 percent between 1993 and 2002. In 2002, 28 percent of curfew arrests involved juveniles under the age of 15, and 31 percent involved females.

SOURCE: Howard N. Snyder, "Juvenile Arrests 2002," *Juvenile Justice Bulletin* (Washington, DC: GPO, U.S. Department of Justice, Office of Juvenile Justice and Delinquency Prevention, September 2004), p. 3.

Myth Fact

The commission of serious, violent crime by juveniles is widespread.

In 2002, there were 276 arrests for every 100,000 juveniles 10 to 17 years of age for murder and nonnegligent manslaughter, forcible rape, robbery, and aggravated assault. If each of those arrests involved a different juvenile (which is very unlikely), then fewer than one-half of 1 percent of all persons aged 10 to 17 in the United States were arrested for one of those four crimes in 2002.

SOURCE: Howard N. Snyder, "Juvenile Arrests 2002," *Juvenile Justice Bulletin* (Washington, DC: GPO, U.S. Department of Justice, Office of Juvenile Justice and Delinquency Prevention, September 2004), p. 4.

FYI

"Child Delinquents"

In 2003, the police arrested about one-half of a million (497,975) youths age 14 and younger. Such very young offenders represented about 5 percent of the total number of juvenile arrestees. These numbers may underestimate the number of child delinquents because in many jurisdictions it is unusual for delinquents under age 12 to be arrested or referred to juvenile court.

SOURCE: Federal Bureau of Investigation, *Crime in the United States 2003*, p. 286, Table 41, www.fbi.gov/ucr/03cius.htm. *OJJDP Research 2000* (Washington, DC: GPO, U.S. Department of Justice, Office of Juvenile Justice and Delinquency Prevention, May 2001), p. 3.

because more arrests are made in those communities and because they know that lower-class communities have fewer resources with which to respond informally to the array of problems experienced there. Consequently, when police have contact with juveniles in lower-class communities, formal responses become more likely because informal responses are believed to be ineffective in most cases. Indeed, research that has examined the effect of neighborhood socioeconomic status has found that as the socioeconomic status of the neighborhood increases, the likelihood that a police-juvenile encounter will end in arrest declines.[31]

The Wishes of the Complainant As noted earlier, many police-juvenile interactions occur because of a citizen complaint to the police. What police do in those situations often depends on whether the complainant is present, what the complainant would like the police to do, and, sometimes, who the complainant is.

The Demeanor of the Youth As one might expect, how youths behave toward the police can influence whether an arrest is made. Interestingly, youths who are either unusually antagonistic or unusually polite are more likely to be arrested. In contrast, youths who are moderately respectful to the police are less likely to be arrested—as long as the offense is not serious.[32]

The Gender of the Offender Gender also appears to influence the decision to arrest, particularly when status offenses are involved. A number of studies have found that female status offenders are more likely to be formally processed than male status offenders.[33]

A juvenile's demeanor can influence arrest decisions. *How would you advise a juvenile to act if he or she is stopped by a police officer?*

When it comes to criminal offenses, however, research results are mixed. Some of the research shows that girls are less likely than boys to be arrested for criminal offenses, even when prior record and seriousness of offense are taken into account.[34] Other research suggests that any gender bias that existed in the past has diminished or disappeared.[35]

The Race and Social Class of the Offender There is strong evidence that a juvenile's race and social class influence police decision making. The evidence is clear that minority and poor youths are represented disproportionately in arrest statistics. For example, according to 2003 UCR data, white youths accounted for 71 percent of all arrests of persons under 18 years of age. They accounted for 69 percent of arrests for index property offenses and about 53 percent of arrests for index violent offenses. In contrast, African American youths accounted for about 27 percent of all arrests of persons under 18 years of age, 28 percent of index property-crime arrests, and approximately 45 percent of index violent-crime arrests. Other racial groups accounted for the remainder of arrests of persons under 18 years of age.[36] Thus, although white youths account for the majority of juvenile arrests, African American youths are arrested in disproportionate numbers, since they comprise only 15.5 percent of the U.S. population under 18 years of age.[37]

The UCR does not report arrests by social class. However, self-report data reveal that the prevalence of delinquency (that is, the proportion of the youth population involved in delinquency) does not differ significantly between social classes when all types of offenses are considered. In other words, the proportions of middle-class and lower-class youths who engage in delinquency are similar. However, when different types of offenses are examined, significant social class differences appear. Middle-class youths have higher rates of involvement in such offenses as stealing from their families, cheating on tests, cutting classes, disorderly conduct, and drunkenness. Lower-class youths, on the other hand, have higher rates of involvement in more serious offenses, such as felony assault and robbery.[38]

POLICE PROCESSING OF JUVENILE OFFENDERS When a police officer encounters a juvenile who has committed an illegal act, the officer must decide what to do. One option is to make an arrest. (In some jurisdictions, this is referred to as "taking into custody.") For practical purposes, an arrest takes place whenever a youth is not free to walk away.

As a general rule, the basis for arresting a juvenile is the same as for arresting an adult. An officer needs to have probable cause. There are, however, several differences between arrests of adults and juveniles. First, the police can arrest juveniles for a wider range of behaviors. For example, juveniles, but not adults, can be arrested for status offenses. (Technically, juveniles are not "arrested" for status offenses, because such offenses are not crimes. Also, because status offenses are not crimes, the apprehension of juveniles for status offenses does not require probable cause.) Second, at least in some jurisdictions, juveniles are given the *Miranda* warnings in the presence of a parent, guardian, or attorney. This is not necessary, however, because the Supreme Court, in *Fare* v. *Michael C.* (1979), ruled that parents or attorneys do not have to be present for juveniles to waive their rights. Third, in many jurisdictions, juveniles are more likely than adults who have committed similar offenses to be detained pending adjudication. In *Schall* v. *Martin* (1984), the Supreme Court ruled that preventive detention of juveniles is acceptable.

Concern about the detention of juveniles generally focuses on the use of preventive detention. Some critics argue that it amounts to punishment before a youth has been found guilty of an offense. The conditions juveniles

Gang Stereotypes

Youth gang members, contrary to popular stereotypes, are not typically male, urban, poor, minority, or from single-parent households. Although they are more likely to live in socially disorganized and marginalized communities, youth gang members come from a variety of backgrounds. One thing they do have in common, however, is that once they join a gang, juveniles engage in high levels of criminal activity.

SOURCE: Finn-Aage Esbensen, "Preventing Adolescent Gang Involvement," *Juvenile Justice Bulletin* (Washington, DC: GPO, U.S. Department of Justice, September 2000), p. 9.

Juveniles and Jail

On a typical day in 2004, 7,083 juveniles were confined in adult jails in the United States—a 7 percent decrease from 2000 and a 9 percent decrease from 1995. Of the 7,083 juveniles confined in adult jails on a typical day in 2004, nearly 90 percent were tried or awaiting trial as adults. In states that allow the jailing of juveniles, statutes usually prevent youths from being placed in cells with adults. This means that jail administrators must provide separate rooms and supervision for juveniles within their facilities. For juveniles, separation often means isolation, which is in turn related to an increased risk of self-destructive behavior. A national study found that the suicide rate for juveniles in adult jails was almost five times the suicide rate for juveniles in the general population, and nearly eight times the suicide rate of juveniles in juvenile detention facilities.

Source: Paige M. Harrison and Allen J. Beck, "Prison and Jail Inmates at Midyear, 2004," *Bureau of Justice Statistics Bulletin* (Washington, DC: GPO, U.S. Department of Justice, April 2005), p. 8, Table 9; Community Research Center, *An Assessment of the National Incidence of Juvenile Suicide in Adult Jails, Lockups, and Juvenile Detention Centers* (Champaign, IL: Community Research Center, 1980).

radical nonintervention A practice based on the idea that youths should be left alone if at all possible, instead of being formally processed.

are sometimes exposed to in detention units and adult jails raise additional concerns.

The exact procedures that the police must follow when taking a juvenile into custody vary from state to state and are specified in state juvenile codes. However, those codes typically require officers to notify a juvenile's parents that the juvenile is in custody. Police often ask parents to come to the police station. Sometimes, an officer transports a youth home prior to any questioning. When an officer feels that detention of a juvenile is appropriate, the juvenile is transported to a juvenile detention facility. If such facilities are not available, the youth may be taken to an adult jail in some jurisdictions. In cases where a juvenile is released to his or her parents, the juvenile and the parents are informed that they will be contacted by the court at a later date about the case. After a juvenile is released, an officer completes the complaint, collecting any additional information needed, and then forwards it to the next stage of the juvenile justice process for further action. When a juvenile is detained in a juvenile detention facility or an adult jail, the processing of the complaint is expedited because juvenile codes require a detention hearing (and therefore, a specific complaint) to determine the appropriateness of detention.

TRENDS IN POLICE PROCESSING OF JUVENILES In 2004, 69.5 percent of all juveniles taken into police custody were referred to juvenile court, 21 percent were handled within the police department and released, and nearly 8 percent were referred to adult or criminal courts.[39] However, an examination of such data over time reveals a trend toward increased formal processing of cases (referral to court) by police agencies. For example, in 1972, approximately 51 percent of youths taken into custody by the police were referred to the juvenile court, 45 percent were handled within the police department and released, and only about 1 percent were referred to criminal courts. Table 10.1 shows that there has been a trend toward

1. Referring more youths to juvenile court.
2. Handling fewer cases within police departments.
3. Referring more cases to criminal courts.

DIVERSION The goal of juvenile diversion programs is to respond to youths in ways that avoid formal juvenile justice processing. Diversion can occur at any stage of the juvenile justice process, but it is most often employed before adjudication.

Diversion programs are based on the understanding that formal responses to youths who violate the law, such as arrest and adjudication, do not always protect the best interests of the youths or the community. Consequently, efforts to divert youths *from* the juvenile justice process by warning and releasing them, as well as efforts to divert youths *to* specific diversionary programs, such as counseling, have long been a part of juvenile justice practice. This is especially true for status offenders. Since the enactment of the Juvenile Justice and Delinquency Act of 1974, which stipulated that status offenders not be placed in secure detention facilities or secure correctional facilities, the number of status offenders diverted from formal juvenile justice processing has increased dramatically.

Today, diversion strategies are of two basic types. Some diversion strategies are based on the idea of radical nonintervention. Other strategies are designed to involve youths, and possibly parents, in a diversionary program. **Radical nonintervention** is based on the idea that youths should be left alone if at all possible, instead of being formally processed. The police practice of warning and releasing some juvenile offenders is an example of radical nonintervention.

| TABLE 10.1 | Percentage Distribution of Juveniles Taken into Police Custody, by Method of Disposition |

	REFERRED TO JUVENILE COURT JURISDICTION	HANDLED WITHIN DEPARTMENT AND RELEASED	REFERRED TO CRIMINAL OR ADULT COURT	REFERRED TO OTHER POLICE AGENCY	REFERRED TO WELFARE AGENCY
1974	47.0	44.4	3.7	2.4	2.5
1975	52.7	41.6	2.3	1.9	1.4
1976	53.4	39.0	4.4	1.7	1.6
1977	53.2	38.1	3.9	1.8	3.0
1978	55.9	36.6	3.8	1.8	1.9
1979	57.3	34.6	4.8	1.7	1.6
1980	58.1	33.8	4.8	1.7	1.6
1981	58.0	33.8	5.1	1.6	1.5
1982	58.9	32.5	5.4	1.5	1.6
1983	57.5	32.8	4.8	1.7	3.1
1984	60.0	31.5	5.2	1.3	2.0
1985	61.8	30.7	4.4	1.2	1.9
1986	61.7	29.9	5.5	1.1	1.8
1987	62.0	30.3	5.2	1.0	1.4
1988	63.1	29.1	4.7	1.1	1.9
1989	63.9	28.7	4.5	1.2	1.7
1990	64.5	28.3	4.5	1.1	1.6
1991	64.2	28.1	5.0	1.0	1.7
1992	62.5	30.1	4.7	1.1	1.7
1993	67.3	25.6	4.8	0.9	1.5
1994	63.2	29.5	4.7	1.0	1.7
1995	65.7	28.4	3.3	0.9	1.7
1996	68.6	23.3	6.2	0.9	0.9
1997	66.9	24.6	6.6	0.8	1.1
1998	69.2	22.2	6.8	0.9	1.0
1999	69.2	22.5	6.4	1.0	0.8
2000	70.8	20.3	7.0	1.1	0.8
2001	72.4	19.0	6.5	1.4	0.7
2002	72.8	18.1	7.0	1.4	0.7
2003	71.0	20.1	7.1	1.2	0.6
2004	69.5	20.8	7.9	1.3	0.5

Note: Because of rounding, percentages may not add to 100.

Source: *Sourcebook of Criminal Justice Statistics Online*, Table 4.26 at www.albany.edu/sourcebook/1995/pdf/t426.pdf.; Federal Bureau of Investigation, *Crime in the United States*, 2002, 2003, and 2004 editions, www.fbi.gov.

The practice of referring juveniles to community agencies for services such as individual or family counseling is an example of a strategy that involves youths in a diversionary program.

Contemporary diversion programs are operated by both juvenile justice and community agencies. Interventions employed in those programs include providing basic casework services to youths; providing individual, family, and group counseling; requiring restitution; and imposing community service.

Recently, a relatively small number of juvenile offenders (estimates suggest more than 120,000 cases a year) have been adjudicated in teen courts or youth courts instead of juvenile courts or adult courts.[40] Teen courts or youth courts are a new way of dealing with relatively young and usually first-time offenders charged with offenses such as theft, misdemeanor assault, disorderly conduct, and possession of alcohol. As of July 2005, there were 1,037 teen court programs in the United States, up from about 50 in 1991.

Teen Courts
To learn more about teen courts, visit the Web site of the National Youth Court Center at **www.youthcourt.net.** *Do you think teen courts are a good idea? Why or why not?*

Teen courts are based on one of four models:

1. Adult judge—An adult serves as judge and rules on legal matters and courtroom procedure. Youths serve as attorneys, jurors, clerks, bailiffs, etc.
2. Youth judge—Similar to the adult judge model, but a youth serves as judge.
3. Tribunal—Youth attorneys present the case to a panel of three youth judges, who decide the appropriate disposition for the defendant. A jury is not used.
4. Peer jury—This model does not use youth attorneys; the case is presented to a youth jury by a youth or adult. The youth jury then questions the defendant directly.

Nearly half of all teen courts use the adult judge model.

Most teen courts do not determine guilt or innocence. Rather they serve as diversion alternatives and youths must admit to the charges against them to qualify for teen court. Figure 10.2 shows the state laws governing the use of teen courts. The most common disposition used in teen court cases is community service. Other frequently used dispositions included victim apology letters, apology essays, teen court jury duty, drug/alcohol classes, and monetary restitution.

Another new juvenile diversion program is restorative justice conferences or family group conferences.[41] Commonly used in Australia and New Zealand and increasingly being used throughout the world, restorative justice conferences bring together juvenile offenders, their victims, and other relevant parties (such as parents or guardians) with trained facilitators to discuss the offense and the harm done to victims and the other relevant parties. As is the

| FIGURE 10.2 | State Laws Governing the Use of Teen Courts |

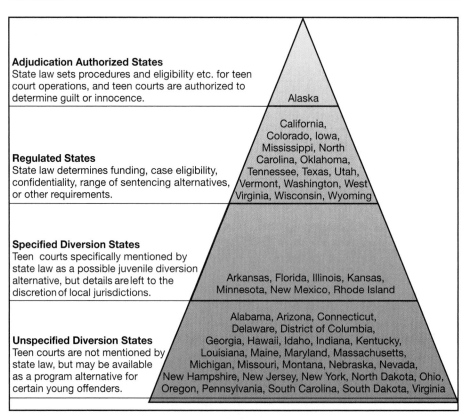

Adjudication Authorized States
State law sets procedures and eligibility etc. for teen court operations, and teen courts are authorized to determine guilt or innocence.

Alaska

Regulated States
State law determines funding, case eligibility, confidentiality, range of sentencing alternatives, or other requirements.

California, Colorado, Iowa, Mississippi, North Carolina, Oklahoma, Tennessee, Texas, Utah, Vermont, Washington, West Virginia, Wisconsin, Wyoming

Specified Diversion States
Teen courts specifically mentioned by state law as a possible juvenile diversion alternative, but details are left to the discretion of local jurisdictions.

Arkansas, Florida, Illinois, Kansas, Minnesota, New Mexico, Rhode Island

Unspecified Diversion States
Teen courts are not mentioned by state law, but may be available as a program alternative for certain young offenders.

Alabama, Arizona, Connecticut, Delaware, District of Columbia, Georgia, Hawaii, Idaho, Indiana, Kentucky, Louisiana, Maine, Maryland, Massachusetts, Michigan, Missouri, Montana, Nebraska, Nevada, New Hampshire, New Jersey, New York, North Dakota, Ohio, Oregon, Pennsylvania, South Carolina, South Dakota, Virginia

Source: Jeffrey A. Butts, Janeen Buck, and Mark B. Coggeshall, *The Impact of Teen Court on Young Offenders* (Washington, DC: U.S. Department of Justice, Office of Juvenile Justice and Delinquency Prevention, The Urban Institute, April 2002), p. 3.

case with teen courts, juvenile offenders who have been screened to participate in restorative justice conferences are generally nonviolent offenders who
commit less-serious offenses and have not had a previous referral.

At the conference, victims and the other relevant parties have an opportunity to explain how they have been affected by the offense and to question the
offending juveniles. At the end of the conference, the participants determine
how the offending juveniles can make amends to the victims for the wrong
done and then sign a reparation agreement. These agreements typically
include an apology and some type of restitution to the victims. They may also
require the offenders to perform community service or complete other requirements such as improving school attendance, finishing homework, or doing
chores at home or school. If an agreement cannot be reached or a juvenile
challenges the allegations, then the matter proceeds to juvenile court.

Advocates of restorative justice conferences and teen courts maintain that the
programs provide greater benefits to all parties involved than does the traditional
juvenile court system. Proponents argue that restorative justice conferences and
teen courts hold juveniles more accountable for their offenses, better enable
offending juveniles to appreciate how their actions negatively affected others, better involve and meet the needs of victims, and create a more supportive community for offending juveniles. Additional benefits include the timelier handling
of cases, cost savings because of the heavy reliance on volunteers, and higher
levels of victim satisfaction. Because of the lack of rigorous studies, it is not possible at this time to determine whether restorative justice conferences and teen
courts are more effective at reducing recidivism than is the traditional juvenile
court system or other juvenile diversion programs. However, based on the
research available, as well as anecdotal evidence, it appears that both restorative
justice conferences and teen courts may be positive alternatives to the traditional
juvenile court process, especially in jurisdictions that do not have a wide variety
of intervention options for young, first-time juvenile offenders.

DETENTION Sometimes a youth is held in a secure detention facility during
processing. There are three primary reasons for this practice: (1) to protect
the community from the juvenile, (2) to ensure that the juvenile appears at a
subsequent stage of processing, and (3) to secure the juvenile's own safety. In
2003, juveniles were held in detention facilities at some point between referral to court and case disposition in 25 percent of all delinquency cases disposed. The percentage of juveniles detained during processing has not changed
very much since 1985.[42] Federal rules require that a juvenile who is detained
in an adult jail or lockup be held for no more than 6 hours and in a separate
area out of sight or sound of adult inmates.[43]

INTAKE SCREENING When the decision to arrest a youth is made, or a social
agency such as a school alleges that an offense has occurred, the next step in
the juvenile justice process is **intake screening.** The purpose of intake screening is to make decisions about the continued processing of cases. Those decisions and others made during juvenile court processing of delinquency cases
in 2002 are shown in Figure 10.3. The location of the intake screening and
the educational background and training of the person who conducts it vary
from jurisdiction to jurisdiction. Traditionally, intake screening has been performed by probation officers. However, in recent years there has been a move
toward involving the prosecuting attorney in the intake process. In fact, in
some jurisdictions, such as Colorado and Washington, intake screening is now
the responsibility of the prosecuting attorney's office.[44] In other states, such
as Michigan, intake screening is done by an intake officer (probation officer)
who works for the juvenile court, although the prosecuting attorney's office
reviews most complaints for legal sufficiency.

Net Widening

Even though diversion programs are frequently touted as a way to reduce the
number of youths involved in juvenile justice, some diversionary strategies contribute to net widening. Net widening
occurs when a program handles youths
who would have been left alone in the
absence of the new program.

intake screening The process by which
decisions are made about the continued
processing of juvenile cases. Decisions might
include dismissing the case, referring the youth
to a diversion program, or filing a petition.

FIGURE 10.3   Juvenile Court Processing of Delinquency Cases, 2002, National Estimates

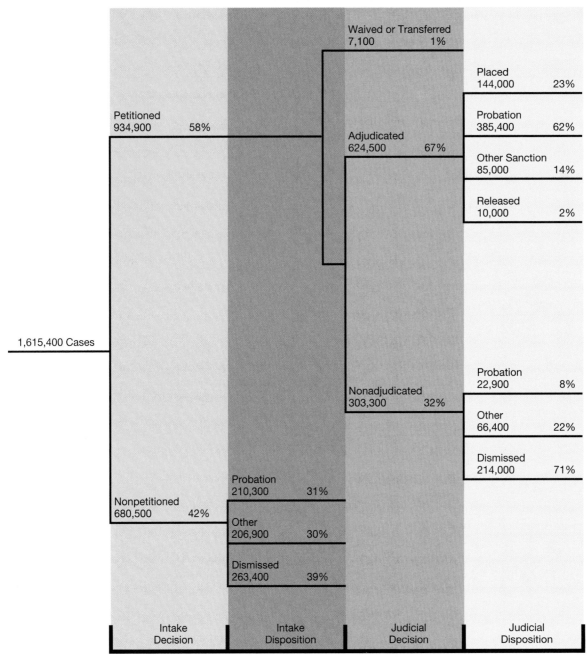

Note: Detail may not add to totals because of rounding.

Source: Howard N. Snyder and Melissa Sickmund, *Juvenile Offenders and Victims: 2006 National Report.* U.S. Department of Justice, Office of Juvenile Justice and Delinquency Prevention, (Pittsburgh, PA: National Center for Juvenile Justice, 2006), p. 177.

petition A legal form of the police complaint that specifies the charges to be heard at the adjudication.

Possible intake decisions might include dismissing the case or having youths and parents in for a conference or an informal hearing to collect additional information for making the intake decision. Other decisions include referral of the youth to a diversion program (for example, informal probation or counseling at a community agency), filing a **petition** (a legal form of the police complaint that specifies the charges to be heard at the adjudication), and waiver or transfer of the case to criminal court.

As in police decision making, a number of factors have been found to influence intake screening decisions. For example, youths who have committed serious offenses, those with prior records, and those who are uncooperative are more likely to have petitions filed. In addition, lower-class minority males, at least in some jurisdictions, are more likely than other groups to receive more formal responses at intake. Finally, there is considerable evidence that female status offenders are likely to be treated more harshly at intake than are their male counterparts, at least in some jurisdictions.[45]

TRANSFER, WAIVER, OR CERTIFICATION TO CRIMINAL COURT Since the early days of the juvenile court, state legislatures have given juvenile court judges statutory authority to transfer certain juvenile offenders to criminal court. In some jurisdictions, transfer is called waiver or certification. **Transfer, waiver, or certification** may occur in cases where youths meet certain age, offense, and (in some jurisdictions) prior-record criteria. For example, in Mississippi, waiver may occur if a youth has reached 13 years of age and has committed any criminal offense. In Michigan, a juvenile must be 14 years of age and must have committed one of a number of felonies specified by law. In many states, before a youth is transferred to an adult criminal court, a separate transfer or waiver hearing must be conducted to determine the waiver's appropriateness.

The judicial waiver process varies from state to state, but at the typical waiver hearing, probable cause must be shown. In addition, in many states the prosecutor must show that

1. The youth presents a threat to the community.
2. Existing juvenile treatment programs would not be appropriate.
3. Programs within the adult system would be more appropriate.

Historically, judicial transfer authority has been exercised infrequently. For example, between 1985 and 2001, the percentage of petition cases transferred to criminal court remained around 1 percent. However, because of changes in the total number of petition cases between 1985 and 2001, the number of delinquency cases waived by juvenile court judges rose about 70 percent between 1985 and 1994 (from 7,100 cases to 12,100 cases), then dropped 54 percent between 1994 and 2001 (from 12,100 cases to 5,600 cases). The net result was that the number of cases judicially waived was 21 percent less in 2000 than in 1985. In 2002, the number of cases waived increased by 27 percent to 7,100, the same number of cases waived in 1985. Between 1985 and 2003, the number of person offense cases waived increased by 23 percent, while waived property offense cases were down 33 percent. Throughout this period, person offense cases were most likely to be judicially waived—except for 1989 through 1992, when drug offense cases were most likely to be waived. In the 7,100 cases waived in 2002, 93 percent of the juveniles were male, 87 percent were 16 or older, and 62 percent were white (35 percent were black).[46]

The number of juvenile cases transferred to criminal court in recent years is actually much larger than the aforementioned data suggest. This is because there are no national statistics available on the number of prosecutorial transfers. Prosecutorial transfers occur in states that have passed legislation giving prosecutors concurrent jurisdiction. In the 15 concurrent jurisdiction states (as of 2004), both the juvenile court and the criminal court have original jurisdiction in cases that meet certain age, offense, and (in some jurisdictions) prior-record criteria. In those states, prosecutors have discretion to file eligible cases in either court. In Florida alone, more than 2,000 juvenile cases were transferred to criminal court in fiscal year 2001 through prosecutorial transfer. Today, because of the availability of prosecutorial transfer, judicial waiver is almost never used in Florida.[47]

Additional developments in this area include (1) an expansion of the number of transfer mechanisms, (2) simplification of the transfer process in some states, including the exclusion of offenders charged with certain offenses

Nathaniel Abraham was 11 when he was charged with first-degree murder for shooting an 18-year-old stranger outside a convenience store in Pontiac, Michigan. *Should youths such as Abraham be transferred to criminal courts for trials? Why or why not?*

transfer, waiver, or certification The act or process by which juveniles who meet specific age, offense, and (in some jurisdictions) prior-record criteria are transferred to criminal court for trial.

Incompetent to Stand Trial

A recent study suggests that thousands of juveniles tried as adults in the United States are incompetent to stand trial because they are emotionally or intellectually unable to contribute to their own defense. When compared with young adults, children ages 11 to 13 were more than three times as likely to be found "seriously impaired" in understanding the judicial process and aiding their own defense. Children 14 or 15 years old were twice as likely to be "seriously impaired" in such awareness and reasoning. Youths age 16 and 17 did not differ from those at least 18 years of age.

SOURCE: Greg Krikorian, "Study: Many Kids Tried as Adults Don't Grasp System," *The Orlando Sentinel*, March 3, 2003, p. A3.

Myth

Greater use of transfer or expansion of transfer criteria will reduce crime because of the adult sanctions that will be applied.

Fact

Youths transferred to criminal court are more likely to commit further crimes than others retained in the juvenile justice system. There is no evidence that transfer has any deterrent effect.

SOURCE: Donna M. Bishop, Charles E. Frazier, Lonn Lanza-Kaduce, and Lawrence Winner, "The Transfer of Juveniles to Criminal Court: Does It Make a Difference?" *Crime and Delinquency* 42 (1996), pp. 171–91; Jeffrey Fagan, "Separating the Men from the Boys: The Comparative Advantage of Juvenile versus Criminal Court Sanctions on Recidivism Among Adolescent Felony Offenders," in James C. Howell, Barry Krisberg, J. David Hawkins, and John Wilson, eds., *A Sourcebook: Serious, Violent, and Chronic Juvenile Offenders* (Thousand Oaks, CA: Sage, 1995), pp. 213–37; Eric Jensen and Linda Metsger, "A Test of the Deterrent Effect of Legislative Waiver on Violent Juvenile Crime," *Crime and Delinquency* 40 (1994), pp. 96–104.

Plea Bargaining

In a nationwide study of plea bargaining in juvenile courts, it was found that "much of the country has either not addressed at all or has not fully developed standards regarding the guilty plea process in juvenile court." It was also discovered that there was considerable variability in the ways that plea bargaining was carried out in various courts. For example, urban courts were more likely to institute formal procedures to regulate plea bargaining than were suburban or rural courts.

SOURCE: Joseph B. Sanborn, Jr., "Pleading Guilty in Juvenile Court," *Justice Quarterly* 9 (1992), pp. 127–50.

from juvenile court jurisdiction, or their mandatory or automatic waiver to criminal court, and (3) the lowering by some states of the maximum age for juvenile court jurisdiction. Statutory exclusion ("legislature transfers") accounts for the largest number of transfers.[48] As for lowering the maximum age, since 1995 all 17-year-olds in at least 10 states (Georgia, Illinois, Louisiana, Massachusetts, Michigan, Missouri, New Hampshire, South Carolina, Texas, and Wisconsin) and all 16- and 17-year-olds in at least three states (Connecticut, New York, and North Carolina) have been subject only to criminal court jurisdiction. Additionally, in 34 states, juveniles who have been convicted as adults must be prosecuted in criminal court for any subsequent offenses (the "Once an adult, always an adult" provision). Those developments reflect a shift in many jurisdictions toward a more punitive orientation toward juvenile offenders. On the other hand, some jurisdictions are moving in the opposite direction with "reverse waivers" and "criminal court blended sentencing." In 25 states, reverse waivers allow juveniles whose cases are handled in criminal courts to petition to have the case heard in juvenile court. Regarding criminal court blended sentencing, 17 states give juveniles convicted in criminal court the opportunity to be sanctioned in the juvenile system.[49]

THE ADJUDICATION HEARING When a petition is filed at intake and the case is not transferred to criminal court, the next step is adjudication. As noted previously, adjudication is the juvenile court equivalent of a trial in criminal court. In some states, such as Michigan, adjudication is now called a trial. It is at adjudication, moreover, that a juvenile begins to develop an official court record.

Before adjudication can take place, several preliminary actions are necessary. A petition must be filed, a hearing date must be set, and the necessary parties (such as the youth, the parents, and witnesses) must be given notice of the hearing. Notice is typically given through a summons or subpoena. A summons, which is an order to appear in court, is issued to the youth; copies are also given to the parents or guardians. The summons specifies the charges and the date, time, and location of the hearing, and it may list the youth's rights, such as a right to an attorney. Subpoenas are issued to witnesses, instructing them to appear on a certain day, time, and place to provide testimony or records.

When charges specified in the petition are contested by a juvenile and the juvenile is represented by an attorney, another critical event often takes place before adjudication—a plea bargain. Plea bargaining, including its problems, was discussed in detail in Chapter 5. Although the extent of plea bargaining in juvenile justice is unknown, it is believed to be a common practice in many juvenile courts.

There are two types of adjudications: contested ones (in which juveniles dispute the charges) and uncontested ones. Contested adjudications are similar to trials in criminal courts, which were described in Chapter 5. They typically employ the same rules of evidence and procedure. Most contested adjudications are bench adjudications, in which the hearing officer—a judge, referee, court master, or commissioner—makes a finding of fact based on the

Uncontested adjudications are generally brief. At the end, the youth or the youth's attorney admits the charges. *Why do you suppose most adjudications are uncontested?*

evidence presented. A **hearing officer** is a lawyer empowered by the juvenile court to hear juvenile cases. In some jurisdictions, contested adjudications are jury trials. However, as noted earlier in this chapter, juveniles do not have a constitutional right to a jury trial, and even in states that give juveniles the right to a jury trial, jury trials are rare.

Like their criminal court counterparts, the vast majority of juvenile court adjudications are uncontested. Uncontested adjudications are generally brief and consist of a reading of the charges, advice of rights, and possibly brief testimony by the youth or other parties, such as a probation officer. After this, the youth, or frequently the youth's attorney, admits the charges. In some states, an uncontested adjudication is called an arraignment.

The majority of cases that are not adjudicated are dismissed. Surprisingly, however, many juveniles whose cases are neither adjudicated nor dismissed are still placed on informal probation or treated in some other way. For example, of the estimated 303,300 delinquency cases filed but not adjudicated in 2002, 71 percent were dismissed. In 8 percent, the juvenile was placed on informal probation, and the remaining 22 percent were disposed of in other ways (see Figure 10.3). However, the majority of cases in which petitions are filed are adjudicated. In 2002, for example, 67 percent of the delinquency cases in juvenile courts were adjudicated (see Figure 10.3). Although 67 percent may not seem like a large percentage, keep in mind that many cases not adjudicated still receive some court supervision, such as informal probation.

DISPOSITION **Disposition** is the juvenile court equivalent of sentencing in criminal court. At the disposition hearing, the court makes its final determination of what to do with the juvenile officially labeled delinquent. Some of the options available to juvenile courts are probation, placement in a diversion program, restitution, community service, detention, placement in foster care, placement in a long-term or short-term residential treatment program, placement with a relative, and placement with the state for commitment to a state facility. In addition, the court may order some combination of those dispositions, such as placement on probation, restitution, and a short stay in detention. However, disposition possibilities are limited by the available options in a particular jurisdiction. In a few jurisdictions, they are also limited by statutory sentencing guidelines. In practice, the disposition options available to most juvenile courts are quite narrow, consisting of probation or

Juvenile Court Cases

The number of juvenile court cases increased 41 percent between 1985 and 2003, to about 1.6 million cases. Between 1997 and 2003, the percentage of homicides decreased 25 percent (1,700 cases in 2002), the percentage of forcible rapes decreased 14 percent (4,700 cases in 2002), the percentage of aggravated assaults decreased 26 percent (47,400 cases in 2002), and the percentage of robberies decreased 36 percent (21,500 cases in 2002). The percentage of property offenses also decreased 27 percent, but the percentage of drug law violations increased 1 percent and the percentage of public order offenses increased 7 percent.

SOURCE: Howard N. Sayder and Melissa Sickmund. *Juvenile Offenders and Victims: 2006 National Report.* U.S. Department of Justice, Office of Juvenile Justice and Delinquency Prevention, (Pittsburgh, PA: National Center for Juvenile Justice, December 2006), p. 157.

hearing officer A lawyer empowered by the juvenile court to hear juvenile cases.

disposition The juvenile court equivalent of sentencing in criminal court. At the disposition hearing, the court makes its final determination of what to do with the juvenile officially labeled delinquent.

incarceration. When incarceration is used, an indeterminate period of commitment or incarceration is the norm.[50]

As part of the disposition, the court also enters various orders regarding the youth's behavior. Those orders consist of rules the youth must follow. Also, the court may enter orders regarding parents, relatives, or other people who live in the home. For example, the court may order parents to attend counseling or a substance abuse treatment program, a boyfriend to move out of the house, or parents to clean up their house and pay for court costs or services provided, such as counseling caseworker services. If parents fail to follow those orders, at least in some jurisdictions, they may be held in contempt of court and placed in jail.

In making the disposition, the hearing officer usually relies heavily on a presentence investigation report (sometimes called a predisposition report), which is completed by a probation officer or an investigator before the disposition. Presentence investigation reports for criminal courts were described in detail in Chapter 6.

The most frequently used disposition in juvenile courts is probation, followed by placement. In 2002, for example, approximately 62 percent of the youths adjudicated delinquent were placed on probation; 23 percent received some type of commitment. Relatively few delinquency cases received other dispositions or were released after adjudication (see Figure 10.3).

Because of recent heightened concerns about violent juvenile offenders, many states have legislatively redefined the juvenile court's mission by de-emphasizing the goal of rehabilitation and stressing the need for public safety, punishment, and accountability in the juvenile justice system. Along with this change in purpose has been a fundamental philosophical change in the focus of juvenile justice, from offender-based dispositions to

CAREERS IN CRIMINAL JUSTICE

Juvenile Probation Officer

My name is Kelly Webster. I am a deputy probation officer (P.O.) with Los Angeles County Probation Department. I work at Camp Scott, a boot camp housing females ages 12–19. Camp Scott is the only female boot camp in L.A. County. Minors sentenced to camp are wards of the court and spend from 4 months to a year incarcerated. They are sentenced to camp for any crime leading up to attempted murder, so their sentences vary.

To become a P.O., a 4-year degree is required, in any subject. I have a B.A. in social welfare from the University of California, Berkeley. However, I never intended on becoming a social worker. My interest has always been in the criminal justice system. I became a P.O. by looking into county job openings upon completing my undergraduate degree. The Probation Department had an opening as a detention services officer in juvenile hall. I worked there for a year before promoting to a P.O. The only difference in the two jobs is the degree required, because of the court report writing.

I work a 56-hour shift, meaning that I work two days and then I have four and a half days off; I sleep at work for two nights. My routine consists of supervising approximately 115 minors at all times. Because camp is structured like the

military, I wear fatigues, as do the minors. Minors must ask permission to speak, salute me when walking by, and march around the facility calling cadences.

During the week, the minors are in school. On the weekends, they are cleaning, receiving visits on Sunday, or writing letters in the dormitory. They do physical training every day and twice on the weekend.

When I am not with the whole group, I have time assigned to counsel my own caseload. I am responsible for about five minors at a time. I write court reports when the minor is scheduled for release, informing the judge of the minor's behavior in camp. I recommend release or more time, depending on how they have progressed. Camp's philosophy is family reunification, so I have as much contact with the minor's family as possible.

What I like most about being a juvenile P.O. is the ability to affect some minors. What I like least about the job is that some of these "hardened" children cannot be helped. It is difficult to hear about what some of these children have endured.

Which aspects of this job would you find most difficult? Why?

offense-based dispositions, which emphasize punishment or incapacitation instead of rehabilitation. These changes are reflected in new disposition or sentencing practices, including (1) the use of *blended sentences,* which combine both juvenile and adult sanctions (see Figure 10.4), (2) the use of

Disposition and Extralegal Factors

Although some research has failed to find evidence that extralegal factors, such as race or social class, influence disposition, the bulk of the research indicates that extralegal factors often play a role in disposition. For example, a number of studies have found that minority and lower-class youths are more likely to receive the most severe dispositions, even when seriousness of offense and prior record are taken into account.

Source: Jeffrey Fagan, Ellen Slaughter, and Richard Hartstone, "Blind Justice: The Impact of Race on the Juvenile Justice Process," *Crime and Delinquency* 33 (1987), pp. 244–58; Belinda R. McCarthy and Brent L. Smith, "The Conceptualization of Discrimination in the Juvenile Justice Process," *Criminology* 24 (1986), pp. 41–64.

FIGURE 10.4	Blended Sentencing Options Create a "Middle Ground" between Traditional Juvenile Sanctions and Adult Sanctions

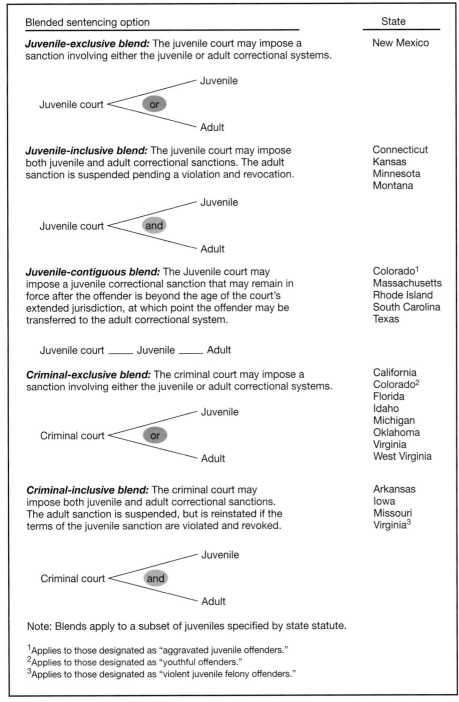

Blended sentencing option	State
Juvenile-exclusive blend: The juvenile court may impose a sanction involving either the juvenile or adult correctional systems.	New Mexico
Juvenile-inclusive blend: The juvenile court may impose both juvenile and adult correctional sanctions. The adult sanction is suspended pending a violation and revocation.	Connecticut Kansas Minnesota Montana
Juvenile-contiguous blend: The Juvenile court may impose a juvenile correctional sanction that may remain in force after the offender is beyond the age of the court's extended jurisdiction, at which point the offender may be transferred to the adult correctional system.	Colorado[1] Massachusetts Rhode Island South Carolina Texas
Criminal-exclusive blend: The criminal court may impose a sanction involving either the juvenile or adult correctional systems.	California Colorado[2] Florida Idaho Michigan Oklahoma Virginia West Virginia
Criminal-inclusive blend: The criminal court may impose both juvenile and adult correctional sanctions. The adult sanction is suspended, but is reinstated if the terms of the juvenile sanction are violated and revoked.	Arkansas Iowa Missouri Virginia[3]

Note: Blends apply to a subset of juveniles specified by state statute.

[1]Applies to those designated as "aggravated juvenile offenders."
[2]Applies to those designated as "youthful offenders."
[3]Applies to those designated as "violent juvenile felony offenders."

Source: "New Laws Have Had a Dramatic Impact on Sentencing for Serious or Violent Juvenile Offenders," *Juvenile Justice Bulletin* (Washington, DC: GPO, U.S. Department of Justice, Office of Juvenile Justice and Delinquency Prevention, 1999 National Report Series, December 1999); Greg Jones and Michael Connelly, "Update on Blended Sentences" (June 2001), www.msccsp.org/publications/blended.html.

mandatory minimum sentences for specific types of offenders or offense categories, and (3) the extension of juvenile court dispositions beyond the offender's age of majority, that is, lengthening the time an offender is held accountable in juvenile court.[51]

Correctional Programs for Juveniles

As noted, when youths are adjudicated, a number of disposition options are available to juvenile courts, although the options typically used in any one jurisdiction are fairly narrow. Three general types of dispositions are

1. Dismissal of the case, which is used in a small percentage of cases.
2. The use of a community-based program.
3. The use of an institutional program.

Because both community-based and institutional correctional programs for adults were the subjects of previous chapters of this book, only the features of those programs that are unique to juveniles will be discussed in the following sections.

COMMUNITY-BASED CORRECTIONAL PROGRAMS FOR JUVENILES

Among the community-based correctional programs for juvenile offenders are diversion, pretrial release, probation, foster care, group home placement, and parole. Some of those programs are designed to provide services to youths in their own homes, while others provide services to youths who have been removed from their homes, at least for short periods of time. Moreover, although all community-based programs are intended to control offenders and provide sanctions for their behavior, they are also designed to accomplish a variety of additional objectives. Those objectives include allowing youths to maintain existing ties with the community, helping them restore ties and develop new and positive ones with the community (reintegration), avoiding the negative consequences of institutional placement, providing a more cost-effective response to offenders, and reducing the likelihood of recidivism. Some of the community-based correctional programs for juveniles are examined in the following sections.

PROBATION Probation is the most frequently used correctional response for youths who are adjudicated delinquent in juvenile courts. Juvenile probation officers are referred to as "the workhorses of the juvenile justice system." In 2002 (the latest year for which data were available), juvenile probation officers processed about 1.6 million cases.[52] Although the actual practice of juvenile probation varies from one jurisdiction to the next, probation officers usually perform four important roles in the juvenile justice process:

1. They perform intake screening.
2. They conduct presentence investigations.
3. They supervise offenders.
4. They provide assistance to youths placed on probation.

In some jurisdictions, all of those roles are performed by the same individual. In other jurisdictions, each probation officer specializes in only one of the roles.

A recent trend in juvenile probation is the development of intensive-supervision (probation) programs, which in some jurisdictions involve home

Nathanial Abraham

On January 13, 2000, 13-year-old Nathaniel Abraham, the youngest American ever convicted of murder as an adult, was sentenced by a family court judge in Pontiac, Michigan, to a 7-year term at a maximum-security juvenile facility. The sentence allows Abraham to be released when he turns 21. In sentencing Abraham, who at age 11 shot and killed a stranger, the judge criticized the growing tendency of the U.S. judicial system to treat children as adults. He believed that the boy had a chance of being rehabilitated.

SOURCE: *Facts on File: World NewsDigest with Index*, 60 no. 3094 (March 23, 2000), p. 196; "Young Killer Gets Another Chance," *The Orlando Sentinel*, January 14, 2000, p. A3.

confinement. Intensive-supervision programs are intended to ensure regular contact between probationers and probation officers. They are also intended to serve as an intermediate response that is more restrictive than standard probation but less restrictive than incarceration. However, like standard probation programs, the frequency of contact between probation officers and probationers varies considerably.[53]

Although there is wide variation in the meaning of intensive supervision, there is some indication that programs that provide frequent supervision of offenders, as well as services, are as effective as incarceration at reducing recidivism.[54] The same research also suggests that intensive-supervision programs are more cost-effective than incarceration, provided they actually divert a sizable number of youths from institutions.

A recent trend in intensive supervision of juveniles is the use of home confinement, which began to be used with juvenile offenders in the 1970s[55] and has grown in popularity since that time. Today, home confinement programs use two mechanisms to monitor youths: frequent probation officer contacts and electronic monitoring. Electronic monitoring requires an offender to wear a tamper-resistant electronic device that automatically notifies the probation department if the juvenile leaves home or another designated location.

The use of home confinement employing electronic monitoring of juvenile offenders began in the 1980s and has grown substantially.[56] However, because electronic monitoring technology is diverse, rapidly developing, and relatively new, little evidence of its effectiveness exists. Still, there are good reasons that some jurisdictions find electronic monitoring attractive:

1. It eases the problem of detention overcrowding.
2. It allows youths to participate in counseling, education, and vocational programs without endangering public safety.
3. It allows youths to live with supervision in a more natural environment than an institution.
4. It allows court workers to better assess the ability of youths to live in the community under standard probation after they leave the program.[57]

Besides probation, juvenile courts in some jurisdictions employ several other types of community-based interventions with juvenile offenders, such as restitution or community service programs, wilderness probation programs, and day treatment programs. In practice, probation is often combined with one of those other community-based interventions.

RESTITUTION Restitution programs, as you may recall, require offenders to compensate victims for damages to property or for physical injuries. The primary goal of restitution programs is to hold youths accountable for their actions. In practice, there are three types of restitution:

1. *Monetary restitution,* a cash payment to the victim for harm done.
2. *Victim-service restitution,* in which the youth provides some service to the victim.
3. *Community-service restitution,* in which the youth provides assistance to a community organization.

Despite the growing popularity of juvenile restitution programs, as well as some programs' effective reduction of recidivism, there are potential problems with some of those programs. Problems include poorly managed, informal programs with low compliance rates; high recidivism rates in some programs; and hearing officers' ordering restitution that is unrealistic to expect juveniles to complete. There is also a potential for net widening, and restitution requirements can be subject to discretionary abuse; some jurisdictions, however, have

OJJDP
Visit the Office of Juvenile Justice and Delinquency Prevention Web site at **www.ojjdp.ncjrs.org** to review the various programs offered by the organization. *Which programs do you think would help deter juvenile crime?*

established restitution guidelines to remedy this problem. Thus, rather than achieving the goals of accountability, offender treatment, and victim compensation, restitution programs may fail to protect community safety. Moreover, they are likely to produce negative perceptions of juvenile justice by both offenders and victims.

WILDERNESS PROBATION (OUTDOOR ADVENTURE) PROGRAMS Wilderness probation or outdoor adventure programs for juvenile offenders are based, in part, on ideas derived from programs such as Outward Bound. (Outward Bound is a company that sells outdoor experiences such as mountain climbing, backpacking, and mountain biking.) A basic assumption of those programs is that learning is best accomplished by acting in an environment where there are consequences for one's actions. Consequently, the programs involve youths in a physically and sometimes emotionally challenging outdoor experience intended to help them develop confidence in themselves, learn to accept responsibility for themselves and others, and develop a relationship of trust with program staff. This is done by engaging youths in a variety of activities, such as camping, backpacking, rock climbing, canoeing, sailing, negotiating rope courses, and a solo experience (spending one or more nights alone in the wilderness).[58]

Evaluations of several wilderness probation programs have shown that they can produce positive effects, such as increases in self-esteem and a decrease in criminal activity both during and after the program.[59] However, research also indicates that the positive effects of the programs may diminish over time or may be no greater than the effects produced by probation programs that provide regular and meaningful contacts between probation officers and probationers.[60]

DAY TREATMENT PROGRAMS Day treatment programs for juvenile offenders operate in a number of jurisdictions around the United States. The programs often target serious offenders who would otherwise be candidates for institutionalization. They provide treatment or services to youths during the day and allow them to return home at night. Because they are viewed as alternatives

Wilderness Probation
You can learn more about wilderness probation programs by accessing The Hope for Youth Web site at **www.hfyny.org.** *What do you think are some of the benefits and drawbacks of wilderness probation?*

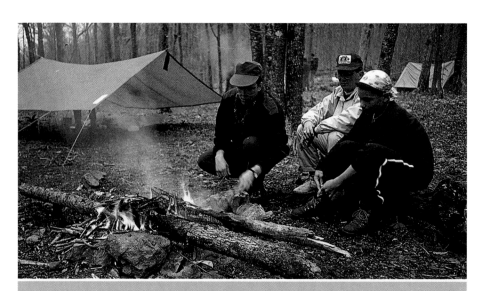

Some juvenile treatment programs strive to provide physically and emotionally challenging experiences to help youthful offenders gain confidence and learn responsibility for their actions. *What are the benefits and drawbacks of these kinds of programs?*

to incarceration, they are believed to be cost-effective. Because they provide highly structured programs for youths during the day, it is assumed that they protect community safety as well. The range of services or treatments can be quite varied and may include academic remediation, individual and group counseling, job skills training, job placement, and social-skills training. Although some evidence suggests that day treatment programs are as effective as, or more effective than, institutional placement, some programs may be no more effective at reducing recidivism than standard probation.[61]

FOSTER HOMES Foster homes are out-of-home placements intended to resemble, as much as possible, a family setting. Foster parents are licensed to provide care for one or more youths (usually one to three) and are paid a daily rate for the costs of care. Foster placement is often used by a court when a youth's home life has been particularly chaotic or harmful. In such a case, foster care is used to temporarily separate the youth from the parents or guardian in an effort to resolve the problems that resulted in the youth's removal. Foster homes are also used to remove youths from particular neighborhoods and for some nonviolent offenders instead of more restrictive placements, such as institutionalization. When used in those ways, they are considered "halfway-in programs." In other instances, foster homes are used as transitions to home and are considered "halfway-out programs."

Although foster homes are widely used by juvenile courts in some jurisdictions, there are few sound evaluations of their effectiveness. The limited research that exists indicates that foster care is generally not effective and may even be counterproductive.

GROUP HOMES Similar to foster homes, group homes are open, nonsecure community-based facilities used in both "halfway-in programs" and "halfway-out

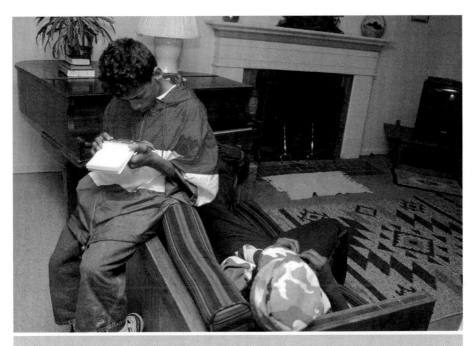

Group homes for delinquent youths are generally less impersonal than institutions and are less expensive than institutional placements. *What are some other advantages of group homes? What are some disadvantages?*

Group Homes

Although group homes are used extensively in juvenile justice, relatively little sound recent research has examined their effectiveness. One well-known, but older, study of a group home program, the Silverlake Experiment, found that youths placed in the program for approximately 6 months were no more likely to commit further crimes than similar youths who were randomly assigned to an institutional placement. In other words, placement in the program was neither more nor less effective than institutionalization at reducing recidivism.

Myth   Fact

Most of the youths housed in juvenile correctional institutions pose an immediate threat to public safety.

As Jerome Miller notes in his book, *Last One Over the Wall: The Massachusetts Experiment in Closing Reform Schools* (1991), in Massachusetts only about 25 percent of youths committed to state correctional facilities had committed offenses against persons. Many of those offenses against persons did not actually involve physical violence or the threat of physical violence. Consequently, many youths placed in correctional facilities, including many of those placed for violent offenses, do not pose a grave threat to public safety.

programs." However, they are somewhat larger and frequently less familylike than foster homes. The purpose of many group homes is to avoid requiring youths to accept "substitute parents," because many youths are in the process of developing emotional independence from parental figures. Nevertheless, group homes are generally less impersonal than institutions and are less expensive than institutional placements. In addition, their location allows residents to take advantage of community services. Youths who live in group homes usually go to school in the home or in the community or work in the community. Treatment typically consists of group or individual counseling provided by group-home staff or outside counselors.

INSTITUTIONAL PROGRAMS FOR JUVENILES

A variety of correctional institutions house juveniles within the United States, including detention centers, adult jails, shelter facilities (some of them are more community based), reception and diagnostic centers, ranches, forestry camps, farms, and training schools. These institutions hold a variety of youths, including those who are status offenders as well as those who have committed violent offenses against others. They are administered by either state or local governments or by private agencies.

JUVENILE CORRECTIONAL INSTITUTIONS What distinguishes institutional programs from their community-based counterparts is that institutional programs typically restrict youths' access to the community more than community-based programs do. Indeed, institutional programs are the most restrictive placements available to juvenile courts. However, juvenile institutions vary in the extent to which they focus on custody and control.

For example, some juvenile institutions employ a variety of security hardware: perimeter fencing or walls, barbed or razor wire, and surveillance and detection devices, such as motion detectors, sound monitors, and security cameras. Those juvenile institutions, classified as secure facilities, closely monitor residents' movement within the facility and restrict residents' access to the community. Most public and private detention centers, reception and diagnostic centers, and state training schools are secure facilities. In contrast, other juvenile institutions rely much less on security devices. Those facilities have no perimeter fencing, and some do not lock entrances or exits at night. Classified as open institutions, they rely more heavily on staff than on physical security. Most private facilities, as well as most public shelters, ranches, forestry camps, and farms, are open institutions.[62]

In addition to differences in the use of security hardware, juvenile correctional institutions also differ in a number of other ways. Some of the institutions are privately operated institutions, although the majority are public institutions. The majority of both private and public institutions are small, housing 40 or fewer residents, although some large, state-operated institutions have a legal capacity of 800 or more. Some institutions are coed; others are single-gender institutions.

Institutions also differ in the average length of time that residents stay in the facility. Typically, youths stay longer in private facilities than in public facilities.

Historically, large juvenile institutions have proven ineffective at preventing youths from offending again. *What do you think could be done to make these institutions more effective?*

However, some private and public facilities are for short-term placements, while others are for long-term placements. Institutions such as detention centers and diagnostic and reception centers are typically for short-term placements. Detention centers usually house youths awaiting adjudication or those who have been adjudicated and are awaiting disposition. In some cases, youths are placed in those institutions for a period of time as a disposition. Other institutions, such as ranches, forestry camps, farms, and training schools, are generally for long-term placements. Youths are placed in them as a result of disposition or possibly assessment at a reception and diagnostic center.

Juvenile institutions also differ in types of programming and quality of care. Almost all juvenile correctional institutions offer basic educational and counseling programs for their residents. Moreover, more than half of all institutions offer family counseling, employment counseling, peer group meetings, a point system, or behavioral contracts. However, there is considerable variability in the extent to which institutions offer more specialized educational or counseling programs for clients and the extent to which residents participate in the programs. For example, research shows that many institutions do not offer vocational training, GED courses, tutoring, suicide prevention, or programs for special offender types, such as violent offenders, sex offenders, or drug offenders.[63]

An examination of the history of juvenile institutions reveals that children have often been subjected to abuse and inhumane treatment in juvenile correctional institutions. Certainly, the overall quality of institutional life in correctional facilities today is vastly improved over that experienced by most youths placed in houses of refuge and early reform and training schools. Many juvenile institutions are administered by competent, caring, and professional administrators, who oversee skilled and caring staff in delivering a variety of high-quality services to their residents. Yet, many of the problems that have historically plagued juvenile correctional institutions are still evident. In a recent study of juvenile correctional institutions,

Boot Camps

In response to the significant increase in juvenile arrests and repeat offenses from the mid-1980s to the mid-1990s, a few states and many localities have established juvenile boot camps, modeled after adult boot camps. Evaluations of juvenile boot camps show they do not reduce the recidivism of graduates any better than incarceration or probation. Some research has found that boot camp graduates are more likely to be rearrested or rearrested more quickly than other offenders. Most boot camp programs have high drop-out rates.

SOURCE: National Mental Health Association, "Juvenile Boot Camps" (2005), www.nmha. org/children/justjuv/bootcamp.cfm

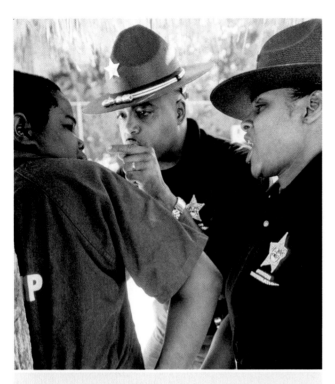

Juvenile boot camps are popular in some jurisdictions. *What are some of the advantages and disadvantages of juvenile boot camps?*

Myth Fact

The increasing use of incarceration for juvenile offenders during the past 15 to 20 years is a response to the growing juvenile crime rate, particularly the growing rate of violent juvenile crime.

The overall juvenile crime rate has been quite stable over time, and the violent juvenile crime rate, as measured by index arrest rates (see Figure 10.5), did not show a significant increase for 15 years, until 1989, well after the trend toward increased incarceration began. Moreover, between 1994 and 2003, arrests for serious violent crimes by juveniles dropped 47 percent. This suggests that the increase in juvenile incarceration is not simply a product of the extent or the seriousness of juvenile crime.

SOURCE: Howard N. Snyder, "Juvenile Arrests 2002," *Juvenile Justice Bulletin* (Washington, DC: GPO, U.S. Department of Justice, Office of Juvenile Justice and Delinquency Prevention, September 2004), p. 5.

for example, researchers learned that approximately 40 percent of the institutions were overcrowded (that is, they did not have enough beds for all of their residents and exceeded standards based on square footage, utility use, or fire codes).[64] Facilities with fewer standard beds were more likely to have transported residents to emergency rooms for treatment of injuries sustained at the institution. Another, older study of the conditions of confinement in American juvenile correctional facilities found overcrowding that resulted in the following substantial deficiencies: a lack of adequate living space, security practices that resulted in escapes or injuries to residents, inadequate health care for residents, and inadequate mechanisms for controlling suicidal behavior. In addition, the study discovered that such "deficiencies were distributed widely across facilities."[65]

Despite the long history of juvenile correctional institutions, there is surprisingly little information on the effectiveness of this response to juvenile offenders. Moreover, what is known is not encouraging. Although there is some indication that effective institutional programs for juveniles exist,[66] the bulk of the evidence indicates that many juvenile institutions have little effect on recidivism. For example, a review of the rearrest rates of youths released in states that rely heavily on institutions found that the percentage of youths rearrested ranged from 51 percent to more than 70 percent.[67] The results may not be surprising, considering the quality of life in many juvenile institutions.

RECENT TRENDS IN JUVENILE INCARCERATION Among recent trends in juvenile incarceration are (1) its increased use (at least until recently), (2) the use of both public and private facilities, (3) the disproportionately large percentage of males and racial or ethnic minorities that are incarcerated, and (4) the increasing number of juveniles being incarcerated in local adult jails and state prisons. Incarceration has become an increasingly popular response to delinquency, though that trend may be moderating somewhat. For example, on October 22, 2003 (the latest year for which data were available), 96,655 juvenile offenders were held in residential placement facilities, 8 percent fewer than in 1997.[68] The District of Columbia had the highest juvenile incarceration rate in 2003 (625 per every 100,000 juveniles in the population), while Vermont had the lowest (72).

Ninety-five percent of juveniles placed in residential facilities in 2003 committed delinquency offenses; only 5 percent committed status offenses. The delinquency offenses included violent person offenses (34 percent of all offenses for which juveniles were incarcerated), property offenses (28 percent), drug offenses 8 percent), and public order offenses (10 percent).

| FIGURE 10.5 | Violent Crime Index Arrest Rates of Juveniles, 1980–2002 |

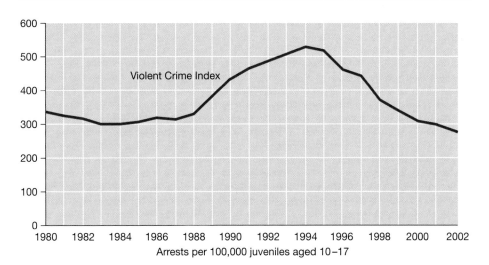

Arrests per 100,000 juveniles aged 10–17

Note: The juvenile violent crime index arrest rate in 2002 was at its lowest level since 1985—47 percent below the peak year of 1994. All the growth in the juvenile violent crime arrest rate that began in the latter part of the 1980s was erased by 2000.

Source: Howard N. Snyder, "Juvenile Arrests 2002," *Juvenile Justice Bulletin* (Washington, DC: GPO, U.S. Department of Justice, Office of Juvenile Justice and Delinquency Prevention, September 2004), p. 5.

Another 15 percent of juveniles were confined for technical violations. Furthermore, whether a juvenile was placed in a public or private facility depended primarily on whether a delinquency or status offense was committed. Of the juveniles who were placed for delinquency offenses, 70 percent were placed in public facilities and 30 percent were placed in private facilities. Conversely, of the juveniles placed for status offenses, 32 percent were placed in public facilities and 68 percent were placed in private facilities. However, states varied greatly in the extent to which they used public or private residential facilities. At one extreme, Mississippi placed 98 percent of its juvenile offenders in public facilities; at the other extreme, Pennsylvania placed 70 percent of its juvenile offenders in private facilities.

A disproportionately large percentage of males and racial or ethnic minorities are incarcerated in juvenile facilities. Although juvenile males comprised half of the U.S. juvenile population aged 10–17 in 2003, 85 percent of all juveniles incarcerated in 2003 were males. However, a larger proportion of females was incarcerated for status offenses (40 percent of females compared to 60 percent of males). About 70 percent of all females incarcerated for status offenses were placed in private as opposed to public facilities.

As for racial and ethnic minorities, in 2003, minorities (that is, nonwhites) comprised about 35 percent of the American population aged 10–17. Yet, minorities accounted for more than 61 percent of all juveniles in custody in 2003. About 65 percent of all juveniles in

FYI

Correctional Facility Conditions

A survey of 984 detention centers, training schools, ranches, farms, and camps holding 65,000 juveniles found that only 20 to 26 percent had adequate bed space, health care, security, or suicide control. The survey discovered that more than 11,000 juveniles committed 18,000 acts of attempted suicide, suicidal gestures, or self-mutilation, and that institutions frequently failed to provide appropriate housing for suicidal juveniles. Nearly half the facilities exceeded their design capacity, and only 24 percent of detained youths were in places that met all living-space standards.

Source: Dale J. Parent, Valerie Leiter, Stephen Kennedy, Lisa Livens, Daniel Wentworth, and Sarah Wilcox, *Conditions of Confinement: Juvenile Detention and Corrections Facilities Research Summary* (Washington, DC: OJJDP, 1994) p. 5.

Myth Fact

A new type of violent juvenile offender, one for whom violence is a way of life—a "superpredator"—emerged in the late 1980s and early 1990s.

Although evidence shows that in the early 1990s, juvenile arrest rates for violent crimes broke out of their historic range and increased to a level greater than in previous generations, the evidence also shows that by 1995 arrest rates for juvenile violence had returned to a level comparable to that of a generation ago. Ironically, because of the myth of the "superpredator," nearly every state legislature made it easier to handle juveniles as adult offenders.

Source: "Challenging the Myths," *1999 National Report Series: Juvenile Justice Bulletin* (Washington, DC: GPO, U.S. Department of Justice, Office of Juvenile Justice and Delinquency Prevention, February 2000).

FIGURE 10.6 | Racial and Ethnic Composition of Inmate Population of Public and Private Juvenile Incarceration Facilities, 2003

Public Facilities

Private Facilities

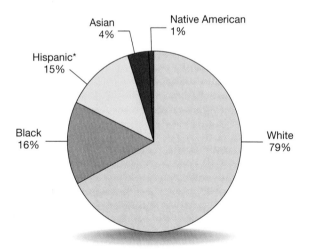

Racial and Ethnic Distribution of 2003 U.S. Population Ages 0–17*

*Note: Persons of Hispanic ethnicity can be of any race; however, most are white.

Source: Melissa Sickmund, "Racial Profile of Juveniles in Residential Placement 2003," Special analysis of OJJDP's Census of Juveniles in Residential Placement 2003 [machine-readable data files].

public facilities and about 55 percent all juveniles in private facilities in 2003 were members of minority groups. Figure 10.6 illustrates the racial and ethnic composition of public and private juvenile incarceration facilities in 2003. Whites are underrepresented in both public and private facilities, blacks are overrepresented in both, Hispanics are overrepresented in public facilities and are underrepresented in private facilities, Asians are underrepresented in both, and Native Americans are overrepresented in both. The Juvenile Justice and Delinquency Prevention Act of 1974, as amended, requires states to determine whether minorities are disproportionately represented in confinement. If over-representation is found, the state must reduce it.

Juveniles have also been increasingly held in local adult jails and state prisons. Those juveniles are not included in the aforementioned total of approximately 96,655 juveniles who were incarcerated. At midyear 2004, local adult jails held 7,083 juveniles, a decrease of about 9 percent from 1995. Eighty-seven percent of the juveniles were being held as adults, and 13 per-cent were being held as juveniles. Another 2,477 juveniles were being held in adult prisons at midyear 2004.[69]

AFTERCARE PROGRAMS Aftercare involves the provision of services to assist youths in successfully making the transition from juvenile institutions to life back in the community. The services are the same as those provided by other types of community-based programs and may include foster care, shelter or group-home placement, home placement, or efforts to help youths live on their own. Parole, too, is one form of aftercare.

Unfortunately, the quality of many aftercare programs is questionable, and in some cases, youths fail to receive any services after institutional release. As in probation, parole supervision, in practice, may involve very little contact between parole officers and parolees. Moreover, large caseloads carried by aftercare workers may prevent the provision of meaningful services.

For those reasons and others (at the time, increasing juvenile crime rates, increasing numbers of juveniles requiring secure care, increasing costs, and the general failure to control or reduce the delinquent behavior of many juve-niles in aftercare), the Office of Juvenile Justice and Delinquency Prevention in the late 1980s initiated an intensive community-based aftercare pilot proj-ect called the Intensive Aftercare Program (IAP).[70] The goal of IAP is to reduce recidivism among high-risk juvenile parolees. The creators of IAP describe it in this way:

> [IAP is a] correctional continuum consisting of three distinct, yet overlapping, segments: pre-release and preparatory planning during incarceration; structured transition that requires the participation of institutional and aftercare staff prior to and following community re-entry; and long-term, reintegrative activi-ties that ensure adequate service delivery and the necessary level of social control.[71]

Table 10.2 shows the specific components of IAP as they are being imple-mented at three of the pilot project sites. To date, the program has not been evaluated to determine whether it is achieving its goal.

In conclusion, twenty-first century juvenile justice in the United States has several important problems to resolve. Many of the problems are the same ones that have plagued juvenile justice since the first specialized insti-tutions for children were established in the early 1800s. The problems include:

1. Providing adequate due process protections to youths at all stages of the juvenile justice process.
2. Continuing to build on knowledge of effective correctional interventions and developing a range of effective and humane correctional responses, from diversion to institutional aftercare programs.
3. Eliminating the abusive treatment of youths placed in correctional programs.

New Prison for Females

In 2000, Florida opened its first maximum-security prison devoted to women ages 13 to 21. The prison, surrounded by razor wire and concrete walls, housed about 50 fe-males who had committed crimes such as murder, armed robbery, drug dealing, and prostitution, as well as some women who had suffered physical and sexual abuse. The goal was to rehabilitate girls. The girls had to attend school and therapy sessions during their 18-month to 3-year stays. Previously, 1 year was the longest sen-tence that could be imposed on a girl committed to a juvenile justice program. The Florida legislature pulled the funding and closed the prison in September 2005, citing continuing problems with mental health services and staff training.

SOURCE: "Girls Get a Prison of Their Own," *The Orlando Sentinel*, March 21, 2000, p. D-3; personal communication with Florida Department of Juvenile Justice (September 19, 2006).

TABLE 10.2	Transition Components of IAP Programming

	IAP SITE		
TRANSITION COMPONENT	COLORADO	NEVADA	VIRGINIA
Early parole planning	Initial plan complete at 30 days after institutional placement; final plan complete at 60 days prior to release.	Initial plan complete at 30 days after institutional placement; final plan complete 30 days prior to furlough.	Initial plan complete 30 days after institutional placement; final plan complete 30 days prior to release.
Multiple perspectives incorporated in plan	Case manager, Institutional staff, youth, parents, and community providers all routinely involved.	Parole officer, institutional community liaison, institutional staff, and youth; parent participation limited.	Parole officer, institutional case manager, youth, interagency "Community Assessment Team," and parent.
Parole officer visits to institution	One to two times per week; routine.	Once per month; routine since spring 1997.	One to two times per month; routine.
Treatment begun in institution and continued in community	Via community providers. Includes multifamily counseling, life skills training, individual counseling, and vocational skills training, done routinely.	Via an institutional-community liaison and parole officers. Includes life skills and drug/alcohol curriculums; done routinely until liaison vacancy.	Via one provider at Hanover only. Drug/alcohol treatment; sporadic use. State policy discourages contract services by community providers for institutionalized youth.
Youth prerelease visits to community	Supervised day trips to community programs, beginning 60 days prior to release.	Not allowed.	Not allowed.
Preparole furlough	Overnight/weekend home passes, beginning 30 days prior to release.	Thirty-day conditional release to community, prior to official parole.	Not allowed.
Transitional residence	Not part of the design, but occurs for some youth.	Not part of the design.	Two group homes in Norfolk; 30- to 60-day length of stay; used for most youth.
Transitional day programming	Two-day-treatment programs in Denver; used for almost all youth during the first few months after release.	One-day-supervison/treatment program; used for most youth.	Day treatment used for youth who do not go to group homes.
Phased supervision levels on parole	Informal system: contact once per week during the first few months, down to once per month later.	Four-phase system: contact four times per week during furlough; three times per week next 90 days; two times per week next 60–90 days; once per week next 30–60 days.	Four-phase system: group home; contact five to seven times per week next 60 days; three to five times per week next 60 days; three times per week last 30 days.

Source: Richard G. Wiebush, Betsy McNulty, and Thao Le, "Implementation of the Intensive Community-Based Aftercare Program," *Juvenile Justice Bulletin* (Washington, DC: GPO, U.S. Department of Justice, Office of Juvenile Justice and Delinquency Prevention, July 2000), p. 9, Table 3.

THINKING CRITICALLY

1. Which of the community-based correctional programs described in the chapter (e.g., restitution, wilderness probation, and day treatment) do you think would be most effective at rehabilitating youths? Why?

2. What do you think are the pros and cons of institutional programs for juveniles?

4. Working out the appropriate balance between community-based and institutional correctional programs.

5. Conducting rigorous evaluations of juvenile justice agencies and programs.

6. Recognizing the limits of correctional responses in solving the juvenile crime problem.

7. Working out an appropriate balance between preventing and correcting delinquency.

1. Describe some of the early institutions used to respond to wayward and criminal youths.

Among the early institutions used to respond to wayward and criminal youths were houses of refuge, placing out, reform schools, industrial schools, and training schools.

2. Explain the effects of some landmark U.S. Supreme Court cases on the juvenile justice system.

Landmark Supreme Court cases on juvenile justice include Ex parte Crouse, People *v.* Turner, Commonwealth *v.* Fisher, Kent *v.* United States, In re Gault, In re Winship, *and* McKeiver *v.* Pennsylvania. *Some of the effects of those cases on juvenile justice are the right to adequate notice of charges, protection against compelled self-incrimination, the right to confront and to cross-examine accusers, and the right to the assistance of counsel.*

3. Identify and describe factors that influence the ways that police process juvenile cases.

Among the factors that influence the ways that police process juvenile cases are (1) the seriousness of the offense, (2) the community, (3) the wishes of the complainant, (4) the demeanor of the youth, (5) the gender of the offender, (6) the race and social class of the offender, and (7) the police organization.

4. Summarize the rationale for the use of diversion in juvenile justice.

Diversion programs in juvenile justice are based on the understanding that formal responses to youths who violate the law, such as arrest and adjudication, do not always protect the best interests of children or the community. Indeed, some formal responses may be harmful to many youths and may increase the likelihood of future delinquent behavior. This is because formal processing may cause youths to develop negative or delinquent self-images, may stigmatize youths in the eyes of significant others, or may subject youths to inhumane treatment.

5. Describe the adjudication hearing in juvenile justice.

There are two types of adjudication: contested ones (in which juveniles dispute the charges) and uncontested ones. Contested adjudications are similar to trials in criminal courts. Most contested adjudications are bench adjudications, in which the hearing officer makes a finding of fact based on the evidence presented. In some jurisdictions, contested adjudications are jury trials. At an uncontested adjudication hearing, the youth, or frequently the youth's attorney, admits to the charges. The vast majority of juvenile court adjudications are uncontested.

6. Describe the disposition hearing and the types of dispositions available to the juvenile court.

The disposition is the juvenile court equivalent of sentencing in criminal court. At the disposition hearing, the court makes its final determination of what to do with the youth who is officially labeled delinquent. At the disposition, the court also enters various orders regarding the youth's behavior. Those orders consist of various rules the youth must follow. Also, the court may enter orders regarding parents, relatives, or other people who live in the home. Dispositions available to the juvenile court include probation, placement in a diversion program, restitution, community service, detention, placement in foster care, placement in a long-term or short-term residential treatment program, placement with a relative, and placement with the state for commitment to a state facility. Not all disposition alternatives are available in all jurisdictions.

7. Identify the types and describe the effectiveness of community-based correctional programs for juveniles.

Community-based correctional programs include diversion, pretrial release, probation, foster care, group home placements, and parole. Evaluations of some programs indicate that they are effective at reducing recidivism or that they are as effective as institutional placement. In contrast, evaluations of other community-based programs indicate that they have little effect on subsequent offenses.

8. Summarize recent trends in juvenile incarceration.

Among recent trends in juvenile incarceration are (1) its increased use (at least until recently), (2) the use of both public and private facilities, (3) the disproportionately large percentage of males and racial or ethnic minorities that are incarcerated, and (4) the increasing number of juveniles being incarcerated in local adult jails and state prisons.

9. Identify the types and describe the effectiveness of institutional programs for juveniles.

In the United States, a variety of correctional institutions house juveniles, including detention centers, adult jails, shelter facilities, reception and diagnostic centers, ranches, forestry camps, farms, and training schools. There is some evidence that small, secure treatment facilities for violent or chronic offenders are effective at reducing recidivism. However, many institutions, *particularly large state institutions, have often been found to have little positive effect on youths' subsequent delinquent behaviors. In fact, they may increase the likelihood that youths will commit further offenses.*

KEY TERMS

juvenile delinquency,
  p. 370
apprenticeship system,
  p. 371
binding-out system,
  p. 371
houses of refuge, p. 371

placing out, p. 372
reform, industrial, or
  training schools,
  p. 373
cottage reformatories,
  p. 373
parens patriae, **p. 375**

adjudication, p. 378
informal juvenile
  justice, p. 379
status offenses, p. 379
radical noninter-
  vention, p. 384
intake screening, p. 387

petition, p. 388
transfer, waiver, or
  certification, p. 389
hearing officer, p. 391
disposition, p. 391

REVIEW QUESTIONS

1. What changes occurred in the sixteenth and seventeenth centuries in the ways the young were viewed?
2. What were the purposes of houses of refuge?
3. What is *parens patriae,* and what was the legal context in which it arose?
4. What was the social and historical context in which the juvenile court was created?
5. Historically, what has been the fundamental difference between the procedures used in juvenile courts and those employed in criminal courts?
6. What is the informal juvenile justice process, and why is it important?
7. What are four typical responses that police officers employ when handling juvenile cases?
8. What are three recent trends in police processing of juveniles?
9. What are two relatively new juvenile diversion alternatives?

10. What are five possible intake decisions that might be made in the juvenile justice process?
11. What are five recent trends in the practice of transferring juvenile cases to criminal court, and what do they suggest about the current orientation of juvenile justice?
12. In practice, what two dispositions are typically available to juvenile court judges in most jurisdictions, and which one is most frequently used?
13. What are three new dispositional or sentencing practices employed by juvenile court judges?
14. What are six objectives of community-based correctional programs for juveniles?
15. What are four problems commonly found in juvenile correctional facilities?
16. What are some important problems that remain unresolved as juvenile justice in the United States enters the twenty-first century?

IN THE FIELD

1. **Debate Juvenile Justice** With fellow students, family members, or friends, debate whether the juvenile justice system ought to be abolished and juvenile offenders treated as adults.
2. **Compare Correctional Facilities** Visit different juvenile correctional facilities in your

community, both community-based facilities and institutional facilities. Compare what you observe at these facilities based on the following criteria:

a. How do terms for similar offenses compare at each facility?

b. How are juveniles treated?

c. Are there educational or rehabilitation opportunities?

d. How does the way of life compare?

ON THE NET

1. **Juvenile Information Center** Go to the Justice Information Center Web site at www.ncjrs. org. Click on Juvenile Justice and then choose one of the documents listed. Read the document and then write a brief summary of it.

2. **Research Parenting Issues** Go to the Parenting Resources for the 21st Century online guide at

http://permanent.access.gpo.gov/lps6447. Select one or more of the major subject headings and then choose one or more of the specific topics to read. Write a report on the delinquency implications of the various parenting issues.

CRITICAL THINKING EXERCIS

1. **The Case of Paul** Paul, a 15-year-old, sexually assaulted, robbed, and killed Billy, an 11-year-old. Billy was missing for 2 days. Paul hid Billy's body for those 2 days in his family's garage before dumping it in a wooded area near the house. Neighbors describe Paul as quiet and introverted. His parents state that he grew increasingly violent after they kept him from a 43-year-old man named Smith who Paul had met in a chat room. Smith was subsequently charged with sexually assaulting Paul. The two apparently had sex in motels five times during the previous 4 months.

a. Should Paul be handled by the justice system (either juvenile or adult) or be diverted, perhaps to a mental health facility? Why?

b. Should he be charged with first-degree murder (as well as the other crimes)? Why or why not?

c. Should he be transferred to criminal court and tried as an adult?

d. If tried as an adult, should he enter a plea of not guilty by reason of insanity? A plea of guilty but insane? Why or why not?

e. If Paul is convicted of any of the charges, what sentence should be imposed? Why?

2. **The Case of James** Seventeen-year-old James lives in a nice lower-middle-class neighborhood in central Florida. A few years ago, James began running with a bad crowd. His parents tried a variety of punishments, to no avail. James was eventually arrested for burglary, theft, and other crimes. A juvenile court judge placed him on probation and ordered him to receive counseling. James violated probation,

stopped going to counseling sessions, and began committing crimes again. After a subsequent arrest, James was ordered into a residential rehabilitation program for several months. After finishing the program, he was placed in a special school, from which he soon ran away. He was next placed in another residential program, one designed for youths "needing more structure." He ran away. After he was caught, a juvenile court judge returned him to the residential program for about 6 months.

James's father states that the rehabilitation programs are a waste of time and money, because they are disorganized and ineffectual. He fears James will kill or be killed, and he wants James to be locked up until the age of 19. However, space is limited in the most secure juvenile institutions. In Florida, youths must commit an average of 12 crimes before they are placed in such institutions.

a. Should James be handled by the justice system (either juvenile or adult) or be diverted? Why?

b. If he is diverted, what type of program would benefit him most? Why?

c. If James is retained in the juvenile justice system, what disposition would be most appropriate and beneficial for him?

To access more information and resources, including study questions, chapter summaries, and links, go to: www.mhhe.com/bohm1.

ENDNOTES

Chapter 1

1. Jay A. Sigler, *Understanding Criminal Law* (Boston: Little, Brown, 1981), p. 3.
2. *Florida v. J. L.*, 529 U.S. 266 (2000).
3. *Illinois v. Wardlow*, 528 U.S. 119 (2000).
4. Herbert Packer, *The Limits of the Criminal Sanction* (Stanford, CA: Stanford University Press, 1968).
5. See, for example, Walter B. Miller, "Ideology and Criminal Justice Policy: Some Current Issues," *Journal of Criminal Law and Criminology* 64 (1973), pp. 141–62.
6. D. Nimmo and J. E. Combs, *Subliminal Politics: Myths and Mythmakers in America* (Englewood Cliffs, NJ: Prentice Hall, 1980), p. 6.
7. Ibid., p. 16.
8. Many of the myths presented in this book were taken from the following sources: Robert M. Bohm and Jeffery T. Walker (eds.), *Demystifying Crime and Criminal Justice* (Los Angeles: Roxbury, 2006); Jeffrey H. Reiman, *The Rich Get Richer and the Poor Get Prison: Ideology, Class, and Criminal Justice,* 7th ed. (Boston: Allyn & Bacon, 2004); Harold E. Pepinsky and Paul Jesilow, *Myths That Cause Crime,* 2nd ed. (Cabin John, MD: Seven Locks, 1985); Kevin N. Wright, *The Great American Crime Myth* (Westport, CT: Greenwood, 1987); also see Robert M. Bohm, "Myths About Criminology and Criminal Justice: A Review Essay," *Justice Quarterly* 4 (1987), pp. 631–42; William Wilbanks, *The Myth of a Racist Criminal Justice System* (Belmont, CA: Wadsworth, 1987); Victor E. Kappeler, Mark Blumberg, and Gary W. Potter, *The Mythology of Crime and Criminal Justice,* 3rd ed. (Prospect Heights, IL: Waveland, 2000); Samuel Walker, *Sense and Nonsense About Crime, and Drugs: A Policy Guide,* 5th ed. (Belmont, CA: Wadsworth, 2000). For a discussion of why these myths exist, see Robert M. Bohm, "Crime, Criminal and Crime Control Policy Myths," *Justice Quarterly* 3 (1986), pp. 193–214.

Chapter 2

1. Material in this section was taken from T. A. Critchley, *A History of Police in England and Wales,* 2nd ed. rev. (Montclair, NJ: Patterson Smith, 1972).
2. Ibid.
3. Patrick Pringle, *Hue and Cry: The Story of Henry and John Fielding and Their Bow Street Runners* (New York: William Morrow, 1965).
4. Material in this section was taken from A. C. Germann, F. Day, and R. Gallati, *Introduction to Law Enforcement and Criminal Justice* (Springfield, IL: Charles C. Thomas, 1962), pp. 54–55.
5. Edward Savage, *Police Records and Recollections, or Boston by Daylight and Gaslights for Two Hundred and Forty Years* (Boston: John P. Dale, 1873).
6. This material came from Carl Sifakis, *The Encyclopedia of American Crime* (New York: Smithmark, 1992), pp. 579–80.
7. Information in this section is from W. Marvin Dulaney, *Black Police in America* (Bloomington: Indiana University Press, 1996).
8. Center for Research on Criminal Justice, *The Iron Fist and the Velvet Glove: An Analysis of the U.S. Police* (Berkeley, CA: Center for Research on Criminal Justice, 1975); Hubert Williams and Patrick V. Murphy, "The Evolving Strategy of Police: A Minority View," *Perspectives on Policing, No. 13* (Washington, DC: U.S. Department of Justice, January 1990).
9. Dulaney, op. cit., p. 2.
10. Thad Sitton, *Texas High Sheriffs* (Austin: Texas Monthly Press, 1988).
11. Adrian N. Anderson, Ralph A. Wooster, David G. Armstrong, and Jeanie R. Stanley, *Texas and Texans* (New York: Glencoe/McGraw-Hill, 1993).
12. Bruce Smith, *Police Systems in the United States* (New York: Harper & Row, 1960), pp. 178–205.
13. *Our Police* (Cincinnati Police Division, 1984).
14. Gene Carte and Elaine Carte, *Police Reform in the United States: The Era of August Vollmer* (Berkeley: University of California Press, 1975).
15. Malcolm K. Sparrow, Mark H. Moore, and David M. Kennedy, *Beyond 911* (New York: Basic Books, 1990).
16. U.S. Department of Justice, *Response Time Analysis: Executive Summary* (Washington, DC: GPO, 1978).
17. Samuel Walker, *The Police in America: An Introduction,* 5th ed. (New York: McGraw-Hill, 2005).
18. Robert C. Trojanowicz and Bonnie Bucqueroux, *Community Policing: A Contemporary Perspective* (Cincinnati: Anderson, 1989); Robert C. Trojanowicz and Bonnie Bucqueroux, *Community Policing: How to Get Started* (Cincinnati: Anderson, 1994).
20. Federal Bureau of Investigation, *Crime in the United States, 2004,* www.fbi.gov/ucr/cius_04/persons_arrested/index.html.
21. Brian A. Reaves, *Federal Law Enforcement Officers, 2004,* U.S. Department of Justice, Bureau of Justice Statistics (Washington, DC, July 2006).

22. Matthew J. Hickman and Brian A. Reaves, *Local Police Departments, 2003* (Washington, DC: Bureau of Justice Statistics, May 2006).

23. V. A. Leonard, *Police Organization and Management* (New York: Foundation Press, 1964).

24. Matthew J. Hickman and Brian A. Reaves, *Sheriffs' Offices 2003* (Washington, DC: Bureau of Justice Statistics, May 2006).

25. Ibid.

26. Ibid.

27. Ibid.; Brian A. Reaves and Matthew J. Hickman, *Census of state and Local Law Enforcement Agencies, 2000* (Washington, DC: Bureau of Justice Statistics, 2002).

28. Reaves, *Federal Law Enforcement Officers, 2004,* op. cit.

29. Ibid.

30. Ibid

31. Kristen Hughes, *Justice Expenditure and Employment in the United States, 2003* (Washington, DC: Bureau of Justice Statistics, April 2006), p. 3, Table 2.

32. Reaves, *Federal Law Enforcement Officers, 2004,* op. cit.

33. Ibid.

34. Material on FLETC is from Reaves and Bauer, *Federal Law Enforcement Officers, 2002,* ibid., p. 11; the Federal Law Enforcement Training Center at www.fletc.gov.

35. Material on the Department of Homeland Security is from the U.S. Department of Homeland Security Web site at www.dhs.gov/dhspublic.

36. *Terrorism in the United States, 1999,* op. cit., p. 10.

37. Material on Homeland Security and the FBI is from the following sources: Rebecca Carr, "FBI Chief: My Agency Can Handle Spying Job," *The Orlando Sentinel,* December 20, 2002, p. A11; Eric Lichtblau, "Pressure on FBI Grows from Within," *The Orlando Sentinel,* December 2, 2002, p. A9; Curt Anderson, "FBI Seeks to Expand Presence Overseas," *The Orlando Sentinel,* March 29, 2003, p. A3; "Senate Confirms Ridge as Head of Homeland Dept," *USA Today,* January 23, 2003, p. 12A.

38. *Terrorism in the United States, 1999,* op. cit.

39. Ibid.

40. U.S. Department of State, Patterns of Global Terrorism 2003 at www.state.gov/s/ct/rls/pgtrpt/2003/c12153.htm (Introduction, p. v).

41. Ibid.

42. Ibid., p. vi–vii.

43. Ibid.

44. Federal Bureau of Investigation at www.fbi.gov/mostwant/topten/fugitives/laden.htm.

45. Kim Bolan, "Canada a Haven for Terrorists," *Vancouver Sun,* June 30, 2003.

46. Michelle Malkin, *Invasion: How America Still Welcomes Terrorists, Criminals, and Other Foreign Menaces to Our Shores* (Washington, DC: Regnery Publishing, Inc., 2001).

47. William Cunningham, John Strauchs, and Clifford Van Meter, *The Hallcrest Report II: Private Security Trends 1970–2000* (McLean, VA: Hallcrest Systems, 1990).

48. Unless indicated otherwise, most of the information in this section is from the *Occupational Outlook Handbook* at http://bls.gov/oco/ocos/159.htm (accessed May 2006).

Chapter 3

1. Keith Haley, "Training," in Gary Cordner and Donna Hale (eds.), *What Works in Policing? Operations and Administration Examined* (Cincinnati: Anderson, 1992).

2. Lee Rainwater, "The Revolt of the Dirty Workers," *Transaction* (November 1967), p. 2.

3. Jerome Skolnick, *Justice Without Trial* (New York: Wiley, 1966).

4. Federal Bureau of Investigation, "Preliminary Statistics for Law Enforcement Officers Killed in 2005" (Press Release, May 15, 2006) at www.fbi.gov/pressrel/pressrel06/leoka.htm; U.S. Department of Justice, Federal Bureau of Investigation, "Law Enforcement Officers Killed & Assaulted 2004," www.fbi.gov/ucr/killed/2004/table1.htm; U.S. Department of Justice, Federal Bureau of Investigation, *Uniform Crimes Reports, 2001, 2000, 1999,* www.fbi.gov/ucr/ucr.htm.

5. "Preliminary Statistics for Law Enforcement Officers Killed in 2005," ibid.

6. "Preliminary Statistics for Law Enforcement Officers Killed in 2005," ibid.; "Law Enforcement Officers Killed & Assaulted 2004," ibid.; *Uniform Crimes Reports, 2003, 2002, 2001, 2000,* op. cit.

7. Ibid.; *Sourcebook of Criminal Justice Statistics, 2001,* www.albany.edu/sourcebook/1995/tost_3.html#3_av, p. 328, Table 3.164.

8. James Q. Wilson, *Varieties of Police Behavior* (Cambridge, MA: Harvard University Press, 1968), pp. 140–227.

9. John Broderick, *Police in a Time of Change* (Morristown, NJ: General Learning Press, 1977), pp. 9–88.

10. William Muir, Jr., *Police: Streetcorner Politicians* (Chicago: University of Chicago Press, 1977).

11. Ellen Hochstedler, "Testing Types: A Review and Test of Police Types," *Journal of Criminal Justice* 9 (1981), pp. 451–66; also see Eugene A. Paoline, "The Myth of a Monolithic Police Culture," in Robert M. Bohm and Jeffery T. Walker (eds.), *Demystifying Crime and Criminal Justice* (Los Angeles: Roxbury, 2006).

12. G. Kelling, T. Pate, D. Dieckman, and C. Brown, *The Kansas City Preventive Patrol Experiment: A Summary Report* (Washington, DC: Police Foundation, 1974).

13. Gary Cordner, "Patrol," in Gary Cordner and Donna Hale (eds.), op. cit.

14. Daniel Mabrey, "Crime Mapping: Tracking the Hotspots," *Crime & Justice International* 18, no. 67 (2002), pp. 31–32.

15. Ibid.

16. James Q. Wilson and Barbara Boland, "The Effect of Police on Crime," *Law and Society Review* 12 (1978), pp. 367–84.

17. George Kelling, *The Newark Foot Patrol Experiment* (Washington, DC: Police Foundation, 1981).

18. Robert C. Trojanowicz, *The Neighborhood Foot Patrol Program in Flint, Michigan* (East Lansing, MI: National Neighborhood Foot Patrol Center, n.d.).

19. Bruce L. Berg and John J. Horgan, *Criminal Investigation*, 3rd ed. (Westerville: Glencoe/McGraw-Hill, 1998).

20. Christine Wicker, "Death Beat," in Keith N. Haley and Mark A. Stallo, *Texas Crime, Texas Justice* (New York: McGraw-Hill, 1996).

21. U.S. Department of Justice, Federal Bureau of Investigations, *Crime in the United States, 2004*, www.fbi.gov/ucr/cius_04/offenses_cleared/index.html.

22. Mark Willman and John Snortum, "Detective Work: The Criminal Investigation Process in a Medium-Size Police Department," *Criminal Justice Review* 9 (1984), pp. 33–39; V. Williams and R. Sumrall, "Productivity Measures in the Criminal Investigation Function," *Journal of Criminal Justice* 10 (1982), pp. 111–22; I. Greenberg and R. Wasserman, *Managing Criminal Investigations* (Washington, DC: U.S. Department of Justice, 1979); P. Greenwood and J. Petersilia, *The Criminal Investigation Process, Vol. I, Summary and Policy Implications* (Washington, DC: U.S. Department of Justice, 1975); B. Greenberg, C. Elliot, L. Kraft, and H. Procter, *Felony Investigation Decision Model: An Analysis of Investigative Elements of Information* (Washington, DC: GPO, 1975).

23. John Conklin, *Robbery and the Criminal Justice System* (New York: J. B. Lippincott, 1972), p. 149.

24. Mike Berry, "Cop's Best Clue—a Fingerprint," *The Orlando Sentinel*, November 8, 2002, p. B1. Integrated Automated Fingerprint System, www.fbi.gov/hq/cjisd/iafis.htm.

25. Hollis Stambaugh, David Beaupre, David Icove, Richard Baker, Waynes Cassady, and Wayne P. Williams, *State and Local Law Enforcement Needs to Combat Local Crime*, National Institute of Justice, August 2000.

26. Ronald T. Holmes, Richard Tewksberry, and Stephen T. Holmes, "Pornography on the Internet," *Law and Order* 45, no. 9 (September 1997).

27. Stambaugh, et al., op. cit.

28. Unless indicated otherwise, information in this section on drug enforcement is from the following sources: Matthew J. Hickman and Brian A. Reaves, "Local Police Departments 2003," U.S. Department of Justice, Bureau of Justice Statistics (Washington, DC: GPO, May 2006), p. 15, Table 29, p. 16, Table 31; Peter Joseph Loughlin, "Does the Civil Asset Forfeiture Reform Act of 2000 Bring a Modicum of Sanity to the Federal Civil Asset Forfeiture System?" at www.malet.com/does_the_civil_asset_forfeiture_.htm; H. Williams, "Drug Control Strategies of United States Law Enforcement," United Nations, Office on Drugs and Crime at www.unodc.org/unodc/en/bulletin/bulletin_1990-01-01_1_page004.html#s005; Scott Ehlers, *Policy Briefing: Asset Forfeiture*, The Drug Policy Foundation (Washington, DC: GPO, 1999); Samuel Walker, *Sense and Nonsense about Crime and Drugs: A Policy Guide*, 5th ed. (Belmont, CA: Wadsworth, 2001), chap. 13; Victor E. Kappeler, Mark Blumberg, and Gary W. Potter, *The Mythology of Crime and Criminal Justice*, 3rd ed. (Prospect Heights, IL: Waveland Press, 2000), chap. 8; "Long-Term Trends in Illicit Drug Use," U.S. Department of Health and Human Services, Office of Applied Studies at www.samhsa.gov/oas/nhsda/2k1nhsda/vol1/chapter9.htm#9.2.

29. Material on research studies based on information in Alfred Blumstein and Joan Petersilia, "NIJ and Its Research Program," *25 Years of Criminal Justice Research* (Washington, DC: The National Institute of Justice, 1994), pp. 10–14.

30. James Q. Wilson and George L. Kelling, "Broken Windows: The Police and Neighborhood Safety," *Atlantic Monthly* 256 (1982), pp. 29–38.

31. Material in this subsection is based on information in the following sources: Community Policing Consortium, *Understanding Community Policing: A Framework for Action*, monograph, www.communitypolicing.org/conpubs.html, January 1998; U.S. Department of Justice, National Institute of Corrections, *Community Justice: Striving for Safe, Secure, and Just Communities* (Louisville, KY: LIS, 1996).

32. See William Oliver, "The Homeland Security Juggernaut: The End of the Community Policing Era?" *Crime & Justice International* 20 (2004), pp. 4–10.

33. *Katz* v. *United States*, 389 U.S. 347 (1967).

34. *United States* v. *Jacobsen*, 466 U.S. 109 (1984).

35. Ibid.

36. Unless indicated otherwise, information in this section is from www.epic.org/privacy/terrorism/hr3162.html, which provides the full text of the USA PATRIOT Act; American Civil Liberties Union, "Surveillance Under the USA PATRIOT Act," www.aclu.org/SafeandFree/SafeandFree.cfm?ID=12263&c=206, April 3, 2003; Electronic Frontier Foundation, "EFF Analysis of the Provisions of the USA PATRIOT Act," www.eff.org/Privacy/Surveillance/ Terrorism militias/20011031_eff_usa_patriot_analysis.htm, October 31, 2001.

37. Department of Justice, "Fact Sheet: USA PATRIOT Act Improvement and Reauthorization Act of 2005" at www.usdoj.gov/opa/pr/2006/March/06_opa_113.html; The American Civil Liberties Union, "The Patriot Act: Where It Stands" at http://action.aclu.org/reformthepatriotact/whereitstands.html.

38. *Dickerson* v. *United States*, 530 U.S. 428 (2000).

Chapter 4

1. W. S. Wilson Huang and Michael S. Vaughn, "Support and Confidence: Public Attitudes Toward the Police," in Timothy J. Flanagan and Dennis R. Longmire (eds.), *Americans View Crime and Justice: A National Public Opinion Survey* (Thousand Oaks, CA: Sage, 1996), pp. 31–45.

2. Humphrey Taylor, "Love Affair with NYPD Has Not Changed Nationwide Attitudes Toward Police," *The Harris Poll* #13, March 20, 2002, at www.harrisinter-active.com/harris_poll/printerfriend/index.asp?PID=290; also see Bureau of Justice Statistics, *Sourcebook of criminal justice statistics Online*, at

www.albany.edu/sourcebook, Tables 2.14, 2.17, 2.24, 2.25, 2.28.

3. *Sourcebook*, op. cit. Table 2.18.

4. Larry Gaines and Victor Kappeler, "Police Selection," in Gary Cordner and Donna Hale (eds.), *What Works in Policing: Operations and Administration Examined* (Cincinnati: Anderson, 1992).

5. Robert B. Mills, "Psychological, Psychiatric, Polygraph, and Stress Evaluation," in Calvin Swank and James Conser (eds.), *The Police Personnel System* (New York: Wiley, 1981).

6. O. W. Wilson and Roy McLaren, *Police Administration* (New York: McGraw-Hill, 1972), p. 261.

7. Albert Reiss, *The Police and the Public* (New Haven, CT: Yale University Press, 1971).

8. Matthew J. Hickman and Brian A. Reaves, *Local Police Departments, 2003*, U.S. Department of Justice, Bureau of Justice Statistics (Washington, DC: GPO, 2006), and U.S. Census Bureau.

9. David Carter, Allen Sapp, and Darrel Stephens, *The State of Police Education: Policy Direction for the 21st Century* (Washington, DC: Police Executive Research Forum, 1989).

10. Information on the Police Corps is from The Police Corps Act, 42 U.S.C., sections 14091 et seq. as amended through November 2, 2002 (Title XX, Subtitle A, of the Violent Crime Control and Law Enforcement Act of 1994); U.S. Department of Justice, Office of the Police Corps at www.ojp.usdoj.gov/opclee/about.html.

11. *Hild* v. *Bruner*, 1980; *Bonsignore* v. *City of New York*, 1981.

12. Jack Gregory, "The Background Investigation and Oral Interview," in Calvin Swank and James Conser (eds.), op. cit.

13. Jerome Skolnick, *Justice Without Trial* (New York: Wiley, 1996).

14. Lawrence W. Sherman and Richard A. Berk, *The Minneapolis Domestic Violence Experiment* (Washington, DC: The Police Foundation, 1984).

15. Steve Lackmeyer and Ken Raymond, "City Leaders Balk at Ban on Police Profiling," *The Oklahoman*, June 3, 2000.

16. Alex Johnson, "Fear and Loathing on the Job," MSNBC, September 4, 2000.

17. NIOSH, "Stress at Work," www.cdc.gov/niosh/stresswk.html.

18. The Word Spy at www.LOGOPHILIA.com/WordSpy/c.html.

19. "10% of Police Shootings Found to Be 'Suicide by Cop,'" *Criminal Justice Newsletter* 29, no. 17 (September 1, 1998), pp. 1–2.

20. Alan Feuer, "Drawing a Bead on a Baffling Endgame: Suicide by Cop," *The New York Times*, June 25, 1998.

21. NIOSH, op. cit.

22. John Dugan and Daniel Breda, "Complaints About Police Officers: A Comparison Among Types and Agencies," *Journal of Criminal Justice* 19 (1991), pp. 165–71.

23. Knapp Commission, *Report on Police Corruption* (New York: George Braziller, 1972).

24. Ellwyn R. Stoddard, "The Informal 'Code' of Police Deviancy: A Group Approach to Blue-Coat Crime," *Journal of Criminal Law, Criminology, and Police Science* 59 (1968), p. 204.

25. Candace McCloy, "Lawsuits Against Police: What Impact Do They Have?" *Criminal Law Bulletin* 20 (1984), pp. 49–56.

26. Federal Bureau of Investigation, *Terrorism in the United States, 1999*, p. 15, at www.fbi.gov/publications/terror/terroris.htm.

27. Ibid.

28. Ibid., p. 16.

29. U.S. State Department, *Patterns of Global Terrorism, 2001*, May 2002, p. v, at www.state.gov/s/ct/rls/pgtrpt/2000/pdf.

30. Ibid., p. 1.

31. *Terrorism in the United States, 1999*, op. cit., p. 15.

32. Ibid., p. i.

33. Ibid.

34. U.S. State Department, *Patterns of Global Terrorism, 2002*, April 2003, p. xiii, at www.state.gov/s/ct/rls/pgtrpt/2002.

35. *Terrorism in the United States, 1999*, op. cit. p. ii.

36. Ibid.

37. Ibid., p. 18.

38. Ibid., p. 19.

39. Ibid., p. 20.

40. Ibid., pp. 25–26.

41. Ibid., p. 16.

42. Ibid., p. 23.

43. Ibid., p. xi.; U.S. Department of State, Country Reports on Terrorism (April 27, 2005), www.state.gov/s/ct/rls/45321.htm.

44. *Terrorism in the United States, 1999*, op. cit., p. 23.

45. Ibid.

46. Ibid., pp. 38–40.

47. Ibid., p. i.

48. See Howard Zinn, *A People's History of the United States* (New York: Harper Colophon, 1980), chap. 4.

49. *Patterns of Global Terrorism, 2002*, op. cit., p. xi.

50. Eric Lichtblau, "Bush Issues Federal Ban on Racial Profiling," *The New York Times*, June 18, 2003.

51. Deborah Orin and David Kadison, "Government Still Knapping as New 9/11 Looms," *New York Post Online Edition*, June 30, 2003.

52. David Johnston, "Report Calls U.S. Agencies Understaffed for Bioterror," *The New York Times*, July 6, 2003.

Chapter 5

1. Administrative Office of the U.S. Courts, Federal Judiciary Web site, "Federal Judicial Vacancies" at www.uscourts.gov/judicialvac.html; Administrative Office of the U.S. Courts, Federal Judiciary Web site, "Judicial Compensation" at www.uscourts.gov/judicialcompensation.html.

2. Administrative Office of the U.S. Courts, Federal Judiciary Web site, "Judicial Business of the United States Courts 2005" at www.uscourts.gov/judbus2005/contents.html.

3. Administrative Office of the U.S. Courts, Federal Judiciary Web site, "About the U.S. Courts," at www.uscourts.gov.

4. "Judicial Business of the United States Courts 2005," op. cit.

5. Administrative Office of the U.S. Courts, Federal Judiciary Web site,"United States Courts of Appeals" at www.uscourts.gov/courtsofappeals.html

6. "Federal Judicial Vacancies," op. cit.; "Judicial Compensation," op. cit.

7. "Federal Judicial Vacancies," op. cit.

8. "Judicial Compensation,"op. cit.

9. Supreme Court of the United States, "2005 Year-End Report on the Federal Judiciary" at www.supremecourtus.gov/publicinfo/publicinfo.html.

10. Material on the state courts is based on information from the following sources: Richard Y. Schauffler, Robert C. LaFountain, Neal B. Kauder, and Shauna M. Strickland, *Examining the Work of State Courts, 2004. A National Perspective from the Court Statistics Project* (Williamsburg, VA: National Center for State Courts, 2005); David B. Rottman, Carol R. Flango, Melissa T. Cantrell, Randall Hansen, Neil LaFountain, *State Court Organization 1998*, U.S. Department of Justice, Bureau of Justice Statistics (Washington, DC: GPO, June 2000); David W. Neubauer, *America's Courts and the Criminal Justice System*, 4th ed. (Pacific Grove, CA: Brooks/Cole, 1992); Christopher Smith, *Courts, Politics, and the Judicial Process* (Chicago: Nelson-Hall, 1993); N. Gary Holten and Lawson L. Lamar, *The Criminal Courts: Structures, Personnel, and Processes* (New York: McGraw-Hill, 1991); Lawrence Baum, *American Courts*, 3rd ed. (Boston: Houghton Mifflin, 1994). U.S. Department of Justice, Bureau of Justice Statistics, *Report to the Nation on Crime and Justice*, 2nd ed. (Washington, DC: GPO, 1988); H. Ted Rubin, *The Courts: Fulcrum of the Justice System* (Santa Monica, CA: Goodyear, 1976); James Eisenstein, Roy Flemming, and Peter Nadulli, *The Contours of Justice: Communities and Their Courts* (Boston: Little, Brown, 1988); Malcolm Feeley, *The Process Is the Punishment: Handling Cases in Lower Criminal Court* (New York: Russell Sage, 1979); Harry P. Stumpf and John H. Culver, *The Politics of State Courts* (New York: Longman, 1992); Paul Wice, *Chaos in the Courthouse: The Inner Workings of the Urban Criminal Courts* (New York: Praeger, 1985).

11. Unless indicated otherwise, material about specialty courts is from C. West Huddleston, III, Karen Freeman-Wilson, Douglas B. Marlowe, and Aaron Roussell, *Painting the Current Picture: A National Report Card on Drug Courts and Other Problem Solving Court Programs in the United States*, Vol. 1, No. 2 (Rockville, MD: National Drug Court Institute, May 2005); "Drug Courts: Overview of Growth, Characteristics, and Results," GAO/GGD-97-106, www.ncjrs.org/txtfiles/dcourts.txt, July 31, 1997; Rottman et al., op. cit., p. 207.

12. John Wolfson and Sherri M. Owens, "Few Pay Back What They Took from Crime Victims," *The Orlando Sentinel*, February 23, 2003, p. B1.

13. Judith S. Kaye, "Making the Case for Hands-On Courts," *Newsweek*, October 11, 1999, p. 13.

14. Maya Bell, "Mentally Ill Get Court of Their Own and Help," *The Orlando Sentinel*, July 13, 1997, p. A-1.

15. "American Court Systems Flow Chart" at www.judicial.state.ia.us/students/6.

16. National Center for State Courts, "Appellate Court: Structure, Jurisdiction and Process," www.ncsconline.org/D_Research/Ct_Struct/Index.html.

17. Ibid.

18. Rubin, op. cit.

19. In addition to the other sources cited, material on the key actors in the court process is from Neubauer, op. cit.; David W. Neubauer, *Judicial Process: Law, Courts and Politics in the United States* (Pacific Grove, CA: Brooks/Cole, 1991); Smith, op. cit.; Holten and Lamar, op. cit.; Baum, op. cit.

20. Material about prosecutors is also taken from David Heilbroner, *Rough Justice: Days and Nights of a Young D.A.* (New York: Pantheon, 1990).

21. Data in this section are from Carol J. DeFrances, "Prosecutors in State Courts, 2001," U.S. Department of Justice, Bureau of Justice Statistics *Bulletin* (Washington, DC: GPO, May 2002).

22. In addition to the other sources cited, material on defense attorneys is from Elizabeth Loftus and E. Ketcham, *For the Defense* (New York: St. Martin's, 1991); Paul Wice, *Judges and Lawyers: The Human Side of Justice* (New York: Harper-Collins, 1991); Paul Wice, *Criminal Lawyers: An Endangered Species* (Newbury Park, CA: Sage, 1978); Seymour Wishman, *Confessions of a Criminal Lawyer* (New York: Penguin, 1982); Lisa J. McIntyre, *The Public Defender: The Practice of Law in the Shadows of Repute* (Chicago: Univ. of Chicago Press, 1987).

23. Data about indigent defense are from Bureau of Justice Statistics, "Indigent Defense Statistics," at www.ojp.usdoj.gov/bjs/id.htm.

24. In addition to the other sources cited, material on judges is from Paul Ryan, Allan Ashman, Bruce D. Sales, and Sandra Shane-DuBow, *American Trial Judges* (New York: Free Press, 1980); Robert Satter, *Doing Justice: A Trial Judge at Work* (New York: Simon & Schuster, 1990); Wice (1991), op. cit.; Wice (1985), op. cit.

25. *Sourcebook of criminal justice statistics* Online, Tables 1.87 and 1.89.

26. In addition to the other sources cited, material on pretrial stages is from Neubauer (1992), op. cit.; Holten and Lamar, op. cit.

27. David C. Steelman, James E. McMillan, and John A. Goerdt, *Caseflow Management: The Heart of Court Management in the New Millennium* (Williamsburg, VA: National Center for State Courts, 2000).

28. G. Thomas Munsterman, Paula L. Hannaford, and G. Marc Whitehead (eds.), *Jury Trial Innovations* (Williamsburg, VA: National Center for State Courts, 1997).

29. Timothy R. Murphy, Paula L. Hannaford, Genevra Kay Loveland, and G. Thomas Munsterman,

Managing Notorious Cases (Williamsburg, VA: National Center for State Courts, 1998).

30. Debbie Salamone Wickhan, "On the Run," *The Orlando Sentinel*, January 7, 2001, p. A-1.

31. Ibid.; Richard Willing, "Skipped bail is taking huge bite," *USA Today* (10/13/2004) at www.usatoday.com/news/nation/2004-10-13-bail-bonds_x.htm.

32. In addition to the other sources cited, material on plea bargaining is from Neubauer (1992), op. cit.; Neubauer (1991), op. cit.; Holten and Lamar, op. cit.; Baum, op. cit.

33. In addition to the other sources cited, material on criminal trials is from Neubauer (1992), op. cit.; Neubauer (1991), op. cit.; Smith, op. cit.; Holten and Lamar, op. cit.

34. In addition to the other sources cited, material on juries is from Rottman et al., op. cit.; Holten and Lamar, op. cit.; Valerie P. Hans and Neil Vidmar, *Judging the Jury* (New York: Plenum, 1986); Harry Kalvan, Jr., and Hans Zeisel, *The American Jury* (Boston: Little, Brown, 1996); James P. Levine, *Juries and Politics* (Pacific Grove, CA: Brooks/Cole, 1992).

35. *Sourcebook of criminal justice statistics* Online, p. 88, Table 1.92.

36. In addition to the other sources cited, material on the trial process is from Satter (1990), op. cit.

37. *Examining the Work of State Courts, 2004*, op. cit.; Jeffrey Rosen, "One Angry Woman: Why Are Hung Juries on the Rise?" *The New Yorker*, February 24 & March 3, 1997, p. 55.

Chapter 6

1. In addition to the other sources cited, material on sentencing and appeals is from David W. Neubauer, *America's Courts and the Criminal Justice System*, 7th ed. (Belmont, CA: Wadsworth, 2002); Christopher Smith, *Courts, Politics, and the Judicial Process* (Chicago: Nelson-Hall, 1993); N. Gary Holten and Lawson L. Lamar, *The Criminal Courts: Structures, Personnel, and Processes* (New York: McGraw-Hill, 1991); Lawrence Baum, *American Courts*, 3rd ed. (Boston: Houghton Mifflin, 1994); David Garland, *Punishment and Modern Society: A Study in Social Theory* (Chicago: Univ. of Chicago Press, 1990); Paul Wice, *Chaos in the Courthouse: The Inner Workings of the Urban Criminal Courts* (New York: Praeger, 1985); John Paul Ryan, Allan Ashman, Bruce D. Sales, and Sandra Shane-DuBow, *American Trial Judges* (New York: Free Press, 1980); Robert Satter, *Doing Justice: A Trial Judge at Work* (New York: Simon & Schuster, 1990); Herbert Packer, *The Limits of the Criminal Sanction* (Stanford, CA: Stanford Univ. Press, 1968).

2. *Weems v. United States*, 217 U.S. 349 (1910); Michael Meltsner, *Cruel and Unusual: The Supreme Court and Capital Punishment.* (New York: Random House, 1973), pp. 173–175; Raymond Paternoster, Capital Punishment in America. (New York: Lexington, 1991), p. 51.

3. Matthew R. Durose and Patrick A. Langan, *Felony Sentences in State Courts, 2002*, U.S. Department

of Justice, Bureau of Justice Statistics *Bulletin* (Washington, DC: GPO, 2004), p. 5.

4. *American Correctional Association 2005 Directory: Adult and Juvenile Correctional Departments, Institutions, Agencies and Probation and Parole Authorities* (Lanham, MD: American Correctional Association, 2005), p. 18.

5. "Sentence Disparity in New York: The Response of Forty-One Judges," *New York Times*, March 30, 1979, p. B3.

6. See Robert M. Bohm, "Retribution and Capital Punishment: Toward a Better Understanding of Death Penalty Opinion," *Journal of Criminal Justice* 20 (1992), pp. 227–35.

7. "New Directions from the Field: Victims' Rights and Services for the 21st Century," U.S. Department of Justice, Office for Victims of Crime, *OVC Bulletin* (Washington, DC: GPO, December 2004).

8. *Report to the Nation 2003: Fiscal Years 2001 and 2002*, U.S. Department of Justice, Office for Victims of Crime, www.ojp.usdoj.gov/ovc/welcovc/reporttonation2003/welcome.html; *Report to the Nation 2005: Fiscal Years 2003 and 2004*, U.S. Department of Justice, Office for Victims of Crime, www.ojp.usdoj.gov/ovc/welcovc/reporttonation2005/welcome.html.

8. *1996 Victims' Rights Sourcebook: A Compilation and Comparison of Victims' Rights Laws*, The National Center for Victims of Crime at www.ncvc.org/resources/reports/sourcebook.

9. "New Directions from the Field: Victims' Rights and Services for the 21st Century," op. cit.

10. "Restorative Justice: An Interview with Visiting Fellow Thomas Quinn," *National Institute of Justice Journal*, No. 235 (March 1998), p. 10.

11. "Ordering Restitution to the Crime Victim," U.S. Department of Justice, Office for Victims of Crime, *Legal Series Bulletin #6* (Washington, DC: GPO, November 2002).

12. Unless indicated otherwise, material about the death penalty is from Robert M. Bohm, *Deathquest II: An Introduction to the Theory and Practice of Capital Punishment in the United States*, 2nd ed. (Cincinnati, OH: Anderson, 2003); James R. Acker, Robert M. Bohm, and Charles S. Lanier (eds.), *America's Experiment with Capital Punishment: Reflections on the Past, Present, and Future of the Ultimate Penal Sanction*, 2nd ed. (Durham, NC: Carolina Academic Press, 2003); Hugo Alan Bedau, *The Death Penalty in America; Current Controversies* (New York: Oxford University Press, 1997); Hugo Adam Bedau (ed.), *The Death Penalty in America*, 3rd ed. (London: Oxford Univ. Press, 1982); William J. Bowers, with Glenn L. Pierce and John McDevitt, *Legal Homicide: Death as Punishment in America, 1864–1982* (Boston: Northeastern Univ. Press, 1984); Raymond Paternoster, *Capital Punishment in America* (New York: Lexington, 1991); Robert M. Bohm, "Humanism and the Death Penalty, with Special Emphasis on the Post-*Furman* Experience," *Justice Quarterly* 6 (1989), pp. 173–95; Victoria Schneider and John Ortiz Smykla, "A Summary Analysis of Executions in the United

States, 1608–1987: The Espy File," in R. M. Bohm (ed.), *The Death Penalty in America: Current Research* (Cincinnati: Anderson, 1991), pp. 1–19.

13. Death Penalty Information Center at www.deathpenaltyinfo.org; AmnestyInternational at web.amnesty.org/library/Index/ENGACT500072002?open&of=ENG-392.

14. Death Penalty Information Center, op. cit.

15. Thomas P. Bonczar and Tracy L. Snell, *Capital Punishment, 2004*, U.S. Department of Justice, Bureau of Justice Statistics Bulletin (Washington, DC: GPO, November 2005), p. 3.

16. Thomas P. Bonczar and Tracy L. Snell, *Capital Punishment, 2003*, U.S. Department of Justice, Bureau of Justice Statistics Bulletin (Washington, DC: GPO, November 2004), p. 16, Appendix table 4 at www.ojp.usdoj.gov/bjs/abstract/cp03.htm.

17. Paternoster, op. cit., pp. 208–9; Barry Scheck, Peter Neufeld, and Jim Dwyer, *Actual Innocence: When Justice Goes Wrong and How to Make It Right* (New York: Penguin Putnam, 2001); James S. Liebman, Jeffrey Fagan, and Valerie West, "A Broken System: Error Rates in Capital Cases, 1973–1995," The Justice Project at www.justice.policy.net/jpreport.html.

18. The Death Penalty Information Center, op. cit.

19. Bonczar and Snell, *Capital Punishment, 2003*, op. cit.

20. Death Penalty Information Center, op. cit.

21. Ibid.

22. Ibid.

23. Gallup Poll, May 19, 2005 (accessed through http://web.lexis-nexis.com).

24. Death Penalty Information Center, op. cit.

25. Robert M. Bohm, *Deathquest II*, op. cit., pp. 242 and 249.

26. "The Shadow over America," *Newsweek*, May 29, 2000, p. 27.

27. Death Penalty Information Center, op. cit.

28. Bohm, *Deathquest II*, op. cit.

29. Survey cited in Edmund F. McGarrell and Marla Sandys, "The Misperception of Public Opinion Toward Capital Punishment: Examining the Spuriousness Explanation of Death Penalty Support," *American Behavioral Scientist* 39 (1996), pp. 500–13, p. 509.

30. Robert M. Bohm, Louise J. Clark, and Adrian F. Aveni, "Knowledge and Death Penalty Opinion: A Test of the Marshall Hypotheses," *Journal of Research in Crime and Delinquency* 28 (1991), pp. 360–87; Robert M. Bohm and Ronald E. Vogel, "A Comparison of Factors Associated with Uninformed and Informed Death Penalty Opinions," *Journal of Criminal Justice* 23 (1994), pp. 125–43; Robert M. Bohm, Ronald E. Vogel, and Albert A. Maisto, "Knowledge and Death Penalty Opinion: A Panel Study," *Journal of Criminal Justice* 21 (1993), pp. 29–45; Robert M. Bohm and Brenda L. Vogel, "More than Ten Years After: The Long-Term Stability of Informed Death Penalty Opinions." *Journal of Criminal Justice* 32 (2004), pp. 307–327.

31. Jeffrey M. Jones, "Understanding Americans' Support for the Death Penalty," The Gallup Organization, Gallup Poll Tuesday *Briefing*, June 3, 2003.

32. Bohm, "Retribution and Capital Punishment," op. cit.; see also Bohm and Vogel, "A Comparison of Factors Associated with Uninformed and Informed Death Penalty Opinions," op. cit.

Chapter 7

1. See Robert Johnson, *Hard Time: Understanding and Reforming the Prison* (Monterey, CA: Brooks/Cole, 1987).

2. Michel Foucault, *Discipline and Punish: The Birth of the Prison* (New York: Pantheon, 1978).

3. See Graeme Newman, *The Punishment Response* (Albany, NY: Harrow and Heston, 1985).

4. Todd R. Clear and George F. Cole, *American Corrections*, 3rd ed. (Belmont, CA: Wadsworth, 1994).

5. Graeme Newman and Pietro Marongiu, "Penological Reform and the Myth of Beccaria," *Criminology* 28 (1990), pp. 325–46.

6. Ibid.

7. Clear and Cole, op. cit.

8. David J. Rothman, *The Discovery of the Asylum: Social Order and Disorder in the New Republic* (Boston: Little, Brown, 1971).

9. See Paul Takagi, "The Walnut Street Jail: A Penal Reform to Centralize the Powers of the State," *Federal Probation* (December 1975), pp. 18–26.

10. Rothman, op. cit.

11. Clear and Cole, op. cit.

12. Nicole Hahn Rafter, "Gender and Justice: The Equal Protection Issue," in L. Goodstein and D. L. MacKenzie (eds.), *The American Prison: Issues in Research and Policy* (New York: Plenum, 1989), pp. 89–109; and see Nicole Hahn Rafter, *Partial Justice: Women in State Prisons, 1800–1935* (Boston: Northeastern University Press, 1985).

13. John Irwin, *Prisons in Turmoil* (Boston: Little, Brown, 1980).

14. Ibid., p. 3.

15. See Robert Martinson, "What Works? Questions and Answers About Prison Reform," *The Public Interest* 42 (1974), pp. 22–54; see also The American Friends Service Committee, *Struggle for Justice: A Report on Crime and Justice in America* (New York: Hill & Wang, 1971).

16. From Charles W. Thomas, "Private Adult Correctional Facility Census: A 'Real-Time' Statistical Profile," www.crim.ufl.edu/pcp, September 4, 2001, Table 1 and Chart 3.

17. Ibid.

18. Ibid.

19. Ibid.

20. Ibid.; James Austin and Gary Coventry, *Emerging Issues on Privatized Prisons* (Washington, DC: U.S. Department of Justice, Bureau of Justice Statistics, February 2001).

21. Doris Layton MacKenzie and James W. Shaw, "The Impact of Shock Incarceration on Technical Violations and New Criminal Activities," *Justice Quarterly* 10 (1993), pp. 463–87; also see Doris Layton MacKenzie and Claire Souryal, *Multisite Evaluation of Shock Incarceration*, National Institute of Justice, November 1994.

22. "Poor Evaluation Brings End to California's Boot Camp," *Criminal Justice Newsletter* 28, no. 15 (August 1, 1997), pp. 1–2.

23. Human Rights Watch World Report 1998: United States, www.hrw.org/worldreport/Back.htm; personal communication.

24. United States Department of Justice, Bureau of Justice Statistics *Bulletin, Prisoners in 1992,* May 1993.

25. Paige M. Harrison and Allen J. Beck, "Prisoners in 2004," U.S. Department of Justice, *Bureau of Justice Statistics Bulletin,* October 2005; Paige M. Harrison and Allen J. Beck, "Prison and Jail Inmates at Midyear 2005," U.S. Department of Justice, Bureau of Justice Statistics *Bulletin,* May 2006.

26. Harrison and Beck, "Prisoners in 2004," op. cit.

27. Ibid.; Harrison and Beck, "Prison and Jail Inmates at Midyear 2005," op. cit.; U.S. Department of Justice, Office of Juvenile Justice and Delinquency Prevention, "Juveniles in Corrections,"*Statistical Briefing Book* at http://ojjdp.ncjrs.org/ojstatbb/corrections/qa08201.asp?qaDate=2003 (accessed May 26, 2006).

28. Harrison and Beck, "Prison and Jail Inmates at Midyear 2005," ibid.

29. Ibid.

30. Ibid.

31. Ibid.

32. James P. Lynch, "A Cross National Comparison of the Length of Custodial Sentences for Serious Crimes," *Justice Quarterly* 10 (1993), pp. 639–60.

33. Nils Christie, *Crime Control as Industry: Toward Gulags Western Style?* (New York: Routledge, 1993).

34. Franklin E. Zimring, "The Great American Lockup," *Washington Post* National Weekly Edition, March 1991, pp. 4–10.

35. Harrison and Beck, "Prison and Jail Inmates at Midyear 2005,"op. cit.

36. See, for example, John Kramer and Darrell Steffensmeir, "Race and Imprisonment Decisions," *Sociological Quarterly* 34 (1993), pp. 357–76; Ronald L. Akers, *Criminological Theories: Introduction and Evaluation,* 2nd ed. (Los Angeles: Roxbury, 1997). For different views, see Edmund F. McGarrell, "Institutional Theory and the Stability of a Conflict Model of the Incarceration Rate," *Justice Quarterly* 10 (1993), pp. 7–28; Cassia Spohn and Jerry Cederblom, "Race and Disparities in Sentencing: A Test of the Liberation Hypothesis," *Justice Quarterly* 8 (1991), pp. 305–27.

37. Federal Bureau of Prisons, "Quick Facts," www.bop.gov/news/quick.jsp#2.

38. The Federal Bureau of Prisons, "Mission Statement," at www.bop.gov.

39. The Federal Bureau of Prisons, "The Bureau in Brief," at www.bop.gov/pubinfo.html.

40. American Correctional Association 2005 Directory: Adult and Juvenile Correctional Departments, Institutions, Agencies and Probation and Parole Authorities (Lanham, MD: American Correctional Association, 2005), calculated from data on p. 56.

41. Francis X. Clines, "A Futuristic Prison Awaits the Hard Core 400." *The New York Times,* national ed., October 17, 1994, p. 1A.

42. Daniel P. Mears and Jamie Watson, "Towards a Fair and Balanced Assessment of Supermax Prisons," *Justice Quarterly* 23 (2006), pp. 232–270; Chase Riveland, "Supermax Prisons: Overview and General Considerations," U.S. Department of Justice, *National Institute of Corrections,* January 1999.

43. Material on Camp Delta is from Andrew Selsky and Jennifer Loven, "3 Gitmo detainees commit suicide, officials report," *The Orlando Sentinel,* June 11, 2006, p. A12; "Profile: Guantanamo Bay," BBC News at http://news.bbc.co.uk/1/hi/world/americas/4720962.stm (June 29, 2006); Matthew Hay Brown, "Detainees Await an Unkown Fate," *The Orlando Sentinel,* July 20, 2003, p. A1; CBS News.com, "Camp Delta: Guantanamo Bay (June 23, 2004), www.cbsnews.com/stories/2003/09/16/60II/main573616.shtml.

44. Harrison and Beck, "Prisoners in 2004," op. cit., p. 4.

45. Ibid., p. 9.

46. *American Correctional Association 2005 Directory,* op. cit., calculated from data on p. 30.

47. Ibid.

48. John Ortiz Smykla and Jimmy J. Williams," Co-Corrections in the United States, 1970–1990: Two Decades of Disadvantages for Women Prisoners," *Women and Criminal Justice* 8 (1996), pp. 61–76.

49. Harrison and Beck, "Prison and Jail Inmates at Midyear 2004," op. cit., p. 7; Harrison and Beck, "Prison and Jail Inmates at Midyear 2005," op. cit., p. 7.

50. Harrison and Beck, "Prison and Jail Inmates at Midyear 2005," op. cit., p. 8.

51. Ibid.

52. John Irwin, *The Jail: Managing the Underclass in American Society* (Berkeley: University of California Press, 1985).

53. John A. Backstrand, Don C. Gibbons, and Joseph F. Jones, "Who Is in Jail: An Examination of the Rabble Hypothesis," *Crime and Delinquency* 38 (1992), pp. 219–29.

54. See Dale K. Sechrest and William C. Collins, *Jail Management and Liability Issues* (Miami: Coral Gables Publishing, 1989).

55. Unless indicated otherwise, information in this section on jail design is from Frank Schmalleger and John Ortiz Smykla, *Corrections in the 21st Century* 3rd ed., (Burr Ridge, IL: McGraw-Hill, 2007), pp. 220–223; *Podular, Direct Supervision Jails: Information Packet,* U.S. Department of Justice, National Institute of Corrections, Jails Division (January 1993) at www.nicic.org/resources/topics/DirectSupervisionJails.aspx; Steve Fishback, "The Design of the New Anchorage Jail," *Alaska Justice Forum* 18, no. 3 (Fall 2001) at www.uaa.alaska.edu/just/forum/f183fa01/c_anchjail.html.

56. Mary Stohr-Gillman, Linda Zupan, Craig Curtis, Ben Menke, and Nicholas Lourich, "The Development of a Behavioral-Based Performance Appraisal System," *American Jails* 5 (1992), pp. 10–16.

57. Jeffrey D. Senese, "Evaluating Jail Reform: A Comparative Analysis of Popular/Direct and Linear Jail Inmate Infractions," *Journal of Criminal Justice* 25 (1997), pp. 61–73; Linda L. Zupan, *Jails: Reform*

and the New Generation Philosophy (Cincinnati: Anderson, 1991); Schmalleger and Smykla, op. cit., p. 223; Fishback, op. cit.

58. *2001 Directory of Direct Supervision Jails*, U.S. Department of Justice, National Institute of Corrections, at www.nicic.orgLibrary/017416.

59. James W. Marquart and Ben M. Crouch, "Coopting the Kept: Using Inmates for Social Control in a Southern Prison," in M. K. Carlie and K. I. Minor (eds.), *Prisons Around the World: Studies in International Penology* (Dubuque, IA: Wm. C. Brown, 1992), pp. 124–38.

60. United States Department of Justice, Bureau of Justice Statistics Special Report, Prison Rule Violators, December 1989.

61. Harrison and Beck, "Prisoners in 2004," op. cit., p. 8, Table 10; Kathleen Maguire, Ann L. Pastore, and Timothy J. Flanagan, *Sourcebook of Criminal Justice Statistics—1992*, U.S. Department of Justice, Bureau of Justice Statistics (Washington, DC: GPO, 1993), pp. 622 and 634, Tables 6.69 and 6.82; "Longer Sentences Mean Older Prisoners and New Set of Problems," *The Orlando Sentinel*, September 1, 1996, p. A-15.

62. Most of the information on the mentally ill is from "Fact Sheet: Criminalization of Americans with Severe Mental Illnesses," Treatment Advocacy Center at www.psychlaws.org/GeneralResources/Fact3.htm; Human Rights Watch, "Ill-Equipped: U.S. Prisons and Offenders with Mental Illness," www.hrw.org/reports/2003/usa1003/.

63. Allen J. Beck and Laura M. Maruschak, "Mental Health Treatment in State Prisons, 2000," U.S. Department of Justice, Bureau of Justice Statistics *Special Report* (Washington, DC: GPO, July 2001).

64. Information in this section about HIV and AIDS is from Laura Maruschak, *HIV in Prisons 2003*, U.S. Department of Justice, Bureau of Justice Statistics *Bulletin*, September 2005.

65. Camp and Camp, *Adult Systems*, op. cit., pp. 130–131; Camille Graham Camp and George M. Camp, *The Corrections Yearbook 1999* (Middletown, CT: Criminal Justice Institute), pp. 39–42.

66. National Institute for Literacy, "FACT SHEET: Corrections Education," January 2001, at www.nifl.gov.

67. For reference, see Anthony Walsh, *Understanding, Assessing, and Counseling the Criminal Justice Client* (Pacific Grove, CA: Brooks/Cole, 1988); also see Patricia van Voorhis, Michael Braswell, and David Lester, *Correctional Counseling and Rehabilitation*, 4th ed. (Cincinnati: Anderson, 2000).

68. Ted Palmer, *A Profile of Correctional Effectiveness and New Directions for Research* (Albany, NY: State University of New York Press, 1994).

69. Johnson, op. cit.

Chapter 8

1. Erving Goffman, *Asylums* (New York: Doubleday, 1961), p. xiii.

2. James B. Jacobs, *Stateville: The Penitentiary in Mass Society* (Chicago: University of Chicago Press, 1977).

3. See Donald Clemmer, *The Prison Community* (New York: Holt, Rinehart & Winston, 1940); Gresham M. Sykes, *The Society of Captives: A Study of a Maximum Security Prison* (Princeton, NJ: Princeton University Press, 1958).

4. Clemmer, op. cit.

5. John Irwin and Donald R. Cressey, "Thieves, Convicts, and the Inmate Culture," *Social Problems* 10 (1962), pp. 142–55. Also see Clarence Schrag, "Some Foundations for a Theory of Corrections," in D. R. Cressey (ed.), *The Prison: Studies in Institutional Organization and Change* (New York: Holt, Rinehart & Winston, 1961), pp. 30–35.

6. See Richard Hawkins and Geoffrey P. Alpert, *American Prison Systems: Punishment and Justice* (Englewood Cliffs, NJ: Prentice Hall, 1989); John Irwin, *Prisons in Turmoil* (Boston: Little, Brown, 1980). Also see Leo Carroll, *Hacks, Blacks, and Cons: Race Relations in a Maximum Security Prison* (Lexington, MA: Heath, 1974); Geoffrey Hunt, Stephanie Riegel, Tomas Morales, and Dan Waldorf, "Changes in Prison Culture: Prison Gangs and the Case of the 'Pepsi Generation,'" *Social Problems* 40 (1993), pp. 398–409; James B. Jacobs, *New Perspectives on Prisons and Imprisonment* (Ithaca, NY: Cornell University Press, 1983).

7. American Correctional Association 2005 Directory: Adult and Juvenile Correctional Departments, Institutions, Agencies and Probation and Parole Authorities (Lanham, MD: American Correctional Association, 2005), p. 60.

8. Lee Bowker, *Prison Victimization* (New York: Elsevier, 1980).

9. Ann Cordilia, *The Making of an Inmate: Prison as a Way of Life* (Cambridge, MA: Schenkman, 1983).

10. Goffman, op. cit., p. 14.

11. Hans Toch, *Living in Prison: The Ecology of Survival* (New York: Free Press, 1977).

12. Robert Johnson, *Hard Time: Understanding and Reforming the Prison* (Monterey, CA: Brooks/Cole, 1987).

13. Irwin, op. cit.

14. David Ward and Gene Kassebaum, "Homosexuality: A Model of Adaptation in a Prison for Women," *Social Problems* 12 (1964), pp. 159–77.

15. Joycelyn Pollock-Byrne, *Women, Prison, and Crime* (Pacific Grove, CA: Brooks/Cole, 1990).

16. Christopher J. Mumola, "Incarcerated Parents and Their Children," U.S. Department of Justice, Bureau of Justice Statistics Special Report (Washington, DC: GPO, August 2000), p. 2, Table 1 and p. 3, Table 4.

17. Phyllis Jo Baunach, *Mothers in Prison* (New Brunswick, NJ: Transaction Books, 1985).

18. Rose Giallombardo, *Society of Women: A Study of a Women's Prison* (New York: Wiley, 1966); Esther Heffernan, *Making It in Prison: The Square, the Cool, and the Life* (New York: Wiley, 1972); Alice M. Propper, *Prison Homosexuality* (Lexington, MA: Heath, 1981).

19. Propper, op. cit.

20. Giallombardo, op. cit.

21. David Ward and Gene Kassebaum, *Women's Prison: Sex and Social Structure* (Chicago: Aldine, 1965).
22. Heffernan, op. cit.; Schrag, op. cit.
23. Gordon Hawkins, *The Prison: Policy and Practice* (Chicago: University of Chicago Press, 1976), p. 85.
24. *American Correctional Association 2005 Directory: Adult and Juvenile Correctional Departments, Institutions, Agencies and Probation and Parole Authorities* (Lanham, MD: American Correctional Association, 2005), calculated from data on pp. 38, 46, and 48. Data from California and Vermont were not available from this source and were obtained directly from the two agencies.
25. Hawkins and Alpert, op. cit.
26. Ibid.
27. Sykes, op. cit.
28. John D. Hewitt, Eric D. Poole, and Robert M. Regoli, "Self-Reported and Observed Rule-Breaking in Prison: A Look at Disciplinary Response," *Justice Quarterly* 3 (1984), pp. 437–47.
29. Hawkins and Alpert, op. cit.
30. Lucien X. Lombardo, *Guards Imprisoned: Correctional Officers at Work*, 2nd ed. (Cincinnati: Anderson, 1989). And see Johnson, op. cit.
31. Barbara A. Owen, "Race and Gender Relations Among Prison Workers," *Crime and Delinquency* 31 (1985), pp. 147–59.
32. American Correctional Association, *Corrections Compendium*, February 2003, p. 11.
33. American Correctional Association, *Corrections Compendiun*, January 2003, p. 9.
34. Jacobs, op. cit., pp. 36–37.
35. "Appendix B: Text of the Prison Litigation Reform Act of 1995" at http://ojjdp.ncjrs.org/PUBS/walls/appen-b.html; The American Civil Liberties Union, "The Prison Litigation Reform Act (PLRA)," at www.aclu.org/prison/gen/14769res20031113.html.
36. *Wilson* v. *Seiter*, 111 S.Ct. 2321 (1991).
37. Hawkins and Alpert, op. cit.
38. ACLU National Prison Project, "Your Rights Regarding Environmental Hazards and Toxic Materials" at www.aclu.org/prison/conditions/14661res20031114.html.
39. Lauren E. Glaze and Seri Palla, "Probation and Parole in the United States, 2004," U.S. Department of Justice, Bureau of Justice Statistics *Bulletin* (Washington, DC: GPO, November 2005), pp. 1 and 8.
40. Unless indicated otherwise, information about recidivism is from Patrick A. Langan and David J. Levin, "Recidivism of Prisoners Released in 1994," U.S. Department of Justice, Bureau of Justice Statistics *Special Report* (Washington, DC: GPO, June 2002). Also see Miles D. Harer, *Recidivism Among Federal Prison Releasees in 1987: A Preliminary Report*, Federal Bureau of Prisons, Office of Research and Evaluation, December 9, 1993; United States Department of Justice, Bureau of Justice Statistics *Special Report, Recidivism of Prisoners Released in 1983*, April 1989; United States Department of Justice, Bureau of Justice Statistics Special Report, *Recidivism of Young Paroletes*, May 1987.

41. *Recidivisn of Prisoners Released in 1983*, op. cit.
42. Ben M. Crouch, "Is Incarceration Really Worse? Analysis of Offenders' Preferences for Prison over Probation," *Justice Quarterly* 10 (1993), pp. 67–88.
43. Kenneth D. Tunnell, "Choosing Crime: Close Your Eyes and Take Your Chances," *Justice Quarterly* 7 (1990), pp. 673–90.
44. Robert Martinson, "What Works? Questions and Answers About Prison Reform," *The Public Interest* 42 (1974), pp. 22–54.
45. Lynne Goodstein, "Inmate Adjustment to Prison and the Transition to Community Life," in R. M. Carter, D. Glaser, and L. T. Wilkins (eds.), *Correctional Institutions*, 3rd ed. (New York: Harper & Row, 1985), pp. 285–302.
46. Francis T. Cullen and Paul Gendreau, "Assessing Correctional Rehabilitation: Policy, Practice, and Prospects," in U.S. Department of Justice, Office of Justice Programs, *Criminal Justice 2000*, vol. 3, at www.ojp.usdoj.gov/nij/criminal_justice2000/vol3_2000.html.

Chapter 9

1. David E. Duffee, "Community Corrections: Its Presumed Characteristics and an Argument for a New Approach," in D. E. Duffee and E. F. McGarrell (eds.), *Community Corrections: A Community Field Approach* (Cincinnati: Anderson, 1990), pp. 1–41.
2. Patricia M. Harris, Todd R. Clear, and S. Christopher Baird, "Have Community Supervision Officers Changed Their Attitudes Toward Their Work?" *Justice Quarterly* 6 (1989), pp. 233–46. And see Robert T. Sigler, "Role Conflict for Adult Probation and Parole Officers: Fact or Myth," *Journal of Criminal Justice* 16 (1988), pp. 121–29.
3. Lauren E. Glaze and Seri Palla, "Probation and Parole in the United States, 2004," U.S. Department of Justice, Bureau of Justice Statistics *Bulletin* (Washington, DC: GPO, November 2005), p. 6, Table 3.
4. David J. Rothman, *Conscience and Convenience: The Asylum and Its Alternatives in Progressive America* (Boston: Little, Brown, 1980), p. 44; www.ohnd.uscourts.gov/U_S_Probation/U_S_Probation_Employment/u_s_probation_employment.html.
5. Tom Condon, "Prison Experiment: Sentenced to Read" at www.ctnow.com/templates/misc/printstory.jsp?slug=hc%2Dcondon1010%2Eartoct10
6. Rolando V. del Carmen, "Legal Issues and Liabilities in Community Corrections," in T. Ellsworth (ed.), *Contemporary Community Corrections* (Prospect Heights, IL: Waveland Press, 1992), pp. 383–407.
7. Jay S. Albanese, Bernadette A. Fiore, Jerie H. Powell, and Janet R. Storti, *Is Probation Working? A Guide for Managers and Methodologists* (New York: University Press of America, 1981), p. 65.
8. Ibid.
9. Joan Petersilia, Susan Turner, James Kahan, and Joyce Peterson, *Granting Felons Probation: Public Risks and Alternatives* (Santa Monica, CA: Rand, 1985).
10. United States Department of Justice, Bureau of Justice Statistics *Special Report, Recidivism of Felons*

on Probation, 1986–89 (Washington, DC: GPO, February 1992).

11. Rothman, op. cit.

12. Association of Paroling Authorities International, "Parole Board Surveys," www.apaintl.org/Publications.html; John C. Runda, Edward E. Rhine, and Robert E. Wetter, *The Practice of Parole Boards* (Lexington, KY: Host Communications Printing, 1994).

13. Ibid.

14. Ibid.

15. Ibid.

16. Ibid.

17. Ibid.

18. Ibid.

19. Ibid.

20. Ibid.

21. Ibid.

22. Ibid.

23. Richard McCleary, *Dangerous Men: The Sociology of Parole* (Beverly Hills, CA: Sage, 1978).

24. Peggy B. Burke, *Abolishing Parole: Why the Emperor Has No Clothes* (Lexington, KY: American Probation and Parole Association, 1995); Peggy B. Burke, "Issues in Parole Release Decision Making," in C. A. Hartjen and E. E. Rhine (eds.), *Correctional Theory and Practice* (Chicago: Nelson-Hall, 1992), pp. 213–32.

25. Association of Paroling Authorities International, "Parole Board Survey 2003," op. cit.; Timothy A. Hughes, Doris James Wilson, and Allen J. Beck, "Trends in State Parole, 1990–2000," U.S. Department of Justice, Bureau of Justice Statistics *Special Report* (Washington, DC: GPO, October 2001), p. 2.

26. Paula M. Ditton and Doris James Wilson, "Truth in Sentencing in State Prisons," U.S. Department of Justice, Bureau of Justice *Special Report* (Washington, DC: GPO, January 1999), p. 3.

27. Burke, *Abolishing Parole*, op. cit.

28. John C. Watkins, Jr., "Probation and Parole Malpractice in a Noninstitutional Setting: A Contemporary Analysis," *Federal Probation* 53 (1989), pp. 29–34 (quotations from p. 30). Also see Rolando V. del Carmen, op. cit.

29. Calculated from Lauren E. Glaze and Seri Palla, "Probation and Parole in the United States, 2004," op. cit., p. 1. Lauren E. Glaze, "Probation and Parole in the United States, 2001," U.S. Department of Justice, Bureau of Justice Statistics *Bulletin* (Washington, DC: GPO, August 2002), p. 1.

30. Jeffrey K. Liker, "Wage and Status Effects of Employment on Affective Well-Being Among Ex-Felons," *American Sociological Review* 47 (1982), pp. 264–83 (quotation from p. 282).

31. Richard A. Berk and David Rauma, "Capitalizing on Nonrandom Assignment to Treatments: A Regression-Discontinuity Evaluation of a Crime-Control Program," *Journal of the American Statistical Association* 78 (1983), pp. 21–27. And see Peter H. Rossi, Richard A. Berk, and K. J. Lenihan, *Money, Work, and Crime: Experimental Evidence* (New York: Academic Press, 1980).

32. Information evaluating parole is from Timothy A. Hughes, Doris James Wilson, and Allen J. Beck, "Trends in State Parole, 1990–2000," U.S. Department of Justice, Bureau of Justice Statistics *Special Report* (Washington, DC: GPO, October 2001), pp. 10–14; Lauren E. Glaze, "Probation and Parole in the United States, 2002," op. cit., p. 6, Table 7; "U.S. Correctional Population Reaches 6.3 Million Men and Women Represents 3.1 Percent of the Adult U.S. Population," U.S. Department of Justice, Bureau of Justice Statistics Press Release, July 23, 2000, at www.ojp.usdoj.gov/bjs/pub/pdf/pp99pr.pdf; "Recidivism of Young Parolees," U.S. Department of Justice, Bureau of Justice Statistics *Special Report* (Washington, DC: GPO, May 1987).

33. Runda et al., op. cit. Also see United States G.A.O., *Intermediate Sanctions: Their Impacts on Prison Crowding, Costs, and Recidivism Are Still Unclear* (Washington, DC: General Accounting Office, 1990).

34. Billie S. Erwin and Lawrence A. Bennett, *New Dimensions in Probation: Georgia's Experience with Intensive Probation Supervision*, United States Department of Justice, National Institute of Justice, Research in Brief (Washington, DC: GPO, 1987), p. 4.

35. Joan Petersilia and Susan Turner, "Comparing Intensive and Regular Supervision for High-Risk Probationers: Early Results from an Experiment in California," *Crime and Delinquency* 36 (1990), pp. 87–111.

36. Joan Petersilia and Susan Turner, *Evaluating Intensive Supervision Probation/Parole: Results of a Nationwide Experiment*, U.S. Department of Justice, National Institute of Justice, Research in Brief (Washington, DC: GPO, 1993). For further detail see Joan Petersilia and Susan Turner, "Intensive Probation and Parole," in M. Tonry and A. J. Reiss (eds.), *Crime and Justice: A Review of Research*, Vol. 17 (Chicago: University of Chicago Press, 1993), pp. 281–335.

37. Dale G. Parent, *Day Reporting Centers for Criminal Offenders: A Descriptive Analysis of Existing Programs*, U.S. Department of Justice, National Institute of Justice, Issues and Practices (Washington, DC: GPO 1990).

38. Paige M. Harrison and Allen J. Beck, "Prison and Jail Inmates at Midyear 2005," U.S. Department of Justice, Bureau of Justice Statistics *Bulletin* (Washington, DC: GPO, May 2006), p. 7, Table 8; Paige M. Harrison and Allen J. Beck, "Prison and Jail Inmates at Midyear 2004," U.S. Department of Justice, Bureau of Justice Statistics *Bulletin* (Washington, DC: GPO, April 2005), p. 7, Table 8.

39. Material in this section is from *How to Use Structured Fines (Day Fines) as an Intermediate Sanction*, U.S. Department of Justice, Bureau of Justice Assistance, November 1996.

40. Harrison and Beck, "Prison and Jail Inmates at Midyear 2005," op. cit.; Harrison and Beck, "Prison and Jail Inmates at Midyear 2004," op. cit.

41. Rolando V. del Carmen and Joseph B. Vaughn, "Legal Issues in the Use of Electronic Surveillance in Probation," in T. Ellsworth (ed.), *Contemporary*

Community Corrections (Prospect Heights, IL: Waveland Press, 1992), p. 426.

42. John P. Conrad, "Concluding Comments: VORP and the Correctional Future," in B. Galaway and J. Hudson (eds.), *Criminal Justice, Restitution, and Reconciliation* (Monsey, NY: Criminal Justice Press, 1990), p. 229.

43. Rene Stutzman, "State Takes Eyes Off Inmates," *The Orlando Sentinel*, December 29, 2002, p. A1; Rene Stutzman, "Ankle Monitors Show a Higher Rate of Success, *The Orlando Sentinel*, December 29, 2002, p. A15; Florida Department of Corrections at www.dc.state.fl.us; Camille Graham Camp and George M. Camp, *The 2001 Corrections Yearbook: Adult Systems* (Middletown, CT: Criminal Justice Institute, 2002), p. 206.

44. David J. Hartmann, Paul C. Friday, and Kevin I. Minor, "Residential Probation: A Seven-Year Follow-Up Study of Halfway House Discharges," *Journal of Criminal Justice* 22 (1994), pp. 503–15.

45. Patrick G. Donnelly and Brian E. Forschner, "Client Success or Failure in a Halfway House," *Federal Probation* 48 (1984), pp. 38–44. Also see R. E. Seiter, H. Bowman Carlson, J. Grandfield, and N. Bernam, *Halfway Houses: National Evaluation Program: Phase I, Summary Report*, U.S. Department of Justice (Washington, DC: GPO, 1977).

46. Edward J. Latessa and Lawrence F. Travis, "Halfway House or Probation: A Comparison of Alternative Dispositions," *Journal of Crime and Justice* 14 (1991), pp. 53–75.

47. Belinda Rodgers McCarthy, Bernard J. McCarthy, Jr., and Matthew C. Leone, *Community-Based Corrections*, 4th ed. (Belmont, CA: Wadsworth, 2001). Unless otherwise noted, the material in the remainder of this section draws on pp. 148–156 of this source.

48. Daniel P. LeClair and Susan Guarino-Ghezzi, "Does Incapacitation Guarantee Public Safety? Lessons from the Massachusetts Furlough and Prerelease Programs," *Justice Quarterly* 8 (1991), pp. 9–36 (quotation from p. 26).

Chapter 10

1. Philippe Aries, *Centuries of Childhood: A Social History of Family Life,* translated by Robert Baldick (New York: Random House, 1962).

2. Barry Krisberg and James F. Austin, *Reinventing Juvenile Justice* (Newbury Park, CA: Sage, 1993), p. 9.

3. Harry Elmer Barnes, *The Story of Punishment*, 2nd ed. (Montclair, NJ: Patterson Smith, 1972).

4. David J. Rothman, *The Discovery of the Asylum* (Boston: Little, Brown, 1971).

5. Thomas J. Bernard, *The Cycle of Juvenile Justice* (New York: Oxford University Press, 1992), p. 63; Rothman, op. cit., p. 207.

6. Robert M. Mennel, *Thorns and Thistles* (Hanover, NH: University Press of New England, 1973); Steven L. Schlossman, *Love and the American Delinquent* (Chicago: University of Chicago Press, 1977).

7. Alexander Pisciotta, "Treatment on Trial: The Rhetoric and Reality of the New York House of Refuge,

1857–1935," *The American Journal of Legal History* 29 (1985), pp. 151–81; Rothman, op. cit., p. 231.

8. Clemens Bartollas and Stuart J. Miller, *Juvenile Justice in America* (Englewood Cliffs, NJ: Regents/Prentice Hall, 1994), p. 136.

9. LaMar T. Empey and Mark C. Stafford, *American Delinquency: Its Meaning and Construction,* 3rd ed. (Belmont, CA: Wadsworth, 1991), p. 368.

10. Belinda R. McCarthy and Bernard J. McCarthy, *Community-Based Corrections,* 2nd ed. (Pacific Grove, CA: Brooks/Cole, 1991), p. 98.

11. Krisberg and Austin, op. cit., pp. 23–24; Hastings Hart, *Preventive Treatment of Neglected Children* (New York: Russell Sage, 1910), p. 70.

12. Bartollas and Miller, op. cit., p. 209; John T. Whitehead and Steven P. Lab, *Juvenile Justice: An Introduction* (Cincinnati: Anderson, 1990), p. 47.

13. Cited in Meda Chesney-Lind and Randall G. Shelden, *Girls, Delinquency, and Juvenile Justice* (Pacific Grove, CA: Brooks/Cole, 1992), p. 111.

14. Anthony M. Platt, *The Child Savers: The Invention of Delinquency* (Chicago: University of Chicago Press, 1969), p. 99.

15. Ibid., pp. 101–102.

16. Bernard, op. cit., pp. 68–69.

17. Ibid., pp. 70–71.

18. Platt, op. cit., pp. 134–36; Bernard, op. cit., p. 73.

19. Empey and Stafford, op. cit, pp. 58–59.

20. Bartollas and Miller, op. cit., p. 92; Empey and Stafford, op. cit., p. 59.

21. Krisberg and Austin, op. cit., p. 30.

22. Bernard, op. cit., p. 96.

23. Ibid., pp. 96–97.

24. Walter Wadlington, Charles H. Whitebread, and Samuel M. Davis, *Cases and Materials on Children in the Legal System* (Mineola, NY: Foundation Press, 1983), p. 202; Bernard, op. cit., p. 110.

25. M. A. Bortner, *Delinquency and Justice: An Age of Crisis* (New York: McGraw-Hill, 1988), p. 60.

26. Bernard, op. cit., p. 141.

27. Howard N. Snyder and Melissa Sickmund, *Juvenile Offenders and Victims: 2006 National Report.* (Pittsburgh, PA: National Center for Juvenile Justice, U.S. Department of Justice, Office of Juvenile Justice and Delinquency Prevention, 2006), p. 177.

28. Ibid., p. 157.

29. Ibid.

30. Douglas A. Smith, "The Organizational Context of Legal Control," *Criminology* 22 (1984), pp. 19–38.

31. Robert J. Sampson, "Effects of Socioeconomic Context on Official Reaction to Juvenile Delinquency," *American Sociological Review* 51 (1986), pp. 876–85; also see A. Cicourel, *The Social Organization of Juvenile Justice* (New York: Wiley, 1968).

32. Donald Black and Albert J. Reiss, "Police Control of Juveniles," *American Sociological Review* 35 (1970), pp. 63–77; Richard J. Lundman, Richard E. Sykes, and John P. Clark, "Police Control of Juveniles: A Replication," in Ralph Weisheit and Robert G. Culbertson (eds.), *Juvenile Delinquency: A Justice Perspective* (Prospect Heights, IL: Waveland Press,

1978), pp. 107–15; Irving Piliavan and Scott Briar, "Police Encounters with Juveniles," *American Journal of Sociology* 70 (1964), pp. 206–14.

33. Marvin D. Krohn, James P. Curry, and Shirley Nelson-Kilger, "Is Chivalry Dead? An Analysis of Changes in Police Dispositions of Males and Females," *Criminology* 21 (1983), pp. 417–37; Katherine Teilmann and Pierre H. Landry, "Gender Bias in Juvenile Justice," *Journal of Research in Crime and Delinquency* 18 (1981), pp. 47–80; see also William G. Staples, "Law and Social Control in Juvenile Justice Dispositions," *Journal of Research in Crime and Delinquency* 24 (1987), pp. 7–22; Meda Chesney-Lind, "Judicial Paternalism and the Female Status Offender: Training Women to Know Their Place," *Crime and Delinquency* 23 (1977), pp. 121–30.

34. Robert J. Sampson, "Sex Differences in Self-Reported Delinquency and Official Records: A Multiple-Group Structural Modeling Approach," *Journal of Quantitative Criminology* 1 (1985), pp. 345–67; Dale Dannefer and Russell K. Schutt, "Race and Juvenile Justice Processing in Court and Police Agencies," *American Journal of Sociology* 87 (1982), pp. 1113–32.

35. Merry Morash, "Establishment of a Juvenile Police Record: The Influence of Individual and Peer Group Characteristics," *Criminology* 22 (1984), pp. 97–111; Krohn et al., op. cit.; D. Elliott and H. L. Voss, *Delinquency and Dropout* (Lexington, MA: Lexington Books, 1974).

36. Federal Bureau of Investigation, *Crime in the United States 2003*, p. 289, Table 43, www.fbi.gov/ucr/03cius.htm.

37. *Statistical Abstract of the United States: 2004–2005*, p. 16, Table No. 15.

38. Delbert S. Elliott and David Huizinga, "Social Class and Delinquent Behavior in a National Youth Panel," *Criminology* 21 (1983), pp. 149–77.

39. *Sourcebook of Criminal Justice Statistics Online*, Table 4.26 at www.albany.edu/sourcebook/1995/pdf/t426.pdf; Federal Bureau of Investigation, *Crime in the United States, 2004*, op. cit., p. 337, Table 68.

40. Information about teen courts or youth courts is from Jeffrey Butts, Dean Hoffman, and Janeen Buck, "Teen Courts in the United States: A Profile of Current Programs," U.S. Department of Justice, Office of Juvenile Justice and Delinquency Prevention, Office of Juvenile Justice and Delinquency Prevention Fact Sheet #118 (Washington, DC: GPO, October 1999); Jeffrey A. Butts and Janeen Buck, "Teen Courts: A Focus on Research," *Juvenile Justice Bulletin* (Washington, DC: GPO, U.S. Department of Justice, Office of Juvenile Justice and Delinquency Prevention, October 2000); Jeffrey A. Butts, Janeen Buck, and Mark B. Coggeshall, *The Impact of Teen Court on Young Offenders* (Washington, DC: The Urban Institute, U.S. Department of Justice, Office of Juvenile Justice and Delinquency Prevention, April 2002); National Youth Court Center at www.youthcourt.net.

41. Information on restorative justice conferences or family group conferences is from Edmund F. McGarrell, "Restorative Justice Conferences as an Early Response to Young Offenders," *Juvenile Justice Bulletin* (Washington, DC: GPO, U.S. Department of Justice, Office of Juvenile Justice and Delinquency Prevention, August 2001); U.S. Department of Justice, Office of Juvenile Justice and Delinquency Prevention, *OJJDP Research 2000* (Washington, DC: GPO, May 2001).

42. Snyder and Sickmund, op. cit., p. 197.

43. Ibid., p. 199; Howard N. Snyder and Melissa Sickmund, *Juvenile Offenders and Victims: 1999 National Report* (Washington, DC: GPO, U.S. Department of Justice, National Center for Juvenile Justice, Office of Juvenile Justice and Delinquency Prevention, September 1999), p. 97.

44. Ted Rubin, "The Emerging Prosecutor Dominance of the Juvenile Court Intake Process," *Crime and Delinquency* 26 (1980), pp. 299–318.

45. For a review of this literature, see Chesney-Lind and Shelden, op. cit., pp. 137–39.

46. From Snyder and Sickmund, 1996, op. cit., p. 186.

47. Ibid., pp. 111 and 113.

48. Ibid., p. 113.

49. Unless indicated otherwise, material in this section is from the following sources: Ibid., pp. 111 and 116; Barry C. Feld, "Criminalizing the American Juvenile Court," in Michael Tonry (ed.), *Crime and Justice: A Review of Research*, Vol. 17 (Chicago: University of Chicago Press, 1993), pp. 197–280; Joseph B. Sanborn, Jr., "Policies Regarding the Prosecution of Juvenile Murderers: Which System and Who Should Decide," *Law & Policy* 18 (1996), pp. 151–78; Joseph B. Sanborn, Jr., "Certification to Criminal Court: The Important Policy Questions of How, When, and Why," *Crime and Delinquency* 40 (1994), pp. 262–81; Howard N. Snyder, "Juvenile Arrests 1995," *Juvenile Justice Bulletin* (Washington, DC: GPO, U.S. Department of Justice, Office of Juvenile Justice and Delinquency Prevention, February 1997), p. 12; Barry C. Feld, "The Juvenile Court Meets the Principle of the Offense: Legislative Changes in Juvenile Waiver Statutes," *Journal of Criminal Law and Criminology* 78 (1987), pp. 471–533; Barry Krisberg, Ira M. Schwartz, Paul Litsky, and James Austin, "The Watershed of Juvenile Justice Reform," *Crime and Delinquency* 32 (1986), pp. 5–38; Donna Hamparian, Linda Estep, Susan M. Muntean, Ramon R. Prestino, Robert G. Swisher, Paul L. Wallace, and Joseph L. White, *Youth in Adult Court: Between Two Worlds* (Washington, DC: OJJDP, 1982); Sickmund, "Juveniles in Court," op. cit., p. 5; and personal communications from Donna M. Bishop and Joseph B. Sanborn, Jr.

50. Martin L. Forst, Bruce A. Fisher, and Robert B. Coates, "Indeterminate and Determinate Sentencing of Juvenile Delinquents: A National Survey of Approaches to Commitment and Release Decision-Making," *Juvenile and Family Court Journal*, Summer 1985, pp. 1–12.

51. Patricia Torbert, Richard Gable, Hunter Hurst IV, Imogene Montgomery, Linda Szymanski, and Douglas Thomas, *State Responses to Serious and Violent Juvenile Crime* (Washington, DC: GPO, U.S.

Department of Justice, Office of Juvenile Justice and Delinquency Prevention, July 1996), chap. 3.

52. Patricia McFall Torbet, "Juvenile Probation: The Workhorse of the Juvenile Justice System," *Juvenile Justice Bulletin* (Washington, DC: GPO, U.S. Department of Justice, Office of Juvenile Justice and Delinquency Prevention, March 1996); Snyder and Sickmund, 2006, op. cit., p. 177.

53. Troy L. Armstrong, "National Survey of Juvenile Intensive Supervision" (Parts I and II), *Criminal Justice Abstracts* 20 (1988), pp. 342–48 (Part I) and 497–523 (Part II).

54. Richard G. Wiebush, "Juvenile Intensive Supervision: The Impact on Felony Offenders Diverted from Institutional Placement," *Crime and Delinquency* 39 (1993), pp. 68–89; William H. Barton and Jeffrey A. Butts, "Viable Options: Intensive Supervision Programs for Juvenile Delinquents," *Crime and Delinquency* 36 (1990), pp. 238–56.

55. Richard A. Ball, Ronald Huff, and Robert Lilly, *House Arrest and Correctional Policy: Doing Time at Home* (Newbury Park, CA: Sage, 1988).

56. See Marc Renzema and David T. Skelton, "Use of Electronic Monitoring in the United States: 1989 Update," National Institute of Justice, Research in Brief (Washington, DC: National Institute of Justice, 1990); Daniel Ford and Annesley K. Schmidt, "Electronically Monitored Home Confinement," National Institute of Justice, Research in Action (Washington, DC: National Institute of Justice, 1985).

57. Joseph B. Vaughn, "A Survey of Juvenile Electronic Monitoring and Home Confinement Programs," *Juvenile and Family Court Journal* 40 (1989), pp. 1–36.

58. Kevin I. Minor and Preston Elrod, "The Effects of a Probation Intervention on Juvenile Offenders' Self-Concepts, Loci of Control, and Perceptions of Juvenile Justice," *Youth and Society* 25 (1994), pp. 490–511; Gerald L. Golins, *Utilizing Adventure Education to Rehabilitate Juvenile Delinquents* (Las Cruces, NM: Educational Resources Information Center, Clearinghouse on Rural Education and Small Schools, 1980).

59. See, for example, R. Callahan, "Wilderness Probation: A Decade Later," *Juvenile and Family Court Journal* 36 (1985), pp. 31–51; John Winterdyk and Ronald Roesch, "A Wilderness Experiential Program as an Alternative for Probationers: An Evaluation," *Canadian Journal of Criminology* 24 (1982), pp. 39–49.

60. H. Preston Elrod and Kevin I. Minor, "Second Wave Evaluation of a Multi-Faceted Intervention for Juvenile Court Probationers," *International Journal of Offender Therapy and Comparative Criminology* 36 (1992), pp. 247–62; John Winterdyk and Curt Griffiths, "Wilderness Experience Programs: Reforming Delinquents or Beating Around the Bush?" *Juvenile and Family Court Journal* 35 (1984), pp. 35–44; Winterdyk and Roesch, op. cit.

61. Ted Palmer, *The Re-Emergence of Correctional Intervention* (Newbury Park, CA: Sage, 1992); Office of Juvenile Justice and Delinquency Prevention, *Project New Pride: Replication* (Washington: OJJDP, 1979); LaMar T. Empey and Maynard L. Erickson, *The Provo Experiment: Evaluating Community Control of Delinquency* (Lexington, MA: Lexington Books, 1972).

62. Terrence P. Thornberry, Stewart E. Tolnay, Timothy J. Flanagan, and Patty Glynn, *Office of Juvenile Justice and Delinquency Prevention Report on Children in Custody 1987: A Comparison of Public and Private Juvenile Custody Facilities* (Washington, DC: OJJDP, 1991).

63. Thornberry et al. (1991), op. cit.; Dale G. Parent, "Conditions of Confinement," *Juvenile Justice*, Vol. 1, No. 1 (Spring/Summer 1993), pp. 2–7, www.ncjrs.org/pdffiles/jjjs93.pdf.

64. Melissa Sickmund, "Juvenile Residential Facility Census, 2000: Selected Findings,"*Juvenile Offenders and Victims National Report Series Bulletin* (Washington, DC: GPO, U.S. Department of Justice, Office of Juvenile Justice and Delinquency Prevention, December 2002), p. 3.

65. Dale G. Parent, Valerie Leiter, Stephen Kennedy, Lisa Livens, Daniel Wentworth, and Sarah Wilcox, *Conditions of Confinement: Juvenile Detention and Corrections Facilities Research Summary* (Washington: OJJDP, 1994), p. 5.

66. See, for example, Barry Krisberg, "Juvenile Justice: Improving the Quality of Care," *National Council on Crime and Delinquency* (San Francisco: NCCD, 1992); Carol J. Garrett, "Effects of Residential Treatment on Adjudicated Delinquents," *Journal of Research in Crime and Delinquency* 22 (1985), pp. 287–308.

67. Barry Krisberg, Robert DeComo, and Norma C. Herrera, *National Juvenile Custody Trends 1978–1989* (Washington: OJJDP, 1992), p. 2; also see Steven Lab and John T. Whitehead, "A Meta-Analysis of Juvenile Correctional Treatment," *Journal of Research in Crime and Delinquency* 26 (1989), pp. 276–95; Norman G. Hoffmann, Ana M. Abrantes, and Ronald Anton, "Criminals, Troubled Youth, or a Bit of Both," *Addiction Professional* 1, no. 4 (July 2003).

68. Unless indicated otherwise, data in this section are from National Center for Juvenile Justice, "Census of Juveniles in Residential Placement Databook" at http://ojjdp.ncjrs.org/ojstatbb/cjrp/asp/Selection.asp; Snyder and Sickmund, 2006, op. cit., chap. 7.

69. Harrison and Beck, "Prison and Jail Inmates at Midyear 2004," op. cit., p. 8, Table 9, and p. 5, Table 5.

70. Richard G. Wiebush, Betsy McNulty, and Thao Le, "Implementation of the Intensive Community-Based Aftercare Program," *Juvenile Justice Bulletin* (Washington, DC: GPO, U.S. Department of Justice, Office of Juvenile Justice and Delinquency Prevention, July 2000).

71. Ibid., p. 2.

Glossary

adjudication The juvenile court equivalent of a trial in criminal court, or the process of rendering a judicial decision regarding the truth of the facts alleged in a petition. (Ch. 10)

administrative segregation The keeping of inmates in secure isolation so that they cannot harm others. (Ch. 7)

aggravating circumstance A factor (for example, the crime was especially heinous, atrocious, or cruel) that increases the degree of an offender's blameworthiness for a criminal act. (Ch. 6)

aggressive patrol The practice of having an entire patrol section make numerous traffic stops and field interrogations. (Ch. 3)

allocution The procedure at a sentencing hearing in which the convicted defendant has the right to address the court before the sentence is imposed. During allocution, a defendant is identified as the person found guilty and has a right to deny or explain information contained in the PSI if his or her sentence is based on it. (Ch. 6)

appellate jurisdiction The power of a court to review a case for errors of law. (Ch. 5)

apprenticeship system The method by which middle- and upper-class children were taught skilled trades by a master. (Ch. 10)

arraignment A pretrial stage to hear the information or indictment and to allow a plea. (Chs. 1, 5)

arrest The seizing and detaining of a person by lawful authority. (Chs. 1, 3)

arrest warrant A written order directing law enforcement officers to arrest a person. The charge or charges against a suspect are specified on the warrant. (Ch. 5)

Auburn system An early system of penology, originating at Auburn Penitentiary in New York, in which inmates worked and ate together in silence during the day and were placed in solitary cells for the evening. (Ch. 7)

bail/bail bond Usually a monetary guarantee deposited with the court to ensure that suspects or defendants will appear at a later stage in the criminal justice process. (Ch. 1, 5)

banishment A punishment, originating in ancient times, that required offenders to leave the community and live elsewhere, commonly in the wilderness. (Ch. 7)

bench trial A trial before a judge without a jury. (Ch. 1)

bench warrant or capias A document that authorizes a suspect's or defendant's arrest for not appearing in court as required. (Ch. 5)

beyond a reasonable doubt The standard of proof necessary to find a defendant guilty in a criminal trial. (Ch. 1)

bifurcated trial A two-stage trial (unlike the one-stage trial in other felony cases) consisting of a guilt phase and a separate penalty phase. (Ch. 6)

binding-out system Practice in which children were "bound over" to masters for care. However, under the binding-out system, masters were not required to teach youths a trade. (Ch. 10)

booking The administrative recording of an arrest. Typically, the suspect's name, the charge, and perhaps the suspect's fingerprints or photograph are entered in the police blotter. (Chs. 1, 5)

classification facility A facility to which newly sentenced offenders are taken so that their security risks and needs can be assessed and they can be assigned to a permanent institution. (Ch. 7)

clear and convincing evidence The standard of proof required in some civil cases and, in federal courts, the standard of proof necessary for a defendant to make a successful claim of insanity. (Ch. 1)

cocorrectional facilities Usually small, minimum-security institutions that house both men and women with the goal of normalizing the prison environment by integrating the daytime activities of the sexes. (Ch. 7)

college academies Schools where students pursue a program that integrates an associate's degree curriculum in law enforcement or criminal justice with the state's required peace officer training. (Ch. 4)

community corrections The subfield of corrections in which offenders are supervised and provided services outside jail or prison.

community policing A contemporary approach to policing that actively involves the community in a working partnership to control and reduce crime. (Ch. 2)

commutations Reductions in sentences, typically granted by a state's governor. (Chs. 6, 8)

complaint A charging document specifying that an offense has been committed by a person or persons named or described; usually used for misdemeanors and ordinance violations. (Ch. 5)

conditional release A form of release that requires that a suspect/defendant maintain contact with a pretrial release program or undergo regular drug monitoring or treatment. (Ch. 5)

confession An admission by a person accused of a crime that he or she committed the offense charged. (Ch. 3)

conjugal visits An arrangement whereby inmates are permitted to visit in private with their spouses or significant others to maintain their personal relationship. (Ch. 7)

constable The peacekeeper in charge of protection in early English towns. (Ch. 2)

constable-watch system A system of protection in early England in which citizens, under the direction of a constable, or chief peacekeeper, were required to guard the city and to pursue criminals. (Ch. 2)

contraband An illegal substance or object. (Ch. 3)

contract security Protective services that a private security firm provides to people, agencies, and companies that do not employ their own security personnel or that need extra protection. (Ch. 2)

convict code A constellation of values, norms, and roles that regulate the way inmates interact with one another and with prison staff. (Ch. 8)

copicide A form of suicide in which a person gets fatally shot after intentionally provoking police officers. (Ch. 4)

cottage reformatories Correctional facilities for youths, first developed in the late 1800s, that were intended to closely parallel family life and remove children from the negative influences of the urban environment. Children in those facilities lived with surrogate parents, who were responsible for the youths' training and education. (Ch. 10)

crime control model One of Packer's two models of the criminal justice process. Politically, it reflects traditional conservative values. In this model, the control of criminal behavior is the most important function of criminal justice. (Ch. 1)

criminal law One of two general types of law practiced in the United States (the other is civil law); "a formal means of social control [that uses] rules . . . interpreted [and enforced] by the courts . . . to set limits to the conduct of the citizens, to guide the officials, and to define . . . unacceptable behavior." (Ch. 1)

criminal sanctions or **criminal punishment** Penalties that are imposed for violating the criminal law. (Ch. 6)

crisis intervention A counselor's efforts to address some crisis in an inmate's life and to calm the inmate. (Ch. 7)

custody level The classification assigned to an inmate to indicate the degree of precaution that needs to be taken when working with that inmate. (Ch. 7)

cybercrime The use of computer technology to commit crime. (Ch. 3)

day reporting centers Facilities that are designed for offenders who would otherwise be in prison or jail and that require offenders to report regularly to confer with staff about supervision and treatment matters. (Ch. 9)

defendant A person against whom a legal action is brought, a warrant is issued, or an indictment is found. (Ch. 1)

deprivation model A theory that the inmate society arises as a response to the prison environment and the painful conditions of confinement. (Ch. 8)

determinate sentence A sentence with a fixed period of incarceration, which eliminates the decision-making responsibility of parole boards. (Ch. 6)

directed patrol Patrolling under guidance or orders on how to use patrol time. (Ch. 3)

discretion The exercise of individual judgment, instead of formal rules, in making decisions. (Ch. 4)

disposition The juvenile court equivalent of sentencing in criminal court. At the disposition hearing, the court makes its final determination of what to do with the juvenile officially labeled delinquent. (Ch. 10)

diversion Organized, systematic efforts to remove individuals from further processing in criminal justice by placing them in alternative programs; diversion may be pretrial or posttrial. (Ch. 9)

doctrine of fundamental fairness The rule that makes confessions inadmissible in criminal trials if they were obtained by means of either psychological manipulation or "third-degree" methods. (Ch. 3)

doctrine of legal guilt The principle that people are not to be held guilty of crimes merely on a showing, based on reliable evidence, that in all probability they did in fact do what they are accused of doing. Legal guilt results only when factual guilt is determined in a procedurally regular fashion, as in a criminal trial, and when the procedural rules designed to protect suspects and defendants and to safeguard the integrity of the process are employed. (Ch. 1)

domestic terrorism The unlawful use, or threatened use, of force or violence by a group or individual based and operating entirely within the United States or its territories without foreign direction committed against persons or property to intimidate or coerce a government, the civilian population, or any segment thereof, in furtherance of political or social objectives. (Ch. 4)

double jeopardy The trying of a defendant a second time for the same offense when jeopardy attached in the first trial and a mistrial was not declared. (Ch. 5)

dual court system The court system in the United States, consisting of one system of state and local courts and another system of federal courts. (Ch. 5)

due process model One of Packer's two models of the criminal justice process. Politically, it embodies traditional liberal values. In this model, the principal goal of criminal justice is at least as much to protect the innocent as it is to convict the guilty. (Ch. 1)

due process of law The procedures followed by courts to ensure that a defendant's constitutional rights are not violated. (Chs. 1, 5)

electronic monitoring An arrangement that allows an offender's whereabouts to be gauged through the use of computer technology. (Ch. 9)

excessive force A measure of coercion beyond that necessary to control participants in a conflict. (Ch. 4)

exclusionary rule The rule that illegally seized evidence must be excluded from trials in federal courts. (Ch. 3)

felonies Serious offenses punishable by confinement in prison for more than 1 year or by death. (Ch. 1)

field interrogation A temporary detention in which officers stop and question pedestrians and motorists they find in suspicious circumstances. (Ch. 3)

flat-time sentencing Sentencing in which judges may choose between probation and imprisonment but have little discretion in setting the length of a prison sentence. Once an offender is imprisoned, there is no possibility of reduction in the length of the sentence. (Ch. 6)

frisking Conducting a search for weapons by patting the outside of a suspect's clothing, feeling for hard objects that might be weapons. (Ch. 1)

full enforcement A practice in which the police make an arrest for every violation of law that comes to their attention. (Ch. 4)

general deterrence The attempt to prevent people in general from engaging in crime by punishing specific individuals and making examples of them. (Chs. 5, 6)

general jurisdiction The power of a court to hear any type of case. (Ch. 5)

GIS crime mapping A technique that involves the charting of crime patterns within a geographic area. (Ch. 3)

good time The number of days deducted from an inmate's sentence by prison authorities for good behavior or for other reasons. (Chs. 6, 8)

grand jury Generally a group of 12 to 23 citizens who meet in closed sessions to investigate charges coming from preliminary hearings or to engage in other responsibilities. A primary purpose of the grand jury is to determine whether there is probable cause to believe that the accused committed the crime or crimes. (Ch. 1, 5)

grand jury indictment A written accusation by a grand jury charging that one or more persons have committed a crime. (Ch. 5)

"grass eaters" Officers who occasionally engage in illegal and unethical activities, such as accepting small favors, gifts, or money for ignoring violations of the law during the course of their duties. (Ch. 4)

habeas corpus A court order requiring that a confined person be brought to court so that his or her claims can be heard. (Ch. 8)

halfway houses Community-based residential facilities that are less secure and restrictive than prison or jail but provide a more controlled environment than other community correctional programs. (Ch. 9)

hands-off philosophy A philosophy under which courts are reluctant to hear prisoners' claims regarding their rights while incarcerated. (Ch. 8)

hearing officer A lawyer empowered by the juvenile court to hear juvenile cases. (Ch. 10)

highway patrol model A model of state law enforcement services in which officers focus on highway traffic safety, enforcement of the state's traffic laws, and the investigation of accidents on the state's roads, highways, and property. (Ch. 2)

home confinement A program that requires offenders to remain in their homes except for approved periods of absence; commonly used in combination with electronic monitoring. (Ch. 9)

houses of refuge The first specialized correctional institutions for youths in the United States. (Ch. 10)

hung jury The result when jurors cannot agree on a verdict. The judge declares a mistrial. The prosecutor must decide whether to retry the case. (Ch. 5)

importation model A theory that the inmate society is shaped by the attributes inmates bring with them when they enter prison. (Ch. 8)

incapacitation The removal or restriction of the freedom of those found to have violated criminal laws. (Chs. 5, 6)

incarceration rate A figure derived by dividing the number of people incarcerated by the population of the area and multiplying the result by 100,000; used to compare incarceration levels of units with different population sizes. (Ch. 7)

indeterminate sentence A sentence with a fixed minimum and maximum term of incarceration, rather than a set period. (Ch. 6)

indictment A document that outlines the charge or charges against a defendant. (Ch. 5)

informal juvenile justice The actions taken by citizens to respond to juvenile offenders without involving the official agencies of juvenile justice. (Ch. 10)

information A document that outlines the formal charge(s) against a suspect, the law(s) that have been violated, and the evidence to support the charge(s). (Ch. 1, 5)

initial appearance A pretrial stage in which a defendant is brought before a lower court to be given notice of the charge(s) and advised of her or his constitutional rights. (Ch. 1)

institution of social control An organization that persuades people, through subtle and not-so-subtle means, to abide by the dominant values of society. (Ch. 1)

intake screening The process by which decisions are made about the continued processing of juvenile cases. Decisions might include dismissing the case, referring the youth to a diversion program, or filing a petition. (Ch. 10)

intensive-supervision probation and parole (ISP) An alternative to incarceration that provides stricter conditions, closer supervision, and more treatment services than do traditional probation and parole. (Ch. 9)

intermediate sanctions Sanctions that, in restrictiveness and punitiveness, lie between traditional probation and traditional imprisonment or, alternatively, between imprisonment and traditional parole. (Ch. 9)

internal affairs investigations unit The police unit that ferrets out illegal and unethical activity engaged in by the police. (Ch. 4)

international terrorism Violent acts dangerous to human life that are a violation of the criminal laws of the United States or any state, or that would be a criminal violation if committed within the jurisdiction of the United States or any state. These acts appear to be intended to intimidate or coerce a civilian population, influence the policy of a government by intimidation or coercion, or affect the conduct of a government by assassination or kidnapping. International terrorist acts occur outside the United States or transcend national boundaries in terms of the means by which they are accomplished, the persons they appear intended to coerce or intimidate, or the locale in which the perpetrators operate or seek asylum. (Ch. 4)

jail A facility, usually operated at the local level, that holds convicted offenders and unconvicted persons for relatively short periods. (Ch. 7)

jailhouse lawyers Inmates skilled in legal matters. (Ch. 8)

job stress The harmful physical and emotional outcomes that occur when the requirements of a job do not match the capabilities, resources, or needs of the worker. (Ch. 4)

jurisdiction A politically defined geographical area; the right or authority of a justice agency to act in regard to a particular subject matter, territory, or person; the authority of a court to hear and decide cases. (Chs. 1, 2, 5)

just deserts The punishment rationale based on the idea that offenders should be punished automatically, simply because they have committed a crime—they "deserve" it—and the idea that the punishment should fit the crime. (Ch. 6)

juvenile delinquency A special category of offense created for youths who, in most U.S. jurisdictions, are persons between the ages of 7 and 18. (Ch. 10)

less-eligibility principle The position that prisoners should receive no service or program superior to the services and programs available to free citizens without charge. (Ch. 7)

lockup A very short-term holding facility that is frequently located in or very near an urban police agency so that suspects can be held pending further inquiry. (Ch. 7)

mandatory release A method of prison release under which an inmate is released after serving a legally required portion of his or her sentence, minus good-time credits. (Ch. 8)

mandatory sentencing Sentencing in which a specified number of years of imprisonment (usually within a range) is provided for particular crimes. (Ch. 6)

"meat eaters" Officers who actively seek ways to make money illegally while on duty. (Ch. 4)

medical model A theory of institutional corrections, popular during the 1940s and 1950s, in which crime was seen as symptomatic of personal illness in need of treatment. (Ch. 7)

mere suspicion The standard of proof with the least certainty; a "gut feeling." With mere suspicion, a law enforcement officer cannot legally even stop a suspect. (Ch. 1)

merit system A system of employment whereby an independent civil service commission, in cooperation with the city personnel section and the police department, sets employment qualifications, performance standards, and discipline procedures. (Ch. 4)

milieu therapy A variant of group therapy that encompasses the total living environment so that the environment continually encourages positive behavioral change. (Ch. 7)

misdemeanors Less serious crimes generally punishable by a fine or by incarceration in jail for not more than 1 year. (Ch. 1)

mitigating circumstance A factor (for example, the defendant has no significant history of prior criminal activity) that reduces the degree of an offender's blameworthiness for a criminal act. (Ch. 6)

myths Beliefs based on emotion rather than analysis. (Ch. 1)

net widening A phenomenon that occurs when the offenders placed in a novel program are not the offenders for whom the program was designed. The consequence is that those in the program receive more severe sanctions than they would have received had the new program remained unavailable. (Ch. 9)

nolle prosequi (*nol. pros.*) The notation placed on the official record of a case when prosecutors elect not to prosecute. (Ch. 5)

nolo contendere Latin for "no contest." When defendants plead nolo, they do not admit guilt but are willing to accept punishment. (Ch. 5)

operational styles The different overall approaches to the police job. (Ch. 3)

original jurisdiction The authority of a court to hear a case when it is first brought to court. (Ch. 5)

panopticon A prison design consisting of a round building with tiers of cells lining the inner circumference and facing a central inspection tower. (Ch. 7)

pardon A "forgiveness" for the crime committed that stops further criminal processing. (Ch. 6)

parens patriae The legal philosophy justifying state intervention in the lives of children when their parents are unable or unwilling to protect them. (Ch. 10)

parole A method of prison release whereby inmates are released at the discretion of a board or other authority before having completed their entire sentences; can also refer to the community supervision received upon release. (Chs. 1, 8, 9)

parole guidelines Structured instruments used to estimate the probability of parole recidivism and to direct the release decisions of parole boards. (Ch. 9)

Peel's Principles of Policing A dozen standards proposed by Robert Peel, the author of the legislation resulting in the formation of the London Metropolitan Police Department. The standards are still applicable to today's law enforcement. (Ch. 2)

penal code The criminal law of a political jurisdiction. (Ch. 1)

Pennsylvania system An early system of U.S. penology in which inmates were kept in solitary cells so that they could study religious writings, reflect on their misdeeds, and perform handicraft work. (Ch. 7)

penology The study of prison management and the treatment of offenders. (Ch. 7)

personal jurisdiction A court's authority over the parties to a lawsuit. (Ch. 5)

petition A legal form of the police complaint that specifies the charges to be heard at the adjudication. (Ch. 10)

placing out The practice of placing children on farms in the Midwest and West to remove them from the supposedly corrupting influences of their parents and the cities. (Ch. 10)

plea bargaining or **plea negotiating** The practice whereby the prosecutor, the defense attorney, the defendant, and—in many jurisdictions—the judge agree on a specific sentence to be imposed if the accused pleads guilty to an agreed-upon charge or charges instead of going to trial. (Chs. 1, 5)

police cadet program A program that combines a college education with agency work experience and academy training. Upon graduation, a cadet is promoted to police officer. (Ch. 4)

posses Groups of able-bodied citizens of a community, called into service by a sheriff or constable to chase and apprehend offenders. (Ch. 2)

preliminary hearing In a felony case, a pretrial stage at which a judge determines whether there is probable cause to support the charge or charges imposed by the prosecutor. (Chs. 1, 5)

preponderance of evidence Evidence that more likely than not outweighs the opposing evidence, or sufficient evidence to overcome doubt or speculation. (Ch. 1)

presentence investigation (PSI) An investigation conducted by a probation agency or other designated authority at the request of a court into the past behavior, family circumstances, and personality of an adult who has been convicted of a crime, to assist the court in determining the most appropriate sentence. (Ch. 9)

presentence investigation reports Reports, often called PSIs or PSIRs, that are used in the federal system and the majority of states to help judges determine the appropriate sentence. They are also used in classifying probationers, parolees, and prisoners according to their treatment needs and security risk. (Ch. 6)

presumptive sentencing Sentencing that allows a judge to retain some sentencing discretion, subject to appellate review. The legislature determines a sentence range for each crime. (Ch. 6)

preventive detention Holding suspects or defendants in jail without giving them an opportunity to post bail, because of the threat they pose to society. (Ch. 5)

preventive patrol Patrolling the streets with little direction; between responses to radio calls, officers are "systematically unsystematic" and observant in an attempt to both prevent and ferret out crime. Also known as *random patrol*. (Ch. 3)

prisonization The process by which an inmate becomes socialized into the customs and principles of the inmate society. (Ch. 8)

privatization The involvement of the private sector in the construction and the operation of confinement facilities. (Ch. 7)

probable cause A standard of proof that requires evidence sufficient to make a reasonable person believe that, more likely than not, the proposed action is justified. (Ch. 1)

probation A sentence in which the offender, rather than being incarcerated, is retained in the community under the supervision of a probation agency and required to abide by certain rules and conditions to avoid incarceration. (Ch. 9)

probation conditions Rules that specify what an offender is and is not to do during the course of a probation sentence. (Ch. 9)

procedural law The body of law that governs the ways substantive laws are administered; sometimes called *adjective* or *remedial* law. (Ch. 1)

proportionality review A review in which the appellate court compares the sentence in the case it is reviewing with penalties imposed in similar cases in the state. The object is to reduce, as much as possible, disparity in death penalty sentencing. (Ch. 6)

proprietary security In-house protective services that a security staff provides for the entity that employs it. (Ch. 2)

protective custody The segregation of inmates for their own safety. (Ch. 7)

public safety officers Police department employees who perform many police services but do not have arrest powers. (Ch. 4)

punishment The imposition of a penalty for criminal wrongdoing. (Ch. 5)

racial profiling The stopping and/or detaining of individuals by law enforcement officers based solely on race. (Ch. 4)

radical nonintervention A practice based on the idea that youths should be left alone if at all possible, instead of being formally processed. (Ch. 10)

reasonable suspicion A standard of proof that is more than a gut feeling. It includes the ability to articulate reasons for the suspicion. With reasonable suspicion, a law enforcement officer is legally permitted to stop and frisk a suspect. (Ch. 1)

recidivism The return to illegal activity after release from incarceration; the return of probationers to crime during or after probation. (Chs. 8, 9)

reform, industrial, or training schools Correctional facilities for youths, first developed in the late 1800s, that focused on custody. Today, those institutions are often called training schools and although they may place more emphasis on treatment, they still rely on custody and control. (Ch. 10)

rehabilitation The attempt to "correct" the personality and behavior of convicted offenders through educational, vocational, or therapeutic treatment and to return them to society as law-abiding citizens. (Chs. 5, 6)

reintegration The process of rebuilding former ties to the community and establishing new ties after release from prison. (Ch. 9)

release on own recognizance (ROR) A release secured by a suspect's written promise to appear in court. (Ch. 5)

restitution Money paid or services provided by a convicted offender to victims, their survivors, or the community to make up for the injury inflicted. (Chs. 6, 9)

retribution A justification for punishment that implies repayment for an offense committed. (Ch. 6)

revenge The punishment rationale expressed by the biblical phrase, "An eye for an eye, and a tooth for a tooth." People who seek revenge want to pay back offenders by making them suffer for what they have done. (Ch. 6)

revocation The repeal of a probation sentence or parole, and substitution of a more restrictive sentence, because of violation of probation or parole conditions. (Ch. 9)

role The rights and responsibilities associated with a particular position in society. (Ch. 3)

role conflict The psychological stress and frustration that results from trying to perform two or more incompatible responsibilities. (Ch. 3)

role expectation The behavior and actions that people expect from a person in a particular role. (Ch. 3)

rules of discovery Rules that mandate that a prosecutor provide defense counsel with any exculpatory evidence (evidence favorable to the accused that has an effect on guilt or punishment) in the prosecutor's possession. (Ch. 5)

searches Exploration or inspections, by law enforcement officers, of homes, premises, vehicles, or persons, for the purpose of discovering evidence of crimes or persons who are accused of crimes. (Ch. 3)

security level A designation applied to a facility to describe the measures taken, both inside and outside, to preserve security and custody. (Ch. 7)

seizures The taking of persons or property into custody in response to violations of the criminal law. (Ch. 3)

selective enforcement The practice of relying on the judgment of the police leadership and rank-and-file officers to decide which laws to enforce. (Ch. 4)

self-incrimination Being a witness against oneself. If forced, it is a violation of the Fifth Amendment. (Ch. 3)

shire reeve In medieval England, the chief law enforcement officer in a territorial area called a shire; later called the sheriff. (Ch. 2)

shock incarceration The placement of offenders in facilities patterned after military boot camps. (Ch. 7)

slave patrols The earliest form of policing in the South. They were a product of the slave codes. (Ch. 2)

snitch system A system in which staff learn from inmate informants about the presence of contraband, the potential for disruptions, and other threats to security. (Ch. 7)

special jurisdiction The power of a court to hear only certain kinds of cases. (Ch. 5)

special or specific deterrence The prevention of individuals from committing crimes again by punishing them. (Ch. 6)

state police model A model of state law enforcement services in which the agency and its officers have the same law enforcement powers as local police but can exercise them anywhere within the state. (Ch. 2)

status offenses Acts that are not crimes when committed by adults but are illegal for minors (for example, truancy or running away from home). (Ch. 10)

structured fines, or day fines Fines that are based on defendants' ability to pay. (Ch. 9)

subject matter jurisdiction The power of a court to hear a particular type of case. (Ch. 5)

subpoena A written order to testify issued by a court officer. (Ch. 5)

sub-rosa economy The secret exchange of goods and services among inmates; the black market of the prison. (Ch. 8)

substantive law The body of law that defines criminal offenses and their penalties. (Ch. 1)

summary or bench trials Trials without a jury. (Chs. 1, 5)

tech prep (technical preparation) A program in which area community colleges and high schools team up to offer 6 to 9 hours of college law enforcement courses in the eleventh and twelfth grades, as well as one or two training certifications, such as police dispatcher or local corrections officer. Students who graduate are eligible for police employment at age 18. (Ch. 4)

technical violations Failure to abide by the technical rules or conditions of probation or parole (for example, not reporting regularly to the probation officer), as distinct from commission of a new criminal act. (Ch. 9)

temporary-release programs Programs that allow jail or prison inmates to leave the facility for short periods to participate in approved community activities. (Ch. 9)

terrorism The systematic use of terror or unpredictable violence against governments, publics, or individuals to attain a political objective; the unlawful use of force and violence against persons or property to intimidate or coerce a government, the civilian population, or any segment thereof, in furtherance of political or social objectives; or premeditated, politically motivated violence perpetrated against noncombatant targets by subnational groups or clandestine agents, usually intended to influence an audience. (Ch. 4)

three I's of police selection Three qualities of the American police officer that seem to be of paramount importance: intelligence, integrity, and interaction skills. (Ch. 4)

tithing system A private self-help protection system in early medieval England, in which a group of 10 families, or a tithing, agreed to follow the law, keep the peace in their areas, and bring law violators to justice. (Ch. 2)

total institution An institutional setting in which persons sharing some characteristics are cut off from the wider society and expected to live according to institutional rules and procedures. (Ch. 8)

traffic accident investigation crews In some agencies, the special units assigned to all traffic accident investigations. (Ch. 3)

transfer, waiver, or certification The act or process by which juveniles who meet specific age, offense, and (in some jurisdictions) prior-record criteria are transferred to criminal court for trial. (Ch. 10)

transportation A punishment in which offenders were transported from their home nation to one of that nation's colonies to work. (Ch. 7)

trial *de novo* A trial in which an entire case is reheard by a trial court of general jurisdiction because there is an appeal and there is no written transcript of the earlier proceeding. (Ch. 5)

unsecured bond An arrangement in which bail is set but no money is paid to the court. (Ch. 5)

venire The pool from which jurors are selected. (Ch. 5)

venue The place of a trial. (Ch. 5)

victim-impact statements Descriptions of the harm and suffering that a crime has caused victims and their survivors. (Ch. 6)

voir dire The process in which potential jurors who might be biased or unable to render a fair verdict are screened out. (Ch. 5)

warrant A written order from a court directing law enforcement officers to conduct a search or to arrest a person. (Ch. 3)

workhouses European forerunners of the modern U.S. prison, where offenders were sent to learn discipline and regular work habits. (Ch. 7)

writ of *certiorari* A written order, from the U.S. Supreme Court to a lower court whose decision is being appealed, to send the records of the case forward for review. (Ch. 5)

writ of *habeas corpus* An order from a court to an officer of the law to produce a prisoner in court to determine if the prisoner is being legally detained or imprisoned. (Ch. 5)

PHOTO CREDITS

PHOTO CREDITS

Case Index

SUBJECT INDEX

SUBJECT INDEX